FORD PICK-UPS AND BRONCO
1976-86 REPAIR MANUAL

Covers all U.S. and Canadian models of
Ford F-100, F-150, F-250, F-350 and
Bronco (1978-86 only); 2 and 4 wheel drive,
gasoline and diesel engines

by Thomas A. Mellon, A.S.E., S.A.E.

PUBLISHED BY **HAYNES NORTH AMERICA. Inc.**

Manufactured in USA
© 1994 Haynes North America, Inc.
ISBN 0-8019-8576-5
Library of Congress Catalog Card No. 93-074301
13 14 15 16 17 9876543210

Haynes Publishing Group
Sparkford Nr Yeovil
Somerset BA22 7JJ England

Haynes North America, Inc
861 Lawrence Drive
Newbury Park
California 91320 USA

ABCDE
FGHIJ
K
2

4M1

Contents

Contents

DRIVE TRAIN **7**

SUSPENSION AND STEERING **8**

BRAKES **9**

BODY AND TRIM **10**

GLOSSARY

MASTER INDEX

SAFETY NOTICE

Proper service and repair procedures are vital to the safe, reliable operation of all motor vehicles, as well as the personal safety of those performing repairs. This manual outlines procedures for servicing and repairing vehicles using safe, effective methods. The procedures contain many NOTES, CAUTIONS and WARNINGS which should be followed, along with standard procedures to eliminate the possibility of personal injury or improper service which could damage the vehicle or compromise its safety.

It is important to note that repair procedures and techniques, tools and parts for servicing motor vehicles, as well as the skill and experience of the individual performing the work vary widely. It is not possible to anticipate all of the conceivable ways or conditions under which vehicles may be serviced, or to provide cautions as to all possible hazards that may result. Standard and accepted safety precautions and equipment should be used when handling toxic or flammable fluids, and safety goggles or other protection should be used during cutting, grinding, chiseling, prying, or any other process that can cause material removal or projectiles.

Some procedures require the use of tools specially designed for a specific purpose. Before substituting another tool or procedure, you must be completely satisfied that neither your personal safety, nor the performance of the vehicle will be endangered.

Although information in this manual is based on industry sources and is complete as possible at the time of publication, the possibility exists that some car manufacturers made later changes which could not be included here. While striving for total accuracy, the authors or publishers cannot assume responsibility for any errors, changes or omissions that may occur in the compilation of this data.

PART NUMBERS

Part numbers listed in this reference are not recommendations by Haynes North America, Inc. for any product brand name. They are references that can be used with interchange manuals and aftermarket supplier catalogs to locate each brand supplier's discrete part number.

SPECIAL TOOLS

Special tools are recommended by the vehicle manufacturer to perform their specific job. Use has been kept to a minimum, but where absolutely necessary, they are referred to in the text by the part number of the tool manufacturer. These tools can be purchased, under the appropriate part number, from your local dealer or regional distributor, or an equivalent tool can be purchased locally from a tool supplier or parts outlet. Before substituting any tool for the one recommended, read the SAFETY NOTICE at the top of this page.

ACKNOWLEDGMENTS

This publication contains material that is reproduced and distributed under a license from Ford Motor Company. No further reproduction or distribution of the Ford Motor Company material is allowed without the express written permission from Ford Motor Company.

1

GENERAL INFORMATION AND MAINTENANCE

HOW TO USE THIS BOOK

Chilton's Repair Manual for 1978–86 Ford Bronco and 1976–86 Ford Pickups is intended to help you learn more about the inner workings of your vehicle while saving you money on its upkeep and operation.

The beginning of the book will likely be referred to the most, since that is where you will find information for maintenance and tune-up. The other sections deal with the more complex systems of your vehicle. Systems (from engine through brakes) are covered to the extent that the average do-it-yourselfer can attempt. This book will not explain such things as rebuilding a differential because the expertise required and the special tools necessary make this uneconomical. It will, however, give you detailed instructions to help you change your own brake pads and shoes, replace spark plugs, and perform many more jobs that can save you money and help avoid expensive problems.

A secondary purpose of this book is a reference for owners who want to understand their vehicle and/or their mechanics better.

Where to Begin

Before removing any bolts, read through the entire procedure. This will give you the overall view of what tools and supplies will be required. So read ahead and plan ahead. Each operation should be approached logically and all procedures thoroughly understood before attempting any work.

If repair of a component is not considered practical, we tell you how to remove the part and then how to install the new or rebuilt replacement. In this way, you at least save labor costs.

Avoiding Trouble

Many procedures in this book require you to "label and disconnect . . ." a group of lines, hoses or wires. Don't be think you can remember where everything goes—you won't. If you hook up vacuum or fuel lines incorrectly, the vehicle may run poorly, if at all. If you hook up electrical wiring incorrectly, you may instantly learn a very expensive lesson.

You don't need to know the proper name for each hose or line. A piece of masking tape on the hose and a piece on its fitting will allow you to assign your own label. As long as you remember your own code, the lines can be reconnected by matching your tags. Remember that tape will dissolve in gasoline or solvents; if a part is to be washed or cleaned, use another method of identification. A permanent felt-tipped marker or a metal scribe can be very handy for marking metal parts. Remove any tape or paper labels after assembly.

Maintenance or Repair?

Maintenance includes routine inspections, adjustments, and replacement of parts which show signs of normal wear. Maintenance compensates for wear or deterioration. Repair implies that something has broken or is not working. A need for a repair is often caused by lack of maintenance. for example: draining and refilling automatic transmission fluid is maintenance recommended at specific intervals. Failure to do this can shorten the life of the transmission/ transaxle, requiring very expensive repairs. While no maintenance program can prevent items from eventually breaking or wearing out, a general rule is true: MAINTENANCE IS CHEAPER THAN REPAIR.

Two basic mechanic's rules should be mentioned here. First, whenever the left side of the vehicle or engine is referred to, it means the driver's side. Conversely, the right side of the vehicle means the passenger's side. Second, screws and bolts are removed by turning counterclockwise, and tightened by turning clockwise unless specifically noted.

Safety is always the most important rule. Constantly be aware of the dangers involved in working on an automobile and take the proper precautions. Please refer to the information in this section regarding SERVICING YOUR VEHICLE SAFELY and the SAFETY NOTICE on the acknowledgment page.

Avoiding the Most Common Mistakes

Pay attention to the instructions provided. There are 3 common mistakes in mechanical work:

1. Incorrect order of assembly, disassembly or adjustment. When taking something apart or putting it together, performing steps in the wrong order usually just costs you extra time; however, it CAN break something. Read the entire procedure before beginning. Perform everything in the order in which the instructions say you should, even if you can't see a reason for it. When you're taking apart something that is very intricate, you might want to draw a picture of how it looks when assembled in order to make sure you get everything back in its proper position. When making adjustments, perform them in the proper order. One adjustment possibly will affect another.

2. Overtorquing (or undertorquing). While it is more common for overtorquing to cause damage, undertorquing may allow a fastener to vibrate loose causing serious damage. Especially when dealing with aluminum parts, pay attention to torque specifications and utilize a torque wrench in assembly. If a torque figure is not available, remember that if you are using the right tool to perform the job, you will probably not have to strain yourself to get a fastener tight enough. The pitch of most threads is so slight that the tension you put on the wrench will be multiplied many times in actual force on what you are tightening.

There are many commercial products available for ensuring that fasteners won't come loose, even if they are not torqued just right (a very common brand is Loctite®). If you're worried about getting something together tight enough to hold, but loose enough to avoid mechanical damage during assembly, one of these products might offer substantial insurance. Before choosing a threadlocking compound, read the label on the package and make sure the product is compatible with the materials, fluids, etc. involved.

3. Crossthreading. This occurs when a part such as a bolt is screwed into a nut or casting at the wrong angle and forced. Crossthreading is more likely to occur if access is difficult. It helps to clean and lubricate fasteners, then to start threading the bolt, spark plug, etc. with your fingers. If you encounter resistance, unscrew the part and start over again at a different angle until it can be inserted and turned several times without much effort. Keep in mind that many parts have tapered threads, so that gentle turning will automatically bring the part you're threading to the proper angle. Don't put a wrench on the part until it's been tightened a couple of turns by hand. If you suddenly encounter resistance, and the part has not seated fully, don't force it. Pull it back out to make sure it's clean and threading properly.

Be sure to take your time and be patient, and always plan ahead. Allow yourself ample time to perform repairs and maintenance.

TOOLS AND EQUIPMENT

▶ See Figures 1 thru 15

Without the proper tools and equipment it is impossible to properly service your vehicle. It would be virtually impossible to catalog every tool that you would need to perform all of the operations in this book. It would be unwise for the amateur to rush out and buy an expensive set of tools on the theory that he/she may need one or more of them at some time.

The best approach is to proceed slowly, gathering a good quality set of those tools that are used most frequently. Don't be misled by the low cost of bargain tools. It is far better to spend a little more for better quality. Forged wrenches, 6 or 12-point sockets and fine tooth ratchets are by far preferable to their less expensive counterparts. As any good mechanic can tell you, there are few worse experiences than trying to work on a vehicle with bad tools. Your monetary savings will be far outweighed by frustration and mangled knuckles.

Begin accumulating those tools that are used most frequently: those associated with routine maintenance and tune-up. In addition to the normal assortment of screwdrivers and pliers, you should have the following tools:

• Wrenches/sockets and combination open end/box end wrenches in sizes ⅛–¾ in. and/or 3mm–19mm ¹³⁄₁₆ in. or ⅝ in. spark plug socket (depending on plug type).

➥If possible, buy various length socket drive extensions. Universal-joint and wobble extensions can be extremely useful, but be careful when using them, as they can change the amount of torque applied to the socket.

• Jackstands for support.
• Oil filter wrench.
• Spout or funnel for pouring fluids.

• Grease gun for chassis lubrication (unless your vehicle is not equipped with any grease fittings)

• Hydrometer for checking the battery (unless equipped with a sealed, maintenance-free battery).

• A container for draining oil and other fluids.

• Rags for wiping up the inevitable mess.

In addition to the above items there are several others that are not absolutely necessary, but handy to have around. These include an equivalent oil absorbent gravel, like cat litter, and the usual supply of lubricants, antifreeze and fluids. This is a basic list for routine maintenance, but only your personal needs and desire can accurately determine your list of tools.

After performing a few projects on the vehicle, you'll be amazed at the other tools and non-tools on your workbench. Some useful household items are: a large turkey baster or siphon, empty coffee cans and ice trays (to store parts), a ball of twine, electrical tape for wiring, small rolls of colored tape for tagging lines or hoses, markers and pens, a note pad, golf tees (for plugging vacuum lines), metal coat hangers or a roll of mechanic's wire (to hold things out of the way), dental pick or similar long, pointed probe, a strong magnet, and a small mirror (to see into recesses and under manifolds).

A more advanced set of tools, suitable for tune-up work, can be drawn up easily. While the tools are slightly more sophisticated, they need not be outrageously expensive. There are several inexpensive tach/dwell meters on the market that are every bit as good for the average mechanic as a professional model. Just be sure that it goes to a least 1200–1500 rpm on the tach scale and that it works on 4, 6 and 8-cylinder engines. The key to these purchases is to make them with an eye towards adaptability and wide range. A basic list of tune-up tools could include:

• Tach/dwell meter.

• Spark plug wrench and gapping tool.

• Feeler gauges for valve adjustment.

• Timing light.

The choice of a timing light should be made carefully. A light which works on the DC current supplied by the vehicle's battery is the best choice; it should have a xenon tube for brightness. On any vehicle with an electronic ignition sys-

Fig. 1 All but the most basic procedures will require an assortment of ratchets and sockets

TCCS1200

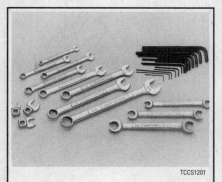

Fig. 2 In addition to ratchets, a good set of wrenches and hex keys will be necessary

TCCS1201

Fig. 3 A hydraulic floor jack and a set of jackstands are essential for lifting and supporting the vehicle

TCCS1202

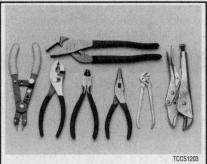

Fig. 4 An assortment of pliers, grippers and cutters will be handy for old rusted parts and stripped bolt heads

TCCS1203

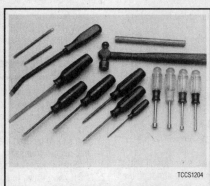

Fig. 5 Various drivers, chisels and prybars are great tools to have in your toolbox

TCCS1204

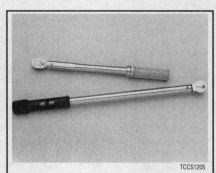

Fig. 6 Many repairs will require the use of a torque wrench to assure the components are properly fastened

TCCS1205

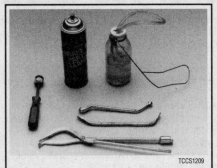

Fig. 7 Although not always necessary, using specialized brake tools will save time

TCCS1209

Fig. 8 A few inexpensive lubrication tools will make maintenance easier

TCCS1210

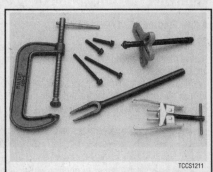

Fig. 9 Various pullers, clamps and separator tools are needed for many larger, more complicated repairs

TCCS1211

Fig. 10 A variety of tools and gauges should be used for spark plug gapping and installation

TCCS1212

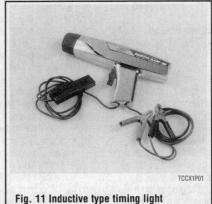

Fig. 11 Inductive type timing light

TCCX1P01

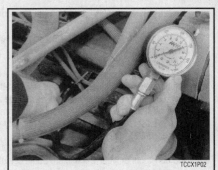

Fig. 12 A screw-in type compression gauge is recommended for compression testing

TCCX1P02

Fig. 13 A vacuum/pressure tester is necessary for many testing procedures

TCCX1P03

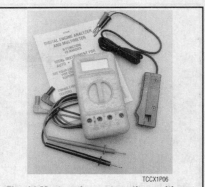

Fig. 14 Most modern automotive multimeters incorporate many helpful features

TCCX1P06

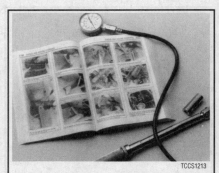

Fig. 15 Proper information is vital, so always have a Chilton Total Car Care manual handy

TCCS1213

tem, a timing light with an inductive pickup that clamps around the No. 1 spark plug cable is preferred.

In addition to these basic tools, there are several other tools and gauges you may find useful. These include:

• Compression gauge. The screw-in type is slower to use, but eliminates the possibility of a faulty reading due to escaping pressure.

• Manifold vacuum gauge.

• 12V test light.

• A combination volt/ohmmeter.

• Induction Ammeter. This is used for determining whether or not there is current in a wire. These are handy for use if a wire is broken somewhere in a wiring harness.

As a final note, you will probably find a torque wrench necessary for all but the most basic work. The beam type models are perfectly adequate, although the newer click types (breakaway) are easier to use. The click type torque wrenches tend to be more expensive. Also keep in mind that all types of torque wrenches should be periodically checked and/or recalibrated. You will have to decide for yourself which better fits your pocketbook, and purpose.

Special Tools

Normally, the use of special factory tools is avoided for repair procedures, since these are not readily available for the do-it-yourself mechanic. When it is possible to perform the job with more commonly available tools, it will be pointed out, but occasionally, a special tool was designed to perform a specific function and should be used. Before substituting another tool, you should be convinced that neither your safety nor the performance of the vehicle will be compromised.

Special tools can usually be purchased from an automotive parts store or from your dealer. In some cases special tools may be available directly from the tool manufacturer.

SERVICING YOUR VEHICLE SAFELY

♦ See Figures 16, 17 and 18

It is virtually impossible to anticipate all of the hazards involved with automotive maintenance and service, but care and common sense will prevent most accidents.

The rules of safety for mechanics range from "don't smoke around gasoline," to "use the proper tool(s) for the job." The trick to avoiding injuries is to develop safe work habits and to take every possible precaution.

Do's

• Do keep a fire extinguisher and first aid kit handy.

• Do wear safety glasses or goggles when cutting, drilling, grinding or prying, even if you have 20–20 vision. If you wear glasses for the sake of vision, wear safety goggles over your regular glasses.

• Do shield your eyes whenever you work around the battery. Batteries contain sulfuric acid. In case of contact with, flush the area with water or a mixture of water and baking soda, then seek immediate medical attention.

• Do use safety stands (jackstands) for any undervehicle service. Jacks are for raising vehicles; jackstands are for making sure the vehicle stays raised until you want it to come down.

• Do use adequate ventilation when working with any chemicals or hazardous materials. Like carbon monoxide, the asbestos dust resulting from some brake lining wear can be hazardous in sufficient quantities.

• Do disconnect the negative battery cable when working on the electrical system. The secondary ignition system contains EXTREMELY HIGH VOLTAGE. In some cases it can even exceed 50,000 volts.

• Do follow manufacturer's directions whenever working with potentially hazardous materials. Most chemicals and fluids are poisonous.

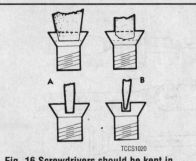

Fig. 16 Screwdrivers should be kept in good condition to prevent injury or damage which could result if the blade slips from the screw

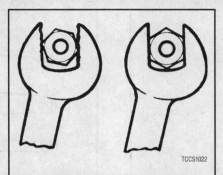

Fig. 17 Using the correct size wrench will help prevent the possibility of rounding off a nut

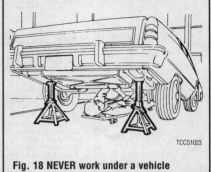

Fig. 18 NEVER work under a vehicle unless it is supported using safety stands (jackstands)

• Do properly maintain your tools. Loose hammerheads, mushroomed punches and chisels, frayed or poorly grounded electrical cords, excessively worn screwdrivers, spread wrenches (open end), cracked sockets, slipping ratchets, or faulty droplight sockets can cause accidents.

• Likewise, keep your tools clean; a greasy wrench can slip off a bolt head, ruining the bolt and often harming your knuckles in the process.

• Do use the proper size and type of tool for the job at hand. Do select a wrench or socket that fits the nut or bolt. The wrench or socket should sit straight, not cocked.

• Do, when possible, pull on a wrench handle rather than push it, and adjust your stance to prevent a fall.

• Do be sure that adjustable wrenches are tightly closed on the nut or bolt and pulled so that the force is on the side of the fixed jaw.

• Do strike squarely with a hammer; avoid glancing blows.

• Do set the parking brake and block the drive wheels if the work requires a running engine.

Don'ts

• Don't run the engine in a garage or anywhere else without proper ventilation—EVER! Carbon monoxide is poisonous; it takes a long time to leave the human body and you can build up a deadly supply of it in your system by simply breathing in a little at a time. You may not realize you are slowly poisoning yourself. Always use power vents, windows, fans and/or open the garage door.

• Don't work around moving parts while wearing loose clothing. Short sleeves are much safer than long, loose sleeves. Hard-toed shoes with neoprene soles protect your toes and give a better grip on slippery surfaces. Watches and jewelry is not safe working around a vehicle. Long hair should be tied back under a hat or cap.

• Don't use pockets for toolboxes. A fall or bump can drive a screwdriver deep into your body. Even a rag hanging from your back pocket can wrap around a spinning shaft or fan.

• Don't smoke when working around gasoline, cleaning solvent or other flammable material.

• Don't smoke when working around the battery. When the battery is being charged, it gives off explosive hydrogen gas.

• Don't use gasoline to wash your hands; there are excellent soaps available. Gasoline contains dangerous additives which can enter the body through a cut or through your pores. Gasoline also removes all the natural oils from the skin so that bone dry hands will suck up oil and grease.

• Don't service the air conditioning system unless you are equipped with the necessary tools and training. When liquid or compressed gas refrigerant is released to atmospheric pressure it will absorb heat from whatever it contacts. This will chill or freeze anything it touches.

• Don't use screwdrivers for anything other than driving screws! A screwdriver used as an prying tool can snap when you least expect it, causing injuries. At the very least, you'll ruin a good screwdriver.

• Don't use an emergency jack (that little ratchet, scissors, or pantograph jack supplied with the vehicle) for anything other than changing a flat! These jacks are only intended for emergency use out on the road; they are NOT designed as a maintenance tool. If you are serious about maintaining your vehicle yourself, invest in a hydraulic floor jack of at least a 1½ ton capacity, and at least two sturdy jackstands.

FASTENERS, MEASUREMENTS AND CONVERSIONS

Bolts, Nuts and Other Threaded Retainers

♦ See Figures 19 and 20

Although there are a great variety of fasteners found in the modern car or truck, the most commonly used retainer is the threaded fastener (nuts, bolts, screws, studs, etc.). Most threaded retainers may be reused, provided that they are not damaged in use or during the repair. Some retainers (such as stretch bolts or torque prevailing nuts) are designed to deform when tightened or in use and should not be reinstalled.

Whenever possible, we will note any special retainers which should be replaced during a procedure. But you should always inspect the condition of a retainer when it is removed and replace any that show signs of damage. Check all threads for rust or corrosion which can increase the torque necessary to achieve the desired clamp load for which that fastener was originally selected. Additionally, be sure that the driver surface of the fastener has not been compromised by rounding or other damage. In some cases a driver surface may become only partially rounded, allowing the driver to catch in only one direction. In many of these occurrences, a fastener may be installed and tightened, but the driver would not be able to grip and loosen the fastener again.

If you must replace a fastener, whether due to design or damage, you must ALWAYS be sure to use the proper replacement. In all cases, a retainer of the

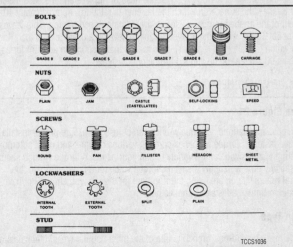

Fig. 19 There are many different types of threaded retainers found on vehicles

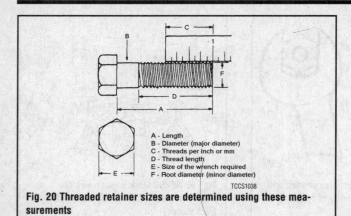

A - Length
B - Diameter (major diameter)
C - Threads per inch or mm
D - Thread length
E - Size of the wrench required
F - Root diameter (minor diameter)

TCCS1038

Fig. 20 Threaded retainer sizes are determined using these measurements

same design, material and strength should be used. Markings on the heads of most bolts will help determine the proper strength of the fastener. The same material, thread and pitch must be selected to assure proper installation and safe operation of the vehicle afterwards.

Thread gauges are available to help measure a bolt or stud's thread. Most automotive and hardware stores keep gauges available to help you select the proper size. In a pinch, you can use another nut or bolt for a thread gauge. If the bolt you are replacing is not too badly damaged, you can select a match by finding another bolt which will thread in its place. If you find a nut which threads properly onto the damaged bolt, then use that nut to help select the replacement bolt.

✷✷ WARNING

Be aware that when you find a bolt with damaged threads, you may also find the nut or drilled hole it was threaded into has also been damaged. If this is the case, you may have to drill and tap the hole, replace the nut or otherwise repair the threads. NEVER try to force a replacement bolt to fit into the damaged threads.

Torque

Torque is defined as the measurement of resistance to turning or rotating. It tends to twist a body about an axis of rotation. A common example of this would be tightening a threaded retainer such as a nut, bolt or screw. Measuring torque is one of the most common ways to help assure that a threaded retainer has been properly fastened.

When tightening a threaded fastener, torque is applied in three distinct areas, the head, the bearing surface and the clamp load. About 50 percent of the measured torque is used in overcoming bearing friction. This is the friction between the bearing surface of the bolt head, screw head or nut face and the base material or washer (the surface on which the fastener is rotating). Approximately 40 percent of the applied torque is used in overcoming thread friction. This leaves only about 10 percent of the applied torque to develop a useful clamp load (the force which holds a joint together). This means that friction can account for as much as 90 percent of the applied torque on a fastener.

TORQUE WRENCHES

♦ See Figure 21

In most applications, a torque wrench can be used to assure proper installation of a fastener. Torque wrenches come in various designs and most automotive supply stores will carry a variety to suit your needs. A torque wrench should be used any time we supply a specific torque value for a fastener. Again, the general rule of "if you are using the right tool for the job, you should not have to strain to tighten a fastener" applies here.

Beam Type

The beam type torque wrench is one of the most popular types. It consists of a pointer attached to the head that runs the length of the flexible beam (shaft) to a scale located near the handle. As the wrench is pulled, the beam bends and the pointer indicates the torque using the scale.

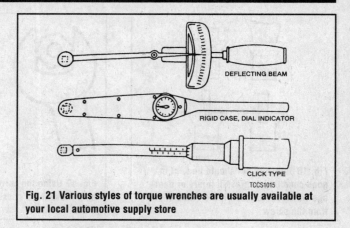

DEFLECTING BEAM

RIGID CASE, DIAL INDICATOR

CLICK TYPE

TCCS1015

Fig. 21 Various styles of torque wrenches are usually available at your local automotive supply store

Click (Breakaway) Type

Another popular design of torque wrench is the click type. To use the click type wrench you pre-adjust it to a torque setting. Once the torque is reached, the wrench has a reflex signaling feature that causes a momentary breakaway of the torque wrench body, sending an impulse to the operator's hand.

Pivot Head Type

♦ See Figure 22

Some torque wrenches (usually of the click type) may be equipped with a pivot head which can allow it to be used in areas of limited access. BUT, it must be used properly. To hold a pivot head wrench, grasp the handle lightly, and as you pull on the handle, it should be floated on the pivot point. If the handle comes in contact with the yoke extension during the process of pulling, there is a very good chance the torque readings will be inaccurate because this could alter the wrench loading point. The design of the handle is usually such as to make it inconvenient to deliberately misuse the wrench.

➤ **It should be mentioned that the use of any U-joint, wobble or extension will have an effect on the torque readings, no matter what type of wrench you are using. For the most accurate readings, install the socket directly on the wrench driver. If necessary, straight extensions (which hold a socket directly under the wrench driver) will have the least effect on the torque reading. Avoid any extension that alters the length of the wrench from the handle to the head/driving point (such as a crow's foot). U-joint or wobble extensions can greatly affect the readings; avoid their use at all times.**

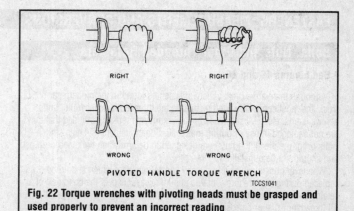

RIGHT   RIGHT

WRONG   WRONG

PIVOTED HANDLE TORQUE WRENCH

TCCS1041

Fig. 22 Torque wrenches with pivoting heads must be grasped and used properly to prevent an incorrect reading

Rigid Case (Direct Reading)

A rigid case or direct reading torque wrench is equipped with a dial indicator to show torque values. One advantage of these wrenches is that they can be held at any position on the wrench without affecting accuracy. These wrenches are often preferred because they tend to be compact, easy to read and have a great degree of accuracy.

TORQUE ANGLE METERS

Because the frictional characteristics of each fastener or threaded hole will vary, clamp loads which are based strictly on torque will vary as well. In most applications, this variance is not significant enough to cause worry. But, in certain applications, a manufacturer's engineers may determine that more precise clamp loads are necessary (such is the case with many aluminum cylinder heads). In these cases, a torque angle method of installation would be specified. When installing fasteners which are torque angle tightened, a predetermined seating torque and standard torque wrench are usually used first to remove any compliance from the joint. The fastener is then tightened the specified additional portion of a turn measured in degrees. A torque angle gauge (mechanical protractor) is used for these applications.

Standard and Metric Measurements

▶ **See Figure 23**

Throughout this manual, specifications are given to help you determine the condition of various components on your vehicle, or to assist you in their installation. Some of the most common measurements include length (in. or cm/mm), torque (ft. lbs., inch lbs. or Nm) and pressure (psi, in. Hg, kPa or mm Hg). In most cases, we strive to provide the proper measurement as determined by the manufacturer's engineers.

Though, in some cases, that value may not be conveniently measured with what is available in your toolbox. Luckily, many of the measuring devices which are available today will have two scales so the Standard or Metric measurements may easily be taken. If any of the various measuring tools which are available to you do not contain the same scale as listed in the specifications, use the accompanying conversion factors to determine the proper value.

The conversion factor chart is used by taking the given specification and multiplying it by the necessary conversion factor. For instance, looking at the first line, if you have a measurement in inches such as "free-play should be 2 in." but your ruler reads only in millimeters, multiply 2 in. by the conversion factor of 25.4 to get the metric equivalent of 50.8mm. Likewise, if the specification was given only in a Metric measurement, for example in Newton Meters (Nm), then look at the center column first. If the measurement is 100 Nm, multiply it by the conversion factor of 0.738 to get 73.8 ft. lbs.

CONVERSION FACTORS

LENGTH–DISTANCE

Inches (in.)	x 25.4	= Millimeters (mm)	x .0394	= Inches
Feet (ft.)	x .305	= Meters (m)	x 3.281	= Feet
Miles	x 1.609	= Kilometers (km)	x .0621	= Miles

VOLUME

Cubic Inches (in3)	x 16.387	= Cubic Centimeters	x .061	= in3
IMP Pints (IMP pt.)	x .568	= Liters (L)	x 1.76	= IMP pt.
IMP Quarts (IMP qt.)	x 1.137	= Liters (L)	x .88	= IMP qt.
IMP Gallons (IMP gal.)	x 4.546	= Liters (L)	x .22	= IMP gal.
IMP Quarts (IMP qt.)	x 1.201	= US Quarts (US qt.)	x .833	= IMP qt.
IMP Gallons (IMP gal.)	x 1.201	= US Gallons (US gal.)	x .833	= IMP gal.
Fl. Ounces	x 29.573	= Milliliters	x .034	= Ounces
US Pints (US pt.)	x .473	= Liters (L)	x 2.113	= Pints
US Quarts (US qt.)	x .946	= Liters (L)	x 1.057	= Quarts
US Gallons (US gal.)	x 3.785	= Liters (L)	x .264	= Gallons

MASS–WEIGHT

Ounces (oz.)	x 28.35	= Grams (g)	x .035	= Ounces
Pounds (lb.)	x .454	= Kilograms (kg)	x 2.205	= Pounds

PRESSURE

Pounds Per Sq. In. (psi)	x 6.895	= Kilopascals (kPa)	x .145	= psi
Inches of Mercury (Hg)	x .4912	= psi	x 2.036	= Hg
Inches of Mercury (Hg)	x 3.377	= Kilopascals (kPa)	x .2961	= Hg
Inches of Water (H₂O)	x .07355	= Inches of Mercury	x 13.783	= H₂O
Inches of Water (H₂O)	x .03613	= psi	x 27.684	= H₂O
Inches of Water (H₂O)	x .248	= Kilopascals (kPa)	x 4.026	= H₂O

TORQUE

Pounds–Force Inches (in-lb)	x .113	= Newton Meters (N·m)	x 8.85	= in-lb
Pounds–Force Feet (ft-lb)	x 1.356	= Newton Meters (N·m)	x .738	= ft-lb

VELOCITY

Miles Per Hour (MPH)	x 1.609	= Kilometers Per Hour (KPH)	x .621	= MPH

POWER

Horsepower (Hp)	x .745	= Kilowatts	x 1.34	= Horsepower

FUEL CONSUMPTION*

Miles Per Gallon IMP (MPG)	x .354	= Kilometers Per Liter (Km/L)		
Kilometers Per Liter (Km/L)	x 2.352	= IMP MPG		
Miles Per Gallon US (MPG)	x .425	= Kilometers Per Liter (Km/L)		
Kilometers Per Liter (Km/L)	x 2.352	= US MPG		

*It is common to covert from miles per gallon (mpg) to liters/100 kilometers (1/100 km), where mpg (IMP) x 1/100 km = 282 and mpg (US) x 1/100 km = 235.

TEMPERATURE

Degree Fahrenheit (°F) = (°C x 1.8) + 32
Degree Celsius (°C) = (°F − 32) x .56

TCCS1044

Fig. 23 Standard and metric conversion factors chart

SERIAL NUMBER IDENTIFICATION

Vehicle

▶ **See Figures 24 thru 28**

The vehicle identification plate is located on the driver's side door pillar. There are three lines of information on the plate, which consists of arrangements of letters and numbers.

The first line from the top of the warranty number, which is a code that identifies the series of vehicle, the engine, and assembly plant, and the numerical sequence in which the vehicle was built.

The second line of numbers contains codes that identify the wheelbase (inches), color, model code, trim code, body type code, transmission code and the rear axle code.

The third line gives the maximum gross vehicle weight (GVW) inch lbs., the certified net horsepower @ rpm, and the D.S.O. number, which is the district to which the vehicle was delivered and if applicable, specially ordered, factory installed equipment.

A VIN number is also affixed to the top of the dashboard, on the driver's side.

VIN codes prior to 1981 are comprised of 13 digits and letters. The code, beginning in 1981 includes 17 digits and letters.

Additionally, a Vehicle Emission Control Information (VECI) label is found under the hood. This label contains the vehicle's vacuum diagram and tune-up specifications.

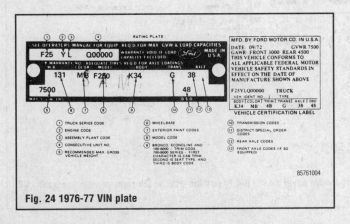

Fig. 24 1976-77 VIN plate

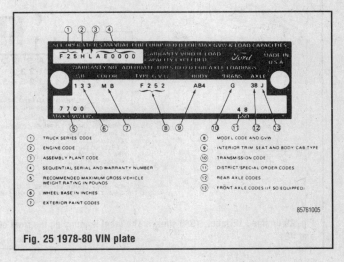

Fig. 25 1978-80 VIN plate

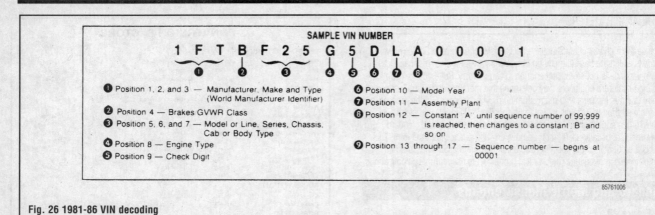

SAMPLE VIN NUMBER

1 F T B F 2 5 G 5 D L A 0 0 0 0 1

① Position 1, 2, and 3 — Manufacturer, Make and Type (World Manufacturer Identifier)

② Position 4 — Brakes/GVWR Class

③ Position 5, 6, and 7 — Model or Line, Series, Chassis, Cab or Body Type

④ Position 8 — Engine Type

⑤ Position 9 — Check Digit

⑥ Position 10 — Model Year

⑦ Position 11 — Assembly Plant

⑧ Position 12 — Constant "A" until sequence number of 99,999 is reached, then changes to a constant "B" and so on

⑨ Position 13 through 17 — Sequence number — begins at 00001

Fig. 26 1981-86 VIN decoding

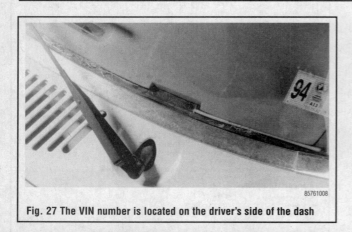

Fig. 27 The VIN number is located on the driver's side of the dash

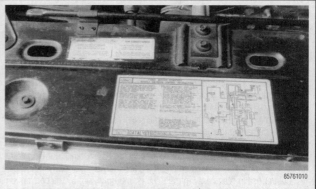

Fig. 28 Vehicle Emission Control Information (VECI) label

Engine

♦ See Figures 29 and 30

The engine identification tag identifies the cubic inch displacement of the engine, the model year, the year and month in which the engine was built, where it was built and the change level number. The change level is usually the number one (1), unless there are parts on the engine that will not be completely interchangeable and will require minor modification.

The engine identification tag is located under the ignition coil attaching bolt on all engines except the diesels. The diesel engine I.D. number is stamped on the front of the block in front of the left cylinder head.

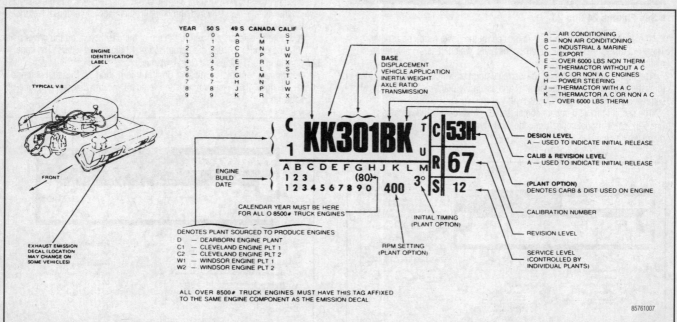

Fig. 29 Engine I.D. label, 1980 shown. The label is found on the front of the valve cover on the 6-4.9L; on the front of the right valve cover on the V6 and V8

ENGINE CODES

Engine	76	77	78	79	80	81	82	83	84–86
V6-232							3	3	
V8-255							D		
6-300	B	B	B	B	E	E	E	9, Y②	Y
6-300HD				K					
V8-302				G	F	F	F	F	F
V8-351W	H	H	H	H	G	W	W	G	G③
V8-351M		H	H	H					
V8-360	Y								
V8-390	H								
V8-400			S	S	S	Z			
V8-420①								1	I
V8-460	A	A	A	A	A			L	L

① International-Harvester built Diesel
② 9 code set up for LP gas
③ 1985–86: H

85761C01

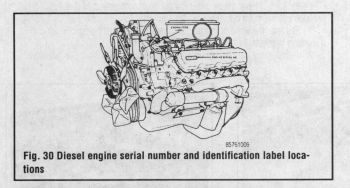

Fig. 30 Diesel engine serial number and identification label locations

Transmission

▶ See Figures 31 and 32

The transmission identification letter is located on a metal tag or plate attached to the case or it is stamped directly on the transmission case.

TRANSMISSION CODE CHART

Code	Description
B (1976–78)	Warner T-85-3 Speed
C	Ford-Manual-3 Speed
D	Warner T-89-3 Speed
E	Warner T-87-3 Speed
F	Warner T-18-4 Speed
A (1976–86)	New Process 435-4 Speed
P	Warner T-19-4 Speed
B (1979–86)	Clark-4 Speed O.D.
G	Automatic C4
W	Automatic C5
P	Automatic C6 thru 1977
K	Automatic C6 1978–86
J	Automatic FMX
T	Automatic Overdrive

85761C02

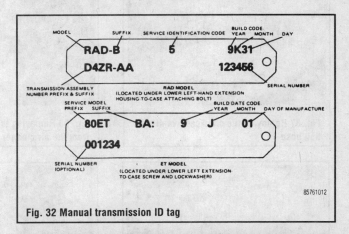

Fig. 31 Automatic transmission ID tag; C4 shown

Fig. 32 Manual transmission ID tag

Drive Axle

The drive axle code is found stamped on a flat surface on the axle tube, next to the differential housing, or, on a tag secured by one of the differential housing cover bolts.

ROUTINE MAINTENANCE

→All maintenance procedures included in this section refer to both gasoline and diesel engines except where noted.

Air Cleaner

The standard air cleaner on carbureted engines is a paper element type, with an oil bath air cleaner available as an option on some engines.

The paper cartridge should be replaced according to the Preventive Maintenance Schedule at the end of this section.

→Check the air filter more often if the vehicle is operated under severe dusty conditions and replace or clean it as necessary.

REMOVAL & INSTALLATION

Carbureted Engines with a Paper Element

♦ See Figures 34 thru 42

1. Open the engine compartment hood.
2. Remove the wing nut holding the air cleaner assembly to the top of the carburetor.
3. Disconnect the crankcase ventilation hose at the air cleaner and remove the entire air cleaner assembly from the carburetor.

4. Remove and discard the old filter element, and inspect the condition of the air cleaner mounting gasket. Replace the gasket as necessary.

→A crankcase ventilation filter or breather element is located in the side of the air cleaner body. The filter should be replaced rather than cleaned. Simply pull the old filter out of the body every 20,000 miles (or more frequently if the vehicle has been used in extremely dusty conditions) and push a new filter into place.

5. Install the air cleaner body on the carburetor so that the word **FRONT** faces toward the front of the vehicle.
6. Place the new filter element in the air cleaner body and install the cover and tighten the wing nut. If the word **TOP** appears on the element, make sure that the side that the word appears on is facing up when the element is in place.
7. Connect the crankcase ventilation hose to the air cleaner.

Carbureted Engines with an Oil Bath Element

♦ See Figure 43

Periodically, check the oil reservoir for an accumulation of dirt. Also, check the element mesh for a buildup of dirt and other foreign particles.

1. Remove the wing nuts that hold the air cleaner to the carburetor and mounting brackets. Lift the assembly from the engine.
2. Remove the air cleaner cover and drain the old oil from the reservoir.

Fig. 34 Removing the wing nut from the air cleaner

Fig. 35 Removing the top vacuum hoses from the air cleaner

Fig. 36 Removing the air filter element

Fig. 37 Removing the crankcase ventilation hose

Fig. 38 Removing the side vacuum hoses from the air cleaner

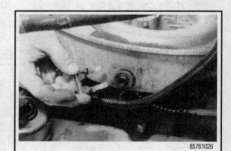
Fig. 39 Removing retaining clip for the breather element

Fig. 40 Removing felt washer from the breather element

Fig. 41 Removing the breather element

Fig. 42 Removing the air cleaner assembly

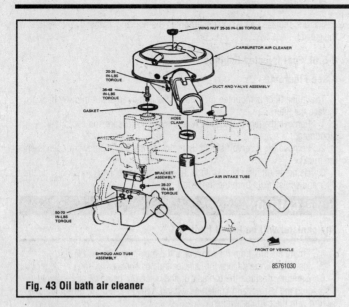

Fig. 43 Oil bath air cleaner

3. Clean all parts in a safe, non-flammable solvent and rinse them thoroughly with clean water. Dispose of all old oil and oily water properly.

4. Dry all parts thoroughly with compressed air, or allow them to air dry completely.

5. Inspect the gasket. If it is at all questionable, replace it.

6. Saturate the mesh element in clean engine oil. The best way is to immerse it in an oil-filled tub.

7. Fill the reservoir to the FULL mark with clean engine oil. The best oil to use is determined by the temperature. Above 32 degrees F, (0 deg. C) use SAE 30W; below 32 deg. F, use SAE 20W.

8. When you're all done, replace the assembly on the engine.

8-5.0L EFI Engine

♦ See Figure 44

1. Loosen the two clamps that secure the hose assembly to the air cleaner.
2. Remove the two screws that attach the air cleaner to the bracket.
3. Disconnect the hose and inlet tube from the air cleaner.
4. Remove the screws attaching the air cleaner cover.
5. Remove the air filter and tubes.
6. Installation is the reverse of removal. Don't overtighten the hose clamps! A torque of 12-15 in. lb. is sufficient.

Diesel Engines

1. Open the engine compartment hood.
2. Remove the wing nut holding the air cleaner assembly.
3. Remove and discard the old filter element, and inspect the condition of the air cleaner mounting gasket. Replace the gasket as necessary.

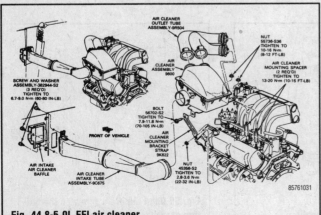

Fig. 44 8-5.0L EFI air cleaner

4. Place the new filter element in the air cleaner body and install the cover and tighten the wing nut.

Fuel Filter

REMOVAL & INSTALLATION

❊❊ CAUTION

NEVER SMOKE WHEN WORKING AROUND OR NEAR GASOLINE! MAKE SURE THAT THERE IS NO IGNITION SOURCE NEAR YOUR WORK AREA!

Carburetor Mounted Filters

♦ See Figures 45 and 46

Several different types of carbureted-mounted filters are used. Some filters screw into the float chamber with a rubber fuel line sliding onto the nipple on the filter. Others screw into the float chamber and a steel fuel line screws into the filter. The Holley 4180 carburetor has a small filter element, sometimes bronze; sometimes paper, which is located behind the float chamber inlet nut. Replacement of these filters is to be performed on a COLD engine only.

1. Wait until the engine is cold. Disconnect the negative battery cable.
2. Remove the air cleaner assembly.
3. Place some absorbent rags under the filter or float chamber inlet nut.
4. On those so equipped, remove the hose clamp and slide the rubber hose from the filter, then unscrew the filter from the bowl. Or, hold the filter with one wrench while unscrewing the fuel line from the filter with another, then, unscrew the filter from the bowl. Or, on the 4180, using 2 wrenches, disconnect the fuel line from the fuel inlet nut, then, unscrew the inlet nut and remove the gaskets, filter element and spring from the bowl.

❊❊ CAUTION

It is possible for gasoline to spray in all directions when disconnecting the fuel line! For this reason, wearing eye protection is recommended during this procedure.

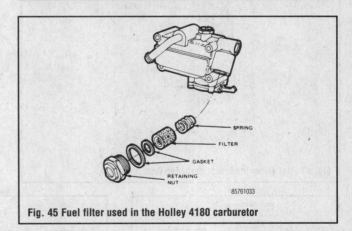

Fig. 45 Fuel filter used in the Holley 4180 carburetor

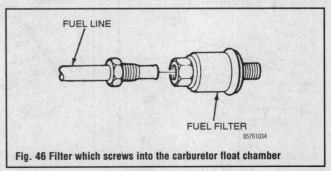

Fig. 46 Filter which screws into the carburetor float chamber

5. Coat the threads of the new filter, or the inlet nut, with non-hardening, gasoline-proof sealer, or, use Teflon tape on the threads, and screw it into place by hand. Tighten it snugly with the wrench.

✳✳ WARNING

Do not overtighten the filter! The threads in the carburetor bowl are soft metal and are easily stripped! You DON'T want to damage these threads!!

6. Connect the hose or fuel line to the new filter or inlet nut. Most replacement filters come with a new hose and clamps. Use them.
7. Remove the fuel-soaked rags, wipe up any spilled fuel and start the engine. Check the filter connections for leaks.

Fuel Pump Mounted Cartridge Type Filter

▶ **See Figure 47**

The 8-360 and 8-390 engines, and some 6-300 engines used a fuel pump mounted filter. The filter element is found inside a screw-on housing. To replace the filter, simply unscrew the housing, discard the fuel, filter and

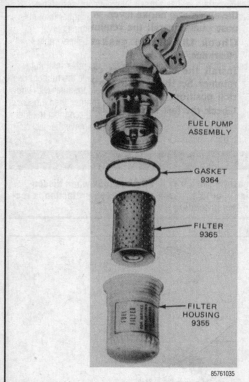

Fig. 47 Fuel pump mounted, cartridge type fuel filter

gasket and replace them. Don't overtighten the housing as that would distort the gasket.

8-5.0L Fuel Injected Engines

▶ **See Figure 48**

The inline filter is mounted on the left side frame rail about midway back. To replace the filter:
1. Remove the fuel tank cap to relieve system pressure and avoid fuel siphoning.
2. Remove the reservoir shield by removing the 3 or 4 screws (depends on the truck).
3. Using an oil filter type wrench, unscrew the lower reservoir and slide the filter and canister out from the frame rail.

✳✳ CAUTION

The canister will be full of fuel!

4. Empty the fuel from the canister and remove the filter and O-ring.
5. Install a new cartridge in the canister and position a new O-ring in the groove.
6. Carefully position the canister on the reservoir, being careful to avoid dislodging the O-ring, and tighten it by hand. When hand tight, give it another ⅙ turn with the oil filter wrench.

➡**The rubber grommet on the cartridge will seat on the housing stud as the O-ring is compressed.**

Diesel Engines

▶ **See Figure 49**

The diesel engine uses a one-piece spin-on fuel filter. Do not add fuel to the new fuel filter. Allow the engine to draw fuel through the filter.
1. Remove the spin-on filter by unscrewing it counterclockwise with your hands or a strap wrench.
2. Clean the filter mounting surface.
3. Coat the gasket or the replacement filter with clean diesel fuel. This helps ensure a good seal.
4. Tighten the filter by hand until the gasket touches the filter mounting surface.
5. Tighten the filter an additional ½ turn.

➡**After changing the fuel filter, the engine will purge the trapped air as it runs. The engine may run roughly and smoke excessively until the air is cleared from the system.**

Fuel/Water Separator

REMOVAL & INSTALLATION

▶ **See Figure 50**

The diesel engine is equipped with a fuel/water separator in the fuel supply line. A Water in Fuel indicator light is provided on the instrument panel to alert the driver. The light should glow when the ignition switch is in the Start position

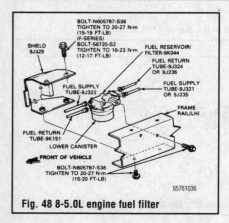

Fig. 48 8-5.0L engine fuel filter

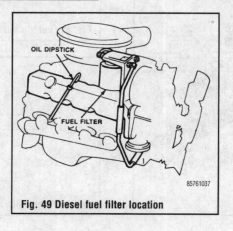

Fig. 49 Diesel fuel filter location

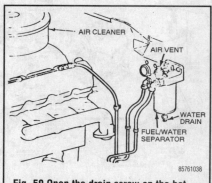

Fig. 50 Open the drain screw on the bottom of the water separator to drain

to indicate proper light and water sensor function. If the light glows continuously while the engine is running, the water must be drained from the separator as soon as possible to prevent damage to the fuel injection system.

1. Shut off the engine. Failure to shut the engine off before draining the separator will cause air to enter the system.

2. Unscrew the vent on the top center of the separator unit 2½ to 3 turns.

3. Unscrew the drain screw on the bottom of the separator 1½ to 2 turns and drain the water into an appropriate container.

4. After the water is completely drained, close the water drain fingertight.

5. Tighten the vent until snug, then turn it an additional ¼ turn.

6. Start the engine and check the Water in Fuel indicator light; it should not be lit. If it is lit and continues to stay so, there is a problem somewhere else in the fuel system.

→All but very early production models have a drain hose connected to separator which allows water to drain directly into a container placed underneath the vehicle.

PCV Valve

REMOVAL & INSTALLATION

♦ See Figures 51 and 52

Check the PCV valve according to the Preventive Maintenance Schedule at the end of this section to see if it is free and not gummed up, stuck or blocked. To check the valve, remove it from the engine and work the valve by sticking a screwdriver in the crankcase side of the valve. It should move. It is possible to clean the PCV valve by soaking it in a solvent and blowing it out with compressed air. This can restore the valve to some level of operating order. This should be used only as an emergency measure. Otherwise the valve should be replaced.

Evaporative Canister

REMOVAL & INSTALLATION

♦ See Figure 53

The fuel evaporative emission control canister should be inspected for damage or leaks at the hose fittings every 24,000 miles. Repair or replace any old or

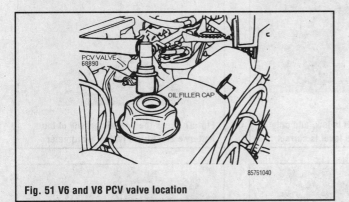

Fig. 51 V6 and V8 PCV valve location

cracked hoses. Replace the canister if it is damaged in any way. The canister is located under the hood, to the right of the engine. For more detailed canister service, see Section 4.

Battery

PRECAUTIONS

Always use caution when working on or near the battery. Never allow a tool to bridge the gap between the negative and positive battery terminals. Also, be careful not to allow a tool to provide a ground between the positive cable/terminal and any metal component on the vehicle. Either of these conditions will cause a short circuit, leading to sparks and possible personal injury.

Do not smoke or all open flames/sparks near a battery; the gases contained in the battery are very explosive and, if ignited, could cause severe injury or death.

All batteries, regardless of type, should be carefully secured by a battery hold-down device. If not, the terminals or casing may crack from stress during vehicle operation. A battery which is not secured may allow acid to leak, making it discharge faster. The acid can also eat away at components under the hood.

Always inspect the battery case for cracks, leakage and corrosion. A white corrosive substance on the battery case or on nearby components would indicate a leaking or cracked battery. If the battery is cracked, it should be replaced immediately.

GENERAL MAINTENANCE

Always keep the battery cables and terminals free of corrosion. Check and clean these components about once a year.

Keep the top of the battery clean, as a film of dirt can help discharge a battery that is not used for long periods. A solution of baking soda and water may be used for cleaning, but be careful to flush this off with clear water. DO NOT let any of the solution into the filler holes. Baking soda neutralizes battery acid and will de-activate a battery cell.

Batteries in vehicles which are not operated on a regular basis can fall victim to parasitic loads (small current drains which are constantly drawing current from the battery). Normal parasitic loads may drain a battery on a vehicle that is in storage and not used for 6–8 weeks. Vehicles that have additional accessories such as a phone or an alarm system may discharge a battery sooner. If the vehicle is to be stored for longer periods in a secure area and the alarm system is not necessary, the negative battery cable should be disconnected to protect the battery.

Remember that constantly deep cycling a battery (completely discharging and recharging it) will shorten battery life.

BATTERY FLUID

♦ See Figure 54

Check the battery electrolyte level at least once a month, or more often in hot weather or during periods of extended vehicle operation. On non-sealed batteries, the level can be checked either through the case (if translucent) or by removing the cell caps. The electrolyte level in each cell should be kept filled to the split ring inside each cell, or the line marked on the outside of the case.

If the level is low, add only distilled water through the opening until the level is correct. Each cell must be checked and filled individually. Distilled water

Fig. 52 Removing the PCV valve

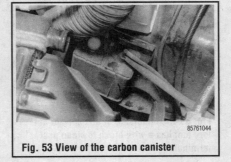

Fig. 53 View of the carbon canister

Fig. 54 Maintenance-free batteries usually contain a built-in hydrometer to check fluid level

should be used, because the chemicals and minerals found in most drinking water are harmful to the battery and could significantly shorten its life.

If water is added in freezing weather, the vehicle should be driven several miles to allow the water to mix with the electrolyte. Otherwise, the battery could freeze.

Although some maintenance-free batteries have removable cell caps, the electrolyte condition and level on all sealed maintenance-free batteries must be checked using the built-in hydrometer "eye." The exact type of eye will vary. But, most battery manufacturers, apply a sticker to the battery itself explaining the readings.

➡ **Although the readings from built-in hydrometers will vary, a green eye usually indicates a properly charged battery with sufficient fluid level. A dark eye is normally an indicator of a battery with sufficient fluid, but which is low in charge. A light or yellow eye usually indicates that electrolyte has dropped below the necessary level. In this last case, sealed batteries with an insufficient electrolyte must usually be discarded.**

Checking the Specific Gravity

♦ **See Figures 55, 56 and 57**

A hydrometer is required to check the specific gravity on all batteries that are not maintenance-free. On batteries that are maintenance-free, the specific gravity is checked by observing the built-in hydrometer "eye" on the top of the battery case.

☀ CAUTION

Battery electrolyte contains sulfuric acid. If you should splash any on your skin or in your eyes, flush the affected area with plenty of clear water. If it lands in your eyes, get medical help immediately.

The fluid (sulfuric acid solution) contained in the battery cells will tell you many things about the condition of the battery. Because the cell plates must be kept submerged below the fluid level in order to operate, the fluid level is extremely important. And, because the specific gravity of the acid is an indication of electrical charge, testing the fluid can be an aid in determining if the battery must be replaced. A battery in a vehicle with a properly operating charging system should require little maintenance, but careful, periodic inspection should reveal problems before they leave you stranded.

At least once a year, check the specific gravity of the battery. It should be between 1.20 and 1.26 on the gravity scale. Most auto stores carry a variety of inexpensive battery hydrometers. These can be used on any non-sealed battery to test the specific gravity in each cell.

The battery testing hydrometer has a squeeze bulb at one end and a nozzle at the other. Battery electrolyte is sucked into the hydrometer until the float is lifted from its seat. The specific gravity is then read by noting the position of the float. If gravity is low in one or more cells, the battery should be slowly charged and checked again to see if the gravity has come up. Generally, if after charging, the specific gravity between any two cells varies more than 50 points (0.50), the battery should be replaced, as it can no longer produce sufficient voltage to guarantee proper operation.

CABLES

♦ **See Figures 58, 59, 60 and 61**

Once a year (or as necessary), the battery terminals and the cable clamps should be cleaned. Loosen the clamps and remove the cables, negative cable first. On top post batteries, the use of a puller specially made for this purpose is recommended. These are inexpensive and available in most parts stores. Side terminal battery cables are secured with a small bolt.

Clean the cable clamps and the battery terminal with a wire brush, until all corrosion, grease, etc., is removed and the metal is shiny. It is especially important to clean the inside of the clamp thoroughly (an old knife is useful here), since a small deposit of oxidation there will prevent a sound connection and inhibit starting or charging. Special tools are available for cleaning these parts, one type for conventional top post batteries and another type for side terminal batteries. It is also a good idea to apply some dielectric grease to the terminal, as this will aid in the prevention of corrosion.

After the clamps and terminals are clean, reinstall the cables, negative cable last; DO NOT hammer the clamps onto battery posts. Tighten the clamps

Fig. 55 On non-sealed batteries, the fluid level can be checked by removing the cell caps

Fig. 56 If the fluid level is low, add only distilled water until the level is correct

Fig. 57 Check the specific gravity of the battery's electrolyte with a hydrometer

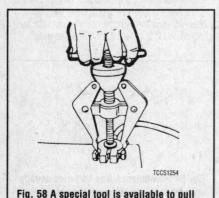

Fig. 58 A special tool is available to pull the clamp from the post

Fig. 59 The underside of this special battery tool has a wire brush to clean post terminals

Fig. 60 Place the tool over the battery posts and twist to clean until the metal is shiny

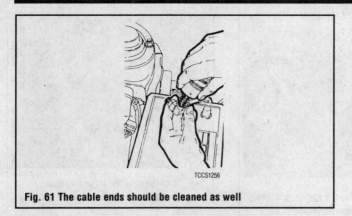

Fig. 61 The cable ends should be cleaned as well

securely, but do not distort them. Give the clamps and terminals a thin external coating of grease after installation, to retard corrosion.

Check the cables at the same time that the terminals are cleaned. If the cable insulation is cracked or broken, or if the ends are frayed, the cable should be replaced with a new cable of the same length and gauge.

CHARGING

> ⁂ **CAUTION**
>
> The chemical reaction which takes place in all batteries generates explosive hydrogen gas. A spark can cause the battery to explode and splash acid. To avoid personal injury, be sure there is proper ventilation and take appropriate fire safety precautions when working with or near a battery.

A battery should be charged at a slow rate to keep the plates inside from getting too hot. However, if some maintenance-free batteries are allowed to discharge until they are almost "dead," they may have to be charged at a high rate to bring them back to "life." Always follow the charger manufacturer's instructions on charging the battery.

REPLACEMENT

When it becomes necessary to replace the battery, select one with an amperage rating equal to or greater than the battery originally installed. Deterioration and just plain aging of the battery cables, starter motor, and associated wires makes the battery's job harder in successive years. This makes it prudent to install a new battery with a greater capacity than the old.

Belts

INSPECTION

▶ **See Figures 62, 63, 64, 65 and 66**

Inspect the belts for signs of glazing or cracking. A glazed belt will be perfectly smooth from slippage, while a good belt will have a slight texture of fabric visible. Cracks will usually start at the inner edge of the belt and run outward. All worn or damaged drive belts should be replaced immediately. It is best to replace all drive belts at one time, as a preventive maintenance measure, during this service operation.

ADJUSTMENTS

▶ **See Figures 67 thru 72**

Alternator Belt

1. Holding the alternator in place to maintain tension, tighten the adjusting arm bolt. Recheck the belt tension. When the belt is properly tensioned, tighten the alternator mounting bolt.

Power Steering Drive Belt

6-300 (4.9L)

1. Hold a ruler perpendicularly to the drive belt at its longest run, test the tightness of the belt by pressing it firmly with your thumb. The deflection should not exceed ¼ inch.

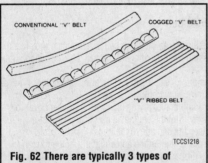

Fig. 62 There are typically 3 types of accessory drive belts found on vehicles today

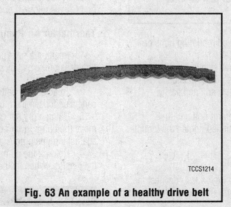

Fig. 63 An example of a healthy drive belt

Fig. 64 Deep cracks in this belt will cause flex, building up heat that will eventually lead to belt failure

Fig. 65 The cover of this belt is worn, exposing the critical reinforcing cords to excessive wear

Fig. 66 Installing too wide a belt can result in serious belt wear and/or breakage

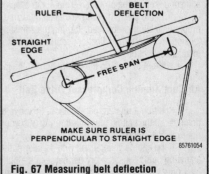

Fig. 67 Measuring belt deflection

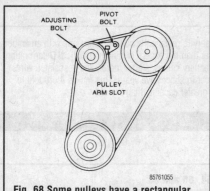

Fig. 68 Some pulleys have a rectangular slot to aid in adjusting the belt

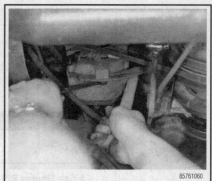

Fig. 69 On some V8s, it's easier to access the adjusting bolt from underneath

Fig. 70 Loosening the adjusting and mounting bolts on 1983-86 power steering pumps

Fig. 71 Adjusting the air conditioning compressor belt on later model trucks

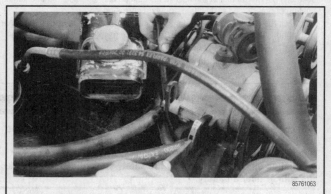

Fig. 72 Adjusting the Thermactor® pump belt

2. To adjust the belt tension, loosen the adjusting and mounting bolts on the front face of the steering pump cover plate (hub side).

3. Using a pry bar or broom handle on the pump hub, move the power steering pump toward or away from the engine until the proper tension is reached. Do not pry against the reservoir as it is relatively soft and easily deformed.

4. Holding the pump in place, tighten the adjusting arm bolt and then recheck the belt tension. When the belt is properly tensioned tighten the mounting bolts.

V8 ENGINE

1. Position a ruler perpendicular to the drive belt at its longest run. Test the tightness of the belt by pressing it firmly with your thumb. The deflection should be about ¼ inch.

2. To adjust the belt tension, loosen the three bolts in the three elongated adjusting slots at the power steering pump attaching bracket.

3. Turn the steering pump drive belt adjusting nut as required until the proper deflection is obtained. Turning the adjusting nut clockwise will increase tension and decrease deflection; counterclockwise will decrease tension and increase deflection.

4. Without disturbing the pump, tighten the three attaching bolts.

Air Conditioning Compressor Drive Belt

1. Position a ruler perpendicular to the drive belt at its longest run. Test the tightness of the belt by pressing it firmly with your thumb. The deflection should not exceed ¼ inch.

2. If the engine is equipped with an idler pulley, loosen the idler pulley adjusting bolt(s), insert a pry bar between the pulley and the engine (or in the idler pulley adjusting slot), and adjust the tension accordingly. If the engine is

not equipped with an idler pulley, the alternator must be moved to accomplish this adjustment, as outlined under Alternator (Fan Drive) Belt.

3. When the proper tension is reached, tighten the idler pulley adjusting bolt (if so equipped) or the alternator adjusting and mounting bolts.

Thermactor Air Pump Drive Belt

1. Position a ruler perpendicular to the drive belt at its longest run. Test the tightness of the belt by pressing it firmly with your thumb. The deflection should be about ¼ inch.

2. To adjust the belt tension, loosen the adjusting arm bolt slightly. If necessary, also loosen the mounting belt slightly.

3. Using a pry bar or broom handle, pry against the pump rear cover to move the pump toward or away from the engine as necessary. Do not pry against the pump housing itself, as damage to the housing may result.

4. Holding the pump in place, tighten the adjusting arm bolt and recheck the tension. When the belt is properly tensioned, tighten the mounting bolt.

Hoses

▶ See Figures 73, 74, 75 and 76

✳✳ CAUTION

On models equipped with an electric cooling fan, disconnect the negative battery cable, or fan motor wiring harness connector before replacing any radiator/heater hose. The fan may come on, under certain circumstances, even though the ignition is Off.

Inspect the condition of the radiator and heater hoses periodically. Early spring and at the beginning of the fall or winter, when you are performing other maintenance, are good times. Make sure the engine and cooling system are cold. Visually inspect for cracking, rotting or collapsed hoses, replace as necessary. Run your hand along the length of the hose. If a weak or swollen spot is noted when squeezing the hose wall, replace the hose.

Fig. 73 The cracks developing along this hose are a result of age-related hardening

Fig. 74 A hose clamp that is too tight can cause older hoses to separate and tear on either side of the clamp

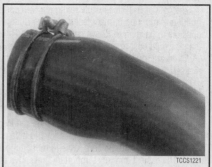

Fig. 75 A soft spongy hose (identifiable by the swollen section) will eventually burst and should be replaced

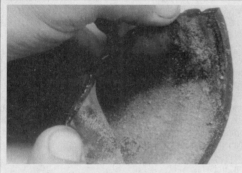

Fig. 76 Hoses are likely to deteriorate from the inside if the cooling system is not periodically flushed

REMOVAL & INSTALLATION

▶ See Figure 77

1. Drain the cooling system into a suitable container (if the coolant is to be reused).

✳✳ CAUTION

When draining the coolant, keep in mind that cats and dogs are attracted by the ethylene glycol antifreeze, and are quite likely to drink any that is left in an uncovered container or in puddles on the ground. This will prove fatal in sufficient quantity. Always drain the coolant into a sealable container. Coolant should be reused unless it is contaminated or several years old.

2. Loosen the hose clamps at each end of the hose that requires replacement.
3. Twist, pull and slide the hose off the radiator, water pump, thermostat or heater connection.

Fig. 77 Removing the upper radiator hose

4. Clean the hose mounting connections. Position the hose clamps on the new hose.
5. Coat the connection surfaces with a water resistant sealer and slide the hose into position. Make sure the hose clamps are located beyond the raised bead of the connector (if equipped) and centered in the clamping area of the connection.
6. Tighten the clamps to 20-30 inch lbs. Do not overtighten.
7. Fill the cooling system.
8. Start the engine and allow it to reach normal operating temperature. Check for leaks.

Air Conditioning System

SYSTEM SERVICE & REPAIR

➡ **It is recommended that the A/C system be serviced by an EPA Section 609 certified automotive technician utilizing a refrigerant recovery/recycling machine.**

The do-it-yourselfer should not service his/her own vehicle's A/C system for many reasons, including legal concerns, personal injury, environmental damage and cost.

According to the U.S. Clean Air Act, it is a federal crime to service or repair (involving the refrigerant) a Motor Vehicle Air Conditioning (MVAC) system for money without being EPA certified. It is also illegal to vent R-12 and R-134a refrigerants into the atmosphere. State and/or local laws may be more strict than the federal regulations, so be sure to check with your state and/or local authorities for further information.

➡ **Federal law dictates that a fine of up to $25,000 may be levied on people convicted of venting refrigerant into the atmosphere.**

When servicing an A/C system you run the risk of handling or coming in contact with refrigerant, which may result in skin or eye irritation or frostbite. Although low in toxicity (due to chemical stability), inhalation of concentrated refrigerant fumes is dangerous and can result in death; cases of fatal cardiac arrhythmia have been reported in people accidentally subjected to high levels of refrigerant. Some early symptoms include loss of concentration and drowsiness.

➡ **Generally, the limit for exposure is lower for R-134a than it is for R-12. Exceptional care must be practiced when handling R-134a.**

Also, some refrigerants can decompose at high temperatures (near gas heaters or open flame), which may result in hydrofluoric acid, hydrochloric acid and phosgene (a fatal nerve gas).

It is usually more economically feasible to have a certified MVAC automotive technician perform A/C system service on your vehicle.

R-12 Refrigerant Conversion

If your vehicle still uses R-12 refrigerant, one way to save A/C system costs down the road is to investigate the possibility of having your system converted to R-134a. The older R-12 systems can be easily converted to R-134a refrigerant by a certified automotive technician by installing a few new components and changing the system oil.

The cost of R-12 is steadily rising and will continue to increase, because it is no longer imported or manufactured in the United States. Therefore, it is often possible to have an R-12 system converted to R-134a and recharged for less than it would cost to just charge the system with R-12.

If you are interested in having your system converted, contact local automotive service stations for more details and information.

PREVENTIVE MAINTENANCE

Although the A/C system should not be serviced by the do-it-yourselfer, preventive maintenance should be practiced to help maintain the efficiency of the vehicle's A/C system. Be sure to perform the following:

• The easiest and most important preventive maintenance for your A/C system is to be sure that it is used on a regular basis. Running the system for five minutes each month (no matter what the season) will help ensure that the seals and all internal components remain lubricated.

➡**Some vehicles automatically operate the A/C system compressor whenever the windshield defroster is activated. Therefore, the A/C system would not need to be operated each month if the defroster was used.**

• In order to prevent heater core freeze-up during A/C operation, it is necessary to maintain proper antifreeze protection. Be sure to properly maintain the engine cooling system.

• Any obstruction of or damage to the condenser configuration will restrict air flow which is essential to its efficient operation. Keep this unit clean and in proper physical shape.

➡**Bug screens which are mounted in front of the condenser (unless they are original equipment) are regarded as obstructions.**

• The condensation drain tube expels any water which accumulates on the bottom of the evaporator housing into the engine compartment. If this tube is obstructed, the air conditioning performance can be restricted and condensation buildup can spill over onto the vehicle's floor.

SYSTEM INSPECTION

Although the A/C system should not be serviced by the do-it-yourselfer, system inspections should be performed to help maintain the efficiency of the vehicle's A/C system. Be sure to perform the following:

The easiest and often most important check for the air conditioning system consists of a visual inspection of the system components. Visually inspect the system for refrigerant leaks, damaged compressor clutch, abnormal compressor drive belt tension and/or condition, plugged evaporator drain tube, blocked condenser fins, disconnected or broken wires, blown fuses, corroded connections and poor insulation.

A refrigerant leak will usually appear as an oily residue at the leakage point in the system. The oily residue soon picks up dust or dirt particles from the surrounding air and appears greasy. Through time, this will build up and appear to be a heavy dirt impregnated grease.

For a thorough visual and operational inspection, check the following:

• Check the surface of the radiator and condenser for dirt, leaves or other material which might block air flow.

• Check for kinks in hoses and lines. Check the system for leaks.
• Make sure the drive belt is properly tensioned. During operation, make sure the belt is free of noise or slippage.
• Make sure the blower motor operates at all appropriate positions, then check for distribution of the air from all outlets.

➡**Remember that in high humidity, air discharged from the vents may not feel as cold as expected, even if the system is working properly. This is because moisture in humid air retains heat more effectively than dry air, thereby making humid air more difficult to cool.**

Windshield Wipers

ELEMENT (REFILL) CARE & REPLACEMENT

◆ **See Figures 78, 79 and 80**

For maximum effectiveness and longest element life, the windshield and wiper blades should be kept clean. Dirt, tree sap, road tar and so on will cause streaking, smearing and blade deterioration if left on the glass. It is advisable to wash the windshield carefully with a commercial glass cleaner at least once a month. Wipe off the rubber blades with the wet rag afterwards. Do not attempt to move wipers across the windshield by hand; damage to the motor and drive mechanism will result.

To inspect and/or replace the wiper blade elements, place the wiper switch in the **LOW** speed position and the ignition switch in the **ACC** position. When the wiper blades are approximately vertical on the windshield, turn the ignition switch to **OFF**.

Examine the wiper blade elements. If they are found to be cracked, broken or torn, they should be replaced immediately. Replacement intervals will vary with usage, although ozone deterioration usually limits element life to about one year. If the wiper pattern is smeared or streaked, or if the blade chatters across the glass, the elements should be replaced. It is easiest and most sensible to replace the elements in pairs.

If your vehicle is equipped with aftermarket blades, there are several different types of refills and your vehicle might have any kind. Aftermarket blades and arms rarely use the exact same type blade or refill as the original equipment.

Regardless of the type of refill used, be sure to follow the part manufacturer's instructions closely. Make sure that all of the frame jaws are engaged as the refill is pushed into place and locked. If the metal blade holder and frame are allowed to touch the glass during wiper operation, the glass will be scratched.

Tires and Wheels

Common sense and good driving habits will afford maximum tire life. Make sure that you don't overload the vehicle or run with incorrect pressure in the tires. Either of these will increase tread wear. Fast starts, sudden stops and sharp cornering are hard on tires and will shorten their useful life span.

➡**For optimum tire life, keep the tires properly inflated, rotate them often and have the wheel alignment checked periodically.**

Inspect your tires frequently. Be especially careful to watch for bubbles in the tread or sidewall, deep cuts or underinflation. Replace any tires with bubbles in

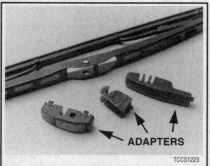

TCCS1223

Fig. 78 Most aftermarket blades are available with multiple adapters to fit different vehicles

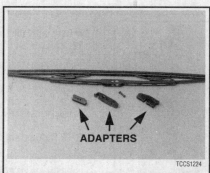

TCCS1224

Fig. 79 Choose a blade which will fit your vehicle, and that will be readily available next time you need blades

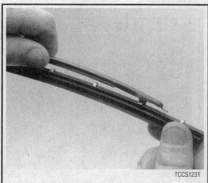

TCCS1231

Fig. 80 When installed, be certain the blade is fully inserted into the backing

the sidewall. If cuts are so deep that they penetrate to the cords, discard the tire. Any cut in the sidewall of a radial tire renders it unsafe. Also look for uneven tread wear patterns that may indicate the front end is out of alignment or that the tires are out of balance.

TIRE ROTATION

▶ **See Figure 81**

Tires must be rotated periodically to equalize wear patterns that vary with a tire's position on the vehicle. Tires will also wear in an uneven way as the front steering/suspension system wears to the point where the alignment should be reset.

Rotating the tires will ensure maximum life for the tires as a set, so you will not have to discard a tire early due to wear on only part of the tread. Regular rotation is required to equalize wear.

When rotating "unidirectional tires," make sure that they always roll in the same direction. This means that a tire used on the left side of the vehicle must not be switched to the right side and vice-versa. Such tires should only be rotated front-to-rear or rear-to-front, while always remaining on the same side of the vehicle. These tires are marked on the sidewall as to the direction of rotation; observe the marks when reinstalling the tire(s).

Some styled or "mag" wheels may have different offsets front to rear. In these cases, the rear wheels must not be used up front and vice-versa. Furthermore, if these wheels are equipped with unidirectional tires, they cannot be rotated unless the tire is remounted for the proper direction of rotation.

➡**The compact or space-saver spare is strictly for emergency use. It must never be included in the tire rotation or placed on the vehicle for everyday use.**

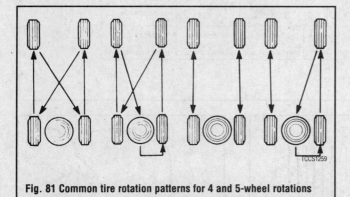

Fig. 81 Common tire rotation patterns for 4 and 5-wheel rotations

TIRE DESIGN

▶ **See Figure 82**

For maximum satisfaction, tires should be used in sets of four. Mixing of different brands or types (radial, bias-belted, fiberglass belted) should be avoided. In most cases, the vehicle manufacturer has designated a type of tire on which the vehicle will perform best. Your first choice when replacing tires should be to use the same type of tire that the manufacturer recommends.

When radial tires are used, tire sizes and wheel diameters should be selected to maintain ground clearance and tire load capacity equivalent to the original specified tire. Radial tires should always be used in sets of four.

✳ CAUTION

Radial tires should never be used on only the front axle.

When selecting tires, pay attention to the original size as marked on the tire. Most tires are described using an industry size code sometimes referred to as P-Metric. This allows the exact identification of the tire specifications, regardless of the manufacturer. If selecting a different tire size or brand, remember to check the installed tire for any sign of interference with the body or suspension while the vehicle is stopping, turning sharply or heavily loaded.

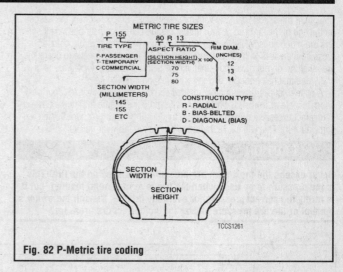

Fig. 82 P-Metric tire coding

Snow Tires

Good radial tires can produce a big advantage in slippery weather, but in snow, a street radial tire does not have sufficient tread to provide traction and control. The small grooves of a street tire quickly pack with snow and the tire behaves like a billiard ball on a marble floor. The more open, chunky tread of a snow tire will self-clean as the tire turns, providing much better grip on snowy surfaces.

To satisfy municipalities requiring snow tires during weather emergencies, most snow tires carry either an M + S designation after the tire size stamped on the sidewall, or the designation "all-season." In general, no change in tire size is necessary when buying snow tires.

Most manufacturers strongly recommend the use of 4 snow tires on their vehicles for reasons of stability. If snow tires are fitted only to the drive wheels, the opposite end of the vehicle may become very unstable when braking or turning on slippery surfaces. This instability can lead to unpleasant endings if the driver can't counteract the slide in time.

Note that snow tires, whether 2 or 4, will affect vehicle handling in all non-snow situations. The stiffer, heavier snow tires will noticeably change the turning and braking characteristics of the vehicle. Once the snow tires are installed, you must re-learn the behavior of the vehicle and drive accordingly.

➡**Consider buying extra wheels on which to mount the snow tires. Once done, the "snow wheels" can be installed and removed as needed. This eliminates the potential damage to tires or wheels from seasonal removal and installation. Even if your vehicle has styled wheels, see if inexpensive steel wheels are available. Although the look of the vehicle will change, the expensive wheels will be protected from salt, curb hits and pothole damage.**

TIRE STORAGE

If they are mounted on wheels, store the tires at proper inflation pressure. All tires should be kept in a cool, dry place. If they are stored in the garage or basement, do not let them stand on a concrete floor; set them on strips of wood, a mat or a large stack of newspaper. Keeping them away from direct moisture is of paramount importance. Tires should not be stored upright, but in a flat position.

INFLATION & INSPECTION

▶ **See Figures 83 thru 88**

The importance of proper tire inflation cannot be overemphasized. A tire employs air as part of its structure. It is designed around the supporting strength of the air at a specified pressure. For this reason, improper inflation drastically reduces the tire's ability to perform as intended. A tire will lose some air in day-to-day use; having to add a few pounds of air periodically is not necessarily a sign of a leaking tire.

Two items should be a permanent fixture in every glove compartment: an accurate tire pressure gauge and a tread depth gauge. Check the tire pressure (including the spare) regularly with a pocket type gauge. Too often, the gauge on the end of the air hose at your corner garage is not accurate because it suffers too much abuse. Always check tire pressure when the tires are cold, as pressure increases with temperature. If you must move the vehicle to check the tire inflation, do not drive more than a mile before checking. A cold tire is generally one that has not been driven for more than three hours.

A plate or sticker is normally provided somewhere in the vehicle (door post, hood, tailgate or trunk lid) which shows the proper pressure for the tires. Never counteract excessive pressure build-up by bleeding off air pressure (letting some air out). This will cause the tire to run hotter and wear quicker.

✳✳ CAUTION

Never exceed the maximum tire pressure embossed on the tire! This is the pressure to be used when the tire is at maximum loading, but it is rarely the correct pressure for everyday driving. Consult the owner's manual or the tire pressure sticker for the correct tire pressure.

Once you've maintained the correct tire pressures for several weeks, you'll be familiar with the vehicle's braking and handling personality. Slight adjustments in tire pressures can fine-tune these characteristics, but never change the cold pressure specification by more than 2 psi. A slightly softer tire pressure will give a softer ride but also yield lower fuel mileage. A slightly harder tire will give crisper dry road handling but can cause skidding on wet surfaces. Unless you're fully attuned to the vehicle, stick to the recommended inflation pressures.

All automotive tires have built-in tread wear indicator bars that show up as ½ in. (13mm) wide smooth bands across the tire when 1⁄16 in. (1.5mm) of tread remains. The appearance of tread wear indicators means that the tires should be replaced. In fact, many states have laws prohibiting the use of tires with less than this amount of tread.

You can check your own tread depth with an inexpensive gauge or by using a Lincoln head penny. Slip the Lincoln penny (with Lincoln's head upside-down) into several tread grooves. If you can see the top of Lincoln's head in 2 adjacent grooves, the tire has less than 1⁄16 in. (1.5mm) tread left and should be replaced. You can measure snow tires in the same manner by using the "tails" side of the Lincoln penny. If you can see the top of the Lincoln memorial, it's time to replace the snow tire(s).

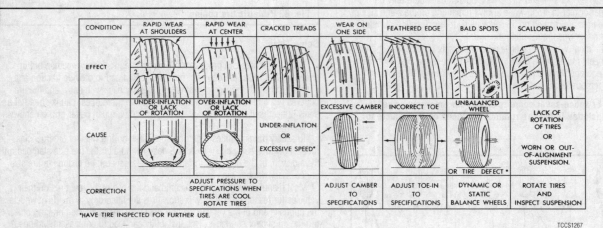

Fig. 83 Common tire wear patterns and causes

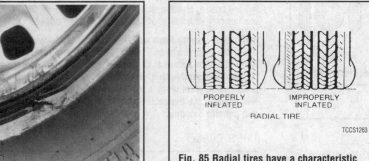

Fig. 85 Radial tires have a characteristic sidewall bulge; don't try to measure pressure by looking at the tire. Use a quality air pressure gauge

Fig. 86 Tread wear indicators will appear when the tire is worn

Fig. 84 Tires with deep cuts, or cuts which bulge, should be replaced immediately

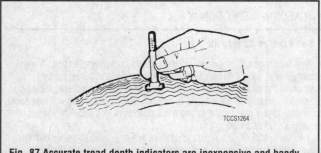

Fig. 87 Accurate tread depth indicators are inexpensive and handy

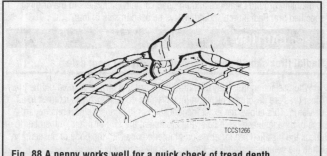

Fig. 88 A penny works well for a quick check of tread depth

FLUIDS AND LUBRICANTS

▶ See Figure 89

Fluid Disposal

Used fluids, such as engine oil, antifreeze, transmission oils and brake fluid are hazardous as waste material and must be disposed of properly.

Before draining any fluids, consult with your local municipal government. In may areas, waste oils are being accepted as part of the recycling program. A number of service stations, repair facilities and auto parts stores are accepting these waste fluids for recycling.

Be sure of the recycling center's policies before draining any fluids, as many will not accept different fluids that have been mixed together, such as oil and antifreeze.

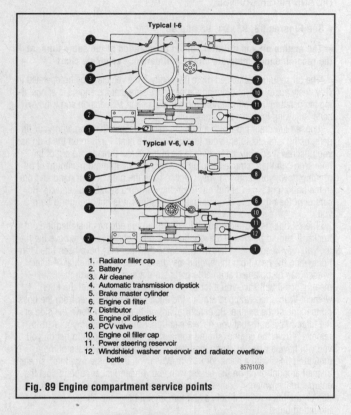

Typical I-6

Typical V-6, V-8

1. Radiator filler cap
2. Battery
3. Air cleaner
4. Automatic transmission dipstick
5. Brake master cylinder
6. Engine oil filter
7. Distributor
8. Engine oil dipstick
9. PCV valve
10. Engine oil filler cap
11. Power steering reservoir
12. Windshield washer reservoir and radiator overflow bottle

85761078

Fig. 89 Engine compartment service points

Fuel and Engine Oil Recommendations

▶ See Figure 90

GASOLINE ENGINES

The recommended oil viscosities for sustained temperatures ranging from below 0°F (−18°C) to above 32°F (0°C) are listed in this section. They are broken down into multi-viscosities and single viscosities. Multiviscosity oils are recommended because of their wider range of acceptable temperatures and driving conditions.

When adding oil to the crankcase or changing the oil or filter, it is important that oil of an equal quality to original equipment be used in your truck. The use of inferior oils may void the warranty, damage your engine, or both.

The SAE (Society of Automotive Engineers) grade number of oil indicates the viscosity of the oil (its ability to lubricate at a given temperature). The lower the SAE number, the lighter the oil; the lower the viscosity, the easier it is to crank the engine in cold weather but the less the oil will lubricate and protect the engine in high temperatures. This number is marked on every oil container.

Oil viscosities should be chosen from those oils recommended for the lowest anticipated temperatures during the oil change interval. Due to the need for an oil that embodies both good lubrication at high temperatures and easy cranking

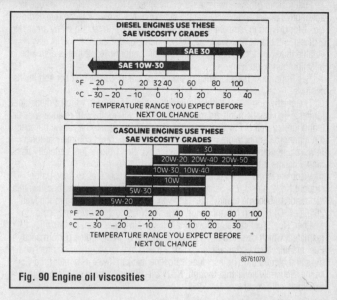

Fig. 90 Engine oil viscosities

in cold weather, multigrade oils have been developed. Basically, a multigrade oil is thinner at low temperatures and thicker at high temperatures. For example, a 10W-40 oil (the W stands for winter) exhibits the characteristics of a 10 weight (SAE 10) oil when the truck is first started and the oil is cold. Its lighter weight allows it to travel to the lubricating surfaces quicker and offer less resistance to starter motor cranking than, say, a straight 30 weight (SAE 30) oil. But after the engine reaches operating temperature, the 10W-40 oil begins acting like straight 40 weight (SAE 40) oil, its heavier weight providing greater lubrication with less chance of foaming than a straight 30 weight oil.

The API (American Petroleum Institute) designations, also found on the oil container, indicates the classification of engine oil used under certain given operating conditions. Only oils designated for use Service SG heavy duty detergent should be used in your truck. Oils of the SG type perform may functions inside the engine besides their basic lubrication. Through a balanced system of metallic detergents and polymeric dispersants, the oil prevents high and low temperature deposits and also keeps sludge and dirt particles in suspension. Acids, particularly sulfuric acid, as well as other by-products of engine combustion are neutralized by the oil. If these acids are allowed to concentrate, they can cause corrosion and rapid wear of the internal engine parts.

✳✳ CAUTION

Non-detergent motor oils or straight mineral oils should not be used in your Ford gasoline engine.

DIESEL ENGINES

Engine Oil

Diesel engines require different engine oil from those used in gasoline engines. Besides doing the things gasoline engine oil does, diesel oil must also deal with increased engine heat and the diesel blow-by gases, which create sulfuric acid, a high corrosive.

Under the American Petroleum Institute (API) classifications, gasoline engine oil codes begin with an **S**, and diesel engine oil codes begin with a **C**. This first letter designation is followed by a second letter code which explains what type of service (heavy, moderate, light) the oil is meant for. For example, the top of a typical oil can will include: API SERVICES SG, CD. This means the oil in the can is a superior, heavy duty engine oil when used in a diesel engine.

Many diesel manufacturers recommend an oil with both gasoline and diesel engine API classifications.

➡**Ford specifies the use of an engine oil conforming to API service categories of both SG and CD. DO NOT use oils labeled as only SG or only CD as they could cause engine damage.**

Fuel

Fuel makers produce two grades of diesel fuel, No. 1 and No. 2, for use in automotive diesel engines. Generally speaking, No. 2 fuel is recommended over No. 1 for driving in temperatures above 20°F (−7°C). In fact, in many areas, No. 2 diesel is the only fuel available. By comparison, No. 2 diesel fuel is less volatile than No. 1 fuel, and gives better fuel economy. No. 2 fuel is also a better injection pump lubricant.

Two important characteristics of diesel fuel are its cetane number and its viscosity.

The cetane number of a diesel fuel refers to the ease with which a diesel fuel ignites. High cetane numbers mean that the fuel will ignite with relative ease or that it ignites well at low temperatures. Naturally, the lower the cetane number, the higher the temperature must be to ignite the fuel. Most commercial fuels have cetane numbers that range from 35 to 65. No. 1 diesel fuel generally has a higher cetane rating than No. 2 fuel.

Viscosity is the ability of a liquid, in this case diesel fuel, to flow. Using straight No. 2 diesel fuel below 20°F (−7°C) can cause problems, because this fuel tends to become cloudy, meaning wax crystals begin forming in the fuel. 20°F (−7°C) is often call the cloud point for No. 2 fuel. In extremely cold weather, No. 2 fuel can stop flowing altogether. In either case, fuel flow is restricted, which can result in no start condition or poor engine performance. Fuel manufacturers often winterize No. 2 diesel fuel by using various fuel additives and blends (no. 1 diesel fuel, kerosene, etc.) to lower its winter time viscosity. Generally speaking, though, No. 1 diesel fuel is more satisfactory in extremely cold weather.

➡**No. 1 and No. 2 diesel fuels will mix and burn with no ill effects, although the engine manufacturer recommends one or the other. Consult the owner's manual for information.**

Depending on local climate, most fuel manufacturers make winterized No. 2 fuel available seasonally.

Many automobile manufacturers publish pamphlets giving the locations of diesel fuel stations nationwide. Contact the local dealer for information.

Do not substitute home heating oil for automotive diesel fuel. While in some cases, home heating oil refinement levels equal those of diesel fuel, many times they are far below diesel engine requirements. The result of using dirty home heating oil will be a clogged fuel system, in which case the entire system may have to be dismantled and cleaned.

One more word on diesel fuels. Don't thin diesel fuel with gasoline in cold weather. The lighter gasoline, which is more explosive, will cause rough running at the very least, and may cause extensive damage to the fuel system if enough is used.

Engine

OIL LEVEL CHECK

▶ **See Figure 91**

Check the engine oil level every time you fill the gas tank. The oil level should be above the ADD mark and not above the FULL mark on the dipstick.

Make sure that the dipstick is inserted into the crankcase as far as possible and that the vehicle is resting on level ground. Also, allow a few minutes after turning off the engine for the oil to drain into the pan or an inaccurate reading will result.

1. Open the hood and remove the engine oil dipstick.
2. Wipe the dipstick with a clean, lint-free rag and reinsert it. Be sure to insert it all the way.
3. Pull out the dipstick and note the oil level. It should be between the **SAFE** (MAX) mark and the **ADD** (MIN) mark.
4. If the level is below the lower mark, replace the dipstick and add fresh oil to bring the level within the proper range. Do not overfill.
5. Recheck the oil level and close the hood.

➡**Use a multi-grade oil with API classification SF.**

OIL AND FILTER CHANGE

▶ **See Figures 92, 93, 94, 95 and 96**

➡**The engine oil and oil filter should be changed at the same time, at the recommended intervals on the maintenance schedule chart.**

The oil should be changed more frequently if the vehicle is being operated in very dusty areas. Before draining the oil, make sure that the engine is at operating temperature. Hot oil will hold more impurities in suspension and will flow better, allowing the removal of more oil and dirt.

Loosen the drain plug with a wrench, then, unscrew the plug with your fingers, using a rag to shield your fingers from the heat. Push in on the plug as you unscrew it so you can feel when all of the screw threads are out of the hole. You can then remove the plug quickly with the minimum amount of oil running down your arm and you will also have the plug in your hand and not in the bottom of a pan of hot oil. Drain the oil into a suitable receptacle. Be careful of the oil. If it is at operating temperatures it is hot enough to burn you.

The oil filter is located on the left side of all the engines installed in Ford trucks. It should be changed every time the oil is changed. To remove the filter, you may need an oil filter wrench since the filter may have been fitted too tightly and the heat from the engine may have made it even tighter. A filter wrench can be obtained at an auto parts store and is well worth the investment, since it will save you a lot of grief. Loosen the filter with the filter wrench. With a rag wrapped around the filter, unscrew the filter from the boss on the side of the engine. Be careful of hot oil that will run down the side of the filter. Make sure that you have a pan under the filter before you start to remove it from the engine; should some of the hot oil happen to get on you, you will have a place to dump the filter in a hurry. Wipe the base of the mounting boss with a clean, dry cloth. When you install the new filter, smear a small amount of oil on the gasket with your finger, just enough to coat the entire surface, where it comes in contact with the mounting plate. When you tighten the filter, rotate it only a half turn after it comes in contact with the mounting boss.

Before installing the oil pan drain plug, clean the threads and wrap them with Teflon® tape. DO NOT OVERTIGHTEN THE DRAIN PLUG! Overtightening will strip the threads in the pan. The drain plug torque is 20-25 ft. lbs.

Fig. 91 Engine oil dipstick on a the 8-302

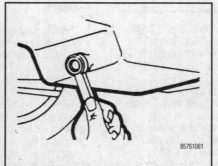
Fig. 92 Loosen, but do not remove, the drain plug on the bottom of the oil pan. Get your drain pan ready

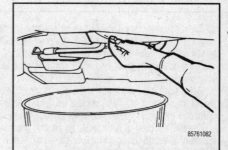
Fig. 93 Unscrew the plug by hand. Keep an inward pressure on the plug as you unscrew it so the oil won't escape until you pull it away

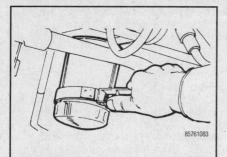

Fig. 94 Move the drain pan underneath the oil filter. Use a strap wrench to remove the filter—remember it is filled with hot, dirty oil

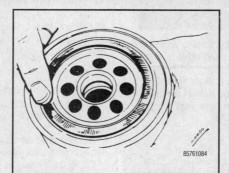

Fig. 95 Wipe clean engine oil around the rubber gasket of the new filter. This helps to ensure a good seal

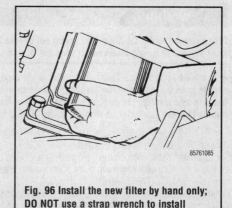

Fig. 96 Install the new filter by hand only; DO NOT use a strap wrench to install

Transmission

FLUID RECOMMENDATIONS

Manual Transmissions:
- All models — SAE 85W/90 gear oil

Automatic Transmissions:
- C4 — Type F
- C5 — Type H
- C6 — 1976 Type F; 1977-86 Dexron®II
- AOD — Dexron®II ATF

LEVEL CHECK

Automatic Transmissions

♦ See Figures 97 and 98

It is very important to maintain the proper fluid level in an automatic transmission. If the level is either too high or too low, poor shifting operation and internal damage are likely to occur. For this reason a regular check of the fluid level is essential.

1. Drive the vehicle for 15-20 minutes to allow the transmission to reach operating temperature.
2. Park the truck on a level surface, apply the parking brake and leave the engine idling. Shift the transmission and engage each gear, then place the gear selector in **P** (PARK).
3. Wipe away any dirt in the areas of the transmission dipstick to prevent it from falling into the filler tube. Withdraw the dipstick, wipe it with a clean, lint-free rag and reinsert it until it seats.
4. Withdraw the dipstick and note the fluid level. It should be between the upper (FULL) mark and the lower (ADD) mark.
5. If the level is below the lower mark, use a funnel and add fluid in small quantities through the dipstick filler neck. Keep the engine running while adding fluid and check the level after each small amount. Do not overfill.

Manual Transmission

♦ See Figure 99

The fluid level should be checked every 6 months/6,000 miles, whichever comes first.

1. Park the truck on a level surface, turn off the engine, apply the parking brake and block the wheels.
2. Remove the filler plug from the side of the transmission case with a proper size wrench. The fluid level should be even with the bottom of the filler hole.
3. If additional fluid is necessary, add it through the filler hole using a siphon pump or squeeze bottle.
4. Replace the filler plug; do not overtighten.

DRAIN AND REFILL

Automatic Transmission

♦ See Figures 100 thru 106

C4 AND C5

1. Raise the truck and support on jackstands.
2. Place a drain pan under the transmission.
3. Disconnect the filler tube from the pan to drain most of the fluid.
4. Loosen the pan attaching bolts and drain the remaining fluid from the transmission.
5. When the fluid has drained to the level of the pan flange, remove the remaining pan bolts working from the rear and both sides of the pan to allow it to drop and drain slowly.
6. When all of the fluid has drained, remove the pan and clean it thoroughly. Discard the pan gasket.
7. Remove the filter and screen.

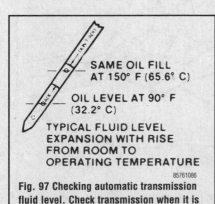

Fig. 97 Checking automatic transmission fluid level. Check transmission when it is warmed to operating temperature

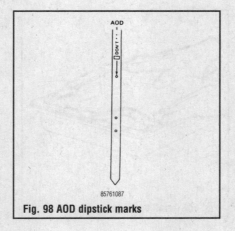

Fig. 98 AOD dipstick marks

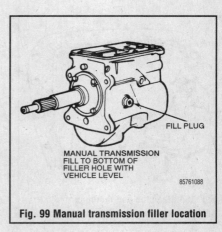

Fig. 99 Manual transmission filler location

✳✳ WARNING

When removing the C4 filter, be careful not to lose the throttle pressure limit valve and spring when separating the filter from the valve body.

➤Some C4 units have a torque converter drain plug. If yours does, it can be seen by removing the inspection plate from the front of the bell-housing and rotating the converter until it comes into view. Ford recommends that the converter be drained every 30,000 miles.

8. Place a new gasket on the pan, and install the pan on the transmission. Tighten the attaching bolts to 12-16 ft. lbs.

9. Clean the threads on the filler tube nut and wrap them with Teflon® tape or coat them with non-hardening sealer. Connect the tube, tightening the nut securely. DO NOT OVERTIGHTEN!

10. Clean the threads on the converter drain plug and wrap them with Teflon® tape or coat them with non-hardening sealer. Install the drain plug tightening it securely. DO NOT OVERTIGHTEN!

11. Add three 3 quarts of fluid through the transmission through the filler tube; 5 quarts if the converter was drained.

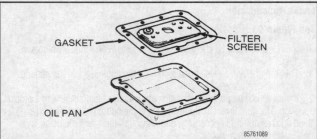

Fig. 100 Automatic transmission filters are found above the transmission oil pan

12. Lower the vehicle. Start the engine and move the gear selector through shift pattern. Allow the engine to reach normal operating temperature.

13. Check the transmission fluid. Add fluid, if necessary, to maintain correct level.

C6 AND FMX

1. Raise the truck and support on jackstands.
2. Place a drain pan under the transmission.
3. Loosen the pan attaching bolts and drain the fluid from the transmission.
4. When the fluid has drained to the level of the pan flange, remove the remaining pan bolts working from the rear and both sides of the pan to allow it to drop and drain slowly.
5. When all of the fluid has drained, remove the pan and clean it thoroughly. Discard the pan gasket.
6. Place a new gasket on the pan, and install the pan on the transmission. Tighten the attaching bolts to 12-16 ft. lbs.
7. Add three 3 quarts of fluid to the transmission through the filler tube.
8. Lower the vehicle. Start the engine and move the gear selector through shift pattern. Allow the engine to reach normal operating temperature.
9. Check the transmission fluid. Add fluid, if necessary, to maintain correct level.

Manual Transmission

➤If the vehicle was operated in deep water, it's a good idea to drain and refill the transmission as soon afterward as possible

1. Place a suitable drain pan under the transmission.
2. Remove the drain plug and allow the gear lube to drain out.
3. Replace the drain plug, remove the filler plug and fill the transmission to the proper level with the required fluid. A kitchen-type baster is a good tool for this job if a squeeze-type gear oil bottle is no available.
4. Reinstall the filler plug.

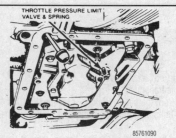

Fig. 101 C4 throttle pressure limit valve and spring. They are held in place by the filter. The valve is installed with the large end towards the valve body; the spring fits over the valve stem

Fig. 102 Many late model have no drain plug. Loosen the pan bolts and allow one corner of the pan to hang so that the fluid will drain out

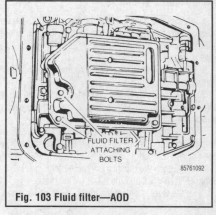

Fig. 103 Fluid filter—AOD

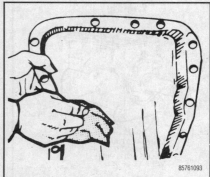

Fig. 104 Clean the pan thoroughly with a safe solvent and allow it to dry

Fig. 105 Install a new pan gasket

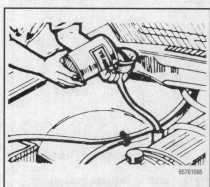

Fig. 106 Fill the transmission with required amount of fluid. Do not overfill

Transfer Case

FLUID RECOMMENDATIONS

- Dana 21 — SAE 50W engine oil
- NP203 — below 32°F (0°C) SAE 30W engine oil; above 32°F SAE 50W engine oil
- NP205 — 1976-77 SAE 50W engine oil; 1978 and later SAE 90W gear oil
- NP208 — Dexron®II ATF
- Borg-Warner1345 — Dexron®II ATF

LEVEL CHECK

Position the vehicle on level ground. Remove the transfer case fill plug located on the left side of the transfer case. The fluid level should be up to the fill hole. If lubricant doesn't run out when the plug is removed, add lubricant until it does run out and then replace the fill plug.

DRAIN AND REFILL

➧ See Figure 107

The transfer case is serviced at the same time and in the same manner as the transmission. On all but the NP203, clean the area around the filler and drain plugs and remove the filler plug on the side of the transfer case. Remove the drain plug on the bottom of the transfer case and allow the lubricant to drain completely. Clean and install the drain plug.

On the NP203, loosen the front and rear housing bolts and allow the fluid to drain. Tighten the bolts.

Add the proper lubricant. Install the filler plug.

Front (4WD) and Rear Axles

LEVEL CHECK

➧ See Figure 108

Clean the area around the fill plug, which is located in the housing cover, before removing the plug. The lubricant level should be maintained to the bottom of the fill hole with the axle in its normal running position. If lubricant does not appear at the hole when the plug is removed, additional lubricant should be added. Use hypoid gear lubricant SAE 80 or 90.

➡If the differential is of the limited slip type, be sure and use special limited slip differential additive.

DRAIN AND REFILL

Drain and refill the front and rear axle housing every 24,000 miles, or every day if the vehicle is operated in deep water.

For the Ford 9 in. rear axle, remove the oil with a suction gun through the filler hole. On all other axles, loosen the differential cover bolts and let the fluid drain out. Refill the axle housings with the proper oil. Be sure to clean the area around the filler plug before removing the plug. See the section on level checks.

Cooling System

➧ See Figures 109, 110 and 111

✱✱ CAUTION

Never remove the radiator cap under any conditions while the engine is running! Failure to follow these instructions could result in damage to the cooling system or engine and/or personal injury. To avoid having scalding hot coolant or steam blow out of the radiator, use extreme care when removing the radiator cap from a hot radiator. Wait until the engine has cooled, then wrap a thick cloth around the radiator cap and turn it slowly to the first stop. Step back while the pressure is released from the cooling system. When you are sure the pressure has been released, press down on the radiator cap (still have the cloth in position) turn and remove the radiator cap.

At least once every 2 years, the engine cooling system should be inspected, flushed, and refilled with fresh coolant. If the coolant is left in the system too long, it loses its ability to prevent rust and corrosion. If the coolant has too much water, it won't protect against freezing.

The pressure cap should be looked at for signs of age or deterioration. Fan belt and other drive belts should be inspected and adjusted to the proper tension. (See checking belt tension).

Hose clamps should be tightened, and soft or cracked hoses replaced. Damp spots, or accumulations of rust or dye near hoses, water pump or other areas, indicate possible leakage, which must be corrected before filling the system with fresh coolant.

CHECK THE RADIATOR CAP

➧ See Figure 112

While you are checking the coolant level, check the radiator cap for a worn or cracked gasket. It the cap doesn't seal properly, fluid will be lost and the engine will overheat.

Worn caps should be replaced with a new one.

CLEAN RADIATOR OF DEBRIS

➧ See Figure 113

Periodically clean any debris, leaves — paper, insects, etc. — from the radiator fins. Pick the large pieces off by hand. The smaller pieces can be washed away with water pressure from a hose.

Carefully straighten any bent radiator fins with a pair of needle nose pliers. Be careful, the fins are very soft. Don't wiggle the fins back and forth too much. Straighten them once and try not to move them again.

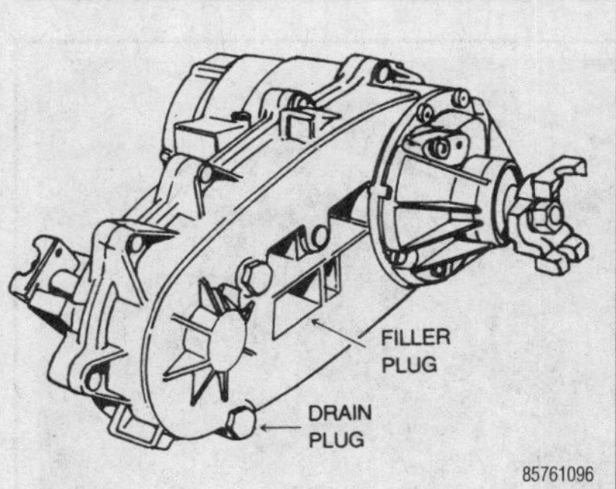

Fig. 107 Transfer case filler and drain plug locations—NP208 shown

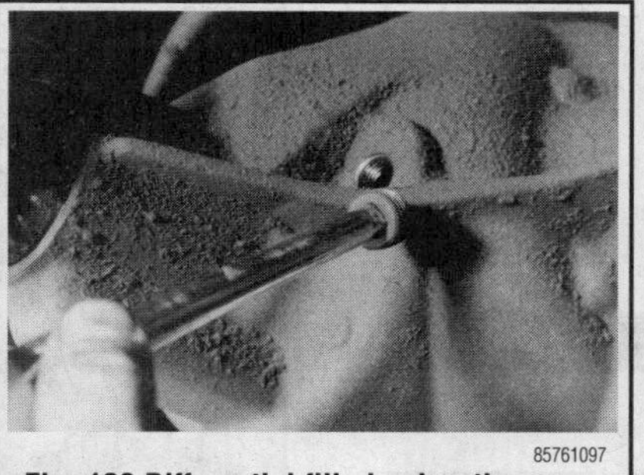

Fig. 108 Differential fill plug location; Ford 8.8 in. rear axle shown. 4x4 front axle has a square-headed plug located on the differential cover

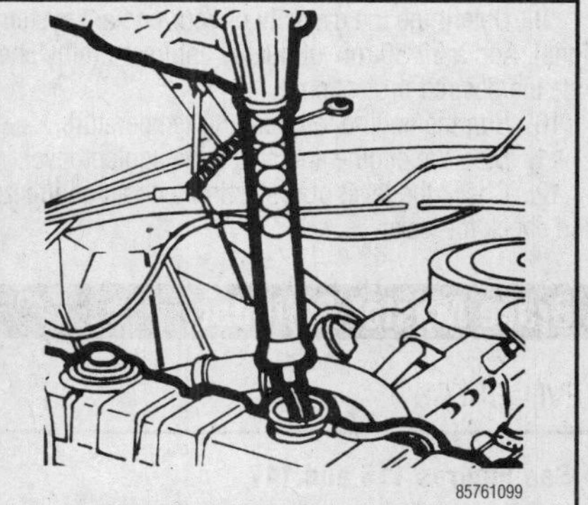

Fig. 109 Check antifreeze protection with an inexpensive tester

Fig. 110 Coolant level check

Fig. 111 The system should be pressure tested once a year

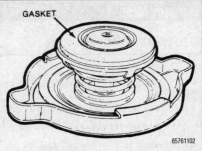

Fig. 112 Check the radiator cap gasket for cracks or wear

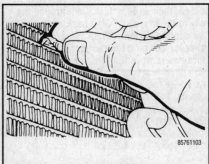

Fig. 113 Keep the radiator fins clear of debris for maximum cooling

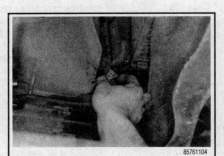

Fig. 114 Open the radiator petcock to drain the cooling system. Spray first with penetrating oil

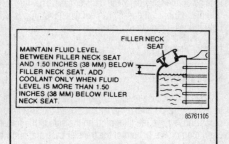

Fig. 115 On vehicles without a coolant recovery system, fill the radiator as shown

DRAIN AND REFILL THE COOLING SYSTEM

▶ See Figures 114 and 115

Completely draining and refilling the cooling system every two years at least will remove accumulated rust, scale and other deposits. Coolant in late model trucks is a 50/50 mixture of ethylene glycol and water for year round use. Use a good quality antifreeze with water pump lubricants, rust inhibitors and other corrosion inhibitors along with acid neutralizers.

1. Drain the existing antifreeze and coolant. Open the radiator and engine drain petcocks, or disconnect the bottom radiator hose, at the radiator outlet.

➡ Before opening the radiator petcock, spray it with some penetrating lubricant.

2. Close the petcock or reconnect the lower hose.
3. Add a can of quality radiator flush and fill the system with water.
4. Idle the engine until the upper radiator hose gets hot.
5. Drain the system again.
6. Repeat this process until the drained water is clear and free of scale.
7. Close all petcocks and connect all the hoses.
8. If equipped with a coolant recovery system, flush the reservoir with water and leave empty.
9. Determine the capacity of your coolant system (see capacities specifications). Add a 50/50 mix of quality antifreeze (ethylene glycol) and water to provide the desired protection.
10. Run the engine to operating temperature.
11. Stop the engine and check the coolant level.
12. Check the level of protection with an antifreeze tester, replace the cap and check for leaks.

Brake Master Cylinder

LEVEL CHECK

▶ See Figures 116 and 117

The master cylinder reservoir is located under the hood, on the left side firewall. Before removing the master cylinder reservoir cap, make sure the vehicle is resting on level ground and clean all dirt away from the top of the master cylinder. Pry off the retaining clip or unscrew the holddown bolt and remove the cap. The brake fluid level should be within ¼ inch (6mm) of the top of the reservoir.

If the level of the brake fluid is less than half the volume of the reservoir, it is advised that you check the brake system for leaks. Leaks in the hydraulic brake system most commonly occur at the wheel cylinder.

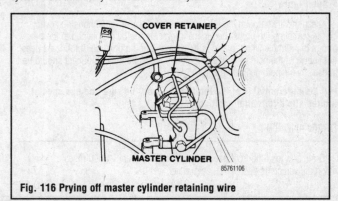

Fig. 116 Prying off master cylinder retaining wire

Fig. 117 Checking the brake fluid level in the master cylinder

There is a rubber diaphragm in the top of the master cylinder cap. As the fluid level lowers in the reservoir due to normal brake shoe wear or leakage, the diaphragm takes up the space. This is to prevent the loss of brake fluid out the vented cap and contamination by dirt. After filling the master cylinder to the proper level with heavy duty brake fluid, but before replacing the cap, fold the rubber diaphragm up into the cap, then replace the cap in the reservoir and tighten the retaining bolt or snap the retaining clip into place.

Hydraulic Clutch Reservoir

LEVEL CHECK

The hydraulic fluid reservoirs on these systems are mounted on the firewall. Fluid level checks are performed like those on the brake hydraulic system. The proper fluid level is indicated by a step on the reservoir. Keep the reservoir topped up with DOT 3 brake fluid; do not overfill.

❊❊ CAUTION

Carefully clean the top and sides of the reservoir before opening, to prevent contamination of the system with dirt, etc. Remove the reservoir diaphragm before adding fluid, and replace after filling.

Manual Steering Gear

LUBRICANT RECOMMENDATION

- F100-350 2-wheel drive — chassis lube
- F100 4-wheel drive — SAE 90W gear oil

LEVEL CHECK

2-Wheel Drive

1. Center the steering wheel.
2. Remove the steering gear housing filler plug.
3. Remove the lower cover-to-housing attaching bolt.
4. With a clean punch or similar object, clean out or push the loose lubricant in the filler plug hole and cover-to-housing attaching bolt hole inward.
5. Slowly turn the steering wheel to the left until the linkage reaches its stop. Lubricant should rise within the cover lower bolt hole.
6. Slowly turn the steering wheel to the right until the linkage reaches its stop. Lubricant should rise within the filler plug hole.
7. If lubricant does not rise in both of the holes, add steering gear lubricant until it comes out both the holes during the check.
8. Install the lower cover-to-housing attaching bolt and the filler plug.

4-Wheel Drive

1. Remove the filler plug from the sector shaft cover.
2. Check to see if the lubricant level is visible in the filler plug tower. If the lubricant is visible, install the filler plug. If the lubricant is not visible, add gear

lubricant until the lubricant is visible about 1 inch (25mm) from the top of the hole in the filler plug tower.
3. Replace the filler plug.

Power Steering Reservoir

FLUID RECOMMENDATIONS

- 1976-82 — Type F ATF
- 1983-86 — Dexron®II ATF

LEVEL CHECK

▶ See Figure 118

Position the vehicle on level ground. Run the engine until the fluid is at normal operating temperature. Turn the steering wheel all the way to the left and right several times. Position the wheels in the straight ahead position, then shut off the engine. Check the fluid level on the dipstick which is attached to the reservoir cap. The level should be between the ADD and FULL marks on the dipstick. Add fluid accordingly. Do not overfill. Use power steering fluid.

Chassis Greasing

▶ See Figures 119, 120 and 121

The vehicle should be greased according to the intervals in the Preventive Maintenance Schedule at the end of this section.

2-Wheel Drive Front Wheel Bearings

➡ **For wheel bearing service on 4-wheel drive trucks, see Section 7.**

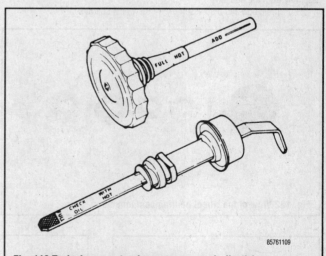

Fig. 118 Typical power steering pump reservoir dipsticks

Fig. 119 Connecting rod-to-Pitman arm ball joint grease fitting; 1978 Bronco shown

Fig. 120 Connecting rod-to-tie rod ball joint grease fitting; 1978 Bronco shown

Fig. 121 Tie rod end ball joint grease fitting, driver's side; 1978 Bronco shown

REPACKING

▶ **See Figures 122, 123, 124, 125 and 126**

Before handling the bearings, there are a few things that you should remember to do and not to do.

Remember to DO the following:
- Remove all outside dirt from the housing before exposing the bearing.
- Treat a used bearing as gently as you would a new one.
- Work with clean tools in clean surroundings.
- Use clean, dry canvas gloves, or at least clean, dry hands.
- Clean solvents and flushing fluids are a must.
- Use clean paper when laying out the bearings to dry.
- Protect disassembled bearings from rust and dirt. Cover them up.
- Use clean rags to wipe bearings.
- Keep the bearings in oil-proof paper when they are to be stored or are not in use.
- Clean the inside of the housing before replacing the bearing.

Do NOT do the following:
- Don't work in dirty surroundings.
- Don't use dirty, chipped or damaged tools.
- Try not to work on wooden work benches or use wooden mallets.
- Don't handle bearings with dirty or moist hands.
- Do not use gasoline for cleaning; use a safe solvent.
- Do not spin-dry bearings with compressed air. They will be damaged.
- Do not spin dirty bearings.
- Avoid using cotton waste or dirty cloths to wipe bearings.
- Try not to scratch or nick bearing surfaces.
- Do not allow the bearing to come in contact with dirt or rust at any time.

1. Raise and support the front end on jackstands.
2. Remove the wheel cover. Remove the wheel.
3. Remove the caliper from the disc and wire it to the underbody to prevent damage to the brake hose. See Chapter 9
4. Remove the grease cap from the hub. Then, remove the cotter pin, nut lock, adjusting nut and flat washer from the spindle. Remove the outer bearing assembly from the hub.
5. Pull the hub and disc assembly off the wheel spindle.

6. Remove and discard the old grease retainer. Remove the inner bearing cone and roller assembly from the hub.
7. Clean all grease from the inner and outer bearing cups with solvent. Inspect the cups for pits, scratches, or excessive wear. If the cups are damaged, remove them with a drift.
8. Clean the inner and outer cone and roller assemblies with solvent and shake them dry. If the cone and roller assemblies show excessive wear or damage, replace them with the bearing cups as a unit.
9. Clean the spindle and the inside of the hub with solvent to thoroughly remove all old grease.
10. Covering the spindle with a clean cloth, brush all loose dirt and dust from the brake assembly. Remove the cloth carefully so as to not get dirt on the spindle.
11. If the inner and/or outer bearing cups were removed, install the replacement cups on the hub. Be sure that the cups seat properly in the hub.
12. It is imperative that all old grease be removed from the bearings and surrounding surfaces before repacking.
13. Install the hub and disc on the wheel spindle. To prevent damage to the grease retainer and spindle threads, keep the hub centered on the spindle.
14. Install the outer bearing cone and roller assembly and the flat washer on the spindle. Install the adjusting nut.
15. Adjust the wheel bearings by torquing the adjusting nut to 17-25 ft. lbs. with the wheel rotating to seat the bearing. Then back off the adjusting nut ½ turn. Retighten the adjusting nut to 10-15 in. lbs. Install the locknut so that the castellations are aligned with the cotter pin hole. Install the cotter pin. Bend the ends of the cotter pin around the castellations of the locknut to prevent interference with the radio static collector in the grease cap. Install the grease cap.

✷✷ WARNING

New bolts must be used when servicing floating caliper units. The upper bolt must be tightened first. For floating caliper units, see Caliper Assembly Service in the Brake Chapter. For sliding caliper units, see Shoe and Lining Replacement in the Brake Section.

16. Install the wheels.
17. Install the wheel cover.

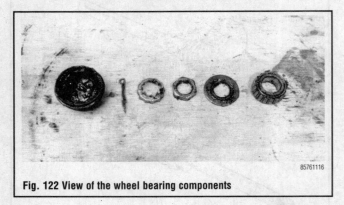

Fig. 122 View of the wheel bearing components

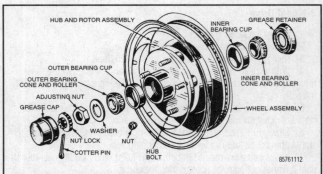

Fig. 123 Front hub, bearing, and grease seal with disc brakes— 2WD

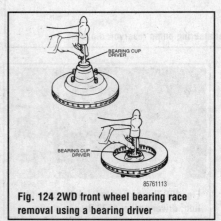

Fig. 124 2WD front wheel bearing race removal using a bearing driver

Fig. 125 Packing the front wheel bearing

Fig. 126 2WD front wheel bearing race installation

TOWING THE VEHICLE

If your truck has to be towed by a tow truck, it can be towed forward for any distance with the driveshaft connected as long as it is done fairly slowly. Otherwise disconnect the driveshaft at the rear axle and tie it up. On F-250HD and F-350, the rear axle shafts can be removed and the hub covered to prevent lubricant loss. If your 4-wheel drive truck has to be towed backward, remove the front axle driving hubs, or disengage the lock-out hubs to prevent the front differential from rotating. If the drive hubs are removed, improvise a cover to keep out dust and dirt.

JACKING

▶ **See Figure 127**

It is very important to be careful about running the engine, on vehicles equipped with limited slip differentials, while the vehicle is up on the jack. This is because when the drive train is engaged, power is transmitted to the wheel with the best traction and the vehicle will drive off the jack if one drive wheel is in contact with the floor, resulting in possible damage or injury.

Jack a Ford truck from under the axles, radius arms, or spring hangers and the frame. Be sure and block the diagonally opposite wheel. Place jackstands under the vehicle at the points mentioned or directly under the frame when you are going to work under the vehicle.

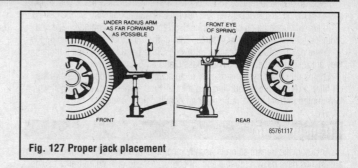

Fig. 127 Proper jack placement

TRAILER TOWING

Factory trailer towing packages are available on most trucks. However, if you are installing a trailer hitch and wiring on your truck, there are a few thing that you should know.

Trailer Weight

Trailer weight is the first, and most important, factor in determining whether or not your vehicle is suitable for towing the trailer you have in mind. The horsepower-to-weight ratio should be calculated. The basic standard is a ratio of 35:1. That is, 35 pounds of GVW for every horsepower.

To calculate this ratio, multiply you engine's rated horsepower by 35, then subtract the weight of the vehicle, including passengers and luggage. The resulting figure is the ideal maximum trailer weight that you can tow. One point to consider: a numerically higher axle ratio can offset what appears to be a low trailer weight. If the weight of the trailer that you have in mind is somewhat higher than the weight you just calculated, you might consider changing your rear axle ratio to compensate.

Hitch Weight

There are three kinds of hitches: bumper mounted, frame mounted, and load equalizing.

Bumper mounted hitches are those which attach solely to the vehicle's bumper. Many states prohibit towing with this type of hitch, when it attaches to the vehicle's stock bumper, since it subjects the bumper to stresses for which it was not designed. Aftermarket rear step bumpers, designed for trailer towing, are acceptable for use with bumper mounted hitches.

Frame mounted hitches can be of the type which bolts to two or more points on the frame, plus the bumper, or just to several points on the frame. Frame mounted hitches can also be of the tongue type, for Class I towing, or, of the receiver type, for Classes II and III.

Load equalizing hitches are usually used for large trailers. Most equalizing hitches are welded in place and use equalizing bars and chains to level the vehicle after the trailer is hooked up.

The bolt-on hitches are the most common, since they are relatively easy to install.

Check the gross weight rating of your trailer. Tongue weight is usually figured as 10% of gross trailer weight. Therefore, a trailer with a maximum gross weight of 2,000 lb. will have a maximum tongue weight of 200 lb. Class I trailers fall into this category. Class II trailers are those with a gross weight rating of 2,000-3,500 lb., while Class III trailers fall into the 3,500-6,000 lb. category. Class IV trailers are those over 6,000 lb. and are for use with fifth wheel trucks, only.

When you've determined the hitch that you'll need, follow the manufacturer's installation instructions, exactly, especially when it comes to fastener torques.

The hitch will subjected to a lot of stress and good hitches come with hardened bolts. Never substitute an inferior bolt for a hardened bolt.

Wiring

Wiring the truck for towing is fairly easy. There are a number of good wiring kits available and these should be used, rather than trying to design your own. All trailers will need brake lights and turn signals as well as tail lights and side marker lights. Most states require extra marker lights for overly wide trailers. Also, most states have recently required backup lights for trailers, and most trailer manufacturers have been building trailers with back-up lights for several years.

Additionally, some Class I, most Class II and just about all Class III trailers will have electric brakes.

Add to this number an accessories wire, to operate trailer internal equipment or to charge the trailer's battery, and you can have as many as seven wires in the harness.

Determine the equipment on your trailer and buy the wiring kit necessary. The kit will contain all the wires needed, plus a plug adapter set which included the female plug, mounted on the bumper or hitch, and the male plug, wired into, or plugged into the trailer harness.

When installing the kit, follow the manufacturer's instructions. The color coding of the wires is standard throughout the industry.

One point to note, some domestic vehicles, and most imported vehicles, have separate turn signals. On most domestic vehicles, the brake lights and rear turn signals operate with the same bulb. For those vehicles with separate turn signals, you can purchase an isolation unit so that the brake lights won't blink whenever the turn signals are operated, or, you can go to your local electronics supply house and buy four diodes to wire in series with the brake and turn signal bulbs. Diodes will isolate the brake and turn signals. The choice is yours. The isolation units are simple and quick to install, but far more expensive than the diodes. The diodes, however, require more work to install properly, since they require the cutting of each bulb's wire and soldering in place of the diode.

One final point, the best kits are those with a spring loaded cover on the vehicle mounted socket. This cover prevents dirt and moisture from corroding the terminals. Never let the vehicle socket hang loosely. Always mount it securely to the bumper or hitch.

Engine Cooling

One of the most common, if not THE most common, problem associated with trailer towing is engine overheating.

With factory installed trailer towing packages, a heavy duty cooling system is usually included. Heavy duty cooling systems are available as optional equipment on most trucks, with or without a trailer package. If you have one of these extra-capacity systems, you shouldn't't have any overheating problems.

If you have a standard cooling system, without an expansion tank, you'll definitely need to get an aftermarket expansion tank kit, preferably one with at least a 2 quart capacity. These kits are easily installed on the radiator's overflow hose, and come with a pressure cap designed for expansion tanks.

Another helpful accessory is a Flex Fan. These fan are large diameter units are designed to provide more airflow at low speeds, with blades that have deeply cupped surfaces. The blades then flex, or flatten out, at high speed, when less cooling air is needed. These fans are far lighter in weight than stock fans, requiring less horsepower to drive them. Also, they are far quieter than stock fans.

If you do decide to replace your stock fan with a flex fan, note that if your truck has a fan clutch, a spacer between the flex fan and water pump hub will be needed.

Aftermarket engine oil coolers are helpful for prolonging engine oil life and reducing overall engine temperatures. Both of these factors increase engine life.

While not absolutely necessary in towing Class I and some Class II trailers, they are recommended for heavier Class II and all Class III towing.

Engine oil cooler systems consist of an adapter, screwed on in place of the oil filter, a remote filter mounting and a multi-tube, finned heat exchanger, which is mounted in front of the radiator or air conditioning condenser.

Transmission

An automatic transmission is usually recommended for trailer towing. Modern automatics have proven reliable and, of course, easy to operate, in trailer towing.

The increased load of a trailer, however, causes an increase in the temperature of the automatic transmission fluid. Heat is the worst enemy of an automatic transmission. As the temperature of the fluid increases, the life of the fluid decreases.

It is essential, therefore, that you install an automatic transmission cooler.

The cooler, which consists of a multi-tube, finned heat exchanger, is usually installed in front of the radiator or air conditioning compressor, and hooked in-line with the transmission cooler tank inlet line. Follow the cooler manufacturer's installation instructions.

Select a cooler of at least adequate capacity, based upon the combined gross weights of the truck and trailer.

Cooler manufacturers recommend that you use an aftermarket cooler in addition to, and not instead of, the present cooling tank in your truck's radiator. If you do want to use it in place of the radiator cooling tank, get a cooler at least two sizes larger than normally necessary.

➡ **A transmission cooler can, sometimes, cause slow or harsh shifting in the transmission during cold weather, until the fluid has a chance to come up to normal operating temperature. Some coolers can be purchased with or retrofitted with a temperature bypass valve which will allow fluid flow through the cooler only when the fluid has reached operating temperature, or above.**

CAPACITIES—PICK-UPS
Crankcase and Cooling System (qts.)

Year	Engine	Crankcase Oil and Filter Change	Cooling System					
			Standard System		Extra Cooling		With A/C	Super Cooling
			Man. Trans.	Auto. Trans.	Man. Trans.	Auto. Trans.		
1976	300 eng., F-100 4 x 2	6.0	12.5	14.5	14.5	14.5	—	—
	F-150/250 4 x 4	6.0	14.5	14.5	16.5	16.5	—	—
	F-150/250 4 x 2	6.0	12.5	12.5	14.5	14.5	—	—
	F-350	6.0	14.5	14.5	14.5	14.5	14.5	—
	302 eng., F-100 4 x 2	6.0	15.0	15.0	17.5	17.5	17.5	—
	360 eng., F-100 4 x 2	6.0	19.5	22.0	22.5	22.5	24.0	24.0
	F-150/250 4 x 2	6.0	19.5	19.5	22.0	22.5	24.0	24.0
	F-100/150 4 x 4	6.0	16.5	16.5	16.5	16.5	16.5	—
	F-250 4 x 4	6.0	16.5	16.5	16.5	16.5	16.5	18.5
	F-350	6.0	22.5	22.5	24.0	24.0	24.0	—
1977	300 eng., F-100 4 x 2	6.0	12.5	14.5	14.5	14.5	—	—
	F-150/250 4 x 4	6.0	14.5	14.5	14.5	14.5	—	—
	F-350	6.0	14.5	14.5	14.5	14.5	—	—
	302 eng., F-100 4 x 2	6.0	15.5	17.5	15.5	17.5	17.5	—
	351 eng., F-100 4 x 2	6.0	19.5	22.0	19.5	19.5	22.0	24.0
	F-150/250 4 x 2	6.0	19.5	19.5	19.5	19,5	22.0	24.0
	F-150/250 4 x 4	6.0	22.0	22.0	22.0	22.0	22.0	24.0
	F-350	6.0	22.0	22.0	22.0	22.0	22.0	—
	400 eng., F-100/150/250/350	6.0	22.0	22.0	22.0	22.0	22.0	24.0
	460 eng., F-150/250/350	6.0	22.5	22.5	22.5	22.5	22.5	—
1978–86	300 eng., F-100/250/350	6.0	13.0	14.0	13.0	14.0	17.0	14.0
	232, 255, 302 eng., F-100/150	6.0	15.0②	15.0②	15.0	18.0	18.0	11.0
	351 eng., F-100, F-150/350	6.0	17.0	—	17.0	—	—	16.0
	400 eng., F-250/350	6.0	18.0	—	18.0	—	18.0	24.0
	460 eng., F-150/350, 250	6.0	24.0③	24.0③	24.0③	24.0③	24.0③	24.0③
	420 Diesel, All	10.0	29.0	29.0	29.0	29.0	29.0	29.0

SRW—Single Rear Wheels
DRW—Dual Rear Wheels
① 6.0 4 x 4
② 10.0 qts. 1983 and later
③ 18 qts. 1983 and later

85761C04

CAPACITIES CHART—BRONCO

Year	Engine	Crankcase With Filter (qts.)	Transmission (pts.) Manual	Transmission (pts.) Automatic ⑥	Transfer Case (pts.)	Axle (pts.) Front	Axle (pts.) Rear	Gasoline Tank (gals.) Main	Gasoline Tank (gals.) Auxiliary	Cooling System (qts.)
1978–79	8-351M	6	7.0	26.4	4.0①	5.8	6.5⑧	25.0②	—	20.0③
	8-400	6	7.0	26.4	4.0①	5.8	6.5⑧	25.0②	—	22.0④
1980–81	6-300	6	7.0⑨	26.8	6.5	4.0	6.5⑧	25.0②	—	13.0⑤
	8-302	6	7.0⑨	26.8	6.5	4.0	6.5⑧	25.0②	—	13.0⑥
	8-351W	6	7.0⑨	26.8	6.5	4.0	6.5⑧	25.0②	—	15.0⑦
1982–86	6-300	6	7.0⑨	26.8	7.0	4.0	6.5⑧	25.0②	—	13.0⑤
	8-302	6	7.0⑨	26.8	7.0	4.0	6.5⑧	25.0②	—	13.0⑥
	8-351W	6	7.0⑨	26.8	7.0	4.0	6.5⑧	25.0②	—	15.0⑦

① Full-time unit: 9.0
② Optional tank: 32.0
③ Extra cooling package, air conditioning, automatic transmission or trailer towing package: 22.0
Super Cooling package: 24.0
④ Super Cooling package: 24.0
⑤ Air conditioning or Super Cooling package: 14.0
⑥ Extra Cooling package with auto. trans.; air conditioning; Super Cooling package: 14.0
⑦ Air conditioning or Super Cooling package: 16.0
⑧ With locking differential, use Lubricant Ford part #ESW-M2C119-A or equivalent
⑨ 4-speed overdrive available from 1981: 4.5

85761C08

PREVENTIVE MAINTENANCE SCHEDULE

Model/Interval	Item	Service
1976		
Every 5 months or 5,000 miles	Brakes	Inspect
	Crankcase	Change oil and filter
	Differential	Check level
	Chassis fittings	Lubricate
	Transmission, automatic	Adjust bands, check level
	Transmission, manual	Check level
	Air cleaner oil bath	Clean and refill
	Power steering	Check level
	Idle speed	Adjust
	Throttle kickdown exc. F-100	Check
	Throttle solenoid-off speed	Check
Every 6 months	Cooling system	Inspect, change coolant
Every 15 months or 15,000 miles	Brake master cylinder	Check level
	Parking brake linkage	Oil with 10W
	Air cleaner element	Replace
	Air cleaner temperature valve	Check
	Choke system	Inspect
	Distributor cap and rotor	Inspect
	Distributor wick	Oil with 10W
	Drive belts	Check & adjust
	EGR system	Clean and inspect
	Fuel filter	Replace
	Ignition timing	Adjust
	Intake manifold, 302 V8	Torque
	Manifold heat riser	Inspect
	PCV system	Inspect
	Spark plugs	Replace
	Spark plug wires	Inspect
	Thermactor system	Inspect
	Free running hubs	Clean and repack
Every 20 months or 20,000 miles	Front wheel bearings	Clean and repack
	Rear wheel bearings, Dana axle	Clean and repack
Every 25 months or 25,000 miles	Differential, Dana	Change lubricant
	Transmission, 4-speed	Change lubricant
	Transfer case	Change lubricant
Every 30 months or 30,000 miles	Air cleaner crankcase filter	Replace
	EEC canister	Inspect
	Fuel vapor system	Inspect
	PCV valve	Replace
1977 and Later F-100 Only		
Every 6 months	Cooling system	Change coolant
Every 7 months or 7,500 miles	Crankcase	Change oil and filter
	Drive belts	Check and adjust
	Idle speed and TSP-off speed	Adjust
	Ignition timing	Check and adjust
	Chassis fittings	Lubricate
	Clutch linkage	Inspect and oil
	Transmission, automatic	Adjust bands, check level
Every 15 months or 15,000 miles	Exhaust system heat shields	Inspect

85761C09

PREVENTIVE MAINTENANCE SCHEDULE

Model/Interval	Item	Service
Every 22 months or 22,500 miles	Spark plugs	Replace
	Exhaust control valve, 300cid	inspect
	PCV Valve	Replace
	Idle mixture	Adjust
	Choke system	Inspect
	Thermactor delay valve	Inspect
Every 30 months or 30,000 miles	Air cleaner element	Replace
	Air cleaner crankcase filter	Replace
	Air cleaner temperature control valve	Check
	Fuel vapor system	Inspect
	Front wheel bearings	Clean and repack
	Brakes	Inspect
	Brake master cylinder	Check level
1977 and Later Bronco F-150, 250, 350 (Except Diesel)		
Every 6 months or 6,000 miles	Crankcase	Change oil & filter
	Cooling System	Change coolant
	Idle speed and TSP-off speed	Adjust
	Ignition timing	Adjust
	Decel throttle control system	Check
	Chassis fittings	Lubricate
	4 x 4 power cylinder	Lubricate
	Clutch linkage	Inspect and oil
	Exhaust system heat shields	Inspect
	Transmission, automatic	Adjust bands, check level
Every 15 months or 15,000 miles	Spark plugs	Replace
	Exhaiust control valve	Check & lubricate
	Drive belts	Check and adjust
	Air cleaner temperature control	Check
	Choke system	Check
	Thermactor system	Check
	Crankcase breathe cap	Clean
	EGR system	Clean and inspect
	PCV system	Clean and inspect
Every 30 months or 30,000 miles	PCV valve	Replace
	Air cleaner element	Replace
	Air cleaner crankcase filter	Replace
	Fuel vapor system	Inspect
	Brake master cylinder	Check
	Brakes	Inspect
	Free-running hubs	Clean and repack
	Front wheel bearings	Clean and repack
	Rear wheel bearings, Dana axles	Clean and repack
6.9L Diesel Models		
Every 6 months or 5,000 miles	Crankcase	Change oil and filter
	Idle speed	Check and adjust
	Throttle linkage	Check operation
	Fuel/water separator	Drain water
	U-joints	Lubricate
	Front axle spindles	Lubricate
Every 6 months or 15,000 miles	Fuel filter	Replace
	Drive belts	Check/adjust
	Steering linkage	Lubricate
Every year	Coolant	Check condition/Replace
	Cooling hoses, clamps	Check condition/Replace

85761C9A

ENGLISH TO METRIC CONVERSION: MASS (WEIGHT)

Current **mass** measurement is expressed in pounds and ounces (lbs. & ozs.). The metric unit of mass (or weight) is the kilogram (kg). Even although this table does not show conversion of masses (weights) larger than 15 lbs, it is easy to calculate larger units by following the data immediately below.

To convert ounces (oz.) to grams (g): multiply th number of ozs. by 28
To convert grams (g) to ounces (oz.): multiply the number of grams by .035

To convert pounds (lbs.) to kilograms (kg): multiply the number of lbs. by .45
To convert kilograms (kg) to pounds (lbs.): multiply the number of kilograms by 2.2

lbs	kg	lbs	kg	oz	kg	oz	kg
0.1	0.04	0.9	0.41	0.1	0.003	0.9	0.024
0.2	0.09	1	0.4	0.2	0.005	1	0.03
0.3	0.14	2	0.9	0.3	0.008	2	0.06
0.4	0.18	3	1.4	0.4	0.011	3	0.08
0.5	0.23	4	1.8	0.5	0.014	4	0.11
0.6	0.27	5	2.3	0.6	0.017	5	0.14
0.7	0.32	10	4.5	0.7	0.020	10	0.28
0.8	0.36	15	6.8	0.8	0.023	15	0.42

ENGLISH TO METRIC CONVERSION: TEMPERATURE

To convert Fahrenheit (°F) to Celsius (°C): take number of °F and subtract 32; multiply result by 5; divide result by 9

To convert Celsius (°C) to Fahrenheit (°F): take number of °C and multiply by 9; divide result by 5; add 32 to total

Fahrenheit (F)		Celsius (C)		Fahrenheit (F)		Celsius (C)		Fahrenheit (F)		Celsius (C)	
°F	°C	°C	°F	°F	°C	°C	°F	°F	°C	°C	°F
−40	−40	−38	−36.4	80	26.7	18	64.4	215	101.7	80	176
−35	−37.2	−36	−32.8	85	29.4	20	68	220	104.4	85	185
−30	−34.4	−34	−29.2	90	32.2	22	71.6	225	107.2	90	194
−25	−31.7	−32	−25.6	95	35.0	24	75.2	230	110.0	95	202
−20	−28.9	−30	−22	100	37.8	26	78.8	235	112.8	100	212
−15	−26.1	−28	−18.4	105	40.6	28	82.4	240	115.6	105	221
−10	−23.3	−26	−14.8	110	43.3	30	86	245	118.3	110	230
−5	−20.6	−24	−11.2	115	46.1	32	89.6	250	121.1	115	239
0	−17.8	−22	−7.6	120	48.9	34	93.2	255	123.9	120	248
1	−17.2	−20	−4	125	51.7	36	96.8	260	126.6	125	257
2	−16.7	−18	−0.4	130	54.4	38	100.4	265	129.4	130	266
3	−16.1	−16	3.2	135	57.2	40	104	270	132.2	135	275
4	−15.6	−14	6.8	140	60.0	42	107.6	275	135.0	140	284
5	−15.0	−12	10.4	145	62.8	44	112.2	280	137.8	145	293
10	−12.2	−10	14	150	65.6	46	114.8	285	140.6	150	302
15	−9.4	−8	17.6	155	68.3	48	118.4	290	143.3	155	311
20	−6.7	−6	21.2	160	71.1	50	122	295	146.1	160	320
25	−3.9	−4	24.8	165	73.9	52	125.6	300	148.9	165	329
30	−1.1	−2	28.4	170	76.7	54	129.2	305	151.7	170	338
35	1.7	0	32	175	79.4	56	132.8	310	154.4	175	347
40	4.4	2	35.6	180	82.2	58	136.4	315	157.2	180	356
45	7.2	4	39.2	185	85.0	60	140	320	160.0	185	365
50	10.0	6	42.8	190	87.8	62	143.6	325	162.8	190	374
55	12.8	8	46.4	195	90.6	64	147.2	330	165.6	195	383
60	15.6	10	50	200	93.3	66	150.8	335	168.3	200	392
65	18.3	12	53.6	205	96.1	68	154.4	340	171.1	205	401
70	21.1	14	57.2	210	98.9	70	158	345	173.9	210	410
75	23.9	16	60.8	212	100.0	75	167	350	176.7	215	414

2

ENGINE PERFORMANCE AND TUNE-UP

TUNE-UP PROCEDURES

In order to extract the full measure of performance and economy from your engine it is essential that it be properly tuned at regular intervals. A regular tune-up will keep your vehicle's engine running smoothly and will prevent the annoying minor breakdowns and poor performance associated with an untuned engine.

A complete tune-up should be performed every 12,000 miles or twelve months, whichever comes first. This interval should be halved if the vehicle is operated under severe conditions, such as trailer towing, prolonged idling, continual stop and start driving, or if starting or running problems are noticed. It is assumed that the routine maintenance described in Chapter 1 has been kept up, as this will have a decided effect on the results of a tune-up. All of the applicable steps of a tune-up should be followed in order, as the result is a cumulative one.

If the specifications on the tune-up sticker in the engine compartment disagree with the Tune-Up Specifications chart in this chapter, the figures on the sticker must be used. The sticker often reflects changes made during the production run.

Spark Plugs

A typical spark plug consists of a metal shell surrounding a ceramic insulator. A metal electrode extends downward through the center of the insulator and protrudes a small distance. Located at the end of the plug and attached to the side of the outer metal shell is the side electrode. The side electrode bends in at a 90 degree angle so that its tip is even with, and parallel to, the tip of the center electrode. The distance between these two electrodes (measured in thousandths of an inch) is called the spark plug gap. The spark plug does not actually produce a spark but merely provides a gap across which the current can arc. The coil produces anywhere from 20,000 to 40,000 volts which travels to the distributor where it is distributed through the spark plug wires to the spark plugs. The current passes along the center electrode and jumps the gap to the side electrode, and, in so doing, ignites the air/fuel mixture in the combustion chamber.

SPARK PLUG HEAT RANGE

▶ **See Figure 1**

Spark plug heat range is the ability of the plug to dissipate heat. The longer the insulator (or the farther it extends into the engine), the hotter the plug will operate; the shorter the insulator (the closer the electrode is to the block's cooling passages) the cooler it will operate. A plug that absorbs little heat and remains too cool will quickly accumulate deposits of oil and carbon since it is not hot enough to burn them off. This leads to plug fouling and consequently to misfiring. A plug that absorbs too much heat will have no deposits but, due to the excessive heat, the electrodes will burn away quickly and might possibly lead to preignition or other ignition problems. Preignition takes place when plug tips get so hot that they glow sufficiently to ignite the air/fuel mixture before the actual spark occurs. This early ignition will usually cause a pinging during low speeds and heavy loads.

The general rule of thumb for choosing the correct heat range when picking a spark plug is: if most of your driving is long distance, high speed travel, use a colder plug; if most of your driving is stop and go, use a hotter plug. Original equipment plugs are generally a good compromise between the 2 styles and most people never have the need to change their plugs from the factory-recommended heat range.

REMOVAL & INSTALLATION

▶ **See Figures 2, 3, 4 and 5**

A set of spark plugs usually requires replacement after about 20,000–30,000 miles (32,000–48,000 km), depending on your style of driving. In normal operation plug gap increases about 0.001 in. (0.025mm) for every 2500 miles (4000 km). As the gap increases, the plug's voltage requirement also increases. It requires a greater voltage to jump the wider gap and about two to three times as much voltage to fire the plug at high speeds than at idle. The improved air/fuel ratio control of modern fuel injection combined with the higher voltage output of modern ignition systems will often allow an engine to run significantly longer on a set of standard spark plugs, but keep in mind that efficiency will drop as the gap widens (along with fuel economy and power).

When you're removing spark plugs, work on one at a time. Don't start by removing the plug wires all at once, because, unless you number them, they may become mixed up. Take a minute before you begin and number the wires with tape.

➡ **On models equipped with electronic ignition, apply a small amount of silicone dielectric compound (D7AZ-19A331-A or the equivalent) to the inside of the terminal boots whenever an ignition wire is disconnected from the plug, or coil/distributor cap connection.**

1. Twist the spark plug boot and remove the boot and wire from the plug. Do not pull on the wire itself as this will damage the wire.

2. If possible, use a brush or gag to clean the area around the spark plug. Make sure that all the dirt is removed so that none will enter the cylinder after the plug is removed.

3. Remove the spark plug using the proper size socket. Truck models use either a ⅝ inch or ¹³⁄₁₆ inch size socket depending on the engine. Turn the socket counterclockwise to remove the plug. Be sure to hold the socket straight on the plug to avoid breaking the plug, or rounding off the hex on the plug.

4. Once the plug is out, check the plug to determine engine condition. This is crucial since plug readings are vital signs of engine condition.

5. Use a round wire feeler gauge to check the plug gap. The correct size gauge should pass through the electrode gap with a slight drag. If you're in doubt, try one size smaller and one larger. The smaller gauge should go through easily while the larger one shouldn't go through at all. If the gap is incorrect, use the electrode bending tool on the end of the gauge to adjust the gap. When adjusting the gap, always bend the side electrode. The center electrode is non-adjustable.

6. Squirt a drop of penetrating oil on the threads of the new plug and install it. Don't oil the threads too heavily. Turn the plug in clockwise by hand until it is snug.

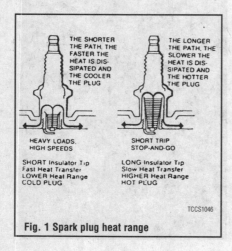

THE SHORTER THE PATH. THE FASTER THE HEAT IS DISSIPATED AND THE COOLER THE PLUG

THE LONGER THE PATH. THE SLOWER THE HEAT IS DISSIPATED AND THE HOTTER THE PLUG

HEAVY LOADS.
HIGH SPEEDS

SHORT TRIP
STOP-AND-GO

SHORT Insulator Tip
Fast Heat Transfer
LOWER Heat Range
COLD PLUG

LONG Insulator Tip
Slow Heat Transfer
HIGHER Heat Range
HOT PLUG

TCCS1046

Fig. 1 Spark plug heat range

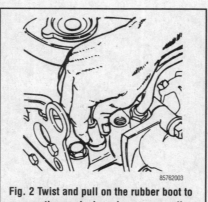

85762003

Fig. 2 Twist and pull on the rubber boot to remove the spark plug wires; never pull on the wire itself

85762038

Fig. 3 Removing a spark plug; 8-302 shown

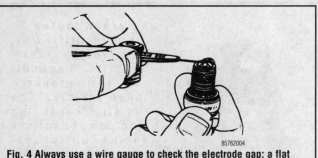

Fig. 4 Always use a wire gauge to check the electrode gap; a flat feeler gauge may not give the proper reading

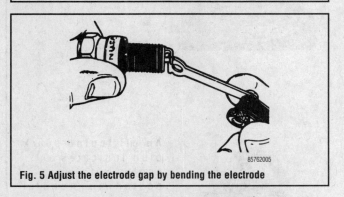

Fig. 5 Adjust the electrode gap by bending the electrode

7. When the plug is finger tight, tighten it with a wrench. If you don't have a torque wrench, tighten the plug until snug (do not over tighten).

8. Install the plug boot firmly over the plug. Proceed to the next plug.

INSPECTION & GAPPING

▶ See Figures 6, 7, 8 and 9

Check the plugs for deposits and wear. If they are not going to be replaced, clean the plugs thoroughly. Remember that any kind of deposit will decrease the efficiency of the plug. Plugs can be cleaned on a spark plug cleaning machine, which can sometimes be found in service stations, or you can do an acceptable job of cleaning with a stiff brush. If the plugs are cleaned, the electrodes must be filed flat. Use an ignition points file, not an emery board or the like, which will leave deposits. The electrodes must be filed perfectly flat with sharp edges; rounded edges reduce the spark plug voltage by as much as 50%.

Check spark plug gap before installation. The ground electrode (the L-shaped one connected to the body of the plug) must be parallel to the center electrode and the specified size wire gauge (please refer to the Tune-Up Specifications chart for details) must pass between the electrodes with a slight drag.

➡NEVER adjust the gap on a used platinum type spark plug.

Always check the gap on new plugs as they are not always set correctly at the factory. Do not use a flat feeler gauge when measuring the gap on a used plug, because the reading may be inaccurate. A round-wire type gapping tool is the best way to check the gap. The correct gauge should pass through the electrode gap with a slight drag. If you're in doubt, try one size smaller and one larger. The smaller gauge should go through easily, while the larger one shouldn't go through at all. Wire gapping tools usually have a bending tool attached. Use that to adjust the side electrode until the proper distance is obtained. Absolutely never attempt to bend the center electrode. Also, be careful not to bend the side electrode too far or too often as it may weaken and break off within the engine, requiring removal of the cylinder head to retrieve it.

Spark Plug Wires

CHECKING AND REPLACING SPARK PLUG CABLES

Visually inspect the spark plug cables for burns, cuts, or breaks in the insulation. Check the spark plug boots and the nipples on the distributor cap and coil. Replace any damaged wiring. If no physical damage is obvious, the wires can be checked with an ohmmeter for excessive resistance.

When installing a new set of spark plug cables, replace the cables on at a time so there will be no mix-up. Start by replacing the longest cable first. Install the boot firmly over the spark plug. Route the wire exactly the same as the original. Insert the nipple firmly into the tower on the distributor cap. Repeat the process for each cable.

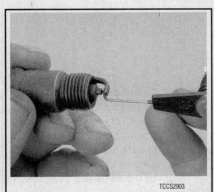

Fig. 6 Checking the spark plug gap with a feeler gauge

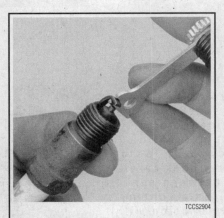

Fig. 7 Adjusting the spark plug gap

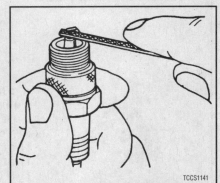

Fig. 8 If the standard plug is in good condition, the electrode may be filed flat— WARNING: do not file platinum plugs

A normally worn spark plug should have light tan or gray deposits on the firing tip.

A carbon fouled plug, identified by soft, sooty, black deposits, may indicate an improperly tuned vehicle. Chec the air cleaner, ignition components and engine control system.

This spark plug has been **left in the engine too long,** as evidenced by the extreme gap- Plugs with such an extreme gap can cause misfiring and stumbling accompanied by a noticeable lack of power.

An oil fouled spark plug indicates an engine with worn poston rings and/or bad valve seals allowing excessive oil to enter the chamber.

A physically damaged spark plug may be evidence of severe detonation in that cylinder. Watch that cylinder carefully between services, as a continued detonation will not only damage the plug, but could also damage the engine.

A bridged or almost bridged spark plug, identified by a build up between the electrodes caused by excessive carbon or oil build-up on the plug.

Fig. 9 Inspect the spark plug to determine engine running conditions

TCCA1P40

TUNE-UP SPECIFICATIONS

When analyzing compression test results, look for uniformity among cylinders rather than specific pressure.

Year	Engine No. Cyl. Displacement (cu. in.)	Spark Plugs Orig. Type	Spark Plugs Gap (in.)	Distributor Point Dwell (deg.)	Distributor Point Gap (in.)	Ignition Timing (deg.) Man.	Ignition Timing (deg.) Auto.	Intake Valve Opens (deg.)	Fuel Pump Pressure (psi)	Idle Speed (rpm) ▲ Man.	Idle Speed (rpm) ▲ Auto.
1976	6-300	BRF-42B	0.044	Electronic	Electronic	②	②	12B	4-6	②	650
	8-302	ARF-42B	0.044	Electronic	Electronic	12B	6B	16B	4-6	850/550	650
	8-360	BRF-42B	②	Electronic	Electronic	②	②	13B	4-6	②	②
	8-390	BRF-42B	②	Electronic	Electronic	②	13B	13B	4-6	②	②
	8-460	ARF-52B	②	Electronic	Electronic	—	12B	12B	4-6	—	650
1977	6-300	BRF-42B	0.044④	Electronic	Electronic	②	②	12B	5-7	②	②
	8-302	ASF-42B	0.044	Electronic	Electronic	②	②	16B	6-8	②	②
	8-351	ASF-42B	0.044	Electronic	Electronic	②	②	—	6-8	②	②
	8-400	ASF-42B	0.044	Electronic	Electronic	②	②	—	6-8	②	②
	8-460	ASF-42B	0.044	Electronic	Electronic	②	②	—	5-7	②	②

▲ Where two figures are separated by a slash, the lower of the two is the rpm with the idle solenoid disconnected.
① Breakerless ignition available in 1974
② See underhood specifications sticker
③ With underhood sticker #659-6B
④ Engines built after 11/15/76: 0.054
⑤ With Exhaust Emission—TDC
⑥ Transistor Ignition—TDC
⑦ Transistor Ignition —22-24
⑧ Transistor Ignition .020
⑨ Auto. Trans.—0.030
⑩ With exhaust emission:
  Man. Trans.—625
  Auto. Trans.—550
  Without exhaust emission:
  Man. Trans.—550
  Auto. Trans.—475

5762C01

TUNE-UP SPECIFICATIONS 1978-80

(For 1979 and 1980 Tune-Up Specifications consult the Vehicle Emissions Control Label, which is located on the engine of the vehicle. This decal will contain a calibration number which when used in conjunction with the chart below will yield the required tune-up information. If the information given in this chart disagrees with the information on the decal, use the information on the decal.)

Calibration	Spark Plug Gap	Ignition Timing	Fast Idle RPM High Cam	Fast Idle RPM Kick Down	Curb Idle rpm A/C① Off/On	Curb Idle rpm Non A/C	Tsp Off rpm A/C	Tsp Off rpm Non A/C
9-87G-R0	.042-.046	8°BTDC	2700	—	—	600	—	—
9-97J-R0	.042-.046	8°BTDC	—	1600	650	—	—	—
9-97J-R11	.042-.046	8°BTDC	—	1600	650	—	—	—

① Only for A/C-TSP equipped. A/C compressor electromagnetic clutch deenergized.

85762C02

TUNE-UP SPECIFICATIONS 1981

(For 1981 Tune-Up Specifications consult the Vehicle Emissions Control Label, which is located on the engine of the vehicle. This decal will contain a calibration number which when used in conjunction with the chart below will yield the required tune-up information. If the information given in this chart disagrees with the information on the decal, use the information on the decal.)

Calibration Number	Engine	Spark Plug Gap	Ignition Timing °BTDC	Timing RPM	Fast Idle rpm High CAM	Fast Idle rpm Kick Down	Curb Idle rpm A/C On	Curb Idle rpm A/C Off	Curb Idle rpm Non A/C
1-57G-R1	4.1L	.042-.046	4	800	2200	—	—	—	750
1-57G-R10	4.1L	.042-.046	4	800	2050	—	—	—	700
1-58-R0	4.1L	.042-.046	10	800	2000	—	—	—	575
1-51D-R0	4.9L	.042-.046	6	800	—	1400	700	600	600
1-51D-R10	4.9L	.042-.046	6	800	—	1250	650	550	550
1-51D-R12	4.9L	.042-.046	6	800	—	1250	650	550	550
1-51E-R0	4.9L	.042-.046	6	800	—	1400	700	600	600
1-51F-R0	4.9L	.042-.046	6	800	—	1250	650	550	550
1-51G-R0	4.9L	.042-.046	6	800	—	1250	650	550	550
1-51H-R0	4.9L	.042-.046	6	800	—	1250	650	550	550
1-51K-R0	4.9L	.042-.046	6	800	—	1250	650	550	550
1-51L-R0	4.9L	.042-.046	6	800	—	1250	650	550	550
1-51E-R10	4.9L	.042-.046	6	800	—	1400	700	600	600
1-51F-R10	4.9L	.042-.046	6	800	—	1250	650	550	550
1-51G-R10	4.9L	.042-.046	6	800	—	1250	650	550	550
1-51H-R10	4.9L	.042-.046	6	800	—	1250	650	550	550
1-51K-R10	4.9L	.042-.046	6	800	—	1250	650	550	550
1-51L-R10	4.9L	.042-.046	6	800	—	1250	650	550	550
1-51S-R0	4.9L	.042-.046	6	800	—	1400	700	600	600
1-51S-R10	4.9L	.042-.046	6	800	—	1250	650	550	550
1-51T-R0	4.9L	.042-.046	6	800	—	1250	650	550	550
1-52G-R0	4.9L	.042-.046	10	800	—	1400	—	—	500
1-52H-R0	4.9L	.042-.046	10	800	—	1250	—	—	500
1-52K-R0	4.9L	.042-.046	10	800	—	1250	—	—	500
1-52L-R0	4.9L	.042-.046	10	800	—	1250	—	—	500
1-52G-R10	4.9L	.042-.046	10	800	—	1400	—	—	500
1-52H-R10	4.9L	.042-.046	10	800	—	1250	—	—	500
1-52K-R10	4.9L	.042-.046	10	800	—	1250	—	—	500
1-52L-R10	4.9L	.042-.046	10	800	—	1250	—	—	500
1-52S-R0	4.9L	.042-.046	10	800	—	1400	—	—	500
1-52T-R0	4.9L	.042-.046	10	800	—	1250	—	—	550
5-77-R1	4.9L	.042-.046	10	800	—	1500	—	—	600(A)
5-78-R1	4.9L	.042-.046	10	800	—	1500	—	—	700(M)
9-77J-R12	4.9L	.042-.046	12	800	1600	—	—	—	700
9-77S-R10	4.9L	.042-.046	10	800	1600	—	—	—	700
9-78J-R0	4.9L	.042-.046	12	800	1600	1500	—	—	550
9-78J-R11	4.9L	.042-.046	12	800	2200	—	—	—	550
1-53D-R0	5.0L	.042-.046	8	800	2050	—	—	—	700
1-53F-R0	5.0L	.042-.046	8	800	2050	—	—	—	650
1-53G-R0	5.0L	.042-.046	8	800	2050	—	—	—	650

85762C03

TUNE-UP SPECIFICATIONS 1981

(For 1981 Tune-Up Specifications consult the Vehicle Emissions Control Label, which is located on the engine of the vehicle. This decal will contain a calibration number which when used in conjunction with the chart below will yield the required tune-up information. If the information given in this chart disagrees with the information on the decal, use the information on the decal.)

Calibration Number	Engine	Spark Plug Gap	Ignition Timing °BTDC	Timing RPM	Fast Idle rpm High CAM	Fast Idle rpm Kick Down	Curb Idle rpm A/C On	Curb Idle rpm A/C Off	Curb Idle rpm Non A/C
1-53H-R0	5.0L	.042-.046	8	800	2050	-	-	-	650
1-53K-R0	5.0L	.042-.046	8	800	2050	-	-	-	650
1-53D-R10	5.0L	.042-.046	8	800	2200	-	-	-	700
1-53G-R10	5.0L	.042-.046	8	800	2050	-	-	-	650
1-53K-R10	5.0L	.042-.046	8	800	2050	-	-	-	650
1-53D-R12	5.0L	.042-.046	8	800	2050	-	-	-	650
1-53F-R11	5.0L	.042-.046	8	800	2050	-	-	-	650
1-53G-R12	5.0L	.042-.046	8	800	2050	-	-	-	650
1-53H-R11	5.0L	.042-.046	8	800	2050	-	-	-	650
1-53K-R13	5.0L	.042-.046	8	800	2050	-	-	-	650
1-54D-R1	5.0L	.042-.046	8	800	2000	-	-	-	575
1-54K-R0	5.0L	.042-.046	8	800	1850	-	-	-	525
1-54F-R0	5.0L	.042-.046	8	800	2000	-	-	-	575
1-54G-R0	5.0L	.042-.046	8	800	2000	-	-	-	575
1-54H-R0	5.0L	.042-.046	8	800	2000	-	-	-	575
1-54L-R2	5.0L	.042-.046	8	800	2000	-	-	-	575
1-54P-R0	5.0L	.042-.046	-	-	1350	-	-	-	-
1-54R-R0	5.0L	.042-.046	-	-	1350	-	-	-	-
1-54P-R10	5.0L	.042-.046	-	-	1350	-	-	-	-
1-54R-R10	5.0L	.042-.046	-	-	1200	-	-	-	-
7-79-R1	5.0L	.042-.046	6	800	-	1250	-	-	750
7-80-R0	5.0L	.042-.046	6	800	-	1500	-	-	650
1-59A-R0	5.8L	.042-.046	10	800	2000	-	650	-	650
1-59H-R0	5.8L	.042-.046	10	800	2000	-	650	-	650
1-59K-R0	5.8L	.042-.046	10	800	2000	-	650	-	650
1-59A-R10	5.8L	.042-.046	10	800	2000	-	650	-	650
1-59B-R10	5.8L	.042-.046	10	800	2000	-	650	-	650
1-59G-R10	5.8L	.042-.046	10	800	1850	-	600	-	600
1-59H-R10	5.8L	.042-.046	6	800	1850	-	600	-	600
1-59K-R10	5.8L	.042-.046	6	800	1850	-	600	-	600
1-60A-R0	5.8L	.042-.046	6	800	2200	-	-	-	-
1-60B-R0	5.8L	.042-.046	6	800	2200	-	-	-	-
1-60H-R1	5.8L	.042-.046	6	800	2000	-	625	550	550
1-60J-R0	5.8L	.042-.046	6	800	2000	-	625	550	550
1-60K-R1	5.8L	.042-.046	6	800	2000	-	625	550	550
1-60A-R10	5.8L	.042-.046	6	800	1850	-	575	500	500
1-60B-R10	5.8L	.042-.046	6	800	1850	-	575	500	500
1-60H-R10	5.8L	.042-.046	6	800	1850	-	575	500	500

85762CA3

TUNE-UP SPECIFICATIONS 1981

(For 1981 Tune-Up Specifications consult the Vehicle Emissions Control Label, which is located on the engine of the vehicle. This decal will contain a calibration number which when used in conjunction with the chart below will yield the required tune-up information. If the information given in this chart disagrees with the information on the decal, use the information on the decal.)

Calibration Number	Engine	Spark Plug Gap	Ignition Timing °BTDC	Timing RPM	Fast Idle rpm High CAM	Fast Idle rpm Kick Down	Curb Idle rpm A/C On	Curb Idle rpm A/C Off	Curb Idle rpm Non A/C
1-60J-R10	5.8L	.042-.046	6	800	1850	-	575	500	500
1-60K-R10	5.8L	.042-.046	6	800	1850	-	575	500	500
1-63T-R0	5.8L	.042-0.46	-	-	1700	-	-	-	-
1-64A-R0	5.8L	.042-0.46	8	800	2000	-	625	550	550
1-64G-R1	5.8L	.042-0.46	10	600	2000	-	625	550	550
1-64H-R2	5.8L	.042-0.46	10	600	2000	-	625	550	550
1-64R-R1	5.8L	.042-0.46	-	-	1650	-	-	-	-
1-64S-R0	5.8L	.042-0.46	-	-	1500	-	-	-	-
1-64T-R0	5.8L	.042-0.46	-	-	1500	-	-	-	-
7-76J-R11	5.8L	.042-0.46	6	800	1700	-	-	-	600
9-71J-R10	5.8L	.042-0.46	10	800	1750	-	-	-	600
9-71J-R11	5.8L	.042-0.46	10	800	1750	-	-	-	600
9-72J-R11	5.8L	.042-0.46	10	800	2000	-	-	-	600
9-72J-R12	5.8L	.042-0.46	10	800	2000	-	-	-	600
9-83G-R12	6.1L	.042-0.46	6	800	2200	-	-	-	600
9-83H-R11	6.1L	.042-0.46	6	800	2500	-	-	-	600
9-83H-R14	6.1L	.042-0.46	2	800	2500	-	-	-	600
9-73J-R11	6.6L	.042-0.46	6	800	1750	-	-	-	600
9-73J-R12	6.6L	.042-0.46	6	800	1750	-	-	-	600
9-74J-R11	6.6L	.042-0.46	3	800	2000	-	-	-	600
9-74J-R12	6.6L	.042-0.46	6	800	2000	-	-	-	600
9-87G-R11	7.0L	.042-0.46	6	800	2700	-	-	-	600
9-97J-R0	7.5L	.042-0.46	8	800	1600	-	-	-	600
7-93J-R0	7.8L	.038-0.42	10	800	2500	-	650	650	600
7-95J-R0	8.8L	.038-0.42	10	800	2500	-	-	-	600

85762CB3

TUNE-UP SPECIFICATIONS 1982

(For 1982 Tune-Up Specifications consult the Vehicle Emissions Control Label, which is located on the engine of the vehicle. This decal will contain a calibration number which when used in conjunction with the chart below will yield the required tune-up information. If the information given in this chart disagrees with the information on the decal, use the information on the decal.)

Calibration	Engine	Spark Plug Gap	Ignition Timing	Fast Idle rpm	Curb Idle rpm
2-54R-R0	5.0L	.042-.046	—	1350	—
2-54X-R1	5.0L	.042-.046	12° BTDC	2100	650
1-63T-R1	5.8L	.042-.046	—	1700	—
1-63T-R10B	5.8L	.042-.046	—	1700	—
1-64H-R2	5.8L	.042-.046	10° BTDC	2000	625
1-64R-R1	5.8L	.042-.046	—	1650	—
1-64S-R0	5.8L	.042-.046	—	1650	—
1-64T-R0	5.8L	.042-.046	—	1650	—
1-64T-R10	5.8L	.042-.046	—	1650	—
2-63Y-R10B	5.8L	.042-.046	—	1700	—
2-64X-R0	5.8L	.042-.046	14° BTDC	2000	625
2-64Y-R10B	5.8L	.042-.046	—	1650	—
9-77J-R12	4.9L	.042-.046	12° BTDC	1600	—
9-77G-R10	4.9L	.042-.046	10° BTDC	1600	—
9-78J-R0	4.9L	.042-.046	12° BTDC	1600	—
9-78J-R11	4.9L	.042-.046	12° BTDC	1600	—
2-75J-R17	5.8L	.042-.046	5° BTDC	1500	700①
2-76J-R17	5.8L	.042-.046	5° BTDC	1500	—
7-75J-R14	5.8L	.042-.046	6° BTDC	1500	700①
7-76J-R11	5.8L	.042-.046	6° BTDC	1700	—
7-76J-R13	5.8L	.042-.046	12° BTDC	1600	500
7-76J-R14	5.8L	.042-.046	6° BTDC	1700	—
7-76J-R15	5.8L	.042-.046	6° BTDC	1700	—
9-83G-R12	6.1L	.042-.046	6° BTDC	2200	600
9-83H-R11	6.1L	.042-.046	6° BTDC	2500	600
9-83H-R14	6.1L	.042-.046	2° BTDC	2500	600
9-73J-R11	6.6L	.042-.046	6° BTDC	1750	600④
9-73J-R12	6.6L	.042-.046	6° BTDC	1750	600④
9-73J-R13	6.6L	.042-.046	6° BTDC	1750	600④
9-73J-R14	6.6L	.042-.046	6° BTDC	1750	—
9-74J-R11	6.6L	.042-.046	6° BTDC	2000	—
9-74J-R12	6.6L	.042-.046	6° BTDC	2000	—
9-74J-R13	6.6L	.042-.046	3° BTDC	2000	—
9-74J-R14	6.6L	.042-.046	6° BTDC	2000	—
9-87G-R11	7.0L	.042-.046	6° BTDC	—	600
9-97J-R12	7.5L	.042-.046	8° BTDC	—	650

① A/C on—50 RPM Less is NON A/C
② A/C on—600 NON A/C
③ 100 RPM Less for NON A/C or A/C off
④ NON A/C

TUNE-UP SPECIFICATIONS 1983

(For 1983 Tune-Up Specifications consult the Vehicle Emissions Control Label, which is located on the engine of the vehicle. This decal will contain a calibration number which when used in conjunction with the chart below will yield the required tune-up information. If the information given in this chart disagrees with the information on the decal, use the information on the decal.)

Calibration	Engine	Spark Plug Gap	Ignition Timing	Fast Idle rpm	Curb Idle rpm
3-55D-R00	3.8L	.042-.046	2° BTDC	1300	550
3-56D-R00	3.8L	.042-.046	10° BTDC	2200	550
3-51D-R00	4.9L	.042-.046	6° BTDC	1600	700②
3-51E-R01	4.9L	.042-.046	6° BTDC	1600	700②
2-63Y-R12	5.8L	.042-.046	—	1700	750
2-64X-R00	5.8L	.042-.046	14° BTDC	2000	625③
2-64Y-R11	5.8L	.042-.046	—	1650	600
2-64Y-R12	5.8L	.042-.046	10° BTDC	1650	600②
5-77-R01	4.9L	.042-.046	10° BTDC	1500	600②
5-78-R01	4.9L	.042-.046	10° BTDC	1500	600②
9-77J-R12	4.9L	.042-.046	12° BTDC	1600	700
9-77S-R10	4.9L	.042-.046	10° BTDC	1600	700
9-78J-R00	4.9L	.042-.046	12° BTDC	1600	550
9-78J-R11	4.9L	.042-.046	12° BTDC	1600	550
7-79-R01	5.0L	.042-.046	6° BTDC	1250	750
7-80-R00	5.0L	.042-.046	6° BTDC	1600	650
2-75A-R10	5.8L	.042-.046	8° BTDC	1500	650
2-75J-R20	5.8L	.042-.046	8° BTDC	1500	650
2-76A-R10	5.8L	.042-.046	8° BTDC	1500	650
2-76J-R20	5.8L	.042-.046	8° BTDC	1500	650
9-83G-R12	6.1L	.042-.046	6° BTDC	2200	600
9-83G-R14	6.1L	.042-.046	6° BTDC	1600	600
9-83H-R11	6.1L	.042-.046	6° BTDC	2500	600
9-83H-R14	6.1L	.042-.046	2° BTDC	2500	600
9-87G-R11	7.0L	.042-.046	6° BTDC	2700	600
9-97J-R13	7.5L	.042-.046	8° BTDC	1600	600
9-98S-R00	7.5L	.042-.046	6° BTDC	1500	600

① 600—Non A/C or A/C off
② 550—A/C off and Non A/C
③ 700—Manual Trans.

8576C C05

8576C C04

TUNE-UP SPECIFICATIONS 1984

(For 1984 Tune-Up Specifications consult the Vehicle Emissions Control Label, which is located on the engine of the vehicle. This decal will contain a calibration number which when used in conjunction with the chart below will yield the required tune-up information. If the information given in this chart disagrees with the information on the decal, use the information on the decal.)

Calibration	Engine	Spark Plug Gap	Ignition Timing	Fast Idle rpm	Curb Idle rpm
4-51D-R01	4.9L	.042-.046	10° BTDC	1600	600-700[1]
4-51E-R00	4.9L	.042-.046	10° BTDC	1600	600-700[1]
4-51K-R00	4.9L	.042-.046	10° BTDC	1600	600-700[1]
4-51L-R00	4.9L	.042-.046	10° BTDC	1600	600-700[1]
4-51R-R00	4.9L	.042-.046	10° BTDC	1600	600-700[1]
4-51S-R00	4.9L	.042-.046	10° BTDC	1600	600-700[1]
4-51S-R01	4.9L	.042-.046	10° BTDC	1600	600-700[1]
4-51S-R02	4.9L	.042-.046	10° BTDC	1600	600-700[1]
4-51T-R00	4.9L	.042-.046	10° BTDC	1600	600-700[1]
4-51Z-R00	4.9L	.042-.046	10° BTDC	1600	600-700[1]
4-51L-R00	4.9L	.042-.046	10° BTDC	1600	600-700[1]
4-52R-R00	4.9L	.042-.046	10° BTDC	1600	600-700[1]
4-52S-R00	4.9L	.042-.046	10° BTDC	1600	600-700[1]
4-52T-R00	4.9L	.042-.046	10° BTDC	1600	600-700[1]
4-52W-R00	4.9L	.042-.046	10° BTDC	1600	600-700[1]
4-53F-R00	5.0L	.042-.046	8° BTDC	2100	800[2]
4-53F-R10	5.0L	.042-.046	8° BTDC	2100	800[2]
4-53G-R00	5.0L	.042-.046	8° BTDC	2100	800[2]
4-53G-R10	5.0L	.042-.046	8° BTDC	2100	800[2]
4-53K-R00	5.0L	.042-.046	8° BTDC	2100	800[2]
4-53K-R10	5.0L	.042-.046	8° BTDC	2100	800[2]
4-53Z-R00	5.0L	.042-.046	8° BTDC	2100	800[2]
4-53Z-R10	5.0L	.042-.046	8° BTDC	2100	800[2]
4-54E-R00	5.0L	.042-.046	8° BTDC	2100	800[2]
4-53E-R10	5.0L	.042-.046	8° BTDC	2100	800[2]
4-54J-R00	5.0L	.042-.046	8° BTDC	2100	800[2]
4-54J-R10	5.0L	.042-.046	8° BTDC	2100	800[2]
4-54L-R00	5.0L	.042-.046	8° BTDC	2100	800[2]
4-54L-R10	5.0L	.042-.046	8° BTDC	2100	800[2]
4-54R-R00	5.0L	.042-.046	10° BTDC	2000	575
4-54R-R10	5.0L	.042-.046	10° BTDC	2000	575
4-54T-R00	5.0L	.042-.046	10° BTDC	2000	575
4-54T-R10	5.0L	.042-.046	10° BTDC	2000	575
4-54W-R00	5.0L	.042-.046	12° BTDC	2100	675[4]
4-54W-R10	5.0L	.042-.046	12° BTDC	2100	675[4]
4-63H-R00	5.0L	.042-.046	10° BTDC	2000	750
4-64H-R00	5.8L	.042-.046	10° BTDC	2000	600
4-64T-R00	5.8L	.042-.046	10° BTDC	2000	600
4-64Y-R00	5.8L	.042-.046	10° BTDC	2000	600
5-77-R01	4.9L	.042-.046	10° BTDC	1500	600[1]

85762C06

TUNE-UP SPECIFICATIONS 1984

(For 1984 Tune-Up Specifications consult the Vehicle Emissions Control Label, which is located on the engine of the vehicle. This decal will contain a calibration number which when used in conjunction with the chart below will yield the required tune-up information. If the information given in this chart disagrees with the information on the decal, use the information on the decal.)

Calibration	Engine	Spark Plug Gap	Ignition Timing	Fast Idle rpm	Curb Idle rpm
5-78-R01	4.9L	.042-.046	10° BTDC	1500	600[1]
9-77J-R12	4.9L	.042-.046	12° BTDC	1600	700[1]
9-78J-R00	4.9L	.042-.046	12° BTDC	1600	550
9-78J-R11	4.9L	.042-.046	12° BTDC	1600	550
7-79-R01	5.0L	.042-.046	6° BTDC	1500	750[6]
7-80-R00	5.0L	.042-.046	6° BTDC	1500	750[6]
2-75A-R10	5.8L	.042-.046	8° BTDC	1500	800[7]
2-75J-R20	5.8L	.042-.046	8° BTDC	1500	700[1]
2-76A-R10	5.8L	.042-.046	8° BTDC	1500	800[6]
2-76J-R20	5.8L	.042-.046	8° BTDC	1500	700[1]
9-83G-R12	6.1L	.042-.046	6° BTDC	2200	600
9-83G-R14	6.1L	.042-.046	6° BTDC	1600	600
9-83H-R11	6.1L	.042-.046	6° BTDC	2500	600
9-83G-R11	7.0L	.042-.046	6° BTDC	2700	600
9-97J-R10	7.5L	.042-.046	8° BTDC	1600	800[7]
3-98S-R10	7.5L	.042-.046	8° BTDC	1600	800[7]
4-98S-R00	7.5L	.042-.046	8° BTDC	1600	800[7]
4-37A-R00	2.0L	—	—	1450	725-775
4-37B-R00	2.0L	—	—	1450	725-775
3-47D-R00	2.2L	—	—	1450	780-830
4-68J-R00	6.9L	—	—	—	650-700
4-68X-R00	6.9L	—	—	—	650-700

[1] 550-650 RPM—Auto. Trans. in DRIVE
[2] 700—Non A/C or A/C off
[3] 700—Non A/C or A/C off
[4] 700—Manual Trans.
[5] 600—TSP off
[6] 650—"D" auto. trans.; 525—TSP off
[7] 650—DRIVE

85762CA6

TUNE-UP SPECIFICATIONS 1985-86

(For 1985-86 Tune-Up Specifications consult the Vehicle Emissions Control Label, which is located on the engine of the vehicle. This decal will contain a calibration number which when used in conjunction with the chart below will yield the required tune-up information. If the information given in this chart disagrees with the information on the decal, use the information on the decal.)

Calibration	Engine	Spark Plug Gap	Ignition Timing	Fast Idle rpm	Curb Idle rpm
4-51R-R00	4.9L	.042-.046	10° BTDC	1600	600-700①
4-51S-R02	4.9L	.042-.046	10° BTDC	1600	600-700①
4-51T-R00	4.9L	.042-.046	10° BTDC	1600	600-700①
4-52G-R02	4.9L	.042-.046	10° BTDC	1600	600-700①
4-52G-R10	4.9L	.042-.046	10° BTDC	1600	600-700①
4-52L-R00	4.9L	.042-.046	10° BTDC	1600	600-700①
4-52L-R10	4.9L	.042-.046	10° BTDC	1600	600-700①
4-52R-R00	4.9L	.042-.046	10° BTDC	1600	600-700①
4-52S-R00	4.9L	.042-.046	10° BTDC	1600	600-700①
4-52S-R10	4.9L	.042-.046	10° BTDC	1600	600-700①
4-52T-R00	4.9L	.042-.046	10° BTDC	1600	600-700①
5-51D-R00	4.9L	.042-.046	10° BTDC	1600	600-700①
5-51E-R00	4.9L	.042-.046	10° BTDC	1600	600-700①
5-51F-R00	4.9L	.042-.046	10° BTDC	1600	600-700①
5-51H-R00	4.9L	.042-.046	10° BTDC	1600	600-700①
5-51K-R00	4.9L	.042-.046	10° BTDC	1600	600-700①
5-51L-R00	4.9L	.042-.046	10° BTDC	1600	600-700①
5-51V-R00	4.9L	.042-.046	10° BTDC	1600	600-700①
5-51Z-R00	4.9L	.042-.046	10° BTDC	1600	600-700①
5-52E-R00	4.9L	.042-.046	10° BTDC	1600	600-700①
5-52K-R00	4.9L	.042-.046	10° BTDC	1600	600-700①
5-52W-R00	4.9L	.042-.046	10° BTDC	1600	600-700①
5-52Y-R00	4.9L	.042-.046	10° BTDC	1600	600-700①
4-54R-R12	5.0L	.042-.046	10° BTDC	2000	575D
4-54R-R13	5.0L	.042-.046	10° BTDC	2000	575D
4-54R-R14	5.0L	.042-.046	10° BTDC	2000	575D
5-53D-R00	5.0L	.042-.046	10° BTDC	—	—
5-53D-R01	5.0L	.042-.046	10° BTDC	—	—
5-53F-R00	5.0L	.042-.046	8° BTDC	—	—
5-53F-R01	5.0L	.042-.046	8° BTDC	—	—
5-53H-R00	5.0L	.042-.046	8° BTDC	—	—
5-53H-R01	5.0L	.042-.046	10° BTDC	—	—
5-54Q-R00	5.0L	.042-.046	10° BTDC	—	—
5-54Q-R01	5.0L	.042-.046	10° BTDC	—	—
5-54S-R00	5.0L	.042-.046	10° BTDC	—	—
5-54S-R01	5.0L	.042-.046	10° BTDC	—	—
5-54W-R00	5.0L	.042-.046	10° BTDC	—	—
5-54X-R00	5.0L	.042-.046	10° BTDC	—	—
4-64G-R00	5.8L(F)	.042-.046	10° BTDC	1900	650D
4-64G-R02	5.8L(F)	.042-.046	10° BTDC	1900	650D
4-64G-R02	5.8L(E)	.042-.046	10° BTDC	1900	650D

85762G07

TUNE-UP SPECIFICATIONS 1985-86

(For 1985-86 Tune-Up Specifications consult the Vehicle Emissions Control Label, which is located on the engine of the vehicle. This decal will contain a calibration number which when used in conjunction with the chart below will yield the required tune-up information. If the information given in this chart disagrees with the information on the decal, use the information on the decal.)

Calibration	Engine	Spark Plug Gap	Ignition Timing	Fast Idle rpm	Curb Idle rpm
4-64T-R00	5.8L(F)	.042-.046	10° BTDC	2000	600D
4-64T-R00	5.8L(E)	.042-.046	10° BTDC	2000	600D
4-64Z-R10	5.8L(F)	.042-.046	14° BTDC	1900	650D
4-64Z-R10	5.8L(E)	.042-.046	14° BTDC	1900	650D
5-63H-R00	5.8L	.042-.046	10° BTDC	2000	700
5-63Y-R00	5.8L	.042-.046	10° BTDC	2000	700

85762CA7

① 550-650 in Drive A/T

FIRING ORDERS

◆ **See Figures 10, 11, 12, 13 and 14**

➡**To avoid confusion, remove and tag the spark plug wires one at a time, for replacement.**

If a distributor is not keyed for installation with only one orientation, it could have been removed previously and rewired. The resultant wiring would hold the correct firing order, but could change the relative placement of the plug towers in relation to the engine. For this reason it is imperative that you label all wires before disconnecting any of them. Also, before removal, compare the current wiring with the accompanying illustrations. If the current wiring does not match, make notes in your book to reflect how your engine is wired.

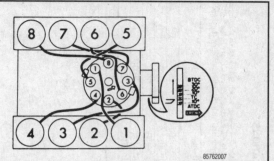
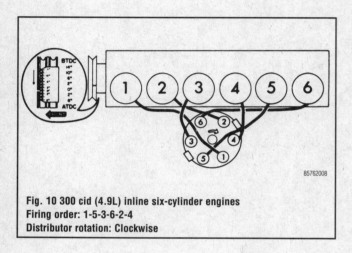

Fig. 12 255 cid (4.2L), 302 cid (5.0L), 360 cid (5.9L), 390 cid (6.5L), 460 cid (7.5L) V8 engines
Firing order: 1-5-4-2-6-3-7-8
Distributor rotation: Counterclockwise

Fig. 10 300 cid (4.9L) inline six-cylinder engines
Firing order: 1-5-3-6-2-4
Distributor rotation: Clockwise

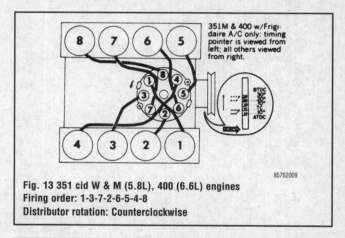

Fig. 13 351 cid W & M (5.8L), 400 (6.6L) engines
Firing order: 1-3-7-2-6-5-4-8
Distributor rotation: Counterclockwise

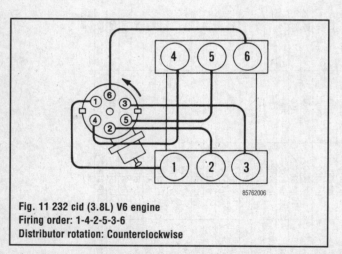

Fig. 11 232 cid (3.8L) V6 engine
Firing order: 1-4-2-5-3-6
Distributor rotation: Counterclockwise

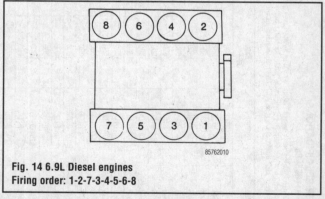

Fig. 14 6.9L Diesel engines
Firing order: 1-2-7-3-4-5-6-8

DURA SPARK ELECTRONIC IGNITION SYSTEMS

Carbureted Engines

BASIC OPERATING PRINCIPLES

The Ford Solid State Ignition is a pulse triggered, transistor controlled breakerless ignition system. With the ignition switch **ON**, the primary circuit is on and the ignition coil is energized. When the armature spokes approach the magnetic pick-up coil assembly, they induce a voltage which tells the amplifier to turn the coil primary current off. A timing circuit in the amplifier module will turn the current on again after the coil field has collapsed. When the current is

on, it flows from the battery through the ignition switch, the primary windings of the ignition coil, and through the amplifier module circuits to ground. When the current is off, the magnetic field built up in the ignition coil is allowed to collapse, inducing a high voltage into the second windings of the coil. High voltage is produced each time the field is thus built up and collapsed.

Although the systems are basically the same, Ford refers to their solid state ignition in several different ways. 1976 systems are referred to simply as Breakerless systems. In 1977, Ford named their ignition system Dura Spark I and Dura Spark II. In 1982 Ford dropped the Dura Spark I and introduced the Dura Spark III. This system is based on Electronic Engine Control (EEC). The EEC system controls spark advance in response to various engine sensors. This includes a crankshaft position sensor which replaces the stator and armature assembly in the distributor. Dura Spark II is the version used in all states except California. Dura Spark I and III are the systems used in California V8's only. Basically, the only difference between the two is that the coil charging currents are higher in the California vehicles. This is necessary to fire the leaner fuel/air mixtures required by California's stricter emission laws. The difference in coils alters some of the test values.

Ford has used several different types of wiring harness on their solid state ignition systems, due to internal circuitry changes in the electronic module. Wire continuity and color have not been changed, but the arrangement of the terminals in the connectors is different for each year. Schematics of the different years are included here, but keep in mind that the wiring in all diagrams has been simplified and as a result, the routing of your wiring may not match the wiring in the diagram. However, the wire colors and terminal connections are the same.

Wire color coding is critical to servicing the Ford Solid State Ignition. Battery current reaches the electronic module through either the white or red wire, depending on whether the engine is cranking or running. When the engine is cranking, battery current is flowing through the white wire. When the engine is running, battery current flows through the red wire. All distributor signals flow through the orange and purple wires. The green wire carries primary current from the coil to the module. The black wire is a ground between the distributor and the module. In 1976, the blue wire was dropped when the zener diode was added to the module. The orange and purple wires which run from the stator to the module must always be connected to the same color wire at the module. If these connections are crossed, polarity will be reversed and the system will be thrown out of phase. Some replacement wiring harnesses were sold with the wiring crossed, which complicates the problem considerably. As previously noted, the black wire is the ground wire. The screw which grounds the black wire, also, of course, grounds the engine primary circuit. If this screw is loose, dirty, or corroded, a seemingly incomprehensible ignition problem will develop. Several other cautions should be noted here. Keep in mind that on vehicles equipped with catalytic converters, any test that requires removal of a spark plug wire while the engine is running should be kept to a thirty second maximum. Any longer than this may damage the converter. In the event you are testing spark plug wires, do not pierce them. Test the wires at their terminals only.

TROUBLESHOOTING THE FORD SOLID STATE IGNITION SYSTEM

▶ See Figure 15

➡Ford has substantially altered their 1978–86 electronic ignition test procedure. Due to the sensitive nature of the system and the complexity of the test procedures, it is recommended that you refer to your dealer if you suspect a problem in your 1978–86 electronic ignition system. The system can, of course, be tested by substituting known good components (module, stator, etc.).

This system, which at first appears to be extremely complicated, is actually quite simple to diagnose and repair. Diagnosis does, however, require the use of a voltmeter and an ohmmeter. You will also need several jumper wires with both blade ends and alligator clips.

The symptoms of a defective component within the solid state system are exactly the same as those you would encounter in a conventional system. Some of these symptoms are:
- Hard or no starting
- Rough idle
- Poor fuel economy
- Engine misses while under load or while accelerating

If you suspect a problem in your ignition system, first perform a spark intensity test to pinpoint the problem. Using insulated pliers, hold the end of one of the spark plug leads about ½ inch (12.7mm) away from the engine block or other good ground, and crank the engine. If you have a nice, fat spark, then your problem is not in the ignition system. If you have no spark or a very weak spark, then proceed to the following tests.

Stator Test

▶ See Figure 16

To test the stator (also known as the magnetic pickup assembly), you will need an ohmmeter. Run the engine until it reaches operating temperature, then turn the ignition switch to the off position. Disconnect the wire harness from the distributor. Connect the ohmmeter between the orange and purple wires. Resistance should be 400–800Ω. Next, connect the ohmmeter between the black wire and a good ground on the engine. Operate the vacuum advance either by hand or with an external vacuum source. Resistance should be Ω. Finally, connect the ohmmeter between the orange wire and ground, and then purple wire and ground. Resistance should be over 70,000Ω in both cases. If any of your ohmmeter readings differ from the above specifications, then the stator is defective and must be replaced as a unit.

If the stator is good, then either the electronic module or the wiring connections must be checked next. Because of its complicated electronic nature, the module itself cannot be checked, except by substitution. If you have access to a module which you know to be good, then perform a substitution test at this time. If this cures the problem, then the original module is faulty and must be replaced. If it does not cure the problem or if you cannot locate a known good module, then disconnect the two wiring harnesses from the module, and, using a voltmeter, check the following circuits.

➡Make no tests at the module side of the connectors.

1. Starting circuit: Connect the voltmeter leads to ground and to the corresponding female socket of the white male lead from the module (you will need a jumper wire with a blade end). Crank the engine over. The voltage should be between 8 and 12 volts.

2. Running circuit: Turn the ignition switch to the ON position. Connect the voltmeter leads to ground and the corresponding female socket of the red male lead from the module. Voltage should be battery voltage plus or minus 0.1 volts.

3. Coil circuit: Leave the ignition switch ON. Connect the voltmeter leads to ground and to the corresponding female socket of the green male lead from the module. Voltage should be battery voltage plus or minus 0.1 volts.

If any of the preceding readings are incorrect, inspect and repair any loose, broken, frayed or dirty connections. If this doesn't solve the problem, perform a battery source test.

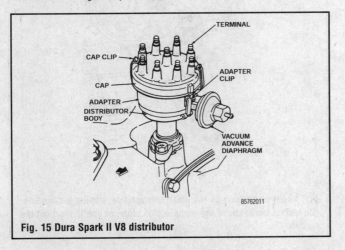

Fig. 15 Dura Spark II V8 distributor

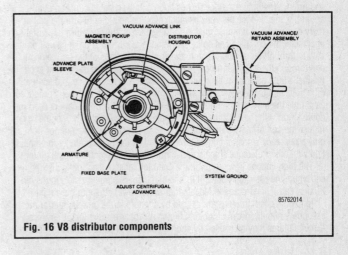

Fig. 16 V8 distributor components

Battery Source Test

To make this test, do not disconnect the coil.

Connect the voltmeter leads to the BAT terminal at the coil and a good ground. Connect a jumper wire from the DEC terminal at the coil to a good ground. Make sure all lights and accessories are off. Turn the ignition to the **ON** position. Check the voltage. If the voltage is below 4.9 volts (11 volts for Dura Spark I), then check the primary wiring for broken strands, cracked or frayed wires, or loose or dirty terminals. Repair or replace any defects. If, however, the voltage is above 7.9 volts (14 volts for Dura Spark I), then you have a problem in the resistance wiring and it must be replaced.

It should be noted here that if you do have a problem in your electronic ignition system, most of the time it will be a case of loose, dirty or frayed wires. The electronic module, being completely solid state, is not ordinarily subject to failure. It is possible for the unit to fail, of course, but as a general rule, the source of an ignition system probably will be somewhere else in the circuit.

IGNITION COIL TEST

The ignition coil must be diagnosed separately from the rest of the ignition system.

1. Primary resistance is measured between the two primary (low voltage) coil terminals, with the coil connector disconnected and the ignition switch off. Primary resistance should be 0.3-1.0Ω.

2. On Dura Spark ignitions, the secondary resistance is measured between the BATT and high voltage (secondary) terminals of the ignition coil with the ignition off, and the wiring from the coil disconnected. Secondary resistance must be 8,000-11,500Ω.

3. If resistance tests are okay, but the coil is still suspected, test the coil on a coil tester by following the test equipment manufacturer's instructions for a standard coil. If the reading differs from the original test, check for a defective harness.

SPARK PLUG WIRE RESISTANCE

Resistance on these wires must not exceed 5,000Ω per foot. To properly measure this, remove the wires from the plugs, and remove the distributor cap. Measure the resistance through the distributor cap at that end. Do not pierce any ignition wire for any reason. Measure only from the two ends.

→Silicone grease must be re-applied to the spark plug wires whenever they are removed. When removing the wires from the spark plugs, a special tool should be used. do not pull on the wires. Grasp and twist the boot to remove the wire. Whenever the high tension wires are removed from the plugs, coil, or distributor, silicone grease must be applied to the boot before reconnection. Use a clean small screwdriver blase to coat the entire interior surface with Ford silicone grease D7AZ-19A331-A, Dow Corning #111, or General Electric G-627.

SYSTEM OPERATION

With the ignition switch **ON**, the primary circuit is on and the ignition coil is energized. When the armature spokes approach the magnetic pickup coil assembly, they induce the voltage which tells the amplifier to turn the coil primary current off. A timing circuit in the amplifier module will turn the current on again after the coil field has collapsed. When the current is on, it flows from the battery through the ignition switch, the primary windings of the ignition coil, and through the amplifier module circuits to ground. When the current is off, the magnetic field built up in the ignition coil is allowed to collapse, inducing a high voltage into the secondary windings of the coil. High voltage is produced each time the field is thus built up and collapsed. When DuraSpark is used in conjunction with the EEC, the EEC computer tells the DuraSpark module when to turn the coil primary current off or on. In this case, the armature position is only a reference signal of engine timing, used by the EEC computer in combination with other reference signals to determine optimum ignition spark timing.

The high voltage flows through the coil high tension lead to the distributor cap where the rotor distributes it to one of the spark plug terminals in the distributor cap. This process is repeated for every power stroke of the engine.

Ignition system troubles are caused by a failure in the primary and/or the secondary circuit; incorrect ignition timing; or incorrect distributor advance. Circuit failures may be caused by shorts, corroded or dirty terminals, loose connections, defective wire insulation, cracked distributor cap or rotor, defective pick-up coil assembly or amplifier module, defective distributor points or fouled spark plugs.

If an engine starting or operating trouble is attributed to the ignition system, start the engine and verify the complaint. On engines that will not start, be sure that there is gasoline in the fuel tank and the fuel is reaching the cylinders. Then locate the ignition system problem using the following procedures.

TROUBLESHOOTING DURASPARK II

The following procedures can be used to determine whether the ignition system is working or not. If these procedures fail to correct the problem, a full troubleshooting procedure should be performed.

Preliminary Checks

◆ See Figures 17 and 18

1. Check the battery's state of charge and connections.
2. Inspect all wires and connections for breaks, cuts, abrasions, or burn spots. Repair as necessary.
3. Unplug all connectors one at a time and inspect for corroded or burned contacts. Repair and plug connectors back together. DO NOT remove the dielectric compound in the connectors.
4. Check for loose or damaged spark plug or coil wires. A wire resistance check is given at the end of this section. If the boots or nipples are removed on 8mm ignition wires, reline the inside of each with new silicone dielectric compound (Motorcraft WA-10).

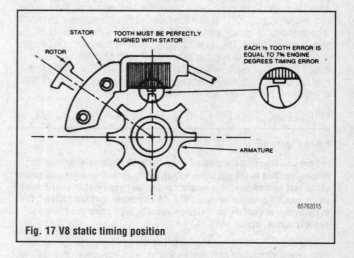

Fig. 17 V8 static timing position

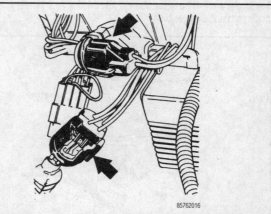

Fig. 18 When working on the electronic ignition, unplug the module connectors here. Leave the module side alone or you'll short out the module

Special Tools

♦ See Figures 19 and 20

To perform the following tests, two special tools are needed; the ignition test jumper shown in the illustration and a modified spark plug. Use the illustration to assembly the ignition test jumper. The test jumper must be used when performing the following tests. The modified spark plug is basically a spark plug with the side electrode removed. Ford makes a special tool called a Spark Tester for this purpose, which besides not having a side electrode is equipped with a spring clip so that it can be grounded to engine metal. It is recommended that the Spark Tester be used as there is less chance of being shocked.

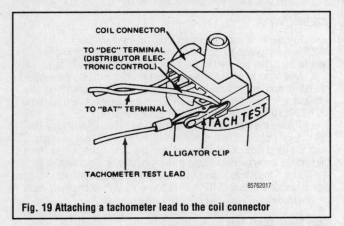

Fig. 19 Attaching a tachometer lead to the coil connector

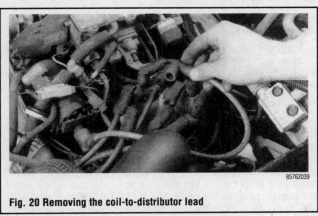

Fig. 20 Removing the coil-to-distributor lead

Run Mode Spark Test

♦ See Figures 21, 22, 23 and 24

➡The wire colors given here are the main colors of the wires, not the dots or hashmarks.

STEP 1

1. Remove the distributor cap and rotor from the distributor.
2. With the ignition off, turn the engine over by hand until one of the teeth on the distributor armature aligns with the magnet in the pickup coil.
3. Remove the coil wire from the distributor cap. Install the modified spark plug (see Special Tools, above) in the coil wire terminal and using heavy gloves and insulated pliers, hold the spark plug shell against the engine block.
4. Turn the ignition to RUN (not START) and tap the distributor body with a screwdriver handle. There should be a spark at the modified spark plug or at the coil wire terminal.
5. If a good spark is evident, the primary circuit is OK: perform the Start Mode Spark Test. If there is no spark, proceed to STEP 2.

STEP 2

1. Unplug the module connector(s) which contain(s) the green and black module leads.

Fig. 21 Removing the distributor cap

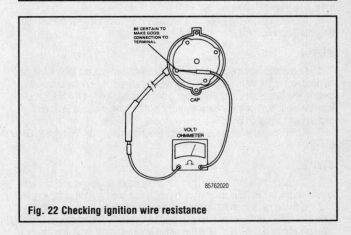

Fig. 22 Checking ignition wire resistance

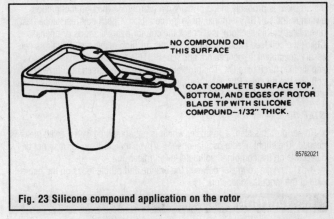

Fig. 23 Silicone compound application on the rotor

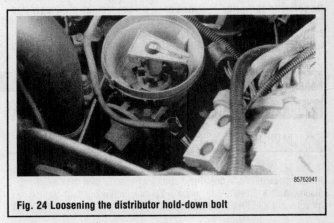

Fig. 24 Loosening the distributor hold-down bolt

2. In the harness side of the connector(s), connect the special test jumper (see Special Tools, above) between the leads which connect to the green and black leads of the module pig tails. Use paper clips on connector socket holes to make contact. Do not allow clips to ground.

3. Turn the ignition switch to RUN (not START) and close the test jumper switch. Leave closed for about 1 second, then open. Repeat several times. There should be a spark each time the switch is opened.

4. If there is no spark, the problem is probably in the primary circuit through the ignition switch, the coil, the green lead or the black lead, or the ground connection in the distributor; Perform STEP 3. If there is a spark, the primary circuit wiring and coil are probably OK. The problem is probably in the distributor pick-up, the module red wire, or the module: perform STEP 6.

STEP 3

1. Disconnect the test jumper lead from the black lead and connect it to a good ground. Turn the test jumper switch on and off several times as in STEP 2.

2. If there is no spark, the problem is probably in the green lead, the coil, or the coil feed circuit: perform STEP 5.

3. If there is spark, the problem is probably in the black lead or the distributor ground connection: perform STEP 4.

STEP 4

1. Connect an ohmmeter between the black lead and ground. With the meter on its lowest scale, there should be no measurable resistance in the circuit. If there is resistance, check the distributor ground connection and the black lead from the module. Repair as necessary, remove the ohmmeter, plug in all connections and repeat STEP 1.

2. If there is no resistance, the primary ground wiring is OK: perform STEP 6.

STEP 5

1. Disconnect the test jumper from the green lead and ground and connect it between the TACH-TEST terminal of the coil and a good ground to the engine.

2. With the ignition switch in the RUN position, turn the jumper switch on. Hold it on for about 1 second then turn it off as in Step 2. Repeat several times. There should be a spark each time the switch in turned off. If there is no spark, the problem is probably in the primary circuit running through the ignition switch to the coil BAT terminal, or in the coil itself. Check coil resistance (test given later in this section), and check the coil for internal shorts or opens. Check the coil feed circuit for opens, shorts, or high resistance. Repair as necessary, reconnect all connectors and repeat STEP 1. If there is spark, the coil and its feed circuit are OK. The problem could be in the green lead between the coil and the module. Check for an open or short, repair as necessary, reconnect all connectors and repeat STEP 1.

STEP 6

To perform this step, a voltmeter which is not combined with a dwell meter is needed. The slight needle oscillations (½ V) you'll be looking for may not be detectable on the combined voltmeter/dwell meter unit.

1. Connect a voltmeter between the orange and purple leads on the harness side of the module connectors.

❊❊ CAUTION

On catalytic converter equipped cars, disconnect the air supply line between the Thermactor by-pass valve and the manifold before cranking the engine with the ignition off. This will prevent damage to the catalytic converter. After testing, run the engine for at least 3 minutes before reconnecting the by-pass valve, to clear excess fuel from the exhaust system.

2. Set the voltmeter on its lowest scale and crank the engine. The meter needle should oscillate slightly (about ½ V). If the meter does not oscillate, check the circuit through the magnetic pick-up in the distributor for open, shorts, shorts to ground and resistance. Resistance between the orange and purple leads should be 400-1,000Ω, and between each lead and ground should be more than 70,000Ω. Repair as necessary, reconnect all connectors and repeat STEP 1.

If the meter oscillates, the problem is probably in the power feed to the module (red wire) or in the module itself: proceed to STEP 7.

STEP 7

1. Remove all meters and jumpers and plug in all connectors.

2. Turn the ignition switch to the RUN position and measure voltage between the battery positive terminal and engine ground. It should be 12 volts.

3. Next, measure voltage between the red lead of the module and engine ground. To mark this measurement, it will be necessary to pierce the red wire with a straight pin and connect the voltmeter to the straight pin and to ground. DO NOT ALLOW THE STRAIGHT PIN TO BE GROUNDED!

4. The two readings should be within one volt of each other. If not within one volt, the problem is in the power feed to the red lead. Check for shorts, open, or high resistance and correct as necessary. After repairs, repeat Step 1. If the readings are within one volt, the problem is probably in the module. Replace it with a good module and repeat STEP 1. If this corrects the problem, reconnect the old module and repeat STEP 1. If the problem returns, permanently install the new module.

Start Mode Spark Test

➡ **The wire colors given here are the main colors of the wires, not the dots or hashmarks.**

1. Remove the coil wire from the distributor cap. Install the modified spark plug mentioned under Special Tools, above, in the coil wire and ground it to engine metal either by its spring clip (Spark Tester) or by holding the spark plug shell against the engine block with insulated pliers.

➡ **See CAUTION under STEP 6 of Run Mode Spark Test, above.**

2. Have an assistant crank the engine using the ignition switch and check for spark. If there is good spark, the problem is probably in distributor cap, rotor, ignition cables or spark plugs. If there is no spark, proceed to Step 3.

3. Measure the battery voltage. Next, measure the voltage at the white wire of the module while cranking the engine. To mark this measurement, it will be necessary to pierce the white wire with a straight pin and connect the voltmeter to the straight pin and to ground. DO NOT ALLOW THE STRAIGHT PIN TO BE GROUNDED. The battery voltage and the voltage at the white wire should be within 1 volt of each other. If the readings are not within 1 volt of each other, check and repair the feed through the ignition switch to the white wire. Recheck for spark (Step 1). If the readings are within 1 volt of each other, or if there is still no spark after the power feed to white wire is repaired, proceed to Step 4.

4. Measure the coil BAT terminal voltage while cranking the engine. The reading should be within 1 volt of battery voltage. If the readings are not within 1 volt of each other, check and repair the feed through the ignition switch to the coil. If the readings are within 1 volt of each other, the problem is probably in the ignition module. Substitute another module and repeat the test for spark (Step 1).

TFI-IV ELECTRONIC IGNITION SYSTEM

5.0L Fuel Injected Engines

SYSTEM OPERATION

The TFI-IV ignition system features a universal distributor using no centrifugal or vacuum advance. The distributor has a die cast base which incorporates an integrally mounted TFI (Thick Film Integrated) ignition module, a "Hall Effect" vane switch stator assembly and provision for fixed octane adjustment. The TFI system uses an E-Core ignition coil in lieu of the Dura Spark coil. No distributor calibration is required and initial timing is not a normal adjustment, since advance etc. is controlled by the EEC-IV system.

ADJUSTMENTS

The air gap between the armature and magnetic pick-up coil in the distributor is not adjustable, nor are there any adjustment for the amplifier module.

Inoperative components are simply replaced. Any attempt to connect components outside the vehicle may result in component failure.

TROUBLESHOOTING THE TFI-IV SYSTEM

◆ **See Figure 25**

➡**After performing any test which requires piercing a wire with a straight pin, remove the straight pin and seal the holes in the wire with silicone sealer.**

Ignition Coil Secondary Voltage

1. Disconnect the secondary (high voltage) coil wire from the distributor cap and install a spark tester between the coil wire and ground.
2. Crank the engine. A good, strong spark should be noted at the spark tester. If spark is noted, but the engine will not start, check the spark plugs, spark plug wiring, and fuel system. If there is no spark at the tester: Check the ignition coil secondary wire resistance; it should be no more than 5,000Ω per foot. Inspect the ignition coil for damage and/or carbon tracking. With the distributor cap removed, verify that the distributor shaft turns with the engine; if it does not, repair the engine as required. If the fault was not found proceed to the next test.

Ignition Coil Primary Circuit Switching

1. Insert a small straight pin in the wire which runs from the coil negative (–) terminal to the TFI module, about 1 inch from the module.

✳✳ WARNING

The pin must not touch ground!

2. Connect a 12 VDC test lamp between the straight pin and an engine ground.
3. Crank the engine, noting the operation of the test lamp. If the test lamp flashes, proceed to the next test. If the test lamp lights but does not flash, proceed to the Wiring Harness test. If the test lamp does not light at all, proceed to the Primary Circuit Continuity test.

Ignition Coil Resistance

Refer to the General Testing for an explanation of the resistance tests. Replace the ignition coil if the resistance is out of the specification range.

Wiring Harness

1. Disconnect the wiring harness connector from the TFI module; the connector tabs must be PUSHED to disengage the connector. Inspect the connector for damage, dirt, and corrosion.

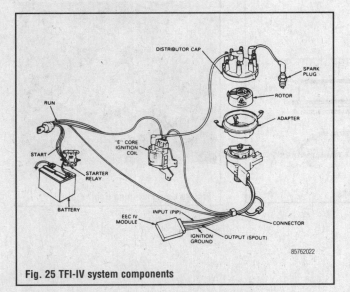

Fig. 25 TFI-IV system components

2. Attach the negative lead of a voltmeter to the base of the distributor. Attach the other voltmeter lead to a small straight pin. With the ignition switch in the RUN position, insert the straight pin into the No. 1 terminal of the TFI module connector. Note the voltage reading. With the ignition switch in the RUN position, move the straight pin to the No. 2 connector terminal. Again, note the voltage reading. Move the straight pin to the No. 3 connector terminal, then turn the ignition switch to the START position. Note the voltage reading then turn the ignition OFF.
3. The voltage readings should all be at least 90% of the available battery voltage. If the readings are okay, proceed to the Stator Assembly and Module test. If any reading is less than 90% of the battery voltage, inspect the wiring, connectors, and/or ignition switch for defects. if the voltage is low only at the No. 1 terminal, proceed to the ignition coil primary voltage test.

Stator Assembly and Module

1. Remove the distributor from the engine.
2. Remove the TFI module from the distributor.
3. Inspect the distributor terminals, ground screw, and stator wiring for damage. Repair as necessary.
4. Measure the resistance of the stator assembly, using an ohmmeter. If the ohmmeter reading is 800-975Ω, the stator is okay, but the TFI module must be replaced. If the ohmmeter reading is less than 800Ω or more than 975Ω, the TFI module is okay, but the stator module must be replaced.
5. Repair as necessary and install the TFI module and the distributor.

TFI Module

1. Remove the distributor cap from the distributor, and set it aside (spark plug wires intact).
2. Disconnect the TFI harness connector.
3. Remove the distributor.
4. Remove the two TFI module retaining screws.
5. To disengage the modules terminals from the distributor base connector, pull the right side of the module down the distributor mounting flange and then back up. Carefully pull the module toward the flange and away from the distributor.

✳✳ WARNING

Step 5 must be followed EXACTLY; failure to do so will result in damage to the distributor module connector pins.

6. Coat the TFI module baseplate with a thin layer of silicone grease (FD7AZ-19A331-A or its equivalent).
7. Place the TFI module on the distributor base mounting flange. Position the module assembly toward the distributor bowl and carefully engage the distributor connector pins. Install and torque the two TFI module retaining screws to 9-16 in.lb.
8. Install the distributor assembly.
9. Install the distributor cap and check the engine timing.

Primary Circuit Continuity

This test is performed in the same manner as the previous Wiring Harness test, but only the No. 1 terminal conductor is tested (ignition switch in Run position). If the voltage is less than 90% of the available battery voltage, proceed to the coil primary voltage test.

Ignition Coil Primary Voltage

1. Attach the negative lead of a voltmeter to the distributor base.
2. Turn the ignition switch ON and connect the positive voltmeter lead to the negative (–) ignition coil terminal. Note the voltage reading and turn the ignition OFF. If the voltmeter reading is less than 90% of the available battery voltage, inspect the wiring between the ignition module and the negative (–) coil terminal, then proceed to the last test, which follows.

Ignition Coil Supply Voltage

1. Attach the negative lead of a voltmeter to the distributor base.
2. Turn the ignition switch ON and connect the positive voltmeter lead to the

positive (+) ignition coil terminal. Note the voltage reading then turn the ignition OFF. If the voltage reading is at least 90% of the battery voltage, yet the engine will still not run; first, check the ignition coil connector and terminals for corro-

sion, dirt, and/or damage; second, replace the ignition switch if the connectors and terminal are okay.

3. Connect any remaining wiring.

IGNITION TIMING

Ignition timing is the measurement, in degrees of crankshaft rotation, of the point at which the spark plugs fire in each of the cylinders. It is measured in degrees before or after Top Dead Center (TDC) of the compression stroke.

Ideally, the air/fuel mixture in the cylinder will be ignited by the spark plug just as the piston passes TDC of the compression stroke. If this happens, the piston will be beginning the power stroke just as the compressed and ignited air/fuel mixture starts to expand. The expansion of the air/fuel mixture then forces the piston down on the power stroke and turns the crankshaft.

Because it takes a fraction of a second for the spark plug to ignite the mixture in the cylinder, the spark plug must fire a little before the piston reaches TDC. Otherwise, the mixture will not be completely ignited as the piston passes TDC and the full power of the explosion will not be used by the engine.

The timing measurement is given in degrees of crankshaft rotation before the piston reaches TDC (BTDC, or Before Top Dead Center). If the setting for the ignition timing is 5 degrees BTDC, each spark plug must fire 5 degrees before each piston reaches TDC. This only holds true, however, when the engine is at idle speed.

As the engine speed increases, the pistons go faster. The spark plugs have to ignite the fuel even sooner if it is to be completely ignited when the piston reaches TDC.

With the Dura Spark II system, the distributor has a means to advance the timing of the spark as the engine speed increases. This is accomplished by centrifugal weights within the distributor and a vacuum diaphragm mounted on the side of the distributor. It is necessary to disconnect the vacuum lines from the diaphragm when the ignition timing is being set.

With the TFI-IV system, ignition timing is calculated at all phases of vehicle operation by the TFI module. Therefore, no provision for adjustment is provided.

If the ignition is set too far advanced (BTDC), the ignition and expansion of the fuel in the cylinder will occur too soon and tend to force the piston down while it is still traveling up. This causes engine ping. If the ignition spark is set too far retarded after TDC (ATDC), the piston will have already passed TDC and started on its way down when the fuel is ignited. This will cause the piston to be forced down for only a portion of its travel. This will result in poor engine performance and lack of power.

The timing is best checked with a timing light. This device is connected in series with the No. 1 spark plug. The current that fires the spark plug also causes the timing light to flash.

There is a notch on the crankshaft pulley on all 6-cyl. engines. A scale of

degrees of crankshaft rotation is attached to the engine block in such a position that the notch will pass close by the scale. On the V8 engines, the scale is located on the crankshaft pulley and a pointer is attached to the engine block so that the scale will pass close by. When the engine is running, the timing light is aimed at the mark on the crankshaft pulley and the scale.

Ignition Timing Adjustment

▶ See Figures 26, 27 and 28

With the Dura Spark II system, only an initial timing adjustment is possible. Ignition timing is not considered to be a part of tune-up or routine maintenance.

With the TFI-IV system, no ignition timing adjustment is possible and none should be attempted.

IGNITION TIMING CHECK

1. Locate the timing marks on the crankshaft pulley and the front of the engine.
2. Clean the timing marks so that you can see them.
3. Mark the timing marks with a piece of chalk or with paint. Color the mark on the scale that will indicate the correct timing when it is aligned with the mark on the pulley or the pointer. It is also helpful to mark the notch in the pulley or the tip of the pointer with a small dab of color.
4. Attach a tachometer to the engine.
5. Attach a timing light according to the manufacturer's instructions. If the timing light has three wires, one is attached to the No. 1 spark plug with an adapter. The other wires are connected to the battery. The red wire goes to the positive side of the battery and the black wire is connected to the negative terminal of the battery.
6. Disconnect the vacuum line to the distributor at the distributor and plug the vacuum line. A golf tee does a fine job.
7. Check to make sure that all of the wires clear the fan and then start the engine.
8. Adjust the idle to the correct setting.
9. Aim the timing light at the timing marks. If the marks that you put on the flywheel or pulley and the engine are aligned with the light flashes, the timing is correct. Turn off the engine and remove the tachometer and the timing light. If the mark are not in alignment, replace the ignition module.

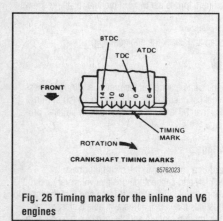

Fig. 26 Timing marks for the inline and V6 engines

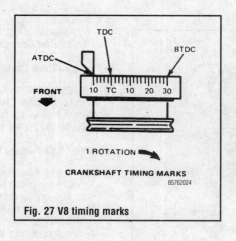

Fig. 27 V8 timing marks

Fig. 28 Using a timing light

IDLE SPEED AND MIXTURE

Carbureted Engines

♦ See Figures 29 thru 35

IDLE SPEED ADJUSTMENT

1976

1. Remove the air cleaner and plug the vacuum lines.
2. Set the parking brake and block the wheels.
3. Connect a tachometer according to the manufacturer's instructions.
4. Run the engine to normalize underhood temperatures.
5. Check, and if necessary, reset the ignition timing.
6. Make certain that the choke plate is fully open.
7. Place the manual transmission in neutral; the automatic in Drive. Block the wheels.
8. Turn the solenoid adjusting screw in or out to obtain the specified idle speed. The idle speed is the higher of the two rpm figures on the underhood specification sticker.
9. Disconnect the solenoid lead wire. Place the automatic transmission in neutral.
10. Turn the solenoid off adjusting screw to obtain the solenoid off rpm. This is the lower of the two rpm figures on the underhood specifications sticker.
11. Connect the solenoid lead wire and open the throttle slightly to allow the solenoid plunger to extend.
12. Stop the engine, replace the air cleaner and connect the vacuum lines. Check the idle speed. Readjust if necessary with the air cleaner installed.

1977–86

1. Block the wheels and apply parking brake.
2. Run engine until normal operating temperature is reached.

3. Place the vehicle in Park or Neutral, A/C in Off position, and set parking brake.
4. Remove air cleaner.
5. Disconnect and plug decel throttle control kicker diaphragm vacuum hose.
6. Connect a slave vacuum hose from an engine manifold vacuum source to the decel throttle control kicker.
7. Run engine at approximately 2,500 rpm for 15 seconds, then release the throttle.
8. If decel throttle control rpm is not within plus or minus 50 rpm of specification, adjust the kicker.
9. Disconnect the slave vacuum hose and allow engine to return to curb idle.
10. Adjust curb idle, if necessary, using the curb idle adjusting screw.
11. Rev the engine momentarily, recheck curb idle and adjust if necessary.
12. Reconnect the decel throttle control vacuum hose to the diaphragm.
13. Reinstall the air cleaner.

IDLE MIXTURE ADJUSTMENT

1976–86

➡ For this procedure, Ford recommends a propane enrichment procedure. This requires special equipment not available to the general public. In lieu of this equipment the following procedure may be followed to obtain satisfactory idle mixture.

1. Block the wheels, set the parking brake and run the engine to bring it to normal operating temperature.
2. Disconnect the hose between the emission canister and the air cleaner.
3. On engines equipped with the Thermactor air injection system, the routing of the vacuum lines connected to the dump valve will have to be temporarily changed. Mark them for reconnection before switching them.

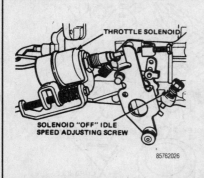

Fig. 29 Autolite 2150 with solenoid throttle positioner

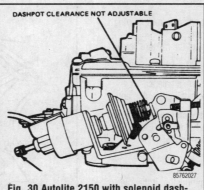

Fig. 30 Autolite 2150 with solenoid dashpot throttle positioner

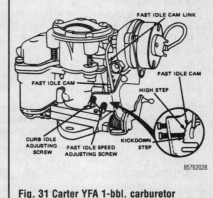

Fig. 31 Carter YFA 1-bbl. carburetor

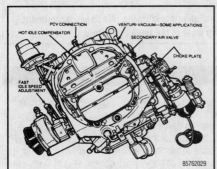

Fig. 32 Autolite 4300 4-bbl. carburetor. Some models do not have a throttle solenoid

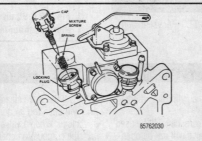

Fig. 33 Some 1980 and later 2150 2-bbl. models have metal plugs and caps in place of the plastic limiter caps on the idle mixture adjusting screws. They should be carefully removed before attempting any adjustments

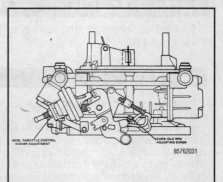

Fig. 34 Curb idle screw locations on the 4180C 4-bbl. carburetor

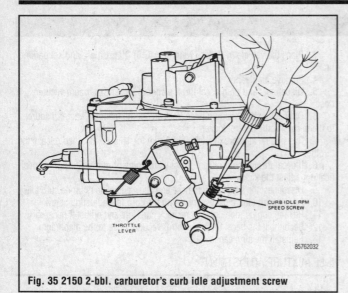

Fig. 35 2150 2-bbl. carburetor's curb idle adjustment screw

4. For dump valves with one or two vacuum lines at the side, disconnect and plug the lines.

5. For dump valves with one vacuum line at the top, check the line to see if it is connected to the intake manifold or an intake manifold source such as the carburetor or distributor vacuum line. If not, remove and plug the line at the dump valve and connect a temporary length of vacuum hose from the dump valve fitting to a source of intake manifold vacuum.

6. Remove the limiter caps from the mixture screws by CAREFULLY cutting them with a sharp knife.

7. Place the transmission in neutral and run the engine at 2500 rpm for 15 seconds.

8. Place the automatic transmission in Drive; the manual in neutral.

9. Adjust the idle speed to the higher of the two figures given on the underhood sticker.

10. Turn the idle mixture screws to obtain the highest possible rpm, leaving the screws in the leanest position that will maintain this rpm.

11. Repeat steps 7 through 10 until further adjustment of the mixture screws does not increase the rpm.

12. Turn the screws in until the lower of the two idle speed figures is reached. Turn the screws in ¼ turn increments each to insure a balance.

13. Turn the engine off and remove the tachometer. Reinstall all equipment.

➡**Rough idle, that cannot be corrected by normal service procedures on 1977 and later models, may be cause by leakage between the EGR valve body and diaphragm. To determine if this is the cause:**

14. Tighten the EGR bolts to 15 ft. lbs. Connect a vacuum gauge to the intake manifold.

15. Lift to exert a sideways pressure on the diaphragm housing. If the idle changes or the reading on the vacuum gauge varies, replace the EGR valve.

Fuel Injected Engines

These engines have idle speed controlled by the TFI-IV/EEC-IV system and no adjustment is possible.

VALVE LASH

Valve adjustment determines how far the valves enter the cylinder and how long they stay open and closed.

If the valve clearance is too large, part of the lift of the camshaft will be used in removing the excessive clearance. Consequently, the valve will not be opening as far as it should. This condition has two effects: the valve train components will emit a tapping sound as they take up the excessive clearance and the engine will perform poorly because the valves don't open fully and allow the proper amount of gases to flow into and out of the engine.

6.9L V8 Diesel

➧ **See Figure 36**

CURB IDLE ADJUSTMENT

1. Place the transmission in neutral or park.
2. Bring the engine up to normal operating temperature.
3. Idle speed is measured with manual transmission in neutral and automatic transmission in Drive with the wheels blocked and parking brake ON.
4. Check the curb idle speed, using a magnetic pickup tachometer suitable for diesel engines. The part number of the Ford tachometer is Rotunda 99-0001. Adjust the idle speed to 600-700 rpm.

➡**Always check the underhood emissions control information sticker for the latest idle and adjustment specifications.**

5. Place the transmission in neutral or park and momentarily speed up the engine. Allow the rpm to drop to idle and recheck the idle speed. Readjust if necessary.

FAST IDLE ADJUSTMENT

1. Place the transmission in neutral or park.
2. Start the engine and bring up to normal operating temperatures.
3. Disconnect the wire from the fast idle solenoid.
4. Apply battery voltage to activate the solenoid plunger.
5. Speed up the engine momentarily to set the plunger.
6. The fast idle should be between 850-900 rpm. Adjust the fast idle by turning the solenoid plunger in or out.
7. Speed up the engine momentarily and recheck the fast idle. Readjust if necessary.
8. Remove the battery voltage from the solenoid and reconnect the solenoid wire.

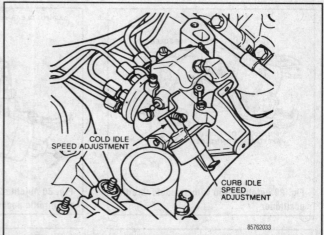

Fig. 36 6.9L diesel injection pump showing idle speed adjustment. Pump is mounted on top front of the intake manifold

If the valve clearance is too small, the intake valve and the exhaust valves will open too far and they will not fully seal on the cylinder head when they close. When a valve seats itself on the cylinder head, it does two things: it seals the combustion chamber so that none of the gases in the cylinder escape and it cools itself by transferring some of the heat it absorbs from the combustion in the cylinder to the cylinder head and to the engine's cooling system. If the valve clearance is too small, the engine will run poorly because of the gases escaping from the combustion chamber. The valves will also become overheated and will warp, since they cannot transfer heat unless they are touching the valve seat in the cylinder head.

➡ **While all valve adjustments must be made as accurately as possible, it is better to have the valve adjustment slightly loose than slightly tight as a burned valve may result from overly tight adjustments.**

Hydraulic valve lifters operate with zero clearance in the valve train, and because of this the rocker arms are nonadjustable. The only means by which valve system clearances can be altered is by installing over or undersize pushrods; but, because of the hydraulic lifter's natural ability to compensate for slack in the valve train, all components of all the valve system should be checked for wear if there is excessive play in the system.

Adjustment

ADJUSTABLE ROCKER ARMS

▶ **See Figure 37**

Inline Six Cylinder Engines

▶ **See Figure 38**

1. Crank the engine until the TDC mark on the crankshaft damper is aligned with timing pointer on the cylinder front cover.
2. Scribe a mark on the damper at this point.
3. Scribe two more marks on the damper, each equally spaced from the first mark (see illustration).
4. With the engine on TDC of the compression stroke, (mark A aligned with the pointer) back off the rocker arm adjusting nut until there is end-play in the pushrod. Tighten the adjusting nut until all clearance is removed, then tighten the adjusting nut one additional turn. To determine when all clearance is removed from the rocker arm, turn the pushrod with the fingers. When the pushrod can no longer be turned, all clearance has been removed.
5. Repeat this procedure for each valve, turning the crankshaft ⅓ turn to the next mark each time and following the engine firing order of 1-5-3-6-2-4.

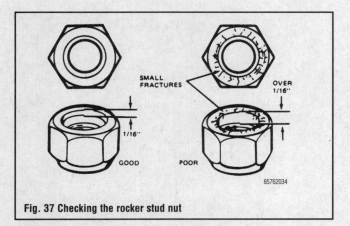

Fig. 37 Checking the rocker stud nut

Gasoline V8 Engines

▶ **See Figures 39 and 40**

1. Crank the engine until the No. 1 cylinder is at TDC of the compression stroke and the timing pointer is aligned with the mark on the crankshaft damper.
2. Scribe a mark on the damper at this point.
3. Scribe two additional marks on the damper (see illustration).
4. With the timing pointer aligned with mark 1 on the damper, back off the rocker arm adjusting nut on the following valves until there is end-play in the

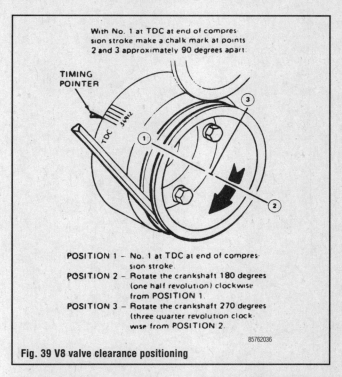

STEP 1 - SET NO. 1 PISTON ON T.D.C. AT END OF COMPRESSION STROKE ADJUST NO. 1 INTAKE AND EXHAUST

STEP 4 - CHECK NO. 6 INTAKE AND EXHAUST

STEP 2 - CHECK NO. 5 INTAKE AND EXHAUST

STEP 5 - CHECK NO. 2 INTAKE AND EXHAUST

STEP 3 - CHECK NO. 3 INTAKE AND EXHAUST

STEP 6 - CHECK NO. 4 INTAKE AND EXHAUST

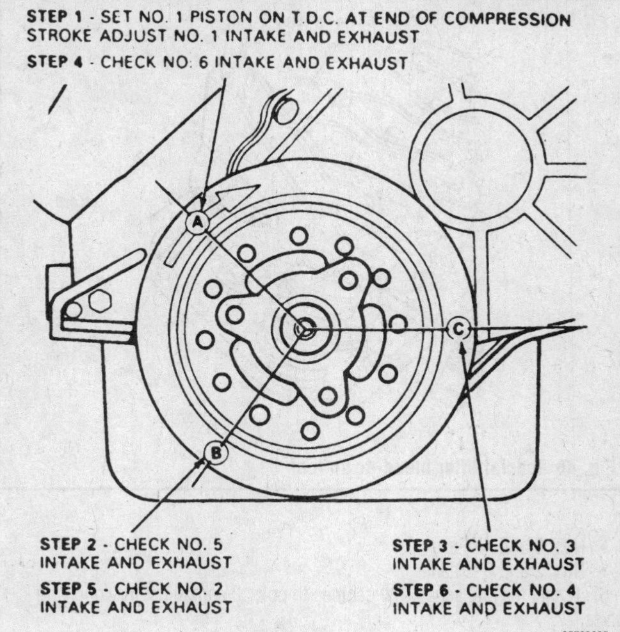

Fig. 38 6-300 valve clearance adjustment positions

With No. 1 at TDC at end of compression stroke make a chalk mark at points 2 and 3 approximately 90 degrees apart.

TIMING POINTER

POSITION 1 — No. 1 at TDC at end of compression stroke.

POSITION 2 — Rotate the crankshaft 180 degrees (one half revolution) clockwise from POSITION 1.

POSITION 3 — Rotate the crankshaft 270 degrees (three quarter revolution clockwise from POSITION 2.

Fig. 39 V8 valve clearance positioning

pushrod. Tighten the adjusting nut until all clearance is removed, then tighten the adjusting nut one additional turn. To determine when all clearance is removed from the rocker arm, turn the pushrod with the fingers. When the pushrod can no longer be turned, all clearance has been removed.

- Nos. 1, 7 and 8 Intake
- Nos. 1, 5 and 4 Exhaust

5. Rotate the crankshaft 180 degrees to point 2 and adjust the following valves:

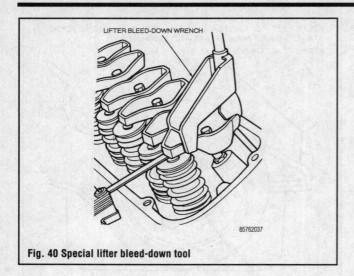

LIFTER BLEED-DOWN WRENCH

85762037

Fig. 40 Special lifter bleed-down tool

- Nos. 5 and 4 Intake
- Nos. 2 and 6 Exhaust

6. Rotate the crankshaft 270 degrees to point 3 and adjust the following valves:
- Nos. 2, 3 and 6 Intake
- Nos. 7, 3 and 8 Exhaust

NON-ADJUSTABLE ROCKER ARMS

Gasoline V8 Engines

1. Crank the engine until the No. 1 cylinder is at TDC of the compression stroke and the timing pointer is aligned with the mark on the crankshaft damper.
2. Scribe a mark on the damper at this point.
3. Scribe two additional marks on the damper (see illustration).
4. With the timing pointer aligned with mark 1 on the damper, tighten the following valves on the specified torque:
- 255, 302, 360, 390 and 460: Nos. 1, 7 and 8 Intake; Nos. 1, 5 and 4 Exhaust
- 351, 400: Nos. 1, 4 and 8 Intake; Nos. 1,3 and 7 Exhaust
5. Rotate the crankshaft 180 degrees to point 2 and tighten the following valves:
- 255, 302, 360, 390 and 460: Nos. 5 and 4 Intake; Nos. 2 and 6 Exhaust
- 351, 400: Nos. 3 and 7 Intake; Nos. 6 and 6 Exhaust
6. Rotate the crankshaft 270 degrees to point 3 and tighten the following valves:
- 255, 302, 360, 390 and 460: Nos. 2, 3 and 6 Intake; Nos. 7, 3 and 8 Exhaust
- 351, 400: Nos. 2, 5 and 6 Intake; Nos. 4, 5 and 8 Exhaust
7. Rocker arm tightening specifications are:
- Except 460: tighten the nut until it contacts the rocker shoulder, then torque to 18-20 ft. lbs.
- 460: tighten the nut until it contacts the rocker shoulder, then torque to 18-22 ft. lbs.

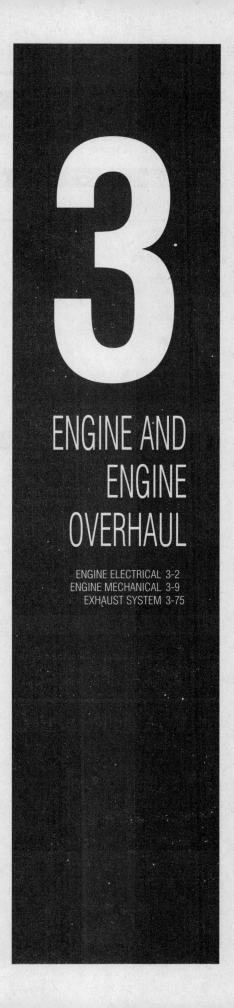

3

ENGINE AND ENGINE OVERHAUL

ENGINE ELECTRICAL

➡Two ignition systems are used across these models and years. All carbureted engines use the Dura Spark system. The fuel injected 5.0L engine uses the TFI-IV system.

Ignition Coil

REMOVAL & INSTALLATION

♦ See Figure 1

Dura Spark System

1. Disconnect the battery ground.
2. Pull off plastic wire connector from the coil.
3. Loosen the coil bracket tightening bolt and slide the coil from the bracket.
4. Installation is the reverse of removal.

TFI-IV System

1. Disconnect the battery ground.
2. Unplug the coil-to-distributor cap wire and pull off plastic connector from the coil.
3. Remove the retaining screws and remove the coil.
4. Installation is the reverse of removal.

Ignition Module

REMOVAL & INSTALLATION

Dura Spark System

♦ See Figures 2 and 3

Removing the module, on all models, is a matter of simply pulling apart the connectors and removing the fasteners that attach it to the fender or firewall. When unplugging the connectors, pull them apart with a firm, straight pull. NEVER PRY THEM APART! To pry them apart will cause damage. When reconnecting them, coat the mating ends with silicone dielectric grease to waterproof the connection. Press the connectors together firmly to overcome any vacuum lock caused by the grease.

➡If the locking tabs weaken or break, don't replace the unit. Just secure the connection with electrical tape or tie straps.

TFI-IV System

1. Remove the distributor cap.
2. Remove the TFI harness connector.
3. Remove the distributor from the engine.
4. Place the distributor on a clean work area and remove the two module attaching screws.
5. Pull the right side of the module down the distributor mounting flange and then back up to disengage the module terminals in the distributor base. The module may then be pulled towards the flange and away from the distributor.

❋❋ WARNING

Do not attempt to lift the module from the mounting surface prior to moving the entire TFI module toward the distributor flange as this will break the pins at the connector.

To install:

6. Coat the mounting flange on the distributor with a 1/32 in. layer of silicone grease.
7. Carefully position the module on the flange and slide it into position, engaging the connector pins.
8. Install the mounting screws and tighten them to 30 inch lbs.
9. Install the distributor and cap.
10. Connect the wiring, start the engine and check the ignition timing.

Distributor

REMOVAL

Except TFI-IV

♦ See Figures 4 and 5

1. Remove the air cleaner assembly, taking note of the hose locations.
2. Disconnect the distributor wiring connector from the vehicle wiring harness.
3. Noting the position of the vacuum line(s) on the distributor diaphragm, disconnect the lines at the diaphragm. Unsnap the two distributor cap retaining clamps and remove the cap, rotor and adapter.

➡If it is necessary to disconnect ignition wires from the cap to get enough room to remove the distributor, make sure to label every wire and the cap for easy and accurate reinstallation.

4. Rotate the engine to align any pole on the armature with the pole on the stator.
5. Install the rotor. Using chalk or paint, carefully mark the position of the distributor rotor in relation to the distributor housing and mark the position of the distributor housing in relation to the engine block. When this is done, you should have a line on the distributor housing directly in line with the tip of the rotor and another line on the engine block directly in line with the mark on the distributor housing. This is very important because the distributor must be installed in the exact same location from which it was removed, if correct ignition timing is to be maintained.
6. Remove the distributor holddown bolt and clamp. Remove the distributor from the engine. Make sure that the oil pump (intermediate) driveshaft does not come out with the distributor. If it does, remove it from the distributor shaft, coat its lower end with heavy grease, and reinsert it, making sure that it fully engages the oil pump drive.

➡Do not disturb the engine while the distributor is removed. If you turn the engine over with the distributor removed, you will have to retime the engine.

85763360

Fig. 1 Dura Spark ignition coil on a 1978 Bronco with the 8-351M

85763003

Fig. 2 Dura Spark module on a 1981 F-150

85763361

Fig. 3 Dura Spark ignition module on a 1978 Bronco

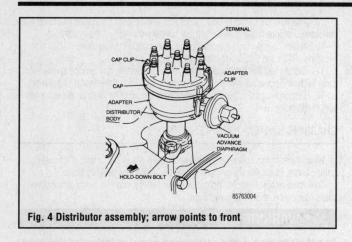

Fig. 4 Distributor assembly; arrow points to front

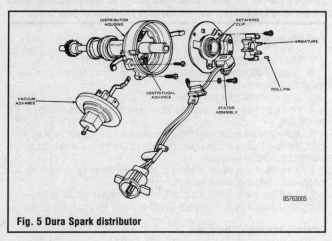

Fig. 5 Dura Spark distributor

TFI-IV Systems

♦ **See Figure 6**

1. Disconnect the primary wiring connector from the distributor.
2. Mark the position of the cap's No.1 terminal on the distributor base.

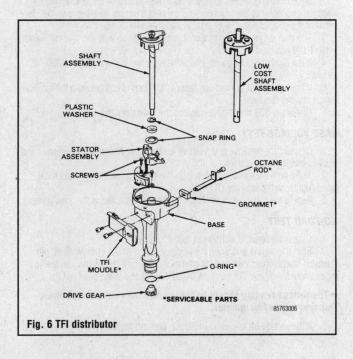

Fig. 6 TFI distributor

3. Unclip and remove the cap. Remove the adapter.
4. Remove the rotor.
5. Remove the TFI connector.
6. Matchmark the distributor base and engine for installation reference.
7. Remove the holddown bolt and lift out the distributor.

INSTALLATION—ENGINE NOT ROTATED

Except TFI-IV

1. If the engine was not cranked (disturbed) when the distributor was removed, position the distributor in the block with the armature and stator poles aligned, the rotor aligned with the mark previously scribed on the distributor body and the marks on the distributor body and cylinder block in alignment. If the stator and armature poles cannot be aligned by rotating the distributor, pull the distributor out just far enough to disengage the drive gear and rotate the distributor shaft to engage a different gear tooth.
2. Install the distributor holddown bolt and clamp finger tight.
3. Install the distributor cap and wires.
4. Connect the distributor wiring connector to the wiring harness. Tighten the holddown bolt.
5. Install the air cleaner, if removed.
6. Check the ignition timing as outlined in Section 2.

TFI-IV System

1. If the engine was not cranked (disturbed) when the distributor was removed, position the distributor in the block with the rotor aligned with the mark previously scribed on the distributor body and the marks on the distributor body and cylinder block in alignment. Continue rotating the shaft so that the leading edge of the vane is centered on the vane switch assembly.

➡ **If the vane and vane switch cannot be aligned by rotating the distributor body in the engine, pull the distributor out just far enough to disengage the gears and rotate the shaft to engage a different gear tooth. Repeat Step 1.**

2. Install and finger tighten the holddown bolt.
3. Connect the TFI and primary wiring.
4. Install the rotor, if not already done.

➡ **Coat the brass portions of the rotor with a 1/32 inch thick coating of silicone dielectric compound.**

5. Install the cap and adapter (as necessary). Install the wires and start the engine.
6. Check and set the ignition timing.
7. Tighten the holddown bolt to 25 ft. lbs.

INSTALLATION—CRANKSHAFT OR CAMSHAFT ROTATED

Except TFI-IV

♦ **See Figure 7**

If the engine is cranked (disturbed) with the distributor removed, it will now be necessary to retime the engine.
1. Rotate the engine so that No.1 piston is at TDC of the compression stroke.
2. Align the timing marks to the correct ignition timing shown on the underhood decal.
3. Install the distributor with the rotor in the No.1 firing position and any armature pole aligned with a stator pole.

➡ **Make sure that the oil pump intermediate shaft properly engages the distributor shaft. It may be necessary to rotate the engine after the distributor gear is partially engaged in order to engage the oil pump intermediate shaft and fully seat the distributor in the block.**

4. If it was necessary to rotate the engine to align the oil pump, repeat Steps 1, 2 and 3.
5. Install the holddown bolt finger tight.
6. Install the distributor cap and wires.
7. Connect the distributor wiring connector to the wiring harness. Tighten the holddown bolt.
8. Install the air cleaner, if removed.

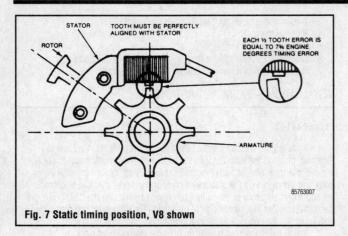

Fig. 7 Static timing position, V8 shown

9. Check the ignition timing as outlined in Section 2.
10. When everything is set, tighten the holddown bolt to 25 ft. lbs.

TFI-IV System

1. Rotate the engine so that the No.1 piston is at TDC of the compression stroke.
2. Align the timing marks so that the engine is set at the ignition timing shown on the underhood sticker.
3. Install the rotor on the shaft and rotate the shaft so that the rotor tip points to the No.1 mark made on the distributor base.
4. Continue rotating the shaft so that the leading edge of the vane is centered on the vane switch assembly.
5. Position the distributor in the block and rotate the distributor body to align the leading edge of the vane and vane switch. Verify that the rotor tip points to the No.1 firing position.

➡**If the vane and vane switch cannot be aligned by rotating the distributor body in the engine, pull the distributor out just far enough to disengage the gears and rotate the shaft to engage a different gear tooth. Repeat Steps 3, 4 and 5.**

6. Install and finger tighten the holddown bolt.
7. Connect the TFI and primary wiring.
8. Install the rotor, if not already done.

➡**Coat the brass portions of the rotor with a ¹⁄₃₂ inch thick coating of silicone dielectric compound.**

9. Install the cap and adapter (as necessary). Install the wires and start the engine.
10. Check and set the ignition timing.
11. Tighten the holddown bolt to 25 ft. lbs.

Alternator

ALTERNATOR PRECAUTIONS

To prevent damage to the alternator and regulator, the following precautions should be taken when working with the electrical system.
1. Never reverse the battery connections.
2. Booster batteries for starting must be connected properly: positive-to-positive and negative-to-ground.
3. Disconnect the battery cables before using a fast charger; the charger has a tendency to force current through the diodes in the opposite direction for which they were designed. This burns out the diodes.
4. Never use a fast charger as a booster for starting the vehicle.
5. Never disconnect the voltage regulator while the engine is running.
6. Avoid long soldering times when replacing diodes or transistors. Prolonged heat is damaging to AC generators.
7. Do not use test lamps of more than 12 volts (V) for checking diode continuity.
8. Do not short across or ground any of the terminals on the AC generator.

9. The polarity of the battery, generator, and regulator must be matched and considered before making any electrical connections within the system.
10. Never operate the alternator on an open circuit. Make sure that all connections within the circuit are clean and tight.
11. Disconnect the battery terminals when performing any service on the electrical system. This will eliminate the possibility of accidental reversal of polarity.
12. Disconnect the battery ground cable if arc welding is to be done on any part of the truck.

CHARGING SYSTEM TROUBLESHOOTING

When performing charging system tests, turn off all lights and electrical components. Place the transmission in **P** and apply the parking brake.
To ensure accurate meter indications, the battery terminal posts and battery cable clamps must be clean and tight.

❋❋ WARNING

Do not make jumper wire connections except as instructed. Incorrect jumper wire connections can damage the regulator or fuse links.

Preliminary Inspection

1. Make sure the battery cable connections are clean and tight.
2. Check all alternator and regulator wiring connections. Make sure all connections are clean and secure.
3. Check the alternator belt tension. Adjust, if necessary.
4. Check the fuse link between the starter relay and alternator. Replace if burned out.
5. Make sure the fuses/fuse links to the alternator are not burned or damaged. This could cause an open circuit or high resistance, resulting in erratic or intermittent charging problems.
6. If equipped with heated windshield, make sure the wiring connections to the alternator output control relay are correct and tight.
7. If equipped with heated windshield, make sure the connector to the heated windshield module is properly seated and there are no broken wires.

External Regulator Alternator

CHARGING SYSTEM INDICATOR LIGHT TEST

1. If the charging system indicator light does not come on with the ignition key in the **RUN** position and the engine not running, check the ignition switch-to-regulator I terminal wiring for an open circuit or burned out charging system indicator light. Replace the light, if necessary.
2. If the charging system indicator light does not come on, disconnect the electrical connector at the regulator and connect a jumper wire between the I terminal of the connector and the negative battery cable clamp.
3. The charging system indicator light should go on with the ignition switch in the **RUN** position.
4. If the light does not go on, check the light for continuity and replace, if necessary.
5. If the light is not burned out, there is an open circuit between the ignition switch and the regulator.
6. Check the 500 ohm resistor across the indicator light.

BASE VOLTAGE TEST

1. Connect the negative and positive leads of a voltmeter to the negative and positive battery cable clamps.
2. Make sure the ignition switch is in the **OFF** position and all electrical loads (lights, radio, etc.) are OFF.
3. Record the battery voltage shown on the voltmeter; this is the base voltage.

NO-LOAD TEST

1. Connect a suitable tachometer to the engine.
2. Start the engine and bring the engine speed to 1500 rpm. With no other electrical loads (doors closed, foot off the brake pedal), the reading on the voltmeter should increase, but no more than 2.5 volts above the base voltage.

➡**The voltage reading should be taken when the voltage stops rising. This may take a few minutes.**

3. If the voltage increases as in Step 2, perform the Load Test.

4. If the voltage continues to rise, perform the Over Voltage Tests.

5. If the voltage does not rise to the proper level, perform the Under Voltage Tests.

LOAD TEST

1. With the engine running, turn the blower speed switch to the high speed position and turn the headlights on to high beam.

2. Raise the engine speed to approximately 2000 rpm. The voltmeter reading should be a minimum of 0.5 volts above the base voltage. If not, perform the Under Voltage Tests.

➡ **If the voltmeter readings in the No-Load Test and Load Test are as specified, the charging system is operating properly. Go to the following tests if one or more of the voltage readings differs, and also check for battery drain.**

OVER VOLTAGE TESTS

1. If the voltmeter reading was more than 2.5 volts above the base voltage in the No-Load Test, connect a jumper wire between the voltage regulator base and the alternator frame or housing. Repeat the No-Load Test.

2. If the over voltage condition disappears, check the ground connections on the alternator, regulator and from the engine to the dash panel and to the battery. Clean and securely tighten the connections.

3. If the over voltage condition still exists, disconnect the voltage regulator wiring connector from the voltage regulator. Repeat the No-Load Test.

4. If the over voltage condition disappears (voltmeter reads base voltage), replace the voltage regulator.

5. If the over voltage condition still exists with the voltage regulator wiring connector disconnected, check for a short between circuits A and F in the wiring harness and service, as necessary. Then reconnect the voltage regulator wiring connector.

UNDER VOLTAGE TESTS

1. If the voltage reading was not more than 0.5 volts above the base voltage, disconnect the wiring connector from the voltage regulator and connect an ohmmeter from the F terminal of the connector to ground. The ohmmeter should indicate more than 2.4 ohms.

2. If the ohmmeter reading is less than 2.4 ohms, service the grounded field circuit in the wiring harness or alternator and repeat the Load Test.

❋❋ WARNING

Do not replace the voltage regulator before a shorted rotor coil or field circuit has been serviced. Damage to the regulator could result.

3. If the ohmmeter reading is more than 2.4 ohms, connect a jumper wire from the A to F terminals of the wiring connector and repeat the Load Test. If the voltmeter now indicates more than 0.5 volts above the base voltage, the regulator or wiring is damaged or worn. Perform the S and I Circuit Tests and service the wiring or regulator, as required.

4. If the voltmeter still indicates an under voltage problem, remove the jumper wire from the voltage regulator connector and leave the connector disconnected from the regulator.

5. Disconnect the FLD terminal on the alternator and pull back the protective cover from the BAT terminal. Connect a jumper wire between the FLD and BAT terminals and repeat the Load Test.

6. If the voltmeter indicates a 0.5 volts or more, increase above base voltage, perform the S and I Circuit Tests and service the wiring or regulator, as indicated.

7. If the voltmeter still indicates under voltage, shut the engine OFF and move the positive voltmeter lead to the BAT terminal of the alternator. If the voltmeter now indicates the base voltage, service the alternator. If the voltmeter indicates 0 volts, service the alternator-to-starter relay wire.

REGULATOR S AND I CIRCUIT TESTS

1. Disconnect the voltage regulator wiring connector and install a jumper wire between the A and F terminals.

2. With the engine idling and the negative voltmeter lead connected to the negative battery terminal, connect the positive voltmeter lead to the S terminal and then to the I terminal of the regulator wiring connector.

3. The S circuit voltage reading should be approximately ½ the I circuit reading. If the voltage readings are correct, remove the jumper wire. Replace the voltage regulator and repeat the Load Test.

4. If there is no voltage present, service the faulty wiring circuit. Connect the positive voltmeter lead to the positive battery terminal.

5. Remove the jumper wire from the regulator wiring connector and connect the connector to the regulator. Repeat the Load Test

FUSE LINK CONTINUITY

1. Make sure the battery is okay. (See Section 1)

2. Turn on the headlights or any accessory. If the headlights or accessory do not operate, the fuse link is probably burned out.

3. On some vehicles there are several fuse links. Proceed as in Step 2 to test other fuse links.

4. To test the fuse link that protects the alternator, check for voltage at the BAT terminal of the alternator, using a voltmeter. If there is no voltage, the fuse link is probably burned out.

Integral Regulator/External Fan Alternator

CHARGING SYSTEM INDICATOR LIGHT TEST

Two conditions can cause the charging system indicator light to come on when your truck is running: no alternator output, caused by a damaged alternator, regulator or wiring, or an over voltage condition, caused by a shorted alternator rotor, regulator or wiring.

In a normally functioning system, the charging system indicator light will be OFF when the ignition switch is in the **OFF** position, ON when the ignition switch is in the **RUN** position and the engine not running, and OFF when the ignition switch is in the **RUN** position and the engine is running.

1. If the charging system indicator light does not come on, disconnect the wiring connector from the regulator.

2. Connect a jumper wire between the connector I terminal and the negative battery cable clamp.

3. Turn the ignition switch to the **RUN** position, but leave the engine OFF. If the charging system indicator light does not come on, check for a light socket resistor. If there is a resistor, check the contact of the light socket leads to the flexible printed circuit. If they are good, check the indicator light for continuity and replace if burned out. If the light checks out good, perform the Regulator I Circuit Test.

4. If the indicator light comes on, remove the jumper wire and reconnect the wiring connector to the regulator. Connect the negative voltmeter lead to the negative battery cable clamp and connect the positive voltmeter lead to the regulator A terminal screw. Battery voltage should be indicated. If battery voltage is not indicated, service the A circuit wiring.

5. If battery voltage is indicated, clean and tighten the ground connections to the engine, alternator and regulator. Tighten loose regulator mounting screws to 15–26 inch lbs. (1.7–2.8 Nm).

6. Turn the ignition switch to the **RUN** position with the engine OFF. If the charging system indicator light still does not come on, replace the regulator.

BASE VOLTAGE TEST

1. Connect the negative and positive leads of a voltmeter to the negative and positive battery cable clamps.

2. Make sure the ignition switch is in the **OFF** position and all electrical loads (lights, radio, etc.) are OFF.

3. Record the battery voltage shown on the voltmeter; this is the base voltage.

NO-LOAD TEST

1. Connect a suitable tachometer to the engine.

2. Start the engine and bring the engine speed to 1500 rpm. With no other electrical loads (doors closed, foot off the brake pedal), the reading on the voltmeter should increase, but no more than 2.5 volts above the base voltage.

➡ **The voltage reading should be taken when the voltage stops rising. This may take a few minutes.**

3. If the voltage increases as in Step 2, perform the Load Test.

4. If the voltage continues to rise, perform the Over Voltage Tests.

5. If the voltage does not rise to the proper level, perform the Under Voltage Tests.

LOAD TEST

1. With the engine running, turn the blower speed switch to the high speed position and turn the headlights on to high beam.

2. Raise the engine speed to approximately 2000 rpm. The voltmeter read-

ing should be a minimum of 0.5 volts above the base voltage. If not, perform the Under Voltage Tests.

➡️If the voltmeter readings in the No-Load Test and Load Test are as specified, the charging system is operating properly. Go to the following tests if one or more of the voltage readings differs, and also check for battery drain.

OVER VOLTAGE TESTS

If the voltmeter reading was more than 2.5 volts above base voltage in the No-Load Test, proceed as follows:
  1. Turn the ignition switch to the **RUN** position, but do not start the engine.
  2. Connect the negative voltmeter lead to the alternator rear housing. Connect the positive voltmeter lead first to the alternator output connection at the starter solenoid and then to the regulator A screw head.
  3. If there is greater than 0.5 volts difference between the 2 locations, service the A wiring circuit to eliminate the high resistance condition indicated by excessive voltage drop.
  4. If the over voltage condition still exists, check for loose regulator and alternator grounding screws. Tighten loose regulator grounding screws to 15–26 inch lbs. (1.7–2.8 Nm).
  5. If the over voltage condition still exists, connect the negative voltmeter lead to the alternator rear housing. With the ignition switch in the **OFF** position, connect the positive voltmeter lead first to the regulator A screw head and then to the regulator F screw head. If there are different voltage readings at the 2 screw heads, a malfunctioning grounded brush lead or a grounded rotor coil is indicated; service or replace the entire alternator/regulator unit.
  6. If the same voltage is obtained at both screw heads in Step 5 and there is no high resistance in the ground of the A+ circuit, replace the regulator.

UNDER VOLTAGE TESTS

If the voltmeter reading was not more than 0.5 volts above base voltage, proceed as follows:
  1. Disconnect the electrical connector from the regulator. Connect an ohmmeter between the regulator A and F terminal screws. The ohmmeter reading should be more than 2.4 ohms. If it is less than 2.4 ohms, the regulator has failed. also check the alternator for a shorted rotor or field circuit. Perform the Load Test after servicing.

✳✳ WARNING

Do not replace the voltage regulator before a shorted rotor coil or field circuit has been serviced. Damage to the regulator could result.

  2. If the ohmmeter reading is greater than 2.4 ohms, connect the regulator wiring connector and connect the negative voltmeter lead to the alternator rear housing. Connect the positive voltmeter lead to the regulator A terminal screw. The voltmeter should indicate battery voltage. If there is no voltage, service the A wiring circuit and then perform the Load Test.
  3. If the voltmeter indicates battery voltage, connect the negative voltmeter lead to the alternator rear housing. With the ignition switch in the **OFF** position, connect the positive voltmeter lead to the regulator F terminal screw. The voltmeter should indicate battery voltage. If there is no voltage, there is an open field circuit in the alternator. Service or replace the alternator, then perform the Load Test after servicing.
  4. If the voltmeter indicates battery voltage, connect the negative voltmeter lead to the alternator rear housing. Turn the ignition switch to the **RUN** position, leaving the engine off, and connect the positive voltmeter lead to the regulator F terminal screw. The voltmeter should read 1.5 volts or less. If more than 1.5 volts is indicated, perform the I circuit tests and service the I circuit if needed. If the I circuit is normal, replace the regulator, if needed, and perform the Load Test after servicing.
  5. If 1.5 volts or less is indicated, disconnect the alternator wiring connector. Connect a set of 12 gauge jumper wires between the alternator B+ terminal blades and the mating wiring connector terminals. Perform the Load Test, but connect the positive voltmeter lead to one of the B+ jumper wire terminals. If the voltage increases more than 0.5 volts above base voltage, service the alternator-starter relay wiring. Repeat the Load Test, measuring voltage at the battery cable clamps after servicing.
  6. If the voltage does not increase more than 0.5 volts above base voltage,

connect a jumper wire from the alternator rear housing to the regulator F terminal. Repeat the Load Test with the positive voltmeter lead connected to one of the B+ jumper wire terminals. If the voltage increases more than 0.5 volts, replace the regulator. If the voltage does not increase more than 0.5 volts, service or replace the alternator.

REGULATOR S AND I CIRCUIT TEST

  1. Disconnect the wiring connector from the regulator. Connect a jumper wire between the regulator A terminal and the wiring connector A lead and connect a jumper wire between the regulator F screw and the alternator rear housing.
  2. With the engine idling and the negative voltmeter lead connected to the negative battery terminal, connect the positive voltmeter lead first to the S terminal and then to the I terminal of the regulator wiring connector.
  3. The S circuit voltage should be approximately ½ that of the I circuit. If the voltage readings are correct, remove the jumper wire. Replace the regulator and connect the regulator wiring connector. Perform the Load Test.
  4. If there is no voltage present, remove the jumper wire and service the faulty wiring circuit or alternator.
  5. Connect the positive voltmeter lead to the positive battery terminal and connect the wiring connector to the regulator. Repeat the Load Test.

FUSE LINK CONTINUITY

  1. Make sure the battery is okay (See Section 1).
  2. Turn on the headlights or any accessory. If the headlights or accessory do not operate, the fuse link is probably burned out.
  3. On some vehicles there are several fuse links. Proceed as in Step 2 to test other fuse links.
  4. To test the fuse link that protects the alternator, check for voltage at the BAT terminal of the alternator and A terminal of the regulator, using a voltmeter. If there is no voltage, the fuse link is probably burned out.

FIELD CIRCUIT DRAIN

In all of the Field Circuit Drain test steps, connect the negative voltmeter lead to the alternator rear housing.
  1. With the ignition switch in the **OFF** position, connect the positive voltmeter lead to the regulator F terminal screw. The voltmeter should read battery voltage if the system is operating normally. If less than battery voltage is indicated, go to Step 2.
  2. Disconnect the wiring connector from the regulator and connect the positive voltmeter lead to the wiring connector I terminal. There should be no voltage indicated. If voltage is indicated, service the I lead from the ignition switch to identify and eliminate the voltage source.
  3. If there was no voltage indicated in Step 2, connect the positive voltmeter lead to the wiring connector S terminal. No voltage should be indicated. If no voltage is indicated, replace the regulator.
  4. If there was voltage indicated in Step 3, disconnect the wiring connector from the alternator rectifier connector. Connect the positive voltmeter lead to the regulator wiring connector S terminal. If voltage is indicated, service the S lead to the alternator connector to eliminate the voltage source. If no voltage is indicated, the alternator rectifier assembly is faulty.

REMOVAL & INSTALLATION

▶ See Figures 8 and 9

  1. Open the hood and disconnect the battery ground cable.
  2. Remove the adjusting arm bolt.
  3. Remove the alternator through-bolt. Remove the drive belt from the alternator pulley and lower the alternator.

➡️Some engines are equipped with a ribbed, K-section belt and automatic tensioner. A special tool must be made to remove the tension from the tensioner arm. Loosen the idler pulley pivot and adjuster bolts before using the tool. See the accompanying illustration for tool details.

  4. Label all of the leads to the alternator so that you can install them correctly and disconnect the leads from the alternator.
  5. Remove the alternator from the vehicle.
  6. To install, reverse the above procedure. Torque the pivot bolt to 58 ft. lbs.; the adjusting bolt to 25 ft. lbs.; the wire terminal nuts to 60–90 inch lbs.

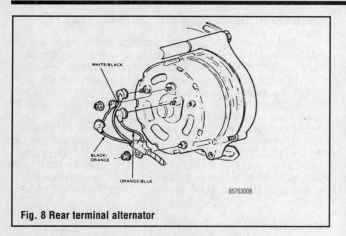

Fig. 8 Rear terminal alternator

Fig. 10 External voltage regulator; 1978 Bronco shown

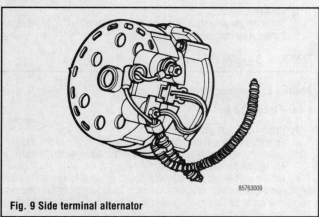

Fig. 9 Side terminal alternator

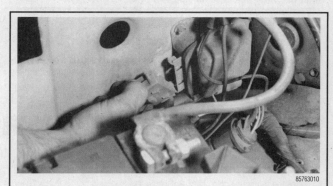

Fig. 11 Disconnecting the wiring from the external regulator; 1983 F-150 shown

BELT TENSION ADJUSTMENT

The fan belt drives the alternator and water pump. If the belt is too loose, it will slip and the alternator will not be able to produce it rated current. Also, the water pump will not operate efficiently and the engine could overheat.

Check the tension of the belt by pushing your thumb down on the longest span of the belt, midway between the pulleys. Belt deflection should be approximately ½ inch (13mm).To adjust the belt tension, proceed as follows:

1. Loosen the alternator mounting bolt and the adjusting arm bolts.
2. Apply pressure on the alternator front housing only, moving the alternator away from the engine to tighten the belt. Do not apply pressure to the rear of the cast aluminum housing of an alternator; damage to the housing could result.
3. Tighten the alternator mounting bolt and the adjusting arm bolts when the correct tension is reached.

Regulator

Trucks through with a rear terminal alternator employ a separate, external regulator, usually mounted on the fender well. Trucks with a side terminal alternator incorporate a regulator found on the back of the alternator. The regulator is not adjustable.

REMOVAL & INSTALLATION

External Regulator

▶ **See Figures 10 and 11**

1. Disconnect the positive terminal of the battery.
2. Unplug the wiring connector at the regulator.
3. Remove the 2 holddown screws, then remove the unit from the vehicle.
4. Install the new voltage regulator using the holddown screws from the old one, or new ones if they are provided with the replacement regulator. Tighten the holddown screws.
5. Connect the wiring to the new regulator.

Integral Regulator

1. Disconnect the positive terminal of the battery.
2. Unplug the wiring connector at the regulator.
3. Remove the 2 holddown screws, then remove the unit from the alternator.
4. Install the new voltage regulator using the holddown screws from the old one, or new ones if they are provided with the replacement regulator. Tighten the holddown screws.
5. Connect the wiring to the new regulator.

Battery

REMOVAL & INSTALLATION

1. Loosen the nuts which secure the cable ends to the battery terminals. Lift the negative battery cables from the terminals first with a twisting motion, then the positive cables. If there is a battery cable puller available, make use of it.

✴✴ WARNING

On vehicles with dual batteries, take great care to avoid grounding the disconnected end of the positive cable linking the two batteries, before the other end is disconnected.

2. Remove the holddown nuts from the battery holddown bracket and remove the bracket and the battery. Lift the battery straight up and out of the vehicle, being sure to keep the battery level to avoid spilling the battery acid.
3. Before installing the battery in the vehicle, make sure that the battery terminals are clean and free from corrosion. Use a battery terminal cleaner on the terminals and on the inside of the battery cable ends. If a cleaner is not available, use coarse grade sandpaper to remove the corrosion. A mixture of baking soda and water poured over the terminals and cable ends will help remove and neutralize any acid buildup.

❄❄ WARNING

Take great care to avoid getting any of the baking soda solution inside the battery. If any solution gets inside the battery a violent reaction will take place and/or the battery will be damaged.

4. Before installing the cables onto the terminals, cut a piece of felt cloth, or something similar into a circle about 3 inch (76mm) across. Cut a hole in the middle about the size of the battery terminals at their base. Push the cloth pieces over the terminals so that they lay flat on the top of the battery. Soak the pieces of cloth with oil. This will keep oxidation to a minimum.

5. Place the battery in the vehicle. Install the cables onto the terminals.

❄❄ WARNING

On vehicles with dual batteries, take great care to avoid grounding the disconnected end of the positive cable linking the two batteries, after the other end is connected.

6. Tighten the nuts on the cable ends.

➡ **See Section 1 for battery maintenance illustrations.**

7. Smear a light coating of grease on the cable ends and tops of the terminals. This will further prevent the buildup of oxidation on the terminals and the cable ends.

8. Install and tighten the nuts of the battery holddown bracket.

Starter

TESTING

Place the transmission in **N** or **P**. Disconnect the vacuum line to the Thermactor® bypass valve, if equipped, before performing any cranking tests. After tests, run the engine for 3 minutes before connecting the vacuum line.

Starter Cranks Slowly

1. Connect jumper cables as shown in the Jump Starting procedure in Section 1. If, with the aid of the booster battery, the starter now cranks normally, check the condition of the battery. Recharge or replace the battery, as necessary. Clean the cables and battery posts and make sure connections are tight.

2. If Step 1 does not correct the problem, clean and tighten the connections at the starter relay and battery ground on the engine. You should not be able to rotate the eyelet terminals easily, by hand. Also make sure the positive cable is not shorted to ground.

3. If the starter still cranks slowly, it must be replaced.

Starter Relay Operates But Starter Doesn't Crank

1. Connect jumper cables as shown in the Jump Starting procedure in Section 1. If, with the aid of the booster battery, the starter now cranks normally, check the condition of the battery. Recharge or replace the battery, as necessary. Clean the cables and battery posts and make sure connections are tight.

2. If Step 1 does not correct the problem, clean and tighten the connections at the starter and relay. Make sure the wire strands are secure in the eyelets.

3. On models with a fender mounted solenoid, if the starter still doesn't crank, it must be replaced.

4. On vehicles with starter mounted solenoid: Connect a jumper cable across terminals B and M of the starter solenoid. If the starter does not operate, replace the starter. If the starter does operate, replace the solenoid.

❄❄ CAUTION

Making the jumper connections could cause a spark. Battery jumper cables or equivalent, should be used due to the high current in the starting system.

Starter Doesn't Crank — Relay Chatters or Doesn't Click

1. Connect jumper cables as shown in the Jump Starting procedure in Section 1. If, with the aid of the booster battery, the starter now cranks normally, check the condition of the battery. Recharge or replace the battery, as necessary. Clean the cables and battery posts and make sure connections are tight.

2. If Step 1 does not correct the problem, remove the push-on connector from the relay (red with blue stripe wire). Make sure the connection is clean and secure and the relay bracket is grounded.

3. If the connections are good, check the relay operation with a jumper wire. Remove the push-on connector from the relay and, using a jumper wire, jump from the now exposed terminal on the starter relay to the main terminal (battery side or battery positive post). If this corrects the problem, check the ignition switch, neutral safety switch and the wiring in the starting circuit for open or loose connections.

4. If a jumper wire across the relay does not correct the problem, replace the relay.

Starter Spins But Doesn't Crank Engine

1. Remove the starter.

2. Check the armature shaft for corrosion and clean or replace, as necessary.

3. If there is no corrosion, replace the starter drive.

REMOVAL & INSTALLATION

Positive Engagement Type

▶ **See Figures 12 and 13**

1. Disconnect the negative battery cable.

2. Firmly apply the parking brake and place blocks in back of the rear wheels. Raise the front of the truck and install jackstands beneath the frame.

3. Tag and disconnect the wiring at the starter.

4. Turn the front wheels fully to the right. On some later models it will be necessary to remove the frame brace. On many models, it will be necessary to remove the two bolts retaining the steering idler arm to the frame to gain access to the starter.

5. Remove the starter mounting bolts and remove the starter.

6. Reverse the above procedure to install. Torque the mounting bolts to 12–15 ft. lbs. on starters with 3 mounting bolts and 15–20 ft. lbs. on starters with 2 mounting bolts. Torque the idler arm retaining bolts to 28–35 ft. lbs. (if removed). Make sure that the nut securing the heavy cable to the starter is snugged down tightly.

Solenoid Actuated Type

1. Disconnect the battery ground cable.

2. Raise the vehicle and disconnect the cables and wires at the starter solenoid.

3. Turn the front wheels to the right and remove the two bolts attaching steering idler arm to the frame.

4. Remove the starter mounting bolts and remove the starter.

5. Installation is the reverse of removal. Torque the mounting bolts to 20 ft. lbs.

Starter Relay

REMOVAL & INSTALLATION

External Fender-Mounter Relay

▶ **See Figure 14**

1. Disconnect the positive battery cable from the battery terminal. With dual batteries, disconnect the connecting cable at both ends.

2. Remove the nut securing the positive battery cable to the relay.

3. Remove the positive cable and any other wiring under that cable.

4. Tag and remove the push-on wires from the front of the relay.

5. Remove the nut and disconnect the cable from the starter side of the relay.

6. Remove the relay attaching bolts and remove the relay.

7. Installation is the reverse of removal.

Fig. 12 View of the starter on the 8-255, 302; other engines are similar

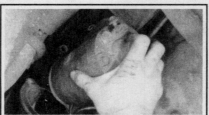

Fig. 13 Removing the starter; be careful, it's heavy

Fig. 14 Fender-mounted starter relay

ENGINE MECHANICAL

GENERAL ENGINE SPECIFICATIONS

Year	Engine ID/VIN	Engine Displacement cu. in. (L)	Fuel System Type	Bore × Stroke (in.)	Compression Ratio	Oil Pressure @ rpm
1976	B	300 (4.9)	1-bbl	4.00 × 3.98	8.4:1	40–60
	G	302 (5.0)	2-bbl	4.00 × 3.00	8.2:1	40–60
	Y	360 (4.9)	2-bbl	4.05 × 3.50	7.2:1	35–60
	H	390 (6.4)	2-bbl	4.05 × 3.78	8.2:1	35–50
	M	390 (6.4)	4-bbl	4.05 × 3.78	8.2:1	35–50
	J	460 (7.5)	4-bbl	4.36 × 3.85	8.0:1	40–65
1977	B	300 (4.9)	1-bbl	4.00 × 3.98	8.4:1	40–60
	G	302 (5.0)	2-bbl	4.00 × 3.00	8.2:1	40–60
	H	351M (5.8)	2-bbl	4.00 × 3.50	8.0:1	50–75
	S	400 (6.6)	2-bbl	4.00 × 4.00	8.0:1	50–75
	J	460 (7.5)	4-bbl	4.36 × 3.85	8.0:1	40–65
1978	B	300 (4.9)	1-bbl	4.00 × 3.98	8.4:1	40–60
	G	302 (5.0)	2-bbl	4.00 × 3.00	8.2:1	40–60
	H	351M (5.8)	2-bbl	4.00 × 3.50	8.0:1	50–75
	H	351W (5.8)	2-bbl	4.00 × 3.50	8.2:1	40–60
	S	400 (6.6)	2-bbl	4.00 × 4.00	8.0:1	50–75
	J	460 (7.5)	4-bbl	4.36 × 3.85	8.0:1	40–65
1979	B	300 (4.9)	1-bbl	4.00 × 3.98	8.4:1	40–60
	K	300HD (4.9)	1-bbl	4.00 × 3.98	8.0:1	40–60
	G	302 (5.0)	2-bbl	4.00 × 3.00	8.2:1	40–60
	H	351M (5.8)	2-bbl	4.00 × 3.50	8.0:1	50–75
	H	351W (5.8)	2-bbl	4.00 × 3.50	8.2:1	40–60
	S	400 (6.6)	2-bbl	4.00 × 4.00	8.0:1	50–75
	J	460 (7.5)	4-bbl	4.36 × 3.85	8.2:1	40–65
1980	B	300 (4.9)	1-bbl	4.00 × 3.98	8.4:1	40–60
	K	300HD (4.9)	1-bbl	4.00 × 3.98	8.0:1	40–60
	G	302 (5.0)	2-bbl	4.00 × 3.00	8.2:1	40–60
	H	351M (5.8)	2-bbl	4.00 × 3.50	8.0:1	50–75
	H	351W (5.8)	2-bbl	4.00 × 3.50	8.2:1	40–60
	S	400 (6.6)	2-bbl	4.00 × 4.00	8.0:1	50–75
	J	460 (7.5)	4-bbl	4.36 × 3.85	8.4:1	50–65
1981	D	255 (4.2)	2-bbl	3.68 × 3.00	8.2:1	40–60
	B	300 (4.9)	1-bbl	4.00 × 3.98	8.4:1	40–60
	G	302 (5.0)	2-bbl	4.00 × 3.00	8.2:1	40–60
	H	351W (5.8)	2-bbl	4.00 × 3.50	8.2:1	40–60
	J	460 (7.5)	4-bbl	4.36 × 3.85	8.4:1	50–65
1982	3	232 (3.8)	2-bbl	3.81 × 3.39	8.7:1	40–60
	D	255 (4.2)	2-bbl	3.68 × 3.00	8.2:1	40–60
	B	300 (4.9)	1-bbl	4.00 × 3.98	8.4:1	40–60
	G	302 (5.0)	2-bbl	4.00 × 3.00	8.2:1	40–60
	H	351W (5.8)	2-bbl	4.00 × 3.50	8.2:1	40–60
	J	460 (7.5)	4-bbl	4.36 × 3.85	8.4:1	50–65

85763C01

GENERAL ENGINE SPECIFICATIONS

Year	Engine ID/VIN	Engine Displacement cu. in. (L)	Fuel System Type	Bore × Stroke (in.)	Compression Ratio	Oil Pressure @ rpm
1983	3	232 (3.8)	2-bbl	3.81 × 3.39	8.7:1	40-60
	9	300 (4.9)	1-bbl LP	4.00 × 3.98	7.5:1	40-60
	Y	300 (4.9)	1-bbl	4.00 × 3.98	8.4:1	40-60
	F	302 (5.0)	2-bbl	4.00 × 3.00	8.2:1	40-60
	G	351W (5.8)	2-bbl	4.00 × 3.50	8.2:1	40-60
	1	420 (6.9)	Diesel	4.00 × 4.18	20.7:1	40-60
	L	460 (7.5)	4-bbl	4.36 × 3.85	8.4:1	50-75
1984	Y	300 (4.9)	1-bbl	4.00 × 3.98	8.4:1	40-60
	F	302 (5.0)	2-bbl	4.00 × 3.00	8.2:1	40-60
	G	351W (5.8)	2-bbl	4.00 × 3.50	8.2:1	40-60
	1	420 (6.9)	Diesel	4.00 × 4.18	20.7:1	40-60
	L	460 (7.5)	4-bbl	4.36 × 3.85	8.4:1	50-75
1985	Y	300 (4.9)	1-bbl	4.00 × 3.98	8.2:1	40-60
	F	302 (5.0)	2-bbl	4.00 × 3.00	8.2:1	40-60
	N	302 (5.0)	EFI	4.00 × 3.00	8.2:1	40-60
	G	351W (5.8)	2-bbl	4.00 × 3.50	8.2:1	40-60
	H	351W (5.8)	4-bbl	4.00 × 3.50	8.2:1	40-60
	1	420 (6.9)	Diesel	4.00 × 4.18	20.7:1	40-60
	L	460 (7.5)	4-bbl	4.36 × 3.85	8.4:1	50-75
1986	Y	300 (4.9)	1-bbl	4.00 × 3.98	8.4:1	40-60
	N	302 (5.0)	EFI	4.00 × 3.00	8.2:1	40-60
	H	351W (5.8)		4.00 × 3.50		40-60
	1	420 (6.9)	Diesel	4.00 × 4.18	20.7:1	40-60
	L	460 (7.5)	4-bbl	4.36 × 3.85	8.4:1	50-75

NOTE: Horsepower and torque are SAE net figures. They are measured at the rear of the transmission with all accessories installed and operating. Since the figures vary when a given engine is installed in different models, some are representative rather than exact.

85763C1A

CAMSHAFT SPECIFICATIONS

All measurements given in inches.

Year	VIN	Engine Displacement cu. in.	Journal Diameter 1	2	3	4	5	Bearing Clearance	Lobe Lift Intake	Exhaust	Camshaft End Play
1976	B	300	2.0170-2.0180	2.0170-2.0180	2.0170-2.0180	2.0170-2.0180	—	0.001-0.003	0.2490	0.2490	0.001-0.007
	G	302	2.0805-2.0815	2.0655-2.0665	2.0505-2.0515	2.0355-2.0365	2.0205-2.0215	0.001-0.003	0.2303	0.2375	0.001-0.007
	Y	360	2.1238-2.1248	2.1238-2.1248	2.1238-2.1248	2.1238-2.1248	2.1238-2.1248	0.001-0.003	0.2470	0.2490	0.001-0.007
	H	390	2.1238-2.1248	2.1238-2.1248	2.1238-2.1248	2.1238-2.1248	2.1238-2.1248	0.001-0.003	0.2470	0.2490	0.001-0.007
	M	390	2.1238-2.1248	2.1238-2.1248	2.1238-2.1248	2.1238-2.1248	2.1238-2.1248	0.001-0.003	0.2470	0.2490	0.001-0.007
	J	460	2.1238-2.1248	2.1238-2.1248	2.1238-2.1248	2.1238-2.1248	2.1238-2.1248	0.001-0.003	0.2530	0.2780	0.001-0.007
1977	B	300	2.0170-2.0180	2.0170-2.0180	2.0170-2.0180	2.0170-2.0180	—	0.001-0.003	0.2490	0.2490	0.001-0.007
	G	302	2.0805-2.0815	2.0655-2.0665	2.0505-2.0515	2.0355-2.0365	2.0205-2.0215	0.001-0.003	0.2375	0.2470	0.001-0.007
	H	351M	2.1248-2.1328	2.1238-2.1248	2.1238-2.1248	2.1238-2.1248	2.1238-2.1248	0.001-0.002	0.2474	0.2500	0.001-0.006
	S	400	2.1248-2.1328	2.1238-2.1248	2.1238-2.1248	2.1238-2.1248	2.1238-2.1248	0.001-0.003	0.2474	0.2500	0.001-0.006
	J	460	2.1238-2.1248	2.1238-2.1248	2.1238-2.1248	2.1238-2.1248	2.1238-2.1248	0.001-0.003	0.2530	0.2780	0.001-0.006
1978	B	300	2.0170-2.0180	2.0170-2.0180	2.0170-2.0180	2.0170-2.0180	—	0.001-0.003	0.2490	0.2490	0.001-0.007
	G	302	2.0805-2.0815	2.0655-2.0665	2.0505-2.0515	2.0355-2.0365	2.0205-2.0215	0.001-0.003	0.2303	0.2375	0.001-0.007
	H	351W	2.0805-2.0815	2.0655-2.0665	2.0505-2.0515	2.0355-2.0365	2.0205-2.0215	0.001-0.002	0.2600	0.2600	0.001-0.007
	H	351M	2.1248-2.1328	2.1238-2.1248	2.1238-2.1248	2.1238-2.1248	2.1238-2.1248	0.001-0.003	0.2474	0.2500	0.001-0.006
	S	400	2.1248-2.1328	2.1238-2.1248	2.1238-2.1248	2.1238-2.1248	2.1238-2.1248	0.001-0.003	0.2474	0.2500	0.001-0.006
	J	460	2.1238-2.1248	2.1238-2.1248	2.1238-2.1248	2.1238-2.1248	2.1238-2.1248	0.001-0.003	0.2530	0.2780	0.001-0.006
1979	B, K	300	2.0170-2.0180	2.0170-2.0180	2.0170-2.0180	2.0170-2.0180	—	0.001-0.003	0.2490	0.2490	0.001-0.007
	G	302	2.0805-2.0815	2.0655-2.0665	2.0505-2.0515	2.0355-2.0365	2.0205-2.0215	0.001-0.003	0.2375	0.2470	0.001-0.007
	H	351W	2.0805-2.0815	2.0655-2.0665	2.0505-2.0515	2.0355-2.0365	2.0205-2.0215	0.001-0.003	0.2600	0.2600	0.001-0.007
	H	351M	2.1248-2.1328	2.1238-2.1248	2.1238-2.1248	2.1238-2.1248	2.1238-2.1248	0.001-0.003	0.2500	0.2500	0.001-0.006
	S	400	2.1248-2.1328	2.1238-2.1248	2.1238-2.1248	2.1238-2.1248	2.1238-2.1248	0.001-0.003	0.2500	0.2500	0.001-0.006
	J	460	2.1238-2.1248	2.1238-2.1248	2.1238-2.1248	2.1238-2.1248	2.1238-2.1248	0.001-0.003	0.2526	0.2780	0.001-0.006

85763C02

CAMSHAFT SPECIFICATIONS

All measurements given in inches.

Year	VIN	Engine Displacement cu. in.	Journal Diameter 1	2	3	4	5	Bearing Clearance	Lobe Lift Intake	Lobe Lift Exhaust	Camshaft End Play
1980	B, K	300	2.0170-2.0180	2.0170-2.0180	2.0170-2.0180	2.0170-2.0180	—	0.001-0.003	0.2490	0.2490	0.001-0.007
	G	302	2.0805-2.0815	2.0655-2.0665	2.0505-2.0515	2.0355-2.0365	2.0205-2.0215	0.001-0.003	0.2375	0.2470	0.001-0.007
	H	351W	2.0805-2.0815	2.0655-2.0665	2.0505-2.0515	2.0355-2.0365	2.0205-2.0215	0.001-0.003	0.2600	0.2600	0.001-0.007
	H	351M	2.1248-2.1328	2.0655-2.0665	2.0505-2.0515	2.0355-2.0365	2.0205-2.0215	0.001-0.003	0.2500	0.2500	0.001-0.006
	S	400	2.1248-2.1328	2.0655-2.0665	2.0505-2.0515	2.0355-2.0365	2.0205-2.0215	0.001-0.003	0.2500	0.2500	0.001-0.006
	J	460	2.1238-2.1248	2.1238-2.1248	2.1238-2.1248	2.1238-2.1248	2.1238-2.1248	0.001-0.003	0.2530	0.2780	0.001-0.006
1981	B	300	2.0170-2.0180	2.0170-2.0180	2.0170-2.0180	2.0170-2.0180	—	0.001-0.003	0.2490	0.2490	0.001-0.007
	G	302	2.0805-2.0815	2.0655-2.0665	2.0505-2.0515	2.0355-2.0365	2.0205-2.0215	0.001-0.003	0.2375	0.2375	0.001-0.007
	H	351W	2.0805-2.0815	2.0655-2.0665	2.0505-2.0515	2.0355-2.0365	2.0205-2.0215	0.001-0.003	0.2600	0.2600	0.001-0.007
	J	460	2.1238-2.1248	2.1238-2.1248	2.1238-2.1248	2.1238-2.1248	2.1238-2.1248	0.001-0.003	0.2530	0.2780	0.001-0.006
1982	3	232	2.0505-2.0515	2.0505-2.0515	2.0505-2.0515	2.0505-2.0515	—	0.001-0.003	0.2400	0.2410	0
	D	255	2.0805-2.0815	2.0655-2.0665	2.0505-2.0515	2.0355-2.0365	2.0205-2.0215	0.001-0.003	0.2375	0.2375	0.001-0.007
	B	300	2.0170-2.0180	2.0170-2.0180	2.0170-2.0180	2.0170-2.0180	—	0.001-0.003	0.2490	0.2490	0.001-0.007
	G	302	2.0805-2.0815	2.0655-2.0665	2.0505-2.0515	2.0355-2.0365	2.0205-2.0215	0.001-0.003	0.2375	0.2470	0.001-0.007
	H	351W	2.0805-2.0815	2.0655-2.0665	2.0505-2.0515	2.0355-2.0365	2.0205-2.0215	0.001-0.003	0.2600	0.2600	0.001-0.007
	J	460	2.1238-2.1248	2.1238-2.1248	2.1238-2.1248	2.1238-2.1248	2.1238-2.1248	0.001-0.003	0.2530	0.2780	0.001-0.006
1983	3	232	2.0505-2.0515	2.0505-2.0515	2.0505-2.0515	2.0505-2.0515	—	0.001-0.003	0.2400	0.2410	0
	Y, 9	300	2.0170-2.0180	2.0170-2.0180	2.0170-2.0180	2.0170-2.0180	—	0.001-0.003	0.2490⊙	0.2490⊙	0.001-0.007
	F	302	2.0805-2.0815	2.0655-2.0665	2.0505-2.0515	2.0355-2.0365	2.0205-2.0215	0.001-0.003	0.2375	0.2474	0.001-0.007
	G	351W	2.0805-2.0815	2.0655-2.0665	2.0505-2.0515	2.0355-2.0365	2.0205-2.0215	0.001-0.003	0.2600	0.2600	0.001-0.007
	1	420 (diesel)	2.0990-2.1000	2.0990-2.1000	2.0990-2.1000	2.0990-2.1000	2.0990-2.1000	0.001-0.005	0.2535	0.2530	0.001-0.009
	L	460	2.1238-2.1248	2.1238-2.1248	2.1238-2.1248	2.1238-2.1248	2.1238-2.1248	0.001-0.003	0.2520	0.2780	0.001-0.006

85763C2A

CAMSHAFT SPECIFICATIONS

All measurements given in inches.

Year	VIN	Engine Displacement cu. in.	Journal Diameter 1	2	3	4	5	Bearing Clearance	Lobe Lift Intake	Lobe Lift Exhaust	Camshaft End Play
1984	Y	300	2.0170-2.0180	2.0170-2.0180	2.0170-2.0180	2.0170-2.0180	—	0.001-0.003	0.2490⊙	0.2490⊙	0.001-0.007
	F	302	2.0805-2.0815	2.0655-2.0665	2.0505-2.0515	2.0355-2.0365	2.0205-2.0215	0.001-0.003	0.2375	0.2474	0.001-0.007
	G	351W	2.0805-2.0815	2.0655-2.0665	2.0505-2.0515	2.0355-2.0365	2.0205-2.0215	0.001-0.003	0.2600	0.2600	0.001-0.007
	1	420 (diesel)	2.0990-2.1000	2.0990-2.1000	2.0990-2.1000	2.0990-2.1000	2.0990-2.1000	0.001-0.005	0.2535	0.2530	0.001-0.009
	L	460	2.1238-2.1248	2.1238-2.1248	2.1238-2.1248	2.1238-2.1248	2.1238-2.1248	0.001-0.003	0.2520	0.2780	0.001-0.006
1985	Y	300	2.0170-2.0180	2.0170-2.0180	2.0170-2.0180	2.0170-2.0180	—	0.001-0.003	0.2490⊙	0.2490⊙	0.001-0.007
	N, F	302	2.0805-2.0815	2.0655-2.0665	2.0505-2.0515	2.0355-2.0365	2.0205-2.0215	0.001-0.003	0.2375	0.2474	0.001-0.007
	H, G	351W	2.0805-2.0815	2.0655-2.0665	2.0505-2.0515	2.0355-2.0365	2.0205-2.0215	0.001-0.003	0.2600	0.2600	0.001-0.007
	1	420 (diesel)	2.0990-2.1000	2.0990-2.1000	2.0990-2.1000	2.0990-2.1000	2.0990-2.1000	0.001-0.005	0.2535	0.2530	0.001-0.009
	L	460	2.1238-2.1248	2.1238-2.1248	2.1238-2.1248	2.1238-2.1248	2.1238-2.1248	0.001-0.003	0.2520	0.2780	0.001-0.006
1986	Y	300	2.0170-2.0180	2.0170-2.0180	2.0170-2.0180	2.0170-2.0180	—	0.001-0.003	0.2490⊙	0.2490⊙	0.001-0.007
	N, F	302	2.0805-2.0815	2.0655-2.0665	2.0505-2.0515	2.0355-2.0365	2.0205-2.0215	0.001-0.003	0.2375	0.2474	0.001-0.007
	H, G	351W	2.0805-2.0815	2.0655-2.0665	2.0505-2.0515	2.0355-2.0365	2.0205-2.0215	0.001-0.003	0.2600	0.2600	0.001-0.007
	1	420 (diesel)	2.0990-2.1000	2.0990-2.1000	2.0990-2.1000	2.0990-2.1000	2.0990-2.1000	0.001-0.005	0.2535	0.2530	0.001-0.009
	L	460	2.1238-2.1248	2.1238-2.1248	2.1238-2.1248	2.1238-2.1248	2.1238-2.1248	0.001-0.003	0.2520	0.2780	0.001-0.006

⊙ F-100/150 2WD w/2.47-1 or 2.75-1 axle ratio and manual transmission, except California

85763C2B

VALVE SPECIFICATIONS

Year	Engine VIN	Engine Displacement cu. in.	Seat Angle (deg.)	Face Angle (deg.)	Spring Test Pressure (lbs. @ in.)	Spring Installed Height (in.)	Stem-to-Guide Clearance (in.) Intake	Stem-to-Guide Clearance (in.) Exhaust	Stem Diameter (in.) Intake	Stem Diameter (in.) Exhaust
1980	B, K	300	45	44	○	○	0.0010-0.0027	0.0010-0.0027	0.3416-0.3423	0.3416-0.3423
	G	302	45	44	○	○	0.0010-0.0027	0.0015-0.0032	0.3416-0.3423	0.3411-0.3418
	H	351W	45	44	○	○	0.0010-0.0027	0.0015-0.0032	0.3416-0.3423	0.3411-0.3418
	H	351M	45	44	215-237 @ 1.39	○	0.0010-0.0027	0.0015-0.0032	0.3416-0.3423	0.3411-0.3418
	S	400	45	44	215-237 @ 1.39	○	0.0010-0.0027	0.0015-0.0032	0.3416-0.3423	0.3411-0.3418
	J	460	45	44	218-240 @ 1.33	1.810	0.0010-0.0027	0.0010-0.0027	0.3416-0.3423	0.3416-0.3423
1981	D	255	45	44	○	○	0.0010-0.0027	0.0015-0.0032	0.3416-0.3423	0.3411-0.3418
	B	300	45	44	○	○	0.0010-0.0027	0.0015-0.0032	0.3416-0.3423	0.3411-0.3418
	G	302	45	44	○	○	0.0010-0.0027	0.0015-0.0032	0.3416-0.3423	0.3411-0.3418
	H	351W	45	44	○	○	0.0010-0.0027	0.0015-0.0032	0.3416-0.3423	0.3411-0.3418
	J	460	45	44	218-240 @ 1.33	1.810	0.0010-0.0027	0.0010-0.0027	0.3416-0.3423	0.3416-0.3423
1982	3	232	45	44	215 @ 1.79	1.700	0.0010-0.0027	0.0015-0.0032	0.3416-0.3423	0.3411-0.3418
	D	255	45	44	○	○	0.0010-0.0027	0.0015-0.0032	0.3416-0.3423	0.3411-0.3418
	B	300	45	44	○	○	0.0010-0.0027	0.0015-0.0032	0.3416-0.3423	0.3411-0.3418
	G	302	45	44	○	○	0.0010-0.0027	0.0015-0.0032	0.3416-0.3423	0.3411-0.3418
	H	351W	45	44	○	○	0.0010-0.0027	0.0015-0.0032	0.3416-0.3423	0.3411-0.3418
	J	460	45	44	218-240 @ 1.33	1.810	0.0010-0.0027	0.0010-0.0027	0.3416-0.3423	0.3416-0.3423
1983	3	232	45	44	215 @ 1.79	1.700	0.0010-0.0027	0.0015-0.0032	0.3416-0.3423	0.3411-0.3418
	9, Y	300	45	44	○	○	0.0010-0.0027	0.0015-0.0032	0.3423-0.3716	0.3411-0.3418
	F	302	45	44	○	○	0.0010-0.0027	0.0015-0.0032	0.3416-0.3423	0.3411-0.3418
	H	351W	45	44	○	○	0.0010-0.0027	0.0015-0.0032	0.3416-0.3423	0.3411-0.3418
	1	420	○	○	60 @ 1.798	1.798	0.0012-0.0029	0.0012-0.0029	0.3717-0.3724	0.3717-0.3724
	L	460	45	44	218-240 @ 1.33	1.810	0.0010-0.0027	0.0010-0.0027	0.3416-0.3423	0.3416-0.3423

85763C3A

VALVE SPECIFICATIONS

Year	Engine VIN	Engine Displacement cu. in.	Seat Angle (deg.)	Face Angle (deg.)	Spring Test Pressure (lbs. @ in.)	Spring Installed Height (in.)	Stem-to-Guide Clearance (in.) Intake	Stem-to-Guide Clearance (in.) Exhaust	Stem Diameter (in.) Intake	Stem Diameter (in.) Exhaust
1976	B	300	45	45	○	1.700	0.0010-0.0027	0.0010-0.0027	0.3416-0.3423	0.3416-0.3423
	G	302	45	44	190-210 @ 1.31	1.690	0.0010-0.0027	0.0015-0.0032	0.3416-0.3423	0.3411-0.3418
	Y	360	45	44	○	1.828 ○	0.0010-0.0027	0.0015-0.0032	0.3711-0.3718	0.3703-0.3706
	H	390	45	44	○	1.828 ○	0.0010-0.0027	0.0015-0.0032	0.3711-0.3718	0.3703-0.3706
	M	390	45	44	○	1.828 ○	0.0010-0.0027	0.0015-0.0032	0.3711-0.3718	0.3703-0.3706
	J	460	45	44	240-265	1.810	0.0010-0.0027	0.0010-0.0027	0.3416-0.3423	0.3416-0.3423
1977	B	300	45	45	○	1.700	0.0010-0.0027	0.0010-0.0027	0.3416-0.3423	0.3416-0.3423
	G	302	45	44	190-210 @ 1.31	1.690	0.0010-0.0027	0.0015-0.0032	0.3416-0.3423	0.3411-0.3418
	H	351M	45	44	○	○	0.0010-0.0027	0.0015-0.0032	0.3416-0.3423	0.3411-0.3418
	S	400	45	44	○	○	0.0010-0.0027	0.0015-0.0032	0.3416-0.3423	0.3411-0.3418
	J	460	45	44	218-240 @ 1.33	2.060	0.0010-0.0027	0.0010-0.0027	0.3416-0.3423	0.3416-0.3423
1978	B	300	45	44	○	○	0.0010-0.0027	0.0010-0.0027	0.3416-0.3423	0.3416-0.3423
	G	302	45	44	○	○	0.0010-0.0027	0.0015-0.0032	0.3416-0.3423	0.3411-0.3418
	H	351W	45	44	○	○	0.0010-0.0027	0.0015-0.0032	0.3416-0.3423	0.3411-0.3418
	H	351M	45	44	○	○	0.0010-0.0027	0.0015-0.0032	0.3416-0.3423	0.3411-0.3418
	S	400	45	44	○	○	0.0010-0.0027	0.0015-0.0032	0.3416-0.3423	0.3411-0.3418
	J	460	45	44	218-240 @ 1.33	2.060	0.0010-0.0027	0.0010-0.0027	0.3416-0.3423	0.3416-0.3423
1979	B, K	300	45	44	○	○	0.0010-0.0027	0.0010-0.0027	0.3416-0.3423	0.3416-0.3423
	G	302	45	44	○	○	0.0010-0.0027	0.0015-0.0032	0.3416-0.3423	0.3411-0.3418
	H	351W	45	44	215-237 @ 1.39	○	0.0010-0.0027	0.0015-0.0032	0.3416-0.3423	0.3411-0.3418
	H	351M	45	44	215-237 @ 1.39	○	0.0010-0.0027	0.0015-0.0032	0.3416-0.3423	0.3411-0.3418
	S	400	45	44	215-237 @ 1.39	○	0.0010-0.0027	0.0015-0.0032	0.3416-0.3423	0.3411-0.3418
	J	460	45	44	218-240 @ 1.33	1.810	0.0010-0.0027	0.0010-0.0027	0.3416-0.3423	0.3416-0.3423

85763C03

CRANKSHAFT AND CONNECTING ROD SPECIFICATIONS

Year	Engine VIN	Engine Displacement (cu. in.)	Main Brg. Journal Dia.	Crankshaft Main Brg. Oil Clearance	Shaft End-play	Thrust on No.	Journal Diameter	Connecting Rod Oil Clearance	Side Clearance
1976	B	300	2.3982–2.3990	0.0008–0.0015	0.004–0.008	5	2.1228–2.1236	0.0008–0.0015	0.006–0.013
	G	302	2.2482–2.2490	①	0.004–0.008	3	2.1228–2.1236	0.0008–0.0015	0.010–0.020
	Y	360	2.7484–2.7492	0.0005–0.0015	0.004–0.010	3	2.4380–2.4388	0.0008–0.0015	0.008–0.025
	H, M	390	2.7484–2.7492	0.0005–0.0015	0.004–0.010	3	2.4380–2.4388	0.0008–0.0015	0.008–0.025
	J	460	2.9994–3.0002	0.0008–	0.004–0.008	3	2.4992–2.5000	0.0008–0.0015	0.010–0.020
1977	B	300	2.3982–2.3990	0.0008–0.0015	0.004–0.008	5	2.1228–2.1236	0.0008–0.0015	0.006–0.013
	G	302	2.2482–2.2490	①	0.004–0.008	3	2.1228–2.1236	0.0008–0.0015	0.010–0.020
	H	351M	2.9994–3.0002	0.0008–0.0015	0.004–0.008	3	2.3103–2.3111	0.0008–0.0015	0.010–0.020
	S	400	2.9994–3.0002	0.0008–0.0015	0.004–0.008	3	2.3103–2.3111	0.0008–0.0015	0.010–0.020
	J	460	2.9994–3.0002	0.0008–0.0015	0.004–0.008	3	2.4992–2.5000	0.0008–0.0015	0.010–0.020
1978	B	300	2.3982–2.3990	0.0008–0.0015	0.004–0.008	5	2.1228–2.1236	0.0008–0.0015	0.006–0.013
	G	302	2.2482–2.2490	①	0.004–0.008	3	2.1228–2.1236	0.0008–0.0015	0.010–0.020
	H	351W	2.9994–3.0002	0.0008–0.0015	0.004–0.008	3	2.3103–2.3111	0.0008–0.0015	0.010–0.020
	H	351M	2.9994–3.0002	0.0008–0.0015	0.004–0.008	3	2.3103–2.3111	0.0008–0.0015	0.010–0.020
	S	400	2.9994–3.0002	0.0008–0.0015	0.004–0.008	3	2.3103–2.3111	0.0008–0.0015	0.010–0.020
	J	460	2.9994–3.0002	0.0008–0.0015	0.004–0.008	3	2.4992–2.5000	0.0008–0.0015	0.010–0.020
1979	B, K	300	2.3982–2.3990	0.0008–0.0015	0.004–0.008	5	2.1228–2.1236	0.0008–0.0015	0.006–0.013
	G	302	2.2482–2.2490	①	0.004–0.008	3	2.1228–2.1238	0.0008–0.0015	0.010–0.020
	H	351W	2.9994–3.0002	0.0008–0.0015	0.004–0.008	3	2.3103–2.3111	0.0008–0.0015	0.010–0.020
	H	351M	2.9994–3.0002	0.0008–0.0015	0.004–0.008	3	2.3103–2.3111	0.0008–0.0015	0.010–0.020
	S	400	2.9994–3.0002	0.0008–0.0015	0.004–0.008	3	2.3103–2.3111	0.0008–0.0015	0.010–0.020
	J	460	2.9994–3.0002	0.0008–0.0015	0.004–0.008	3	2.4992–2.5000	0.0008–0.0015	0.010–0.020

8576C04

VALVE SPECIFICATIONS

Year	Engine VIN	Engine Displacement cu. in.	Seat Angle (deg.)	Face Angle (deg.)	Spring Test Pressure (lbs. @ in.)	Spring Installed Height (in.)	Stem-to-Guide Clearance (in.) Intake	Exhaust	Stem Diameter (in.) Intake	Exhaust
1984	Y	300	45	44	⑨	⑨	0.0010–0.0027	0.0010–0.0027	0.3416–0.3423	0.3416–0.3423
	F	302	45	44	⑨	⑨	0.0010–0.0027	0.0015–0.0032	0.3416–0.3423	0.3411–0.3418
	G	351W	45	44	190–210 @ 1.200	1.798	0.0010–0.0027	0.0015–0.0032	0.3416–0.3423	0.3411–0.3418
	I	420	⑫	⑫	60 @ 1.798	1.798	0.0012–0.0029	0.0012–0.0029	0.3717–0.3724	0.3717–0.3724
	L	460	45	44	218–240 @ 1.33	1.810	0.0010–0.0027	0.0010–0.0027	0.3416–0.3423	0.3416–0.3423
1985	Y	300	45	44	⑨	⑨	0.0010–0.0027	0.0010–0.0027	0.3416–0.3423	0.3416–0.3423
	F, N	302	45	44	⑨	⑨	0.0010–0.0027	0.0015–0.0032	0.3416–0.3423	0.3411–0.3418
	G	351W	45	44	190–210 @ 1.200	1.798	0.0010–0.0027	0.0015–0.0032	0.3416–0.3423	0.3411–0.3418
	I	420	⑫	⑫	60 @ 1.798	1.798	0.0012–0.0029	0.0012–0.0029	0.3717–0.3724	0.3717–0.3724
	L	460	45	44	218–240 @ 1.33	1.810	0.0010–0.0027	0.0010–0.0027	0.3416–0.3423	0.3416–0.3423
1986	Y	300	45	44	⑨	⑨	0.0010–0.0027	0.0010–0.0027	0.3416–0.3423	0.3416–0.3423
	N	302	45	44	⑨	⑨	0.0010–0.0027	0.0015–0.0032	0.3416–0.3423	0.3411–0.3418
	H	351W	45	44	190–210 @ 1.200	1.798	0.0010–0.0027	0.0015–0.0032	0.3416–0.3423	0.3411–0.3418
	I	420	⑫	⑫	60 @ 1.798	1.798	0.0012–0.0029	0.0012–0.0029	0.3717–0.3724	0.3717–0.3724
	L	460	45	44	218–240 @ 1.33	1.810	0.0010–0.0027	0.0010–0.0027	0.3416–0.3423	0.3416–0.3423

① Intake: 187–207 @ 1.300 Exhaust: 182–202 @ 1.180
② F-100 Intake: 90 @ 1.820 Exhaust: 183 @ 1.240
③ F-250 Int. & Ex.: 220 @ 1.380
④ F-100 Exhaust: 1.445
⑤ Intake: 215–237 @ 1.390
⑥ Intake: 215–237 @ 1.250
⑦ Intake: 1.650 Exhaust: 1.820
⑧ Intake: 218–240 @ 1.390 Exhaust: 218–240 @ 1.250 Exhaust: 1.680

Intake: 1.700 Exhaust: 1.580
Intake: 190–210 @ 1.310 Exhaust: 190–210 @ 1.200
Intake: 1.580
Intake: 1.600
Intake: 190–210 @ 1.340 Exhaust: 190–210 @ 1.200
Intake: 1.790
Intake: 1.800
Intake: 192–210 @ 1.360 Exhaust: 190–210 @ 1.200
Intake: 1.780
Intake: 1.600

⑨ Intake: 190–210 @ 1.360 Exhaust: 190–210 @ 1.360
⑩ Intake: 196–212 @ 1.360 Exhaust: 190–210 @ 1.200
⑪ Intake: 30 Exhaust: 37.5
⑫ Intake: 165–175 @ 1.300 Exhaust: 165–175 @ 1.180
⑬ Intake: 166–184 @ 1.240 Exhaust: 166–184 @ 1.070
⑭ Intake: 1.640 Exhaust: 1.470

8576C3B

CRANKSHAFT AND CONNECTING ROD SPECIFICATIONS

Year	Engine VIN	Engine Displacement (cu. in.)	Crankshaft Main Brg. Journal Dia.	Crankshaft Main Brg. Oil Clearance	Crankshaft Shaft End-play	Crankshaft Thrust on No.	Connecting Rod Journal Diameter	Connecting Rod Oil Clearance	Connecting Rod Side Clearance
1980	B, K	300	2.3982-2.3990	0.0008-0.0015	0.004-0.008	5	2.1228-2.1236	0.0008-0.0015	0.006-0.013
	G	302	2.2482-2.2490	⊙	0.004-0.008	3	2.1228-2.1236	0.0008-0.0015	0.010-0.020
	H	351W	2.9994-3.0002	0.0008-0.0015	0.004-0.008	3	2.3103-2.3111	0.0008-0.0015	0.010-0.020
	H	351M	2.9994-3.0002	0.0008-0.0015	0.004-0.008	3	2.3103-2.3111	0.0008-0.0015	0.010-0.020
	S	400	2.9994-3.0002	0.0008-0.0015	0.004-0.008	3	2.3103-2.3111	0.0008-0.0015	0.010-0.020
	J	460	2.9994-3.0002	0.0008-0.0015	0.004-0.008	3	2.4992-2.5000	0.0008-0.0015	0.010-0.020
1981	D	255	2.2482-2.2490	⊙	0.004-0.008	3	2.1228-2.1236	0.0008-0.0015	0.010-0.020
	B	300	2.3982-2.3990	0.0008-0.0015	0.004-0.008	5	2.1228-2.1236	0.0008-0.0015	0.006-0.013
	G	302	2.2482-2.2490	⊙	0.004-0.008	3	2.1228-2.1236	0.0008-0.0015	0.010-0.020
	H	351W	2.9994-3.0002	0.0008-0.0015	0.004-0.008	3	2.3103-2.3111	0.0008-0.0015	0.010-0.020
	J	460	2.9994-3.0002	0.0008-0.0015	0.004-0.008	3	2.4992-2.5000	0.0008-0.0015	0.010-0.020
1982	3	232	2.5190-2.5198	0.0010-0.0014	0.004-0.008	3	2.3103-2.3111	0.0010-0.0014	0.004-0.011
	D	255	2.2482-2.2490	⊙	0.004-0.008	3	2.4992-2.5000	0.0008-0.0015	0.010-0.020
	B	300	2.3982-2.3990	⊙	0.004-0.008	5	2.1228-2.1236	0.0008-0.0015	0.006-0.013
	G	302	2.2482-2.2490	⊙	0.004-0.008	3	2.1228-2.1236	0.0008-0.0015	0.010-0.020
	H	351W	2.9994-3.0002	0.0008-0.0015	0.004-0.008	3	2.3103-2.3111	0.0008-0.0015	0.010-0.020
	J	460	2.9994-3.0002	0.0008-0.0015	0.004-0.008	3	2.4992-2.5000	0.0008-0.0015	0.010-0.020
1983	3	232	2.5190-2.5198	0.0010-0.0014	0.004-0.008	3	2.3103-2.3111	0.0010-0.0014	0.004-0.011
	9, Y	300	2.3982-2.3990	⊙	0.004-0.008	5	2.1228-2.1236	0.0008-0.0015	0.006-0.013
	F	302	2.2482-2.2490	⊙	0.004-0.008	3	2.1228-2.1236	0.0008-0.0015	0.010-0.020
	G	351W	2.9994-3.0002	0.0008-0.0015	0.004-0.008	3	2.3103-2.3111	0.0008-0.0015	0.010-0.020
	1	420	3.1228-3.1236	0.0018-0.0036	0.001-0.009	3	2.4980-2.4990	0.0011-0.0026	0.008-0.020
	L	460	2.9994-3.0002	0.0008-0.0015	0.004-0.008	3	2.4992-2.5000	0.0008-0.0015	0.010-0.020

85763C4A

CRANKSHAFT AND CONNECTING ROD SPECIFICATIONS

Year	Engine VIN	Engine Displacement (cu. in.)	Crankshaft Main Brg. Journal Dia.	Crankshaft Main Brg. Oil Clearance	Crankshaft Shaft End-play	Crankshaft Thrust on No.	Connecting Rod Journal Diameter	Connecting Rod Oil Clearance	Connecting Rod Side Clearance
1984	Y	300	2.3982-2.3990	0.0008-0.0015	0.004-0.008	5	2.1228-2.1236	0.0008-0.0015	0.006-0.013
	F	302	2.2482-2.2490	⊙	0.004-0.008	3	2.1228-2.1236	0.0008-0.0015	0.010-0.020
	G	351W	2.9994-3.0002	0.0008-0.0015	0.004-0.008	3	2.3103-2.3111	0.0008-0.0015	0.010-0.020
	1	420	3.1228-3.1236	0.0018-0.0036	0.001-0.009	3	2.4980-2.4990	0.0011-0.0026	0.008-0.020
	L	460	2.9994-3.0002	0.0008-0.0015	0.004-0.008	3	2.4992-2.5000	0.0008-0.0015	0.010-0.020
1985	Y	300	2.3982-2.3990	0.0008-0.0015	0.004-0.008	5	2.1228-2.1236	0.0008-0.0015	0.006-0.013
	N, F	302	2.2482-2.2490	⊙	0.004-0.008	3	2.1228-2.1236	0.0008-0.0015	0.010-0.020
	H, G	351W	2.9994-3.0002	0.0008-0.0015	0.004-0.008	3	2.3103-2.3111	0.0008-0.0015	0.010-0.020
	1	420	3.1228-3.1236	0.0018-0.0036	0.001-0.009	3	2.4980-2.4990	0.0011-0.0026	0.008-0.020
	L	460	2.9994-3.0002	0.0008-0.0015	0.004-0.008	3	2.4992-2.5000	0.0008-0.0015	0.010-0.020
1986	Y	300	2.3982-2.3990	0.0008-0.0015	0.004-0.008	5	2.1228-2.1236	0.0008-0.0015	0.006-0.013
	N	302	2.2482-2.2490	⊙	0.004-0.008	3	2.1228-2.1236	0.0008-0.0015	0.010-0.020
	H	351W	2.9994-3.0002	0.0008-0.0015	0.004-0.008	3	2.3103-2.3111	0.0008-0.0015	0.010-0.020
	1	420	3.1228-3.1236	0.0018-0.0036	0.001-0.009	3	2.4980-2.4990	0.0011-0.0026	0.008-0.020
	L	460	2.9994-3.0002	0.0008-0.0015	0.004-0.008	3	2.4992-2.5000	0.0008-0.0015	0.010-0.020

⊙ No 1: 0.0001-0.0015
All others: 0.0005-0.0015
② No 1: 0.0008-0.0015
All others: 0.0008-0.0026

85763C4B

PISTON AND RING SPECIFICATIONS
All measurements are given in inches.

Year	Engine VIN	Engine Displacement cu. in.	Piston to Bore Clearance	Ring Side Clearance Top Compression	Ring Side Clearance Bottom Compression	Ring Side Clearance Oil Control	Ring Gap Top Compression	Ring Gap Bottom Compression	Ring Gap Oil Control
1976	B	300	0.0014-0.0022	0.0020-0.0040	0.002-0.004	Snug	0.0100-0.0200	0.010-0.020	0.015-0.055
	G	302	0.0018-0.0026	0.0020-0.0040	0.002-0.004	Snug	0.0100-0.0200	0.010-0.020	0.015-0.055
	Y	360	0.0015-0.0023	0.0020-0.0040	0.002-0.004	Snug	0.0150-0.0230	0.010-0.020	0.015-0.055
	H, M	390	0.0015-0.0023	0.0020-0.0040	0.002-0.004	Snug	0.0150-0.0230	0.010-0.020	0.015-0.055
	J	460	0.0022-0.0030	0.0020-0.0040	0.002-0.004	Snug	0.0100-0.0200	0.010-0.020	0.015-0.055
1977	B	300	0.0014-0.0022	0.0019-0.0036	0.0020-0.0040	Snug	0.0100-0.0200	0.0100-0.0200	0.015-0.055
	G	302	0.0018-0.0026	0.0019-0.0036	0.0020-0.0040	Snug	0.0100-0.0200	0.0100-0.0200	0.015-0.055
	H	351M	0.0014-0.0022	0.0019-0.0036	0.0020-0.0040	Snug	0.0100-0.0200	0.0100-0.0200	0.015-0.055
	S	400	0.0014-0.0022	0.0019-0.0036	0.0020-0.0040	Snug	0.0100-0.0200	0.0100-0.0200	0.015-0.055
	J	460	0.0022-0.0030	0.0025-0.0045	0.0025-0.0045	Snug	0.0100-0.0200	0.0100-0.0200	0.010-0.030
1978	B	300	0.0014-0.0022	0.0019-0.0036	0.0020-0.0040	Snug	0.0100-0.0200	0.0100-0.0200	0.015-0.055
	G	302	0.0018-0.0026	0.0019-0.0036	0.0020-0.0040	Snug	0.0100-0.0200	0.0100-0.0200	0.015-0.055
	H	351W	0.0022-0.0030	0.0019-0.0036	0.0020-0.0040	Snug	0.0100-0.0200	0.0100-0.0200	0.015-0.055
	H	351M	0.0014-0.0022	0.0019-0.0036	0.0020-0.0040	Snug	0.0100-0.0200	0.0100-0.0200	0.015-0.055
	S	400	0.0014-0.0022	0.0019-0.0036	0.0020-0.0040	Snug	0.0100-0.0200	0.0100-0.0200	0.015-0.055
	J	460	0.0022-0.0030	0.0025-0.0045	0.0025-0.0045	Snug	0.0100-0.0200	0.0100-0.0200	0.010-0.030
1979	K, B	300	0.0014-0.0022	0.0019-0.0036	0.0020-0.0040	Snug	0.0100-0.0200	0.0100-0.0200	0.010-0.035
	G	302	0.0018-0.0026	0.0019-0.0036	0.0020-0.0040	Snug	0.0100-0.0200	0.0100-0.0200	0.015-0.035
	H	351W	0.0022-0.0030	0.0019-0.0036	0.0020-0.0040	Snug	0.0100-0.0200	0.0100-0.0200	0.010-0.035
	H	351M	0.0014-0.0022	0.0019-0.0036	0.0020-0.0040	Snug	0.0100-0.0200	0.0100-0.0200	0.010-0.035
	S	400	0.0014-0.0022	0.0019-0.0036	0.0020-0.0040	Snug	0.0100-0.0200	0.0100-0.0200	0.010-0.035
	J	460	0.0022-0.0030	0.0019-0.0036	0.0020-0.0040	Snug	0.0100-0.0200	0.0100-0.0200	0.010-0.035

PISTON AND RING SPECIFICATIONS
All measurements are given in inches.

Year	Engine VIN	Engine Displacement cu. in.	Piston to Bore Clearance	Ring Side Clearance Top Compression	Ring Side Clearance Bottom Compression	Ring Side Clearance Oil Control	Ring Gap Top Compression	Ring Gap Bottom Compression	Ring Gap Oil Control
1980	K, B	300	0.0014-0.0022	0.0019-0.036	0.0020-0.0040	Snug	0.0100-0.0200	0.0100-0.0200	0.010-0.035
	G	302	0.0018-0.0026	0.0019-0.036	0.0020-0.0040	Snug	0.0100-0.0200	0.0100-0.0200	0.010-0.035
	H	351W	0.0018-0.0026	0.0019-0.036	0.0020-0.0040	Snug	0.0100-0.0200	0.0100-0.0200	0.010-0.035
	H	351M	0.0014-0.0022	0.0019-0.036	0.0020-0.0040	Snug	0.0100-0.0200	0.0100-0.0200	0.010-0.035
	S	400	0.0014-0.0022	0.0019-0.036	0.0020-0.0040	Snug	0.0100-0.0200	0.0100-0.0200	0.010-0.035
	J	460	0.0022-0.0030	0.0019-0.036	0.0020-0.0040	Snug	0.0100-0.0200	0.0100-0.0200	0.010-0.035
1981	D	255	0.0018-0.0026	0.0019-0.036	0.0020-0.0040	Snug	0.0100-0.0200	0.0100-0.0200	0.010-0.035
	B	300	0.0014-0.0022	0.0019-0.036	0.0020-0.0040	Snug	0.0100-0.0200	0.0100-0.0200	0.010-0.035
	G	302	0.0018-0.0026	0.0019-0.036	0.0020-0.0040	Snug	0.0100-0.0200	0.0100-0.0200	0.010-0.035
	H	351W	0.0018-0.0026	0.0019-0.036	0.0020-0.0040	Snug	0.0100-0.0200	0.0100-0.0200	0.010-0.035
	J	460	0.0022-0.0030	0.0019-0.036	0.0020-0.0040	Snug	0.0100-0.0200	0.0100-0.0200	0.010-0.035
1982	3	232	0.0014-0.0022	0.0016-0.0037	0.0016-0.037	Snug	0.0100-0.0200	0.0100-0.0200	0.015-0.058
	D	255	0.0018-0.0026	0.0019-0.036	0.0020-0.0040	Snug	0.0100-0.0200	0.0100-0.0200	0.010-0.035
	B	300	0.0014-0.0022	0.0019-0.036	0.0020-0.0040	Snug	0.0100-0.0200	0.0100-0.0200	0.010-0.035
	G	302	0.0018-0.0026	0.0019-0.036	0.0020-0.0040	Snug	0.0100-0.0200	0.0100-0.0200	0.010-0.035
	H	351W	0.0018-0.0026	0.0019-0.036	0.0020-0.0040	Snug	0.0100-0.0200	0.0100-0.0200	0.010-0.035
	J	460	0.0022-0.0030	0.0025-0.0045	0.0025-0.0045	Snug	0.0100-0.0200	0.0100-0.0200	0.010-0.035
1983	3	232	0.0014-0.0022	0.0016-0.0037	0.0016-0.037	Snug	0.0100-0.0200	0.0100-0.0200	0.015-0.058
	9, Y	300	0.0014-0.0022	0.0019-0.036	0.0020-0.0040	Snug	0.0100-0.0200	0.0100-0.0200	0.015-0.055
	F	302	0.0018-0.0026	0.0019-0.036	0.0020-0.0040	Snug	0.0100-0.0200	0.0100-0.0200	0.010-0.035
	G	351W	0.0018-0.0026	0.0019-0.036	0.0020-0.0040	Snug	0.0100-0.0200	0.0100-0.0200	0.010-0.035
	1	420	0.0055-0.0075	0.0020-0.0040	0.0020-0.0040	0.0010-0.0030	0.0140-0.0240	0.0100-0.0240	0.060-0.070
	L	460	0.0022-0.0030	0.0025-0.0045	0.0025-0.0045	Snug	0.0100-0.0200	0.0100-0.0200	0.010-0.035

TORQUE SPECIFICATIONS

All readings in ft. lbs.

Year	Engine VIN	Engine Displacement (cu. in.)	Cylinder Head Bolts	Connecting Rod Bearing Bolts	Main Bearing Bolts	Crankshaft Damper Bolt	Flywheel to Crankshaft Bolts	Manifold Intake	Manifold Exhaust
1976	B	300	70-85	40-45	60-70	130-150	75-85	23-28	23-28
	G	302	65-70	19-24	60-70	70-90	75-85	23-25	18-24
	Y	360	90	40-45	95-105	130-150	75-85	40-45	12-18
	H, M	390	90	40-45	95-105	130-150	75-85	40-45	12-18
	J	460	130-140	40-45	95-105	70-90	75-85	25-30	28-33
1977	B	300	70-85	40-45	60-70	130-150	75-85	22-32	28-33
	G	302	65-72	19-24	60-70	70-90	75-85	23-25	18-24
	H	351M	105	40-45	95-105	70-90	75-85	⊖	18-24
	S	400	105	40-45	95-105	70-90	75-85	⊖	18-24
	J	460	130-140	40-45	95-105	130-150	75-85	22-32	28-33
1978	B	300	70-85	40-45	60-70	130-150	75-85	22-32	28-33
	G	302	65-72	19-24	60-70	70-90	75-85	23-25	18-24
	H	351W	105-112	40-45	95-105	70-90	75-85	23-25	18-24
	H	351M	105	40-45	95-105	70-90	75-85	⊖	18-24
	S	400	105	40-45	95-105	70-90	75-85	⊖	18-24
	J	460	130-140	40-45	95-105	130-150	75-85	22-32	28-33
1979	B, K	300	70-85	40-45	60-70	130-150	75-85	22-32	28-33
	G	302	65-72	19-24	60-70	70-90	75-85	23-25	18-24
	H	351W	105-112	40-45	95-105	70-90	75-85	23-25	18-24
	S	400	95-105	40-45	95-105	70-90	75-85	⊖	18-24
	J	460	130-140	40-45	95-105	70-90	75-85	22-32	28-33
1980	B, K	300	70-85	40-45	60-70	130-150	75-85	22-32	28-33
	G	302	65-72	19-24	60-70	70-90	75-85	23-25	18-24
	H	351W	105-112	40-45	95-105	70-90	75-85	23-25	18-24
	H	351M	95-105	40-45	95-105	70-90	75-85	23-25	18-24
	S	400	95-105	40-45	95-105	70-90	75-85	⊖	18-24
	J	460	130-140	40-45	95-105	130-150	75-85	22-32	28-33
1981	D	255	65-72	19-24	60-70	70-90	75-85	23-25	18-24
	B	300	70-85	40-45	60-70	130-150	75-85	22-32	28-33
	G	302	65-72	19-24	60-70	70-90	75-85	23-25	18-24
	H	351W	105-112	40-45	95-105	70-90	75-85	23-25	18-24
	J	460	130-140*	40-45	95-105	70-90	75-85	22-32	28-33
1982	3	232	74	31-36	65-81	93-121	54-64	⊘	15-22
	D	255	65-72	19-24	60-70	70-90	75-85	23-25	18-24
	B	300	85	40-45	60-70	130-150	75-85	22-32	22-32
	G	302	65-72	19-24	60-70	70-90	75-85	23-25	18-24
	H	351W	105-112	40-45	95-105	70-90	75-85	23-25	18-24
	J	460	130-140	45-50	95-105	70-90	75-85	22-32	28-33

⊕ ³/₈ in.: 22-32
⊖ ⁷/₁₆ in.: 17-25
⊘ Step 1: 5
Step 2: 10
Step 3: 18

85763C06

PISTON AND RING SPECIFICATIONS

All measurements are given in inches.

Year	Engine VIN	Engine Displacement cu. in.	Piston to Bore Clearance	Ring Side Clearance Top Compression	Bottom Compression	Oil Control	Ring Gap Top Compression	Bottom Compression	Oil Control
1984	Y	300	0.0014-0.0022	0.0019-0.0036	0.0020-0.0040	Snug	0.0100-0.0200	0.0100-0.0200	0.015-0.055
	F	302	0.0018-0.0026	0.0019-0.0036	0.0020-0.0040	Snug	0.0100-0.0200	0.0100-0.0200	0.010-0.030
	G	351W	0.0018-0.0026	0.0019-0.0036	0.0020-0.0040	Snug	0.0100-0.0200	0.0100-0.0200	0.010-0.035
	1	420	0.0055-0.0065	0.0020-0.0040	0.0020-0.0040	0.0010-0.0030	0.0140-0.0240	0.0100-0.0240	0.060-0.070
	L	460	0.0022-0.0030	0.0025-0.0045	0.0025-0.0045	Snug	0.0100-0.0200	0.0100-0.0200	0.010-0.035
1985	Y	300	0.0010-0.0018	0.0019-0.0036	0.0020-0.0040	Snug	0.0100-0.0200	0.0100-0.0200	0.015-0.055
	F, N	302	0.0018-0.0026	0.0019-0.0036	0.0020-0.0040	Snug	0.0100-0.0200	0.0100-0.0200	0.015-0.055
	G, H	351W	0.0018-0.0026	0.0019-0.0036	0.0020-0.0040	Snug	0.0100-0.0200	0.0100-0.0200	0.015-0.055
	1	420	0.0055-0.0065	0.0020-0.0040	0.0020-0.0040	0.0010-0.0030	0.0140-0.0240	0.0100-0.0240	0.060-0.070
	L	460	0.0022-0.0030	0.0025-0.0045	0.0025-0.0045	Snug	0.0100-0.0200	0.0100-0.0200	0.010-0.035
1986	Y	300	0.0010-0.0018	0.0019-0.0036	0.0020-0.0040	Snug	0.0100-0.0200	0.0100-0.0200	0.015-0.055
	N	302	0.0018-0.0026	0.0019-0.0036	0.0020-0.0040	Snug	0.0100-0.0200	0.0100-0.0200	0.015-0.055
	H	351W	0.0018-0.0026	0.0019-0.0036	0.0020-0.0040	Snug	0.0100-0.0200	0.0100-0.0200	0.015-0.055
	1	420	0.0055-0.0075	0.0020-0.0040	0.0020-0.0040	0.0010-0.0030	0.0140-0.0240	0.0100-0.0240	0.060-0.070
	L	460	0.0022-0.0030	0.0025-0.0045	0.0025-0.0045	Snug	0.0100-0.0200	0.0100-0.0200	0.010-0.035

85763C5B

TORQUE SPECIFICATIONS
All readings in ft. lbs.

Year	Engine VIN	Engine Displacement (cu. in.)	Cylinder Head Bolts	Connecting Rod Bearing Bolts	Main Bearing Bolts	Crankshaft Damper Bolt	Flywheel to Crankshaft Bolts	Manifold Intake	Manifold Exhaust
1983	3	232	74	31–36	65–81	93–121	54–64	②	15–22
	9, Y	300	85	40–45	60–70	130–150	75–85	22–32	22–32
	F	302	65–72	19–24	60–70	70–90	75–85	23–25	18–24
	G	351W	105–112	40–45	95–105	70–90	75–85	23–25	18–24
	1	420	60	46–51	95	90	38	③	30
	L	460	130–140	45–50	95–105	70–90	75–85	22–32	28–33
1984	Y	300	85	40–45	60–70	130–150	75–85	22–32	22–32
	F	302	65–72	19–24	60–70	70–90	75–85	23–25	18–24
	G	351W	105–112	40–45	95–105	70–90	75–85	23–25	18–24
	1	420	75	46–51	95	90	47	③	30
	L	460	130–140	45–50	95–105	70–90	75–85	22–32	28–33
1985	Y	300	70–85	40–45	60–70	130–150	75–85	22–32	22–32
	F, N	302	65–72	19–24	60–70	70–90	75–85	23–25	18–24
	G, H	351W	105–112	40–45	95–105	70–90	75–85	23–25	18–24
	1	420	80	53	95	90	47	③	30
	L	460	130–140	45–50	95–105	70–90	75–85	22–32	28–33
1986	Y	300	70–85	40–45	60–70	130–150	75–85	22–32	22–32
	N	302	65–72	19–24	60–70	70–90	75–85	23–25	18–24
	H	351W	105–112	40–45	95–105	70–90	75–85	23–25	18–24
	1	420	80	53	95	90	47	③	35
	L	460	130–140	45–50	95–105	70–90	75–85	22–32	28–33

① 3/8 in.: 22–32
  5/16 in.: 17–25
② Step 1: 5
  Step 2: 10
  Step 3: 18
③ 5/16 in.: 14
  3/8 in.: 24
  7/16 in.: 38

85763C6A

Engine Overhaul Tips

Most engine overhaul procedures are fairly standard. In addition to specific parts replacement procedures and complete specifications for your individual engine, this section also is a guide to accept rebuilding procedures. Examples of standard rebuilding practice are shown and should be used along with specific details concerning your particular engine.

Competent and accurate machine shop services will ensure maximum performance, reliability and engine life.

In most instances it is more profitable for the do-it-yourself mechanic to remove, clean and inspect the component, buy the necessary parts and deliver these to a shop for actual machine work.

On the other hand, much of the rebuilding work (crankshaft, block, bearings, piston rods, and other components) is well within the scope of the do-it-yourself mechanic.

TOOLS

The tools required for an engine overhaul or parts replacement will depend on the depth of your involvement. With a few exceptions, they will be the tools found in a mechanic's tool kit. More in-depth work will require any or all of the following:

- a dial indicator (reading in thousandths) mounted on a universal base
- micrometers and telescope gauges
- jaw and screw-type pullers
- scraper
- valve spring compressor
- ring groove cleaner
- piston ring expander and compressor
- ridge reamer
- cylinder hone or glaze breaker
- Plastigage®
- engine stand

The use of most of these tools are illustrated in this section. Many can be rented for a one-time use from a local parts jobber or tool supply house specializing in automotive work.

Occasionally, the use of special tools is called for. See the information on Special Tools and Safety Notice in the front of this book before substituting another tool.

INSPECTION TECHNIQUES

Procedures and specifications are given in this section for inspecting, cleaning and assessing the wear limits of most major components. Other procedures such as Magnaflux® and Zyglo® can be used to locate material flaws and stress cracks. Magnaflux® is a magnetic process applicable only to ferrous materials. The Zyglo® process coats the material with a fluorescent dye penetrant and can be used on any material. Checking for suspected surface cracks can be more readily made using spot check dye. The dye is sprayed onto the suspected area, wiped off and the area sprayed with a developer. Cracks will show up brightly.

OVERHAUL TIPS

Aluminum has become extremely popular for use in engines, due to its low weight. Observe the following precautions when handling aluminum parts:
- Never hot tank aluminum parts (the caustic hot tank solution will eat the aluminum.

• Remove all aluminum parts (identification tag, etc.) from engine parts prior to the tanking.

• Always coat threads lightly with engine oil or anti-seize compounds before installation, to prevent seizure.

• Never overtorque bolts or spark plugs especially in aluminum threads.

Stripped threads in any component can be repaired using any of several commercial repair kits (Heli-Coil®, Microdot®, Keenserts®, etc.).

When assembling the engine, any parts that will be frictional contact must be prelubed to provide lubrication at initial start-up. Any product specifically formulated for this purpose can be used, but engine oil is not recommended as a prelube.

When semi-permanent (locked, but removable) installation of bolts or nuts is desired, threads should be cleaned and coated with Loctite® or other similar, commercial non-hardening sealant.

REPAIRING DAMAGED THREADS

▶ See Figures 15, 16, 17, 18 and 19

Several methods of repairing damaged threads are available. Heli-Coil® (shown here), Keenserts® and Microdot® are among the most widely used. All involve basically the same principle—drilling out stripped threads, tapping the hole and installing a prewound insert—making welding, plugging and oversize fasteners unnecessary.

Two types of thread repair inserts are usually supplied: a standard type for most—Inch Coarse, Inch Fine, Metric Course and Metric Fine thread sizes and a spark lug type to fit most spark plug port sizes. Consult the individual manufacturer's catalog to determine exact applications. Typical thread repair kits will contain a selection of prewound threaded inserts, a tap (corresponding to the outside diameter threads of the insert) and an installation tool. Spark plug inserts usually differ because they require a tap equipped with pilot threads and a combined reamer/tap section. Most manufacturers also supply blister-packed thread repair inserts separately in addition to a master kit containing a variety of taps and inserts plus installation tools.

Before effecting a repair to a threaded hole, remove any snapped, broken or damaged bolts or studs. Penetrating oil can be used to free frozen threads. The offending item can be removed with locking pliers or with a screw or stud extractor. After the hole is clear, the thread can be repaired, as shown in the series of accompanying illustrations.

CHECKING ENGINE COMPRESSION

A noticeable lack of engine power, excessive oil consumption and/or poor fuel mileage measured over an extended period are all indicators of internal engine wear. Worn piston rings, scored or worn cylinder bores, blown head gaskets, sticking or burnt valves and worn valve seats are all possible culprits here. A check of each cylinder's compression will help you locate the problems.

As mentioned earlier, a screw-in type compression gauge is more accurate that the type you simply hold against the spark plug hole, although it takes slightly longer to use. It's worth it to obtain a more accurate reading. Follow the procedures below.

Gasoline Engines

▶ See Figure 20

1. Warm up the engine to normal operating temperature.
2. Remove all the spark plugs.
3. Disconnect the high tension lead from the ignition coil and ground it.
4. Screw the compression gauge into the no.1 spark plug hole until the fitting is snug.

✸✸ WARNING

Be careful not to crossthread the plug hole. On aluminum cylinder heads use extra care, as the threads in these heads are easily ruined.

5. Fully open the throttle either by operating the carburetor throttle linkage by hand or by having an assistant floor the accelerator pedal.
6. While you read the compression gauge, ask the assistant to crank the engine two or three times in short bursts using the ignition switch or a remote starter switch.

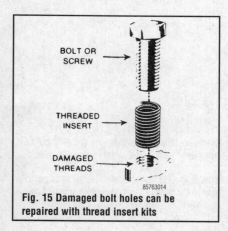

Fig. 15 Damaged bolt holes can be repaired with thread insert kits

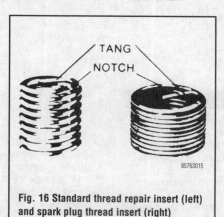

Fig. 16 Standard thread repair insert (left) and spark plug thread insert (right)

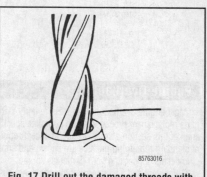

Fig. 17 Drill out the damaged threads with specified drill. Drill completely through the hole or to the bottom of a blind hole

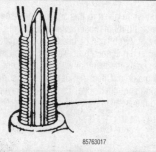

Fig. 18 With the tap supplied, tap the hole to receive the thread insert. Keep the tap well oiled and back it out frequently to avoid clogging the threads

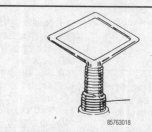

Fig. 19 Screw the threaded insert onto the installation tool until the tang engages the slot. Screw the insert into the tapped hole until it is ¼–½ turn below the top surface. After installation break off the tang with a hammer and punch

Fig. 20 The screw-in type compression gauge is more accurate

7. Read the compression gauge at the end of each series of cranks, and record the highest of these readings. Repeat this procedure for each of the engine's cylinders. Compare the highest reading of each cylinder to the compression pressure specification in the Tune-Up Specifications chart. The specs in this chart are maximum values.

A cylinder's compression pressure is usually acceptable if it is not less than 80% of maximum. The difference between any two cylinders should be no more than 12-14 pounds.

8. If a cylinder is unusually low, pour a tablespoon of clean engine oil into the cylinder through the spark plug hole and repeat the compression test. If the compression comes up after adding the oil, it appears that the cylinder's piston rings or bore are damaged or worn. If the pressure remains low, the valves may not be seating properly (a valve job is needed), or the head gasket may be blown near that cylinder. If compression in any two adjacent cylinders is low, and if the addition of oil doesn't help the compression, there is leakage past the head gasket. Oil and coolant water in the combustion chamber can result from this problem. There may be evidence of water droplets on the engine dipstick when a head gasket has blown.

Diesel Engines

▶ See Figure 21

Checking cylinder compression on diesel engines is basically the same procedure as on gasoline engines except for the following:

1. A special compression gauge adaptor suitable for diesel engines (because these engines have much greater compression pressures) must be used.
2. Remove the injector tubes and remove the injectors from each cylinder.

✳✳ WARNING

Don't forget to remove the washer underneath each injector. Otherwise, it may get lost when the engine is cranked.

3. Disconnect power to the fuel pump.
4. When fitting the compression gauge adaptor to the cylinder head, make sure the bleeder of the gauge (if equipped) is closed.
5. When reinstalling the injector assemblies, install new washers underneath each injector.

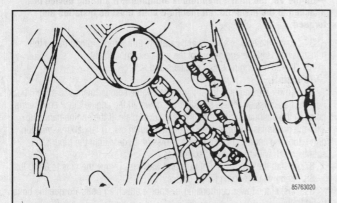

Fig. 21 Diesel engines require a special compression gauge adaptor

Engine

REMOVAL & INSTALLATION

✳✳ WARNING

Disconnect the negative battery cable(s) before beginning any work. Always label all disconnected hoses, vacuum lines and wires, to prevent incorrect reassembly. Do not disconnect any air conditioning lines; escaping refrigerant (Freon®) will freeze any surface it contacts, including skin and eyes and is an environmental hazard. Have the system discharged professionally before required repairs are started.

6-300

1. Drain the cooling system and the crankcase.

✳✳ CAUTION

When draining the coolant, keep in mind that cats and dogs are attracted by the ethylene glycol antifreeze, and are quite likely to drink any that is left in an uncovered container or in puddles on the ground. This will prove fatal in sufficient quantity. Always drain the coolant into a sealable container. Coolant should be reused unless it is contaminated or several years old.

2. Remove the hood.
3. Disconnect the negative battery cable.

➡It's probably not necessary to disconnect any air conditioning lines. Sufficient clearance can be gained simply by dismounting the compressor and laying it aside. If, for some reason, sufficient clearance cannot be achieved, perform the next 2 steps.

4. Discharge the air conditioning system. See Section 1.
5. Disconnect the refrigerant lines at the compressor. Cap all openings at once.
6. Remove the compressor.
7. Disconnect the heater hose from the water pump and coolant outlet housing.
8. Disconnect the flexible fuel line from the fuel pump.
9. Remove the radiator.
10. Remove the fan, water pump pulley, and fan belt.
11. Disconnect the accelerator cable.
12. Disconnect the brake booster vacuum hose at the intake manifold.
13. On trucks with automatic transmission, disconnect the transmission kickdown rod at the bellcrank assembly.
14. Disconnect the exhaust pipe from the exhaust manifold.
15. Disconnect the body ground strap and the battery ground cable from the engine.
16. Disconnect the engine wiring harness at the ignition coil, the coolant temperature sending unit, and the oil pressure sensing unit. Position the wiring harness out of the way.
17. Remove the alternator mounting bolts and position the alternator out of the way.
18. Remove the power steering pump from the mounting brackets and move it to one side, leaving the lines attached.
19. Raise and support the truck on jackstands.
20. Remove the starter.
21. Remove the automatic transmission filler tube bracket, if so equipped.
22. Remove the rear engine plate upper right bolt.
23. On manual transmission equipped trucks:
    a. Remove the flywheel housing lower attaching bolts.
    b. Disconnect the clutch return spring.
24. On automatic transmission equipped trucks:
    a. Remove the converter housing access cover assembly.
    b. Remove the flywheel-to-converter attaching nuts.
    c. Secure the converter in the housing.
    d. Remove the transmission oil cooler lines from the retaining clip at the engine.
    e. Remove the lower converter housing-to-engine attaching bolts.
25. Remove the nut from each of the two front engine mounts.
26. Lower the vehicle and position a jack under the transmission and support it.
27. Remove the remaining bellhousing-to-engine attaching bolts.
28. Attach an engine lifting device and raise the engine slightly and carefully pull it from the transmission. Lift the engine out of the vehicle.
   To install:
29. Place a new gasket on the muffler inlet pipe.
30. Carefully lower the engine into the truck. Make sure that the dowels in the engine block engage the holes in the bellhousing.
31. On manual transmission equipped trucks, start the transmission input shaft into the clutch disc. It may be necessary to adjust the position of the engine or transmission in order for the input shaft to enter the clutch disc. If necessary, turn the crankshaft until the input shaft splines mesh with the clutch disc splines.

32. On automatic transmission equipped trucks, start the converter pilot into the crankshaft. Secure the converter to the flywheel.

33. Install the bellhousing upper attaching bolts. Torque the bolts to 50 ft. lbs.

34. Remove the jack supporting the transmission.

35. Remove the lifting device.

36. Install the engine mount nuts and tighten them to 70 ft. lbs.

37. Install the automatic transmission coil cooler lines bracket, if equipped.

38. Install the remaining bellhousing attaching bolts. Torque them to 50 ft. lbs.

39. Connect the clutch return spring, if so equipped.

40. Install the starter and connect the starter cable.

41. Attach the automatic transmission fluid filler tube bracket, if so equipped.

42. On trucks with automatic transmissions, install the transmission oil cooler lines in the bracket at the cylinder block.

43. Connect the exhaust pipe to the exhaust manifold. Tighten the nuts to 25–35 ft. lbs.

44. Connect the engine ground strap and negative battery cable.

45. On a truck with an automatic transmission, connect the kickdown rod to the bellcrank assembly on the intake manifold.

46. Connect the accelerator linkage.

47. Connect the brake booster vacuum line to the intake manifold.

48. Connect the coil primary wire, oil pressure and coolant temperature sending unit wires, fuel line, heater hoses, and the battery positive cable.

49. Install the alternator on its mounting bracket.

50. Install the power steering pump on its bracket.

51. Install the water pump pulley, spacer, fan, and fan belt. Adjust the belt tension.

52. Install the air conditioning compressor. Connect the refrigerant lines.

53. Install the radiator.

54. Install the condenser and connect the refrigerant lines.

55. Charge the refrigerant system. See Section 1.

56. Connect the upper and lower radiator hoses to the radiator and engine.

57. Connect the automatic transmission oil cooler lines, if so equipped.

58. Install and adjust the hood.

59. Fill the cooling system.

60. Fill the crankcase.

61. Start the engine and check for leaks.

62. Bleed the cooling system.

63. Adjust the clutch pedal free-play or the automatic transmission control linkage.

64. Install the air cleaner.

V6 and Gasoline V8 Engines Except 8-460

1. Remove the hood. See Section 10.
2. Drain the cooling system and crankcase.

✳✳ CAUTION

When draining the coolant, keep in mind that cats and dogs are attracted by the ethylene glycol antifreeze, and are quite likely to drink any that is left in an uncovered container or in puddles on the ground. This will prove fatal in sufficient quantity. Always drain the coolant into a sealable container. Coolant should be reused unless it is contaminated or several years old.

3. Disconnect the battery cables and alternator wiring. Tag the wires.

4. On carbureted engines, remove the air cleaner and intake duct assembly, plus the crankcase ventilation hose. On fuel injected engines, remove the air intake hoses. Remove the PCV tube and carbon canister hose.

5. Disconnect the upper and lower radiator hoses.

➡It's probably not necessary to disconnect any air conditioning lines. Sufficient clearance can be gained simply by dismounting the compressor and laying it aside. If, for some reason, sufficient clearance cannot be achieved, perform the next 2 steps.

6. Discharge the air conditioning system. See Section 1.

7. Disconnect the refrigerant lines at the compressor. Cap all openings immediately.

8. If so equipped, disconnect the automatic transmission oil cooler lines.

9. Remove the fan shroud and lay it over the fan.

10. Remove the radiator.

11. Remove the fan shroud, fan, spacer, pulley and belt.

12. Remove the alternator pivot and adjusting bolts. Remove the alternator.

13. Disconnect the oil pressure sending unit lead from the sending unit. Tag it.

14. Disconnect the fuel tank-to-pump fuel line at the fuel pump and plug or clamp the line.

15. On trucks with the 5.0L EFI engine, depressurize the fuel system (see Section 5) and disconnect the chassis fuel line at the fuel rails.

16. Disconnect the accelerator linkage and speed control linkage at the carburetor.

17. Disconnect the automatic transmission kick-down rod and remove the return spring, if so equipped.

18. Disconnect the power brake booster vacuum hose. Tag it.

19. On 5.0L EFI models, disconnect the throttle bracket from the upper intake manifold and swing it out of the way with the cables still attached.

20. Disconnect the heater hoses from the water pump and intake manifold or tee (EFI).

21. Disconnect the temperature sending unit wire from the sending unit. Tag it.

22. Remove the upper bellhousing-to-engine attaching bolts.

23. Remove the wiring harness from the left rocker arm cover and position the wires out of the way.

24. Disconnect the ground strap from the cylinder block.

25. Disconnect the air conditioning compressor clutch wire. Tag it.

26. Raise the front of the truck and disconnect the starter cable from the starter.

27. Remove the starter.

28. Disconnect the exhaust pipes from the exhaust manifolds.

29. Disconnect the engine mounts from the brackets on the frame.

30. On trucks with automatic transmissions, remove the converter inspection plate and remove the torque converter-to-flywheel attaching bolts.

31. Remove the remaining bellhousing-to-engine attaching bolts.

32. Lower the vehicle and support the transmission with a jack.

33. Install an engine lifting device and shop crane.

➡**On the V6, the intake manifold is aluminum. If a lifting device is attached to the manifold, all manifold bolts must be installed and torqued.**

34. Raise the engine slightly and carefully pull it forward and out of the transmission. Lift the engine out of the engine compartment.

35. Install the engine on an engine stand.

To install:

36. Lower the engine carefully into the engine compartment and slide it back into the transmission. Make sure that the dowel in the engine block engage the holes in the bellhousing through the rear cover plate. If the engine hangs up after the transmission input shaft enters the clutch disc (manual transmission only), turn the crankshaft with the transmission in gear until the input shaft splines mesh with the clutch disc splines.

37. Install the engine mount nuts and washers. Torque the nuts to 80 ft. lbs.

38. Remove the engine lifting device.

39. Install the lower bellhousing-to-engine attaching bolts. Torque the bolts to 50 ft. lbs.

40. Remove the transmission support jack.

41. On trucks with automatic transmissions, install the torque converter-to-flywheel attaching bolts. Torque the bolts to 30 ft. lbs.

42. Install the converter inspection plate. Torque the bolts to 60 inch lbs.

43. Install the starter. Torque the mounting bolts to 20 ft. lbs.

44. Connect the starter cable to the starter.

45. Connect the exhaust pipe to the exhaust manifolds. Tighten the exhaust pipe-to-exhaust manifold nuts to 25–35 ft. lbs.

46. Lower the truck.

47. Install the upper bellhousing-to-engine attaching bolts. Torque the bolts to 50 ft. lbs.

48. Connect the wiring harness at the left rocker arm cover.

49. Connect the ground strap to the cylinder block.

50. Connect the air conditioning compressor clutch wire.

51. Connect the heater hoses at the water pump and intake manifold or tee (EFI).

52. Connect the temperature sending unit wire at the sending unit.
53. Connect the accelerator linkage and speed control linkage at the carburetor or throttle body.
54. Connect the automatic transmission kick-down rod and install the return spring, if so equipped.
55. Connect the power brake booster vacuum hose.
56. On 5.0L EFI models, connect the throttle bracket to the upper intake manifold.
57. Connect the fuel tank-to-pump fuel line at the fuel pump. On 5.0L EFI, connect the chassis fuel line at the fuel rails.
58. Connect the oil pressure sending unit lead to the sending unit.
59. Install the alternator.
60. Connect the refrigerant lines to the compressor.
61. Install the radiator and fan, shroud, fan, spacer, pulley and belt.
62. Connect the upper and lower radiator hoses, and, if so equipped, the automatic transmission oil cooler lines.
63. On carbureted engines, install the air cleaner and intake duct assembly, plus the crankcase ventilation hose. On 5.0L EFI engines, install the air intake hoses, PCV tube and carbon canister hose.
64. Connect the battery and alternator cables.
65. Fill the cooling system and crankcase.
66. Charge the air conditioning system. See Section 1.
67. Install the hood.
If the torque for a particular fastener was not mentioned above, use the following torque values as a guide:
- ¼ inch–20: 6–9 ft. lbs.
- ⁵⁄₁₆ inch-18: 12-18 ft. lbs.
- ⅜ inch-16: 22-32 ft. lbs.
- ⁷⁄₁₆ inch-14: 45-57 ft. lbs.
- ½ inch-13: 55-80 ft. lbs.
- ⁹⁄₁₆ inch: 85-120 ft. lbs.

➡All fasteners are assumed to be at least grade 5.

8-460

1. Remove the hood.
2. Drain the cooling system.

✳✳ CAUTION

When draining the coolant, keep in mind that cats and dogs are attracted by the ethylene glycol antifreeze, and are quite likely to drink any that is left in an uncovered container or in puddles on the ground. This will prove fatal in sufficient quantity. Always drain the coolant into a sealable container. Coolant should be reused unless it is contaminated or several years old.

3. Disconnect the negative battery cable from the block.
4. Remove the air cleaner assembly.
5. Remove the crankcase ventilation hose.
6. Remove the canister hose.
7. Disconnect the upper and lower radiator hoses.
8. Disconnect the transmission oil cooler lines from the radiator.
9. Disconnect the engine oil cooler lines at the oil filter adapter.

✳✳ WARNING

Don't disconnect the lines at the quick-connect fittings behind or at the oil cooler. Disconnecting them may permanently damage them.

➡It's probably not necessary to disconnect any air conditioning lines. Sufficient clearance can be gained simply by dismounting the compressor and laying it aside. If, for some reason, sufficient clearance cannot be achieved, perform the next 2 steps.

10. Discharge the air conditioning system. See Section 1.
11. Disconnect the refrigerant lines at the compressor. Cap the openings at once!
12. Disconnect the refrigerant lines at the condenser. Cap the openings at once!
13. Remove the condenser.
14. Remove the fan shroud from the radiator and position it up, over the fan.

15. Remove the radiator.
16. Remove the fan shroud.
17. Remove the fan, belts and pulley from the water pump.
18. Remove the compressor.
19. Remove the power steering pump from the engine, if so equipped, and position it to one side. Do not disconnect the fluid lines.
20. Disconnect the fuel pump inlet line from the pump and plug the line.
21. Disconnect the oil pressure sending unit wire at the sending unit.
22. Remove the alternator drive belts and disconnect the alternator from the engine, positioning it aside.
23. Disconnect the ground cable from the right front corner of the engine.
24. Disconnect the heater hoses.
25. Remove the transmission fluid filler tube attaching bolt from the right side valve cover and position the tube out of the way.
26. Disconnect all vacuum lines at the rear of the intake manifold.
27. Disconnect the speed control cable at the carburetor, if so equipped.
28. Disconnect the accelerator rod and the transmission kickdown rod and secure them out of the way.
29. Disconnect the engine wiring harness at the connector on the fire wall. Disconnect the primary wire at the coil.
30. Remove the upper flywheel housing-to-engine bolts.
31. Raise the vehicle and disconnect the exhaust pipes at the exhaust manifolds.
32. Disconnect the starter cable and remove the starter. Bring the starter forward and rotate the solenoid outward to remove the assembly.
33. Remove the access cover from the converter housing and remove the flywheel-to-converter attaching nuts.
34. Remove the lower converter housing-to-engine attaching bolts.
35. Remove the engine mount through bolts attaching the rubber insulator to the frame brackets.
36. Lower the vehicle and place a jack under the transmission to support it.
37. Remove the converter housing-to-engine block attaching bolts (left side).
38. Remove the coil and bracket assembly from the intake manifold.
39. Attach an engine lifting device and carefully take up the weight of the engine.
40. Move the engine forward to disengage it from the transmission and slowly lift it from the truck.
To install:
41. Lower the engine slowly into the truck.
42. Slide the engine rearward to engage it with the transmission and slowly lower it onto the supports.
43. Install the engine support nuts and torque them to 74 ft. lbs.
44. Remove the engine lifting device.
45. Install the converter housing-to-engine block upper and left side attaching bolts. Torque the bolts to 50 ft. lbs.
46. Install the coil and bracket assembly on the intake manifold.
47. Remove the jack from under the transmission.
48. Raise the truck.
49. Install the lower converter housing-to-engine attaching bolts. Torque the bolts to 50 ft. lbs.
50. Install the flywheel-to-converter attaching nuts. Torque the nuts to 34 ft. lbs.
51. Install the access cover on the converter housing. Torque the bolts to 60-90 inch lbs.
52. Install the starter.
53. Connect the starter cable.
54. Connect the exhaust pipes at the exhaust manifolds and lower the truck.
55. Connect the engine wiring harness at the connector on the fire wall.
56. Connect the primary wire at the coil.
57. Connect the accelerator rod and the transmission kickdown rod.
58. Connect the speed control cable.
59. Connect all vacuum lines at the rear of the intake manifold.
60. Install the transmission fluid filler tube attaching bolt from the right side valve cover and position the tube out of the way.
61. Connect the heater hoses.
62. Connect the ground cable at the right front corner of the engine.
63. Install the alternator and drive belts.
64. Connect the oil pressure sending unit wire at the sending unit.
65. Connect the fuel pump inlet line at the pump and plug the line.
66. Install the power steering pump and belt.

67. Install air conditioning compressor. Connect the refrigerant lines.
68. Install the fan, belts and pulley on the water pump.
69. Position the fan shroud over the fan.
70. Install the radiator.
71. Attach the fan shroud.
72. Install the condenser.
73. Connect the refrigerant lines at the condenser.
74. Charge the air conditioning system. See Section 1.
75. Connect the engine oil cooler lines at the oil filter adapter.
76. Connect the transmission oil cooler lines at the radiator.
77. Connect the upper and lower radiator hoses.
78. Connect the canister hose.
79. Connect the crankcase ventilation hose.
80. Connect the negative battery cable from the block.
81. Fill the cooling system.
82. Install the air cleaner assembly.
83. Install the hood.

If the torque for a particular fastener was not mentioned above, use the following torque values as a guide:

- ¼ inch-20: 6-9 ft. lbs..
- ⁵⁄₁₆ inch-18: 12-18 ft. lbs.
- ⅜ inch-16: 22-32 ft. lbs.
- ⁷⁄₁₆ inch-14: 45-57 ft. lbs.
- ½ inch-13: 55-80 ft. lbs.
- ⁹⁄₁₆ inch: 85-120 ft. lbs.

➡It is assumed that all fasteners are at least grade 5.

Diesel Engines

1. Remove the hood.
2. Drain the coolant.

❋❋ CAUTION

When draining the coolant, keep in mind that cats and dogs are attracted by the ethylene glycol antifreeze, and are quite likely to drink any that is left in an uncovered container or in puddles on the ground. This will prove fatal in sufficient quantity. Always drain the coolant into a sealable container. Coolant should be reused unless it is contaminated or several years old.

3. Remove the air cleaner and intake duct assembly and cover the air intake opening with a clean rag to keep out the dirt.
4. Remove the upper grille support bracket and upper air conditioning condenser mounting bracket.
5. On vehicles equipped with air conditioning, the system MUST be discharged to remove the condenser.

❋❋ WARNING

DO NOT attempt to do this yourself, unless you are familiar with A/C repair. See Section 1.

6. Remove the radiator fan shroud halves.
7. Remove the fan and clutch assembly as described under water pump removal in this section.
8. Detach the radiator hoses and the transmission cooler lines, if so equipped.
9. Remove the condenser. Cap all openings at once!
10. Remove the radiator.
11. Remove the power steering pump and position it out of the way.
12. Disconnect the fuel supply line heater and alternator wires at the alternator.
13. Disconnect the oil pressure sending unit wire at the sending unit, remove the sender from the firewall and lay it on the engine.
14. Disconnect the accelerator cable and the speed control cable, if so equipped, from the injection pump. Remove the cable bracket with the cables attached, from the intake manifold and position it out of the way.
15. Disconnect the transmission kickdown rod from the injection pump, if so equipped.

16. Disconnect the main wiring harness connector from the right side of the engine and the ground strap from the rear of the engine.
17. Remove the fuel return hose from the left rear of the engine.
18. Remove the two lower transmission-to-engine attaching bolts.
19. Disconnect the heater hoses.
20. Disconnect the water temperature sender wire.
21. Disconnect the overheat light switch wire and position the wire out of the way.
22. Raise the truck and support on it on jackstands.
23. Disconnect the battery ground cables from the front of the engine and the starter cables from the starter.
24. Remove the fuel inlet line and plug the fuel line at the fuel pump.
25. Detach the exhaust pipe at the exhaust manifold.
26. Disconnect the engine insulators from the no. 1 crossmember.
27. Remove the flywheel inspection plate and the four converter-to-flywheel attaching nuts, if equipped with automatic transmission.
28. Remove the jackstands and lower the truck.
29. Support the transmission on a jack.
30. Remove the four upper transmission attaching bolts.
31. Attach an engine lifting sling and remove the engine from the truck.

To install:

32. Lower the engine into truck.
33. Align the converter to the flex plate and the engine dowels to the transmission.
34. Install the engine mount bolts and torque them to 80 ft. lbs.
35. Remove the engine lifting sling.
36. Install the four lower transmission attaching bolts. Torque the bolts to 65 ft. lbs.
37. Remove transmission jack.
38. Raise and support the front end on jackstands.
39. If equipped with automatic transmission, install the four converter-to-flywheel attaching nuts. Torque the nuts to 34 ft. lbs.
40. Install the flywheel inspection plate. Torque the bolts to 60-90 inch lbs.
41. Attach the exhaust pipe at the exhaust manifold.
42. Connect the fuel inlet line.
43. Connect the battery ground cables to the front of the engine.
44. Connect the starter cables at the starter.
45. Lower the truck.
46. Connect the overheat light switch wire.
47. Connect the water temperature sender wire.
48. Connect the heater hoses.
49. Install the two upper transmission-to-engine attaching bolts. Torque the bolts to 65 ft. lbs.
50. Connect the fuel return hose at the left rear of the engine.
51. Connect the main wiring harness connector at the right side of the engine and the ground strap from the rear of the engine.
52. Connect the transmission kickdown rod at the injection pump, if so equipped.
53. Connect the accelerator cable and the speed control cable, if so equipped, at the injection pump.
54. Install the cable bracket with the cables attached, to the intake manifold.
55. Install the oil pressure sending unit.
56. Connect the oil pressure sending unit wire at the sending unit.
57. Connect the fuel supply line heater and alternator wires at the alternator.
58. Install the power steering pump.
59. Install the radiator.
60. Install the condenser.
61. Connect the radiator hoses and the transmission cooler lines, if so equipped.
62. Install the fan and clutch assembly as described under water pump removal in this section.
63. Install the radiator fan shroud halves.
64. On vehicles equipped with air conditioning, charge the system. See Section 1.
65. Install the upper grille support bracket and upper air conditioning condenser mounting bracket.
66. Install the air cleaner and intake duct assembly.
67. Fill the cooling system.
68. Install the hood.

Rocker Covers

REMOVAL & INSTALLATION

6-300 Engine

1. Disconnect the inlet hose at the crankcase filler cap.
2. Remove the air cleaner and inlet tube.
3. Disconnect the accelerator cable and kickdown linkage.
4. Disconnect the fuel line.
5. Remove the ignition coil and wires.
6. Remove the rocker arm cover.
7. Remove and discard the gasket.

To install:

8. Clean the mating surfaces for the cover and head thoroughly.
9. Coat both mating surfaces with gasket sealer and place the new gasket on the head with the locating tabs downward.
10. Place the cover on the head making sure the gasket is evenly seated. Torque the bolts to 48-84 inch lbs.
11. Install the ignition coil and wires.
12. Connect the fuel line.
13. Install the accelerator cable bracket and kickdown linkage.
14. Install the air cleaner and inlet hose.

8-255, 8-302 (Carbureted) or 8-351W Engines

▶ **See Figures 22, 23 and 24**

1. Disconnect the battery ground cable.
2. Remove the air cleaner and inlet duct.
3. Remove the coil.
4. For the right cover, remove the lifting eye and Thermactor® tube; for the left cover, remove the oil filler pipe attaching bolt.
5. Mark and remove the spark plug wires.
6. Remove any vacuum lines, wires or pipes in the way. Make sure that you tag them for identification.
7. Remove the cover bolts and lift off the cover. It may be necessary to break the cover loose by rapping on it with a rubber mallet. NEVER pry the cover off!

To install:

8. Thoroughly clean the mating surfaces of both the cover and head.
9. Coat both mating surfaces with gasket sealer and place the new gasket(s) in the cover(s) with the locating tabs engaging the slots.
10. Place the cover on the head making sure the gasket is evenly seated. Torque the bolts to 10-13 ft. lbs. After 2 minutes, retighten the bolts.
11. Install the vacuum lines, wires and pipes.
12. Install the spark plug wires.
13. For the right cover, install the lifting eye and Thermactor® tube; for the left cover, install the oil filler pipe attaching bolt.
14. Install the coil.
15. Install the air cleaner and inlet duct.
16. Connect the battery ground cable.

8-5.0L EFI Engine

1. Disconnect the battery ground cable.
2. Remove the air cleaner and inlet duct.

3. Remove the coil.
4. For the right cover, remove the lifting eye (except Lightning) and Thermactor® tube; for the left cover, remove the oil filler pipe attaching bolt, and, on Lightning, the lifting eye.
5. Mark and remove the spark plug wires. On the Lightning, remove the upper intake manifold.
6. Remove any vacuum lines, wires or pipes in the way. Make sure that you tag them for identification.
7. Remove the cover bolts and lift off the cover. It may be necessary to break the cover loose by rapping on it with a rubber mallet. NEVER pry the cover off!

To install:

8. Thoroughly clean the mating surfaces of both the cover and head.
9. Coat both mating surfaces with gasket sealer and place the new gasket(s) in the cover(s) with the locating tabs engaging the slots.
10. Place the cover on the head making sure the gasket is evenly seated. Torque the bolts to 10-13 ft. lbs. After 2 minutes, retighten the bolts.
11. Install the vacuum lines, wires and pipes.
12. Install the spark plug wires. On the Lightning, install the upper intake manifold.
13. For the right cover, install the lifting eye (except Lightning) and Thermactor® tube; for the left cover, install the oil filler pipe attaching bolt, and, on Lightning, the lifting eye.
14. Install the coil.
15. Install the air cleaner and inlet duct.
16. Connect the battery ground cable.

8-351M, 8-360, 8-390, and 8-400

1. Disconnect the battery ground cables.
2. Tag and disconnect the spark plug wires.
3. Remove the air cleaner and inlet duct.
4. Remove the crankcase ventilation hose (passenger's side) or oil filler cap and PCV hose (driver's side).
5. Tag and remove any hose or wire left in the way.
6. Remove the holddown bolts and lift off the valve cover. On the passenger's side, this is very difficult on air conditioner equipped trucks. Inside the valve cover there is a baffle under the crankcase vent hose hole. The evaporator case overhangs the cover and the cover must be manuevered so that the baffle clears the rocker arms.

➡ **If the cover(s) will not readily lift off, break it loose by rapping it with a rubber mallet. If that still won't do it, you'll have to carefully pry the cover off, but this will undoubtedly bend the cover lip. Make sure you straighten it before installation**

To install:

7. Thoroughly clean the mating surfaces of both the cover and head. Make sure the cover flanges are straight.
8. Coat both mating surfaces with gasket sealer and place the new gasket on the head.
9. Place the cover on the head making sure the gasket is evenly seated.

➡ **On A/C equipped trucks, this is harder than removal. Torque the bolts to 10-15 ft. lbs.**

10. Install the vacuum lines, wires and pipes.
11. Install the spark plug wires.

Fig. 22 Removing the rocker cover bolts; 8-255, carbureted 8-302 shown

Fig. 23 Lifting off the valve cover; 8-255, carbureted 8-302 shown

Fig. 24 Valve cover gasket locating tabs

12. Install the air cleaner and inlet tube.
13. Connect the battery(ies).
14. Run the engine, check for leaks and retorque the bolts

8-460 Engine

1. Disconnect the battery ground cable(s).
2. Remove the air cleaner and inlet duct.
3. Remove the Thermactor® air supply control valve and bracket.
4. Remove the coil.
5. Disconnect the Thermactor® air control valve-to-air pump hose and tube.
6. Mark and remove the spark plug wires.
7. Remove any vacuum lines, wires or pipes in the way. Make sure that you tag them for identification.
8. Remove the cover bolts and lift off the cover. It may be necessary to break the cover loose by rapping on it with a rubber mallet. NEVER pry the cover off!

To install:
9. Thoroughly clean the mating surfaces of both the cover and head.
10. Place the new cover seal(s) in the cover(s) with the locating tab engaging the slot.
11. Place the cover on the head. Torque the bolts to 6-9 ft. lbs. from right to left.
12. Install the vacuum lines, wires and pipes.
13. Install the spark plug wires.
14. Connect the Thermactor® air control valve-to-air pump hose and tube.
15. Install the coil.
16. Install the Thermactor® air supply control valve and bracket.
17. Install the air cleaner and inlet duct.
18. Connect the battery ground cable(s).

8-6.9L Diesel

1. Disconnect the battery ground cables.
2. Remove the cover bolts and lift off the covers. It may be necessary to break the covers loose by rapping on them with a rubber mallet. NEVER pry a cover off!
3. Clean the mating surfaces of the covers and heads thoroughly, coat the mating surfaces with gasket sealer, place new gaskets in the covers, position the covers on the heads and torque the bolts to 72 inch lbs.

Rocker Arm Shaft

REMOVAL & INSTALLATION

8-360 and 8-390

▶ See Figure 25

1. Remove air cleaner, disconnect spark plug leads and remove leads from the bracket on the valve cover.

2. Remove crankcase ventilation hose from the rocker cover, then remove rocker cover. On the left rocker cover the wiring harness must be removed.
3. On the right side, start at the number 4 cylinder (rearmost) and loosen support bolts in sequence, two turns at a time. Remove the shaft assembly and the baffle plate after all bolts have been loosened. The same procedure is followed on the left bank, except that the bolt loosening sequence starts with the number 5 cylinder (foremost).

✳✳ WARNING

The above bolt loosening procedure must be followed to avoid damage to the rocker arm shaft.

To install:
4. Apply Lubriplate® to the pad end of the rocker arms, to the tip of the valve stems and to both ends of the pushrods.
5. Rotate the engine to 45 degrees past the number 1 cylinder (TDC).
6. With the pushrods in place, position rocker arm shaft assembly and baffle plate on the cylinder head so that the oil holes are on the bottom and the identification notch is down and toward the front on the right bank and toward the rear on the left bank. Tighten support bolts finger tight.
7. On the right bank, start at the number 4 cylinder and tighten the support bolts two turns at a time in sequence (4-3-2-1) until the supports are fully in contact with the cylinder head. Then tighten the bolts to 40-45 ft. lbs. torque. The same procedure is followed on the left bank starting at the number 5 cylinder. This procedure allows time for the hydraulic lifter leakdown and thus prevents damage to the pushrods, valves, and rocker arms.
8. Check valve clearances and adjust if necessary.
9. Install rocker cover, using new gaskets and sealer.
10. Install remaining components.

Rocker Arms

REMOVAL & INSTALLATION

6-300 Engine

▶ See Figure 26

1. Disconnect the rocker cover.
2. Remove the spark plug wires.
3. Remove the distributor cap.
4. Remove the pushrod cover (engine side cover).
5. Loosen the rocker arm bolts until the pushrods can be removed. KEEP THE PUSHRODS IN ORDER, FOR INSTALLATION!
6. Using a magnetic lifter removal tool, remove the lifters. Wipe clean the exterior of each lifter as it's removed and mark it with an indelible marker, so that it can be installed in its original bore.

To install:
7. Coat the bottom surface of each lifter with multi-purpose grease, and coat the rest of the lifter with clean engine oil.
8. Install each lifter in it original bore using the magnetic tool.

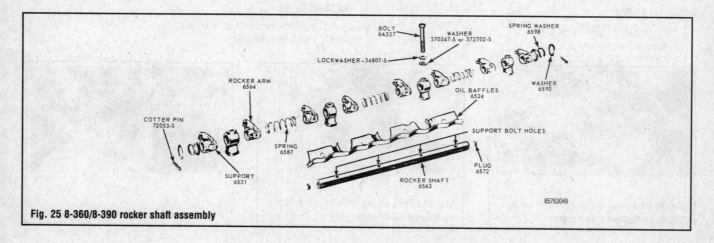

Fig. 25 8-360/8-390 rocker shaft assembly

BOLT 6A527
WASHER 370347-S or 372702-S
LOCKWASHER–34807-S
SPRING WASHER 6598
WASHER 6590
ROCKER ARM 6564
OIL BAFFLES 6524
COTTER PIN 72053-S
SUPPORT BOLT HOLES
SPRING 6587
PLUG 6572
SUPPORT 6531
ROCKER SHAFT 6563

85763049

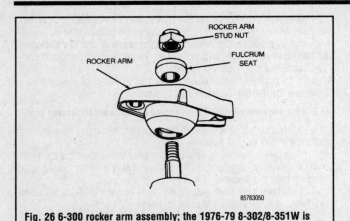

Fig. 26 6-300 rocker arm assembly; the 1976-79 8-302/8-351W is similar

9. Coat each end of each pushrod with multi-purpose grease and install each in its original position. Make sure that each pushrod is properly seated in the lifter socket.

10. Engage the rocker arms with the pushrods and tighten the rocker arm bolts enough to hold the pushrods in place.

11. Adjust the valve clearance as described below.

12. Install the pushrod cover (engine side cover).

13. Install the distributor cap.

14. Install the spark plug wires.

15. Install the rocker arm cover.

8-255, 8-302 Carbureted or 8-351W Engines

▶ **See Figures 26 and 27**

1. Remove the intake manifold.

2. Disconnect the Thermactor® air supply hose at the pump.

3. Remove the rocker arm covers.

4. Loosen the rocker arm fulcrum bolts, fulcrum seats and rocker arms. KEEP ALL PARTS IN ORDER FOR INSTALLATION!

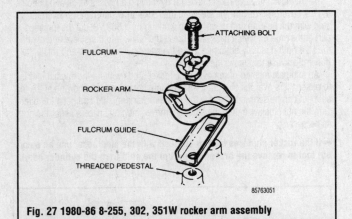

Fig. 27 1980-86 8-255, 302, 351W rocker arm assembly

To install:

5. Apply multi-purpose grease to the valve stem tips, the fulcrum seats and sockets.

6. Install the fulcrum guides, rocker arms, seats and bolts. Torque the bolts to 18–25 ft. lbs.

7. Install the rocker arm covers.

8. Connect the Thermactor® air supply hose at the pump.

9. Install the intake manifold.

8-302 EFI Engines

▶ **See Figures 27, 28, 29 and 30**

1. Remove the upper and lower intake manifolds.

2. Disconnect the Thermactor® air supply hose at the pump.

3. Remove the rocker arm covers.

4. Loosen the rocker arm fulcrum bolts, fulcrum seats and rocker arms. KEEP ALL PARTS IN ORDER FOR INSTALLATION!

To install:

5. Apply multi-purpose grease to the valve stem tips, the fulcrum seats and sockets.

6. Install the fulcrum guides, rocker arms, seats and bolts. Torque the bolts to 18–25 ft. lbs.

7. Install the rocker arm covers.

8. Connect the Thermactor® air supply hose at the pump.

9. Install the intake manifolds.

8-351M, 8-400 and 8-460 Engines

▶ **See Figure 31**

1. Remove the intake manifold.

2. Remove the rocker arm covers.

3. Loosen the rocker arm fulcrum bolts, fulcrum, oil deflector, seat and rocker arms. KEEP EVERYTHING IN ORDER FOR INSTALLATION!

To install:

4. Coat each end of each pushrod with multi-purpose grease.

5. Coat the top of the valve stems, the rocker arms and the fulcrum seats with multi-purpose grease.

6. Rotate the crankshaft by hand until No. 1 piston is at TDC of compression. The firing order marks on the damper will be aligned at TDC with the timing pointer.

7. Install the rocker arms, seats, deflectors and bolts on the following valves:

- No. 1 intake and exhaust
- No. 3 intake
- No. 8 exhaust
- No. 7 intake
- No. 5 exhaust
- No. 8 intake
- No. 4 exhaust

Engage the rocker arms with the pushrods and tighten the rocker arm fulcrum bolts to 18–25 ft. lbs.

8. Rotate the crankshaft on full turn — 360° — and re-align the TDC mark and pointer. Install the parts and tighten the bolts on the following valves:

- No. 2 intake and exhaust
- No. 4 intake
- No. 3 exhaust
- No. 5 intake

Fig. 28 Removing the rocker stud nut; 1983 8-302 shown

Fig. 29 Removing the fulcrum; 1983 8-302 shown

Fig. 30 Removing the rocker arm; 1983 8-302 shown

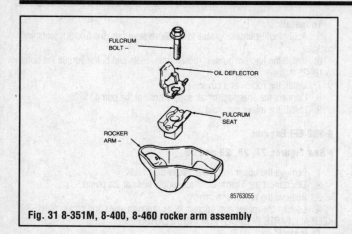

Fig. 31 8-351M, 8-400, 8-460 rocker arm assembly

- No. 6 exhaust
- No. 6 intake
- No. 7 exhaust
9. Install the rocker arm covers.
10. Install the intake manifold.
11. Check the valve clearance as described under Hydraulic Valve Clearance, below.

Diesel Engines

▶ See Figures 32 and 33

1. Disconnect the ground cables from both batteries.
2. Remove the valve cover attaching screws and remove both valve cover.
3. Remove the valve rocker arm post mounting bolts. Remove the rocker arms and posts in order and mark them with tape so they can be installed in their original positions.

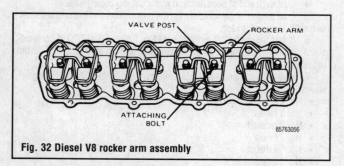

Fig. 32 Diesel V8 rocker arm assembly

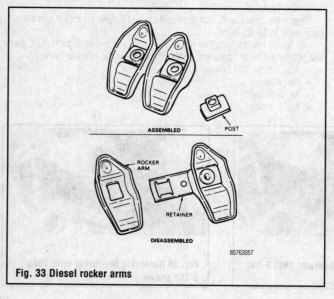

Fig. 33 Diesel rocker arms

4. If the cylinder heads are to be removed, then the pushrods can now be removed. Make a holder for the pushrods out of a piece of wood or cardboard, and remove the pushrods in order. **It is very important that the pushrods be re-installed in their original order.** The pushrods can remain in position if no further disassembly is required.
5. If the pushrods were removed, install them in their original locations. Make sure they are fully seated in the tappet seats.

➡ **The copper colored end of the pushrod goes toward the rocker arm.**

6. Apply a polyethylene grease to the valve stem tips. Install the rocker arms and posts in their original positions.
7. Turn the engine over by hand until the valve timing mark is at the 11:00 position, as viewed from the front of the engine. Install all of the rocker arm post attaching bolts and torque to 27 ft. lbs.
8. Install new valve cover gaskets and install the valve cover. Install the battery cables, start the engine and check for leaks.

Rocker Studs

REMOVAL & INSTALLATION

Gasoline Engines

▶ See Figures 34, 35 and 36

Rocker arm studs which are broken or have damaged threads may be replaced with standard studs. Studs which are loose in the cylinder head must be replaced with oversize studs which are available for service. The amount of oversize and diameter of the studs are as follows:
- 0.006 inch (0.152mm) oversize: 0.3774-0.3781 inch (9.586-9.604mm)
- 0.010 inch (0.254mm) oversize: 0.3814-0.3821 inch (9.688-9.705mm)
- 0.015 inch (0.381mm) oversize: 0.3864-0.3871 inch (9.815-9.832mm)

A tool kit for replacing the rocker studs is available and contains a stud remover and two oversize reamers: one for 0.006 inch (0.152mm) and one for 0.015 inch (0.381mm) oversize studs. For 0.010 inch (0.254mm) oversize studs, use reamer tool T66P-6A527-B. To press the replacement studs into the cylinder head, use the stud replacer tool T69P-6049-D. Use the smaller reamer tool first when boring the hole for oversize studs.

1. Remove the valve rocker cover(s) by moving all hoses aside and unbolting the cover(s). Position the sleeve of the rocker arm stud remover over the stud with the bearing end down. When working on a 302 V8, cut the threaded part of the stud off with a hacksaw. Thread the puller into the sleeve and over the stud until it is fully bottomed. Hold the sleeve with a wrench and rotate the puller clockwise to remove the stud.

An alternate method of removing the rocker studs without the special tool is to put spacers over the stud until just enough threads are left showing at the top so a nut can be screwed onto the top of the rocker arm stud and get a full bite. Turn the nut clockwise until the stud is removed, adding spacers under the nut as necessary.

➡ **If the rocker stud was broken off flush with the stud boss, use an easyout tool to remove the broken off part of the stud from the cylinder head.**

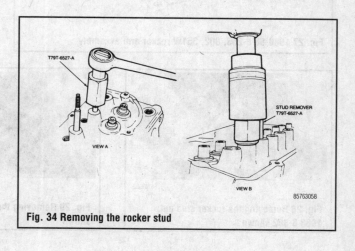

Fig. 34 Removing the rocker stud

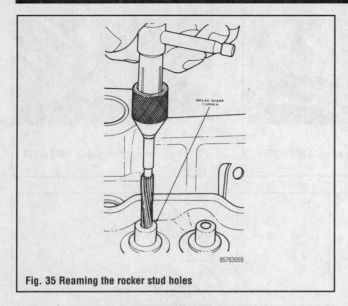

Fig. 35 Reaming the rocker stud holes

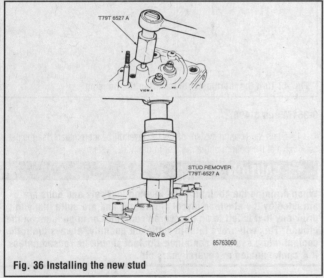

Fig. 36 Installing the new stud

2. If a loose rocker arm stud is being replaced, ream the stud bore for the selected oversize stud.

➡ **Keep all metal particles away from the valves.**

3. Coat the end of the stud with Lubriplate®. Align the stud and installer with the stud bore and top the sliding driver until it bottoms. When the installer contacts the stud boss, the stud is installed to its correct height.

Thermostat

➡ **It is a good practice to check the operation of a new thermostat before it is installed in an engine. Place the thermostat in a pan of boiling water. If it does not open more than ¼ inch (6mm), do not install it in the engine.**

REMOVAL & INSTALLATION

6-300 Engines

♦ **See Figure 37**

1. Drain the cooling system below the level of the coolant outlet housing. Use the petcock valve at the bottom of the radiator to drain the system. It is not necessary to remove any of the hoses.

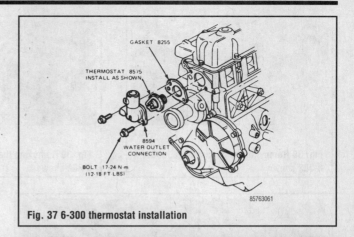

Fig. 37 6-300 thermostat installation

✳✳ CAUTION

When draining the coolant, keep in mind that cats and dogs are attracted by the ethylene glycol antifreeze, and are quite likely to drink any that is left in an uncovered container or in puddles on the ground. This will prove fatal in sufficient quantity. Always drain the coolant into a sealable container. Coolant should be reused unless it is contaminated or several years old.

2. Remove the coolant outlet housing retaining bolts and slide the housing with the hose attached to one side.

3. Remove the thermostat and gasket from the cylinder head and clean both mating surfaces.

4. To install the thermostat, coat a new gasket with water resistant sealer and position it on the outlet of the engine. The gasket must be in place before the thermostat is installed.

5. Install the thermostat with the bridge (opposite end of the spring) inside the elbow connection and turn it to lock it into position.

6. Position the elbow connection onto the mounting surface of the outlet, so that the thermostat flange is resting on the gasket and install the retaining bolts. Torque the bolts to 15 ft. lbs.

7. Fill the radiator and operate the engine until it reaches operating temperature. Check the coolant level and adjust if necessary.

V6-3.8L, 8-255, 8-302 and 8-351W

♦ **See Figures 38, 39, 40, 41 and 42**

1. Drain the cooling system below the level of the coolant outlet housing. Use the petcock valve at the bottom of the radiator to drain the system. It is not necessary to remove any of the hoses.

✳✳ CAUTION

When draining the coolant, keep in mind that cats and dogs are attracted by the ethylene glycol antifreeze, and are quite likely to drink any that is left in an uncovered container or in puddles on the ground. This will prove fatal in sufficient quantity. Always drain the coolant into a sealable container. Coolant should be reused unless it is contaminated or several years old.

2. Disconnect the bypass hoses at the water pump and intake manifold.

3. Remove the bypass tube.

4. Remove the coolant outlet housing retaining bolts, bend the hose and lift the housing with the hose attached to one side.

5. Remove the thermostat and gasket from the intake manifold and clean both mating surfaces.

6. To install the thermostat, coat a new gasket with water resistant sealer and position it on the outlet of the engine. The gasket must be in place before the thermostat is installed.

7. Install the thermostat with the bridge (opposite end of the spring) inside the elbow connection and the thermostat flange positioned in the recess in the manifold.

8. Position the elbow connection onto the mounting surface of the outlet. Torque the bolts to 18 ft. lbs.

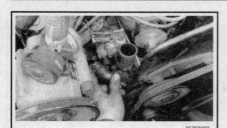

Fig. 38 Removing the bypass hose; 1983 8-302 shown

Fig. 39 Removing the housing bolts; 1983 8-302 shown

Fig. 40 Removing the housing; 1983 8-302 shown

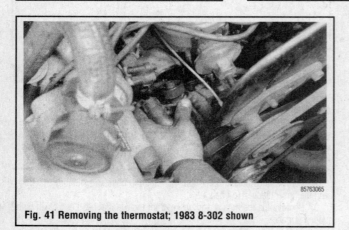

Fig. 41 Removing the thermostat; 1983 8-302 shown

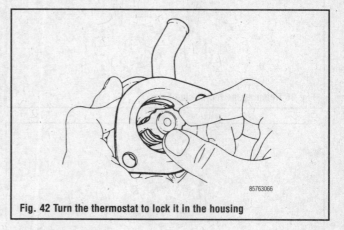

Fig. 42 Turn the thermostat to lock it in the housing

9. Install the bypass tube and hoses.

10. Fill the radiator and operate the engine until it reaches operating temperature. Check the coolant level and adjust if necessary.

8-360 and 8-390

1. Drain the cooling system below the level of the coolant outlet housing. Use the petcock valve at the bottom of the radiator to drain the system. It is not necessary to remove any of the hoses.

※※ CAUTION

When draining the coolant, keep in mind that cats and dogs are attracted by the ethylene glycol antifreeze, and are quite likely to drink any that is left in an uncovered container or in puddles on the ground. This will prove fatal in sufficient quantity. Always drain the coolant into a sealable container. Coolant should be reused unless it is contaminated or several years old.

2. Disconnect the bypass hoses at the water pump and intake manifold.

3. Remove the bypass tube.

4. Remove the coolant outlet housing retaining bolts, bend the hose and lift the housing with the hose attached to one side.

5. Remove the thermostat and gasket from the intake manifold and clean both mating surfaces.

6. To install the thermostat, coat a new gasket with water resistant sealer and position it on the outlet of the engine. The gasket must be in place before the thermostat is installed.

7. Install the thermostat with the bridge (opposite end of the spring) inside the outlet housing and the thermostat flange positioned in the recess in the manifold.

8. Position the outlet housing onto the mounting surface of the manifold. Torque the bolts to 15 ft. lbs.

9. Install the bypass tube and hoses.

10. Fill the radiator and operate the engine until it reaches operating temperature. Check the coolant level and adjust if necessary.

8-351M and 8-400

1. Drain the cooling system below the level of the thermostat. Use the petcock valve at the bottom of the radiator to drain the system.

※※ CAUTION

When draining the coolant, keep in mind that cats and dogs are attracted by the ethylene glycol antifreeze, and are quite likely to drink any that is left in an uncovered container or in puddles on the ground. This will prove fatal in sufficient quantity. Always drain the coolant into a sealable container. Coolant should be reused unless it is contaminated or several years old.

2. Disconnect the vacuum hose connector from the PVS valve located on the thermostat housing.

3. Remove the upper radiator hose.

4. Remove the thermostat housing retaining bolts.

5. Remove the gasket and thermostat from the block and clean both mating surfaces.

To install:

6. Position a new thermostat in the recess in the block with the spring side down.

7. Coat a new gasket with water resistant sealer and position it on the outlet of the engine.

8. Position the thermostat housing onto the mounting surface of the outlet. Torque the bolts to 25 ft. lbs.

9. Install the upper radiator hose.

10. Connect the vacuum hoses

11. Fill the radiator and operate the engine until it reaches operating temperature. Check the coolant level and adjust if necessary.

8-460

1. Drain the cooling system below the level of the thermostat. Use the petcock valve at the bottom of the radiator to drain the system.

When draining the coolant, keep in mind that cats and dogs are attracted by the ethylene glycol antifreeze, and are quite likely to drink any that is left in an uncovered container or in puddles on the ground. This will prove fatal in sufficient quantity. Always drain the coolant into a sealable container. Coolant should be reused unless it is contaminated or several years old.

2. Remove the upper radiator hose.
3. Remove the thermostat housing retaining bolts.
4. Remove the gasket and thermostat from the intake manifold and clean both mating surfaces.
   To install:
5. Position a new thermostat in the recess in the manifold with the spring side down.
6. Coat a new gasket with water resistant sealer and position it on the manifold.
7. Position the thermostat housing onto the mounting surface of the outlet. Torque the bolts to 25 ft. lbs.
8. Install the upper radiator hose.
9. Fill the radiator and operate the engine until it reaches operating temperature. Check the coolant level and adjust if necessary.

Diesel Engines

The factory specified thermostat does not contain an internal bypass. On these engines, an internal bypass is located in the block. The use of any replacement thermostat other than that meeting the manufacturer's specifications will result in engine overheating! Use only thermostats meeting the specifications of Ford part number E5TZ-8575-C or Navistar International part number 1807945-C1.

1. Disconnect both battery ground cables.
2. Drain the coolant to a point below the thermostat housing.

When draining the coolant, keep in mind that cats and dogs are attracted by the ethylene glycol antifreeze, and are quite likely to drink any that is left in an uncovered container or in puddles on the ground. This will prove fatal in sufficient quantity. Always drain the coolant into a sealable container. Coolant should be reused unless it is contaminated or several years old.

3. Remove the alternator and vacuum pump belts
4. Remove the alternator.
5. Remove the vacuum pump and bracket.
6. Remove all but the lowest vacuum pump/alternator mounting casting bolt.
7. Loosen the lowest bolt and pivot the casting outboard of the engine.
8. Remove the thermostat housing attaching bolts, bend the hose and lift the housing up and to one side.
9. Remove the thermostat and gasket.
10. Clean the thermostat housing and block surfaces thoroughly.
11. Coat a new gasket with waterproof sealer and position the gasket on the manifold outlet opening.
12. Install the thermostat in the manifold opening with the spring element end downward and the flange positioned in the recess in the manifold.
13. Place the outlet housing into position and install the bolts. Torque the bolts to 20 ft. lbs.
14. Reposition the casting.
15. Install the vacuum pump and bracket.
16. Install the alternator.
17. Adjust the drive belts.
18. Fill and bleed the cooling system.
19. Connect both battery cables.
20. Run the engine and check for leaks.

Intake Manifold

REMOVAL & INSTALLATION

V6-3.8L and 8-255, 8-302, 8-351W, 8-360 and 8-390

◆ **See Figures 43 thru 53**

1. Drain the cooling system, remove the air cleaner and the intake duct assembly.

When draining the coolant, keep in mind that cats and dogs are attracted by the ethylene glycol antifreeze, and are quite likely to drink any that is left in an uncovered container or in puddles on the ground. This will prove fatal in sufficient quantity. Always drain the coolant into a sealable container. Coolant should be reused unless it is contaminated or several years old.

2. Disconnect the accelerator rod from the carburetor and remove the accelerator retracting spring. Disconnect the automatic transmission kickdown rod at the carburetor, if so equipped.
3. Disconnect the high tension lead and all other wires from the ignition coil.
4. Disconnect the spark plug wires from the spark plugs by grasping the rubber boots and twisting and pulling at the same time. Remove the wires from the brackets on the rocker covers. Remove the distributor cap and spark plug wire assembly.
5. Remove the carburetor fuel inlet line and the distributor vacuum line from the carburetor.
6. Remove the distributor lockbolt and remove the distributor and vacuum lines. See Distributor Removal & Installation.
7. Disconnect the upper radiator hose from the coolant outlet housing and the temperature sending unit wire at the sending unit.

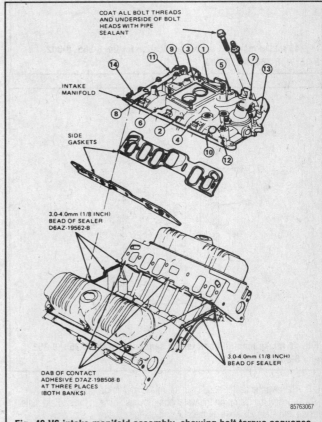

Fig. 43 V6 intake manifold assembly, showing bolt torque sequence

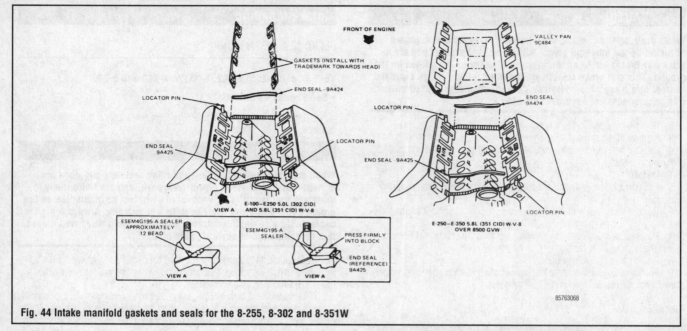

Fig. 44 Intake manifold gaskets and seals for the 8-255, 8-302 and 8-351W

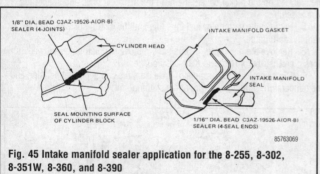

Fig. 45 Intake manifold sealer application for the 8-255, 8-302, 8-351W, 8-360, and 8-390

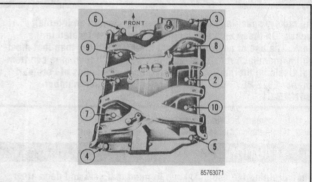

Fig. 47 Intake manifold bolt torque sequence for the 8-360 and 8-390

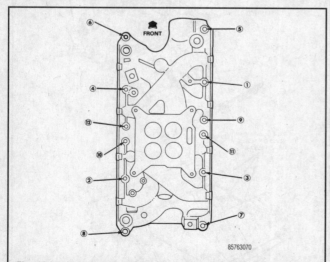

Fig. 46 Intake manifold bolt torque sequence for the 8-255, 8-302 and 8-351W

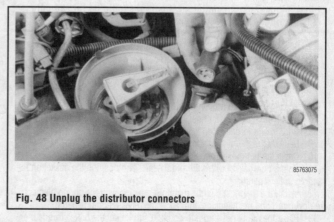

Fig. 48 Unplug the distributor connectors

8. Remove the heater hose from the intake manifold.
9. Loosen the clamp on the water pump bypass hose at the coolant outlet housing and slide the hose off the outlet housing.
10. Disconnect the PCV hose at the rocker cover.
11. If the engine is equipped with the Thermactor® exhaust emission control

system, remove the air pump to cylinder head air hose at the air pump and position it out of the way. Also remove the air hose at the backfire suppressor valve. Remove the air hose bracket from the valve rocker arm cover and position the air hose out of the way.
12. On the 360 and the 390 engines, remove the rocker arm shafts and pushrods. The push rods **must** be reinstalled in their original positions.
13. Remove the intake manifold and carburetor as an assembly. It may be necessary to pry the intake manifold from the cylinder head. There are projection built into the manifold for this purpose. NEVER pry on a gasket surface!

Fig. 49 Mark the distributor body for rotor alignment

Fig. 50 Removing the distributor

Fig. 51 Prying up the intake manifold

Fig. 52 Lifting off the intake manifold

Fig. 53 Removing the front manifold seal

14. Remove all traces of the intake manifold-to-cylinder head gaskets and the two end seals from both the manifold and the other mating surfaces of the engine.

To install:

15. Clean the mating surfaces of the intake manifold, cylinder heads, and block with lacquer thinner or similar solvent. Apply a ⅛ inch (3mm) bead of silicone-rubber RTV sealant at the points shown in the accompanying diagram.

⁕⁕ WARNING

Do not apply sealer to the waffle portions of the seals as the sealer will rupture the end seal material.

16. Position new seals on the block and press the seal locating extensions into the holes in the mating surfaces.

17. Apply a 1⁄16 inch (1.6mm) bead of sealer to the outer end of each manifold seal for the full length of the seal (4 places). Do not apply sealer to the waffle portion of the end seals.

➡**This sealer sets in about 15 minutes, depending on brand, so work quickly but carefully. DO NOT DROP ANY SEALER INTO THE MANIFOLD CAVITY. IT WILL FORM, SET AND PLUG THE OIL GALLERY.**

18. Position the manifold gasket onto the block and heads with the alignment notches under the dowels in the heads. Be sure gasket holes align with head holes.

19. If the temperature sending unit was removed, clean the threads and coat them with electrically conductive sealer.

20. Carefully lower the manifold into position. Run your finger around the front and rear seals to make sure they are in position. If not, remove the manifold and reposition them.

21. Install the manifold nuts and bolts. Following the tightening sequence, first tighten all fasteners to 12 ft. lbs., then to the final torque of 25 ft. lbs.

22. Install all remaining parts, run the engine and check for leaks.

8-351M and 8-400

▸ **See Figures 54, 55 and 56**

1. Drain the cooling system, remove the air cleaner and the intake duct assembly.

Fig. 54 Intake manifold sealer application for the 8-351M and 8-400

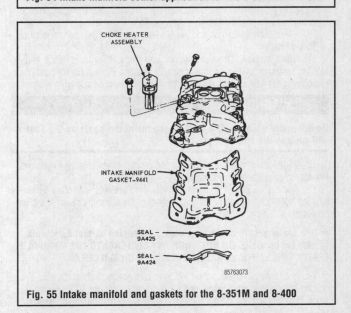

Fig. 55 Intake manifold and gaskets for the 8-351M and 8-400

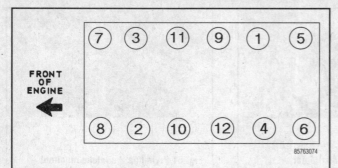

Fig. 56 Intake manifold bolt torque sequence for the 8-351M and 8-400

❈❈ CAUTION

When draining the coolant, keep in mind that cats and dogs are attracted by the ethylene glycol antifreeze, and are quite likely to drink any that is left in an uncovered container or in puddles on the ground. This will prove fatal in sufficient quantity. Always drain the coolant into a sealable container. Coolant should be reused unless it is contaminated or several years old.

2. Disconnect the accelerator rod from the carburetor and remove the accelerator retracting spring. Disconnect the automatic transmission kickdown rod at the carburetor, if so equipped.

3. Disconnect the high tension lead and all other wires from the ignition coil.

4. Disconnect the spark plug wires from the spark plugs by grasping the rubber boots and twisting and pulling at the same time. Remove the wires from the brackets on the rocker covers. Remove the distributor cap and spark plug wire assembly.

5. Remove the carburetor fuel inlet line and the distributor vacuum line from the carburetor.

6. Remove the distributor lockbolt and remove the distributor and vacuum lines. See Distributor Removal & Installation.

7. Disconnect the PCV hose at the rocker cover.

8. If the engine is equipped with the Thermactor® exhaust emission control system, remove the air pump to cylinder head air hose at the air pump and position it out of the way. Also remove the air hose at the backfire suppressor valve. Remove the air hose bracket from the valve rocker arm cover and position the air hose out of the way.

9. Remove the intake manifold and carburetor as an assembly. It may be necessary to pry the intake manifold from the cylinder head. There are projections built into the manifold for this purpose. NEVER pry on a gasket surface!

10. Remove the valley pan and the two end seals from the heads and block.
To install:

11. Clean the mating surfaces of the intake manifold, cylinder heads, and block with lacquer thinner or similar solvent. Apply a ⅛ inch (3mm) bead of silicone-rubber RTV sealant at the points shown in the accompanying diagram.

❈❈ WARNING

Do not apply sealer to the waffle portions of the seals as the sealer will rupture the end seal material.

12. Position new seals on the block and press the seal locating extensions into the holes in the mating surfaces.

13. Apply a ¹⁄₁₆ inch (1.6mm) bead of sealer to the outer end of each manifold seal for the full length of the seal (4 places). Do not apply sealer to the waffle portion of the end seals.

➡This sealer sets in about 15 minutes, depending on brand, so work quickly but carefully. DO NOT DROP ANY SEALER INTO THE MANIFOLD CAVITY. IT WILL FORM, SET AND PLUG THE OIL GALLERY.

14. Your new valley pan gasket will have an instruction sheet showing a change in the sealer application for the pan-to-heads contact. RTV silicone sealer is to be used around the water passages, while non-hardening gasket sealer is to be used everywhere else.

15. Position the valley pan onto the block and heads with the alignment notches and ridge engaged. Be sure gasket holes align with head holes.

16. Carefully lower the manifold into position. Run your finger around the front and rear seals to make sure they are in position. If not, remove the manifold and reposition them.

17. Install the manifold nuts and bolts. Following the tightening sequence, first tighten all fasteners to 12 ft. lbs., then to the final torque of 25 ft. lbs.

18. Install all remaining parts, run the engine and check for leaks.

8-302 EFI Engines

▶ See Figures 57 and 58

➡Discharge fuel system pressure before starting any work that involves disconnecting fuel system lines. See Fuel Supply Manifold removal and installation procedures (Gasoline Fuel System section).

1. To remove the upper manifold: Remove the air cleaner. Disconnect the electrical connectors at the air bypass valve, throttle position sensor and EGR position sensor.

2. Disconnect the throttle linkage at the throttle ball and the AOD transmission linkage from the throttle body. Remove the bolts that secure the bracket to the intake and position the bracket and cables out of the way.

3. Disconnect the upper manifold vacuum fitting connections by removing all the vacuum lines at the vacuum tree (label lines for position identification). Remove the vacuum lines to the EGR valve and fuel pressure regulator.

4. Disconnect the PCV system by disconnecting the hose from the fitting at the rear of the upper manifold.

5. Remove the two canister purge lines from the fittings at the throttle body.

6. Disconnect the EGR tube from the EGR valve by loosening the flange nut.

7. Remove the bolt from the upper intake support bracket to upper manifold. Remove the upper manifold retaining bolts and remove the upper intake manifold and throttle body as an assembly.

8. Clean and inspect all mounting surfaces of the upper and lower intake manifolds.

9. Position a new mounting gasket on the lower intake manifold and install the upper manifold in the reverse order of removal. Mounting bolts are torqued to 12-18 ft. lbs.

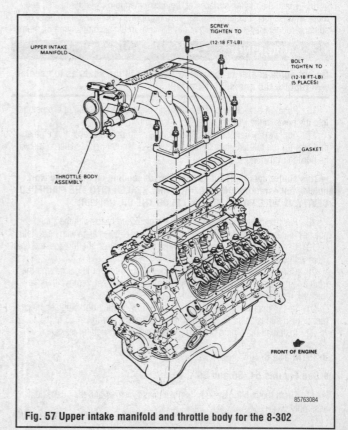

Fig. 57 Upper intake manifold and throttle body for the 8-302

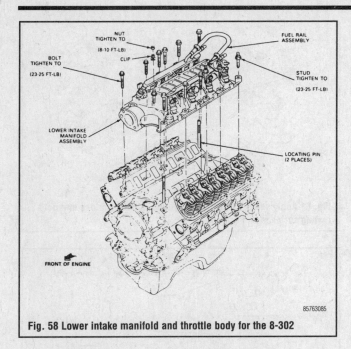

Fig. 58 Lower intake manifold and throttle body for the 8-302

10. To remove the lower intake manifold: Upper manifold and throttle body must be removed first.

11. Drain the cooling system.

❊❊ CAUTION

When draining the coolant, keep in mind that cats and dogs are attracted by the ethylene glycol antifreeze, and are quite likely to drink any that is left in an uncovered container or in puddles on the ground. This will prove fatal in sufficient quantity. Always drain the coolant into a sealable container. Coolant should be reused unless it is contaminated or several years old.

12. Remove the distributor assembly, cap and wires.

13. Disconnect the electrical connectors at the engine, coolant temperature sensor and sending unit, at the air charge temperature sensor and at the knock sensor.

14. Disconnect the injector wiring harness from the main harness assembly. Remove the ground wire from the intake manifold stud. The ground wire must be installed at the same position it was removed from.

15. Disconnect the fuel supply and return lines from the fuel rails.

16. Remove the upper radiator hose from the thermostat housing. Remove the bypass hose. Remove the heater outlet hose at the intake manifold.

17. Remove the air cleaner mounting bracket. Remove the intake manifold mounting bolts and studs. Pay attention to the location of the bolts and studs for reinstallation. Remove the lower intake manifold assembly.

18. Clean and inspect the mounting surfaces of the heads and manifold.

19. Apply a 1/16 inch (1.6mm) bead of RTV sealer to the ends of the manifold seal (the junction point of the seals and gaskets). Install the end seals and intake gaskets on the cylinder heads. The gaskets must interlock with the seal tabs.

20. Install locator bolts at opposite ends of each head and carefully lower the intake manifold into position. Install and tighten the mounting bolts and studs to 23-25 ft. lbs. Install the remaining components in the reverse order of removal.

8-460

▶ See Figures 59 and 60

1. Drain the cooling system and remove the air cleaner assembly.

❊❊ CAUTION

When draining the coolant, keep in mind that cats and dogs are attracted by the ethylene glycol antifreeze, and are quite likely to drink any that is left in an uncovered container or in puddles on the

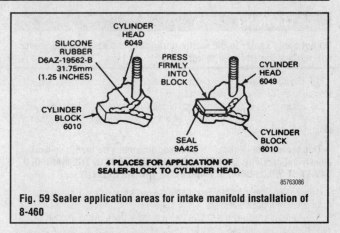

Fig. 59 Sealer application areas for intake manifold installation of 8-460

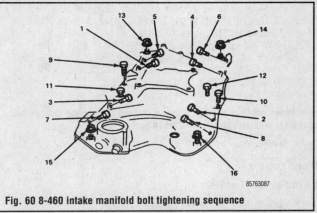

Fig. 60 8-460 intake manifold bolt tightening sequence

ground. This will prove fatal in sufficient quantity. Always drain the coolant into a sealable container. Coolant should be reused unless it is contaminated or several years old.

2. Disconnect the upper radiator hose at the engine.

3. Disconnect the heater hoses at the intake manifold and the water pump. Position them out of the way. Loosen the water pump by-pass hose clamp at the intake manifold.

4. Disconnect the PCV valve and hose at the right valve cover. Disconnect all of the vacuum lines at the rear of the intake manifold and tag them for proper reinstallation.

5. Disconnect the wires at the spark plugs, and remove the wires from the brackets on the valve cover. Disconnect the high tension wire from the coil and remove the distributor cap and wires as an assembly.

6. Disconnect all of the distributor vacuum lines at the carburetor and vacuum control valve and tag them for proper installation. Remove the distributor and vacuum lines as an assembly.

7. Disconnect the accelerator linkage at the carburetor. Remove the speed control linkage bracket, if so equipped, from the manifold and carburetor.

8. Remove the bolts holding the accelerator linkage to the bellcrank and position the linkage and return springs out of the way.

9. Disconnect the fuel line at the carburetor.

10. Disconnect the wiring harness at the coil battery terminal, engine temperature sending unit, oil pressure sending unit, and other connections as necessary. Disconnect the wiring harness from the clips at the left valve cover and position the harness out of the way.

11. Remove the coil and bracket assembly.

12. Remove the intake manifold attaching bolts and lift the manifold and carburetor from the engine as an assembly. It may be necessary to pry the manifold away from the cylinder heads. Do not damage the gasket sealing surfaces.

Installation:

13. Clean the mating surfaces of the intake manifold, cylinder heads and block with lacquer thinner or similar solvent. Apply a 1/8 inch (3mm) bead of silicone-rubber RTV sealant at the points shown in the accompanying diagram.

✳✳ WARNING

Do not apply sealer to the waffle portions of the seals as the sealer will rupture the end seal material.

14. Position the new seals on the block and press the seal locating extensions into the holes in the mating surfaces.

15. Apply a 1/16 inch (1.6mm) bead of sealer to the outer end of each manifold seal for the full length of the seal (4 places). Do not apply sealer to the waffle portion of the end seals.

➡This sealer sets in about 15 minutes, depending on brand, so work quickly but carefully. DO NOT DROP ANY SEALER INTO THE MANIFOLD CAVITY. IT WILL FORM, SET AND PLUG THE OIL GALLERY.

16. Position the manifold gasket onto the block and heads. Be sure gasket holes align with head holes.

17. Lower the manifold into position over the 4 studs. When in position, run your finger around the seal areas to make sure that the seals are still in place.

18. Looking at the torque sequence illustration, install bolts 1 through 10 finger-tight. Then install bolts 11 and 12. Install the nuts on studs 13 through 16. All fasteners should be finger-tight at this point.

19. Tighten bolts 1 through 10, in sequence, to 97-115 inch lbs. (11-13 Nm).

20. Tighten nuts 13 through 16, in sequence, to 53-62 inch lbs. (6-7 Nm).

21. Tighten all bolts and nuts, in sequence, to 20 ft. lbs.

22. Tighten all bolts and nuts, in sequence, to 32 ft. lbs.

23. Install all remaining parts.

➡If the temperature sending unit was removed, clean the threads and coat them with electrically conductive sealer.

24. Run the engine and check for leaks.

Diesel Engines

◆ See Figures 61 and 62

1. Open the hood and remove both battery ground cables.

2. Remove the air cleaner and install clean rags into the air intake of the intake manifold. **It is important that no dirt or foreign objects get into the diesel intake.**

3. Remove the injection pump as described in Section 5 under Diesel Fuel Systems.

4. Remove the fuel return hose from No. 7 and No. 8 rear nozzles and remove the return hose to the fuel tank.

5. Label the positions of the wires and remove the engine wiring harness from the engine.

➡The engine harness ground cables must be removed from the back of the left cylinder head.

6. Remove the bolts attaching the intake manifold to the cylinder heads and remove the manifold.

7. Remove the CDR tube grommet from the valley pan.

8. Remove the bolts attaching the valley pan strap to the front of the engine block, and remove the strap.

9. Remove the valley pan drain plug and remove the valley pan.

10. Apply a 1/8 inch (3mm) bead of RTV sealer to each end of the cylinder block.

➡The RTV sealer should be applied immediately prior to the valley pan installation.

11. Install the valley pan drain plug, CDR tube and new grommet into the valley pan.

12. Install a new O-ring and new back-up ring on the CDR valve.

13. Install the valley pan strap on the front of the valley pan.

14. Install the intake manifold and torque the bolts to 24 ft. lbs. using the sequence shown in the illustration.

15. Reconnect the engine wiring harness and the engine ground wire located to the rear of the left cylinder head.

16. Install the injection pump using the procedure shown in Section 5 under Diesel fuel Systems.

17. Install the no. 7 and no. 8 fuel return hoses and the fuel tank return hose.

18. Remove the rag from the intake manifold and replace the air cleaner. Reconnect the battery ground cables to both batteries.

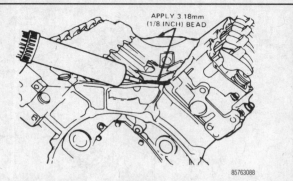

Fig. 61 Apply sealer to the diesel cylinder block-to-intake manifold mating surfaces on each end

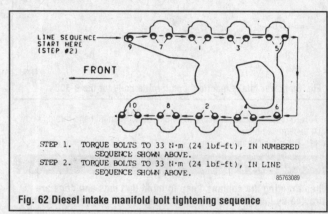

Fig. 62 Diesel intake manifold bolt tightening sequence

19. Run the engine and check for oil and fuel leaks.

➡If necessary, purge the nozzle high pressure lines of air by loosening the connector one half to one turn and cranking the engine until solid stream of fuel, devoid of any bubbles, flows from the connection.

✳✳ CAUTION

Keep eyes and hands away from the nozzle spray. Fuel spraying from the nozzle under high pressure can penetrate the skin.

20. Check and adjust the injection pump timing, as described in Section 5 under Diesel Fuel Systems.

Exhaust Manifold

REMOVAL & INSTALLATION

V6-232

◆ See Figure 63

LEFT SIDE

1. Remove the dipstick bracket.

2. If equipped with cruise control, remove the air cleaner and disconnect the control cable at the carburetor. Remove the servo bracket assembly.

3. Tag and disconnect the spark plug wires.

4. Disconnect the oxygen sensor wire.

5. Raise and support the front end on jackstands.

6. Disconnect the exhaust pipe from the exhaust manifold.

7. Lower the truck.

8. Remove the exhaust manifold attaching bolts and remove the manifold from the cylinder head.

Installation:

9. Install the exhaust manifold in the reverse order of removal.

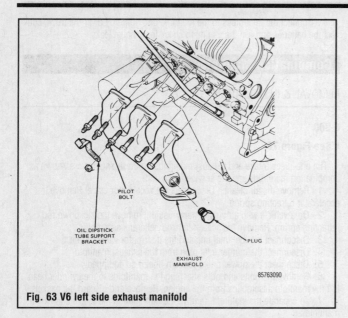

Fig. 63 V6 left side exhaust manifold

→The manifold may warp slightly and all the bolt holes may not align perfectly. The holes in the manifold may be elongated to correct this condition. HOWEVER, do not alter the pilot bolt hole. The pilot bolt is the 3rd from the front. This hole and its corresponding threaded hole in the head must align to properly center the manifold on the head. So, when installing the manifold, instll this bolt first.

Install the pilot bolt, then all the rest of the bolts. Tighten all bolts to 22 ft. lbs., starting from the center and working to both ends alternately. Tighten the exhaust pipe-to-manifold nuts to 24 ft. lbs.

RIGHT SIDE

1. Remove the air cleaner.
2. Remove the transmission dipstick tube.

3. Remove the Thermactor® hose and downstream air tube bracket.
4. Disconnect the coil wires and spark plug wires.
5. Remove the spark plugs and heat shield.
6. Raise and support the truck on jackstands.
7. Disconnect the exhaust pipe from the exhaust manifold.
8. Lower the truck.
9. Remove the exhaust manifold attaching bolts and remove the manifold, inner heat shroud and EGR tube as an assembly, from the cylinder head.
   Installation:
10. Install the exhaust manifold in the reverse order of removal.

→The manifold may warp slightly and all the bolt holes may not align perfectly. The holes in the manifold may be elongated to correct this condition. HOWEVER, do not alter the pilot bolt hole. The pilot bolt is the 4th from the front. This hole and its corresponding threaded hole in the head must align to properly center the manifold on the head. So, when installing the manifold, instll this bolt first.

Install the pilot bolt, then all the rest of the bolts. Tighten all bolts to 22 ft. lbs., starting from the center and working to both ends alternately. Tighten the exhaust pipe-to-manifold nuts to 24 ft. lbs.

8-255, 8-302, 8-351W

▶ See Figures 64, 65, 66, 67 and 68

1. Remove the air cleaner.
2. On the left side, remove the dipstick bracket.
3. Disconnect the exhaust pipe from the exhaust manifold. On the left side, remove the exhaust heat control valve, if so equipped.
4. Remove the exhaust manifold attaching screws and remove the manifold from the cylinder head.
5. Install the exhaust manifold in the reverse order of removal. Apply a light coat of graphite grease to the mating surface of the manifold. Install and tighten the attaching bolts, starting from the center and working to both ends alternately. Tighten to the 24 ft. lbs.

8-351M, 8-400

1. For the right side, remove the air cleaner.
2. For the left side, remove the oil filter and oil dipstick tube bracket.

Fig. 64 Removing the exhaust pipe-to-manifold nuts; 1983 8-302 shown

Fig. 65 Removing the exhaust heat control valve; 1983 8-302 shown

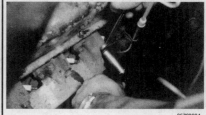

Fig. 66 Unbolting the oil dipstick bracket; 1983 8-302 shown

Fig. 67 Removing the exhaust manifold bolts; 1983 8-302 shown

Fig. 68 Removing the exhaust manifold; 1983 8-302 shown

3. On the left side, you may find it helpful to disconnect the selector lever cross-shaft with a column mounted automatic transmission lever.

4. On either side, tag and disconnect the spark plug wires, just to move them out of the way.

5. Disconnect the exhaust pipe from the exhaust manifold.

6. Remove the exhaust manifold attaching bolts and remove the manifold from the cylinder head.

7. Install the exhaust manifold in the reverse order of removal. Use a new gasket. Install and tighten the attaching bolts, starting from the center and working to both ends alternately. Tighten to 24 ft. lbs.

8-360, 8-390

1. Remove the air cleaner.

2. Remove the dipstick tube assembly.

3. Disconnect the power steering pump bracket from the cylinder block and move it out of the way.

4. Disconnect the exhaust pipe or catalytic converter from the exhaust manifold. Remove and discard the donut gasket.

5. Remove the exhaust manifold attaching screws and remove the manifold from the cylinder head.

6. Install the exhaust manifold in the reverse order of removal. Use a new gasket. Install and tighten the attaching bolts, starting from the center and working to both ends alternately. Tighten to 18 ft. lbs.

8-460

1. On the right side, remove the air cleaner and heat tube.

2. Disconnect the exhaust pipe from the exhaust manifold.

3. Remove the exhaust manifold attaching screws and remove the manifold from the cylinder head.

4. Install the exhaust manifold in the reverse order of removal. Use a new gasket. Install and tighten the attaching bolts, starting from the center and working to both ends alternately. Tighten to 33 ft. lbs.

Diesel Engines

▶ See Figure 69

1. Disconnect the ground cables from both batteries.

2. Jack up the truck and safely support it with jackstands.

3. Disconnect the muffler inlet pipe from the exhaust manifolds.

4. Lower the truck to remove the right manifold. When removing the left manifold, jack the truck up. Bend the tabs on the manifold attaching bolts, then remove the bolts and manifold.

5. Before installing, clean all mounting surfaces on the cylinder heads and the manifold. Apply an anti-seize compound on the manifold both threads and install the left manifold, using a new gasket and new locking tabs.

6. Torque the bolts to specifications and bend the tabs over the flats on the bolt heads to prevent the bolts from loosening.

7. Jack up the truck to install the right manifold. Install the right manifold following procedures 5 and 6 above.

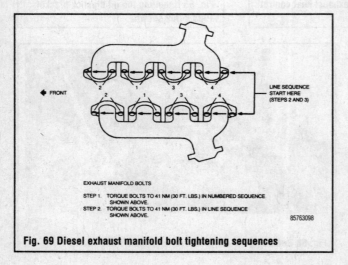

EXHAUST MANIFOLD BOLTS

STEP 1. TORQUE BOLTS TO 41 NM (30 FT. LBS.) IN NUMBERED SEQUENCE
SHOWN ABOVE.
STEP 2. TORQUE BOLTS TO 41 NM (30 FT. LBS.) IN LINE SEQUENCE
SHOWN ABOVE.

85763098

Fig. 69 Diesel exhaust manifold bolt tightening sequences

8. Connect the inlet pipes to the manifold and tighten. Lower the truck, connect the batteries and run the engine to check for exhaust leaks.

Combination Manifold

REMOVAL & INSTALLATION

6-300

▶ See Figure 70

The one-piece intake and exhaust manifolds on these engines are known as combination manifolds and are serviced as a unit.

1. Remove the air cleaner. Disconnect the accelerator cable. Remove the accelerator retracting spring.

2. On a vehicle with automatic transmission, remove the kickdown rod retracting spring. Remove the accelerator rod bellcrank assembly.

3. Disconnect the fuel inlet line and the distributor vacuum line.

4. Disconnect the muffler inlet pipe from the exhaust manifold.

5. Disconnect the power brake vacuum line, if so equipped.

6. Remove the bolts and nuts attaching the manifolds to the cylinder head. Lift the manifold assemblies from the engine. Remove and discard the gaskets.

7. To separate the manifold, remove the nuts joining the intake and exhaust manifolds.

To install:

8. Clean the mating surfaces of the cylinder head and the manifolds.

9. If the intake and exhaust manifolds have been separated, coat the mating surfaces lightly with graphite grease and place the exhaust manifold over the studs on the intake manifold. Install the lockwashers and nuts. Tighten them finger tight.

10. Install a new intake manifold gasket.

11. Coat the mating surfaces lightly with graphite grease. Place the manifold assemblies in position against the cylinder head. Make sure that the gaskets have not become dislodged. Install the attaching nuts and bolts in the proper sequence to 26 ft. lbs. If the intake and exhaust manifolds were separated, tighten the nuts joining them.

12. Position a new gasket on the muffler inlet pipe and connect the inlet pipe to the exhaust manifold.

13. Connect the crankcase vent hose to the intake manifold inlet tube and position the hose clamp.

14. Connect the fuel inlet line and the distributor vacuum line.

15. Connect the accelerator cable and install the retracting spring.

16. On a vehicle with an automatic transmission, install the bellcrank assembly and the kickdown rod retracting spring. Adjust the transmission control linkage.

17. Install the air cleaner.

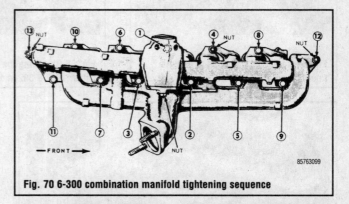

85763099

Fig. 70 6-300 combination manifold tightening sequence

Radiator

REMOVAL & INSTALLATION

▶ See Figures 71 thru 76

1. Drain the cooling system.

Fig. 71 Removing the overflow hose

Fig. 72 Loosening the transmission cooler lines

Fig. 73 Disconnecting the transmission cooler lines

Fig. 74 Disconnecting the upper hose from the radiator

Fig. 75 Removing the upper radiator support bolts

Fig. 76 Removing the radiator. It might be a good idea to unbolt the fan shroud from the radiator first

⁑ CAUTION

When draining the coolant, keep in mind that cats and dogs are attracted by the ethylene glycol antifreeze, and are quite likely to drink any that is left in an uncovered container or in puddles on the ground. This will prove fatal in sufficient quantity. Always drain the coolant into a sealable container. Coolant should be reused unless it is contaminated or several years old.

2. Disconnect the transmission cooling lines from the bottom of the radiator, if so equipped.
3. Remove the retaining bolts at each of the 4 corners of the shroud, if so equipped, and position the shroud over the fan, clear of the radiator.
4. Disconnect the upper and lower hoses from the radiator.
5. Remove the radiator retaining bolts or the upper supports and lift the radiator from the vehicle.
6. Install the radiator in the reverse order of removal. Fill the cooling system and check for leaks.

Engine Fan and Fan Clutch

REMOVAL & INSTALLATION

6-300, 8-360, 8-390, 8-255, 1976-80 8-302, 8-351W Engines

▸ See Figure 77

1. Unbolt the fan shroud and lay it back over the fan.
2. Remove one of the fan-to-hub bolts.
To install:
3. Attach the fan to the hub. The bolts are tightened to 18 ft. lbs.
4. Install the shroud.

V6-232, 8-351M, 8-400, 8-460, 1981-86 8-302, 351W Engines

▸ See Figures 78, 79, 80, 81 and 82

1. Remove the fan shroud and lay it back over the fan.
2. If you need the clearance, remove the radiator.
3. Remove the 4 fan clutch-to-water pump hub bolts and lift off the fan/clutch assembly.
4. Remove the 4 fan-to-clutch bolts and separate the fan from the clutch.

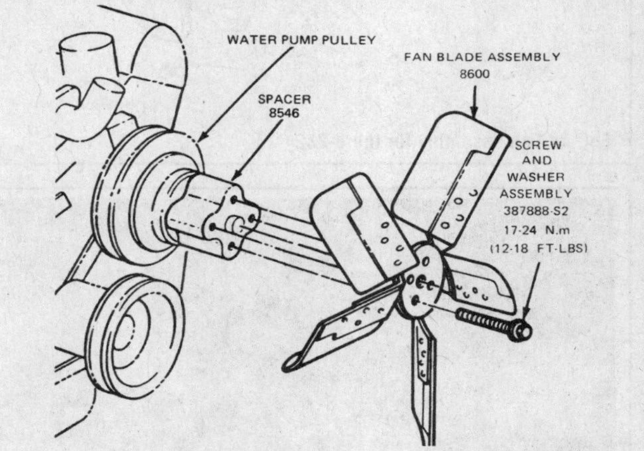

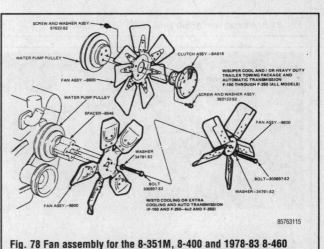

Fig. 77 Fan blade installation for the 1970-86 pick-ups and Bronco w/6-300, 8-255, 8-302, 8-351W, 8-360 and 8-390

Fig. 78 Fan assembly for the 8-351M, 8-400 and 1978-83 8-460

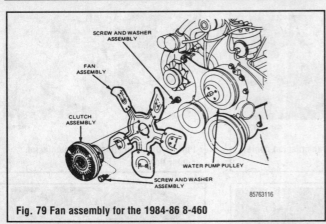

Fig. 79 Fan assembly for the 1984-86 8-460

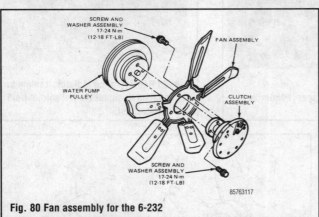

Fig. 80 Fan assembly for the 6-232

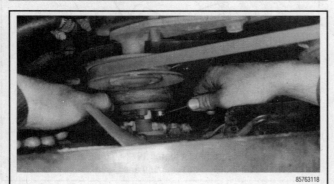

Fig. 81 Removing fan-to-hub bolts; 1983 8-302 shown

Fig. 82 Removing the fan; 1983 8-302 shown

5. Installation is the reverse of removal. Torque the all the bolts to 18 ft. lbs.

Diesel Engine

▶ **See Figure 83**

1. Remove the fan shroud.
2. Turn the large fan clutch-to-hub nut CLOCKWISE (left-handed threads) to remove the fan and clutch from the hub. There are 2 tools made for this purpose, holding tool T84T-6312-A and nut wrench T84T-6312-B.
3. If the fan and clutch have to be separated, remove the fan-to-clutch bolts.

To install:

4. Attach the fan to the clutch. The bolts are tightened to 18 ft. lbs.
5. Install the assembly on the hub and tighten the hub nut to a maximum of 120 ft. lbs., or a minimum of 40 ft. lbs. Remember, the nut is left-handed. Tighten it by turning it COUNTERCLOCKWISE.
6. Install the shroud.

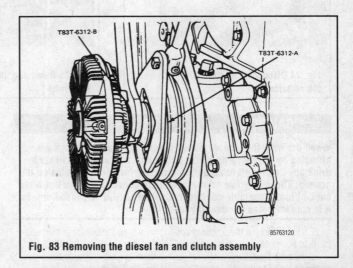

Fig. 83 Removing the diesel fan and clutch assembly

Water Pump

REMOVAL & INSTALLATION

6-300 Engines

1. Drain the cooling system.

✳✳ CAUTION

When draining the coolant, keep in mind that cats and dogs are attracted by the ethylene glycol antifreeze, and are quite likely to drink any that is left in an uncovered container or in puddles on the ground. This will prove fatal in sufficient quantity. Always drain the coolant into a sealable container. Coolant should be reused unless it is contaminated or several years old.

2. Disconnect the lower radiator hose from the water pump.
3. Remove the drive belt, fan, fan spacer, fan shroud, if so equipped, and water pump pulley.
4. Remove the alternator pivot arm from the pump.
5. Disconnect the heater hose at the water pump.
6. Remove the water pump.
7. Before installing the old water pump, clean the gasket mounting surfaces on the pump and on the cylinder block. If a new water pump is being installed, remove the heater hose fitting from the old pump and install it on the new one. Coat the new gaskets with sealer on both sides and install the water pump in the reverse order of removal. Torque the mounting bolts to 14-18 ft. lbs.

V6-232 Engines

▶ **See Figures 84 and 85**

1. Drain the cooling system.

✺✺ CAUTION

When draining the coolant, keep in mind that cats and dogs are attracted by the ethylene glycol antifreeze, and are quite likely to drink any that is left in an uncovered container or in puddles on the ground. This will prove fatal in sufficient quantity. Always drain the coolant into a sealable container. Coolant should be reused unless it is contaminated or several years old.

2. Remove the air cleaner.
3. Remove the bolts securing the fan shroud to the radiator, if so equipped, and position the shroud over the fan.
4. Disconnect the lower radiator hose, heater hose and by-pass hose at the water pump. Remove the drive belts, fan, fan spacer and pulley. Remove the fan shroud, if so equipped.
5. Loosen the alternator pivot bolt and the bolt attaching the alternator adjusting arm to the water pump. Remove the power steering pump bracket from the water pump and position it out of the way.
6. If necessary, remove the air conditioner compressor and bracket. The refrigerant lines should remain connected.

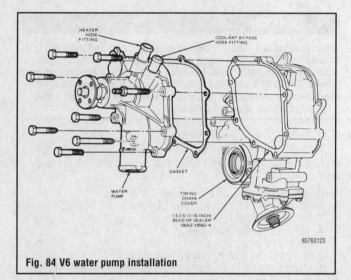

Fig. 84 V6 water pump installation

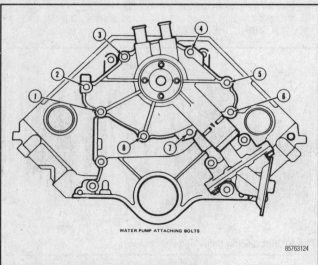

Fig. 85 V6 water pump bolt torque sequence

7. Remove the bolts securing the water pump to the timing chain cover and remove the water pump.
8. Thoroughly clean the mounting surfaces of all gasket material.
9. Install the water pump in the reverse order of removal, using a new gasket. Torque the bolts to 15-22 ft. lbs. in the sequence shown.

8-255, 302, 351W Engines

▶ **See Figures 86, 87, 88, 89 and 90**

1. Drain the cooling system.

✺✺ CAUTION

When draining the coolant, keep in mind that cats and dogs are attracted by the ethylene glycol antifreeze, and are quite likely to drink any that is left in an uncovered container or in puddles on the ground. This will prove fatal in sufficient quantity. Always drain the coolant into a sealable container. Coolant should be reused unless it is contaminated or several years old.

2. Remove the bolts securing the fan shroud to the radiator, if so equipped, and position the shroud over the fan.
3. Disconnect the lower radiator hose, heater hose and by-pass hose at the water pump. Remove the drive belts, fan, fan spacer and pulley. Remove the fan shroud, if so equipped.
4. Loosen the alternator pivot bolt and the bolt attaching the alternator adjusting arm to the water pump. Remove the power steering pump bracket from the water pump and position it out of the way.
5. If necessary, remove the air conditioner compressor and bracket. The refrigerant lines should remain connected.
6. Remove the bolts securing the water pump to the timing chain cover and remove the water pump.
7. Install the water pump in the reverse order of removal, using a new gasket. Torque the bolts to 14-18 ft. lbs.

Fig. 86 Remove the water pump pulley; 1983 8-302 shown

Fig. 87 Removing the bypass hoses; 1983 8-302 shown

Fig. 88 Removing the compressor mounting bracket; 1983 8-302 shown

Fig. 89 Removing the power steering pump; 1983 8-302 shown

Fig. 90 Removing the water pump; 1983 8-302 shown

8-360, 390

1. Drain the cooling system.

✳✳ CAUTION

When draining the coolant, keep in mind that cats and dogs are attracted by the ethylene glycol antifreeze, and are quite likely to drink any that is left in an uncovered container or in puddles on the ground. This will prove fatal in sufficient quantity. Always drain the coolant into a sealable container. Coolant should be reused unless it is contaminated or several years old.

2. Remove the bolts securing the fan shroud to the radiator, if so equipped, and position the shroud over the fan.
3. Disconnect the lower radiator hose, heater hose and by-pass hose at the water pump. Remove the drive belts, fan, fan spacer and pulley. Remove the fan shroud, if so equipped.
4. Loosen the alternator pivot bolt and the bolt attaching the alternator adjusting arm to the water pump. Remove the power steering pump bracket from the water pump and position it out of the way.
5. If necessary, remove the air conditioner compressor and bracket. The refrigerant lines should remain connected.
6. Remove the bolts securing the water pump to the timing chain cover and remove the water pump.
7. Install the water pump in the reverse order of removal, using a new gasket. Torque the bolts to 20-25 ft. lbs.

8-351M, 400, 460

1. Disconnect the battery ground.
2. Drain the cooling system.

✳✳ CAUTION

When draining the coolant, keep in mind that cats and dogs are attracted by the ethylene glycol antifreeze, and are quite likely to drink any that is left in an uncovered container or in puddles on the ground. This will prove fatal in sufficient quantity. Always drain the coolant into a sealable container. Coolant should be reused unless it is contaminated or several years old.

3. Remove the bolts securing the fan shroud to the radiator, if so equipped, and position the shroud over the fan.
4. Remove the fan assembly.
5. Remove the fan shroud.
6. Remove the accessory drive belts and water pump pulley.
7. Remove the alternator and brackets.
8. Remove the compressor and bracket and lay it aside. DO NOT disconnect the refrigerant lines!
9. Remove the power steering pump and brackets. Lay it aside. DO NOT disconnect the fluid lines!
10. Disconnect the heater hose and lower radiator hose from the pump.
11. Remove the bolts securing the water pump to the engine and lift off the water pump.
12. Clean all gasket mounting surfaces thoroughly.

To install:

13. Install the water pump in the reverse order of removal, using a new gasket coated with sealer. Torque the bolts to 12-18 ft. lbs.
14. Install all remaining parts in reverse order. Fill the cooling system, start the engine and check for leaks.

Diesel Engines

▶ See Figures 91 and 92

1. Disconnect both battery ground cables.
2. Drain the cooling system.

✳✳ CAUTION

When draining the coolant, keep in mind that cats and dogs are attracted by the ethylene glycol antifreeze, and are quite likely to drink any that is left in an uncovered container or in puddles on the ground. This will prove fatal in sufficient quantity. Always drain the coolant into a sealable container. Coolant should be reused unless it is contaminated or several years old.

3. Remove the radiator shroud halves.
4. Remove the fan clutch and fan.

➡The fan clutch bolts are left hand thread. Remove them by turning them clockwise.

5. Remove the power steering pump belt.
6. Remove the air conditioning compressor belt.
7. Remove the vacuum pump drive belt.
8. Remove the alternator drive belt.
9. Remove the water pump pulley.
10. Disconnect the heater hose at the water pump.
11. If you're installing a new pump, remove the heater hose fitting from the old pump at this time.
12. Remove the alternator adjusting arm and bracket.
13. Unbolt the air conditioning compressor and position it out of the way. DO NOT DISCONNECT THE REFRIGERANT LINES!

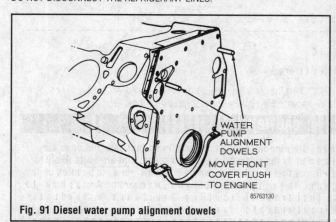

Fig. 91 Diesel water pump alignment dowels

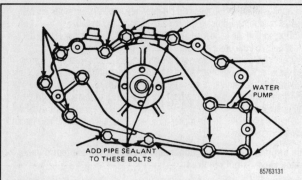

Fig. 92 Diesel water pump installation. The 2 top bolts must be no more than 1¼ in. long

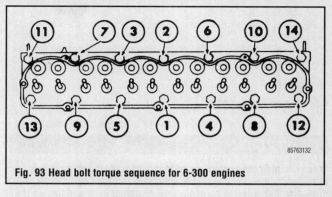

Fig. 93 Head bolt torque sequence for 6-300 engines

14. Remove the air conditioning compressor brackets.

15. Unbolt the power steering pump and bracket and position it out of the way. DO NOT DISCONNECT THE POWER STEERING FLUID LINES!

16. Remove the bolts attaching the water pump to the front cover and lift off the pump.

17. Thoroughly clean the mating surfaces of the pump and front cover.

18. Get a hold of two dowel pins—anything that will fit into 2 mounting bolt holes in the front cover. You'll need these to ensure proper bolt hole alignment when you're installing the water pump.

19. Using a new gasket, position the water pump over the dowel pins and into place on the front cover.

20. Install the attaching bolts. The 2 top center and 2 bottom center bolts must be coated with RTV silicone sealant prior to installation. Also, these 4 bolts are a different length than the other bolts. Torque the bolts to 14 ft. lbs.

21. Install the water pump pulley.

22. Wrap the heater hose fitting threads with Teflon® tape and screw it into the water pump. Torque it to 18 ft. lbs.

23. Connect the heater hose to the pump.

24. Install the power steering pump and bracket. Install the belt.

25. Install the air conditioning compressor bracket.

26. Install the air conditioning compressor. Install the belt.

27. Install the alternator adjusting arm and install the belt.

28. Install the vacuum pump drive belt.

29. Adjust all the drive belts.

30. Install the fan and clutch. Remember that the bolts are left hand thread. Turn them counterclockwise to tighten them. Torque them to 45 ft. lbs.

31. Install the fan shroud halves.

32. Fill and bleed the cooling system.

33. Connect the battery ground cables.

34. Start the engine and check for leaks.

Cylinder Head

REMOVAL & INSTALLATION

6-300

▶ **See Figure 93**

1. Drain the cooling system. Remove the air cleaner. Remove the oil filler tube. Disconnect the battery cable at the cylinder head.

❊❊ CAUTION

When draining the coolant, keep in mind that cats and dogs are attracted by the ethylene glycol antifreeze, and are quite likely to drink any that is left in an uncovered container or in puddles on the ground. This will prove fatal in sufficient quantity. Always drain the coolant into a sealable container. Coolant should be reused unless it is contaminated or several years old.

2. Disconnect the muffler inlet pipe at the exhaust manifold. Pull the muffler inlet pipe down. Remove the gasket.

3. Disconnect the accelerator rod and cable retracting spring. Disconnect the choke control cable if applicable and the accelerator rod at the carburetor.

4. Disconnect the transmission kickdown rod. Disconnect the accelerator linkage at the bellcrank assembly.

5. Disconnect the fuel inlet line at the fuel filter hose, and the distributor vacuum line at the carburetor. Disconnect other vacuum lines as necessary for accessibility and identify them for proper connection.

6. Remove the radiator upper hose at the coolant outlet housing.

7. Disconnect the distributor vacuum line at the distributor. Disconnect the carburetor fuel inlet line at the fuel pump. Remove the lines as an assembly.

8. Disconnect the spark plug wires at the spark plugs and the temperature sending unit wire at the sending unit.

9. Grasp the PCV vent hose near the PCV valve and pull the valve out of the grommet in the valve rocker arm cover. Disconnect the PCV vent hose at the hose fitting in the intake manifold spacer and remove the vent hose and PCV valve.

10. Disconnect the carburetor air vent tube and remove the valve rocker arm cover.

11. Remove the valve rocker arm shaft assembly. Remove the pushrods in sequence so that they can be identified and reinstalled in their original positions.

12. Remove the cylinder head bolts and remove the cylinder head. Do not pry between the cylinder head and the block as the gasket surfaces maybe damaged.

To install:

13. Clean the head and block gasket surfaces. If the cylinder head was removed for a gasket change, check the flatness of the cylinder head and block.

14. Apply sealer to both sides of the new cylinder head gasket. Position the gasket on the cylinder block.

15. Install a new gasket on the flange of the muffler inlet pipe.

16. Lift the cylinder head above the cylinder block and lower it into position using two head bolts installed through the head as guides.

17. Coat the threads of the no. 1 and 6 bolts for the right side of the cylinder head with a small mount of water-resistant sealer. Oil the threads of the remaining bolts. Install, but do not tighten, two bolts at the opposite ends of the head to hold the head and gasket in position.

18. The cylinder head bolts are tightened in 3 progressive steps. Torque them (in the proper sequence) to 55 ft. lbs., then 65 ft. lbs. and finally to 85 ft. lbs.

19. Apply Lubriplate to both ends of the pushrods and install them in their original positions.

20. Install the valve rocker arm shaft assembly.

21. Adjust the valves, as necessary.

22. Install the muffler inlet pipe lockwasher and attaching nuts.

23. Connect the radiator upper hose at the coolant outlet housing.

24. Position the distributor vacuum line and the carburetor fuel inlet line on the engine. Connect the fuel line at the fuel filter hose and install a new clamp. Install the distributor vacuum line at the carburetor. Connect the accelerator linkage at the bellcrank assembly. Connect the transmission kickdown rod.

25. Connect the accelerator rod retracting spring. Connect the choke control cable (if applicable) and the accelerator rod at the carburetor.

26. Connect the distributor vacuum line at the distributor. Connect the carburetor fuel inlet line at the fuel pump. Connect all the vacuum lines using their previous identification for proper connection.

27. Connect the temperature sending unit wire at the sending unit. Connect the spark plug wires. Connect the battery cable at the cylinder head.

28. Fill the cooling system.

29. Install the valve rocker cover. Connect the carburetor air vent tube.

30. Connect the PCV vent hose at the carburetor spacer fitting. Insert the PCV valve with the vent hose attached, into the valve rocker arm cover grommet. Install the air cleaner, start the engine and check for leaks.

V6 Engines

▶ See Figures 94 and 95

1. Drain the cooling system. Disconnect the negative battery cable.

✳✳ CAUTION

When draining the coolant, keep in mind that cats and dogs are attracted by the ethylene glycol antifreeze, and are quite likely to drink any that is left in an uncovered container or in puddles on the ground. This will prove fatal in sufficient quantity. Always drain the coolant into a sealable container. Coolant should be reused unless it is contaminated or several years old.

2. If the right cylinder head is to be removed:

a. Disconnect Thermactor® diverter valve and hose assembly at the bypass valve and downstream air tube.

b. Remove the assembly.

c. Remove the accessory drive idler.

d. Remove the alternator.

e. Remove the Thermactor® pump pulley.

f. Remove the alternator bracket.

g. Remove the PCV valve.

3. If the left cylinder head is being removed:

a. If equipped with air conditioning, remove compressor from its bracket but do not disconnect the refrigerant lines. Move the compressor aside. Remove the mounting bracket from the cylinder head.

b. If equipped with power steering, remove the pump, leaving lines connected. Place the pump aside positioning it so no fluid leaks out. Remove the mounting bracket from the cylinder head.

4. Remove the intake manifold and carburetor as an assembly.

5. Remove the rocker arm cover attaching screws. Loosen the silicone rubber gasket material by inserting a putty knife under the cover flange. Work the cover loose and remove. **The plastic rocker arm covers will break if excessive force is applied when prying loose.**

6. Disconnect the exhaust manifold(s) from the muffler inlet pipe(s).

7. Loosen the rocker arm stud nuts so that the rocker arms can be rotated to the side. Remove the pushrods and identify them so that they can be reinstalled in their original positions.

8. Remove the cylinder head bolts and lift the cylinder head from the block.

To install:

9. Clean the cylinder head, intake manifold, the valve cover and the head gasket surfaces.

10. A specially treated composition head gasket is used. Do not apply sealer to a composition gasket. Position the new gasket over the locating dowels on the cylinder block. Then, position the cylinder head on the block and install the attaching bolts.

11. Apply sealant to the specified cylinder head bolts (short bolts nearest the exhaust manifold), lubricate the remaining bolts and install.

12. Tighten bolts in sequence as follows: 47 ft. lbs., 55 ft. lbs., 63 ft. lbs., 74 ft. lbs. Back-off the bolts 2-3 turns. Repeat tightening sequence.

13. Clean the pushrods. Blow out the oil passage in the rods with compressed air. Check the pushrods for straightness by rolling them on a piece of glass. Never try to straighten a pushrod; always replace it.

14. Apply Lubriplate® to the ends of the pushrods and install them in their original positions.

15. Apply Lubriplate® to the rocker arms and their fulcrum seats and install the rocker arms. Adjust the valves.

➡**If the original valve train components are being reinstalled, a valve clearance check is not required.**

16. Position a new gasket(s) on the muffler inlet pipe(s) as necessary. Connect the exhaust manifold(s) at the muffler inlet pipe(s).

17. Install the intake manifold and related parts.

18. Apply a ⅛-³⁄₁₆ bead of silicone sealant the the rocker arm cover(s). Install within 15 minutes or the sealant will set up.

19. If the right cylinder head was removed:

a. Install the PVC valve.

b. Install the alternator bracket and alternator.

c. Install the Thermactor® pump assembly.

d. Install the accessory drive idler.

e. Install the Thermactor® assembly (diverter valve, hose, and air tube).

20. If the left cylinder head was removed:

a. Attach the A/C compressor mounting bracket. Install the A/C compressor.

b. Attach the power steering pump bracket. Install the power steering pump.

21. Fill the cooling system and check for leaks.

➡**This engine has an aluminium cylinder head and requires a special coolant to prevent corrosion.**

8-255, 302, 351W

▶ See Figure 96

1. Drain the cooling system. Disconnect the negative battery cable.

✳✳ CAUTION

When draining the coolant, keep in mind that cats and dogs are attracted by the ethylene glycol antifreeze, and are quite likely to drink any that is left in an uncovered container or in puddles on the ground. This will prove fatal in sufficient quantity. Always drain the coolant into a sealable container. Coolant should be reused unless it is contaminated or several years old.

2. Remove the intake manifold and carburetor or EFI throttle body.

3. Remove the rocker arm cover(s).

4. If the right cylinder head is to be removed, loosen the alternator adjusting arm bolt and remove the alternator mounting bracket bolt and spacer. Swing the alternator down and out of the way. Remove the ignition coil and the air

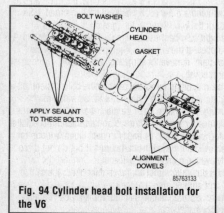

Fig. 94 Cylinder head bolt installation for the V6

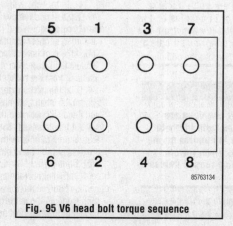

Fig. 95 V6 head bolt torque sequence

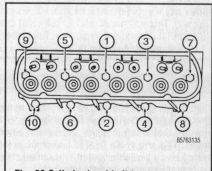

Fig. 96 Cylinder head bolt torque sequence for 8-255, 8-302, 8-351W, 8-351M, 8-360, 8-390, 8-400 and 8-460

cleaner inlet duct from the right cylinder head assembly. Remove the ground strap at rear of head, if equipped. If the engine is equipped with Thermactor exhaust emission control system, remove the air pump and bracket. Disconnect the hose from the rocker arm cover.

5. If the left cylinder head is being removed, remove the bolts fastening the accelerator shaft assembly at the front of the cylinder head. On vehicles equipped with air conditioning, the system must be discharged if the compressor is to be removed. The procedure is best left to an air conditioning specialist. Persons not familiar with A/C systems can be easily injured when working on the systems. If possible remove compressor from its bracket but do not disconnect the refrigerant lines. Move the compressor aside.

6. Disconnect the exhaust manifold(s) from the muffler inlet pipe(s).

7. Loosen the rocker arm stud nuts so that the rocker arms can be rotated to the side. Remove the pushrods and identify them so that they can be reinstalled in their original positions.

8. Remove the cylinder head bolts and lift the cylinder head from the block.

To install:

9. Clean the cylinder head, intake manifold, the valve cover and the head gasket surfaces.

10. A specially treated composition head gasket is used. Do not apply sealer to a composition gasket. Position the new gasket over the locating dowels on the cylinder block. Then, position the cylinder head on the block and install the attaching bolts.

11. The cylinder head bolts are tightened in 3 progressive steps. Tighten all the bolts in the proper sequence to 50 ft. lbs., 60 ft. lbs., and then 72 ft. lbs. for the 8-255 and 302, or, 85 ft. lbs., 95 ft. lbs., then 112 ft. lbs. on the 8-351W.

12. Clean the pushrods. Blow out the oil passage in the rods with compressed air. Check the pushrods for straightness by rolling them on a piece of glass. Never try to straighten a pushrod; always replace it.

13. Apply Lubriplate® to the ends of the pushrods and install them in their original positions.

14. Apply Lubriplate® to the rocker arms and their fulcrum seats and install the rocker arms. Adjust the valves.

15. Position a new gasket(s) on the muffler inlet pipe(s) as necessary. Connect the exhaust manifold(s) at the muffler inlet pipe(s).

16. If the right cylinder head was removed, install the alternator, ignition coil and air cleaner duct on the right cylinder head. Adjust the drive belt. If the left cylinder head was removed, install the accelerator shaft assembly at the front of the cylinder head.

17. Clean the valve rocker arm cover and the cylinder head gasket surfaces. Place the new gaskets in the covers, making sure that the tabs of the gasket engage the notches provided in the cover. Install the compressor. If it was discharged, charge, evaluate,
and leak test the system. Let an air conditioning specialist do this.

18. Install the intake manifold and related parts.

8-351M, 8-400

▶ See Figure 96

1. Drain the cooling system. Disconnect the negative battery cable.

❊❊ CAUTION

When draining the coolant, keep in mind that cats and dogs are attracted by the ethylene glycol antifreeze, and are quite likely to drink any that is left in an uncovered container or in puddles on the ground. This will prove fatal in sufficient quantity. Always drain the coolant into a sealable container. Coolant should be reused unless it is contaminated or several years old.

2. Remove the intake manifold and carburetor.

3. Remove the rocker arm cover(s).

4. If the right cylinder head is to be removed, loosen the alternator adjusting arm bolt and remove the alternator mounting bracket bolt and spacer. Swing the alternator down and out of the way. Remove the ignition coil and the air cleaner inlet duct from the right cylinder head assembly. Remove the ground strap at rear of head, if equipped. If the engine is equipped with Thermactor exhaust emission control system, remove the air pump and bracket. Disconnect the hose from the rocker arm cover.

5. If the left cylinder head is being removed, remove the bolts fastening the accelerator shaft assembly at the front of the cylinder head. On vehicles equipped with air conditioning, the system must be discharged if the compres-

sor is to be removed. The procedure is best left to an air conditioning specialist. Persons not familiar with A/C systems can be easily injured when working on the systems. If possible remove compressor from its bracket but do not disconnect the refrigerant lines. Move the compressor aside.

6. Disconnect the exhaust manifold(s) from the muffler inlet pipe(s).

7. Loosen the rocker arm stud nuts so that the rocker arms can be rotated to the side. Remove the pushrods and identify them so that they can be reinstalled in their original positions.

8. Remove the cylinder head bolts and lift the cylinder head from the block.

To install:

9. Clean the cylinder head, intake manifold, the valve cover and the head gasket surfaces.

10. A specially treated composition head gasket is used. Do not apply sealer to a composition gasket. Position the new gasket over the locating dowels on the cylinder block. Then, position the cylinder head on the block and install the attaching bolts.

11. The cylinder head bolts are tightened in 3 progressive steps. Tighten all the bolts in the proper sequence to 75 ft. lbs., 95 ft. lbs., and then to 105 ft. lbs.

12. Clean the pushrods. Blow out the oil passage in the rods with compressed air. Check the pushrods for straightness by rolling them on a piece of glass. Never try to straighten a pushrod; always replace it.

13. Apply Lubriplate® to the ends of the pushrods and install them in their original positions.

14. Apply Lubriplate® to the rocker arms and their fulcrum seats and install the rocker arms. Adjust the valves.

15. Position a new gasket(s) on the muffler inlet pipe(s) as necessary. Connect the exhaust manifold(s) at the muffler inlet pipe(s).

16. If the right cylinder head was removed, install the alternator, ignition coil and air cleaner duct on the right cylinder head. Adjust the drive belt. If the left cylinder head was removed, install the accelerator shaft assembly at the front of the cylinder head.

17. Clean the valve rocker arm cover and the cylinder head gasket surfaces. Place the new gaskets in the covers, making sure that the tabs of the gasket engage the notches provided in the cover. Install the compressor. If it was discharged, charge, evaluate, and leak test the system. Let an air conditioning specialist do this.

18. Install the intake manifold and related parts.

8-360, 8-390

▶ See Figure 96

1. Drain the cooling system. Disconnect the negative battery cable.

❊❊ CAUTION

When draining the coolant, keep in mind that cats and dogs are attracted by the ethylene glycol antifreeze, and are quite likely to drink any that is left in an uncovered container or in puddles on the ground. This will prove fatal in sufficient quantity. Always drain the coolant into a sealable container. Coolant should be reused unless it is contaminated or several years old.

2. Remove the intake manifold and carburetor.

3. Remove the rocker arm cover(s).

4. If the right cylinder head is to be removed, loosen the alternator adjusting arm bolt and remove the alternator mounting bracket bolt and spacer. Swing the alternator down and out of the way. Remove the ignition coil and the air cleaner inlet duct from the right cylinder head assembly. Remove the ground strap at rear of head, if equipped. If the engine is equipped with Thermactor® exhaust emission control system, remove the air pump and bracket. Disconnect the hose from the rocker arm cover.

5. If the left cylinder head is being removed, remove the bolts fastening the accelerator shaft assembly at the front of the cylinder head. On vehicles equipped with air conditioning, the system must be discharged if the compressor is to be removed. The procedure is best left to an air conditioning specialist. Persons not familiar with A/C systems can be easily injured when working on the systems. If possible remove compressor from its bracket but do not disconnect the refrigerant lines. Move the compressor aside.

6. Disconnect the exhaust manifold(s) from the muffler inlet pipe(s).

7. Loosen the rocker arm stud nuts so that the rocker arms can be rotated to the side. Remove the pushrods and identify them so that they can be reinstalled in their original positions.

8. Remove the cylinder head bolts and lift the cylinder head from the block.

To install:

9. Clean the cylinder head, intake manifold, the valve cover and the head gasket surfaces.

10. A specially treated composition head gasket is used. Do not apply sealer to a composition gasket. Position the new gasket over the locating dowels on the cylinder block. Then, position the cylinder head on the block and install the attaching bolts.

11. The cylinder head bolts are tightened in 3 progressive steps. Tighten all the bolts in the proper sequence to 70 ft. lbs., 80 ft. lbs., and then to 90 ft. lbs.

12. Clean the pushrods. Blow out the oil passage in the rods with compressed air. Check the pushrods for straightness by rolling them on a piece of glass. Never try to straighten a pushrod; always replace it.

13. Apply Lubriplate® to the ends of the pushrods and install them in their original positions.

14. Apply Lubriplate® to the rocker arms and their fulcrum seats and install the rocker arms. Adjust the valves.

15. Position a new gasket(s) on the muffler inlet pipe(s) as necessary. Connect the exhaust manifold(s) at the muffler inlet pipe(s).

16. If the right cylinder head was removed, install the alternator, ignition coil and air cleaner duct on the right cylinder head. Adjust the drive belt. If the left cylinder head was removed, install the accelerator shaft assembly at the front of the cylinder head.

17. Clean the valve rocker arm cover and the cylinder head gasket surfaces. Place the new gaskets in the covers, making sure that the tabs of the gasket engage the notches provided in the cover. Install the compressor. If it was discharged, charge, evaluate, and leak test the system. Let an air conditioning specialist do this.

18. Install the intake manifold and related parts.

8-460

▶ **See Figure 96**

1. Drain the cooling system. Disconnect the negative battery cable.

※※ **CAUTION**

When draining the coolant, keep in mind that cats and dogs are attracted by the ethylene glycol antifreeze, and are quite likely to drink any that is left in an uncovered container or in puddles on the ground. This will prove fatal in sufficient quantity. Always drain the coolant into a sealable container. Coolant should be reused unless it is contaminated or several years old.

2. Remove the intake manifold and carburetor as an assembly.

3. Disconnect the exhaust pipe from the exhaust manifold.

4. Loosen the air conditioning compressor drive belt, if so equipped.

5. Loosen the alternator attaching bolts and remove the bolt attaching alternator bracket to the right cylinder head.

6. Disconnect the air conditioning compressor from the engine and move it aside, out of the way. Do not discharge the air conditioning system.

7. Remove the bolts securing the power steering reservoir bracket to the left cylinder head. Position the reservoir and bracket out of the way.

8. Remove the valve rocker arm covers. Remove the rocker arm bolts, rocker arms, oil deflectors, fulcrums and pushrods in sequence so that they can be reinstalled in their original positions.

9. Remove the cylinder head bolts and lift the head and exhaust manifold off the engine. If necessary, pry at the forward corners of the cylinder head against the casting bosses provided on the cylinder block. Do not damage the gasket mating surfaces of the cylinder head and block by prying against them.

10. Remove all gasket material from the cylinder head and block. Clean all gasket material from the mating surfaces of the intake manifold. If the exhaust manifold was removed, clean the mating surfaces of the cylinder head and exhaust manifold. Apply a thin coat of graphite grease to the cylinder head exhaust port areas and install the exhaust manifold.

11. Position two long cylinder head bolts in the two rear lower bolt holes of the left cylinder head. Place a long cylinder head bolt in the rear lower bolt hole of the right cylinder head. Use rubber bands to keep the bolts in position until the cylinder heads are installed on the cylinder block.

12. Position new cylinder head gaskets on the cylinder block dowels. Do not apply sealer to the gaskets, heads, or block.

13. Place the cylinder heads on the block, guiding the exhaust manifold

studs into the exhaust pipe connections. Install the remaining cylinder head bolts. The longer bolts go in the lower row of holes.

14. Tighten all the cylinder head attaching bolts in the proper sequence in three stages: 80 ft. lbs., 110 ft. lbs., and finally to 140 ft. lbs. When this procedure is used, it is not necessary to retorque the heads after extended use.

15. Make sure that the oil holes in the pushrods are open and install the pushrods in their original positions. Place a dab of Lubriplate® to the ends of the pushrods before installing them.

16. Lubricate® and install the valve rockers. Make sure that the pushrods remain seated in their lifters.

17. Connect the exhaust pipes to the exhaust manifolds.

18. Install the intake manifold and carburetor assembly. Tighten the intake manifold attaching bolts in the proper sequence to 25-30 ft. lbs.

19. Install the air conditioning compressor to the engine.

20. Install the power steering reservoir to the engine.

21. Apply oil-resistant sealer to one side of the new valve cover gaskets and lay the cemented side in place in the valve cover. Install the covers.

22. Install the alternator to the right cylinder head and adjust the alternator drive belt tension.

23. Adjust the air conditioning compressor drive belt tension.

24. Fill the radiator with coolant.

25. Start the engine and check for leaks.

Diesel Engines

▶ **See Figures 97 and 98**

1. Open the hood and disconnect the negative cables from both batteries.

2. Drain the cooling system and remove the radiator fan shroud halves.

※※ **CAUTION**

When draining the coolant, keep in mind that cats and dogs are attracted by the ethylene glycol antifreeze, and are quite likely to drink any that is left in an uncovered container or in puddles on the ground. This will prove fatal in sufficient quantity. Always drain the coolant into a sealable container. Coolant should be reused unless it is contaminated or several years old.

3. Remove the radiator fan and clutch assembly using special tool T83T-6312-A and B. This tool is available through the Owatonna Tool Co. whose address is listed in the front of this boot, or through Ford Dealers. It is also available through many tool rental shops.

➡ **The fan clutch uses a left hand thread and must be removed by turning the nut clockwise.**

4. Label and disconnect the wiring from the alternator.

5. Remove the adjusting bolts and pivot bolts from the alternator and the vacuum pump and remove both units.

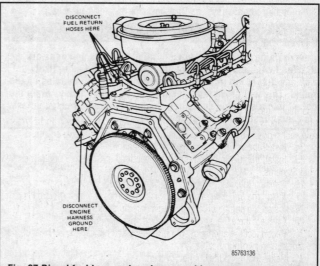

Fig. 97 Diesel fuel hose and engine ground harness connections

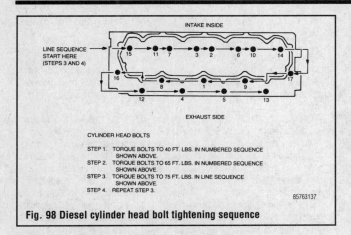

Fig. 98 Diesel cylinder head bolt tightening sequence

6. Remove the fuel filter lines and cap to prevent fuel leakage.

7. Remove the alternator, vacuum pump, and fuel filter brackets with the fuel filter attached.

8. Remove the heater hose from the cylinder head.

9. Remove the fuel injection pump as described in Section 5 under Diesel Fuel Systems.

10. Remove the intake manifold and valley cover.

11. Jack up the truck and safely support it with jackstands.

12. Disconnect the exhaust pipes from the exhaust manifolds.

13. Remove the clamp holding the engine oil dipstick tube in place and the bolt attaching the transmission oil dipstick to the cylinder head.

14. Lower the truck.

15. Remove the engine oil dipstick tube.

16. Remove the valve covers, rocker arms and pushrods. Keep the pushrods in order so they can be returned to their original positions.

17. Remove the nozzles and glow plugs as described in Section 5 under Diesel Fuel Systems.

18. Remove the cylinder head bolts and attach lifting eyes, using special tool T70P-6000 or equivalent, to each end of the cylinder heads.

19. Carefully lift the cylinder heads out of the engine compartment and remove the head gaskets.

➡The cylinder head prechambers may fall out of the heads upon removal.

To install:

20. Position the cylinder head gasket on the engine block and carefully lower the cylinder head in place.

➡Use care in installing the cylinder heads to prevent the prechambers from falling out into the cylinder bores.

21. Install the cylinder head bolt and torque in 4 steps using the sequence shown in the illustration.

➡Lubricate the threads and the mating surfaces of the bolt heads and washers with engine oil.

22. Dip the pushrod ends in clean engine oil and install the pushrods with the copper colored ends toward the rocker arms, making sure the pushrods are fully seated in the tappet pushrod seats.

23. Install the rocker arms and posts in their original positions. Apply Lubriplate® grease to the valve stem tips. Turn the engine over by hand until the timing mark is at the 11 o'clock position as viewed from the front. Install the rocker arm posts, bolts, and torque to 27 ft. lbs. Install the valve covers.

24. Install the valley pan and the intake manifold.

25. Install the fuel injection pump as described in Section 5 under Diesel Fuel Systems.

26. Connect the heater hose to the cylinder head.

27. Install the fuel filter, alternator, vacuum pump, and their drive belts.

28. Install the engine oil and transmission dip stick.

29. Connect the exhaust pipe the the exhaust manifolds.

30. Reconnect the alternator wiring harness and replace the air cleaner. Connect both battery ground cables.

31. Refill and bleed the cooling system.

32. Run the engine and check for fuel, coolant and exhaust leaks.

➡If necessary, purge the high pressure fuel lines of air by loosening the connector one half to one turn and cranking the engine until a solid stream of fuel, free from any bubbles, flows from the connections.

33. Check the injection pump timing. Refer to section 5 for these procedures.

34. Install the radiator fan and clutch assembly using special tools T83T-6312A and B or equivalent.

Valves

REMOVAL & INSTALLATION

◆ **See Figures 99, 100, 101, 102 and 103**

1. Place the head on its side, on blocks of wood or install a pair of head-holding brackets made especially for valve removal.

2. Use a socket slightly larger than the valve stem and keepers, place the socket over the valve stem and gently hit the socket with a plastic hammer to break loose any varnish buildup.

3. Using a valve spring compressor (the locking C-clamp type is the easiest kind to use) compress a valve.

4. Remove the valve keepers, retainer, spring shield and valve spring.

5. Put the parts in a separate container numbered for the cylinder being worked on; do not mix them with other parts removed.

6. Remove and discard the valve stem oil seals. A new seal will be used at assembly time.

7. Remove the valves from the cylinder head and place them, in order, through numbered holes punched in a stiff piece of cardboard or wood valve holding stick.

➡The exhaust valve stems, on some engines, are equipped with small metal caps. Take care not to lose the caps. Make sure to reinstall them at assembly time. Replace any caps that are worn.

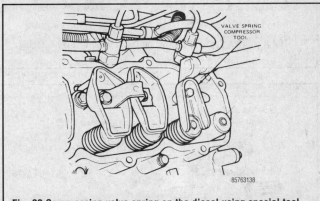

Fig. 99 Compressing valve spring on the diesel using special tool

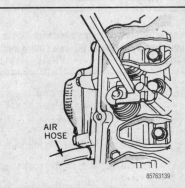

Fig. 100 Compressing gasoline engine valve spring. Note spring compressor position and air hose. Cylinder at TDC

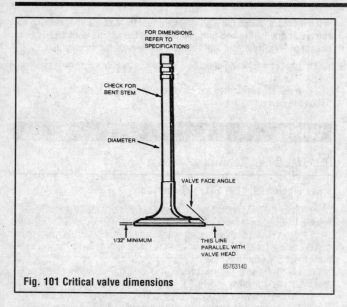

Fig. 101 Critical valve dimensions

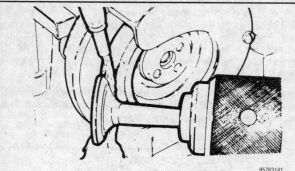

Fig. 102 A well-equipped machine shop can handle valve refacing jobs

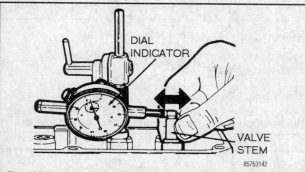

Fig. 103 Measuring valve stem-to-guide clearance. Make sure the indicator is mounted at 90 degrees to the valve stem and as close to the guide as possible

8. Use an electric drill and rotary wire brush to clean the intake and exhaust valve ports, combustion chamber and valve seats. In some cases, the carbon will need to be chipped away. Use a blunt pointed drift for carbon chipping. Be careful around the valve seat areas.

9. Use a wire valve guide cleaning brush and safe solvent to clean the valve guides.

10. Clean the valves with a revolving wires brush. Heavy carbon deposits may be removed with the blunt drift.

➥ When using a wire brush to clean carbon on the valve ports, valves etc., be sure that the deposits are actually removed, rather than burnished.

11. Wash and clean all valve springs, keepers, retaining caps etc., in safe solvent.

12. Clean the head with a brush and safe solvent and wipe dry.

13. Check the head for cracks. Cracks in the cylinder head usually start around an exhaust valve seat because it is the hottest part of the combustion chamber. If a crack is suspected but cannot be detected visually have the area checked with dye penetrant or similar method, have check performed by the machine shop.

14. After all cylinder head parts are reasonably clean, check the valve stem-to-guide clearance. If a dial indicator is not on hand, a visual inspection can give you a fairly good idea if the guide, valve stem or both are worn.

15. Insert the valve into the guide until slight away from the valve seat. Wiggle the valve sideways. A small amount of wobble is normal, excessive wobble means a worn guide or valve stem. If a dial indicator is on hand, mount the indicator so that the stem of the valve is at 90 degrees to the valve stem, as close to the valve guide as possible. Move the valve off the seat, and measure the valve guide-to-stem clearance by rocking the stem back and forth to actuate the dial indicator. Measure the valve stem using a micrometer and compare to specifications to determine whether stem or guide wear is causing excessive clearance.

16. The valve guide, if worn, must be repaired before the valve seats can be resurfaced. Ford supplies valves with oversize stems to fit valve guides that are reamed to oversize for repair. The machine shop will be able to handle the guide reaming for you. In some cases, if the guide is not too badly worn, knurling may be all that is required.

17. Have the valves and valve seats refaced. The valve seats should be a true 45 degrees angle. Remove only enough material to clean up any pits or grooves. Be sure the valve seat is not too wide or narrow. Use a 60 degrees grinding wheel to remove material from the bottom of the seat for raising and a 30 degrees grinding wheel to remove material from the top of the seat to narrow.

18. After the valves are refaced by machine, hand lap them to the valve seat. Clean the grinding compound off and check the position of face-to-seat contact. Contact should be close to the center of the valve face. If contact is close to the top edge of the valve, narrow the seat; if too close to the bottom edge, raise the seat.

19. Valves should be refaced to a true angle of 44 degrees. Remove only enough metal to clean up the valve face or to correct runout. If the edge of a valve head, after machining, is 1/32 inch (0.8mm) or less replace the valve. The tip of the valve stem should also be dressed on the valve grinding machine, however, do not remove more than 0.010 inch (0.254mm).

20. After all valve and valve seats have been machined, check the remaining valve train parts (springs, retainers, keepers, etc.) for wear. Check the valve springs for straightness and tension.

21. Install the valves in the cylinder head.

22. Install new valve stem oil seals (and install exhaust metal caps if so equipped).

23. Using a valve spring compressor (the locking C-clamp type is the easiest kind to use), install the valve keepers, retainer, spring shield and valve spring.

24. Check the valve spring installed height, shim or replace as necessary.

CLEANING AND INSPECTION

▶ **See Figures 104 and 105**

1. With the valves installed to protect the valve seats, remove deposits from the combustion chambers and valve heads with a scraper and a wire brush. Be

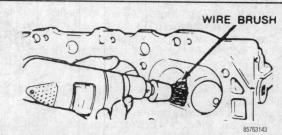

Fig. 104 Removing combustion chamber deposits with a drill-mounted wire brush

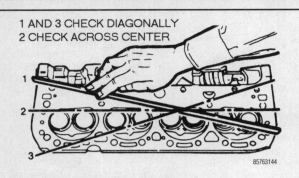

Fig. 105 Checking the cylinder head for warpage

careful not to damage the cylinder head gasket surface. After the valves are removed, clean the valve guide bores with a valve guide cleaning tool. Using cleaning solvent to remove dirt, grease and other deposits, clean all bolts holes; be sure the oil passage is clean (V8 engines).

2. Remove all deposits from the valves with a fine wire brush or buffing wheel.

3. Inspect the cylinder heads for cracks or excessively burned areas in the exhaust outlet ports.

4. Check the cylinder head for cracks and inspect the gasket surface for burrs and nicks. Replace the head if it is cracked.

5. On cylinder heads that incorporate valve seat inserts, check the inserts for excessive wear, cracks, or looseness.

RESURFACING

When the cylinder head is removed, check the flatness of the cylinder head gasket surfaces.

1. Place a straightedge across the gasket surface of the cylinder head. Using feeler gauges, determine the clearance at the center of the straightedge.

2. If warpage exceeds 0.003 inch (0.076mm) in a 6 inch (152mm) span, or 0.006 inch (0.152mm) over the total length, the cylinder head must be resurfaced.

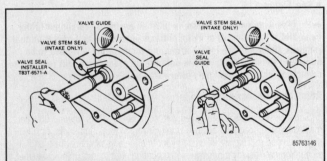

Fig. 106 Installing the valve stem seals on the diesel

3. If necessary to refinish the cylinder head gasket surface, do not plane or grind off more than 0.254mm (0.010 inch) from the original gasket surface.

➡ **When milling the cylinder heads of V6 or V8 engines, the intake manifold mounting position is altered, and must be corrected by milling the manifold flange a proportionate amount. Consult an experienced machinist about this.**

Valve Stem Oil Seals

▶ **See Figures 106 and 107**

When installing valve stem oil seals, ensure that a small amount of oil is able to pass the seal to lubricate the valve stems and guide walls, otherwise, excessive wear will occur.

Valve Springs

CHECKING VALVE SPRINGS

▶ **See Figures 108 and 109**

Place the valve spring on a flat surface next to a carpenter's square. Measure the height of the spring, and rotate the spring against the edge of the square to measure distortion. If the spring height varies (by comparison) by more than 1/16 inch (1.6mm) or if the distortion exceeds 1/16 inch (1.6mm), replace the spring.

Have the valve springs tested for spring pressure at the installed and compressed (installed height minus valve lift) height using a valve spring tester. Springs should be within one pound, plus or minus each other. Replace springs as necessary.

VALVE SPRING INSTALLED HEIGHT

After installing the valve spring, measure the distance between the spring mounting pad and the lower edge of the spring retainer. Compare the measurement to specifications. If the installed height is incorrect, add shim washers between the spring mounting pad and the spring. Use only washers designed for valve springs, available at most parts houses.

Valve Lifters

HYDRAULIC VALVE LIFTER INSPECTION

▶ **See Figures 110, 111, 112 and 113**

➡ **The lifters used on diesel engines require a special test fluid, kerosene is not satisfactory.**

Remove the lifters from their bores and remove any gum and varnish with safe solvent. Check the lifters for concave wear. If the bottom of the lifter is worn concave or flat, replace the lifter. Lifters are built with a convex bottom, flatness indicates wear. If a worn lifter is detected, carefully check the camshaft for wear.

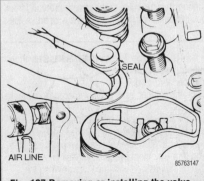

Fig. 107 Removing or installing the valve stem seal on all gasoline engines

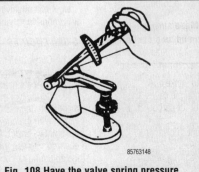

Fig. 108 Have the valve spring pressure checked at a machine shop. Make sure the readings are within specifications

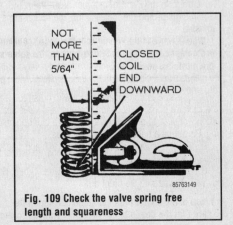

Fig. 109 Check the valve spring free length and squareness

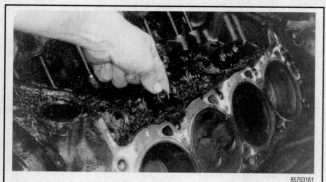

Fig. 110 Removing the valve lifter from a gasoline V8; 1983 8-302 shown

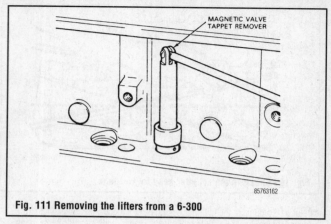

Fig. 111 Removing the lifters from a 6-300

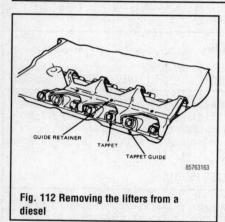

Fig. 112 Removing the lifters from a diesel

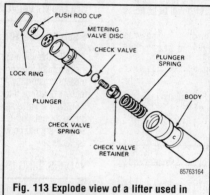

Fig. 113 Explode view of a lifter used in all gasoline engines

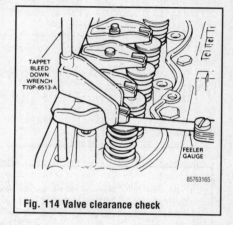

Fig. 114 Valve clearance check

To test lifter leak down, submerge the lifter in a container of kerosene. Chuck a used pushrod or its equivalent into a drill press. Position the container of kerosene so the pushrod acts on the lifter plunger. Pump the lifter with the drill press until resistance increases. Pump several more times to bleed any air from the lifter. Apply very firm, constant pressure to the lifter and observe the rate which fluid bleeds out of the lifter. If the lifter bleeds down very quickly (less than 15 seconds), the lifter should be replaced. If the time exceeds 60 seconds, the lifter is sticking and should be cleaned or replaced. If the lifter is operating properly (leak down time 15-60 seconds) and not worn, lubricate and reinstall in engine.

➡️Always inspect the valve pushrods for wear, straightness and oil blockage. Damaged pushrods will cause erratic valve operation.

VALVE CLEARANCE

Engines with hydraulic lifters require no periodic adjustment to the valve train. In the event of cylinder head removal or any operation that requires disturbing the rocker arms, the rocker arms will have to be adjusted.

When a valve in the engine is in the closed position, the valve lifter is resting on the base circle of the camshaft lobe and the pushrod is in its lowest position. To remove this additional clearance from the valve train, the valve lifter expands to maintain zero clearance in the valve system. When a rocker arm is loosened or removed from the engine, the lifter expands to its fullest travel. When the rocker arm is reinstalled on the engine, the proper valve setting is obtained by tightening the rocker arm to a specified limit. With the lifter fully expanded, and the camshaft lobe is on a high point, excessive torque will required to compress the lifter and obtain the proper setting. Because of this, when any component of the valve system has been removed, a valve adjustment procedure must be followed to ensure that the rocker arm is reinstalled on the engine and tightened with the camshaft lobe for that cylinder at its low position. See VALVE LASH ADJUSTMENT below.

VALVE LASH ADJUSTMENT

▶ See Figure 114

➡️Engines with hydraulic lifters require no periodic adjustment to the valve train. In the event of cylinder head removal or any operation that requires disturbing the rocker arms, the rocker arms will have to be adjusted. These procedures are not tune-up procedures, but rebuild procedures to be performed only after valve train reassembly.

Adjustable Rocker Arms

Some early models are equipped with adjustable rockers whereas the later models are equipped with positive stop type rocker mounting studs. Positive stop equipped rockers are adjusted by turning the adjusting nut down until it stops. You can identify a positive stop mounting stud by determining whether or not the shank portion of the stud that is exposed just above the cylinder head is the same diameter as the threaded portion at the top of the stud, to which the rocker arm retaining nut attaches. If the shank portion is larger than the threaded area, it is a positive stop mounting stud. Use the procedure given below for adjusting the valve lash on positive stop type mounting stud equipped vehicles.

6-300 ENGINES

1. Crank the engine until the TDC mark on the crankshaft damper is aligned with timing pointer on the cylinder front cover.
2. Scribe a mark on the damper at this point.
3. Scribe two more marks on the damper, each equally spaced from the first mark (120 degrees apart).
4. With the engine on TDC of the compression stroke, (mark aligned with the pointer) back off the rocker arm adjusting nut until there is endplay in the pushrod. Tighten the adjusting nut until all clearance is removed, then tighten the adjusting nut one additional turn. To determine when all clearance is removed from the rocker arm, turn the pushrod with the fingers. When the pushrod can no longer be turned, all clearance has been removed.

5. Repeat this procedure for each valve, turning the crankshaft ⅓ turn to the next mark each time and following the engine firing order of 1-5-3-6-2-4.

GASOLINE V8—PREFERRED PROCEDURE

▶ See Figure 115

1. Position the piston(s) on TDC of the compression stroke, using the timing mark on the crankshaft pulley as a reference for starting with the No. 1 cylinder. You can tell if a piston is coming up on its compression stroke by removing the spark plug of the cylinder you are working on and placing your thumb over the hole while the engine is cranked over. Air will try to force its way past your thumb when the piston comes upon the compression stroke. Make sure that the high tension coil wire leading to the distributor is removed before cranking the engine. Remove the valve covers.

2. Starting with No. 1 cylinder, and the piston in the position as mentioned above, apply pressure to slowly bleed down the valve lifter until the plunger is completely bottomed.

3. While holding the valve lifter in the fully collapsed position, check the available clearance between the rocker arm and the valve stem tip. Use a feeler gauge.

4. If the clearance is not within the specified amount, rotate the rocker arm stud nut clockwise to decrease the clearance and counterclockwise to increase the clearance. Normally, one turn of the rocker arm stud nut will vary the clearance by 0.066 inch (1.676mm). Check the break-away torque of each stud nut with a torque wrench, turning it counterclockwise. It should be anywhere from 4.5 to 15 ft. lbs. Replace the nut and/or the stud as necessary.

5. When both valves for the No. 1 cylinder have been adjusted, proceed on to the other valves, following the firing order sequence shown in Section 2 of this book.

6. Replace the valve covers and gaskets.

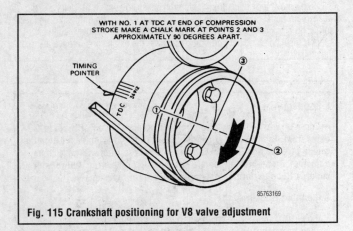

Fig. 115 Crankshaft positioning for V8 valve adjustment

GASOLINE V8—ALTERNATE PROCEDURE

Follow Step 1 of the preferred procedure given above, but instead of collapsing the lifter as in Step 2, loosen the rocker retaining nut until there is endplay present in the pushrod; then tighten the nut to remove all pushrod-to-rocker arm clearance. When the pushrod-to-rocker arm clearance has been eliminated, tighten the stud nut an additional ¾ turn to place the lifter plunger in the desired operating range.

Repeat this procedure for all of the cylinders, using the firing order sequence as a guide. It takes ¼ turn of the crankshaft to bring the next piston in the firing order sequence up to TDC at the end of its compression stroke. Collapsed Tappet Gap Clearance:
- Allowable: 0.071–0.193 inch (1.8–4.9mm)
- Desired: 0.096–0.165 inch (2.4–4.2mm)

Positive Stop Rocker Arms

6-300 ENGINES

▶ See Figures 116 and 117

1. Rotate the crankshaft by hand so that No. 1 piston is at TDC of the compression stroke. Make a chalk mark on the damper at that point, then, make 2

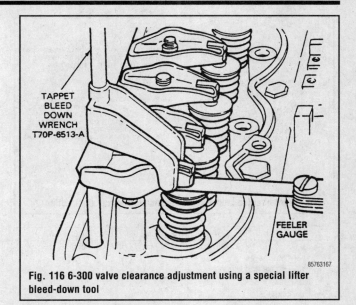

Fig. 116 6-300 valve clearance adjustment using a special lifter bleed-down tool

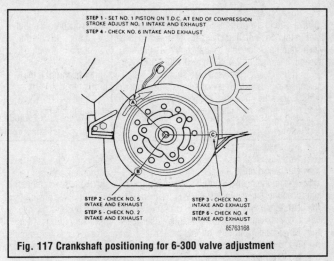

Fig. 117 Crankshaft positioning for 6-300 valve adjustment

more chalk marks about 120 degrees apart, dividing the damper into 3 equal parts. See the accompanying illustration.

2. With No. 1 at TDC, tighten the rocker arm bolts on No. 1 cylinder intake and exhaust to 17–23 ft. lbs. Then, slowly apply pressure, using Lifter Bleed-down wrench T70P-6513-A, or equivalent, to completely bottom the lifter. Take care to avoid excessive pressure that might bend the pushrod. Hold the lifter in this position and check the clearance between the rocker arm and the valve stem tip. Allowable clearance is 2.5–5.0mm (0.10–0.20 in.) with a desired clearance of 3.0–4.5mm (0.125–0.175 in.)

3. If the clearance is less than specified, install a shorter pushrod. If the clearance is greater than specified, install a longer pushrod.

4. Rotate the crankshaft clockwise — viewed from the front — until the next chalk mark is aligned with the timing pointer. Repeat the procedure for No. 5 intake and exhaust.

5. Rotate the crankshaft to the next chalk mark and repeat the procedure for No. 3 intake and exhaust.

6. Repeat the rotation/checking procedure for the remaining valves in firing order, that is: 6–2–4.

GASOLINE V8 ENGINES EXCEPT 8-351M AND 8-400

▶ See Figure 118

1. Rotate the crankshaft by hand so that No. 1 piston is at TDC of the compression stroke. Make a chalk mark on the damper at that point, then, make 2 more chalk marks about 90 degrees apart in a clockwise direction. See the accompanying illustration.

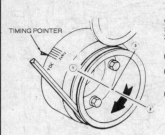

TIMING POINTER

WITH NO 1 AT TDC AT END OF COMPRESSION STROKE MAKE A CHALK MARK AT POINTS 2 AND 3 APPROXIMATELY 90 DEGREES

POSITION 1 - NO. 1 AT TDC AT END OF COMPRESSION STROKE
POSITION 2 - ROTATE THE CRANKSHAFT 180 DEGREES (1/2 REVOLUTION) CLOCKWISE FROM POSITION 1
POSITION 3 - ROTATE THE CRANKSHAFT 270 DEGREES (THREE QUARTER REVOLUTION CLOCK WISE FROM POSITION 2

85763170

Fig. 118 V8 positive stop valve clearance crankshaft positioning

2. With No. 1 at TDC, slowly apply pressure, using Lifter Bleed-down wrench T70P-6513-A, or equivalent, to completely bottom the lifter, on the following valves:
- No. 1 intake and exhaust
- No. 7 intake
- No. 5 exhaust
- No. 8 intake
- No. 4 exhaust

Take care to avoid excessive pressure that might bend the pushrod. Hold the lifter in this position and check the clearance between the rocker arm and the valve stem tip. Allowable clearance is 1.9–4.4mm (0.075–0.175 in.) with a desired clearance of 2.5–3.8mm (0.100-0.150 in.).

3. If the clearance is less than specified, install a shorter pushrod. If the clearance is greater than specified, install a longer pushrod.

4. Rotate the crankshaft clockwise — viewed from the front — 180 degrees, until the next chalk mark is aligned with the timing pointer. Repeat the procedure for:
- No. 5 intake
- No. 2 exhaust
- No. 4 intake
- No. 6 exhaust

5. Rotate the crankshaft to the next chalk mark — 90 degrees — and repeat the procedure for:
- No. 2 intake
- No. 7 exhaust
- No. 3 intake and exhaust
- No. 6 intake
- No. 8 exhaust

8-351M, 8-400 ENGINES

1. Rotate the crankshaft by hand so that No. 1 piston is at TDC of the compression stroke. Make a chalk mark on the damper at that point, then, make 2 more chalk marks about 90 degrees apart in a clockwise direction.

2. With No. 1 at TDC, slowly apply pressure, using Lifter Bleed-down wrench T70P-6513-A, or equivalent, to completely bottom the lifter, on the following valves:
- No. 1 intake and exhaust
- No. 4 intake
- No. 3 exhaust
- No. 8 intake
- No. 7 exhaust

Take care to avoid excessive pressure that might bend the pushrod. Hold the lifter in this position and check the clearance between the rocker arm and the valve stem tip. Allowable clearance is 2.5–5.0mm (0.098–0.198 in.) with a desired clearance of 3.1–4.4mm (0.123–0.173 in.).

3. If the clearance is less than specified, install a shorter pushrod. If the clearance is greater than specified, install a longer pushrod.

4. Rotate the crankshaft clockwise — viewed from the front — 180 degrees, until the next chalk mark is aligned with the timing pointer. Repeat the procedure for:
- No. 3 intake
- No. 2 exhaust
- No. 7 intake
- No. 6 exhaust

5. Rotate the crankshaft to the next chalk mark — 90 degrees — and repeat the procedure for:
- No. 2 intake
- No. 4 exhaust
- No. 5 intake and exhaust
- No. 6 intake
- No. 8 exhaust

Oil Pan

REMOVAL & INSTALLATION

6-300 Engines

▶ See Figure 119

1. Drain the crankcase and also drain the cooling system.

✳✳ CAUTION

When draining the coolant, keep in mind that cats and dogs are attracted by the ethylene glycol antifreeze, and are quite likely to drink any that is left in an uncovered container or in puddles on the ground. This will prove fatal in sufficient quantity. Always drain the coolant into a sealable container. Coolant should be reused unless it is contaminated or several years old.

2. Remove the radiator.
3. Remove the dipstick.
4. Raise the vehicle on a hoist.
5. Remove the engine front support insulator to support bracket nuts and washers on both supports. Raise the front of the engine with a transmission jack and wood block and place 1 inch (25mm) thick wood blocks between the front support insulators and support brackets. Lower the engine and remove the transmission jack.

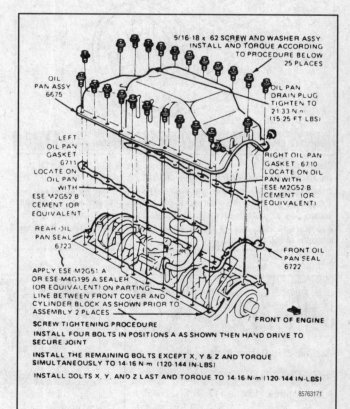

Fig. 119 6-300 oil pan installation

6. Remove the oil pan attaching screws and lower the oil pan onto the crossmember. Remove the two bolts attaching the oil pump pick-up tube to the oil pump. Lower the assembly from the oil pump. Leave it on the bottom of the oil pan. Remove the oil pan and gaskets. Remove the inlet tube and screen from the oil pan.

Installation:

7. Clean the gasket surfaces of the oil pump, oil pan and cylinder block. Remove the rear main bearing cap to oil pan seal and cylinder front cover to oil pan seal. Clean the seal grooves.

8. Apply oil-resistant sealer in the cavities between the bearing cap and cylinder block. Install a new seal in the rear main bearing cap and apply a bead of oil-resistant sealer to the tapered ends of the seal.

9. Install new side gaskets on the oil pan with oil-resistant sealer. Install a new oil pan to cylinder front cover seal on the front cover.

10. Clean the inlet tube and screen assembly and place it in the oil pan.

11. Position the oil pan under the engine. Install the inlet tube and screen assembly on the oil pump with a new gasket. Tighten the bolts to 5-7 ft. lbs. Position the oil pan against the cylinder block and install the attaching bolts. Tighten the bolts in sequence to 10-12 ft. lbs.

12. Raise the engine with a transmission jack and remove the wood blocks from the engine front supports. Lower the engine until the front support insulators are positioned on the support brackets. Install the washers and nuts on the insulator studs and tighten the nuts.

13. Install the starter and connect the starter cable.

14. Lower the vehicle. Install the radiator.

15. Fill the crankcase and cooling system.

16. Start the engine and check for coolant and oil leaks.

V6-232

➡This engine uses RTV silicone sealer in place of a solid pan gasket.

1. Disconnect the battery ground.
2. Remove the oil dipstick.
3. Remove the air cleaner.
4. Remove the bolts attaching the fan shroud to the radiator and position the shroud over the fan.
5. Remove the oil filter.
6. Remove the head pipes from the vehicle.
7. Disconnect the shift linkage at the transmission.
8. Remove the nuts and lockwashers attaching the engine to the engine support insulators.
9. If equipped with an automatic transmission, disconnect the oil cooler line at the left side of the radiator.
10. Raise the engine as high as possible and place wood blocks between the engine and engine supports.
11. Drain the crankcase.

❋❋ CAUTION

The EPA warns that prolonged contact with used engine oil may cause a number of skin disorders, including cancer! You should make every effort to minimize your exposure to used engine oil. Protective gloves should be worn when changing the oil. Wash your hands and any other exposed skin areas as soon as possible after exposure to used engine oil. Soap and water, or waterless hand cleaner should be used.

12. Remove the oil pan attaching bolts and lower the oil pan onto the crossmember.

13. Remove the oil pickup tube and lower the pick-up tube and screen into the oil pan.

14. Remove the oil pan from the vehicle.

Installation:

15. Clean oil pan, inlet tube and gasket surfaces. Inspect the gasket sealing surface for damages and distortion due to overtightening of the bolts. Repair and straighten as required.

16. Place the oil pan on the crossmember. Using a new gasket, install the pickup tube and screen. Make sure that the support bracket engages the No. 2 main bearing cap bolt. Tighten the pick-up tube bolts and nuts to 20 ft. lbs.

17. Install a new rear pan seal in the block. Work the end tabs of the seal into the gaps bewteen the raer main cap and the block.

18. Place a ⅛ in. bead of RTV silicone gasket sealer along the seam where the front cover and block meet. Place a bead of sealer to each end of the rear pan seal at the end tabs.

19. Run a ⅛ in. bead of RTV sealer along the block mating surfaces. At the front cover, increase the width of the bead to ¼ in.

20. Position the oil pan to the cylinder block and install the attaching bolts. Tighten to 8 ft. lbs.

21. Install all remaining components in the reverse order of removal.

8-255, 8-302 (carbureted) and 8-351W

▶ See Figures 120 thru 126

1. Remove the oil dipstick (on pan entry models only).

2. Remove the bolts attaching the fan shroud to the radiator and position the shroud over the fan.

3. Remove the nuts and lockwashers attaching the engine support insulators to the chassis bracket.

4. If equipped with an automatic transmission, disconnect the oil cooler line at the left side of the radiator.

5. Raise the engine and place wood blocks under the engine supports.

6. Drain the crankcase.

❋❋ CAUTION

The EPA warns that prolonged contact with used engine oil may cause a number of skin disorders, including cancer! You should make every effort to minimize your exposure to used engine oil. Protective gloves should be worn when changing the oil. Wash your hands and any other exposed skin areas as soon as possible after exposure to used engine oil. Soap and water, or waterless hand cleaner should be used.

7. Remove the oil pan attaching bolts and lower the oil pan onto the crossmember.

8. Remove the two bolts attaching the oil pump pickup tube to the oil pump. Remove nut attaching oil pump pickup tube to the number 3 main bearing cap stud. Lower the pick-up tube and screen into the oil pan.

9. Remove the oil pan from the vehicle.

Installation:

10. Clean oil pan, inlet tube and gasket surfaces. Inspect the gasket sealing surface for damages and distortion due to overtightening of the bolts. Repair and straighten as required.

11. Position a new oil pan gasket and seal to the cylinder block.

Fig. 120 Removing the engine mount bolts; 8-302 shown

Fig. 121 Wood blocks in position; 8-302 shown

Fig. 122 Removing the front pickup tube-to-pump bolt; 8-302 shown

Fig. 123 Removing the rear pickup tube-to-pump bolt; 8-302 shown

85763175

Fig. 124 Removing the pickup tube-to-bearing cap nut; 8-302 shown

85763176

Fig. 125 Removing the pan; 8-302 shown

85763177

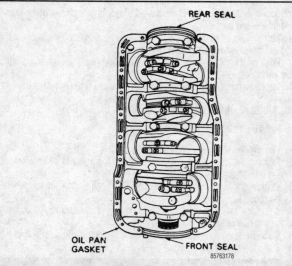

Fig. 126 Oil pan gaskets and seals for the 6-232, 8-255, 8-302 and 8-351W; the 8-351M, 8-400 and 8-460 are similar

85763178

12. Position the oil pick-up tube and screen to the oil pump, and install the lower attaching bolt and gasket loosely. Install nut attaching to number 3 main bearing cap stud.

13. Place the oil pan on the crossmember. Install the upper pick-up tube bolt. Tighten the pick-up tube bolts.

14. Position the oil pan to the cylinder block and install the attaching bolts. Tighten to 10–12 ft. lbs.

8-302 EFI

♦ See Figures 121 thru 127

1. Drain the cooling system.

⁂ CAUTION

When draining the coolant, keep in mind that cats and dogs are attracted by the ethylene glycol antifreeze, and are quite likely to drink any that is left in an uncovered container or in puddles on the ground. This will prove fatal in sufficient quantity. Always drain the coolant into a sealable container. Coolant should be reused unless it is contaminated or several years old.

2. Remove the bolts attaching the fan shroud to the radiator and position the shroud over the fan.

3. Remove the upper intake manifold and throttle body. See Section 5.

4. Remove the nuts and lockwashers attaching the engine support insulators to the chassis bracket.

5. If equipped with an automatic transmission, disconnect the oil cooler line at the left side of the radiator.

6. Remove the exhaust system.

7. Raise the engine and place wood blocks under the engine supports.

8. Drain the crankcase.

⁂ CAUTION

The EPA warns that prolonged contact with used engine oil may cause a number of skin disorders, including cancer! You should make every effort to minimize your exposure to used engine oil. Protective gloves should be worn when changing the oil. Wash your hands and any other exposed skin areas as soon as possible after exposure to used engine oil. Soap and water, or waterless hand cleaner should be used.

9. Support the transmission with a floor jack and remove the transmission crossmember.

10. Remove the oil pan attaching bolts and lower the oil pan onto the crossmember.

11. Remove the two bolts attaching the oil pump pickup tube to the oil pump. Remove nut attaching oil pump pickup tube to the number 3 main bearing cap stud. Lower the pickup tube and screen into the oil pan.

12. Remove the oil pan from the vehicle.

To install:

13. Clean the oil pan, inlet tube and gasket surfaces. Inspect the gasket sealing surface for damages and distortion due to overtightening of the bolts. Repair and straighten as required.

14. Position a new oil pan gasket and seal to the cylinder block.

15. Position the oil pick-up tube and screen to the oil pump, and install the lower attaching bolt and gasket loosely. Install nut attaching to number 3 main bearing cap stud.

16. Place the oil pan on the crossmember. Install the upper pick-up tube bolt. Tighten the pick-up tube bolts.

17. Position the oil pan to the cylinder block and install the attaching bolts. Tighten to 10–12 ft. lbs.

18. Install the transmission crossmember.

19. Raise the engine and remove the blocks under the engine supports. Bolt the engine to the supports.

20. Install the exhaust system.

21. If equipped with an automatic transmission, connect the oil cooler line at the left side of the radiator.

22. Install the nuts and lockwashers attaching the engine support insulators to the chassis bracket.

23. Install the upper intake manifold and throttle body. See Section 5.

24. Install the fan shroud.

25. Fill the crankcase.

26. Fill and bleed the cooling system.

8-360, 8-390

1. Remove the oil dipstick and tube.

2. Drain the crankcase.

⁂ CAUTION

The EPA warns that prolonged contact with used engine oil may cause a number of skin disorders, including cancer! You should make every effort to minimize your exposure to used engine oil. Protective gloves should be worn when changing the oil. Wash your hands and any other exposed skin areas as soon as possible after exposure to used engine oil. Soap and water, or waterless hand cleaner should be used.

3. Remove the oil pan attaching bolts and lower the oil pan onto the axle.

4. Remove the oil pump and pickup tube attaching bolts. Lower the pump and pick-up tube and screen into the oil pan.

5. Rotate the crankshaft so that the throws will clear the pan.

6. Remove the oil pan from the vehicle.

Installation:

7. Clean oil pan, inlet tube and gasket surfaces. Inspect the gasket sealing surface for damages and distortion due to overtightening of the bolts. Repair and straighten as required.

8. Position a new oil pan gasket and seal on the pan using a high-tack gasket sealer.

9. Position a new oil pump gasket on the block, insert the oil pump drive-shaft in the pump and install the pump. DO NOT FORCE IT INTO POSITION! THE SHAFT MAY BE MISASLIGNED!

10. Position the oil pan to the cylinder block and install the attaching bolts. Tighten to 8-10 ft. lbs.

11. Install the dipstick tube and dipstick.

8-351M, 8-400

▶ **See Figures 121 and 126**

1. Raise and support the front end with jackstands placed under the frame rails.

2. Drain the oil.

3. Remove the dipstick and tube.

4. Remove the starter.

5. Unbolt the fan shroud and lay it back over the fan.

6. Remove the engine-to-mount through-bolts.

7. Raise the engine with a jack under the crankshaft damper. Place a wood block between the jack saddle and the damper to protect it. Place blocks cut from a 2x4 piece of lumber between the engine and mounts.

8. Lower the engine onto the blocks and remove the jack.

9. On 4-wheel drive trucks, remove the front wheels and let the drive axle drop to its lowest point.

10. Remove the oil pan bolts and remove the pan.

Installation:

11. Clean the oil pan, inlet tube and gasket surfaces. Inspect the gasket sealing surface for damages and distortion due to overtightening of the bolts. Repair and straighten as required.

12. Position new oil pan gaskets on the pan using a high-tack gasket sealer. Place new seals in the front and rear of the block. Coat the seals with RTV gasket sealer. Coat the block gasket surfaces with non-hardening gasket sealer such as Permatex No.2®

13. Position the pan onto the block and install 2 bolts on each side, finger tight.

14. Install the remaining bolts and torque them to 11-13 ft. lbs. for the 5⁄16 bolts and 7-9 ft. lbs. for the ¼ bolts in a criss-cross pattern.

15. Raise the engine and remove the blocks. Install the engine mount bolts.

16. Install the fan shroud, starter and dipstick tube.

8-460

▶ **See Figures 121, 122, 123 and 126**

1. Raise and support the truck on jackstands. Remove the oil dipstick.

2. Remove the bolts attaching the fan shroud and position it over the fan.

3. Remove the engine support insulators-to-chassis bracket attaching nuts and washers. Disconnect the exhaust pipe at the manifolds.

4. If the vehicle is equipped with an automatic transmission, disconnect the oil cooler line at the left side of the radiator.

5. Raise the engine with a jack placed under the crankshaft damper and a block of wood to act as a cushion. Place wood blocks under the engine supports.

6. Drain the crankcase. Remove the oil filter.

✳✳ CAUTION

The EPA warns that prolonged contact with used engine oil may cause a number of skin disorders, including cancer! You should make every effort to minimize your exposure to used engine oil. Protective gloves should be worn when changing the oil. Wash your hands and any other exposed skin areas as soon as possible after exposure to used engine oil. Soap and water, or waterless hand cleaner should be used.

7. Remove the oil pan attaching screws and lower the oil pan onto the crossmember. Remove the two bolts attaching the oil pump pick-up tube to the oil pump. Lower the assembly from the oil pump. Leave it on the bottom of the oil pan. Remove the oil pan and gaskets. Remove the inlet tube and screen from the oil pan.

To install:

8. In preparation for installation, clean the gasket surfaces of the oil pump, oil pan and cylinder block. Remove the rear main bearing cap-to-oil pan seal and engine front cover-to-oil pan seal. Clean the seal grooves.

9. Position the oil pan front and rear seal on the engine front cover and the rear main bearing cap, respectively. Be sure that the tabs on the seals are over the oil pan gasket.

10. Clean the inlet tube and screen assembly and place it in the oil pan.

11. Position the oil pan under the engine and install the inlet tube and screen assembly on the oil pump with a new gasket. Using new gaskets, position the oil pan against the cylinder block and install the retaining bolts.

12. Install the oil filter.

13. Remove the wood blocks and lower the engine.

14. If the vehicle is equipped with an automatic transmission, connect the oil cooler line at the left side of the radiator.

15. Install the engine support insulators-to-chassis bracket attaching nuts and washers. Connect the exhaust pipe at the manifolds.

16. Install the fan shroud.

17. Install the oil dipstick.

18. Fill the crankcase with oil.

Diesel Engines

▶ **See Figure 127**

1. Disconnect both battery ground cables.

2. Remove the engine oil dipstick.

3. Remove the transmission oil dipstick.

4. Remove the air cleaner and cover the intake opening.

5. Remove the fan and fan clutch.

➡The fan uses left hand threads. Remove them by turning them clockwise.

6. Drain the cooling system.

✳✳ CAUTION

When draining the coolant, keep in mind that cats and dogs are attracted by the ethylene glycol antifreeze, and are quite likely to drink any that is left in an uncovered container or in puddles on the ground. This will prove fatal in sufficient quantity. Always drain the coolant into a sealable container. Coolant should be reused unless it is contaminated or several years old.

7. Disconnect the lower radiator hose.

8. Disconnect the power steering return hose and plug the line and pump.

9. Disconnect the alternator wiring harness.

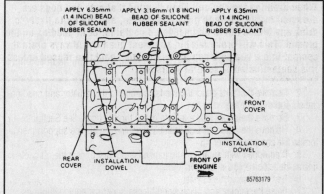

Fig. 127 RTV sealant and dowel location for the diesel oil pan

10. Disconnect the fuel line heater connector from the alternator.
11. Raise and support the front end on jackstand.
12. On trucks with automatic transmission, disconnect the transmission cooler lines at the radiator and plug the lines.
13. Disconnect and plug the fuel pump inlet lines.
14. Drain the crankcase and remove the oil filter.
15. Remove the engine oil filler tube.
16. Disconnect the exhaust pipes at the manifold.
17. Disconnect the muffler inlet pipe from the muffler and remove the pipe.
18. Remove the upper inlet mounting stud from the right exhaust manifold.
19. Unbolt the engine from the No.1 crossmember.
20. Lower the vehicle.
21. Install lifting brackets on the front of the engine.
22. Raise the engine until the transmission contacts the bottom of the firewall.
23. Install wood blocks (2¾ inch on the left side; 2 inch on the right side) between the engine insulators and crossmember.
24. Lower the engine onto the block.
25. Raise and support the front end on jackstand.
26. Remove the flywheel inspection plate.
27. Position fuel pump inlet line No.1 rearward of the crossmember and position the oil cooler lines out of the way
28. Remove the oil pan bolts.
29. Lower the oil pan.

➡ **The oil pan is sealed to the crankcase with RTV silicone sealant in place of a gasket. It may be necessary to separate the pan from the crankcase with a utility knife.**

➡ **The crankshaft may have to be turned to allow the pan to clear the crankshaft throws.**

30. Clean the pan and crankcase mating surfaces thoroughly.
To install:
31. Apply a ⅛ inch bead of RTV silicone sealant to the pan mating surfaces, and a ¼ inch bead on the front and rear covers and in the corners. You have 15 minutes within which to install the pan!
32. Install locating dowels (which you supply) into position.
33. Position the pan on the engine and install the pan bolts loosely.
34. Remove the dowels.
35. Torque the pan bolts to 7 ft. lbs. for ¼ inch-20 bolts; 14 ft. lbs. for ⁵⁄₁₆ inch-18 bolts; 24 ft. lbs. for ⅜ inch-16 bolts.
36. Install the flywheel inspection cover.
37. Lower the truck.
38. Raise the engine and remove the wood blocks.
39. Lower the engine onto the crossmember and remove the lifting brackets.
40. Raise and support the front end on jackstands.
41. Torque the engine-to-crossmember nuts to 70 ft. lbs.
42. Install the upper inlet pipe mounting stud.
43. Install the inlet pipe, using a new gasket.
44. Install the transmission oil filler tube, using a new gasket.
45. Install the oil pan drain plug.
46. Install a new oil filter.
47. Connect the fuel pump inlet line. Make sure that the clip is installed on the crossmember.
48. Connect the transmission cooler lines.
49. Lower the truck.
50. Connect all wiring.
51. Connect the power steering return line.
52. Connect the lower radiator hose.
53. Install the fan and fan clutch.

➡ **The fan uses left hand threads. Install them by turning them counterclockwise.**

54. Remove the cover and install the air cleaner.
55. Install the dipsticks.
56. Fill the crankcase.
57. Fill and bleed the cooling system.
58. Fill the power steering reservoir.
59. Connect the batteries.
60. Run the engine and check for leaks.

Oil Pump

REMOVAL & INSTALLATION

6-300 and V8 Gasoline Engines, exc. the 8-360, 390

▶ **See Figure 128**

1. Remove the oil pan, the oil pump inlet tube and screen assembly. (See Oil Pan Removal.)
2. Remove the oil pump attaching bolts and remove the oil pump gasket and intermediate driveshaft.
To install:
3. Before installing the oil pump, prime it by filling the inlet and outlet port with engine oil and rotating the shaft of the pump to distribute it.
4. Position the new gasket on the pump body and insert the intermediate driveshaft into the pump body.
5. Install the pump and intermediate driveshaft as an assembly. Do not force the pump if it does not seat readily. The driveshaft may be misaligned with the distributor shaft. To align it, rotate the intermediate driveshaft into a new position.
6. Install the oil pump attaching bolts and torque them to 12-15 ft. lbs. on the 6-300; to 20-25 ft. lbs. on the V8s.

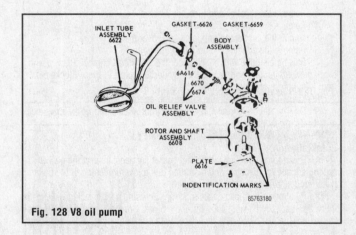

Fig. 128 V8 oil pump

8-360 and 8-390

See the Oil Pan Removal and Installation procedures above.

V6-3.8

1. Remove the oil filter. The oil pump is the assembly to which the oil filter is attached.
2. Remove the pump cover attaching bolts, and the cover.
3. Lift the pump gears out of the pocket in the front cover, and remove the cover gasket and discard.
To install:
4. To install, make sure the gear pocket is lightly packed with petroleum jelly, or liberally coat all gear surfaces with an oil conditioner or a heavy engine oil. **Do not use chassis lubricants.**
5. Install the gears in the cover pocket, making sure the petroleum jelly fills all voids between the gears and the pocket.

✱✱ WARNING

Failure to coat the gears will result in failure of the pump to prime when the engine is started.

6. Position the cover gasket and install the pump cover. Torque the pump cover attaching bolts to 18-22 ft. lbs.

Diesel Engines

◆ **See Figure 129**

1. Remove the oil pan.
2. Remove the oil pick-up tube from the pump.
3. Unbolt and remove the oil pump.
4. Assemble the pick-up tube and pump.
5. Using a new gasket, install the oil pump and torque the bolts to 14 ft. lbs.

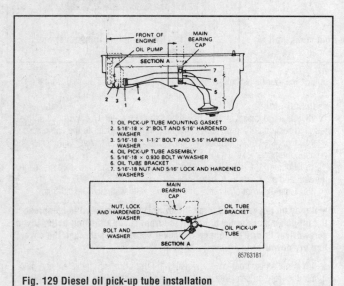

Fig. 129 Diesel oil pick-up tube installation

Fig. 130 Vibration damper bolt removal on gasoline V8s

Crankshaft Pulley (Vibration Damper)

REMOVAL & INSTALLATION

◆ **See Figures 130, 131, 132 and 133**

1. Remove the fan shroud, as required. If necessary, drain the cooling system and remove the radiator. Remove drive belts from pulley.

✳✳ CAUTION

When draining the coolant, keep in mind that cats and dogs are attracted by the ethylene glycol antifreeze, and are quite likely to drink any that is left in an uncovered container or in puddles on the ground. This will prove fatal in sufficient quantity. Always drain the coolant into a sealable container. Coolant should be reused unless it is contaminated or several years old.

2. On those engines with a separate pulley, remove the retaining bolts and separate the pulley from the vibration damper.
3. Remove the vibration damper/pulley retaining bolt from the crankshaft end.
4. Using a puller, remove the damper/pulley from the crankshaft.
5. Upon installation, align the key slot of the pulley hub to the crankshaft key. Complete the assembly in the reverse order of removal. Torque the retaining bolts to the specifications found in the Torque Specifications Chart.

Timing Chain Front Cover and Oil Seal

REMOVAL & INSTALLATION

V6 and Gasoline V8 Except 8-460

◆ **See Figures 134, 135, 136, 137 and 138**

1. Drain the cooling system and the crankcase.

✳✳ CAUTION

When draining the coolant, keep in mind that cats and dogs are attracted by the ethylene glycol antifreeze, and are quite likely to drink any that is left in an uncovered container or in puddles on the ground. This will prove fatal in sufficient quantity. Always drain the coolant into a sealable container. Coolant should be reused unless it is contaminated or several years old.

2. Disconnect the upper and lower radiator hoses from the water pump, transmission oil cooler lines from the radiator, and remove the radiator.
3. Disconnect the heater hose from the water pump. Slide the water pump by-pass hose clamp toward the water pump.
4. Loosen the alternator pivot bolt and the bolt which secures the alternator adjusting arm to the water pump. Position the alternator out of the way.
5. Remove the power steering pump and air conditioning compressor from their mounting brackets, if so equipped.
6. Remove the bolts holding the fan shroud to the radiator, if so equipped. Remove the fan, spacer, pulley and drive belts.

Fig. 131 Removing the pulleys from the damper

Fig. 132 Using a puller

Fig. 133 Lifting off the damper once it breaks free using the puller

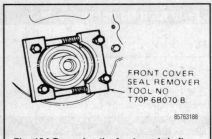

Fig. 134 Removing the front crankshaft seal on the gasoline V8s

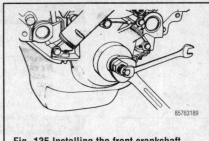

Fig. 135 Installing the front crankshaft seal on the gasoline V8s

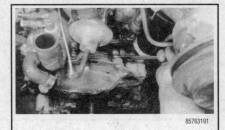

Fig. 136 Removing the front cover bolts; 8-302 shown

Fig. 137 Lifting off the front cover

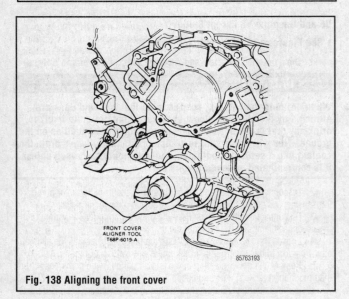

Fig. 138 Aligning the front cover

7. Remove the crankshaft pulley from the crankshaft damper. Remove the damper attaching bolt and washer and remove the damper with a puller. On the 360 or 390 engines, remove the sleeve with a puller.

8. If equipped with a mechanical fuel pump, disconnect the fuel pump outlet line at the fuel pump. Remove the fuel pump attaching bolts and lay the pump to one side with the fuel inlet line still attached.

9. Remove the oil level dipstick and the bolt holding the dipstick tube to the exhaust manifold on the 8-255 and 8-302.

10. Remove the oil pan-to-cylinder front cover attaching bolts. Use a sharp, thin cutting blade to cut the oil pan gasket flush with the cylinder block. Remove the front cover and water pump as an assembly.

11. Discard the front cover gasket.

12. Place the front seal removing tool (Ford part no. T70P-6B070-A or equivalent) into the front cover plate and over the front of the seal. Tighten the two through bolts to force the seal puller under the seal flange, then alternately

tighten the four puller bolts a half turn at a time to pull the oil seal from the cover.

Installation:

13. Coat the gasket surface of the oil pan with sealer. Cut and position the required sections of a new seal on the oil pan. Apply sealer to the corners.

14. Coat the gasket surfaces of the cylinder block and cover with sealer and position the new gasket on the block.

15. Position the front cover on the cylinder block. Use care not to damage the seal and gasket or lose them.

16. Coat the front cover attaching screws with sealer and install them.

➡ **It may be necessary to force the front cover downward to compress the oil pan seal in order to install the front cover attaching bolts. Use a screwdriver or drift to engage the cover screw holes through the cover and pry downward.**

17. Coat a new front cover oil seal with Lubriplate® or equivalent and place it onto the front oil seal alignment and installation tool (Ford part no. T70P-6B070-A or equivalent). Place the tool and the seal onto the end of the crankshaft and push it toward the engine until the seal starts into the front cover.

18. Place the installation screw, washer, and nut onto the end of the crankshaft, then thread the screw into the crankshaft. Tighten the nut against the washer and tool to force the seal into the front cover plate. Remove the tool.

19. Apply Lubriplate® or equivalent to the oil seal rubbing surface of the vibration damper inner hub to prevent damage to the seal. Coat the front of the crankshaft with engine oil for damper installation.

20. To install the damper, line up the damper keyway with the key on the crankshaft, then install the damper onto the crankshaft. Install the cap screw and washer, and tighten the screw to 80 ft. lbs. Install the crankshaft pulley.

21. Assemble the rest of the engine in the reverse order of disassembly.

8-460

▶ **See Figures 138 and 139**

1. Drain the cooling system and crankcase.

✳✳ CAUTION

When draining the coolant, keep in mind that cats and dogs are attracted by the ethylene glycol antifreeze, and are quite likely to drink any that is left in an uncovered container or in puddles on the ground. This will prove fatal in sufficient quantity. Always drain the coolant into a sealable container. Coolant should be reused unless it is contaminated or several years old.

2. Remove the radiator shroud and fan.

3. Disconnect the upper and lower radiator hoses, and the automatic transmission oil cooler lines from the radiator.

4. Remove the radiator upper support and remove the radiator.

5. Loosen the alternator attaching bolts and air conditioning compressor idler pulley and remove the drive belts with the water pump pulley. Remove the bolts attaching the compressor support to the water pump and remove the bracket (support), if so equipped.

6. Remove the crankshaft pulley from the vibration damper. Remove the bolt and washer attaching the crankshaft damper and remove the damper with a puller. Remove the woodruff key from the crankshaft.

7. Loosen the by-pass hose at the water pump, and disconnect the heater return tube at the water pump.

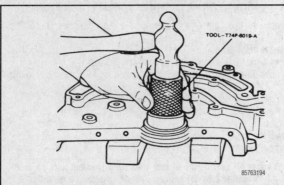

Fig. 139 Installing oil seal into 8-460 front cover; tool makes it easier to drive in seal evenly

8. Disconnect and plug the fuel inlet and outlet lines at the fuel pump, and remove the fuel pump.

9. Remove the bolts attaching the front cover to the cylinder block. Cut the oil pan seal flush with the cylinder block face with a thin knife blade prior to separating the cover from the cylinder block. Remove the cover and water pump as an assembly. Discard the front cover gasket and oil pan seal.

10. Transfer the water pump if a new cover is going to be installed. Clean all of the gasket sealing surfaces on both the front cover and the cylinder block.

11. Coat the gasket surface of the oil pan with sealer. Cut and position the required sections of a new seal on the oil pan. Apply sealer to the corners.

12. Drive out the old front cover oil seal with a pin punch. Clean out the seal recess in the cover. coat a new seal with Lubriplate® or equivalent grease. Install the seal, making sure the seal spring remains in the proper position. A front cover seal tool, Ford part no. T72J-117 or equivalent, makes installation easier.

13. Coat the gasket surfaces of the cylinder block and cover with sealer and position the new gasket on the block.

14. Position the front cover on the cylinder block. Use care not to damage the seal and gasket or mislocate them.

15. Coat the front cover attaching screws with sealer and install them.

➡ **It may be necessary to force the front cover downward to compress the oil pan seal in order to install the front cover attaching bolts. Use a screwdriver or drift to engage the cover screw holes through the cover and pry downward.**

16. Assemble and install the remaining components in the reverse order of removal. Tighten the front cover bolts to 15-20 ft. lbs., the water pump attaching screws to 12-15 ft. lbs., the crankshaft damper to 70-90 ft. lbs., the crankshaft pulley to 35-50 ft. lbs., fuel pump to 19-27 ft. lbs., the oil pan bolts to 9-11 ft. lbs. for the 5/16 inch screws and to 7-9 ft. lbs. for the 1/4 inch screws, and the alternator pivot bolt to 45-57 ft. lbs.

CHECKING TIMING CHAIN DEFLECTION

▶ **See Figure 140**

To measure timing chain deflection, rotate the crankshaft clockwise to take up slack on the left side of chain. Choose a reference point and measure the distance from this point and the chain. Rotate the crankshaft in the opposite direction to take up slack on the right side of the chain. Force the left (slack) side of the chain out and measure the distance to the reference point chosen earlier. The difference between the two measurements is the deflection.

The deflection measurement should not exceed 1/2 inch (13mm). The timing chain should be replaced if the deflection measurement exceeded the specified limit.

CAMSHAFT ENDPLAY MEASUREMENT

The camshaft gears used on some engines are easily damaged if pried upon while the valve train load is on the camshaft. Loosen the rocker arm nuts or rocker arm shaft support bolts before checking the camshaft endplay.

Push the camshaft toward the rear of engine, install and zero a dial indicator, then pry between the camshaft gear and the block to pull the camshaft forward. If the endplay is excessive, check for correct installation of the spacer. If the spacer is installed correctly, replace the thrust plate.

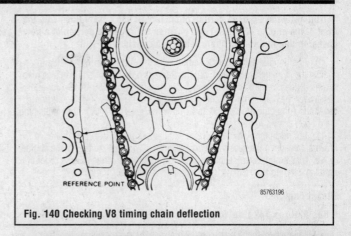

Fig. 140 Checking V8 timing chain deflection

Timing Gear Front Cover and Oil Seal

REMOVAL & INSTALLATION

6-300 Engine

▶ **See Figure 141**

1. Drain the cooling system and disconnect the radiator upper hose at the coolant outlet elbow and remove the two upper radiator retaining bolts.

✸✸ CAUTION

When draining the coolant, keep in mind that cats and dogs are attracted by the ethylene glycol antifreeze, and are quite likely to drink any that is left in an uncovered container or in puddles on the ground. This will prove fatal in sufficient quantity. Always drain the coolant into a sealable container. Coolant should be reused unless it is contaminated or several years old.

2. Raise the vehicle and drain the crankcase.

3. Remove the splash shield and the automatic transmission oil cooling lines, if so equipped, then remove the radiator.

4. Loosen and remove the fan belt, fan and pulley.

5. Use a gear puller to remove the crankshaft pulley damper.

6. Remove the cylinder front cover retaining bolts and gently pry the cover away from the block. Remove the gasket.

7. Drive out the old seal with a pin punch from the rear of the cover. Clean out the recess in the cover.

8. Coat the new seal with grease and drive it into the cover until it is fully seated. Check the seal to make sure that the spring around the seal is in the proper position.

9. Clean the cylinder front cover and the gasket surface of the cylinder block. Apply an oil-resistant sealer to the new front cover gasket and install the gasket onto the cover.

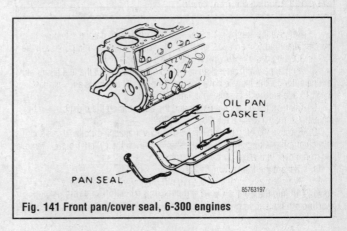

Fig. 141 Front pan/cover seal, 6-300 engines

➡️**Trim away the exposed portion of the old oil pan gasket flush with the front of the engine block. Cut and position the required portion of a new gasket to the oil pan and apply sealer to both sides.**

10. Position the front cover assembly over the end of the crankshaft and against the cylinder block. Start, but do not tighten, the cover and pan attaching screws. Slide a front cover alignment tool (Ford part no. T68P-6019-A or equivalent) over the crank stub and into the seal bore of the cover. Tighten all front cover attaching bolts to 12-18 ft. lbs. ; oil pan screws to 10-15 ft. lbs., tightening the oil pan screws first.

11. Lubricate the hub of the crankshaft damper pulley with Lubriplate® to prevent damage to the seal during installation or on initial starting of the engine.

12. Install and assemble the remaining components in the reverse order of removal, starting from Step 4. Start the engine and check for leaks.

Diesel Engines

▶ **See Figures 142 thru 149**

1. Disconnect both battery ground cables. Drain the cooling system.

✳️✳️ CAUTION

When draining the coolant, keep in mind that cats and dogs are attracted by the ethylene glycol antifreeze, and are quite likely to drink any that is left in an uncovered container or in puddles on the ground. This will prove fatal in sufficient quantity. Always drain the coolant into a sealable container. Coolant should be reused unless it is contaminated or several years old.

2. Remove the air cleaner and cover the air intake on the manifold with clean rags. Do not allow any foreign material to enter the intake.

3. Remove the radiator fan shroud halves.

4. Remove the fan and fan clutch assembly. You will need a puller or ford tool No. T83T-6312-A for this.

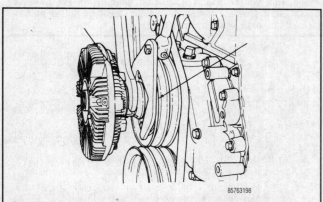

Fig. 142 Removing the diesel fan clutch using a puller (arrows)

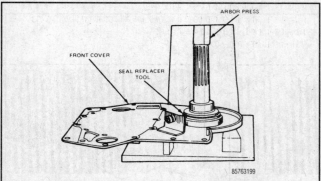

Fig. 143 Diesel front oil seal removal and installation using an arbor press

➡️**The nut is a left hand thread; remove by turning the nut clockwise.**

5. Remove the injection pump as described in Section 5 under Diesel Fuel Systems.

6. Remove the water pump.

7. Jack up the truck and safely support it with jackstands.

8. Remove the crankshaft pulley and vibration damper as described in this section.

9. Remove the engine ground cables at the front of the engine.

10. Remove the five bolts attaching the engine front cover to the engine block and oil pan.

11. Lower the truck.

12. Remove the front cover.

➡️**The front cover oil seal on the diesel must be driven out with an arbor press and a 3¼ inch (82.5mm) spacer. Take the cover to a qualified machinist or engine specialist for this procedure. See also steps 14 and 15.**

13. Remove all old gasket material from the front cover, engine block, oil pan sealing surfaces and water pump surfaces.

14. Coat the new front oil seal with Lubriplate® or equivalent grease.

15. The new seal must be installed using a seal installation tool, Ford part no. T83T-6700-A or an arbor press. A qualified machinist or engine specialist can handle seal installation as well as removal. When the seal bottoms out on the front cover surface, it is installed at the proper depth.

16. Install alignment dowels into the engine block to align the front cover and gaskets. These can be made out of round stock. Apply a gasket sealer to the engine block sealing surfaces, then install the gaskets on the block.

17. Apply a ⅛ inch (3mm) bead of RTV sealer on the front of the engine block as shown in the illustration. Apply a ¼ inch (6mm) bead of RTV sealer on the oil pan.

18. Install the front cover immediately after applying RTV sealer. The sealer will begin to cure and lose its effectiveness unless the cover is installed quickly.

19. Install the water pump gasket on the engine front cover. Apply RTV sealer to the four water pump bolts illustrated. Install the water pump and hand tighten all bolts.

✳️✳️ WARNING

The two top water pump bolts must be no more than 1¼ inch (31.75 mm) long bolts any longer will interfere with (hit) the engine drive gears.

20. Torque the water pump bolts to 19 ft. lbs. Torque the front cover bolts to specifications according to bolt size (see Torque Specifications chart).

21. Install the injection pump adaptor and injection pump as described in Section 5 under Diesel Fuel System.

22. Install the heater hose fitting in the pump using pipe sealant, and connect the heater hose to the water pump.

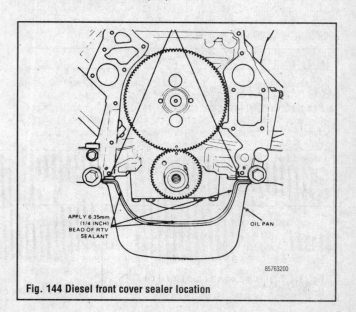

Fig. 144 Diesel front cover sealer location

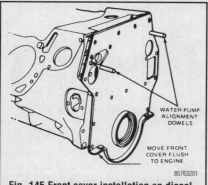

Fig. 145 Front cover installation on diesel, showing water pump alignment dowels

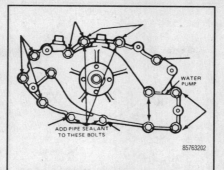

Fig. 146 Diesel water pump-to-front cover installation. The two top pump bolts must be no more than 1¼ in. long

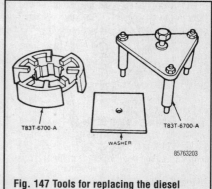

Fig. 147 Tools for replacing the diesel front seal

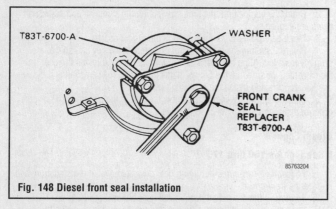

Fig. 148 Diesel front seal installation

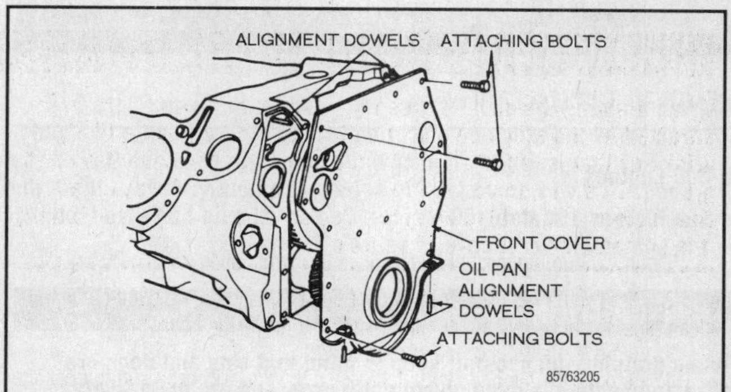

Fig. 150 Fuel pump eccentric removal on the V8

23. Jack up the truck and safely support it with jackstands.
24. Lubricate the front of the crankshaft with clean engine oil. Apply RTV sealant to the engine side of the retaining bolt washer to prevent oil seepage past the keyway. Install the crankshaft vibration damper using Ford Special tools T83T-6316B. Torque the damper-to-crankshaft bolt to 90 ft. lbs.
25. Install the remaining engine components in the reverse order of removal.

Timing Chain

MEASURING TIMING GEAR BACKLASH

Use a dial indicator installed on block to measure timing gear backlash. Hold the gear firmly against the block while making the measurement. If excessive backlash exists, replace both gears.

REMOVAL & INSTALLATION

V6 and Gasoline V8 Engines

▶ **See Figures 150, 151, 152 and 153**

1. Remove the front cover.

Fig. 149 Diesel front cover dowel alignment

2. Rotate the crankshaft counterclockwise to take up the slack on the left side of the chain.
3. Establish a reference point on the cylinder block and measure from this point to the chain.
4. Rotate the crankshaft in the opposite direction to take up the slack on the right side of the chain.
5. Force the left side of the chain out with your fingers and measure the distance between the reference point and the chain. The timing chain deflection is the difference between the two measurements. If the deflection exceeds ½ inch (13mm), replace the timing chain and sprockets.

To replace the timing chain and sprockets:

6. Turn the crankshaft until the timing marks on the sprockets are aligned vertically.
7. Remove the camshaft sprocket retaining screw and remove the fuel pump eccentric and washers.
8. Alternately slide both of the sprockets and timing chain off the crankshaft and camshaft until free of the engine.
9. Position the timing chain on the sprockets so that the timing marks on the sprockets are aligned vertically. Alternately slide the sprockets and chain onto the crankshaft and camshaft sprockets.
10. Install the fuel pump eccentric washers and attaching bolt on the camshaft sprocket. Tighten to 40-45 ft. lbs.
11. Install the front cover.

Fig. 151 V8 timing chain removal

Fig. 152 Crankshaft sprocket removal

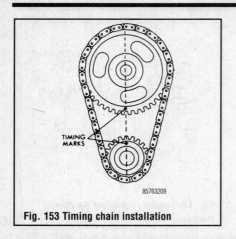

Fig. 153 Timing chain installation

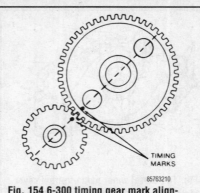

Fig. 154 6-300 timing gear mark alignment

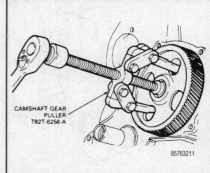

Fig. 155 Removing the camshaft gear from the 6-300

Timing Gears

REMOVAL & INSTALLATION

6-300 Engines

♦ See Figures 154 thru 159

1. Drain the cooling system and remove the front cover.

✳✳ CAUTION

When draining the coolant, keep in mind that cats and dogs are attracted by the ethylene glycol antifreeze, and are quite likely to drink any that is left in an uncovered container or in puddles on the ground. This will prove fatal in sufficient quantity. Always drain the coolant into a sealable container. Coolant should be reused unless it is contaminated or several years old.

2. Crank the engine until the timing marks on the camshaft and crankshaft gears are aligned.

3. Use a gear puller to removal both of the timing gears.

4. Before installing the timing gears, be sure that the key and spacer are properly installed. Align the gear key way with the key and install the gear on the camshaft. Be sure that the timing marks line up on the camshaft and the crankshaft gears and install the crankshaft gear.

5. Install the front cover, and assemble the rest of the engine in the reverse order of disassembly. Fill the cooling system.

Diesel Engines

♦ See Figures 160 thru 170

1. Follow the procedures for timing gear cover removal and installation, and remove the front cover.

2. To remove the crankshaft gear, install gear puller (Ford part) no. T83T-6316-A or equivalent, and using a breaker bar to prevent the crankshaft from rotating, remove the crankshaft gear. To install the crankshaft gear use tool (Ford

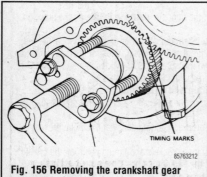

Fig. 156 Removing the crankshaft gear from the 6-300

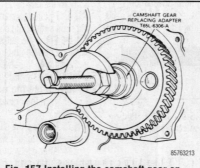

Fig. 157 Installing the camshaft gear on the 6-300

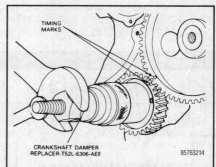

Fig. 158 Installing the crankshaft gear on the 6-300

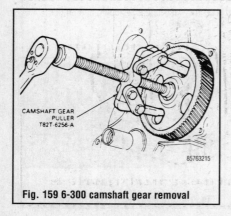

Fig. 159 6-300 camshaft gear removal

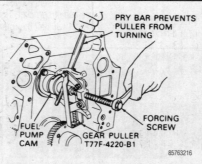

Fig. 160 Removing the diesel fuel pump cam

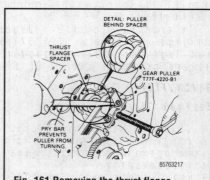

Fig. 161 Removing the thrust flange spacer on the diesel

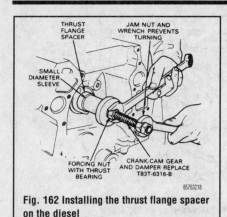

Fig. 162 Installing the thrust flange spacer on the diesel

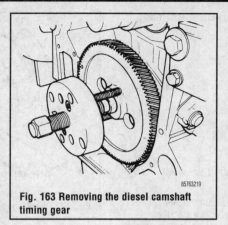

Fig. 163 Removing the diesel camshaft timing gear

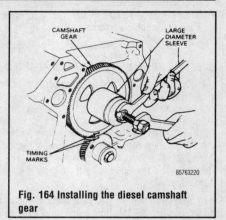

Fig. 164 Installing the diesel camshaft gear

Fig. 165 Special installation tool used on diesel crankshaft gear

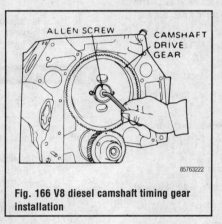

Fig. 166 V8 diesel camshaft timing gear installation

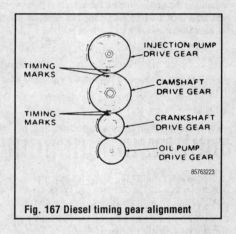

Fig. 167 Diesel timing gear alignment

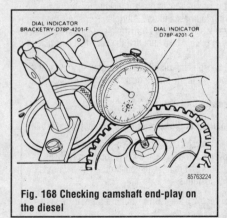

Fig. 168 Checking camshaft end-play on the diesel

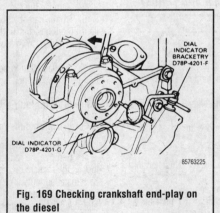

Fig. 169 Checking crankshaft end-play on the diesel

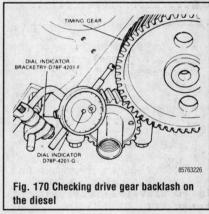

Fig. 170 Checking drive gear backlash on the diesel

part) no. T83T-6316-B or equivalent while aligning the timing marks, and press the gear into place.

3. The camshaft gear may be removed by taking out the Allen screw and installing a gear puller, Ford part no. T83T-6316-A or equivalent and removing the gear. The gear may be replaced by using tool (Ford part) no. T83T-6316-B or equivalent. Torque the Allen screw to 12-18 ft. lbs.

CRANKSHAFT DRIVE GEAR

▶ See Figure 171

1. Complete the front cover removal procedures.
2. Install the crankshaft drive gear remover Tool T83T-6316-A, and using a breaker bar to prevent crankshaft rotation, or flywheel holding Tool T74R-6375-A, remove the crankshaft gear.
3. Install the crankshaft gear using Tool T83T-6316-B aligning the crankshaft drive gear timing mark with the camshaft drive gear timing mark.

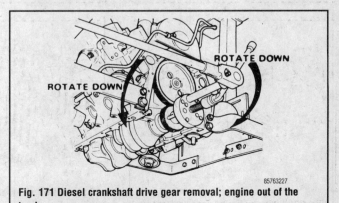

Fig. 171 Diesel crankshaft drive gear removal; engine out of the truck

➡The gear may be heated to 300-350 °F for ease of installation. Heat it in an oven. Do not use a torch.

4. Complete the front cover installation procedures.

INJECTION PUMP DRIVE GEAR AND ADAPTER

1. Disconnect the battery ground cables from both batteries. Remove the air cleaner and install an intake opening cover.
2. Remove the injection pump. Remove the bolts attaching the injection pump adapter to the engine block, and remove the adapter.
3. Remove the engine front cover. Remove the drive gear.
4. Clean all gasket and sealant surfaces of the components removed with a suitable solvent and dry them thoroughly.
5. Install the drive gear in position, aligning all the drive gear timing marks.

➡To determine that the No. 1 piston is at TDC of the compression stroke, position the injection pump drive gear dowel at the 4 o'clock position. The scribe line on the vibration damper should be at TDC. Use extreme care to avoid disturbing the injection pump drive gear, once it is in position.

6. Install the engine front cover. Apply a ⅛ inch (3mm) bead of RTV Sealant along the bottom surface of the injection pump adapter.

➡RTV should be applied immediately prior to adapter installation.

7. Install the injection pump adaptor. Apply sealer to the bolt threads before assembly.

➡With the injection pump adapter installed, the injection pump drive gear cannot jump timing.

8. Install all removed components. Run the engine and check for leaks.

➡If necessary, purge the high pressure fuel lines of air by loosening the connector one half to one turn and crank the engine until a solid flow of fuel, free of air bubbles, flows from the connection.

CAMSHAFT DRIVE GEAR, FUEL PUMP CAM, SPACER AND THRUST PLATE

▶ See Figures 172 and 173

1. Complete the front cover removal procedures.
2. Remove the camshaft allen screw.
3. Install a gear puller, Tool T83T-6316-A and remove the gear. Remove the fuel supply pump, if necessary.
4. Install a gear puller, Tool T77E-4220-B and shaft protector T83T-6316-A and remove the fuel pump cam and spacer, if necessary.
5. Remove the bolts attaching the thrust plate, and remove the thrust plate, if necessary.
6. Install a new thrust plate, if removed.
7. Install the spacer and fuel pump cam against the camshaft thrust flange, using installation sleeve and replacer Tool T83T-6316-B, if removed.
8. Install the camshaft drive gear against the fuel pump cam, aligning the timing mark with the timing mark on the crankshaft drive gear, using installation sleeve and replacer Tool T83T-6316-B.

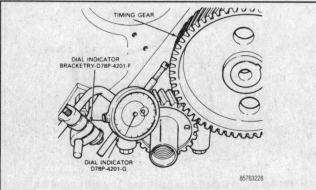

Fig. 172 Checking timing gear backlash on the diesel

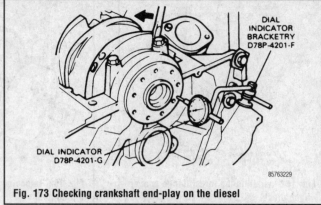

Fig. 173 Checking crankshaft end-play on the diesel

9. Install the camshaft allen screw and tighten to 18 ft. lbs.
10. Install the fuel pump, if removed.
11. Install the front cover, following the previous procedure.

Camshaft

REMOVAL & INSTALLATION

6-300

1. Remove the grille, radiator, and timing cover.
2. Remove the distributor, fuel pump, oil pan and oil pump.
3. Align the timing marks. Unbolt the camshaft thrust plate, working through the holes in the camshaft gear.
4. Loosen the rocker arms, remove the pushrods, take off the side cover and remove the valve lifters with a magnet.
5. Remove the camshaft very carefully to prevent nicking the bearings.
6. Oil the camshaft bearing journals and use Lubriplate® or something similar on the lobes. Install the camshaft, gear, and thrust plate, aligning the gear marks. Tighten down the thrust plate. Make sure that the camshaft end-play is not excessive.
7. The last item to be replaced is the distributor. The rotor should be at the firing position for no. 1 cylinder, with the timing gear marks aligned.

V6 and V8 Including Diesel

➡Ford recommends removing the diesel engine for camshaft removal.

1. Remove the intake manifold and valley pan, if so equipped.
2. Remove the rocker covers, and either remove the rocker arm shafts or loosen the rockers on their pivots and remove the pushrods. The pushrods must be reinstalled in their original positions.
3. Remove the valve lifters in sequence with a magnet. They must be replaced in their original positions.
4. Remove the timing chain/gear cover and timing chain (timing gear on V8 diesel) and sprockets.
5. In addition to the radiator and air conditioning condenser, if so equipped, it may be necessary to remove the front grille assembly and the hood lock assembly to gain the necessary clearance to slide the camshaft out of the front of the engine. On the V6-232, remove the camshaft thrust button and spring. Remove the camshaft thrust plate attaching screws and carefully slide the camshaft out of its bearing bores. Use extra caution not to scratch the camshaft lobes.

➡Camshaft removal tools, Ford part no. T65L-6250-A and adaptor 14-0314 are needed to remove the diesel camshaft.

6. Coat the camshaft with engine oil liberally before installing it. Slide the camshaft into the engine very carefully so as not to scratch the bearing bores with the camshaft lobes. Install the camshaft thrust plate and tighten the attaching screws to 9-12 ft. lbs. Measure the camshaft end-play. If the end-play is more than 0.009 inch (0.228mm), replace the thrust plate. Assemble the remaining components in the reverse order of removal.

CHECKING CAMSHAFT

Camshaft Lobe Lift

▶ **See Figure 174**

Check the lift of each lobe in consecutive order and make a note of the reading.

1. Remove the fresh air inlet tube and the air cleaner. Remove the heater hose and crankcase ventilation hoses. Remove valve rocker arm cover(s).

2. Remove the rocker arm stud nut or fulcrum bolts, fulcrum seat and rocker arm.

3. Remove the pushrod from the valve tappet socket. Install a dial indicator D78P-4201-B or equivalent so that the actuating point of the indicator is in the push rod socket (or the indicator ball socket adaptor tool 6565-AB is on the end of the push rod if the push rod is not removed) and in the same plane as the push rod movement.

4. Disconnect the I terminal and the S terminal at the starter relay. Install an auxiliary starter switch between the battery and S terminals of the start relay (or crank the engine by hand). Crank the engine with the ignition switch off. Turn the crankshaft over until the tappet is on the base circle of the camshaft lobe. At this position, the push rod will be in its lowest position.

5. Zero the dial indicator. Continue to rotate the crankshaft slowly until the push rod is in the fully raised position.

6. Compare the total lift recorded on the dial indicator with the specification shown on the Camshaft Specification chart.

To check the accuracy of the original indicator reading, continue to rotate the crankshaft until the indicator reads zero. If the wear on any lobe is beyond specified limits listed, the camshaft and the valve tappets operating on the worn lobe(s) must be replaced.

7. Remove the dial indicator and auxiliary starter switch.

8. Install the rocker arm, fulcrum seat and stud nut or fulcrum bolts. Check the valve clearance. Adjust if required (refer to procedure in this section).

9. Install the valve rocker arm cover(s) and the air cleaner.

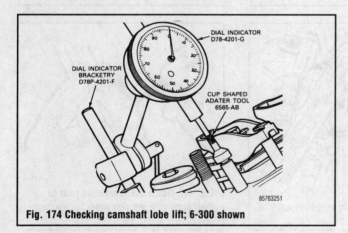

Fig. 174 Checking camshaft lobe lift; 6-300 shown

Camshaft End-Play

▶ **See Figure 175**

➡ **On all gasoline V8 engines, prying against the aluminum-nylon camshaft sprocket, with the valve train load on the camshaft, can break or damage the sprocket. Therefore, the rocker arm adjusting nuts must be backed off, or the rocker arm and shaft assembly must be loosened sufficiently to free the camshaft. After checking the camshaft end play, check the valve clearance. Adjust if required (refer to procedure in this section).**

1. Push the camshaft toward the rear of the engine. Install a dial indicator (Tool D78P-4201-F, -G or equivalent so that the indicator point is on the camshaft sprocket attaching screw.

2. Zero the dial indicator. Position a prybar between the camshaft gear and the block. Pull the camshaft forward and release it. Compare the dial indicator reading with the specifications.

3. If the end play is excessive, check the spacer for correct installation before it is removed. If the spacer is correctly installed, replace the thrust plate.

4. Remove the dial indicator.

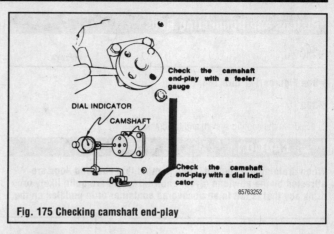

Fig. 175 Checking camshaft end-play

CAMSHAFT BEARING REPLACEMENT

▶ **See Figure 176**

1. Remove the engine following the procedures in this section and install it on a work stand.

2. Remove the camshaft, flywheel and crankshaft, following the appropriate procedures. Push the pistons to the top of the cylinder.

3. Remove the camshaft rear bearing bore plug. Remove the camshaft bearings with Tool T65L-6250-A or equivalent.

4. Select the proper size expanding collet and back-up nut and assemble on the mandrel. With the expanding collet collapsed, install the collet assembly in the camshaft bearing and tighten the back-up nut on the expanding mandrel until the collet fits the camshaft bearing.

5. Assemble the puller screw and extension (if necessary) and install on the expanding mandrel. Wrap a cloth around the threads of the puller screw to protect the front bearing or journal. Tighten the pulling nut against the thrust bearing and pulling plate to remove the camshaft bearing. Be sure to hold a wrench on the end of the puller screw to prevent it from turning.

6. To remove the front bearing, install the puller from the rear of the cylinder block.

7. Position the new bearings at the bearing bores, and press them in place with tool T65L-6250-A or equivalent. Be sure to center the pulling plate and puller screw to avoid damage to the bearing. Failure to use the correct expanding collet can cause severe bearing damage. Align the oil holes in the bearings with the oil holes in the cylinder block before pressing bearings into place.

➡ **Be sure the front bearing is installed 0.020-0.035 inch (0.508-0.889mm) for the in-line six cylinder engines, 0.005-0.020 inch (0.127-0.508mm) for the gasoline V8, 0.040-0.060 inch (1.016-1.524mm) for the diesel V8, below the front face of the cylinder block.**

8. Install the camshaft rear bearing bore plug.

9. Install the camshaft, crankshaft, flywheel and related parts, following the appropriate procedures.

10. Install the engine in the truck, following procedures described earlier in this section.

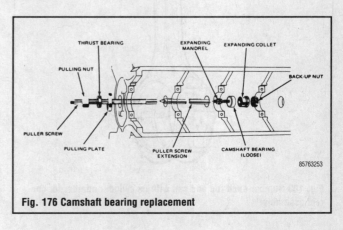

Fig. 176 Camshaft bearing replacement

Pistons and Connecting Rods

REMOVAL

▶ See Figures 177 thru 184

6-300

1. Drain the cooling system and the crankcase.

❊❊ CAUTION

When draining the coolant, keep in mind that cats and dogs are attracted by the ethylene glycol antifreeze, and are quite likely to drink any that is left in an uncovered container or in puddles on the ground. This will prove fatal in sufficient quantity. Always drain the coolant into a sealable container. Coolant should be reused unless it is contaminated or several years old.

2. Remove the cylinder head.
3. Remove the oil pan, the oil pump inlet tube and the oil pump.
4. Turn the crankshaft until the piston to be removed is at the bottom of its travel and place a cloth on the piston head to collect filings. Using a ridge reaming tool, remove any ridge of carbon or any other deposit from the upper cylinder walls where piston travel ends. Do not cut into the piston ring travel area more than 1/32 inch (0.8mm) while removing the ridge.
5. Mark all of the connecting rod caps so that they can be reinstalled in the original positions from which they are removed and remove the connecting rod bearing cap. Also identify the piston assemblies as they, too, must be reinstalled in the same cylinder from which removed.

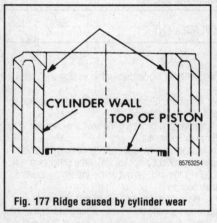
Fig. 177 Ridge caused by cylinder wear

Fig. 178 Sometimes it's necessary to break free the bearing cap using a hammer and BRASS or WOOD drift

Fig. 179 Bearing cap removal

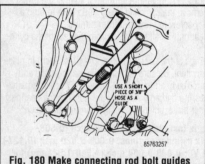
Fig. 180 Make connecting rod bolt guides out of rubber tubing; these also protect the cylinder walls and crank journal from scratches

Fig. 181 Push the piston assembly out with a hammer handle

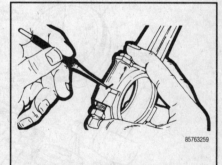
Fig. 182 Match the connecting rods to their caps with a scribe mark for reassembly

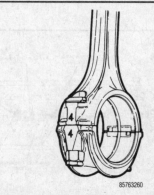
Fig. 183 Number each rod and cap with its cylinder number for correct assembly

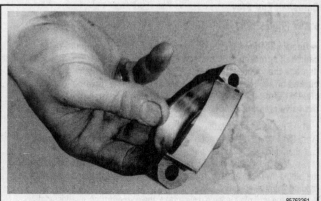
Fig. 184 Removing the bearing cap insert

6. With the bearing caps removed, the connecting rod bearing bolts are potentially damaging to the cylinder walls during removal. To guard against cylinder wall damage, install 4 inch (101.6mm) or 5 inch (127mm) lengths of ⅜ inch (9.5mm) rubber tubing onto the connecting rod bolts. These will also protect the crankshaft journal from scratches when the connecting rod is installed, and will serve as a guide for the rod.

7. Squirt some clean engine oil into each cylinder before removing the pistons. Using a wooden hammer handle, push the connecting rod and piston assembly out of the top of the cylinder (pushing from the bottom of the rod). Be careful to avoid damaging both the crank journal and the cylinder wall when removing the rod and piston assembly.

V6 and V8 Engines Including Diesel

1. Drain the cooling system and the crankcase.

❄❄ CAUTION

When draining the coolant, keep in mind that cats and dogs are attracted by the ethylene glycol antifreeze, and are quite likely to drink any that is left in an uncovered container or in puddles on the ground. This will prove fatal in sufficient quantity. Always drain the coolant into a sealable container. Coolant should be reused unless it is contaminated or several years old.

2. Remove the intake manifold.
3. Remove the cylinder heads.
4. Remove the oil pan.
5. Remove the oil pump.
6. Turn the crankshaft until the piston to be removed is at the bottom of its travel, then place a cloth on the piston head to collect filings.
7. Remove any ridge of deposits at the end of the piston travel from the upper cylinder bore, using a ridge reaming tool. Do not cut into the piston ring travel area more than 1/32 inch (0.8mm) when removing the ridge.
8. Make sure that all of the connecting rod bearing caps can be identified, so they will be reinstalled in their original positions.
9. Turn the crankshaft until the connecting rod that is to be removed is at the bottom of its stroke and remove the connecting rod nuts and bearing cap.
10. With the bearing caps removed, the connecting rod bearing bolts are potentially damaging to the cylinder walls during removal. To guard against cylinder wall damage, install four or five inch lengths of ⅜ inch (0.8mm) rubber tubing onto the connecting rod bolts. These will also protect the crankshaft journal from scratches when the connecting rod is installed, and will serve as a guide for the rod.
11. Squirt some clean engine oil into each cylinder before removing the piston assemblies. Using a wooden hammer handle, push the connecting rod and piston assembly out of the top of the cylinder (pushing from the bottom of the rod). Be careful to avoid damaging both the crank journal and the cylinder wall when removing the rod and piston assembly.
12. Remove the bearing inserts from the connecting rod and cap if the bearings are to be replace, and place the cap onto the piston/rod assembly from which it was removed.

➡The connecting rod and bearing caps are numbered from 1 to 4 in the right bank and from 5 to 8 in in the left bank, beginning at the front of the engine. The numbers on the rod and cap must be on the same side when they are installed in the cylinder bore. Also, the largest chamfer at the bearing end of the rod should be positioned toward the crank pin thrust face of the crankshaft and the notch in the head of the piston faces toward the front of the engine.

PISTON AND ROD DISASSEMBLY

◗ **See Figures 185, 186 and 187**

All of the Ford gasoline engines covered in this guide utilize pressed-in wrist pins, which can only be removed by an arbor press. The diesel pistons are removed in the same way, only the pistons are heated before the wrist pins are pressed out. On both gasoline and diesel engines, the piston/connecting rod assemblies should be taken to an engine specialist or qualified machinist for piston removal and installation.

A piston ring expander is necessary for removing the piston rings without damaging them; any other method (screwdriver blades, pliers, etc.) usually results in the rings being bent, scratched or distorted, or the piston itself being

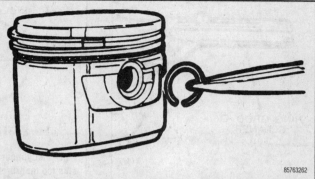
Fig. 185 Use needle-nose or snapring pliers to remove the piston pin clips

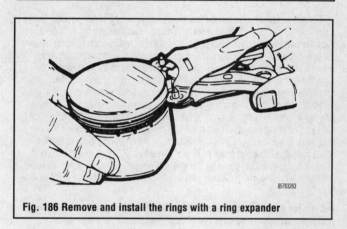
Fig. 186 Remove and install the rings with a ring expander

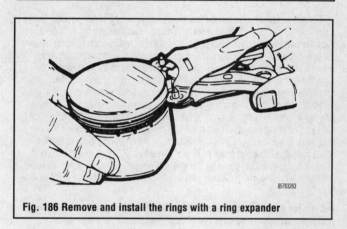
Fig. 187 Press wrist pins in and out with an arbor press. This applies to all engines covered in this manual

damaged. When the rings are removed, clean the ring grooves using an appropriate ring groove cleaning tool, using care not to cut too deeply.

CLEANING AND INSPECTION

◗ **See Figures 188, 189 and 190**

Thoroughly clean all carbon and varnish from the piston with solvent.

❄❄ WARNING

Do not use a wire brush or caustic solvent (acids, etc.) on pistons.

Inspect the pistons for scuffing, scoring, cracks, pitting, or excessive ring groove wear. If these are evident, the piston must be replaced.

Fig. 188 Clean the ring grooves with this tool or the edge of an old ring.

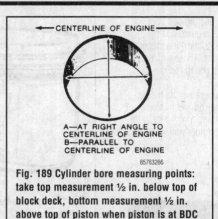

Fig. 189 Cylinder bore measuring points: take top measurement ½ in. below top of block deck, bottom measurement ½ in. above top of piston when piston is at BDC

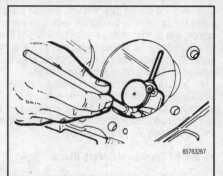

Fig. 190 Measure cylinder bore with a dial gauge

The piston should also be checked in relation to the cylinder diameter. Using a telescoping gauge and micrometer, or a dial gauge, measure the cylinder bore diameter perpendicular (90 degrees) to the piston pin, 2½ inch (64mm) below the cylinder block deck (surface where the block mates with the heads). Then, with the micrometer, measure the piston, perpendicular to its wrist pin on the skirt. the difference between the two measurements is the piston clearance. If the clearance is within specifications or slightly below (after the cylinders have been bored or hones), finish honing is all that is necessary. If the clearance is excessive, try to obtain a slightly larger piston to bring clearance to within specifications. If this is not possible, obtain the first oversize piston and hone (or if necessary, bore) the cylinder to size. Generally, if the cylinder bore is tapered 0.005 inch (0.127mm) or more or is out-of-round 0.003 inch (0.076mm) or more, it is advisable to rebore for the smallest possible oversize piston and rings.

After measuring, mark pistons with a felt tip pen for reference and for assembly.

➡**Cylinder honing and/or boring should be performed by a reputable, professional mechanic with the proper equipment. In some cases, clean-up honing can be done with the cylinder block in the car, but most excessive honing and all cylinder boring must be done with the block stripped and removed from the truck. Before honing the diesel cylinders, the piston oil cooling jets must be removed. This procedure should be handled by a diesel specialist, as special tools are needed. Jets cannot be reused; new jets should be fitted.**

Measuring the Old Pistons

▶ **See Figure 191**

Check used piston-to-cylinder bore clearance as follows:
1. Measure the cylinder bore diameter with a telescope gauge.
2. Measure the piston diameter. When measuring the pistons for size or taper, measurements must be made with the piston pin removed.
3. Subtract the piston diameter from the cylinder bore diameter to determine piston-to-bore clearance.
4. Compare the piston-to-bore clearances obtained with those clearances recommended. Determine if the piston-to-bore clearance is in the acceptable range.

5. When measuring taper, the largest reading must be at the bottom of the skirt.

Selecting New Pistons

1. If the used piston is not acceptable, check the service piston size and determine if a new piston can be selected. (Service pistons are available in standard, high limit and standard oversize.
2. If the cylinder bore must be reconditioned, measure the new piston diameter, then hone the cylinder bore to obtain the preferred clearance.
3. Select a new piston and mark the piston to identify the cylinder for which it was fitted. (On some vehicles, oversize pistons may be found. These pistons will be 0.010 inch (0.254mm) oversize).

CYLINDER HONING

▶ **See Figures 192 and 193**

1. When cylinders are being honed, follow the manufacturer's recommendations for the use of the hone.
2. Occasionally, during the honing operation, the cylinder bore should be thoroughly cleaned and checked for correct fit with the selected piston.
3. When finish-honing a cylinder bore, the hone should be moved up and down at a sufficient speed to obtain a very fine uniform surface finish in a cross-hatch pattern of approximately 45-65 degrees included angle. The finish marks should be clean but not sharp, free from imbedded particles and torn or folded metal.
4. Permanently mark the piston for the cylinder to which it has been fitted and proceed to hone the remaining cylinders.

✳✳ **WARNING**

Handle the pistons with care. Do not attempt to force the pistons through the cylinders until the cylinders have been honed to the correct size. Pistons can be distorted through careless handling.

Fig. 191 Check piston diameter at these points with a micrometer

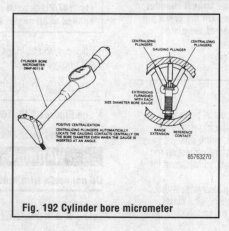

Fig. 192 Cylinder bore micrometer

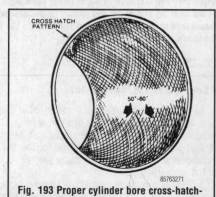

Fig. 193 Proper cylinder bore cross-hatching after honing

5. Thoroughly clean the bores with hot water and detergent. Scrub well with a stiff bristle brush and rinse thoroughly with hot water. It is extremely essential that a good cleaning operation be performed. If any of the abrasive material is allowed to remain in the cylinder bores, it will rapidly wear the new rings and cylinder bores. The bores should be swabbed several times with light engine oil and a clean cloth and then wiped with a clean dry cloth. CYLINDERS SHOULD NOT BE CLEANED WITH KEROSENE OR GASOLINE! Clean the remainder of the cylinder block to remove the excess material spread during the honing operation.

PISTON RING END GAP

▶ **See Figure 194**

Piston ring end gap should be checked while the rings are removed from the pistons. Incorrect end gap indicates that the wrong size rings are being used; ring breakage could occur.

Compress the piston rings to be used in a cylinder, one at a time, into that cylinder. Squirt clean oil into the cylinder, so that the rings and the top 2 inch (51mm) of cylinder wall are coated. Using an inverted piston, press the rings approximately 1 inch (25mm) below the deck of the block (on diesels, measure ring gap clearance with the ring positioned at the bottom of ring travel in the bore). Measure the ring end gap with the feeler gauge, and compare to the Ring Gap chart in this section. Carefully pull the ring out of the cylinder and file the ends squarely with a fine file to obtain the proper clearance.

PISTON RING SIDE CLEARANCE CHECK AND RING INSTALLATION

▶ **See Figures 195, 196 and 197**

Check the pistons to see that the ring grooves and oil return holes have been properly cleaned. Slide a piston ring into its groove, and check the side clearance with a feeler gauge. On gasoline engines, make sure you insert the gauge between the ring and its lower land (lower edge of the groove), because any wear that occurs forms a step at the inner portion of the lower land. On diesels, insert the gauge between the ring and the upper land. If the piston grooves have worn to the extent that relatively high steps exist on the lower land, the piston should be replaced, because these will interfere with the operation of the new rings and ring clearance will be excessive. Piston rings are not furnished in oversize widths to compensate for ring groove wear.

Install the rings on the piston, lowest ring first, using a piston ring expander. There is a high risk of breaking or distorting the rings, or scratching the piston, if the rings are installed by hand or other means.

Position the rings on the piston; spacing of the various piston ring gaps is crucial to proper oil retention and even cylinder wear. When installing new rings, refer to the installation diagram furnished with the new parts.

CONNECTING ROD BEARING INSPECTION

Connecting rod bearings for the engines covered in this guide consist of two halves or shells which are interchangeable in the rod and cap. When the shells are placed in position, the ends extend slightly beyond the rod and cap surfaces so that with the rod bolts torqued the shells will be clamped tightly in place to insure positive seating and to prevent turning. A tang holds the shells in place.

➡**The ends of the bearing shells must never be filed flush with the mating surfaces of the rod and cap.**

If a rod bearing becomes noisy or is worn so that its clearance on the crank journal is sloppy, a new bearing of the correct undersize must be selected and installed since there is no provision for adjustment.

❋❋ WARNING

Under no circumstances should the rod end or cap be filed to adjust the bearing clearance, nor should shims of any kind be used.

Inspect the rod bearings while the rod assemblies are out of the engine. If the shells are scored or show flaking, they should be replaced. If they are in good shape, check for proper clearance on the crank journal (see below). Any scoring or ridges on the crank journal means the crankshaft must be reground and fitted with undersized bearings, or replaced.

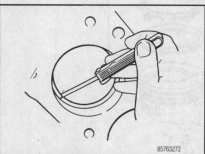

Fig. 194 Check piston ring end gap with a feeler gauge, with the ring positioned in the cylinder one inch below the deck of the block

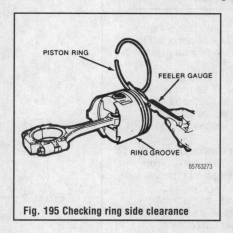

Fig. 195 Checking ring side clearance

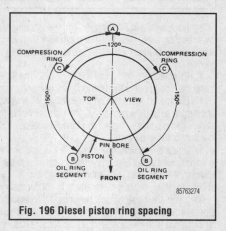

Fig. 196 Diesel piston ring spacing

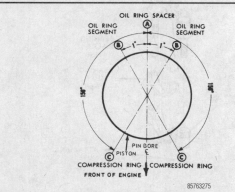

Fig. 197 Gasoline engine piston ring spacing

CHECKING BEARING CLEARANCE AND REPLACING BEARINGS

▶ **See Figures 198 and 199**

➡**Make sure connecting rods and their caps are kept together, and that the caps are installed in the proper direction.**

Replacement bearings are available in standard size, and in undersizes for reground crankshaft. Connecting rod-to-crankshaft bearing clearance is checked using Plastigage® at either the top or bottom of each crank journal. Plastigage® has a range of 0 to 0.003 inch (0.076mm).

1. Remove the rod cap with the bearing shell. Completely clean the bearing shell and the crank journal, and blow any oil from the oil hole in the crankshaft.

➡**The journal surfaces and bearing shells must be completely free of oil, because Plastigage® is soluble in oil.**

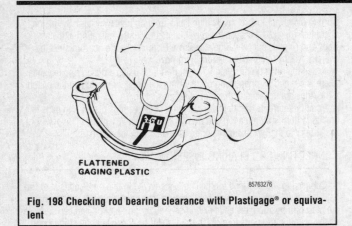

Fig. 198 Checking rod bearing clearance with Plastigage® or equivalent

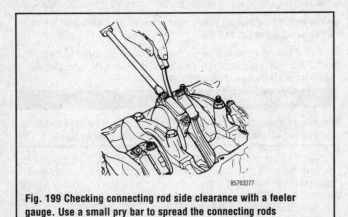

Fig. 199 Checking connecting rod side clearance with a feeler gauge. Use a small pry bar to spread the connecting rods

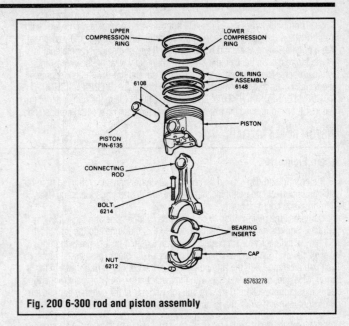

Fig. 200 6-300 rod and piston assembly

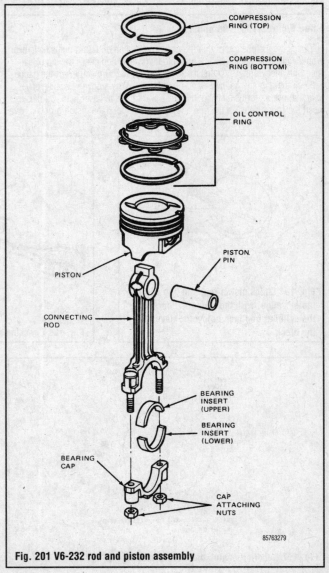

Fig. 201 V6-232 rod and piston assembly

2. Place a strip of Plastigage® lengthwise along the bottom center of the lower bearing shell, then install the cap with shell and torque the bolt or nuts to specification. DO NOT TURN the crankshaft with the Plastigage® installed in the bearing.

3. Remove the bearing cap with the shell. The flattened Plastigage® will be found sticking to either the bearing shell or crank journal. Do not remove it yet.

4. Use the printed scale on the Plastigage® envelope to measure the flattened material at its widest point. The number within the scale which most closely corresponds to the width of the Plastigage® indicated bearing clearance in thousandths of an inch.

5. Check the specifications chart in this section for the desired clearance. It is advisable to install a new bearing if clearance exceeds 0.003 inch (0.076mm); however, if the bearing is in good condition and is not being checked because of bearing noise, bearing replacement is not necessary.

6. If you are installing new bearings, try a standard size, then each undersize in order until one is found that is within the specified limits when checked for clearance with Plastigage®. Each under size has its size stamped on it.

7. When the proper size shell is found, clean off the Plastigage® material from the shell, oil the bearing thoroughly, reinstall the cap with its shell and torque the rod bolt nuts to specification.

➡With the proper bearing selected and the nuts torqued, it should be possible to move the connecting rod back and forth freely on the crank journal as allowed by the specified connecting rod end clearance. If the rod cannot be moved, either the rod bearing is too far undersize or the rod is misaligned.

PISTON AND CONNECTING ROD ASSEMBLY AND INSTALLATION

◆ See Figures 200 thru 206

Install the connecting rod to the piston making sure piston installation notches and any marks on the rod are in proper relation to one another. Lubricate the wrist pin with clean engine oil and install the pin into the rod and piston assembly by using an arbor press as required. Install the wrist pin

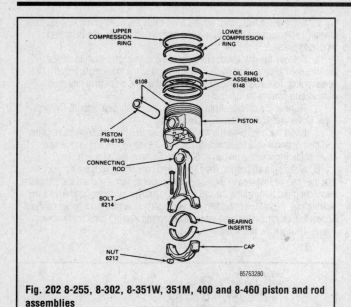

Fig. 202 8-255, 8-302, 8-351W, 351M, 400 and 8-460 piston and rod assemblies

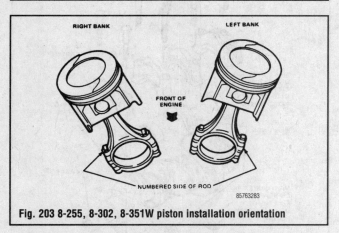

Fig. 203 8-255, 8-302, 8-351W piston installation orientation

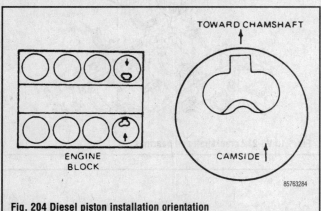

Fig. 204 Diesel piston installation orientation

Fig. 205 Tap the piston assembly into the cylinder with a wooden hammer handle

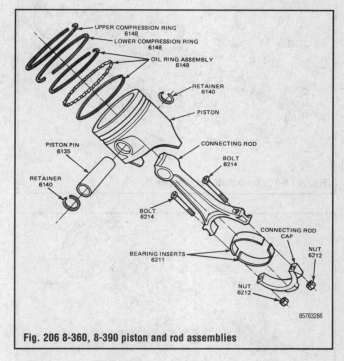

Fig. 206 8-360, 8-390 piston and rod assemblies

on all but the 8-360/390. On these engines, the V-shaped indentation faces inwards (towards the center of the engine. This assumes that the dimple(s) or other markings on the connecting rods are in correct relation to the piston notch(s).

4. From beneath the engine, coat each crank journal with clean oil. Pull the connecting rod, with the bearing shell in place, into position against the crank journal.

5. Remove the rubber hoses. Install the bearing cap and cap nuts and torque to specification.

➡ When more than one rod and piston assembly is being installed, the connecting rod cap attaching nuts should only be tightened enough to keep each rod in position until all have been installed. This will ease the installation of the remaining piston assemblies.

6. Check the clearance between the sides of the connecting rods and the crankshaft using a feeler gauge. Spread the rods slightly with a screwdriver to insert the gauge. If clearance is below the minimum tolerance, the rod may be machined to provide adequate clearance. If clearance is excessive, substitute an unworn rod, and recheck. If clearance is still outside specifications, the crankshaft must be welded and reground, or replaced.

7. Replace the oil pump if removed, and the oil pan.
8. Install the cylinder head(s) and intake manifold.

snaprings if equipped, and rotate them in their grooves to make sure they are seated. To install the piston and rod assemblies:

1. Make sure the connecting rod big bearings (including end cap) are of the correct size and properly installed.

2. Fit rubber hoses over the connecting rod bolt to protect the crankshaft journals, as in the Piston Removal procedure. Coat the rod bearings with clean oil.

3. Using the proper ring compressor, insert the piston assembly into the cylinder so that the notch in the top of the piston faces the front of the engine

Crankshaft and Main Bearings

REMOVAL & INSTALLATION

♦ **See Figures 207 thru 213**

Engine Removed

1. With the engine removed from the vehicle and placed in a work stand, disconnect the spark plug wires from the spark plugs and remove the wires and bracket assembly from the attaching stud on the valve rocker arm cover(s) if so equipped. Disconnect the coil to distributor high tension lead at the coil. Remove the distributor cap and spark plug wires as an assembly. Remove the spark plugs to allow easy rotation of the crankshaft.

2. Remove the fuel pump and oil filter. Slide the water pump by-pass hose clamp (if so equipped) toward the water pump. Remove the alternator and mounting brackets.

3. Remove the crankshaft pulley from the crankshaft vibration damper. Remove the capscrew and washer from the end of the crankshaft. Install a universal puller, Tool T58P-6316-D or equivalent on the crankshaft vibration damper and remove the damper.

4. Remove the cylinder front cover and crankshaft gear, refer to Cylinder Front Cover and Timing Chain in this section.

5. Invert the engine on the work stand. Remove the clutch pressure plate and disc (manual shift transmission). Remove the flywheel and engine rear cover plate. Remove the oil pan and gasket. Remove the oil pump.

6. Make sure all bearing caps (main and connecting rod) are marked so that they can be installed in their original locations. Turn the crankshaft until the connecting rod from which the cap is being removed is down, and remove the bearing cap. Push the connecting rod and piston assembly up into the cylinder. Repeat this procedure until all the connecting rod bearing caps are removed.

7. Remove the main bearings caps.

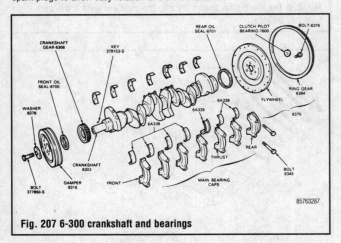

Fig. 207 6-300 crankshaft and bearings

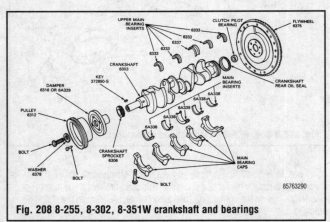

Fig. 208 8-255, 8-302, 8-351W crankshaft and bearings

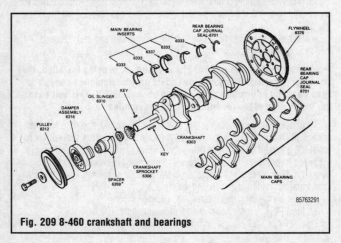

Fig. 209 8-460 crankshaft and bearings

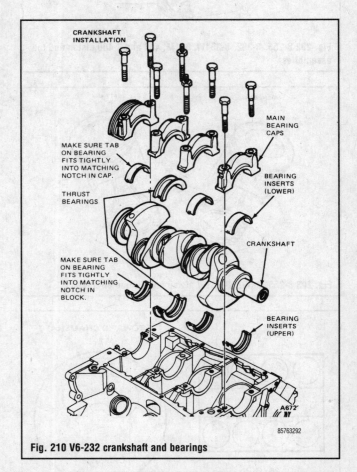

Fig. 210 V6-232 crankshaft and bearings

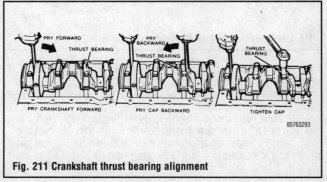

Fig. 211 Crankshaft thrust bearing alignment

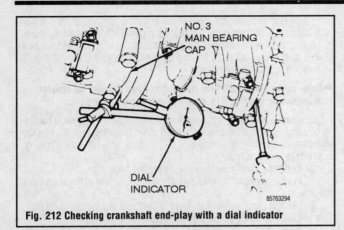

Fig. 212 Checking crankshaft end-play with a dial indicator

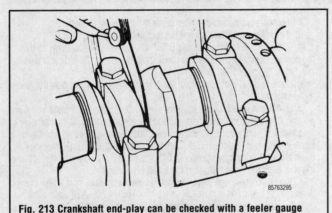

Fig. 213 Crankshaft end-play can be checked with a feeler gauge

8. Carefully lift the crankshaft out of the block so that the thrust bearing surfaces are not damaged. Handle the crankshaft with care to avoid possible fracture to the finished surfaces.

9. Remove the rear journal seal from the block and rear main bearing cap.

10. Remove the main bearing inserts from the block and bearing caps.

11. Remove the connecting rod bearing inserts from the connecting rods and caps.

To install:

12. If the crankshaft main bearing journals have been refinished to a definite undersize, install the correct undersize bearings. Be sure the bearing inserts and bearing bores are clean. Foreign material under the inserts will distort the bearing and cause a failure.

13. Place the upper main bearing inserts in position in the bores with the tang fitting in the slot. Be sure the oil holes in the bearing inserts are aligned with the oil holes in the cylinder block.

14. Install the lower main bearing inserts in the bearing caps.

15. Clean the rear journal oil seal groove and the mating surfaces of the block and rear main bearing cap.

16. Dip the lip-type seal halves in clean engine oil. Install the seals in the bearing cap and block with the undercut side of the seal toward the front of the engine.

➡**This procedure applies only to engines with two piece rear main bearing oil seals. Those having one piece seals will be installed after the crankshaft is in place.**

17. Carefully lower the crankshaft into place. Be careful not to damage the bearing surfaces.

MAIN BEARING REPLACEMENT

♦ **See Figures 214 and 215**

Engine in the Truck

1. With the oil pan, oil pump and spark plugs removed, remove the cap from the main bearing needing replacement and remove the bearing from the cap.

2. Make a bearing roll-out pin, using a bent cotter pin as shown in the illustration. Install the end of the pin in the oil hole in the crankshaft journal.

3. Rotate the crankshaft clockwise as viewed from the front of the engine. This will roll the upper bearing out of the block.

4. Lube the new upper bearing with clean engine oil and insert the plain end between the crankshaft and the indented or notched side of the block. Roll the bearing into place, making sure that the oil holes are aligned. Remove the roll pin from the oil hole.

5. Lube the new lower bearing and install it in the main bearing cap. Install the main bearing cap onto the block, making sure it is positioned in proper direction with the matchmarks in alignment.

6. Torque the main bearing cap to specification.

➡**See Crankshaft Installation for thrust bearing alignment.**

CRANKSHAFT CLEANING AND INSPECTION

♦ **See Figures 216 and 217**

➡**Handle the crankshaft carefully to avoid damage to the finish surfaces.**

1. Clean the crankshaft with solvent, and blow out all oil passages with compressed air. Clean the oil seal contact surface at the rear of the crankshaft with solvent to remove any corrosion, sludge or varnish deposits.

2. Use crocus cloth to remove any sharp edges, burrs or other imperfections which might damage the oil seal during installation or cause premature seal wear.

➡**Do not polish the seal surfaces. A finely polished surface may produce poor sealing or cause premature seal wear.**

3. Inspect the main and connecting rod journals for cracks, scratches, grooves or scores.

4. Measure the diameter of each journal at least four places to determine out-of-round, taper or undersize condition.

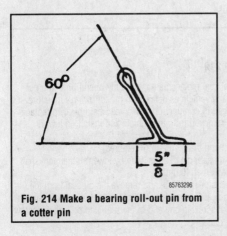

Fig. 214 Make a bearing roll-out pin from a cotter pin

Fig. 215 Install the roll-out pin in the crankshaft journal's oil hole

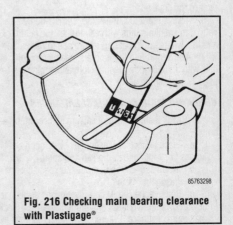

Fig. 216 Checking main bearing clearance with Plastigage®

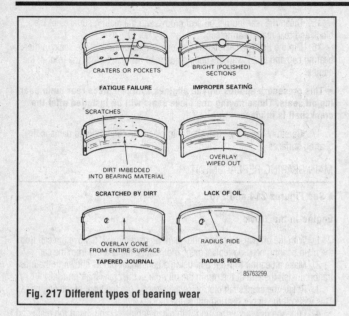

Fig. 217 Different types of bearing wear

5. On an engine with a manual transmission, check the fit of the clutch pilot bearing in the bore of the crankshaft. A needle roller bearing and adapter assembly is used as a clutch pilot bearing. It is inserted directly into the engine crank shaft. The bearing and adapter assembly cannot be serviced separately. A new bearing must be installed whenever a bearing is removed.

6. Inspect the pilot bearing, when used, for roughness, evidence of over-heating or loss of lubricant. Replace if any of these conditions are found.

7. Inspect the rear oil seal surface of the crankshaft for deep grooves, nicks, burrs, porosity, or scratches which could damage the oil seal lip during installation. Remove all nicks and burrs with crocus cloth.

Main Bearings

1. Clean the bearing inserts and caps thoroughly in solvent, and dry them with compressed air.

➡**Do not scrape varnish or gum deposits from the bearing shells.**

2. Inspect each bearing carefully. Bearings that have a scored, chipped, or worn surface should be replaced.

3. The copper-lead bearing base may be visible through the bearing overlay in small localized areas. This may not mean that the bearing is excessively worn. It is not necessary to replace the bearing if the bearing clearance is within recommended specifications.

4. Check the clearance of bearings that appear to be satisfactory with Plastigage® or its equivalent. Fit the new bearings following the procedure Crankshaft and Main Bearings removal and installation, they should be reground to size for the next undersize bearing.

5. Regrind the journals to give the proper clearance with the next undersize bearing. If the journal will not clean up to maximum undersize bearing available, replace the crankshaft.

6. Always reproduce the same journal shoulder radius that existed originally. Too small a radius will result in fatigue failure of the crankshaft. Too large a radius will result in bearing failure due to radius ride of the bearing.

7. After regrinding the journals, chamfer the oil holes, then polish the journals with a #320 grit polishing cloth and engine oil. Crocus cloth may also be used as a polishing agent.

CHECKING MAIN BEARING CLEARANCES

1. Check the clearance of each main bearing by using the following procedure:

a. Place a piece of Plastigage® or its equivalent, on bearing surface across full width of bearing cap and about ¼ inch (6mm) off center.

b. Install cap and tighten bolts to specifications. Do not turn crankshaft while Plastigage® is in place.

c. Remove the cap. Using Plastigage® scale; check width of Plastigage® at widest point to get the minimum clearance. Check at narrowest point to get maximum clearance. Difference between readings is taper of journal.

d. If clearance exceeds specified limits, try a 0.001 inch (0.0254mm) or 0.002 inch (0.051mm) undersize bearing in combination with the standard bearing. Bearing clearance must be within specified limits. If undersize bearings do not bring clearance within desired limits, refinish crankshaft journal, then install undersize bearings.

➡**Refer to Rear Main Oil Seal removal and installation, for special instructions in applying RTV sealer to rear main bearing cup.**

2. Install all the bearing caps except the thrust bearing cap (no. 3 bearing on all except the 6-300 which use the no. 5 as the thrust bearing). BE sure the main bearing caps are installed in their original locations. Tighten the bearing cap bolts to specifications.

3. Install the thrust bearing cap with the bolts finger tight.

4. Pry the crankshaft forward against the thrust surface of the upper half of the bearing.

5. Hold the crankshaft forward and pry the thrust bearing cap to the rear. This will align the thrust surfaces of both halves of the bearing.

6. Retain the forward pressure on the crankshaft. Tighten the cap bolts to specifications.

7. Check the crankshaft end play using the following procedures:

a. Force the crankshaft toward the rear of the engine.

b. Install a dial indicator (tools D78P-4201-F, -G or equivalent) so that the contact point rests against the crankshaft flange and the indicator axis is parallel to the crankshaft axis.

c. Zero the dial indicator. Push the crankshaft forward and note the reading on the dial.

d. If the end play exceeds the wear limit listed in the Crankshaft and Connecting Rod Specifications chart, replace the thrust bearing. If the end play is less than the minimum limit, inspect the thrust bearing faces for scratches, burrs, nicks, or dirt. If the thrust faces are not damaged or dirty, then they probably were not aligned properly. Lubricate and install the new thrust bearing and align the faces following the listed procedures.

8. On engines with one piece rear main bearing oil seal, coat a new crankshaft rear oil seal with oil and install using Tool T65P-6701-A or equivalent. Inspect the seal to be sure it was not damaged during installation.

9. Install new bearing inserts in the connecting rods and caps. Check the clearance of each bearing, following the procedure listed.

10. After the connecting rod bearings have been fitted, apply a light coat of engine oil to the journals and bearings.

11. Turn the crankshaft throw to the bottom of its stroke. Push the piston all the way down until the rod bearing seats on the crankshaft journal.

12. Install the connecting rod cap. Tighten the nuts to specification.

13. After the piston and connecting rod assemblies have been installed, check the side clearance with a feeler gauge between the connecting rods on each connecting rod crankshaft journal. Refer to Crankshaft and Connecting Rod specifications chart in this section.

Rear Main Oil Seal

➡**The 6-300 and the diesel use a one-piece rear main seal. Replacement of this seal requires the removal of the transmission. All other engines use a two-piece seal which may be replaced with the engine and transmission in place.**

REPLACEMENT

Two-Piece Seal

♦ **See Figures 218 and 219**

If the crankshaft rear oil seal replacement is the only operation being performed, it can be done in the vehicle as detailed in the following procedure. If the oil seal is being replaced in conjunction with a rear main bearing replacement, the engine must be removed from the vehicle and install on a work stand.

1. Remove the oil pan and the oil pump (if required).

2. Loosen all the main bearing cap bolts, thereby lowering the crankshaft slightly but not to exceed ¹⁄₃₂ inch (0.8mm).

3. Remove the rear main bearing cap, and remove the oil seal from the bearing cap and cylinder block. On the block half of the seal use a seal removal tool, or install a small metal screw in one end of the seal, and pull on the screw

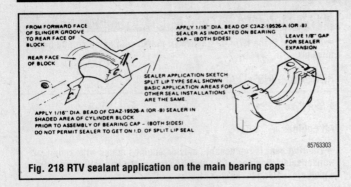

Fig. 218 RTV sealant application on the main bearing caps

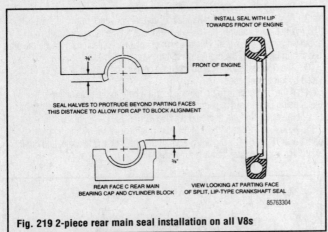

Fig. 219 2-piece rear main seal installation on all V8s

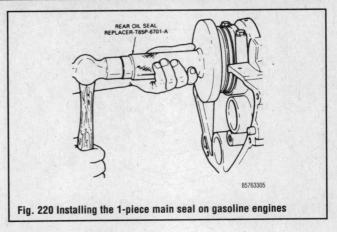

Fig. 220 Installing the 1-piece main seal on gasoline engines

to remove the seal. Exercise caution to prevent scratching or damaging the crankshaft seal surfaces.

4. Remove the oil seal retaining pin from the bearing cap if so equipped. The pin is not used with the split-lip seal.

5. Carefully clean the seal groove in the cap and block with a brush and solvent such as lacquer thinner, spot remover, trichloroethylene, or equivalent. Also, clean the area thoroughly, so that no solvent touches the seal.

6. Dip the split lip-type seal halves in clean engine oil.

7. Carefully install the upper seal (cylinder block) into its groove with undercut side of the seal toward the FRONT of the engine, by rotating it on the seal journal of the crankshaft until approximately ⅜ inch (9.5mm) protrudes below the parting surface. Be sure no rubber has been shaved from the outside diameter of the seal by the bottom edge of the groove. Do not allow oil to get on the sealer area.

8. Tighten the remaining bearing cap bolts to the specifications listed in the Torque chart at the beginning of this section.

9. Install the lower seal in the rear main bearing cap under undercut side of seal toward the FRONT of the engine, allow the seal to protrude approximately ⅜ inch (9.5mm) above the parting surface to mate with the upper seal when the cap is installed.

10. Apply an even ¹⁄₁₆ inch (1.6mm) bead of RTV silicone rubber sealer, to the areas, following the procedure given in the illustration.

➡ **This sealer sets up in 15 minutes.**

11. Install the rear main bearing cap. Tighten the cap bolts to specifications.

12. Install the oil pump and oil pan. Fill the crankcase with the proper amount and type of oil.

13. Operate the engine and check for oil leaks.

One-Piece Seal

GASOLINE ENGINES

▶ **See Figure 220**

If the crankshaft rear oil seal replacement is the only operation being performed, it can be done in the vehicle as detailed in the following procedure. If the oil seal is being replaced in conjunction with a rear main bearing replacement, the engine must be removed from the vehicle and install on a work stand.

1. Remove the starter.

2. Remove the transmission from the vehicle, following procedures in Section 6.

3. On manual shift transmission, remove the pressure plate and cover assembly and the clutch disc following the procedure in Section 7.

4. Remove the flywheel attaching bolts and remove the flywheel and engine rear cover plate.

5. Use an awl to punch two holes in the crankshaft rear oil seal. Punch the holes on opposite sides of the crankshaft and just above the bearing cap to cylinder block split line. Install a sheet metal screw in each hole. Use two large screwdrivers or small pry bars and pry against both screws at the same time to remove the crankshaft rear oil seal. It may be necessary to place small blocks of wood against the cylinder block to provide a fulcrum point for the pry bars. Use caution throughout this procedure to avoid scratching or otherwise damaging the crankshaft oil seal surface.

6. Clean the oil seal recess in the cylinder block and main bearing cap.

7. Clean, inspect and polish the rear oil seal rubbing surface on the crankshaft. Coat the new oil seal and the crankshaft with a light film of engine oil. Start the seal in the recess with the seal lip facing forward and install it with a seal driver. Keep the tool straight with the centerline of the crankshaft and install the seal until the tool contacts the cylinder block surface. Remove the tool and inspect the seal to be sure it was not damaged during installation.

8. Install the engine rear cover plate. Position the flywheel on the crankshaft flange. Coat the threads of the flywheel attaching bolts with oil-resistant sealer and install the bolts. Tighten the bolts in sequence across from each other to the specifications listed in the Torque chart at the beginning of this Section.

9. On a manual shift transmission, install the clutch disc and the pressure plate assembly following the procedure in Section 7.

10. Install the transmission, following the procedure in Section 7.

DIESEL ENGINES

▶ **See Figures 221, 222 and 223**

1. Remove the transmission, clutch and flywheel assemblies.

2. Remove the engine rear cover.

3. Using an arbor press and a 4⅛ inch (104.775mm) diameter spacer, press out the rear oil seal from the cover.

4. To install, clean the rear cover and engine block surfaces. Remove all traces of old RTV sealant from the oil pan and rear cover sealing surface by cleaning with a suitable solvent and drying thoroughly.

5. Coat the new rear oil seal with Lubriplate® or equivalent. Using an arbor press and spacer, install the new seal into the cover.

➡ **The seal must be installed from the engine block side of the rear cover, flush with the seal bore inner surface.**

6. Install a seal pilot, Ford part no. T83T-6701B or equivalent onto the crankshaft.

7. Apply gasket sealant to the engine block gasket surfaces, and install the rear cover gasket to the engine.

8. Apply a ¼ inch (6mm) bead of RTV sealant onto the oil pan sealing surface, immediately after rear cover installation.

9. Push the rear cover into position on the engine and install the cover bolts. Torque to specification.

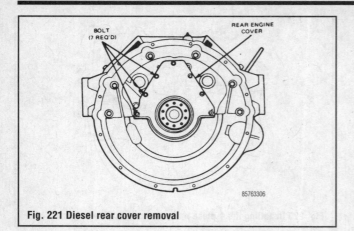

Fig. 221 Diesel rear cover removal

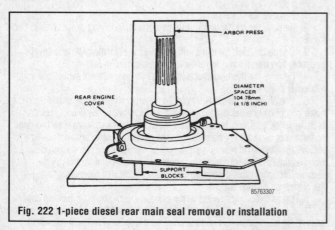

Fig. 222 1-piece diesel rear main seal removal or installation

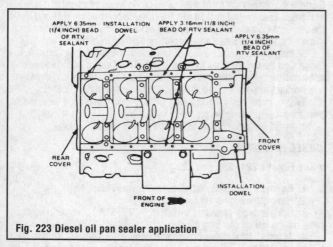

Fig. 223 Diesel oil pan sealer application

10. Position the flywheel on the crankshaft flange. Coat the threads of the flywheel attaching bolts with sealant and install the bolts and flexplate, if equipped. Torque the bolts to specification, alternating across from each bolt.

11. Install the clutch and transmission. Run the engine and check for oil leaks.

Flywheel/Flex Plate and Ring Gear

➡Flex plate is the term for a flywheel mated with an automatic transmission.

REMOVAL & INSTALLATION

◗ **See Figure 224**

All Engines

➡The ring gear is replaceable only on engines mated with a manual transmission. Engines with automatic transmissions have ring gears which are welded to the flex plate.

1. Remove the transmission and transfer case.
2. Remove the clutch, if equipped, or torque converter from the flywheel. The flywheel bolts should be loosened a little at a time in a cross pattern to avoid warping the flywheel. On cars with manual transmissions, replace the pilot bearing in the end of the crankshaft if removing the flywheel.
3. The flywheel should be checked for cracks and glazing. It can be resurfaced by a machine shop.
4. If the ring gear is to be replaced, drill a hole in the gear between two teeth, being careful not to contact the flywheel surface. Using a cold chisel at this point, crack the ring gear and remove it.
5. Polish the inner surface of the new ring gear and heat it in an oven to about 600 °F (316 °C). Quickly place the ring gear on the flywheel and tap it into place, making sure that it is fully seated.

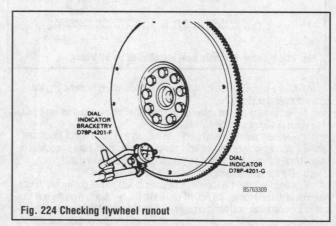

Fig. 224 Checking flywheel runout

✳✳ WARNING

Never heat the ring gear past 800 °F (426 °C), or the tempering will be destroyed.

6. Position the flywheel on the end of the crankshaft. Torque the bolts a little at a time, in a cross pattern, to the torque figure shown in the Torque Specifications Chart.
7. Install the clutch or torque converter.
8. Install the transmission and transfer case.

Completing the Rebuilding Process

Fill the oil pump with oil, to prevent cavitating (sucking air) on initial engine start up. Install the oil pump and the pickup tube on the engine. Coat the oil pan gasket as necessary, and install the gasket and the oil pan. Mount the flywheel and the crankshaft vibration damper or pulley on the crankshaft.

➡**Always use new bolts when installing the flywheel. Inspect the clutch shaft pilot bushing in the crankshaft. If the bushing is excessively worn, remove it with an expanding puller and a slide hammer, and tap a new bushing into place.**

Position the engine, cylinder head side up. Lubricate the lifters, and install them into their bores. Install the cylinder head, and torque it as specified. Insert the pushrods (where applicable), and install the rocker shaft(s) (if so equipped) or position the rocker.

Install the intake and exhaust manifolds, the carburetor(s), the distributor and spark plugs. Mount all accessories and install the engine in the truck. Fill the radiator with coolant, and the crankcase with high quality engine oil.

EXHAUST SYSTEM

✳✳ CAUTION

When working on exhaust systems, ALWAYS wear protective goggles! Avoid working on a hot exhaust system!

Muffler, Catalytic Converter, Inlet and Outlet Pipes

REMOVAL & INSTALLATION

➡**The following applies to exhaust systems using clamped joints. Some models use welded joints at the muffler. These joints will, of course, have to be cut.**

1. Raise and support the truck on jackstands.
2. Remove the U-clamps securing the muffler and outlet pipe.
3. Disconnect the muffler and outlet pipe bracket and insulator assemblies.
4. Remove the muffler and outlet pipe assembly. It may be necessary to heat the joints to get the parts to come off. Special tools are available to aid in breaking loose the joints.
5. On Super Cab and Crew Cab models, remove the extension pipe.

BREAK-IN PROCEDURE

Start the engine, and allow it to run at low speed for a few minutes, while checking for leaks. Stop the engine, check the oil level, and fill as necessary. Restart the engine, and fill the cooling system to capacity. Check and adjust the ignition timing. Run the engine at low to medium speed (800-2,500 rpm) for approximately ½ hour, and retorque the cylinder head bolts. Road test the truck, and check again for leaks.

➡**Some gasket manufacturers recommend not retorquing the cylinder head(s) due to the composition of the head gasket. Follow the directions in the gasket set.**

6. Disconnect the catalytic converter bracket and insulator assembly.

➡**For rod and insulator type hangers, apply a soap solution to the insulator surface and rod ends to allow easier removal of the insulator from the rod end. Don't use oil-based or silicone-based solutions since they will allow the insulator to slip back off once it's installed.**

7. Remove the catalytic converter.
8. On models with Managed Thermactor Air, disconnect the MTA tube assembly.
9. Remove the inlet pipe assembly.
10. Install the components making sure that all the components in the system are properly aligned before tightening any fasteners. Make sure all tabs are indexed and all parts are clear of surrounding body panels. See the accompanying illustrations for proper clearances and alignment. Observe the following torque specifications:
    - Inlet pipe-to-manifold: 35 ft. lbs.
    - MTA U-bolt: 60-96 inch lbs.
    - Inlet pipe or converter-to-muffler or extension: 45 ft. lbs.
    - Hanger bracket and insulator-to-frame: 24 ft. lbs.
    - Bracket and insulator-to-exhaust: 15 ft. lbs.
    - Flat flange bolts (8-460 and diesel) 30 ft. lbs.

TORQUE SPECIFICATIONS

Component	U.S.	Metric
Alternator adjusting bolt		
6-300	24–40 ft. lbs.	33–54 Nm
8-302/351W/351M/400/460	24–40 ft. lbs.	33–54 Nm
Alternator bracket-to-block or head		
6-232	30–40 ft. lbs.	41–54 Nm
6-300	30–45 ft. lbs.	41–61 Nm
8-420	24–39 ft. lbs.	33–53 Nm
Alternator pivot bolt		
6-232	45–57 ft. lbs.	61–76 Nm
8-302/351W/351M/400	45–57 ft. lbs.	61–76 Nm
8-360/390/460	45–57 ft. lbs.	61–76 Nm
8-420	28–53 ft. lbs.	40–68 Nm
Camshaft sprocket-to-camshaft		
6-232	15–22 ft. lbs.	20–30 Nm
8-255/302/351W/351M/400/460	40–45 ft. lbs.	54–61 Nm
8-360/390	45–57 ft. lbs.	61–76 Nm
8-420	12–18 ft. lbs.	17–24 Nm
Camshaft thrust plate bolts		
8-255/302/351W/351M/400/460	9–12 ft. lbs.	13–17 Nm
Carburetor mounting nuts		
6-232	9–11 ft. lbs.	13–17 Nm
6-300	12–15 ft. lbs.	17–20 Nm
8-255/302/351W/351M/400/460	12–15 ft. lbs.	17–20 Nm
Connecting rod nuts		
6-232	31–36 ft. lbs.	42–49 Nm
6-300	40–45 ft. lbs.	54–61 Nm
8-255/302	19–24 ft. lbs.	26–33 Nm
8-351W		
1976–77	19–24 ft. lbs.	26–33 Nm
1978–86	40–45 ft. lbs.	54–61 Nm
8-351M/400	40–45 ft. lbs.	54–61 Nm
8-360/390	40–45 ft. lbs.	54–61 Nm
8-420		
1983–84		
Step 1	38 ft. lbs.	50 Nm
Step 2	46–51 ft. lbs.	62–68 Nm
1985–86		
Step 1	38 ft. lbs.	50 Nm
Step 2	49–54 ft. lbs.	66–70 Nm
8-460		
1976–82	40–45 ft. lbs.	54–61 Nm
1983–86	45–50 ft. lbs.	61–67 Nm
Cylinder head bolts		
6-232		
Step 1	47 ft. lbs.	62 Nm
Step 2	55 ft. lbs.	75 Nm
Step 3	63 ft. lbs.	90 Nm
Step 4	74 ft. lbs.	102 Nm
Step 5	Back off all bolts 2–3 turns	
Step 6	Repeat Steps 1–4	
6-300		
Step 1	55 ft. lbs.	75 Nm
Step 2	65 ft. lbs.	88 Nm
Step 3	70–85 ft. lbs.	95–115 Nm

85763250

TORQUE SPECIFICATIONS

Component	U.S.	Metric
8-255		
Step 1	55–65 ft. lbs.	75–88 Nm
Step 2	65–72 ft. lbs.	88–97 Nm
8-302		
1976–77		
Step 1	50 ft. lbs.	67 Nm
Step 2	60 ft. lbs.	82 Nm
Step 3	65–70 ft. lbs.	88–95 Nm
1978–86		
Step 1	55–65 ft. lbs.	75–88 Nm
Step 2	65–72 ft. lbs.	88–97 Nm
8-351W		
1976–77		
Step 1	50 ft. lbs.	67 Nm
Step 2	60 ft. lbs.	82 Nm
Step 3	65–70 ft. lbs.	88–95 Nm
1978–86		
Step 1	85 ft. lbs.	115 Nm
Step 2	95 ft. lbs.	129 Nm
Step 3	105–112 ft. lbs.	143–151 Nm
8-351M/400		
Step 1	75 ft. lbs.	102 Nm
Step 2	95 ft. lbs.	129
Step 3	105 ft. lbs.	143 Nm
8-360/390		
Step 1	70 ft. lbs.	95 Nm
Step 2	80 ft. lbs.	110 Nm
Step 3	90 ft. lbs.	122 Nm
8-420		
1983		
Step 1	43 ft. lbs.	65 Nm
Step 2	60 ft. lbs.	82 Nm
1984		
Step 1	40 ft. lbs.	55 Nm
Step 2	65 ft. lbs.	88 Nm
Step 3	75 ft. lbs.	102 Nm
Step 4	Back off 1 turn	Back off 1 turn
Step 5	75 ft. lbs.	102 Nm
1985–86		
Step 1	40 ft. lbs.	55 Nm
Step 2	70 ft. lbs.	95 Nm
Step 3	80 ft. lbs.	95 Nm
Step 4	Back off 1 turn	Back off 1 turn
Step 5	80 ft. lbs.	110 Nm
8-460		
Step 1	80 ft. lbs.	110 Nm
Step 2	110 ft. lbs.	149 Nm
Step 3	130–140 ft. lbs.	177–189 Nm
Damper-to-crankshaft		
6-232	93–121 ft. lbs.	125–165 Nm
6-300	130–150 ft. lbs.	177–203 Nm
8-255/302/351W	70–90 ft. lbs.	94–122 Nm
8-351M/400	130–150 ft. lbs.	177–203 Nm
8-360/390	90 ft. lbs.	122 Nm
8-420	70–90 ft. lbs.	94–122 Nm
8-460		

85763350A

TORQUE SPECIFICATIONS

Component	U.S.	Metric
Engine front cover		
6-232	15–22 ft. lbs.	20–30 Nm
6-300	12–18 ft. lbs.	17–24 Nm
8-255/302/351W/351M/400	12–18 ft. lbs.	17–24 Nm
8-360/390	10–15 ft. lbs.	14–20 Nm
8-420		
1/4 in.	7 ft. lbs.	8 Nm
5/16 in	14 ft. lbs.	19 Nm
8-460		
1976–77	15–20 ft. lbs.	20–27 Nm
1978	12–18 ft. lbs.	17–24 Nm
1979	15–21 ft. lbs.	20–28 Nm
1980–81		
5/16 in.	12–18 ft. lbs.	17–24 Nm
7/16 in.	45–55 ft. lbs.	61–75 Nm
1982–86	15–21 ft. lbs.	20–28 Nm
Engine side cover		
6-300	15–20 ft. lbs.	20–27 Nm
Exhaust manifold-to-cylinder head		
6-232	15–22 ft. lbs.	20–30 Nm
6-300		
1976–77	23–28 ft. lbs.	32–38 Nm
1978–81	28–3 ft. lbs.	38–45 Nm
1982–86	22–32 ft. lbs.	30–43 Nm
8-255/302/351W/351M/400	18–24 ft. lbs.	24–32 Nm
8-360/390	12–18 ft. lbs.	17–24 Nm
8-420		
1983–85	30 ft. lbs.	41 Nm
1986	35 ft. lbs.	48 Nm
8-460	28–33 ft. lbs.	38–45 Nm
Exhaust pipe-to-manifold		
6-232	20–25 ft. lbs.	26–35 Nm
6-300	25–35 ft. lbs.	35–48 Nm
8-255/302/351W	25–30 ft. lbs.	35–41 Nm
8-360/390/420	25–35 ft. lbs.	35–48 Nm
Flywheel-to-crankshaft		
6-232	54–64 ft. lbs.	73–87 Nm
6-300	75–85 ft. lbs.	102–115 Nm
8-255/302/351W/351M/400	75–85 ft. lbs.	102–115 Nm
8-360/390	75–85 ft. lbs.	102–115 Nm
8-420		
1983	38 ft. lbs.	53 Nm
1984–86	47 ft. lbs.	64 Nm
8-460	75–85 ft. lbs.	102–115 Nm
Fuel pump mounting bolts		
6-232	15–22 ft. lbs.	20–30 Nm
6-300	12–18 ft. lbs.	17–24 Nm
8-255/302/351W	19–27 ft. lbs.	26–36 Nm
8-351M/400		
Nut	14–20 ft. lbs.	17–26 Nm
Bolt	10–15 ft. lbs.	13–20 Nm
8-360/390	19–27 ft. lbs.	26–36 Nm
8-460	19–27 ft. lbs.	26–36 Nm

85763550B

TORQUE SPECIFICATIONS

Component	U.S.	Metric
Intake manifold-to-cylinder head		
6-232		
Step 1	5 ft. lbs.	7 Nm
Step 2	10 ft. lbs.	14 Nm
Step 3	18 ft. lbs.	24 Nm
6-300		
1976–77	28–33 ft. lbs.	38–45 Nm
1978–86	22–32 ft. lbs.	30–43 Nm
8-255/302/351W	23–25 ft. lbs.	31–34 Nm
8-351M/400		
3/8 in.	22–32 ft. lbs.	30–43 Nm
5/16 in.	17–25 ft. lbs.	23–34 Nm
8-360/390	40–45 ft. lbs.	54–61 Nm
8-420		
5/16 in.	14 ft. lbs.	19 Nm
7/16 in.	24 ft. lbs.	33 Nm
3/7 in.	38 ft. lbs.	52 Nm
8-460		
1976–77	28–33 ft. lbs.	38–45
1978–86	22–32 ft. lbs.	30–43 Nm
Intake-to-exhaust manifold		
6-300	28–33 ft. lbs.	38–45 Nm
Main bearing cap bolts		
6-232	65–81 ft. lbs.	88–110 Nm
6-300	60–70 ft. lbs.	82–95 Nm
8-255	60–70 ft. lbs.	82–95 Nm
8-302	60–70 ft. lbs.	82–95 Nm
8-351W		
1976–77	60–70 ft. lbs.	82–95 Nm
1978–86	95–105 ft. lbs.	129–143 Nm
8-351M/400	95–105 ft. lbs.	129–143 Nm
8-360/390	95–105 ft. lbs.	129–143 Nm
8-420		
Step 1	75 ft. lbs.	102 Nm
Step 2	95 ft. lbs.	129 Nm
8-460	95–105 ft. lbs.	129–143 Nm
Oil filter adapter-to-block or cover		
6-232	18–22 ft. lbs.	24–30 Nm
6-300 HD	38–42 ft. lbs.	52–57 Nm
8-255/302/351W/351M/400	20–30 ft. lbs.	27–41 Nm
8-360/390	17–25 ft. lbs.	23–34 Nm
8-460		
1976–79	20–30 ft. lbs.	27–41 Nm
1980–81	40–60 ft. lbs.	54–82 Nm
1982–86	40–50 ft. lbs.	54–68 Nm
Oil filter center bolt		
8-460	40–50 ft. lbs.	54–68 Nm
Oil pan bolts		
6-232	7–9 ft. lbs.	10–12 Nm
6-300		
1976–84	10–15 ft. lbs.	13–20 Nm
1985–86	10–12 ft. lbs.	14–16 Nm
8-255	9–11 ft. lbs.	12–15 Nm
8-302/351W	9–11 ft. lbs.	12–15 Nm
8-360/390		
1976–80	7–9 ft. lbs.	10–12 Nm
1/4 in. bolts	8–11 ft. lbs.	11–15 Nm
5/16 in. bolts 1981–86	9–11 ft. lbs.	12–15 Nm

85763590C

TORQUE SPECIFICATIONS

Component	U.S.	Metric
8-351M/400		
¼ in.	7-9 ft. lbs.	10-12 Nm
5/16 in.	11-13 ft. lbs.	15-18 Nm
8-360/390	8-10 ft. lbs.	11-14 Nm
8-420		
¼ in.	7 ft. lbs.	10 Nm
5/16 in.	14 ft. lbs.	19 Nm
8-460		
¼ in.	9-11 ft. lbs.	12-15 Nm
5/16 in.	7-9 ft. lbs.	10-12 Nm
Oil pan drain plug		
6-232/300	15-25 ft. lbs.	20-34 Nm
8-255/302/351W/351M/400	15-25 ft. lbs.	20-34 Nm
8-360/390	15-25 ft. lbs.	20-34 Nm
8-420	28 ft. lbs.	38 Nm
8-460	15-25 ft. lbs.	20-34 Nm
Oil pickup tube-to-pump		
6-300	10-15 ft. lbs.	13-20 Nm
8-255/302/351W	10-15 ft. lbs.	13-20 Nm
8-360/390	Press fit	
8-460		
1976-79	12-18 ft. lbs.	17-24 Nm
1980-86		
Oil pump cover plate		
6-300	6-14 ft. lbs.	8-19 Nm
8-460	6-10 ft. lbs.	8-14 Nm
Oil pump-to-block		
6-300		
1976-84	10-15 ft. lbs.	13-20 Nm
1985-86	10-12 ft. lbs.	14-16 Nm
8-255/302/351W	22-32 ft. lbs.	30-43 Nm
8-351M/400	17-27 ft. lbs.	23-37 Nm
8-360/390	22-32 ft. lbs.	30-43 Nm
8-460	22-32 ft. lbs.	30-43 Nm
Pulley-to-damper		
6-232	20-28 ft. lbs.	27-38 Nm
6-300	35-50 ft. lbs.	48-68 Nm
8-255/302/351W/351M/400	35-50 ft. lbs.	48-68 Nm
8-460	35-50 ft. lbs.	48-68 Nm
Rocker arm cover		
6-232	36-60 inch lbs.	4-7 Nm
6-300		
1976-84	48-84 inch lbs.	5-9 Nm
1985-86	70-105 inch lbs.	8-12 Nm
8-255/302/351W/351M/400	36-60 inch lbs.	4-7 Nm
8-360/390	48-84 inch lbs.	5-9 Nm
8-420	72 inch lbs.	8 Nm
8-460	60-72 inch lbs.	7-8 Nm

85763500

TORQUE SPECIFICATIONS

Component	U.S.	Metric
Rocker arm stud/nut		
6-232		
Step 1	5-11 ft. lbs.	7-15 Nm
Step 2	18-26 ft. lbs.	24-35 Nm
6-300	17-23 ft. lbs.	23-31 Nm
8-255	18-25 ft. lbs.	24-34 Nm
8-302/351W		
1976-78	17-23 ft. lbs.	23-31 Nm
1979-86	18-25 ft. lbs.	24-34 Nm
8-351M/400/460	18-25 ft. lbs.	24-34 Nm
Rocker shaft support-to-head		
8-360/390	40-45 ft. lbs.	54-61 Nm
Spark plugs		
6-232	17-22 ft. lbs.	23-30 Nm
6-300		
1976-79	15-25 ft. lbs.	20-34 Nm
1980-86	10-15 ft. lbs.	13-20 Nm
8-255/302/351W/351M/400	10-15 ft. lbs.	13-20 Nm
8-360/390	10-15 ft. lbs.	13-20 Nm
8-460		
1976-78	10-15 ft. lbs.	13-20 Nm
1979-86	5-10 ft. lbs.	7-14 Nm
Thermostat housing bolts		
6-232	15-22 ft. lbs.	20-30 Nm
6-300	12-15 ft. lbs.	16-20 Nm
8-255	9-12 ft. lbs.	12-16 Nm
8-302		
1976-79	12-15 ft. lbs.	16-20 Nm
1980-86	9-12 ft. lbs.	12-16 Nm
8-351W		
1976-79	23-28 ft. lbs.	32-38 Nm
1890-86	9-12 ft. lbs.	12-16 Nm
8-360/390	23-28 ft. lbs.	32-38 Nm
8-351M/400	20 ft. lbs.	27 Nm
8-420	23-28 ft. lbs.	32-38 Nm
8-460		
1976-78	10-15 ft. lbs.	13-20 Nm
1979-81	12-18 ft. lbs.	17-24 Nm
1982-83	10-15 ft. lbs.	13-20 Nm
1984-86	10-15 ft. lbs.	13-20 Nm
Water pump mounting bolts		
6-232	15-22 ft. lbs.	20-30 Nm
6-300	15-20 ft. lbs.	20-27 Nm
1976-79	12-18 ft. lbs.	17-24 Nm
1980-86	12-18 ft. lbs.	17-24 Nm
8-255/302/351W	12-18 ft. lbs.	17-24 Nm
8-351M/400	20-25 ft. lbs.	26-35 Nm
8-360/390	14 ft. lbs.	19 Nm
8-420	12-18 ft. lbs.	17-24 Nm
8-460	15-21 ft. lbs.	20-28 Nm
1979-81	12-18 ft. lbs.	17-24 Nm
1982-83	15-21 ft. lbs.	20-28 Nm
1984-86		

85763500E

ENGINE MECHANICAL SPECIFICATIONS

Component	U.S.	Metric
Camshaft bearing ID		
6-232	2.0525-2.0535 in.	52.1335-52.1589mm
8-255		
No. 1	2.0825-2.0835 in.	52.8955-52.9209mm
No. 2	2.0675-2.0685 in.	52.5145-52.5399mm
No. 3	2.0525-2.0535 in.	52.1335-52.1589mm
No. 4	2.0375-2.0385 in.	51.7525-51.7779mm
No. 5	2.0225-2.0235 in.	51.3715-51.3969mm
6-300 No. 1 through 4	2.0190-2.0200 in.	51.2826-51.3080mm
8-302		
No. 1	2.0825-2.0835 in.	52.8955-52.9209mm
No. 2	2.0675-2.0685 in.	52.5145-52.5399mm
No. 3	2.0525-2.0535 in.	52.1335-52.1589mm
No. 4	2.0375-2.0385 in.	51.7525-51.7779mm
No. 5	2.0225-2.0235 in.	51.3715-51.3969mm
8-351W		
No. 1	2.0825-2.0835 in.	52.8955-52.9209mm
No. 2	2.0675-2.0685 in.	52.5145-52.5399mm
No. 3	2.0525-2.0535 in.	52.1335-52.1589mm
No. 4	2.0375-2.0385 in.	51.7525-51.7779mm
No. 5	2.0225-2.0235 in.	51.3715-51.3969mm
8-351M		
No. 1	2.1258-2.1268 in.	53.9953-54.0207mm
No. 2	2.0675-2.0685 in.	52.5145-52.5399mm
No. 3	2.0525-2.0535 in.	52.1335-52.1589mm
No. 4	2.0375-2.0385 in.	51.7525-51.7779mm
No. 5	2.0225-2.0235 in.	51.3715-51.3969mm
8-360 No. 1 through 5	2.1258-2.1268 in.	53.9953-54.0207mm
8-390 No. 1 through 5	2.1258-2.1268 in.	53.9953-54.0207mm
8-400		
No. 1	2.1258-2.1268 in.	53.9953-54.0207mm
No. 2	2.0675-2.0685 in.	52.5145-52.5399mm
No. 3	2.0525-2.0535 in.	52.1335-52.1589mm
No. 4	2.0375-2.0385 in.	51.7525-51.7779mm
No. 5	2.0225-2.0235 in.	51.3715-51.3969mm
8-420 No. 1 through 5		
1983	2.0990-2.1000 in.	53.3146-53.3400mm
1984	2.1010-2.1045 in.	53.3654-53.4543mm
1985-86	2.1020-2.1055 in.	53.3908-53.4797mm
8-460 No. 1 through 5	2.1258-2.1268 in.	53.9953-54.0207mm
Camshaft end-play		
6-232	0	0
8-255	0.0010-0.0070 in.	0.0254-0.1778mm
6-300		
1976-85	0.0010-0.0070 in.	0.0254-0.1778mm
1986	0.0010-0.0090 in.	0.0254-0.2286mm
8-302	0.0010-0.0070 in.	0.0254-0.1778mm
8-351W	0.0010-0.0060 in.	0.0254-0.1524mm
8-351M	0.0010-0.0060 in.	0.0254-0.1524mm
8-360	0.0010-0.0050 in.	0.0254-0.1270mm
8-390	0.0010-0.0050 in.	0.0254-0.1270mm
8-400	0.0010-0.0060 in.	0.0254-0.1524mm
8-420	0.0010-0.0050 in.	0.0254-0.1270mm
8-460		
1976-85	0.0010-0.0070 in.	0.0254-0.1778mm
1986	0.0010-0.0060 in.	0.0254-0.1524mm

85763C99

ENGINE MECHANICAL SPECIFICATIONS

Component	U.S.	Metric
Camshaft front bearing location①		
6-232	—	—
8-255	0.0050-0.0200 in.	0.1270-0.5080mm
6-300		
1976-77	0.0030-0.0050 in.	0.0762-0.1270mm
1978-86	0.0200-0.0350 in.	0.5080-0.8890mm
8-302	0.0050-0.0200 in.	0.1270-0.5080mm
8-351W	0.0050-0.0200 in.	0.1270-0.5080mm
8-351M	0.0400-0.0600 in.	1.0160-1.5240mm
8-360	0.0050-0.0200 in.	0.1270-0.5080mm
8-390	0.0050-0.0200 in.	0.1270-0.5080mm
8-400	0.0400-0.0600 in.	1.0160-1.5240mm
8-420	0.0400-0.0600 in.	1.0160-1.5240mm
8-460	0.0400-0.0600 in.	1.0160-1.5240mm
Camshaft journal-to-bearing clearance		
6-232	0.0010-0.0030 in.	0.0254-0.0762mm
8-255	0.0010-0.0030 in.	0.0254-0.0762mm
6-300	0.0010-0.0030 in.	0.0254-0.0762mm
8-302	0.0010-0.0030 in.	0.0254-0.0762mm
8-351W	0.0010-0.0030 in.	0.0254-0.0762mm
8-351M	0.0010-0.0030 in.	0.0254-0.0762mm
8-360	0.0010-0.0030 in.	0.0254-0.0762mm
8-390	0.0010-0.0030 in.	0.0254-0.0762mm
8-400	0.0010-0.0030 in.	0.0254-0.0762mm
8-420	0.0010-0.0055 in.	0.0254-0.1397mm
8-460	0.0010-0.0030 in.	0.0254-0.0762mm
Camshaft journal diameter		
6-232 No. 1 through 4	2.0505-2.0515 in.	52.0827-52.1081mm
8-255		
No. 1	2.0805-2.0815 in.	52.8447-52.8701mm
No. 2	2.0655-2.0665 in.	52.4637-52.4891mm
No. 3	2.0505-2.0515 in.	52.0827-52.1081mm
No. 4	2.0355-2.0365 in.	51.7017-51.7271mm
No. 5	2.0205-2.0215 in.	51.3207-51.3461mm
6-300 No. 1 through 4	2.0170-2.0180 in.	51.2318-51.2572mm
8-302		
No. 1	2.0805-2.0815 in.	52.8447-52.8701mm
No. 2	2.0655-2.0665 in.	52.4637-52.4891mm
No. 3	2.0505-2.0515 in.	52.0827-52.1081mm
No. 4	2.0355-2.0365 in.	51.7017-51.7271mm
No. 5	2.0205-2.0215 in.	51.3207-51.3461mm
8-351W		
No. 1	2.0805-2.0815 in.	52.8447-52.8701mm
No. 2	2.0655-2.0665 in.	52.4637-52.4891mm
No. 3	2.0505-2.0515 in.	52.0827-52.1081mm
No. 4	2.0355-2.0365 in.	51.7017-51.7271mm
No. 5	2.0205-2.0215 in.	51.3207-51.3461mm
8-351M		
No. 1	2.1248-2.1328 in.	53.9699-54.1731mm
No. 2	2.0655-2.0665 in.	52.4637-52.2489mm
No. 3	2.0505-2.0515 in.	52.0827-52.1081mm
No. 4	2.0355-2.0365 in.	51.7017-51.7271mm
No. 5	2.0205-2.0215 in.	51.3207-51.3461mm
8-360 No. 1 through 5	2.1238-2.1248 in.	53.9445-53.9699mm
8-390 No. 1 through 5	2.1238-2.1248 in.	53.9445-53.9699mm

8576399A

ENGINE MECHANICAL SPECIFICATIONS

Component	U.S.	Metric
8-400		
No. 1	2.1248–2.1328 in.	53.9699–54.1731mm
No. 2	2.0655–2.0665 in.	52.4637–52.2489mm
No. 3	2.0505–2.0515 in.	52.0827–52.1081mm
No. 4	2.0355–2.0365 in.	51.7017–51.7271mm
No. 5	2.0205–2.0215 in.	51.3207–51.3461mm
8-420		
1983	2.1000–2.1055 in.	53.3400–53.4797mm
1984–85	2.1020–2.1100 in.	53.3908–53.5940mm
1986	2.1030–2.1110 in.	53.4162–53.6194mm
8-460 No. 1 through 5	2.1238–2.1248 in.	53.9445–53.9699mm
Camshaft lobe lift		
6-232		
Intake	0.2400 in.	6.0960mm
Exhaust	0.2410 in.	6.1214mm
8-255 Int. & Exh.	0.2375 in.	6.0325mm
6-300		
Intake	0.2490 in. ②	6.3246mm
Exhaust	0.2490 in. ②	6.3246mm
8-302		
1976–77		
Intake	0.2303 in.	5.8496mm
Exhaust	0.2375 in.	6.0325mm
1978–86		
Intake	0.2375 in.	6.0325mm
Exhaust	0.2474 in.	6.2840mm
8-351W		
1976–77		
Intake	0.2303 in.	5.8496mm
Exhaust	0.2375 in.	6.0325mm
1978–86 Int. & Exh.	0.2600 in.	6.6040mm
8-351M		
Intake	0.2350 in.	5.9690mm
Exhaust	0.2350 in.	5.9690mm
8-360		
Intake	0.2470 in.	6.2738mm
Exhaust	0.2490 in.	6.3246mm
8-390		
Intake	0.2470 in.	6.2738mm
Exhaust	0.2490 in.	6.3246mm
8-400		
Intake	0.2472 in.	6.2788mm
Exhaust	0.2500 in.	6.3500mm
8-460		
1976–79		
Intake	0.2530 in.	6.4262mm
Exhaust	0.2780 in.	7.0612mm
1980–86		
Intake	0.2520 in.	6.4008mm
Exhaust	0.2780 in.	7.0612mm

85763998

ENGINE MECHANICAL SPECIFICATIONS

Component	U.S.	Metric
Connecting rod bearing bore ID		
6-232	2.4266–2.4274 in.	61.6356–61.6600mm
8-255	2.2390–2.2398 in.	56.8706–56.8909mm
6-300	2.2750–2.2758 in.	57.7850–57.8053mm
8-302	2.2390–2.2398 in.	56.8706–56.8909mm
8-351W		
1976–77	2.2390–2.2398 in.	56.8706–56.8909mm
1978–86	2.4265–2.4273 in.	61.6331–61.6534mm
8-351M	2.4361–2.4369 in.	61.8769–61.8973mm
8-360	2.5907–2.5915 in.	65.8038–65.8241mm
8-390	2.5907–2.5915 in.	65.8038–65.8241mm
8-420	2.4361–2.4369 in.	61.8769–61.8973mm
1983	2.6905–2.6910 in.	68.3387–68.3514mm
1984–86	2.5001–2.5016 in.	63.5025–63.5406mm
8-460	2.6522–2.6530 in.	67.3659–67.3862mm
Connecting rod lower end bearing clearance		
6-232	0.0010–0.0014 in.	0.0254–0.0356mm
8-255	0.0008–0.0015 in.	0.0020–0.0381mm
6-300	0.0008–0.0015 in.	0.0020–0.0381mm
8-302	0.0008–0.0015 in.	0.0020–0.0381mm
8-351W	0.0008–0.0015 in.	0.0020–0.0381mm
8-351M	0.0008–0.0015 in.	0.0020–0.0381mm
8-360	0.0008–0.0015 in.	0.0020–0.0381mm
8-390	0.0008–0.0015 in.	0.0020–0.0381mm
8-400	0.0008–0.0015 in.	0.0020–0.0381mm
8-420	0.0011–0.0026 in.	0.0279–0.0660mm
8-460	0.0008–0.0015 in.	0.0020–0.0381mm
Connecting rod bend (max.)		
6-232	0.0016 in. ①	0.0406mm②
8-255	0.0120 in.	0.3048mm
6-300	0.0120 in.	0.3048mm
8-302	0.0120 in.	0.3048mm
8-351W	0.0120 in.	0.3048mm
8-351M	0.0120 in.	0.3048mm
8-360	0.0120 in.	0.3048mm
8-390	0.0120 in.	0.3048mm
8-400	0.0120 in.	0.3048mm
8-420	0.0120 in.	0.3048mm
8-460	0.0120 in.	0.3048mm
Connecting rod-to-crankshaft side clearance		
6-232	0.0047–0.0114 in.	0.1194–0.2896mm
8-255	0.0100–0.0200 in.	0.2540–0.5080mm
6-300	0.0060–0.0130 in.	0.1524–0.3302mm
8-302	0.0100–0.0200 in.	0.2540–0.5080mm
8-351W	0.0100–0.0200 in.	0.2540–0.5080mm
8-351M	0.0100–0.0200 in.	0.2540–0.5080mm
8-360	0.0080–0.0250 in.	0.2032–0.6350mm
8-390	0.0080–0.0250 in.	0.2032–0.6350mm
8-400	0.0100–0.0200 in.	0.2540–0.5080mm
8-420		
1983–85	0.0080–0.0200 in.	0.2032–0.5080mm
1986	0.0120–0.0240 in.	0.3048–0.6096mm
8-460	0.0100–0.0200 in.	0.2540–0.5080mm

85763999C

ENGINE MECHANICAL SPECIFICATIONS

Component	U.S.	Metric
Connecting rod journal diameter		
6-232	2.3103-2.3111 in.	58.6816-58.7019mm
8-255	2.1228-2.1236 in.	53.9191-53.9394mm
6-300	2.1228-2.1236 in.	53.9191-53.9394mm
8-302	2.1228-2.1236 in.	53.9191-53.9394mm
8-351W	2.3103-2.3111 in.	58.6816-58.7019mm
8-351M	2.3103-2.3111 in.	58.6816-58.7019mm
8-360	2.4380-2.4388 in.	61.9252-61.945mm
8-390	2.4380-2.4388 in.	61.9252-61.945mm
8-400	2.3103-2.3111 in.	58.6816-58.7019mm
8-420	2.4980-2.4990 in.	63.4492-63.4746mm
8-460	2.4992-2.5000 in.	63.4797-63.5000mm
Connecting rod journal taper ②		
6-232	0.0003 in.	0.0076mm
8-255	0.0006 in.	0.0152mm
6-300	0.0006 in.	0.0152mm
8-302	0.0006 in.	0.0152mm
8-351W	0.0006 in.	0.0152mm
8-351M	0.0006 in.	0.0152mm
8-360	0.0006 in.	0.0152mm
8-390	0.0006 in.	0.0152mm
8-400	0.0006 in.	0.0152mm
8-420	0.0005 in.	0.0127mm
8-460	0.0006 in.	0.0152mm
Connecting rod length (center-to-center)		
6-232	5.9120-5.9150 in.	150.1648-150.2410mm
8-255	5.0885-5.0915 in.	129.2479-129.3241mm
6-300	6.2082-6.2112 in.	157.6883-157.7645mm
8-302	5.0885-5.0915 in.	129.2479-129.3241mm
8-351W	5.9545-5.9575 in.	151.2443-151.3205mm
8-351M	6.5785-6.5815 in.	167.0939-167.1701mm
8-360	6.5380-6.5420 in.	166.0652-166.1668mm
8-390	6.4860-6.4900 in.	164.7444-164.8460mm
8-400	6.5785-6.5815 in.	167.0939-167.1701mm
8-460	6.6035-6.6065 in.	167.7289-167.8051mm
Connecting rod piston pin bore ID		
6-232	0.9096-0.9112 in.	23.1038-23.1445mm
8-255	0.9096-0.9112 in.	23.1038-23.1445mm
6-300	0.9734-0.9742 in.	24.7244-24.7447mm
8-302		
1976-77	0.9104-0.9112 in.	23.1242-23.1445mm
1978-86	0.9096-0.9112 in.	23.1038-23.1445mm
8-351W		
1976-77	0.9104-0.9112 in.	23.1242-23.1445mm
1978-86	0.9096-0.9112 in.	23.1038-23.1445mm
8-351M	0.9726-0.9742 in.	24.7040-24.7447mm
8-360	0.9752-0.9755 in.	24.7701-24.7777mm
8-390	0.9752-0.9755 in.	24.7701-24.7777mm
8-400	0.9726-0.9742 in.	24.7040-24.7447mm
8-460	1.0386-1.0393 in.	26.3804-26.3982mm

85763990

ENGINE MECHANICAL SPECIFICATIONS

Component	U.S.	Metric
Connecting rod twist (max.)		
6-232	0.0030 in. ①	0.0762mm ①
8-255	0.0240 in.	0.6096mm
6-300	0.0240 in.	0.6096mm
8-302	0.0240 in.	0.6096mm
8-351W	0.0240 in.	0.6096mm
8-351M	0.0240 in.	0.6096mm
8-360	0.0240 in.	0.6096mm
8-390	0.0240 in.	0.6096mm
8-400	0.0240 in.	0.6096mm
8-420	0.0240 in.	0.6096mm
8-460	0.0240 in.	0.6096mm
Crankshaft end-play		
6-232	0.0040-0.0080 in.	0.1016-0.2032mm
8-255	0.0040-0.0080 in.	0.1016-0.2032mm
6-300	0.0040-0.0080 in.	0.1016-0.2032mm
8-302	0.0040-0.0080 in.	0.1016-0.2032mm
8-351W	0.0040-0.0080 in.	0.1016-0.2032mm
8-351M	0.0040-0.0080 in.	0.1016-0.2032mm
8-360	0.0040-0.0100 in.	0.1016-0.2032mm
8-390	0.0040-0.0100 in.	0.1016-0.2032mm
8-400	0.0040-0.0080 in.	0.1016-0.2032mm
8-420	0.0010-0.0090 in.	0.0254-0.2286mm
8-460	0.0040-0.0080 in.	0.1016-0.2032mm
Crankshaft thrust bearing journal length		
6-232	1.1703-1.1722 in.	29.7256-29.7734mm
8-255	1.1370-1.1390 in.	28.8798-28.9306mm
6-300	1.1990-1.2010 in.	30.4546-30.5054mm
8-302	1.1370-1.1390 in.	28.8798-28.9306mm
8-351W	1.1370-1.1390 in.	28.8798-28.9306mm
8-351M	1.1370-1.1390 in.	28.8798-28.9306mm
8-360	1.1240-1.1260 in.	28.5496-28.6004mm
8-390	1.1240-1.1260 in.	28.5496-28.6004mm
8-400	1.1370-1.1390 in.	28.8798-28.9306mm
8-420	1.1325-1.1355 in.	28.7655-34.4170mm
8-460	1.1240-1.1260 in.	28.5496-28.6004mm
Cylinder block head gasket surface flatness ①		
6-232	0.0030 in.	0.0762mm
8-255	0.0030 in.	0.0762mm
6-300	0.0030 in.	0.0762mm
8-302	0.0030 in.	0.0762mm
8-351W	0.0030 in.	0.0762mm
8-351M	0.0030 in.	0.0762mm
8-360	0.0030 in.	0.0762mm
8-390	0.0030 in.	0.0762mm
8-400	0.0030 in.	0.0762mm
8-420	0.0030 in.	0.0762mm
8-460	0.0030 in.	0.0762mm
Cylinder bore diameter		
6-232	3.8100 in.	96.7740mm
8-255	3.6800-3.6835 in.	93.4720-93.5609mm
6-300	4.0000-4.0048 in.	101.6000-101.7219mm
8-302	4.0004-4.0052 in.	101.6102-101.7321mm
8-351W	4.0000-4.0048 in.	101.6000-101.7219mm
8-351M	4.0000-4.0048 in.	101.6000-101.7219mm

85763996E

ENGINE MECHANICAL SPECIFICATIONS

Component	U.S.	Metric
8-360	4.0500-4.0536 in.	102.8700-102.9614mm
8-390	4.0500-4.0536 in.	102.8700-102.9614mm
8-400	4.0000-4.0048 in.	101.6000-101.7219mm
8-420		
1983	4.0000-4.0010 in.	101.6000-101.6254mm
1984-86	3.9995-4.0015 in.	101.5873-101.6381mm
8-460	4.3600-4.3636 in.	110.7440-110.8354mm
Cylinder bore max. taper		
6-232	0.0020 in.	0.0508mm
8-255	0.0010 in.	0.0254mm
6-300	0.0010 in.	0.0254mm
8-302	0.0010 in.	0.0254mm
8-351W	0.0010 in.	0.0254mm
8-351M	0.0010 in.	0.0254mm
8-360	0.0010 in.	0.0254mm
8-390	0.0010 in.	0.0254mm
8-400	0.0010 in.	0.0254mm
8-420	0.0050 in.	0.1270mm
8-460	0.0010 in.	0.0254mm
Cylinder bore out-of-round (max.)		
6-232	0.0020 in.	0.0508mm
8-255	0.0015 in.	0.0381mm
6-300	0.0015 in.	0.0381mm
8-302	0.0015 in.	0.0381mm
8-351W	0.0015 in.	0.0381mm
8-351M	0.0015 in.	0.0381mm
8-360	0.0015 in.	0.0381mm
8-390	0.0015 in.	0.0381mm
8-400	0.0015 in.	0.0381mm
8-420	0.0020 in.	0.0508mm
8-460	0.0015 in.	0.0381mm
Cylinder head gasket surface flatness ①		
6-232	0.0070 in.	0.1778mm
8-255	0.0030 in.	0.0762mm
6-300	0.0060 in.	0.1524mm
8-302	0.0030 in.	0.0762mm
8-351W	0.0030 in.	0.0762mm
8-351M	0.0030 in.	0.0762mm
8-360	0.0030 in.	0.0762mm
8-390	0.0030 in.	0.0762mm
8-400	0.0030 in.	0.0762mm
8-420	0.0030 in.	0.0762mm
8-460	0.0030 in.	0.0762mm
Flywheel ring gear lateral runout		
6-232		
Manual transmission	0.0250 in.	0.6350mm
Automatic transmission	0.0700 in.	1.7780mm
8-255		
Manual transmission	0.0300 in.	0.7620mm
Automatic transmission	0.0600 in.	1.5240mm
6-300		
Manual transmission	0.0400 in.	1.0160mm
Automatic transmission	0.0600 in.	1.5240mm

85763991F

ENGINE MECHANICAL SPECIFICATIONS

Component	U.S.	Metric
8-302		
Manual transmission	0.0300 in.	0.7620mm
Automatic transmission	0.0600 in.	1.5240mm
8-351W		
Manual transmission	0.0300 in.	0.7620mm
Automatic transmission	0.0600 in.	1.5240mm
8-351M		
Manual transmission	0.0300 in.	0.7620mm
Automatic transmission	0.0600 in.	1.5240mm
8-360		
Manual transmission	0.0400 in.	1.0160mm
Automatic transmission	0.0750 in.	1.9050mm
8-390		
Manual transmission	0.0400 in.	1.0160mm
Automatic transmission	0.0750 in.	1.9050mm
8-400		
Manual transmission	0.0300 in.	0.7620mm
Automatic transmission	0.0600 in.	1.5240mm
8-420	0.0080 in.	0.2032mm
8-460	0.0600 in.	1.5240mm
Flywheel clutch face runout		
6-232	0.0050 in.	0.1270mm
8-255	0.0100 in.	0.2540mm
6-300	0.0100 in.	0.2540mm
8-302	0.0100 in.	0.2540mm
8-351W	0.0100 in.	0.2540mm
8-351M	0.0100 in.	0.2540mm
8-360	0.0100 in.	0.2540mm
8-390	0.0100 in.	0.2540mm
8-400	0.0100 in.	0.2540mm
8-420	—	—
8-460		
Lifter-to-bore clearance		
6-232	0.0007-0.0027 in.	0.0178-0.0686mm
8-255	0.0007-0.0027 in.	0.0178-0.0686mm
6-300	0.0007-0.0027 in.	0.0178-0.0686mm
8-302	0.0007-0.0027 in.	0.0178-0.0686mm
8-351W	0.0007-0.0027 in.	0.0178-0.0686mm
8-351M	0.0007-0.0027 in.	0.0178-0.0686mm
8-360	0.0007-0.0027 in.	0.0178-0.0686mm
8-390	0.0007-0.0027 in.	0.0178-0.0686mm
8-400	0.0007-0.0027 in.	0.0178-0.0686mm
8-420		
8-460	0.0007-0.0027 in.	0.0178-0.0686mm
Lifter bore diameter		
6-232	0.8752-0.8767 in.	22.2301-22.2682mm
8-255	0.8752-0.8767 in.	22.2301-22.2682mm
6-300	0.8752-0.8767 in.	22.2301-22.2682mm
8-302	0.8752-0.8767 in.	22.2301-22.2682mm
8-351W	0.8752-0.8767 in.	22.2301-22.2682mm
8-351M	0.8752-0.8767 in.	22.2301-22.2682mm
8-360	0.8752-0.8767 in.	22.2301-22.2682mm
8-390	0.8752-0.8767 in.	22.2301-22.2682mm
8-400	0.8752-0.8767 in.	22.2301-22.2682mm
8-460	0.8752-0.8767 in.	22.2301-22.2682mm

85763996G

ENGINE MECHANICAL SPECIFICATIONS

Component	U.S.	Metric
Lifter collapsed gap		
6-232	0.0880–0.1890 in.	2.2352–4.8006mm
8-255	0.0980–0.1980 in.	2.4892–5.0292mm
6-300	0.1000–0.2000 in.	2.5400–5.0800mm
8-302		
1976–77	0.0900–0.1900 in.	2.2860–4.8260mm
1978–86	0.0960–0.1650 in.	2.4384–4.1910mm
8-351W		
1976–77	0.1060–0.2060 in.	2.6924–5.2324mm
1978–86	0.1230–0.1730 in.	3.1242–4.3942mm
8-351M	0.0750–0.1750 in.	1.9050–4.4450mm
8-360	0.0800–0.1800 in.	2.0320–4.5720mm
8-390	0.0800–0.1800 in.	2.0320–4.5720mm
8-400	0.0750–0.1750 in.	1.9050–4.4450mm
8-460	0.0750–0.1750 in.	1.9050–4.4450mm
Lifter diameter		
6-232	0.8740–0.8745 in.	22.1996–22.2123mm
8-255	0.8740–0.8745 in.	22.1996–22.2123mm
6-300	0.8740–0.8745 in.	22.1996–22.2123mm
8-302	0.8740–0.8745 in.	22.1996–22.2123mm
8-351W	0.8740–0.8745 in.	22.1996–22.2123mm
8-351M	0.8740–0.8745 in.	22.1996–22.2123mm
8-360	0.8740–0.8745 in.	22.1996–22.2123mm
8-390	0.8740–0.8745 in.	22.1996–22.2123mm
8-400	0.8740–0.8745 in.	22.1996–22.2123mm
8-460	0.8740–0.8745 in.	22.1996–22.2123mm
Lifter leakdown rate		
6-232	20–200 sec. @ 0.125 in./3.175mm plunger travel ⑥	
8-255	10–50 sec. max. @ 0.0625 in./1.586mm plunger travel	
6-300	5–50 sec. max. @ 0.0625 in./1.586mm plunger travel	
8-302	5–50 sec. max. @ 0.0625 in./1.586mm plunger travel	
8-351W	5–50 sec. max. @ 0.0625 in./1.586mm plunger travel	
8-351M	5–50 sec. max. @ 0.0625 in./1.586mm plunger travel	
8-360	5–50 sec. max. @ 0.0625 in./1.586mm plunger travel	
8-390	5–50 sec. max. @ 0.0625 in./1.586mm plunger travel	
8-400	5–50 sec. max. @ 0.0625 in./1.586mm plunger travel	
8-420	12–90 sec. max. @ 0.125 in./3.175mm plunger travel ⑥	
8-460	5–50 sec. max. @ 0.0625 in./1.586mm plunger travel	
Main bearing bore diameter		
6-232	2.5200–2.5212 in.	64.0080–64.0385mm
8-255		
No. 1	2.2483–2.2505 in.	57.1068–57.1627mm
No. 2, 3, 4, 5	2.2487–2.2505 in.	57.1170–57.1627mm
6-300	2.3990–2.4005 in.	60.9346–60.9727mm
8-302		
1976–77	2.2490–2.2505 in.	57.1246–57.1627mm
1978–86		
No. 1	2.2483–2.2505 in.	57.1068–57.1627mm
No. 2, 3, 4, 5	2.2487–2.2505 in.	57.1170–57.1627mm
8-351W	3.0002–3.0017 in.	76.2051–76.2432mm
8-351M	3.0002–3.0017 in.	76.2051–76.2432mm
8-360	2.7489–2.7507 in.	69.8221–69.8678mm
8-390		

8576399H

ENGINE MECHANICAL SPECIFICATIONS

Component	U.S.	Metric
	2.7489–2.7507 in.	69.8221–69.8678mm
8-400	3.0002–3.0017 in.	76.2051–76.2432mm
8-420	3.1246–3.1272 in.	79.3648–79.4309mm
8-460		
1976–77		
No. 1	3.0002–3.0017 in.	76.2051–76.2432mm
No. 2, 3, 4, 5	3.0002–3.0028 in.	76.2051–76.2711mm
1978–86	3.0002–3.0017 in.	76.2051–76.2432mm
Main bearing clearance		
6-232	0.0010–0.0014 in.	0.0254–0.0356mm
8-255		
No. 1	0.0001–0.0015 in.	0.0025–0.0381mm
No. 2, 3, 4, 5	0.0005–0.0015 in.	0.0127–0.0381mm
6-300	0.0008–0.0015 in.	0.0127–0.0381mm
8-302		
1976–77	0.0008–0.0015 in.	0.0127–0.0381mm
1978–86		
No. 1	0.0001–0.0015 in.	0.0025–0.0381mm
No. 2, 3, 4, 5	0.0005–0.0015 in.	0.0127–0.0381mm
8-351W	0.0008–0.0015 in.	0.0127–0.0381mm
8-351M	0.0008–0.0015 in.	0.0127–0.0381mm
8-360	0.0005–0.0015 in.	0.0127–0.0381mm
8-390	0.0005–0.0015 in.	0.0127–0.0381mm
8-400	0.0008–0.0015 in.	0.0127–0.0381mm
8-420	0.0018–0.0036 in.	0.0457–0.0914mm
8-460		
1976–77		
No. 1	0.0008–0.0015 in.	0.0127–0.0381mm
No. 2, 3, 4, 5	0.0008–0.0015 in.	0.0127–0.0660mm
1978–86	0.0008–0.0015 in.	0.0127–0.0381mm
Main bearing journal diameter		
6-232	2.5190–2.5198 in.	63.9826–64.0029mm
8-255	2.2482–2.2490 in.	57.1043–57.1246mm
6-300	2.3982–2.3990 in.	60.9143–60.9346mm
8-302	2.2482–2.2490 in.	57.1043–57.1246mm
8-351W	2.9994–3.0002 in.	76.1848–76.2051mm
8-351M	2.9994–3.0002 in.	76.1848–76.2051mm
8-360	2.7484–2.7492 in.	69.8094–69.8297mm
8-390	2.7484–2.7492 in.	69.8094–69.8297mm
8-400	2.9994–3.0002 in.	76.1848–76.2051mm
8-420	3.1228–3.1236 in.	79.3191–79.3394mm
8-460	2.9994–3.0002 in.	76.1848–76.2051mm
Main bearing journal runout (max.)		
6-232	0.002 in.	0.0508mm
8-255	0.002 in.	0.0508mm
6-300	0.002 in.	0.0508mm
8-302	0.002 in.	0.0508mm
8-351W	0.002 in.	0.0508mm
8-351M	0.002 in.	0.0508mm
8-360	0.002 in.	0.0508mm
8-390	0.002 in.	0.0508mm
8-400	0.002 in.	0.0508mm
8-420	0.002 in.	0.0508mm
8-460	0.002 in.	0.0508mm

8576399I

ENGINE MECHANICAL SPECIFICATIONS

Component	U.S.	Metric
Oil pump outer race-to-housing clearance		
6-232	0.0010-0.0130 in.	0.0254-0.3302mm
8-255	0.0010-0.0130 in.	0.0254-0.3302mm
6-300	0.0010-0.0130 in.	0.0254-0.3302mm
8-302	0.0010-0.0130 in.	0.0254-0.3302mm
8-351W	0.0010-0.0130 in.	0.0254-0.3302mm
8-351M	0.0010-0.0130 in.	0.0254-0.3302mm
8-360	0.0010-0.0130 in.	0.0254-0.3302mm
8-390	0.0010-0.0130 in.	0.0254-0.3302mm
8-400	0.0010-0.0130 in.	0.0254-0.3302mm
8-460	0.0010-0.0130 in.	0.0254-0.3302mm
Oil pump relief valve-to-housing clearance		
6-232	0.0017-0.0029 in.	0.0432-0.0737mm
8-255	0.0015-0.0029 in.	0.0381-0.0737mm
6-300	0.0015-0.0029 in.	0.0381-0.0737mm
8-302	0.0015-0.0029 in.	0.0381-0.0737mm
8-351W	0.0015-0.0029 in.	0.0381-0.0737mm
8-351M	0.0015-0.0030 in.	0.0381-0.0762mm
8-360	0.0015-0.0029 in.	0.0381-0.0737mm
8-390	0.0015-0.0029 in.	0.0381-0.0737mm
8-400	0.0015-0.0030 in.	0.0381-0.0762mm
8-460	0.0015-0.0029 in.	0.0381-0.0737mm
Oil pump relief valve spring pressure		
6-232	15.2-17.1 lbs. @ 1.20 in.	6.9-7.8kg @ 3.05 mm
8-255	10.6-12.2 lbs. @ 1.70 in.	4.8-5.5kg @ 4.32mm
6-300	20.6-22.6 lbs. @ 2.49 in.	9.3-10.25kg @ 6.32mm
8-302	10.6-12.2 lbs. @ 1.70 in.	4.8-5.5kg @ 4.32mm
8-351W	18.2-20.2 lbs. @ 2.49 in.	8.3-9.2kg @ 6.32mm
8-351M	20.6-22.6 lbs. @ 2.49 in.	9.3-10.25kg @ 6.32mm
8-360	8.7-9.5 lbs. @ 1.56 in.	3.9-4.3kg @ 3.96mm
8-390	8.7-9.5 lbs. @ 1.56 in.	3.9-4.3kg @ 3.96mm
8-400	20.6-22.6 lbs. @ 2.49 in.	9.3-10.25kg @ 6.32mm
8-460	20.6-22.6 lbs. @ 2.49 in.	9.3-10.25kg @ 6.32mm
Oil pump rotor end clearance		
6-232	—	
8-255	0.0010-0.0040 in.	0.0254-0.1016mm
6-300	0.0010-0.0040 in.	0.0254-0.1016mm
8-302	0.0010-0.0040 in.	0.0254-0.1016mm
8-351W	0.0040 max.	0.1016 max.
8-351M	0.0010-0.0040 in.	0.0254-0.1016mm
8-360	0.0010-0.0040 in.	0.0254-0.1016mm
8-390	0.0040 max.	0.1016 max.
8-400	0.0010-0.0040 in.	0.0254-0.1016mm
8-460	0.0010-0.0040 in.	0.0254-0.1016mm
Piston diameter (centerline)		
6-232		
Coded red	3.8059-3.8101 in.	96.7613-96.7765mm
Coded blue	3.8107-3.8113 in.	96.7918-96.8070mm
0.004 OS	3.8119-3.8125 in.	96.8223-96.8375mm
8-255		
Coded red	3.6784-3.6790 in.	93.4314-93.4466mm
Coded blue	3.6798-3.6804 in.	93.4669-93.4823mm
0.003 OS	3.6812-3.6818 in.	93.5025-93.5177mm

ENGINE MECHANICAL SPECIFICATIONS

Component	U.S.	Metric
Main bearing journal taper ①		
6-232	0.0003 in.	0.0076mm
8-255	0.0005 in.	0.0127mm
6-300	0.0005 in.	0.0127mm
8-302	0.0006 in.	0.0152mm
8-351W	0.0005 in.	0.0127mm
8-351M	0.0005 in.	0.0127mm
8-360	0.0050 in.	0.1270mm
8-390	0.0050 in.	0.1270mm
8-400	0.0005 in.	0.0127mm
8-420	0.0005 in.	0.0127mm
8-460	0.0006 in.	0.0152mm
Main bearing thrust face runout		
6-232	0.0010 in.	0.0254mm
8-255	0.0010 in.	0.0254mm
6-300	0.0010 in.	0.0254mm
8-302	0.0010 in.	0.0254mm
8-351W	0.0010 in.	0.0254mm
8-351M	0.0010 in.	0.0254mm
8-360	0.0010 in.	0.0254mm
8-390	0.0010 in.	0.0254mm
8-400	0.0010 in.	0.0254mm
8-420	0.0010 in.	0.0254mm
8-460	0.0010 in.	0.0254mm
Oil pump gear backlash		
6-232	0.0080-0.0120 in.	0.2032-0.3048mm
8-255	0	
6-300	0	
8-302	0	
8-351W	0	
8-351M	0	
8-360	0	
8-390	0	
8-400	0	
8-420	0	
8-460	0	
Oil pump gear end height (beyond housing)		
6-232	0.0020-0.0055 in.	0.0508-0.1397mm
Oil pump gear radial clearance		
6-232	0.0020-0.0050 in.	0.0508-0.1270mm
Oil pump driveshaft-to-housing clearance		
6-232	0.0015-0.0030 in.	0.0381-0.0762mm
8-255	0.0015-0.0029 in.	0.0381-0.0737mm
6-300	0.0015-0.0029 in.	0.0381-0.0737mm
8-302	0.0015-0.0029 in.	0.0381-0.0737mm
8-351W	0.0015-0.0029 in.	0.0381-0.0737mm
8-351M	0.0015-0.0029 in.	0.0381-0.0737mm
8-360	0.0015-0.0030 in.	0.0381-0.0762mm
8-390	0.0015-0.0029 in.	0.0381-0.0737mm
8-400	0.0015-0.0030 in.	0.0381-0.0762mm
8-460	0.0015-0.0029 in.	0.0381-0.0737mm
Oil pump idler gear-to-idler shaft clearance		
6-232	0.0004-0.0017 in.	0.01020-0.0432mm

85763999K

85763991

ENGINE MECHANICAL SPECIFICATIONS

Component	U.S.	Metric
6-300		
1976-79		
Coded red	3.9984–3.9990 in.	101.5594–101.5764mm
Coded blue	3.9996–4.0002 in.	101.5898–101.6051mm
0.003 OS	4.0008–4.0014 in.	101.6203–101.6356mm
Coded yellow	4.0020–4.0026 in.	101.6508–101.6660mm
1980-86		
Coded red	3.9982–3.9988 in.	101.5543–101.5695mm
Coded blue	3.9994–4.0000 in.	101.5848–101.6000mm
0.003 OS	4.0008–4.0014 in.	101.6203–101.6356mm
8-302		
Coded red	3.9984–3.9990 in.	101.5594–101.5746mm
Coded blue	3.9996–4.0002 in.	101.5898–101.6051mm
0.003 OS	4.0008–4.0014 in.	101.6203–101.6356mm
Coded yellow	4.0020–4.0026 in.	101.6508–101.6660mm
8-351W		
Coded red	3.9978–3.9984 in.	101.5441–101.5594mm
Coded blue	3.9990–3.9996 in.	101.5746–101.5898mm
0.003 OS	4.0002–4.0008 in.	101.6051–101.6203mm
Coded yellow	4.0020–4.0026 in.	101.6508–101.6660mm
8-351M		
Coded red	3.9982–3.9988 in.	101.5543–101.5695mm
Coded blue	3.9994–4.0000 in.	101.5848–101.6000mm
0.003 OS	4.0006–4.0012 in.	101.6152–101.6305mm
8-360		
Coded red	4.0484–4.0490 in.	102.8294–102.8446mm
Coded blue	4.0496–4.0502 in.	102.8598–102.8751mm
0.003 OS	4.0508–4.0514 in.	102.8903–102.9056mm
8-390		
Coded red	4.0484–4.0490 in.	102.8294–102.8446mm
Coded blue	4.0496–4.0502 in.	102.8598–102.8751mm
0.003 OS	4.0508–4.0514 in.	102.8903–102.9056mm
8-400		
Coded red	3.9982–3.9988 in.	101.5543–101.5695mm
Coded blue	3.9994–4.0000 in.	101.5848–101.6000mm
0.003 OS	4.0006–4.0012 in.	101.6152–101.6305mm
8-420		
Standard	3.9935–3.9945 in.	101.4349–101.4603mm
OS	3.9945–3.9955 in.	101.4349–101.4857mm
8-460		
Coded red	4.3585–4.3591 in.	110.7059–110.7211mm
Coded blue	4.3597–4.3603 in.	110.7364–110.7516mm
0.003 OS	4.3609–4.3615 in.	110.7669–110.7821mm
Piston-to-bore clearance		
6-232	0.0014–0.0022 in.	0.0356–0.0559mm
8-255	0.0018–0.0026 in.	0.0457–0.0660mm
6-300		
1976-84	0.0014–0.0022 in.	0.0356–0.0559mm
1985-86	0.0010–0.0018 in.	0.0254–0.0457mm
8-302	0.0018–0.0026 in.	0.0457–0.0660mm
8-351W	0.0018–0.0026 in.	0.0457–0.0660mm
8-351M	0.0014–0.0022 in.	0.0356–0.0559mm
8-360	0.0015–0.0023 in.	0.0381–0.0584mm
8-390	0.0015–0.0023 in.	0.0381–0.0584mm
8-400	0.0014–0.0022 in.	0.0356–0.0559mm
8-420	0.0055–0.0075 in.	0.1397–0.1905mm
8-460	0.0022–0.0030 in.	0.0559–0.0762mm

8576399L

ENGINE MECHANICAL SPECIFICATIONS

Component	U.S.	Metric
Piston height above crankcase		
8-420	0.0100–0.0310 in.	
Piston pin bore diameter in piston		
6-232	0.9122–0.9128 in.	23.1699–23.1851mm
8-255	0.9123–0.9126 in.	23.1724–23.1800mm
6-300	0.9753–0.9756 in.	24.7726–24.7802mm
8-302	0.9122–0.9126 in.	23.1699–23.1800mm
8-351W	0.9124–0.9127 in.	23.1750–23.1826mm
8-351M	0.9754–0.9757 in.	24.7752–24.7828mm
8-360	0.9752–0.9755 in.	24.7701–24.7777mm
8-390	0.9752–0.9755 in.	24.7701–24.7777mm
8-400	0.9754–0.9757 in.	24.7752–24.7828mm
8-420	1.1104–1.1106 in.	28.2042–28.2092mm
8-460	1.0402–1.0405 in.	26.4211–26.4287mm
Piston pin diameter		
6-232	0.9119–0.9124 in.	23.1623–23.1750mm
8-255		
Standard	0.9120–0.9123 in.	23.1648–23.1724mm
0.001 OS	0.9130–0.9133 in.	23.1902–23.1978mm
0.002 OS	0.9140–0.9143 in.	23.2156–23.2232mm
6-300		
Standard	0.9750–0.9753 in.	24.7650–24.7726mm
0.001 OS	0.9760–0.9763 in.	24.7904–24.7980mm
0.002 OS	0.9770–0.9773 in.	24.8158–24.8234mm
8-302		
Standard	0.9120–0.9123 in.	23.1648–23.1724mm
0.001 OS	0.9130–0.0133 in.	23.1902–23.1978mm
0.002 OS	0.9140–0.9143 in.	23.2156–23.2232mm
8-351W		
Standard	0.9120–0.9123 in.	23.1648–23.1724mm
0.001 OS	0.9130–0.9133 in.	23.1902–23.1978mm
0.002 OS	0.9140–0.9143 in.	23.2156–23.2232mm
8-351M	0.9745–0.9754 in.	24.7523–24.7752mm
8-360		
Standard	0.9749–0.9754 in.	24.7627–24.7752mm
0.001 OS	0.9760–0.9763 in.	24.7904–24.7980mm
0.002 OS	0.9770–0.9773 in.	24.8158–24.8234mm
8-390		
Standard	0.9749–0.9754 in.	24.7627–24.7752mm
0.001 OS	0.9760–0.9763 in.	24.7904–24.7980mm
0.002 OS	0.9770–0.9773 in.	24.8158–24.8234mm
8-400		
Standard	0.9749–0.9754 in.	24.7627–24.7752mm
0.001 OS	0.9760–0.9763 in.	24.7904–24.7980mm
0.002 OS	0.9745–0.9754 in.	24.7523–24.7752mm
8-420	1.1099–1.1101 in.	28.1915–28.1965mm
8-460		
Standard	1.0398–1.0403 in.	26.4109–26.4236mm
0.001 OS	1.0410–1.0413 in.	26.4414–26.4490mm
0.002 OS	—	
Piston pin length		
6-232	3.0120–3.0390 in.	76.5048–77.1906mm
8-255	3.0100–3.0400 in.	76.4540–77.2160mm
6-300	3.1500–3.1700 in.	80.0100–80.5180mm
8-302	3.0100–3.0400 in.	76.4540–77.2160mm
8-351W	3.0100–3.0400 in.	76.4540–77.2160mm
8-351M	3.1500–3.1700 in.	80.0100–80.5180mm
8-360	3.1500–3.1700 in.	80.0100–80.5180mm
8-390	3.1500–3.1700 in.	80.0100–80.5180mm
8-400	3.1500–3.1700 in.	80.0100–80.5180mm
8-420	2.7050–2.7150 in.	68.7070–68.9610mm
8-460	3.2900–3.3200 in.	83.5660–84.3280mm

8576399M

ENGINE MECHANICAL SPECIFICATIONS

Component	U.S.	Metric
Piston pin-to-piston bore clearance		
6-232	0.0002-0.0005 in.	0.0051-0.0127mm
8-255	0.0002-0.0004 in.	0.0051-0.0102mm
6-300	0.0002-0.0004 in.	0.0051-0.0102mm
8-302	0.0002-0.0004 in.	0.0051-0.0102mm
8-351W	0.0003-0.0005 in.	0.0076-0.0127mm
8-351M	0.0003-0.0005 in.	0.0076-0.0127mm
8-360	0.0001-0.0003 in.	0.0025-0.0076mm
8-390	0.0001-0.0003 in.	0.0025-0.0076mm
8-400	0.0003-0.0005 in.	0.0076-0.0127mm
8-420	0.0003-0.0007 in.	0.0076-0.0178mm
8-460	0.0002-0.0004 in.	0.0051-0.0102mm
Piston pin-to-rod clearance		
6-232	②	②
8-255	interference fit	
6-300	interference fit	
8-302	interference fit	
8-351W	interference fit	
8-351M	interference fit	
8-360	0.0002-0.0005 in.	0.0051-0.0127mm
8-390	0.0002-0.0005 in.	0.0051-0.0127mm
8-400	interference fit	
8-420	interference fit	
8-460	0.0004-0.0009 in.	0.0102-0.0229mm
Piston ring diameter		
8-420	4.0000 in.	
Piston ring end gap		
6-232 Top	0.0100-0.0200 in.	0.2540-0.5080mm
6-232 2nd	0.0100-0.0200 in.	0.2540-0.5080mm
6-232 Oil	0.0150-0.0583 in.	0.3810-1.4808mm
8-255 Top	0.0100-0.0200 in.	0.2540-0.5080mm
8-255 2nd	0.0100-0.0200 in.	0.2540-0.5080mm
8-255 Oil	0.0100-0.0350 in.	0.2540-0.8890mm
6-300 Top	0.0100-0.0200 in.	0.2540-0.5080mm
6-300 2nd	0.0100-0.0200 in.	0.2540-0.5080mm
6-300 Oil	0.0150-0.0550 in.	0.3810-1.3970mm
8-302 Top	0.0100-0.0200 in.	0.2540-0.5080mm
8-302 2nd	0.0100-0.0200 in.	0.2540-0.5080mm
8-302 Oil	0.0150-0.0550 in.	0.3810-1.3970mm
8-351W Top	0.0100-0.0200 in.	0.2540-0.5080mm
8-351W 2nd	0.0100-0.0200 in.	0.2540-0.5080mm
8-351W Oil	0.0150-0.0550 in.	0.3810-1.3970mm
8-351M Top	0.0100-0.0200 in.	0.2540-0.5080mm
8-351M 2nd	0.0100-0.0200 in.	0.2540-0.5080mm
8-351M Oil	0.0150-0.0550 in.	0.3810-1.3970mm

8576399N

ENGINE MECHANICAL SPECIFICATIONS

Component	U.S.	Metric
8-360 Top	0.0150-0.0230 in.	0.2540-0.5080mm
8-360 2nd	0.0100-0.0200 in.	0.2540-0.5080mm
8-360 Oil	0.0150-0.0550 in.	0.3810-1.3970mm
8-390 Top	0.0150-0.0230 in.	0.2540-0.5080mm
8-390 2nd	0.0100-0.0200 in.	0.2540-0.5080mm
8-390 Oil	0.0150-0.0550 in.	0.3810-1.3970mm
8-400 Top	0.0100-0.0200 in.	0.2540-0.5080mm
8-400 2nd	0.0100-0.0200 in.	0.2540-0.5080mm
8-400 Oil	0.0150-0.0550 in.	0.3810-1.3970mm
8-420 Top	0.0140-0.0240 in.	0.3556-0.6096mm
8-420 2nd	0.0100-0.0240 in.	0.2540-0.6096mm
8-420 Oil	0.0600-0.0700 in.	1.5240-1.7780mm
8-460 Top	0.0100-0.0200 in.	0.2540-0.5080mm
8-460 2nd	0.0100-0.0200 in.	0.2540-0.5080mm
8-460 Oil 1976-77	0.0150-0.0550 in.	0.3810-1.3970mm
8-460 Oil 1978	0.0100-0.0300 in.	0.2540-0.7620mm
8-460 Oil 1979-86	0.0100-0.0350 in.	0.2540-0.8890mm
Piston ring groove width		
6-232 Top	0.0800-0.0809 in.	2.0320-2.0549mm
6-232 2nd	0.0800-0.0809 in.	2.0320-2.0549mm
6-232 Oil	0.1587-0.1596 in.	4.0310-4.0538mm
8-255 Top	0.0800-0.0810 in.	2.0320-2.0574mm
8-255 2nd	0.0800-0.0810 in.	2.0320-2.0574mm
8-255 Oil	0.1880-0.1890 in.	4.7752-4.8006mm
6-300 Top	0.0800-0.0810 in.	2.0320-2.0574mm
6-300 2nd	0.0800-0.0810 in.	2.0320-2.0574mm
6-300 Oil	0.1880-0.1890 in.	4.7752-4.8006mm
8-302 Top	0.0800-0.0810 in.	2.0320-2.0574mm
8-302 2nd	0.0800-0.0810 in.	2.0320-2.0574mm
8-302 Oil	0.1880-0.1890 in.	4.7752-4.8006mm
8-351W Top	0.0800-0.0810 in.	2.0320-2.0574mm
8-351W 2nd	0.0800-0.0810 in.	2.0320-2.0574mm
8-351W Oil	0.1880-0.1890 in.	4.7752-4.8006mm
8-351M Top	0.0800-0.0810 in.	2.0320-2.0574mm
8-351M 2nd	0.0800-0.0810 in.	2.0320-2.0574mm
8-351M Oil	0.1880-0.1890 in.	4.7752-4.8006mm
8-360 Top	0.0800-0.0810 in.	2.0320-2.0574mm
8-360 2nd	0.0960-0.0970 in.	2.4384-2.4638mm
8-360 Oil	0.1880-0.1890 in.	4.7752-4.8006mm
8-390 Top	0.0800-0.0810 in.	2.0320-2.0574mm
8-390 2nd	0.0960-0.0970 in.	2.4384-2.4638mm
8-390 Oil	0.1880-0.1890 in.	4.7752-4.8006mm

85763390

ENGINE MECHANICAL SPECIFICATIONS

Component	U.S.	Metric
8-400		
Top	0.0800–0.0810 in.	2.0320–2.0574mm
2nd	0.0800–0.0810 in.	2.0320–2.0574mm
Oil	0.1880–0.1890 in.	4.7752–4.8006mm
8-460		
Top	0.0805–0.0815 in.	2.0447–2.0701mm
2nd	0.0805–0.0815 in.	2.0447–2.0701mm
Oil	0.1880–0.1890 in.	4.7752–4.8006mm
Piston ring side clearance		
6-232		
Top	0.0016–0.0037 in.	0.0406–0.0940mm
2nd	0.0016–0.0037 in.	0.0406–0.0940mm
Oil	snug	snug
8-255		
Top	0.0019–0.0036 in.	0.0483–0.0914mm
2nd	0.0020–0.0040 in.	0.0508–0.1016mm
Oil	snug	snug
6-300		
1976–77		
Top	0.0020–0.0040 in.	0.0508–0.1016mm
1978–86		
2nd	0.0019–0.0036 in.	0.0483–0.0914mm
Oil	0.0020–0.0040 in.	0.0508–0.1016mm
8-302		
Top	0.0020–0.0040 in.	0.0508–0.1016mm
1976–77		
2nd	0.0019–0.0036 in.	0.0483–0.0914mm
1978–86		
Oil	0.0020–0.0040 in.	0.0508–0.1016mm
8-351W		
Top	0.0020–0.0040 in.	0.0508–0.1016mm
1976–77		
2nd	0.0019–0.0036 in.	0.0483–0.0914mm
1978–86		
Oil	0.0020–0.0040 in.	0.0508–0.1016mm
8-351M		
Top	0.0019–0.0036 in.	0.0483–0.0914mm
2nd	0.0020–0.0040 in.	0.0508–0.1016mm
Oil	snug	snug
8-360		
Top	0.0020–0.0040 in.	0.0508–0.1016mm
2nd	0.0020–0.0040 in.	0.0508–0.1016mm
Oil	snug	snug
8-390		
Top	0.0020–0.0040 in.	0.0508–0.1016mm
2nd	0.0020–0.0040 in.	0.0508–0.1016mm
Oil	snug	snug
8-400		
Top	0.0019–0.0036 in.	0.0483–0.0914mm
2nd	0.0020–0.0040 in.	0.0508–0.1016mm
Oil	snug	snug
8-420		
Top	0.0020–0.0040 in.	0.0508–0.1016mm
2nd	0.0020–0.0040 in.	0.0508–0.1016mm
Oil	0.0010–0.0030 in.	0.0254–0.0762mm

85763399P

ENGINE MECHANICAL SPECIFICATIONS

Component	U.S.	Metric
8-460		
Top	0.0020–0.0040 in.	0.0508–0.1016mm
2nd	0.0020–0.0040 in.	0.0508–0.1016mm
Oil	snug	—
8-460		
1976–77		
Top	0.0019–0.0036 in.	0.0483–0.0914mm
2nd	0.0020–0.0040 in.	0.0508–0.1016mm
Oil	snug	—
1978–81		
Top	0.0019–0.0036 in.	0.0483–0.0914
2nd	0.0020–0.0040 in.	0.0508–0.1016mm
Oil	snug	—
1982–86		
Top	0.0025–0.0045 in.	0.0635–0.1143mm
2nd	0.0025–0.0045 in.	0.0635–0.1143mm
Oil	snug	—
Piston ring width		
6-232		
Top	0.0772–0.0783 in.	1.9601–1.9889mm
2nd	0.0772–0.0783 in.	1.9601–1.9889mm
Oil	—	—
8-255		
Top	0.0770–0.0780 in.	1.9558–1.9812mm
2nd	0.0770–0.0780 in.	1.9558–1.9812mm
Oil	—	—
6-300		
Top	0.0770–0.0780 in.	1.9558–1.9812mm
1976–77		
2nd	0.0774–0.0781 in.	1.9660–1.9837mm
1978–86		
Oil	0.0770–0.0780 in.	1.9558–1.9812mm
8-302		
Top	0.0770–0.0780 in.	1.9558–1.9812mm
2nd	0.0770–0.0780 in.	1.9558–1.9812mm
Oil	—	—
8-351W		
Top	0.0770–0.0780 in.	1.9558–1.9812mm
2nd	0.0770–0.0780 in.	1.9558–1.9812mm
Oil	—	—
8-351M		
Top	0.0770–0.0780 in.	1.9558–1.9812mm
2nd	0.0770–0.0780 in.	1.9558–1.9812mm
Oil	—	—
8-360		
Top	0.0770–0.0780 in.	1.9558–1.9812mm
2nd	0.0770–0.0780 in.	1.9558–1.9812mm
Oil	—	—
8-390		
Top	0.0770–0.0780 in.	1.9558–1.9812mm
2nd	0.0770–0.0780 in.	1.9558–1.9812mm
Oil	—	—
8-400		
Top	0.0770–0.0780 in.	1.9558–1.9812mm
2nd	0.0770–0.0780 in.	1.9558–1.9812mm
Oil	—	—

85763399Q

ENGINE MECHANICAL SPECIFICATIONS

Component	U.S.	Metric
8-460		
Top	0.0770–0.0780 in.	1.9558–1.9812mm
2nd	0.0770–0.0780 in.	1.9558–1.9812mm
Oil	—	—
Pushrod runout (max.)		
6-232	0.0150 in.	0.3810mm
8-255	0.0150 in.	0.3810mm
6-300	0.0150 in.	0.3810mm
8-302	0.0150 in.	0.3810mm
8-351W	0.0150 in.	0.3810mm
8-351M	0.0150 in.	0.3810mm
8-360	0.0200 in.	0.5080mm
8-390	0.0200 in.	0.5080mm
8-400	0.0150 in.	0.3810mm
8-420	0.0150 in.	0.3810mm
8-460	0.0150 in.	0.3810mm
Rocker arm bore diameter		
8-360/390	0.8425–0.8440 in.	21.3995–21.4376mm
Rocker arm lift ratio		
6-232	1.73:1	
8-255	1.61:1	
6-300	1.62:1	
8-302	1.61:1	
8-351W	1.61:1	
8-351M	1.73:1	
8-360	1.73:1	
8-390	1.73:1	
8-400	1.73:1	
8-420	1.73:1	
8-460	1.73:1	
Rocker arm shaft OD		
8-360/390	0.8390–0.0400 in.	21.3106–1.0160mm
Rocker arm-to-shaft clearance		
8-360/390	0.0020–0.0050 in.	0.0508–0.1270mm
Timing chain deflection (max.)		
6-232	0.5000 in.	12.7000mm
8-255	0.5000 in.	12.7000mm
6-300	—	—
8-302	0.5000 in.	12.7000mm
8-351W	0.5000 in.	12.7000mm
8-351M	0.5000 in.	12.7000mm
8-360	0.5000 in.	12.7000mm
8-390	0.5000 in.	12.7000mm
8-400	0.5000 in.	12.7000mm
8-460	0.5000 in.	12.7000mm
Timing gears (sprockets) assembled face runout (max.)		
6-232	0.0050 in.	0.1270mm
8-255	0.0050 in.	0.1270mm
6-300 Camshaft	0.0060 in.	0.1270mm
Crankshaft	0.0030 in.	0.1270mm
8-302	0.0050 in.	0.1270mm
8-351W	0.0050 in.	0.1270mm
8-351M	0.0050 in.	0.1270mm
8-360	0.0050 in.	0.1270mm
8-390	0.0050 in.	0.1270mm
8-400	0.0050 in.	0.1270mm
8-460	0.0050 in.	0.1270mm

8576399R

ENGINE MECHANICAL SPECIFICATIONS

Component	U.S.	Metric
Timing gear backlash		
6-300	0.0020–0.0040 in.	0.0508–0.1016mm
8-420	0.0055–0.0100 in.	0.1397–0.2540mm
Valve face angle		
6-232	44 deg.	
8-255	44 deg.	
6-300	44 deg.	
8-302	44 deg.	
8-351W	44 deg.	
8-351M	44 deg.	
8-360	44 deg.	
8-390	44 deg.	
8-400	44 deg.	
8-420 Intake	30 deg.	
Exhaust	37.5 deg.	
8-460	44 deg.	
Valve face minimum margin		
6-232	0.0625 in.	1.5875mm
8-255	0.0625 in.	1.5875mm
6-300	0.0625 in.	1.5875mm
8-302	0.0625 in.	1.5875mm
8-351W	0.0625 in.	1.5875mm
8-351M	0.0625 in.	1.5875mm
8-360	0.0625 in.	1.5875mm
8-390	0.0625 in.	1.5875mm
8-400	0.0625 in.	1.5875mm
8-420	0.0625 in.	1.5875mm
8-460	0.0625 in.	1.5875mm
Valve face runout (max.)		
6-232	0.0020 in.	0.0508mm
8-255	0.0020 in.	0.0508mm
6-300	0.0020 in.	0.0508mm
8-302	0.0020 in.	0.0508mm
8-351W	0.0020 in.	0.0508mm
8-360	0.0020 in.	0.0508mm
8-390	0.0020 in.	0.0508mm
8-400	0.0020 in.	0.0508mm
8-420	0.0020 in.	0.0508mm
8-460	0.0020 in.	0.0508mm
Valve guide bore		
6-232	0.3433–0.3443 in.	8.7198–8.7452mm
8-255	0.3433–0.3443 in.	8.7198–8.7452mm
6-300	0.3433–0.3443 in.	8.7198–8.7452mm
8-302	0.3433–0.3443 in.	8.7198–8.7452mm
8-351W	0.3433–0.3443 in.	8.7198–8.7452mm
8-351M	0.3433–0.3443 in.	8.7198–8.7452mm
8-360	0.3728–0.3738 in.	9.4691–9.4945mm
8-390	0.3728–0.3738 in.	9.4691–9.4945mm
8-400	0.3433–0.3443 in.	8.7198–8.7452mm
8-420 Intake	0.3736–0.3746 in.	9.4894–9.5148mm
Exhaust	0.3736–0.3746 in.	9.4894–9.5148mm
8-460	0.3433–0.3443 in.	8.7198–8.7452mm

8576399S

ENGINE MECHANICAL SPECIFICATIONS

Component	U.S.	Metric
Valve head diameter		
6-232		
Intake	1.7900 in.	45.4660mm
Exhaust	1.4700 in.	37.3380mm
8-255		
Intake	1.6900-1.6940 in.	42.9260-43.0276mm
Exhaust	1.4390-1.4630 in.	36.5506-37.1602mm
6-300		
Intake		
1976-81	1.7720-1.7900 in.	45.0088-45.4660mm
1982-86	1.7690-1.7930 in.	44.9326-45.5422mm
Exhaust	1.5510-1.5690 in.	39.3954-39.8526mm
8-302		
1976-77		
Intake	1.7730-1.7910 in.	45.0342-45.4914mm
Exhaust	1.4530-1.4680 in.	36.9062-37.2872mm
1978-80		
Intake	1.7700-1.7940 in.	44.9580-45.5676mm
Exhaust	1.4390-1.4630 in.	36.5506-37.1602mm
1981-86		
Intake	1.6900-1.6940 in.	42.9260-43.0276mm
Exhaust	1.4390-1.4630 in.	36.9062-37.2872mm
8-351W		
1976-77		
Intake	1.7730-1.7910 in.	45.0342-45.4914mm
Exhaust	1.4530-1.4680 in.	36.9062-37.2872mm
1978-80		
Intake	1.7700-1.7940 in.	44.9580-45.5676mm
Exhaust	1.4390-1.4630 in.	36.5506-37.1602mm
1981-86		
Intake	1.7700-1.7940 in.	44.9580-45.5676mm
Exhaust	1.4390-1.4630 in.	36.9062-37.2872mm
8-351M		
Intake	2.0320-2.0500 in.	51.6128-52.0700mm
Exhaust	1.6495-1.6595 in.	41.8973-42.1513mm
8-360		
Intake	2.0220-2.0370 in.	51.3588-51.7398mm
Exhaust	1.5510-1.5665 in.	39.3954-39.7764mm
8-390		
Intake	2.0220-2.0370 in.	51.3588-51.7398mm
Exhaust	1.5510-1.5665 in.	39.3954-39.7764mm
8-400		
Intake	2.0320-2.0500 in.	51.6128-52.0700mm
Exhaust	1.6495-1.6595 in.	41.8973-42.1513mm
8-460		
Intake	2.0750-2.0900 in.	52.7050-53.0860mm
Exhaust	1.6460-1.6610 in.	41.8084-42.1894mm
Valve head recession in deck		
8-420		
Intake	0.0420-0.0520 in.	
Exhaust	0.0430-0.0550 in.	

ENGINE MECHANICAL SPECIFICATIONS

Component	U.S.	Metric
Valve seat angle		
6-232	45 deg.	
8-255	45 deg.	
6-300	45 deg.	
8-351W	45 deg.	
8-351M	45 deg.	
8-360	45 deg.	
8-390	45 deg.	
8-400	45 deg.	
8-420		
Intake	30 deg.	
Exhaust	37.5 deg.	
8-460	45 deg.	
Valve seat runout (max.)		
6-232	0.0030 in.	0.0762mm
8-255	0.0020 in.	0.0508mm
6-300	0.0020 in.	0.0508mm
8-302	0.0015 in.	0.0381mm
8-351W	0.0020 in.	0.0508mm
8-351M	0.0020 in.	0.0508mm
8-360	0.0015 in.	0.0381mm
8-390	0.0015 in.	0.0381mm
8-400	0.0020 in.	0.0508mm
8-420	0.0020 in.	0.0508mm
8-460	0.0015 in.	0.0381mm
Valve seat width		
6-232 Int. & Exh.	0.0600-0.0800 in.	1.5240-2.0320mm
8-255 Int. & Exh.	0.0600-0.0800 in.	1.5240-2.0320mm
6-300		
Intake	0.0600-0.0800 in.	1.5240-2.0320mm
Exhaust	0.0700-0.0900 in.	1.7780-2.2860mm
8-302 Int. & Exh.	0.0600-0.0800 in.	1.5240-2.0320mm
8-351W Int. & Exh.	0.0600-0.0800 in.	1.5240-2.0320mm
8-351M		
Intake	0.0600-0.0800 in.	1.5240-2.0320mm
Exhaust	0.0700-0.0900 in.	1.7780-2.2860mm
8-360		
Intake	0.0600-0.0800 in.	1.5240-2.0320mm
Exhaust	0.0700-0.0900 in.	1.7780-2.2860mm
8-390		
Intake	0.0600-0.0800 in.	1.5240-2.0320mm
Exhaust	0.0700-0.0900 in.	1.7780-2.2860mm
8-400		
Intake	0.0600-0.0800 in.	1.5240-2.0320mm
Exhaust	0.0700-0.0900 in.	1.7780-2.2860mm
8-420 Int. & Exh.	0.0650-0.0950 in.	1.6510-2.4130mm
8-460 Int. & Exh.	0.0600-0.0800 in.	1.5240-2.0320mm
Valve spring compression pressure		
6-232 Int. & Exh.	215 lbs. @ 1.790 in.	97.5kg @ 45.46mm
8-255		
Intake	190-212 lbs. @ 1.360 in.	86-96kg @ 34.54mm
Exhaust	190-212 lbs. @ 1.200 in.	86-96kg @ 30.48mm

ENGINE MECHANICAL SPECIFICATIONS

Component	U.S.	Metric
6-300		
1976–83		
Intake	187–207 lbs. @ 1.300 in.	85–94kg @ 33.02mm
Exhaust	182–202 lbs. @ 1.180 in.	82–92kg @ 29.97mm
1984		
Intake	165–175 lbs. @ 1.300 in.	75–79kg @ 33.02mm
Exhaust	165–175 lbs. @ 1.180 in.	75–79kg @ 29.97mm
1985–86		
Intake	166–184 lbs. @ 1.240 in.	75–83kg @ 31.50mm
Exhaust	166–184 lbs. @ 1.070 in.	75–83kg @ 27.18mm
8-302		
1976–78		
Intake	190–210 lbs. @ 1.310 in.	86–95kg @ 33.27mm
Exhaust	190–210 lbs. @ 1.340 in.	86–95kg @ 34.04mm
1979		
Intake	192–212 lbs. @ 1.360 in.	87–96kg @ 34.54mm
Exhaust	190–210 lbs. @ 1.200 in.	86–95kg @ 30.48mm
1980–86		
Intake	196–212 lbs. @ 1.360 in.	89–96kg @ 34.54mm
Exhaust	190–210 lbs. @ 1.200 in.	86–95kg @ 30.48mm
8-351W		
1976–77		
Intake	190–210 lbs. @ 1.310 in.	86–95kg @ 33.27mm
Exhaust	190–210 lbs. @ 1.340 in.	86–95kg @ 34.04mm
1978		
Intake	190–210 lbs. @ 1.340 in.	86–95kg @ 34.04mm
Exhaust	190–210 lbs. @ 1.200 in.	86–95kg @ 30.48mm
1979–83		
Intake	190–210 lbs. @ 1.360 in.	86–95kg @ 34.54mm
Exhaust	190–210 lbs. @ 1.200 in.	86–95kg @ 30.48mm
1984–86		
Intake	190–210 lbs. @ 1.200 in.	86–95kg @ 30.48mm
Exhaust	190–210 lbs. @ 1.200 in.	86–95kg @ 30.48mm
8-351M		
Intake	215–237 lbs. @ 1.390 in.	98–108kg @ 35.31mm
Exhaust	215–237 lbs. @ 1.250 in.	98–108kg @ 31.75mm
8-360		
F-100 exhaust	175–194 lbs. @ 1.240 in.	79–88kg @ 31.50mm
All others	209–231 lbs. @ 1.318 in.	95–105kg @ 33.48mm
8-390		
F-100 exhaust	175–194 lbs. @ 1.240 in.	79–88kg @ 31.50mm
All others	209–231 lbs. @ 1.318 in.	95–105kg @ 33.48mm
8-400		
Intake	218–240 lbs. @ 1.390 in.	99–109kg @ 35.31mm
Exhaust	218–240 lbs. @ 1.250 in.	99–109kg @ 31.75mm
8-420 Int. & Exh.	60 lbs. @ 1.798 in.	27kg @ 45.67mm
460		
1976–77 Int. & Exh.	240–265 lbs. @ 1.330 in.	109–120kg @ 33.78mm
1978–86 Int. & Exh.	218–240 lbs. @ 1.330 in.	99–109kg @ 33.78mm
Valve spring free length (approx.)		
8-255		
Intake	2.0400 in.	51.8160mm
Exhaust	1.8500 in.	46.9900mm
6-300		
1976–83		
Intake	1.9900 in.	50.5460mm
Exhaust	1.8700 in.	47.4980mm

8576399V

ENGINE MECHANICAL SPECIFICATIONS

Component	U.S.	Metric
1984		
Intake	1.9700 in.	50.0380mm
Exhaust	1.8700 in.	47.4980mm
1985–86		
Intake	1.9600 in.	49.7840mm
Exhaust	1.7800 in.	45.2120mm
8-302		
1976–77		
Intake	1.9400 in.	49.2760mm
Exhaust	1.8500 in.	46.9900mm
1978		
Intake	1.9400 in.	49.2760mm
Exhaust	1.8700 in.	47.4980mm
1979–86		
Intake	2.0400 in.	51.8160mm
Exhaust	1.8500 in.	46.9900mm
8-351W		
1976–77		
Intake	2.0600 in.	52.3240mm
Exhaust	2.1200 in.	53.8480mm
1978		
Intake	2.0600 in.	52.3240mm
Exhaust	1.8700 in.	47.4980mm
1979–86		
Intake	2.0400 in.	51.8160mm
Exhaust	1.8500 in.	46.9900mm
8-351M Int. & Exh.	2.0600 in.	52.3240mm
8-360		
F-100 exhaust	2.0000 in.	50.8000mm
All others	2.1200 in.	53.8480mm
8-390		
F-100 exhaust	2.0000 in.	50.8000mm
All others	2.1200 in.	53.8480mm
8-400 Int. & Exh.	2.0600 in.	52.3240mm
8-420 Int. & Exh.	2.0400 in.	51.8160mm
8-460		
1976–77 Int. & Exh.	2.0300 in.	51.5620mm
1978 Int. & Exh.	2.0680 in.	52.5277mm
1979–86 Int. & Exh.	2.0600 in.	52.3240mm
Valve spring installed height ①		
6-232	1 45/64–1 25/32 in.	43.2594–45.2438mm
8-255		
Intake	1 43/64–1 45/64 in.	42.4656–43.2594mm
Exhaust	1 37/64–1 39/64 in.	40.0844–40.8781mm
6-300		
1976–84		
Intake	1 11/16–1 23/32 in.	42.8625–43.6563mm
Exhaust	1 9/16–1 19/32 in.	39.6875–40.4813mm
1985–86		
Intake	1 39/64–1 43/64 in.	40.8940–42.4180mm
Exhaust	1 7/16–1 1/2 in.	36.5760–38.1000mm

8576399W

ENGINE MECHANICAL SPECIFICATIONS

Component	U.S.	Metric
8-390		
Intake	0.3711–0.3718 in.	9.4259–9.4437mm
Exhaust	0.3703–0.3706 in.	9.4056–9.4132mm
8-400		
Intake	0.3416–0.3423 in.	8.6766–8.6944mm
Exhaust	0.3411–0.3418 in.	8.6639–8.6817mm
8-420 Int. & Exh.	0.3717–0.3724 in.	9.4412–9.4590mm
8-460 Int. & Exh.	0.3416–0.3423 in.	8.6766–8.6944mm
Valve stem-to-guide clearance		
6-232		
Intake	0.0010–0.0027 in.	0.0254–0.0686mm
Exhaust	0.0015–0.0032 in.	0.0381–0.0813mm
8-255		
Intake	0.0010–0.0027 in.	0.0254–0.0686mm
Exhaust	0.0015–0.0032 in.	0.0381–0.0813mm
6-300		
Intake	0.0010–0.0027 in.	0.0254–0.0686mm
Exhaust	0.0015–0.0032 in.	0.0381–0.0813mm
8-302		
Intake	0.0010–0.0027 in.	0.0254–0.0686mm
Exhaust		
1976-77	0.0010–0.0027 in.	0.0254–0.0686mm
1978-86	0.0010–0.0027 in.	0.0254–0.0686mm
8-351W		
Intake	0.0010–0.0027 in.	0.0254–0.0686mm
Exhaust	0.0015–0.0032 in.	0.0381–0.0813mm
8-351M		
Intake	0.0010–0.0027 in.	0.0254–0.0686mm
Exhaust	0.0015–0.0032 in.	0.0381–0.0813mm
8-360		
Intake	0.0010–0.0027 in.	0.0254–0.0686mm
Exhaust	0.0015–0.0032 in.	0.0381–0.0813mm
8-390		
Intake	0.0010–0.0027 in.	0.0254–0.0686mm
Exhaust	0.0015–0.0032 in.	0.0381–0.0813mm
8-400		
Intake	0.0010–0.0027 in.	0.0254–0.0686mm
Exhaust	0.0015–0.0032 in.	0.0381–0.0813mm
8-420 Int. & Exh.	0.0010–0.0027 in.	0.0254–0.0686mm
8-460		
Intake	0.0012–0.0029 in.	0.0305–0.0737mm
Exhaust	0.0010–0.0027 in.	0.0254–0.0686mm

① Distance from the front face of the block to the front edge of the bearing
② Per inch (25.4mm)
③ In any 6 in. (152.400mm)
④ Pad to retainer
⑤ Per inch
⑥ 50 lbs. (23kg) load, filled with leak-down test fluid
⑦ 1800 lbs. (817kg) press fit
⑧ F-150 2-wd with 2.47:1 or 2.75:1 axle ratio and man. trans., exc. Calif.: 0.2470 in. (6.2736mm)

8576399Y

ENGINE MECHANICAL SPECIFICATIONS

Component	U.S.	Metric
8-302		
1976-78		
Intake	1 43/64–1 45/64 in.	42.4656–43.2594mm
Exhaust	1 19/32–1 39/64 in.	40.4813–40.8781mm
1979-86		
Intake	1 43/64–1 45/64 in.	42.4656–43.2594mm
Exhaust	1 37/64–1 39/64 in.	40.0844–40.8781mm
8-351W		
1976-78		
Intake	1 49/64–1 13/16 in.	44.8469–46.0375mm
Exhaust	1 13/16–1 27/32 in.	46.0375–46.8313mm
1979-86		
Intake	1 49/64–1 51/64 in.	44.8469–45.6406mm
Exhaust	1 37/64–1 39/64 in.	40.0844–40.8781mm
8-351M Int. & Exh.	1 13/16–1 27/32 in.	46.0375–46.8313mm
8-360		
F-100 exhaust	1 21/32–1 11/16 in.	42.0688–42.8625mm
All others	1 13/16–1 27/32 in.	46.0375–46.8313mm
8-390		
8-400 Int. & Exh.	1 13/16–1 27/32 in.	46.0375–46.8313mm
8-460	1 51/64–1 53/64 in.	45.6406–46.4344mm
Valve spring out-of-square (max.)		
6-232	5/64 in.	1.9844mm
6-255	5/64 in.	1.9844mm
6-300	5/64 in.	1.9844mm
8-302	5/64 in.	1.9844mm
8-351W	5/64 in.	1.9844mm
8-351M	5/64 in.	1.9844mm
8-360	5/64 in.	1.9844mm
8-390	5/64 in.	1.9844mm
8-400	5/64 in.	1.9844mm
8-420	5/64 in.	1.9844mm
8-460	5/64 in.	1.9844mm
Valve stem diameter (standard)		
6-232		
Intake	0.3416–0.3423 in.	8.6766–8.6944mm
Exhaust	0.3411–0.3418 in.	8.6639–8.6817mm
8-255		
Intake	0.3416–0.3423 in.	8.6766–8.6944mm
Exhaust	0.3411–0.3418 in.	8.6639–8.6817mm
6-300		
Intake	0.3416–0.3423 in.	8.6766–8.6944mm
Exhaust	0.3411–0.3418 in.	8.6639–8.6817mm
8-302		
Intake	0.3416–0.3423 in.	8.6766–8.6944mm
Exhaust	0.3411–0.3418 in.	8.6639–8.6817mm
8-351W		
Intake	0.3416–0.3423 in.	8.6766–8.6944mm
Exhaust	0.3411–0.3418 in.	8.6639–8.6817mm
8-351M		
Intake	0.3416–0.3423 in.	8.6766–8.6944mm
Exhaust	0.3411–0.3418 in.	8.6639–8.6817mm
8-360		
Intake	0.3711–0.3718 in.	9.4259–9.4437mm
Exhaust	0.3703–0.3706 in.	9.4056–9.4132mm

8576399X

USING A VACUUM GAUGE

White needle = steady needle   **Dark needle = drifting needle**

The vacuum gauge is one of the most useful and easy-to-use diagnostic tools. It is inexpensive, easy to hook up, and provides valuable information about the condition of your engine.

Indication: Normal engine in good condition

Gauge reading: Steady, from 17–22 in./Hg.

Indication: Sticking valve or ignition miss

Gauge reading: Needle fluctuates from 15–20 in./Hg. at idle

Indication: Late ignition or valve timing, low compression, stuck throttle valve, leaking carburetor or manifold gasket.

Gauge reading: Low (15–20 in./Hg.) but steady

Indication: Improper carburetor adjustment, or minor intake leak at carburetor or manifold

NOTE: Bad fuel injector O-rings may also cause this reading.

Gauge reading: Drifting needle

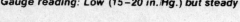

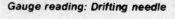

Indication: Weak valve springs, worn valve stem guides, or leaky cylinder head gasket (vibrating excessively at all speeds).

NOTE: A plugged catalytic converter may also cause this reading.

Gauge reading: Needle fluctuates as engine speed increases

Indication: Burnt valve or improper valve clearance. The needle will drop when the defective valve operates.

Gauge reading: Steady needle, but drops regularly

Indication: Choked muffler or obstruction in system. Speed up the engine. Choked muffler will exhibit a slow drop of vacuum to zero.

Gauge reading: Gradual drop in reading at idle

Indication: Worn valve guides

Gauge reading: Needle vibrates excessively at idle, but steadies as engine speed increases

TCCS3C01

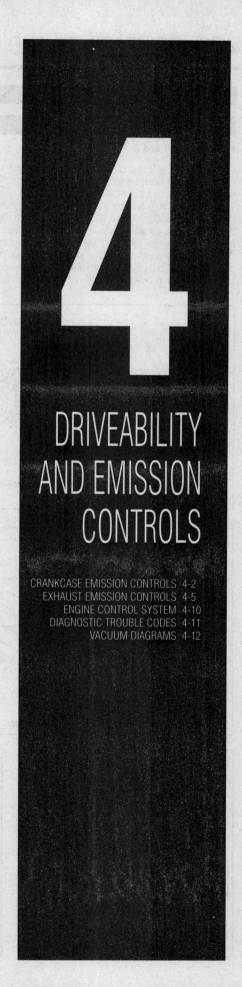

4

DRIVEABILITY AND EMISSION CONTROLS

CRANKCASE EMISSION CONTROLS

Crankcase Ventilation System

▶ See Figures 1 and 2

The crankcase emission control equipment consists of a positive crankcase ventilation (PCV) valve, a closed oil filler cap, a crankcase ventilation filter and the hoses that connect this equipment.

When the engine is running, a small portion of the gases which are formed in the combustion chamber leak by the piston rings and enter the crankcase. Since these gases are under pressure they tend to escape from the crankcase and enter into the atmosphere. If these gases are allowed to remain in the crankcase for any length of time, they would contaminate the engine oil and cause sludge to build up. If the gases are allowed to escape into the atmosphere, they would pollute the air, as they contain unburned hydrocarbons. The crankcase emission control equipment recycles these gases back into the engine combustion chamber, where they are burned.

Crankcase gases are recycled in the following manner. While the engine is running, clean filtered air is drawn into the crankcase through the intake air filter and then through a hose leading to the oil filler cap. As the air passes through the crankcase it picks up the combustion gases and carries them out of the crankcase, up through the PCV valve and into the air cleaner. After they enter the intake manifold they are drawn into the combustion chamber and are burned.

The most critical component of the system is the PCV valve. This vacuum-controlled valve regulates the amount of gases which are recycled into the combustion chamber. At low engine speeds the valve is partially closed, limiting the flow of gases into the intake manifold. As engine speed increases, the valve opens to admit greater quantities of the gases into the intake manifold. If the valve should become blocked or plugged, the gases will be prevented from escaping the crankcase by the normal route. Since these gases are under pressure, they will find their own way out of the crankcase. This alternate route is usually a weak oil seal or gasket in the engine. As the gas escapes past the gasket, it also creates an oil leak. Additionally, if the valve is improperly functioning and allowing excessive gas flow into the intake manifold at low engine speed, such as at idle, idle loping or rough engine idle will result. If idle loping or a rough engine idle is present, inspect the PCV system for proper operation prior to making any adjustments or repairs. Besides causing oil leaks and poor idle quality, an improperly operating PCV system allows these gases to remain in the crankcase for an extended period of time, promoting the formation of sludge in the engine.

TROUBLESHOOTING

1. With the engine running, pull the PCV valve with hose attached, from the valve rocker cover rubber grommet.
2. A hissing noise should be heard as air passes through the valve and a strong vacuum should be felt when you place a finger over the valve inlet if the valve is working properly. While you have your finger over the PCV valve inlet, check for vacuum leaks in the hose and at the connections. Replace any leaking hoses found in the system.
3. With the engine off, remove the hose at the PCV valve. Shake the PCV valve. With the PCV valve removed from the engine, a metallic clicking noise should be heard when it is shaken. This indicates that the valve inside the PCV valve is free to operate. If no noise is heard, replace the PCV valve.

REPLACEMENT

▶ See Figures 3, 4 and 5

1. Disconnect the crankcase vent hose from the air cleaner.
2. Remove the air cleaner and duct assembly from the engine.
3. Inspect the PCV system vacuum hoses for cracks or deterioration and replace as required.
4. To remove the PCV valve from the engine, pull upward on the PCV valve and hose to remove the PCV valve from the grommet in the rocker cover.

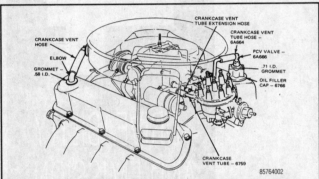

Fig. 1 Crankcase ventilation system components—1978 8-351 and 8-400 engines

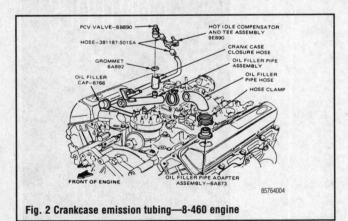

Fig. 2 Crankcase emission tubing—8-460 engine

Fig. 3 Removing the crankcase ventilation hose

Fig. 4 Removing the air cleaner assembly

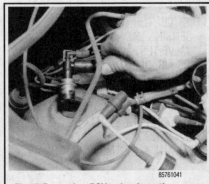

Fig. 5 Removing PCV valve from the rocker cover

5. Remove the PCV valve from the hose. Inspect the PCV valve as outlined above. If the PCV valve is in question, replace it.

To install:

6. If the PCV valve hose was removed, connect it to the intake manifold.
7. Connect the PCV valve to its hose.

8. Install the PCV valve into the rubber grommet in the rocker cover.
9. Install the air cleaner assembly and reconnect the crankcase vent hose, if removed.
10. Start the engine and check for vacuum leaks.

EVAPORATIVE EMISSION CONTROLS

General Information

▶ **See Figure 6**

Changes in atmospheric temperature cause fuel tanks to breathe; that is, the air within the tank expands and contracts with outside temperature changes. As the temperature rises, air escapes through the tank vent tube or the vent in the tank cap. The air which escapes contains gasoline vapors. In a similar manner on carbureted engines, the gasoline which fills the carburetor float bowl expands when the engine is stopped. Engine heat causes this expansion. The vapors escape through the air cleaner.

The Evaporative Emission Control System provides a sealed fuel system with the capability to store and condense fuel vapors. The system has three parts: a fill control vent system; a vapor vent and storage system; and a pressure and vacuum relief system (special fill cap).

The fill control vent system is a modification to the fuel tank. It uses a dome air space within the tank which is 10–12% of the tank's volume. The air space is sufficient to provide for the thermal expansion of the fuel. The space also serves as part of the in-tank vapor vent system.

The in-tank vent system consists of the domed air space previously described and a vapor separator assembly. The separator assembly is mounted to the top of the fuel tank and is secured by a cam-lockring, similar to the one which secures the fuel sending unit. Foam material fills the vapor separator assembly. The foam material separates raw fuel and vapors, thus retarding the entrance of fuel into the vapor line.

The vapor separator is an orifice valve located in the dome of the tank. The restricted size of the orifice, 0.050 in. (1.27mm) tends to allow only vapor to pass out of the tank. The orifice valve is connected to the vent line which runs forward to the carbon filled canister in the engine compartment.

The sealed filler cap has a pressure-vacuum relief valve. Under normal operating conditions, the filler cap operates as a check valve, allowing air to enter the tank to replace the fuel consumed. At the same time, it prevents vapors from escaping through the cap. In case of excessive pressure within the tank, the filler cap valve opens to relieve the pressure.

Because the filler cap is sealed, fuel vapors have only one place through which they may escape: the vapor separator assembly at the top of the fuel tank. The vapors pass through the foam material and continue through a single vapor line which leads to a canister in the engine compartment. The canister is filled with activated charcoal.

Another vapor line runs from the top of the carburetor float chamber or the intake manifold, or the throttle body, to the charcoal canister.

As the fuel vapors (hydrocarbons), enter the charcoal canister, they are absorbed by the charcoal. The air is dispelled through the open bottom of the charcoal canister, leaving the hydrocarbons trapped within the charcoal. When the engine is started, vacuum causes fresh air to be drawn into the canister from its open bottom. The fresh air passes through the charcoal picking up the hydrocarbons which are trapped there and feeding them into the engine for burning with the fuel mixture.

System Inspection

Physical damage, leaks, and missing items are the major answers when diagnosing the evaporative emission control system. Visually inspect the vapor and vacuum lines and connections for looseness, pinching, leakage, or other damage. Remember to include the lines at the top of the canister during your inspection. If vacuum hoses or fuel vapor lines are hard, cracked or deteriorated, replace the lines or hoses. Inspect the carbon canister for cracks and replace if damage is present.

The fuel cap contains an integral pressure and vacuum relief valve. The vacuum valve acts to allow air into the fuel tank to replace the fuel as it is used, while preventing vapors from escaping the tank through the atmosphere. The vacuum relief valve opens after a vacuum of -0.5 psi. The pressure valve acts as a backup pressure relief valve in the event the normal venting system is overcome by excessive generation of internal pressure or restriction of the normal venting system. The pressure relief range is 1.6–2.1 psi over atmospheric pressure. Fill cap damage or contamination that stops the pressure vacuum valve from working may result in deformation of the fuel tank.

➡ **Use of an aftermarket fuel filler cap other than an authorized Ford/Motorcraft or equivalent service part could result in damage to the fuel system or improper system operation if not properly designed for pressure and vacuum relief.**

Carbon Canister

▶ **See Figures 7, 8 and 9**

The carbon filled canister acts as a storage system for the fuel vapors vented from the tank, and where equipped, the carburetor. The outlet of the canister is connected to the air cleaner so that the stored vapors can be drawn into the engine and burned during combustion. Inspect the canister assembly for cracks or damage periodically, replacing unit if defects are found. At least every 24,000 miles, inspect the evaporative emission hoses for cracks or deterioration, and replace as required.

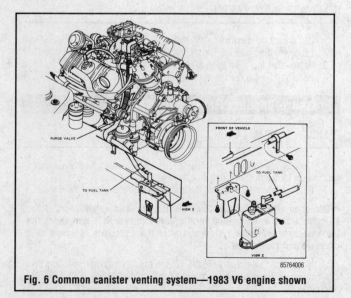

Fig. 6 Common canister venting system—1983 V6 engine shown

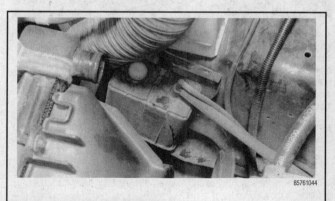

Fig. 7 Carbon canister mounting

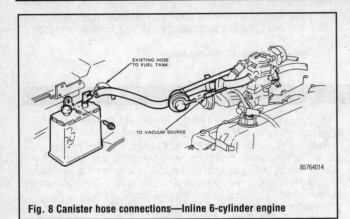

Fig. 8 Canister hose connections—Inline 6-cylinder engine

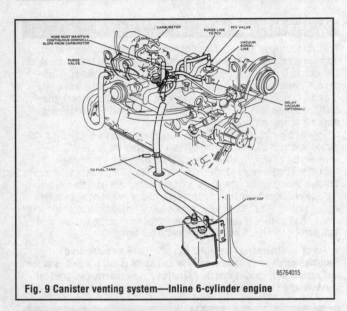

Fig. 9 Canister venting system—Inline 6-cylinder engine

REMOVAL & INSTALLATION

1. Disconnect the negative battery cable.
2. Label and carefully disconnect the vapor hoses from the carbon canister.
3. Remove the canister attaching screws. Lift the canister from the engine compartment, noting its orientation.
4. Installation is the reverse of the removal procedure.

Fuel Tank Vapor Separator/Rollover Valve Assembly

All fuel tank vapor valves make use of a small orifice that tends to allow only vapor and not liquid fuel to pass into the line running forward to the vapor storage canister. This assembly mounts directly to the fuel tank using a rubber grommet. Fuel vapors trapped in the sealed fuel tank are vented through the orifice vapor valve assembly in the top of the tank. The vapors leave the valve assembly through a single vapor line and continue to the carbon canister for storage, until they are purged to the engine.

REMOVAL & INSTALLATION

1. Disconnect the negative battery cable.
2. Drain and remove the fuel tank from the vehicle. Refer to 3.
3. Remove the vapor orifice and rollover valve assembly from the rubber grommet in the fuel tank.
4. Installation is the reverse of the removal procedure.

Purge Control Valve

REMOVAL & INSTALLATION

1. Disconnect the negative battery cable.
2. Label and disconnect the hoses from the purge control valve.
3. Remove the purge control valve from the engine.
4. Installation is the reverse of the removal procedure.

Carburetor Fuel Bowl Thermal Vent Valve

The thermal vent valve is inserted in the carburetor-to-canister vent line and is closed when the engine compartment is cold. This prevents fuel tank vapors generated when the fuel tank heats up before the engine compartment does from being vented through the carburetor fuel bowl. This effect may occur when sunlight strikes a vehicle which has been sitting out all night, and begins to warm the fuel tank. With the thermal vent valve closed, the vapors can not enter the carburetor fuel bowl vent (now open), but must be routed to the carbon canister. As the engine compartment warms up during normal engine operation, the thermal vent valve opens. When the engine is turned off again, the fuel vent valve or solenoid vent valve opens, allowing vapors to flow through the open thermal vent valve and into the carbon canister. As the thermal vent valve cools, it again closes and the cycle begins again.

TESTING

Inspect the valve for air flow and compare to the desired results at the specific temperature. At 90°F, the vent valve should be fully closed, and at 120°F, the vent valve is fully open. If the performance of the valve differs from the desired results, replace the valve.

Vacuum/Thermostatic Bowl Vent Valves

These valves are used in the evaporative emission system to control vapor flow from the carburetor bowl to the carbon canister. With either valve, the flow path from the carburetor bowl to the carbon canister is closed by manifold vacuum, when the engine is running. The thermostatic valve closes the bowl to canister flow path when the temperature of the valve is 90°F or less. When the temperature of the valve is 120°F or more, the valve is open unless closed by manifold vacuum.

TESTING

The vacuum vent valve should flow air when no vacuum is applied and should not flow air with vacuum applied at the vacuum nipple. This test also applies to the vacuum/thermostatic vent valve when it is at a temperature of 120°F or more. At a temperature of 90°F or less, the valve should not pass vacuum.

REMOVAL & INSTALLATION

1. Disconnect the negative battery cable.
2. Label and disconnect the hoses from the fuel bowl thermal vent valve.
3. Remove the fuel bowl thermal vent valve.
4. Installation is the reverse of the removal procedure.

Pressure/Vacuum Relief Fuel Cap

REMOVAL & INSTALLATION

1. Unscrew the fuel filler cap. The cap has a pre-vent feature that allows the tank to vent for the first ¾ turn before unthreading.
2. Remove the screw retaining the fuel cap tether and remove the fuel cap.

➠Use of an aftermarket fuel filler cap other than an authorized Ford/Motorcraft or equivalent service part could result in damage to the fuel system or improper system operation if not properly designed for pressure and vacuum relief.

3. Installation is the reverse of the removal procedure. When installing the cap, continue to turn clockwise until the ratchet mechanism gives off 3 or more loud clicks.

EXHAUST EMISSION CONTROLS

Thermactor System

▶ **See Figure 10**

Most 1976–86 models are equipped with a Thermactor emission control system. The Thermactor emission control system makes use of a belt driven air pump to inject fresh air into the hot exhaust stream through the engine exhaust ports. The result is the extended burning of those fumes which were not completely ignited in the combustion chamber, and the subsequent reduction of the hydrocarbon and carbon monoxide content of the exhaust emissions into harmless carbon dioxide and water.

The Thermactor system is composed of the following components:
1. Air supply pump (belt driven)
2. Air control valves
3. Check valves
4. Air manifolds (internal or external)
5. Air supply tubes (on external manifolds only)

Air for the Thermactor system is cleaned by means of a centrifugal filter fan mounted on the air pump driveshaft. The air filter does not require a replaceable element.

To prevent excessive pressure, the air pump is equipped with a pressure relief valve which uses a replaceable plastic plug to control the pressure setting.

The pump supplies air under pressure, into the exhaust system thus lowering the exhaust emissions due to combustion. The belt driven air pump takes air in through an impeller-type centrifugal air filter fan, thus eliminating the need for a separate air filter. Dust and dirt particles cannot enter the pump because these heavier than air contaminants are thrown from the air intake by centrifugal force. The Thermactor air pump has sealed bearings which are lubricated for the life of the unit, and preset rotor vane and bearing clearances, which do not require any periodic adjustments.

The air supply from the pump is controlled by the air by-pass valve, sometimes called a dump valve. During deceleration, the air bypass valve opens, momentarily diverting the air supply through a silencer and into the atmosphere, thus preventing backfires within the exhaust system.

A check valve is incorporated in the air inlet side of the air manifolds. Its purpose is to prevent exhaust gases from backing up into the Thermactor system. This valve is especially important in the event of drive belt failure, and during deceleration, when the air by-pass valve is dumping the air supply.

The air manifolds and air supply tubes channel the air from the Thermactor air pump into the exhaust ports of each cylinder, thus completing the cycle of the Thermactor system.

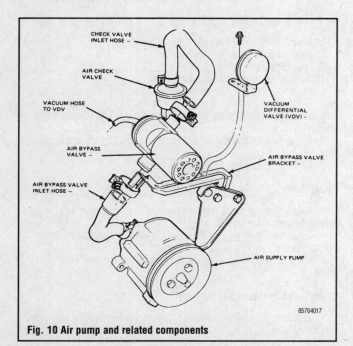

Fig. 10 Air pump and related components

COMPONENT TESTING

Air Supply Pump Functional Check

1. Check and, if necessary, adjust the belt tension. Press at the mid-point of the belt's longest straight run. You should be able to depress the belt about ½ in. (13mm) at most.
2. Run the engine to normal operating temperature and let it idle.
3. Disconnect the air supply hose from the bypass control valve. If the pump is operating properly, airflow should be felt at the pump outlet. The flow should increase as you increase the engine speed. The pump is not serviceable and should be replaced if it is not functioning properly.

Air Supply Control Valve

▶ **See Figure 11**

The Air Supply Control Valve is used in the thermactor system, to direct air pump output to the exhaust manifold or downstream to the catalyst system depending upon the engine control strategy.
1. Start the engine and allow to idle. Disconnect the inlet hose at the valve.
2. Verify that air flow is being supplied to the inlet by disconnecting the air supply hose at the inlet.
3. Verify the presence of air flow with the engine at 1500 rpm. Reconnect the air supply hose at the valve inlet.
4. Disconnect the air supply hoses at outlets "A" and "B" as shown in the appropriate illustration.
5. Remove the vacuum line at the nipple.
6. Accelerate the engine at 1500 rpm. Air flow should be heard and felt at outlet "B" with little or no air flow at outlet "A".
7. With the engine at 1500 rpm, connect a direct vacuum line from any manifold vacuum fitting to the air control valve vacuum nipple. Air flow should be heard and felt at outlet "A" with little or no air flow at outlet "B".
8. Restore all connections. If the desired conditions above are not met, replace the air control valve.

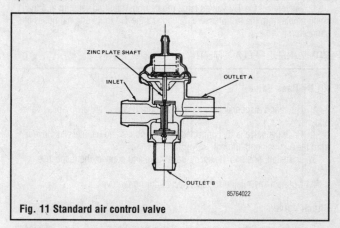

Fig. 11 Standard air control valve

Thermactor Idle Vacuum (TIV) Valve

▶ **See Figure 12**

The Thermactor Idle Vacuum (TIV) valve vents the vacuum signal to the atmosphere when a preset manifold vacuum or pressure is exceeded. It is used to divert thermactor air flow during extended idle conditions to limit exhaust temperature.
1. Disconnect both vacuum nipples of the TIV valve.
2. Install a vacuum hose from the manifold vacuum source to the small nipple of the TIV valve. Perform the appropriate test below as determined by the decal on the valve.

TIV VALVE CODED ASH OR RED

1. Firmly set the parking brake and block the wheels.
2. With the engine at idle, in Neutral, place your fingers over the TIV valve

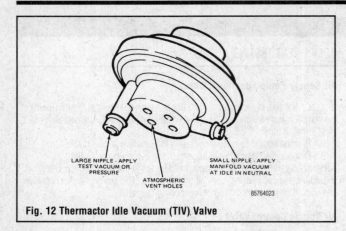

LARGE NIPPLE - APPLY TEST VACUUM OR PRESSURE

ATMOSPHERIC VENT HOLES

SMALL NIPPLE - APPLY MANIFOLD VACUUM AT IDLE IN NEUTRAL

85764023

Fig. 12 Thermactor Idle Vacuum (TIV) Valve

atmospheric vent holes as seen in the illustration. If no vacuum is present, replace the TIV valve.

3. While the engine is still idling, apply the vacuum listed below, to the large nipple from a test source. If vacuum is still sensed when placing fingers over vent holes, the TIV is defective and must be replaced.

- ASH marked valve–1.5-3.0 in. Hg of vacuum
- RED marked valve–3.5-4.5 in. Hg of vacuum

4. Disconnect the TIV large nipple from the manifold vacuum and the TIV small nipple from the test vacuum. Reconnect the TIV valve to the original hoses or connectors.

TIV VALVE CODED TUR

1. Firmly set the parking brake and block the wheels.
2. With the engine at idle, in Neutral, place your fingers over the TIV valve atmospheric vent holes as seen in the illustration. If no vacuum is present, replace the TIV valve.
3. While the engine is running at idle, apply a pressure of 1.5-2.5 in. Hg to the valve's large nipple from a test source. If vacuum is not sensed when placing finger over the vent holes, the TIV is defective and must be replaced.
4. Disconnect the TIV valve's large nipple from manifold vacuum and the small nipple from the test pressure. Reconnect the TIV to its original hoses and connectors.

COMPONENT REPLACEMENT

Air By-Pass Valve

1. Label and disconnect the air and vacuum hoses at the air by-pass valve body.
2. Once the valve is disconnected from all hoses and retainers, remove it from the engine compartment.
3. To install, position the air by-pass valve and connect the respective hoses.
4. Connect any retainers disconnected during removal.

Check Valve

1. Disconnect the air supply hose at the valve. Use a 1¼"; crowfoot wrench. The valve has a standard, right hand pipe thread.
2. Clean the threads on the air manifold adapter (air supply tube on the V8 engines) with a wire brush. Do not blow compressed air through the check valve in either direction.
3. Install the check valve and tighten.
4. Connect the air supply hose.

Air Manifold

1. Disconnect the air supply hose at the check valve, position the hose out of the way and remove the valve.
2. Loosen all of the air manifold-to-cylinder head tube coupling nuts (compression fittings). Inspect the air manifold for damaged threads and fittings and for leaking connections. Repair or replace as required. Clean the manifold and associated parts with kerosene. Do not dry the parts with compressed air.

3. Position the air manifold on the cylinder head. Be sure that all of the tube coupling nuts are aligned with the cylinder head.
4. Screw each coupling nut into the cylinder head, one or two threads. Tighten the tube coupling nuts.
5. Install the check valve and tighten it.
6. Connect the air supply hose to the check valve.

Air Supply Tube

V8 ENGINE ONLY

1. Disconnect the air supply hose at the check valve and position the hose out of the way.
2. Remove the check valve.
3. Remove the air supply tube bolt and seal washer.
4. Carefully remove the air supply tube and seal washer from the cylinder head. Inspect the air supply tube for evidence of leaking threads or seal surfaces. Examine the attaching bolt head, seal washers, and supply tube surface for leaks. Inspect the attaching bolt and cylinder head threads for damage. Clean the air supply tube, seal washers, and bolt with kerosene. Do not dry the parts with compressed air.
5. Install the seal washer and air supply tube on the cylinder head. Be sure that it is positioned in the same manner as before removal.
6. Install the seal washer and mounting bolt. Tighten the bolt.
7. Install the check valve and tighten it.
8. Connect the air supply hose to the check valve.

Air Nozzle

6-CYLINDER ENGINES ONLY

Normally, air nozzles should be replaced during cylinder head reconditioning. A nozzle may be replaced, however, without removing the cylinder head, by removing the air manifold and using a hooked tool.

Clean the nozzle with kerosene and a stiff brush. Inspect the air nozzles for eroded tips.

Air Pump and Filter Fan

1. Loosen the air pump attaching bolts.
2. Remove the drive pulley attaching bolts and pull the pulley off the air pump shaft.
3. Pry the outer disc loose, then remove the centrifugal filter fan. Care must be used to prevent foreign matter from entering the air intake hole, especially if the fan breaks during removal. Do not attempt to remove the metal drive hub.
4. Install the new filter fan by drawing it into position with the pulley bolts.

Air Pump

1. Disconnect the air outlet hose at the air pump.
2. Loosen the pump belt tension adjuster.
3. Disengage the drive belt.
4. Remove the mounting bolt and air pump.
5. Position the air pump on the mounting bracket and install the mounting bolt.
6. Place the drive belt in the pulley and attach the adjusting arm to the air pump.
7. Adjust the drive belt tension and tighten the adjusting arm and mounting bolts.
8. Connect the air outlet hose to the air pump.

Relief Valve

Do not disassemble the air pump on the truck to replace the relief valve, but remove the pump from the engine.

1. Remove the relief valve on the pump housing and hold it in position with a block of wood.
2. Use a hammer to lightly tap the wood block until the relief valve is seated.

Relief Valve Pressure Setting Plug

1. Compress the locking tabs inward (together) and remove the plastic pressure setting plug.

2. Before installing the new plug, be sure that the plug is the correct one. The plugs are color coded.

3. Insert the plug in the relief valve hole and push in until it snaps into place.

Catalytic Converters

The catalytic converter, mounted in the trucks exhaust system is a muffler-shaped device containing a ceramic honeycomb shaped material coated with alumina and impregnated with catalytically active precious metals such as platinum, palladium and rhodium.

The catalyst's job is to reduce air pollutants by oxidizing hydrocarbons (HC) and carbon monoxide (CO). Catalysts containing palladium and rhodium also oxidize nitrous oxides (NOx).

On some trucks, the catalyst is also fed by the secondary air system, via a small supply tube in the side of the catalyst.

No maintenance is possible on the converter, other than keeping the heat shield clear of flammable debris, such as leaves and twigs.

Other than external damage, the only significant damage possible to a converter is through the use of leaded gasoline, or by way of a too rich fuel/air mixture. Both of these problems will ruin the converter through contamination of the catalyst and will eventually plug the converter causing loss of power and engine performance. When this occurs, the catalyst must be replaced. For Removal and Installation procedures, please refer to Section 3 of this manual.

Exhaust Gas Recirculation (EGR) System

SPACER ENTRY EGR SYSTEM

▶ **See Figures 13 and 14**

In this system, a vacuum operated EGR flow valve is attached to the carburetor spacer. A passage in the carburetor spacer mates with a hole in the mounting face of the EGR valve or the intake manifold. The most common system allows exhaust gases to flow from the exhaust crossover, through the control valve and through the spacer into the intake manifold below the carburetor. For those engines where exhaust gases cannot be picked up from the exhaust crossover (6 cylinder) as described above, the gases are picked up from the choke stove located on the exhaust manifold or directly from the exhaust manifold. The exhaust gases are routed to the carburetor spacer through steel tubing.

The vacuum signal which operates the EGR valve originates at the EGR vacuum port in the carburetor. This signal is controlled by at least one, and sometimes two, series of valves.

A water temperature sensing valve (the EGR PVS) which is closed until the water temperature reaches either 60°F (15.5°C) or 125°F (52°C), depending on application, is normally used.

The position of the EGR vacuum port in the carburetor and calibration of the EGR valve can be varied to give the required modulation of EGR during acceleration and low speed cruise conditions. However, a more complicated system using a second series valve is sometimes needed to provide control of EGR for engine operation at high speed cruise conditions. The second valve, the high speed modulator valve, is controlled as a function of vehicle speed.

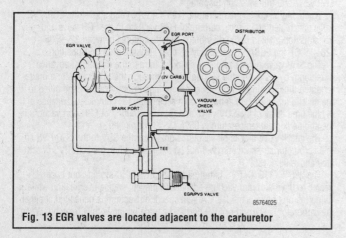

Fig. 13 EGR valves are located adjacent to the carburetor

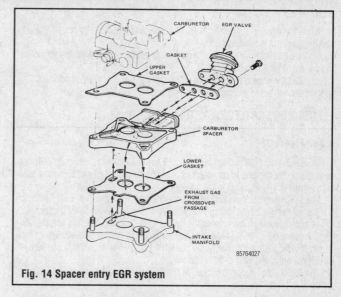

Fig. 14 Spacer entry EGR system

The high speed EGR modulator subsystem consists of a speed sensor, an electronic module and a solenoid vacuum valve. The speed sensor, driven by the speedometer cable, provides an AC signal in relation to engine speed, to the electronic module. The electronic module processes the information from the speed sensor and sends a signal to the high speed modulator (vacuum solenoid) valve. When the vehicle speed exceeds the module trigger speed, the solenoid vacuum valve closes which, in turn, causes the EGR valve to close.

EGR Valve Cleaning

Remove the EGR valve for cleaning. Do not strike or pry on the valve diaphragm housing or supports, as this may damage the valve operating mechanism and/or change the valve calibration. Check orifice hole in the EGR valve body for deposits. A small hand drill of no more than 0.060"; (1.5mm) diameter may be used to clean the hole if plugged. Extreme care must be taken to avoid enlarging the hole or damaging the surface of the orifice plate. Clean the cavity and passages in the main body of the valve.

EGR Supply Passages and Carburetor Space Cleaning

Remove the carburetor and carburetor spacer on engines so equipped. Clean the supply tube with a small power driven rotary type wire brush. Clean the exhaust gas passages in the spacer using a suitable wire brush and/or scraper. The machined holes in the spacer can be cleaned by using a suitable round wire brush. Hard encrusted material should be probed loose first, then brushed out.

Exhaust Gas Channel Cleaning

Clean the exhaust gas channel, where applicable, in the intake manifold, using a suitable carbon scraper. Clean the exhaust gas entry port in the intake manifold by hand passing a suitable drill bit through the holes to auger out the deposits. Do not use a wire brush. The manifold riser bore(s) should be suitably plugged during the above action to prevent any of the residue from entering the induction system.

EGR System Testing

VALVE FUNCTION TEST

With the engine at idle, apply 8 in. Hg of vacuum to the EGR valve. The valve stem should move opening the valve and the engine should roughen. If the valve stem moves but the engine does not roughen, remove and clean the inlet and outlet ports with a wire brush. Do not use sandblasting or gasoline to clean the EGR valve because they will damage the valve.

With the engine at idle, trap 4 in. Hg of vacuum in the valve and hold it. Vacuum should not drop more than 1 in. Hg in 30 seconds. If so, replace the valve.

SEAT TEST

When the valve is suspected of leaking, which is indicated by rough idle or stalling, perform the following:

1. Insert a blocking gasket with no flow holes between the valve and mounting base and retighten the valve.

2. Start the engine and observe idle quality. If the engine idle improves, replace the valve and remove the blocking gasket.

ELECTRONIC EGR (EEGR) SYSTEM

♦ See Figure 15

The Electronic EGR system (EEGR) is found in all systems in which EGR flow is controlled according to computer commands by means of an EGR valve position sensor (EVP) attached to the valve.

The EEGR valve is operated by a vacuum signal from the dual EGR Solenoid Valves, or the electronic vacuum regulator which actuates the valve diaphragm.

As supply vacuum overcomes the spring load, the diaphragm is actuated lifting the pintle off of its seat allowing the exhaust gas to flow. The amount of flow is directly proportional to the pintle position. The EVP sensor sends an electrical signal notify the EEC of its position.

The EEGR valve is not serviceable. The EVP sensor must be serviced separately.

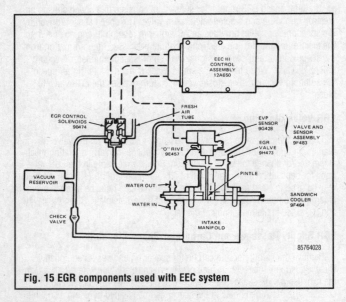

Fig. 15 EGR components used with EEC system

INTEGRAL BACKPRESSURE (IBP) EGR SYSTEM

The Integral Backpressure (IBP) EGR system combines inputs of EGR port vacuum and backpressure into one unit. The valve requires both inputs for proper operation. The valve won't operate on vacuum alone.

There are two types of backpressure valves: the poppet type and the tapered pintle type.

PORTED EGR VALVE

The ported EGR valve is operated by engine vacuum alone. A vacuum signal from the carburetor activates the EGR valve diaphragm. As the vacuum signal increase it gradually opens the valve pintle allowing exhaust gases to flow. The amount of flow is directly proportional to the pintle position.

Functional Check–Signal Response

Check that all a vacuum lines are properly routed and all connections are secure. If vacuum hoses are cracked, crimped or broken replace them.

1. When the engine is cold there should be no vacuum to operate the valve. If there is vacuum check the PVS or TVS for function and replace as required.

2. There should be no vacuum at the valve at warm curb idle.

Thermostatically Controlled Air Cleaner System

This system consists of a heat shroud which is integral with the right side exhaust manifold, a hot air hose and a special air cleaner assembly equipped with a thermal sensor and vacuum motor and air valve assembly.

The temperature of the carburetor intake air is thermostatically controlled by means of a valve plate and a vacuum override built into a duct assembly attached to the air cleaner. The exhaust manifold shroud tube is attached to the shroud over the exhaust manifold for the source of heated air.

The thermal sensor is attached to the air valve actuating lever, along with the vacuum motor lever, both of which control the position of the air valve to supply either heated air from the exhaust manifold or cooler air from the engine compartment.

During the warm-up period, when the under-the-hood temperatures are low, the thermal sensor doesn't exert enough tension on the air valve actuating lever to close (heat off) the air valve. Thus, the carburetor receives heated air from around the exhaust manifold.

As the temperature of the air entering the air cleaner approaches approximately 110°F (43°C), the thermal sensor begins to push on the air valve actuating lever and overcome the spring tension which holds the air valve in the open (heat on) position. The air valve begins to move to the closed (heat off) position, allowing only under-the-hood air to enter the air cleaner.

The air valve in the air cleaner will also open, regardless of the air temperature, during heavy acceleration to obtain maximum airflow through the air cleaner. The extreme decrease in intake manifold vacuum during heavy acceleration permits the vacuum motor to override the thermostatic control. This opens the system to both heated air and air from the engine compartment.

HEATED AIR INTAKE TEST

1. With the engine completely cold, look inside the cold air duct and make sure that the valve plate is fully in the up position (closing the cold air duct).

2. Start the engine and bring it to operating temperature.

3. Stop the engine and look inside the cold air duct again. The valve plate should be down, allowing an opening from the cold air duct into the air cleaner.

4. If the unit appears to be malfunctioning, remove it and examine it to make sure that the springs are not broken or disconnected, and replace the thermostat if all other parts appear intact and properly connected.

EGR/Coolant Spark Control (CSC) System

The EGR/CSC system is used on most 1976 and later models. It regulates both distributor spark advance and the EGR valve operation according to coolant temperature by sequentially switching vacuum signals.

The major EGR/CSC system components are:

1. 95°F (35°C) EGR/PVS valve;
2. Spark Delay Valve (SDV);
3. Vacuum check valve.

When the engine coolant temperature is below 82°F (28°C), the EGR/PVS valve admits carburetor EGR port vacuum (occurring at about 2,500 rpm) directly to the distributor advance diaphragm, through the one-way check valve.

At the same time, the EGR/PVS valve shuts off carburetor EGR vacuum to the EGR valve and transmission diaphragm.

When engine coolant temperature is 95°F (35°C) and above, the EGR/PVS valve is actuated and directs carburetor EGR vacuum to the EGR valve and transmission instead of the distributor. At temperatures between 82–95°F (28–35°C), the EGR/PVS valve may be open, closed, or in mid-position.

The SDV valve delay carburetor spark vacuum to the distributor advance diaphragm by restricting the vacuum signal through the SDV valve for a predetermined time. During normal acceleration, little or not vacuum is admitted to the distributor advance diaphragm until acceleration is completed, because of (1) the time delay of the SDV valve and (2) the rerouting of EGR port vacuum if the engine coolant temperature is 95°F (35°C) or higher.

The check valve blocks off vacuum signal from the SDV to the EGR/PVS so that carburetor spark vacuum will not be dissipated when the EGR/PVS is actuated above 95°F (35°C).

The 235°F (113°C) PVS is not part of the EGR/CSC system, but is connected to the distributor vacuum advance to prevent engine overheating while idling (as on previous models). At idle speed, no vacuum is generated at either the carburetor spark port or EGR port and engine timing is fully retarded. When engine coolant temperature reaches 235°F (113°C), however, the valve is actuated to admit intake manifold vacuum to the distributor advance diaphragm. This advances the engine timing and speeds up the engine. The increase in coolant flow and fan speed lowers engine temperature.

Ported Vacuum Switch Valve (PVS)

The PVS valve is a temperature sensing valve found on the distributor vacuum advance line, and is installed in the coolant outlet elbow. During prolonged periods of idle, or any other situation which causes engine operating temperatures to be higher than normal, the valve, which under normal conditions simply connects the vacuum advance diaphragm to its vacuum source within the carburetor, closes the normal source vacuum port and engages an alternate source vacuum port. This alternate source is from the intake manifold which, under idle conditions, maintains a high vacuum. This increase in vacuum supply to the distributor diaphragm advances the timing, increasing the idle speed. The increase in idle speed causes a directly proportional increase in the operation of the cooling system. When the engine has cooled sufficiently, the vacuum supply is returned to its normal source, the carburetor.

DISTRIBUTOR TEMPERATURE SENSING VACUUM CONTROL VALVE TEST

1. Check the routing and connection of all the vacuum hoses.
2. Attach a tachometer to the engine.
3. Bring the engine up to the normal operating temperature. The engine must not be overheated.
4. Note the engine rpm, with the transmission in Neutral, and the throttle at curb idle.
5. Disconnect the vacuum hose from the intake manifold at the temperature sensing valve. Plug or clamp the hose.
6. Note the idle rpm with the hose disconnected. If there is no change in rpm, the valve is good. If there is a drop of 100 or more rpm, the valve should be replaced. Replace the vacuum line.
7. Check to make sure that the all season coolant mixture meets specifications and that the correct radiator cap is in place and functioning.
8. Block the radiator airflow to induce a higher-than-normal temperature condition.
9. Continue to operate the engine until the temperature or heat indicator shows above normal.

If the engine speed, by this time, has increased 100 or more rpm, the temperature sensing valve is satisfactory. If not, it should be replaced.

Bypass Air Idle Speed Control

The air bypass solenoid is used to control the engine idle speed and is operated by the EEC module.

The valve allows air to pass around the throttle plates to control:
- Cold engine fast idle
- Cold starting
- Dashpot operation
- Over-temperature idle boost
- Engine load correction

The valve is not serviceable and correction is by replacement only.

Emissions Maintenance Warning Light (EMW)

DESCRIPTION

All light trucks with gasoline engines built for sale outside of California employ this device.

The EMW consists of an instrument panel mounted amber light imprinted with the word EGR, EMISS, or EMISSIONS. The light is connected to a sensor module located under the instrument panel. The purpose is the warn the driver that the 60,000 mile emission system maintenance is required on the vehicle. Specific emission system maintenance requirements are listed in the truck's owner's manual maintenance schedule.

RESETTING THE LIGHT

1. Turn the key to the OFF position.
2. Lightly push a Phillips screwdriver through the 0.2"; diameter hole labeled RESET, and lightly press down and hold it.
3. While maintaining pressure with the screwdriver, turn the key to the RUN position. The EMW lamp will light and stay lit as long as you keep pressure on the screwdriver. Hold the screwdriver down for about 5 seconds.
4. Remove the screwdriver. The lamp should go out within 2-5 seconds. If not, repeat steps 1-3.
5. Turn the key OFF.
6. Turn the key to the RUN position. The lamp will light for 2-5 seconds and then go out. If not, repeat the rest procedure.

➡ **If the light comes on between 15,000 and 45,000 miles or between 75,000 and 105,000 miles, you'll have to replace the 1,000 hour pre-timed module.**

Oxygen Sensor

♦ **See Figure 16**

An oxygen sensor is used on most later models and is mounted on the exhaust manifold. The sensor protrudes into the exhaust stream and monitors the oxygen content of the exhaust gases. The oxygen sensor produces a low voltage that is determined by the amount of unburned O_2 in the exhaust. The ECM monitors this low voltage signal and issues a command to adjust for a too rich or too lean fuel mixture.

No attempt should ever be made to measure the output voltage of the oxygen sensor. The current drain of a conventional voltmeter would be such that the sensor would become permanently damaged. No jumpers, test leads, or any other connections should ever be made to the sensor.

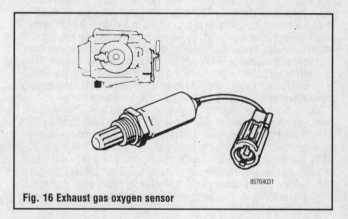

85764031

Fig. 16 Exhaust gas oxygen sensor

REMOVAL & INSTALLATION

The oxygen sensor must be replaced every 30,000 miles (48,000 km). The sensor may be difficult to remove when the engine temperature is below 120°F (48°C). Excessive force may damage the threads in the exhaust manifold or pipe; follow the procedure carefully.
1. Locate the oxygen sensor. It protrudes from the center of the exhaust manifold and looks somewhat like a spark plug.
2. Disconnect the electrical connector from the oxygen sensor.
3. Spray a commercial penetrating oil onto the the sensor threads and let it soak in.
4. Carefully remove the sensor.
To install:
5. Coat the new sensor's threads with anti-seize compound made for oxygen sensors. This is not conventional anti-seize paste. The use of regular anti-seize compound may render the sensor inoperative.
6. Installation torque is 30 ft. lbs. (42 Nm).
7. Reconnect the electrical connector. Be careful not to damage the connector.

ENGINE CONTROL SYSTEM

General Information

Ford vehicles employ the 4th generation Electronic Engine Control system, commonly designated EEC-IV, to manage fuel, ignition and emissions on vehicle engines.

The Engine Control Assembly (ECA) is given responsibility for the operation of the emission control devices, cooling fans, ignition and advance and in some cases, automatic transmission functions. Because the EEC-IV oversees both the ignition timing and the fuel injector operation, a precise air/fuel ratio will be maintained under all operating conditions. The ECA is a microprocessor or small computer which receives electrical inputs from several sensors, switches and relays on and around the engine.

Based on combinations of these inputs, the ECA controls outputs to various devices concerned with engine operation and emissions. The engine control assembly relies on the signals to form a correct picture of current vehicle operation. If any of the input signals is incorrect, the ECA reacts to what ever picture is painted for it. For example, if the coolant temperature sensor is inaccurate and reads too low, the ECA may see a picture of the engine never warming up. Consequently, the engine settings will be maintained as if the engine were cold. Because so many inputs can affect one output, correct diagnostic procedures are essential on these systems.

One part of the ECA is devoted to monitoring both input and output functions within the system. This ability forms the core of the self-diagnostic system. If a problem is detected within a circuit, the controller will recognize the fault, assign it an identification code, and store the code in a memory section. Depending on the year and model, the fault code(s) may be represented by two or three digit numbers. The stored code(s) may be retrieved during diagnosis.

While the EEC-IV system is capable of recognizing many internal faults, certain faults will not be recognized. Because the computer system sees only electrical signals, it cannot sense or react to mechanical or vacuum faults affecting engine operation. Some of these faults may affect another component which will set a code. For example, the ECA monitors the output signal to the fuel injectors, but cannot detect a partially clogged injector. As long as the output driver responds correctly, the computer will read the system as functioning correctly. However, the improper flow of fuel may result in a lean mixture. This would, in turn, be detected by the oxygen sensor and noticed as a constantly lean signal by the ECA. Once the signal falls outside the pre-programmed limits, the engine control assembly would notice the fault and set an identification code.

Additionally, the EEC-IV system employs adaptive fuel logic. This process is used to compensate for normal wear and variability within the fuel system. Once the engine enters steady-state operation, the engine control assembly watches the oxygen sensor signal for a bias or tendency to run slightly rich or lean. If such a bias is detected, the adaptive logic corrects the fuel delivery to bring the air/fuel mixture towards a centered or 14.7:1 ratio. This compensating shift is stored in a non-volatile memory which is retained by battery power even with the ignition switched off. The correction factor is then available the next time the vehicle is operated.

➡️**If the battery cable(s) is disconnected for longer than 5 minutes, the adaptive fuel factor will be lost. After repair it will be necessary to drive the truck at least 10 miles to allow the processor to relearn the correct factors. The driving period should include steady-throttle open road driving if possible. During the drive, the vehicle may exhibit driveability symptoms not noticed before. These symptoms should clear as the ECA computes the correction factor. The ECA will also store Code 19 indicating loss of power to the controller.**

The CHECK ENGINE or SERVICE ENGINE SOON dashboard warning lamp is referred to as the Malfunction Indicator Lamp (MIL). The lamp is connected to the engine control assembly and will alert the driver to certain malfunctions within the EEC-IV system. When the lamp is lit, the ECA has detected a fault and stored an identity code in memory. The engine control system will usually enter either FMEM or HLOS mode and driveability will be impaired.

The light will stay on as long as the fault causing it is present. Should the fault self-correct, the MIL will extinguish but the stored code will remain in memory.

Under normal operating conditions, the MIL should light briefly when the ignition key is turned **ON**. As soon as the ECA receives a signal that the engine is cranking, the lamp will be extinguished. The dash warning lamp should remain out during the entire operating cycle.

Diagnosis and Testing

Diagnosis of a driveability problem requires attention to detail and following the diagnostic procedures in the correct order. Resist the temptation to begin extensive testing before completing the preliminary diagnostic steps. The preliminary or visual inspection must be completed in detail before diagnosis begins. In many cases this will shorten diagnostic time and often cure the problem without electronic testing.

VISUAL INSPECTION

This is possibly the most critical step of diagnosis. A detailed examination of all connectors, wiring and vacuum hoses can often lead to a repair without further diagnosis. Performance of this step relies on the skill of the technician performing it; a careful inspector will check the undersides of hoses as well as the integrity of hard-to-reach hoses blocked by the air cleaner or other components. Wiring should be checked carefully for any sign of strain, burning, crimping or terminal pull-out from a connector.

Checking connectors at components or in harnesses is required; usually, pushing them together will reveal a loose fit. Pay particular attention to ground circuits, making sure they are not loose or corroded. Remember to inspect connectors and hose fittings at components not mounted on the engine, such as the evaporative canister or relays mounted on the fender aprons. Any component or wiring in the vicinity of a fluid leak or spillage should be given extra attention during inspection.

Additionally, inspect maintenance items such as belt condition and tension, battery charge and condition and the radiator cap carefully. Any of these very simple items may affect the system enough to set a fault.

READING FAULTS OR FAULT CODES

▶ **See Figure 17**

If a code was set before a problem self-corrected (such as a momentarily loose connector), the code will be erased if the problem does not reoccur within 80 warm-up cycles. Codes will be output and displayed as numbers on the hand scan tool, i.e. 23. If the codes are being read through the dashboard warning lamp, the codes will be displayed as groups of flashes separated by pauses. Code 23 would be shown as two flashes, a pause and three more flashes. A longer pause will occur between codes.

In all cases, the codes 11 or 111 are used to indicate PASS during testing. Note that the PASS code may appear, followed by other stored codes. These are codes from the continuous memory and may indicate intermittent faults, even though the system does not presently contain the fault. The PASS designation only indicates the system passes all internal tests at the moment.

Although stored codes may be read through the flashing of the CHECK ENGINE or SERVICE ENGINE SOON lamp, the use of hand-held scan tools such as Ford's Self-Test Automatic Readout (STAR) tester or the second generation SUPER STAR II tester or their equivalent is highly recommended. There are

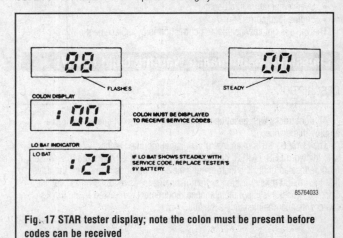

Fig. 17 STAR tester display; note the colon must be present before codes can be received

many manufacturers of these tools; the purchaser must be certain that the tool is proper for the intended use.

The scan tool allows any stored faults to be read from the engine controller memory. Use of the scan tool provides additional data during troubleshooting but does not eliminate the use of the charts. The scan tool makes collecting information easier; the data must be correctly interpreted by an operator familiar with the system. To retrieve the codes using a hand-held scan tool, follow the instructions provided by the manufacturer.

CLEARING CODES

Continuous Memory Codes

These codes are retained in memory for 80 warm-up cycles. To clear the codes for the purposes of testing or confirming repair, perform the KOEO test. When the fault codes begin to be displayed, de-activate the test by either disconnecting the jumper wire (meter, MIL or message center) or releasing the test button on the hand scanner. Stopping the test during code transmission will erase the Continuous Memory. Do not disconnect the negative battery cable to clear these codes; the Keep Alive memory will be cleared and a new code, 19, will be stored for loss of ECA power.

Keep Alive Memory

The Keep Alive Memory (KAM) contains the adaptive factors used by the processor to compensate for component tolerances and wear. It should not be routinely cleared during diagnosis. If an emissions related part is replaced during repair, the KAM must be cleared. Failure to clear the KAM may cause severe driveability problems since the correction factor for the old component will be applied to the new component.

To clear the Keep Alive Memory, disconnect the negative battery cable for at least 5 minutes. After the memory is cleared and the battery reconnected, the vehicle must be driven at least 10 miles so that the processor may relearn the needed correction factors. The distance to be driven depends on the engine and vehicle, but all drives should include steady-throttle cruise on open roads. Certain driveability problems may be noted during the drive because the adaptive factors are not yet functioning.

The diagnostic trouble codes listed below apply to the 1985–86 5.0L EFI V-8 engine.

DIAGNOSTIC TROUBLE CODES

- **Code 11**—System pass
- **Code 12**—RPM unable to reach upper test limit
- **Code 13**—RPM unable to reach lower test limit
- **Code 14**—Pip circuit failure
- **Code 15**—ECA read only memory test failed
- **Code 15**—ECA keep alive memory test failed
- **Code 16**—IDM signal not received
- **Code 18**—SPOUT circuit open or spark angle word failure
- **Code 18**—IDM circuit failure or SPOUT circuit grounded
- **Code 19**—Failure in ECA internal voltage
- **Code 21**—ECT out ot self test range
- **Code 22**—BP sensor out of self test range
- **Code 22**—BP sensor or MAP out of range
- **Code 23**—TP sensor out of self test range
- **Code 24**—ACT sensor out of self test range
- **Code 25**—Knock not sensed during dynamic test
- **Code 26**—VAF/MAF out of self test range
- **Code 26**—TOT out of self test range
- **Code 26**—TOT sensor out of self test range (E-400)
- **Code 28**—Loss of IDM, right side
- **Code 29**—Insufficient input from vehicle speed sensor
- **Code 31**—PFE, EVP or EVR circuit below minimum voltage
- **Code 32**—EVP voltage below closed limit
- **Code 33**—EGR valve opening not detected
- **Code 34**—EVP voltage above closed limit
- **Code 35**—PFE or EVP circuit above closed limit
- **Code 41**—HEGO sensor circuit indicates system lean
- **Code 41**—No HEGO switching detected
- **Code 42**—HEGO sensor circuit indicates system rich
- **Code 44**—Thermactor air system inoperative–right side
- **Code 45**—Thermactor air upstream during self test
- **Code 45**—Coil 1,2 or 3 failure
- **Code 46**—Thermactor air not bypassed during self test
- **Code 47**—4WD switch closed (E40D)
- **Code 48**—Loss of IDM, left side
- **Code 49**—1–2 shift error (E40D)
- **Code 51**—ECT/ACT reads –40°F or circuit open
- **Code 52**—Power steering pressure switch circuit open
- **Code 52**—Power steering pressure switch always open or closed
- **Code 53**—TP circuit above maximum voltage
- **Code 54**—ACT sensor circuit open
- **Code 56**—VAF or MAF circuit above maximum voltage
- **Code 56**—TOT reads –40°F or circuit open (E40D)
- **Code 59**—2–3 shift error (E40D)
- **Code 61**—ECT reads 254°F or circuit grounded
- **Code 63**—TP circuit below minimum voltage
- **Code 64**—ACT sensor grounded or input reads 254°F
- **Code 65**—Overdrive cancel switch open, no change seen (E40D)

- **Code 66**—MAF sensor input below minimum voltage
- **Code 66**—TOT grounded or reads 290°F (E40D)
- **Code 67**—Neutral/drive switch open or A/C on
- **Code 67**—Clutch switch circuit failure
- **Code 67**—MLP sensor out of range or A/C on (E40D)
- **Code 69**—3–4 shift error
- **Code 72**—Insufficient MAF/MAP change during dynamic test
- **Code 73**—Insufficient TP change during dynamic test
- **Code 74**—Brake on/off switch failure or not actuated
- **Code 77**—Operator error
- **Code 79**—A/C on during self test
- **Code 79**—A/C or defrost on during self test
- **Code 81**—Air management 2 circuit failure
- **Code 82**—Air management 1 circuit failure
- **Code 84**—EGR vacuum solenoid circuit failure
- **Code 85**—Canister purge solenoid circuit failure
- **Code 86**—Shift solenoid circuit failure
- **Code 87**—Fuel pump primary circuit failure
- **Code 88**—Loss of dual plug input control
- **Code 89**—Converter clutch solenoid circuit failure
- **Code 91**—Shift solenoid 1 circuit failure (E40D)
- **Code 92**—Shift solenoid 2 circuit failure (E40D)
- **Code 93**—Coast clutch solenoid circuit failure (E40D)
- **Code 94**—Converter clutch solenoid circuit failure (E40D)
- **Code 95**—Fuel pump secondary circuit failure— ECA to ground
- **Code 96**—Fuel pump secondary circuit failure—battery to ECA
- **Code 97**—Overdrive cancel indicator light—circuit failure(E40D)
- **Code 98**—Electronic pressure control driver open in ECA (E40D)
- **Code 98**—Hard fault present
- **Code 99**—Electronic pressure control circuit failure (E40D)
- **Code 111**—System pass
- **Code 112**—ACT sensor circuit grounded or reads 254° F
- **Code 113**—ACT sensor circuit open or reads –40° F
- **Code 114**—ACT outside test limits during KOEO or KOER tests
- **Code 116**—ECT outside test limits during KOEO or KOER tests
- **Code 117**—ECT sensor circuit grounded
- **Code 117**—ECT sensor circuit below minimum voltage or reads 254°F
- **Code 118**—ECT sensor circuit open
- **Code 118**—ECT sensor circuit below maximum voltage or reads –40°F
- **Code 121**—Closed throttle voltage higher or lower than expected
- **Code 122**—TP sensor circuit below minimum voltage
- **Code 123**—TP sensor circuit above maximum voltage
- **Code 126**—BP or MAP sensor higher or lower than expected
- **Code 128**—MAP vacuum circuit failure
- **Code 129**—Insufficient MAF or MAP change during dynamic responded test
- **Code 144**—No HEGO switching detected
- **Code 167**—Insufficient TP change during dynamic response test

- **Code 171**—Fuel system at adaptive limit, HEGO unable to switch
- **Code 172**—HEGO shows system always lean
- **Code 173**—HEGO shows system always rich
- **Code 174**—HEGO switching time is slow
- **Code 179**—Fuel at lean adaptive limit at part throttle; system rich
- **Code 181**—Fuel at rich adaptive limit at part throttle; system lean
- **Code 182**—Fuel at lean adaptive limit at idle; system rich
- **Code 183**—Fuel at rich adaptive limit at idle; system lean
- **Code 211**—PIP circuit fault
- **Code 212**—Loss of IDM input to ECA or SPOUT circuit grounded
- **Code 213**—Spout circuit open
- **Code 224**—Erratic IDM input to processor
- **Code 225**—Knocked not sensed during dynamic response test
- **Code 311**—Thermactor air system inoperative
- **Code 312**—Thermactor air upstream during self test
- **Code 313**—Thermactor air not bypassed during self test
- **Code 327**—EVP or DPFE circuit below minimum voltage
- **Code 328**—EGR closed voltage higher than expected
- **Code 332**—Insufficient EGR flow detected
- **Code 334**—EGR closed voltage higher than expected
- **Code 337**—EVP or DPFE circuit above maximum voltage
- **Code 411**—Cannot control rpm during KOER low rpm check
- **Code 412**—Cannot control rpm during KOER high rpm check
- **Code 452**—Insufficient input from vehicle speed sensor
- **Code 511**—EEC processor ROM test failed
- **Code 512**—EEC processor Keep Alive Memory test failed
- **Code 513**—Failure in EEC processor internal voltage
- **Code 519**—Power steering pressure switch circuit open
- **Code 521**—Power steering pressure switch did not change state
- **Code 525**—Vehicle in gear or A/C on during self test
- **Code 536**—Brake on/off circuit failure, switch not actuated during KOER test

- **Code 538**—Insufficient RPM change during KOER dynamic response test
- **Code 538**—Operator error
- **Code 542**—Fuel pump secondary circuit failure: ECA to ground
- **Code 543**—Fuel pump secondary circuit failure: Battery to ECA
- **Code 552**—Air management 1 circuit failure
- **Code 553**—Air management 2 circuit failure
- **Code 556**—Fuel pump primary circuit failure
- **Code 558**—EGR vacuum regulator circuit failure
- **Code 565**—Canister purge circuit failure
- **Code 569**—Canister purge 2 circuit failure
- **Code 617**—1–2 shift error (E40D)
- **Code 618**—2–3 shift error (E40D)
- **Code 619**—3–4 shift error (E40D)
- **Code 621**—Shift solenoid 1 circuit failure
- **Code 622**—Shift solenoid 2 circuit failure
- **Code 624**—EPC solenoid or driver circuit failure
- **Code 625**—EPC driver open in ECA
- **Code 626**—Coast clutch solenoid circuit failure (E40D)
- **Code 627**—Converter clutch solenoid circuit failure (E40D)
- **Code 628**—Converter clutch error (E40D)
- **Code 629**—Converter clutch control circuit failure
- **Code 631**—Overdrive cancel indicator light circuit failure
- **Code 632**—Overdrive cancel switch not changing states (E40D)
- **Code 633**—4WD switch is closed
- **Code 634**—MLP sensor voltage out ot self test range, A/C on
- **Code 636**—TOT sensor voltage out of self test range
- **Code 637**—TOT sensor circuit above maximum voltage
- **Code 638**—TOT sensor circuit below minimum voltage
- **Code 654**—MLP sensor not in park position
- **Code 998**—Hard fault present

VACUUM DIAGRAMS

Below is a listing of vacuum diagrams for most of the engine and emissions package combinations covered by this manual. Because vacuum circuits will vary based on various engine and vehicle options, always refer first to the vehicle emission control information label, if present. Should the label be missing, or should the vehicle be equipped with a different engine from the truck's original equipment, refer to the diagrams below for the same or similar configuration.

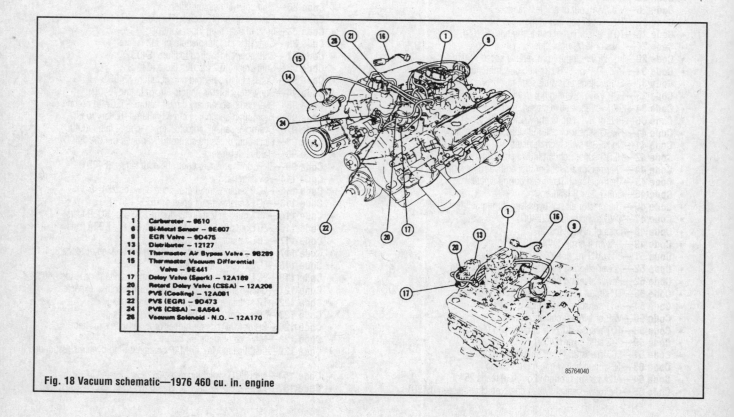

1	Carburetor — 9510
6	Bi-Metal Sensor — 9E607
9	EGR Valve — 9D475
13	Distributor — 12127
14	Thermactor Air Bypass Valve — 9B289
15	Thermactor Vacuum Differential Valve — 9E441
17	Delay Valve (Spark) — 12A189
20	Retard Delay Valve (CSSA) — 12A206
21	PVS (Cooling) — 12A091
22	PVS (EGR) — 9D473
24	PVS (CSSA) — 8A564
26	Vacuum Solenoid - N.O. — 12A170

Fig. 18 Vacuum schematic—1976 460 cu. in. engine

85764040

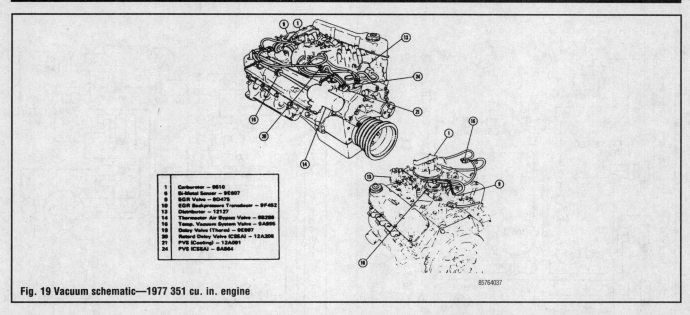

1	Carburetor — 9510
6	Bi-Metal Sensor — 9E607
9	EGR Valve — 9D475
10	EGR Backpressure Transducer — 9F452
13	Distributor — 12127
14	Thermactor Air Bypass Valve — 9B289
16	Temp. Vacuum System Valve — 9A996
19	Delay Valve (Thermal) — 9E007
20	Retard Delay Valve (CSSA) — 12A206
21	PVS (Cooling) — 12A091
24	PVS (CSSA) — 8A564

85764037

Fig. 19 Vacuum schematic—1977 351 cu. in. engine

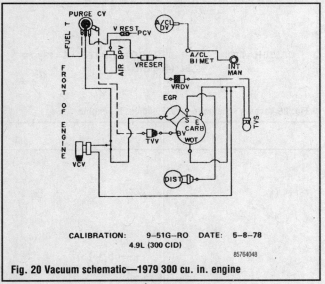

CALIBRATION: 9-51G-RO   DATE: 5-8-78
4.9L (300 CID)

85764048

Fig. 20 Vacuum schematic—1979 300 cu. in. engine

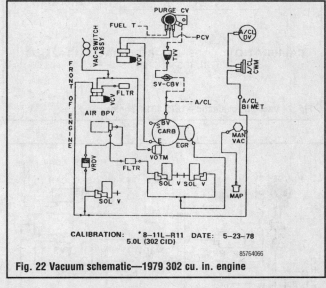

CALIBRATION: *8-11L-R11   DATE: 5-23-78
5.0L (302 CID)

85764066

Fig. 22 Vacuum schematic—1979 302 cu. in. engine

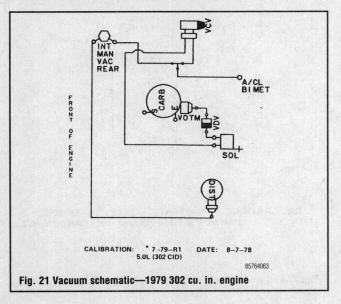

CALIBRATION: *7-79-R1   DATE: 8-7-78
5.0L (302 CID)

85764063

Fig. 21 Vacuum schematic—1979 302 cu. in. engine

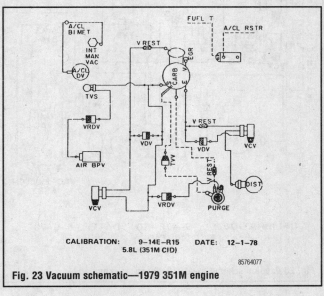

CALIBRATION: 9-14E-R15   DATE: 12-1-78
5.8L (351M CID)

85764077

Fig. 23 Vacuum schematic—1979 351M engine

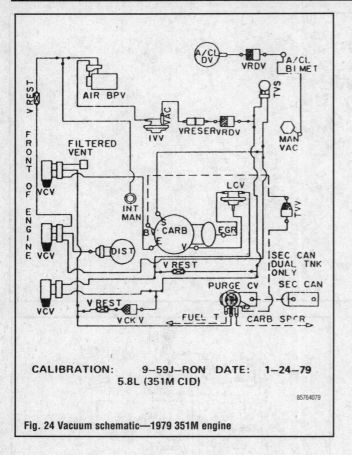

CALIBRATION: 9—59J—RON   DATE: 1—24—79
                 5.8L (351M CID)

85764079

Fig. 24 Vacuum schematic—1979 351M engine

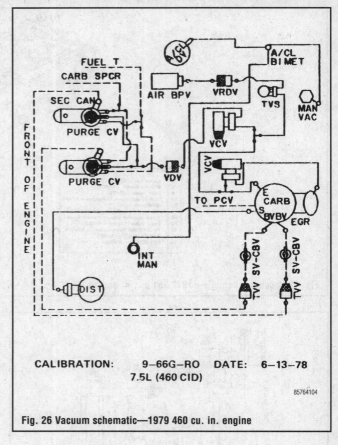

CALIBRATION: 9—66G—RO   DATE: 6—13—78
                 7.5L (460 CID)

85764104

Fig. 26 Vacuum schematic—1979 460 cu. in. engine

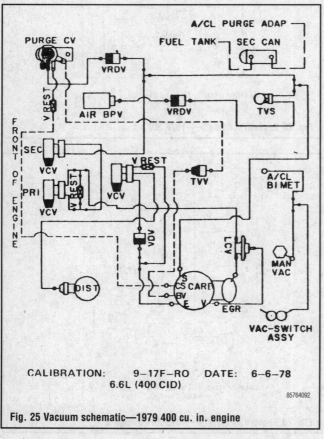

CALIBRATION: 9—17F—RO   DATE: 6-6-78
                 6.6L (400 CID)

85764092

Fig. 25 Vacuum schematic—1979 400 cu. in. engine

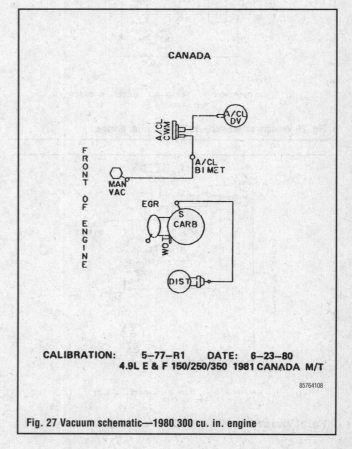

CALIBRATION: 5—77—R1   DATE: 6—23—80
                 4.9L E & F 150/250/350 1981 CANADA M/T

85764108

Fig. 27 Vacuum schematic—1980 300 cu. in. engine

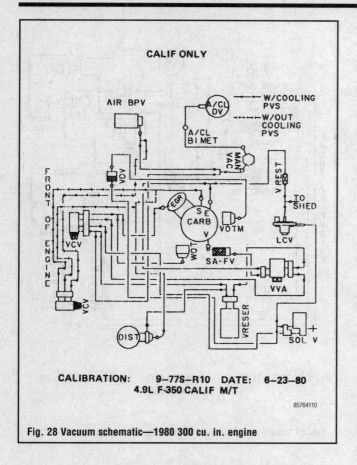

Fig. 28 Vacuum schematic—1980 300 cu. in. engine

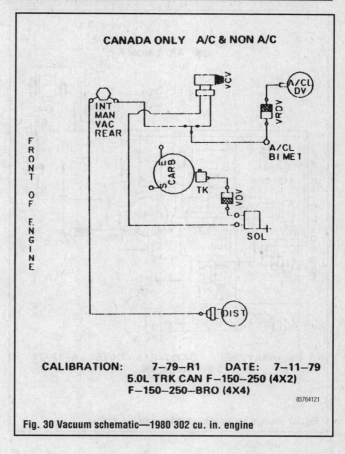

Fig. 30 Vacuum schematic—1980 302 cu. in. engine

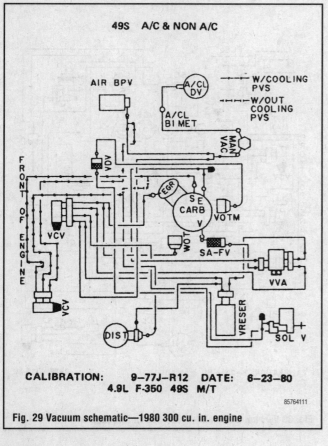

Fig. 29 Vacuum schematic—1980 300 cu. in. engine

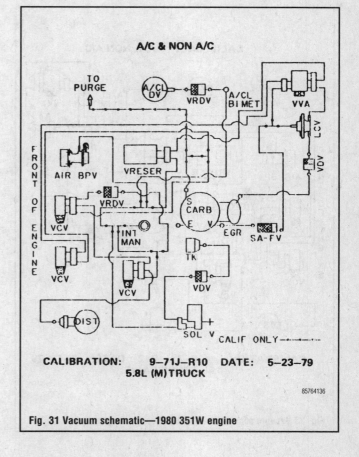

Fig. 31 Vacuum schematic—1980 351W engine

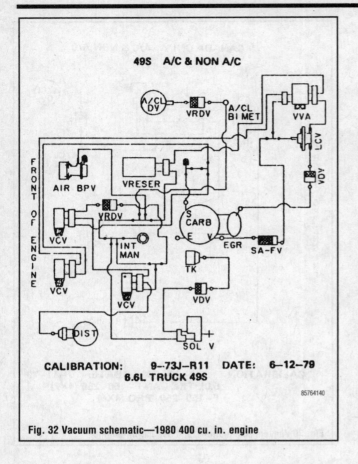

Fig. 32 Vacuum schematic—1980 400 cu. in. engine

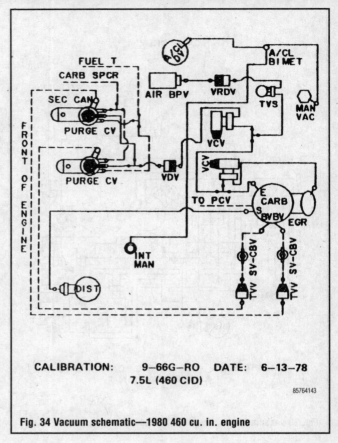

Fig. 34 Vacuum schematic—1980 460 cu. in. engine

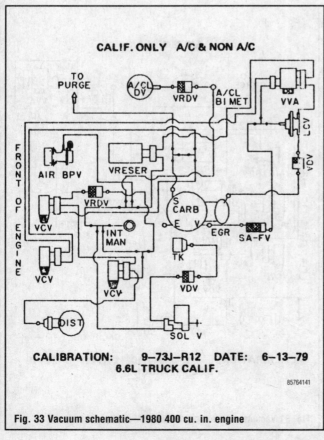

Fig. 33 Vacuum schematic—1980 400 cu. in. engine

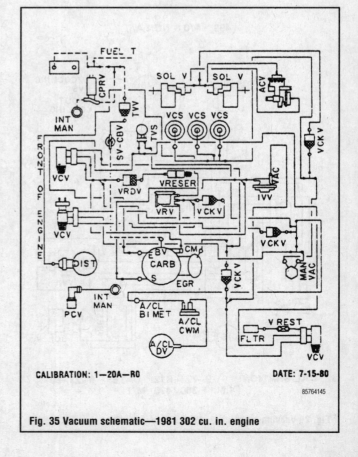

Fig. 35 Vacuum schematic—1981 302 cu. in. engine

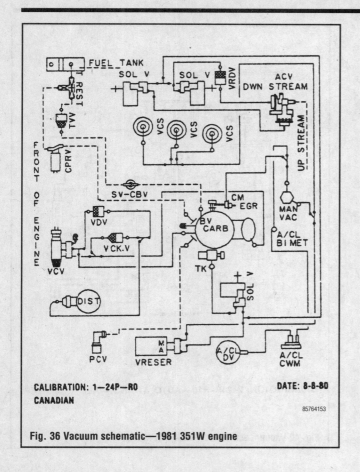

CALIBRATION: 1—24P—R0
CANADIAN

DATE: 8-8-80

85764153

Fig. 36 Vacuum schematic—1981 351W engine

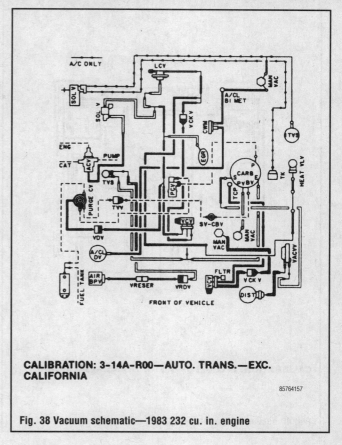

CALIBRATION: 3-14A-R00—AUTO. TRANS.—EXC. CALIFORNIA

85764157

Fig. 38 Vacuum schematic—1983 232 cu. in. engine

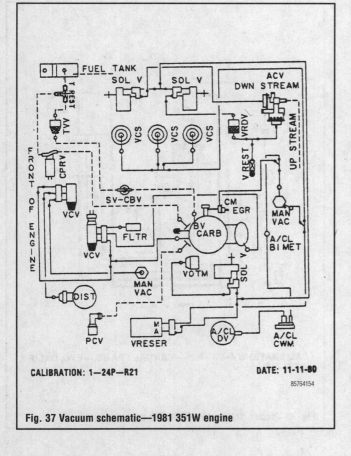

CALIBRATION: 1—24P—R21

DATE: 11-11-80

85764154

Fig. 37 Vacuum schematic—1981 351W engine

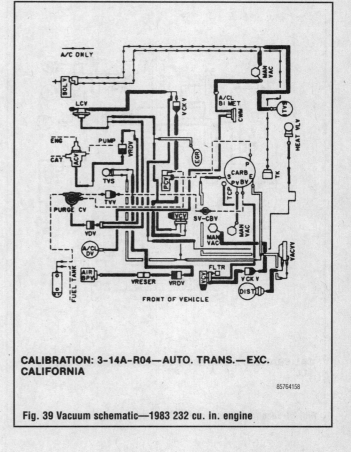

CALIBRATION: 3-14A-R04—AUTO. TRANS.—EXC. CALIFORNIA

85764158

Fig. 39 Vacuum schematic—1983 232 cu. in. engine

CALIBRATION: 2-22A-R17—AUTO. TRANS.—CALIFORNIA

85764164

Fig. 40 Vacuum schematic—1983 302 cu. in. engine

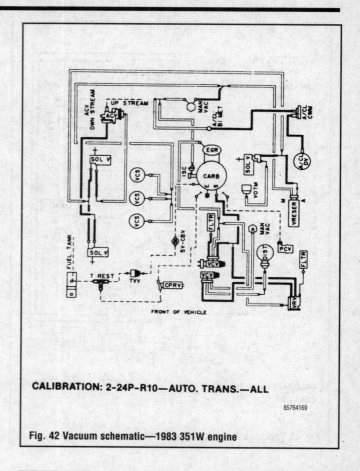

CALIBRATION: 2-24P-R10—AUTO. TRANS.—ALL

85764169

Fig. 42 Vacuum schematic—1983 351W engine

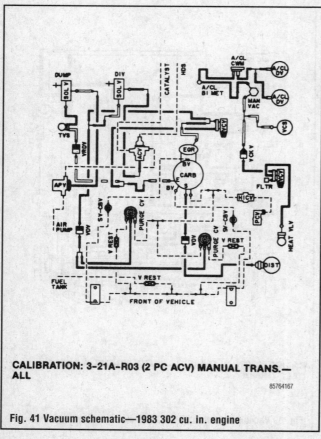

CALIBRATION: 3-21A-R03 (2 PC ACV) MANUAL TRANS.—ALL

85764167

Fig. 41 Vacuum schematic—1983 302 cu. in. engine

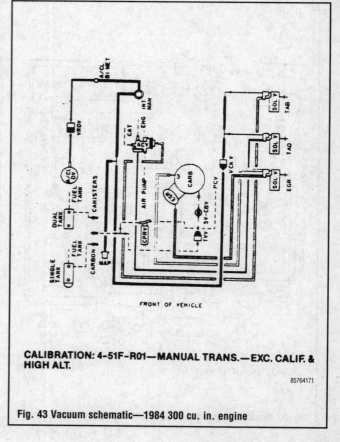

CALIBRATION: 4-51F-R01—MANUAL TRANS.—EXC. CALIF. & HIGH ALT.

85764171

Fig. 43 Vacuum schematic—1984 300 cu. in. engine

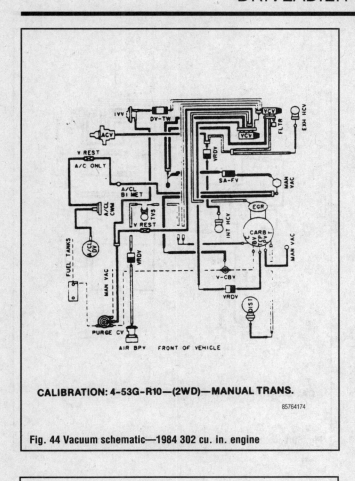

CALIBRATION: 4-53G-R10—(2WD)—MANUAL TRANS.

85764174

Fig. 44 Vacuum schematic—1984 302 cu. in. engine

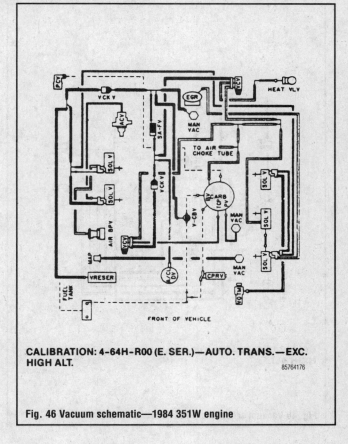

CALIBRATION: 4-64H-R00 (E. SER.)—AUTO. TRANS.—EXC. HIGH ALT.

85764176

Fig. 46 Vacuum schematic—1984 351W engine

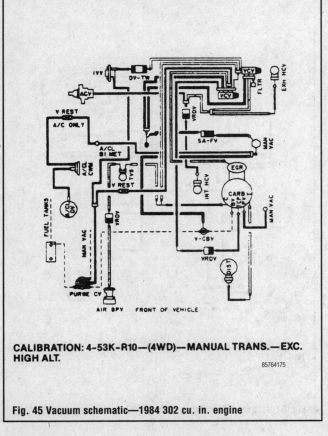

CALIBRATION: 4-53K-R10—(4WD)—MANUAL TRANS.—EXC. HIGH ALT.

85764175

Fig. 45 Vacuum schematic—1984 302 cu. in. engine

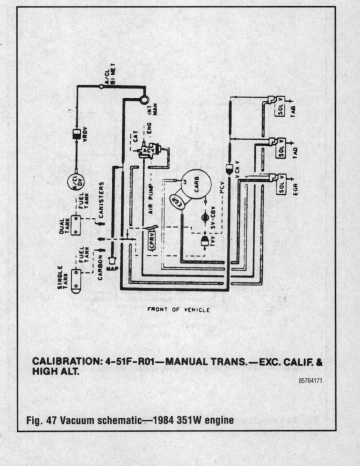

CALIBRATION: 4-51F-R01—MANUAL TRANS.—EXC. CALIF. & HIGH ALT.

85764171

Fig. 47 Vacuum schematic—1984 351W engine

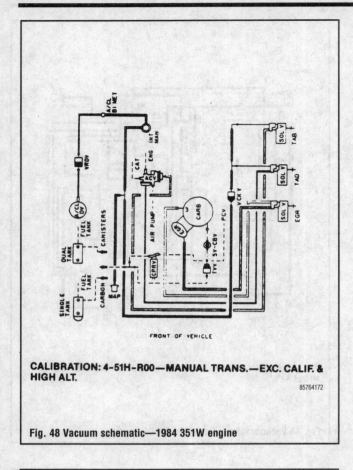

CALIBRATION: 4-51H-R00—MANUAL TRANS.—EXC. CALIF. & HIGH ALT.

85764172

Fig. 48 Vacuum schematic—1984 351W engine

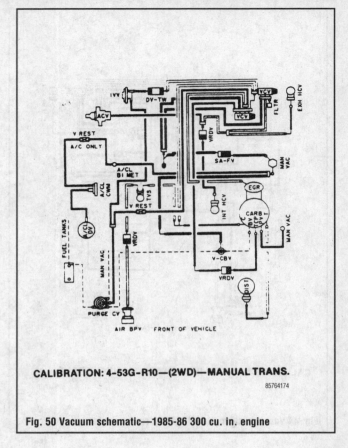

CALIBRATION: 4-53G-R10—(2WD)—MANUAL TRANS.

85764174

Fig. 50 Vacuum schematic—1985-86 300 cu. in. engine

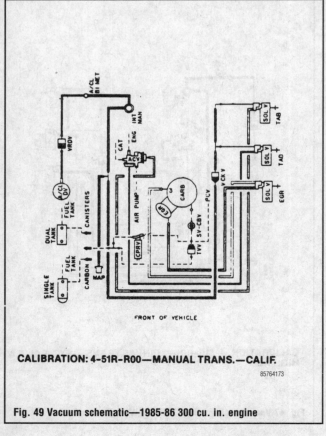

CALIBRATION: 4-51R-R00—MANUAL TRANS.—CALIF.

85764173

Fig. 49 Vacuum schematic—1985-86 300 cu. in. engine

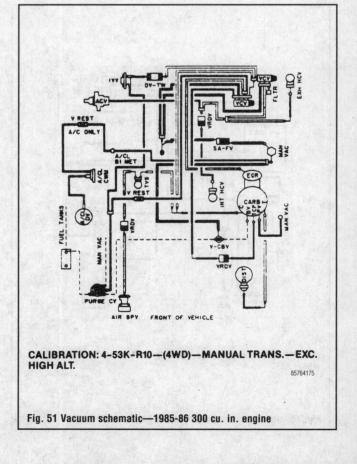

CALIBRATION: 4-53K-R10—(4WD)—MANUAL TRANS.—EXC. HIGH ALT.

85764175

Fig. 51 Vacuum schematic—1985-86 300 cu. in. engine

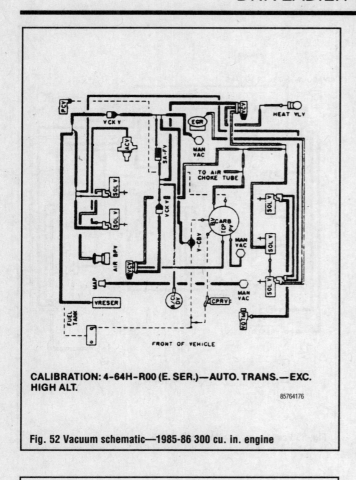

CALIBRATION: 4-64H-R00 (E. SER.)—AUTO. TRANS.—EXC. HIGH ALT.

85764176

Fig. 52 Vacuum schematic—1985-86 300 cu. in. engine

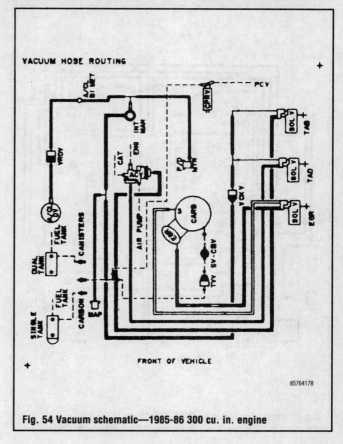

85764178

Fig. 54 Vacuum schematic—1985-86 300 cu. in. engine

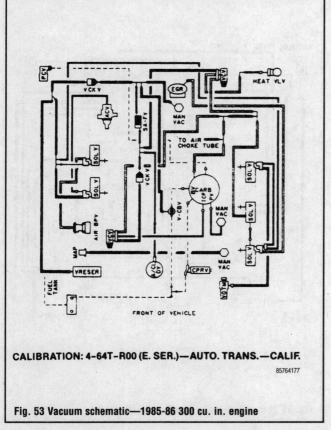

CALIBRATION: 4-64T-R00 (E. SER.)—AUTO. TRANS.—CALIF.

85764177

Fig. 53 Vacuum schematic—1985-86 300 cu. in. engine

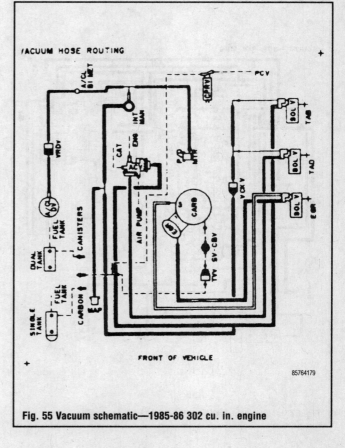

85764179

Fig. 55 Vacuum schematic—1985-86 302 cu. in. engine

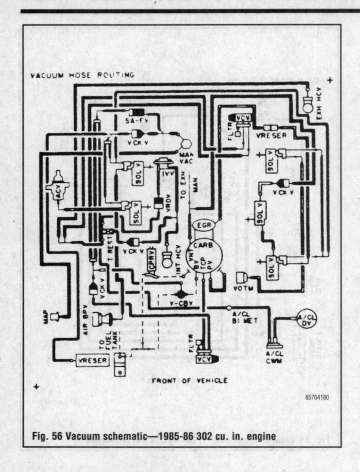

Fig. 56 Vacuum schematic—1985-86 302 cu. in. engine

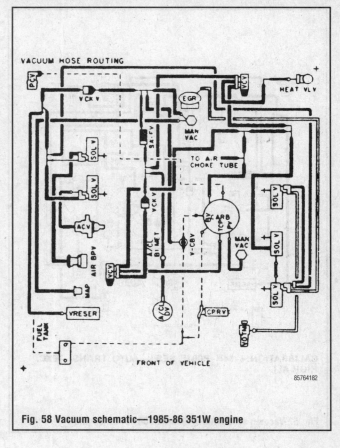

Fig. 58 Vacuum schematic—1985-86 351W engine

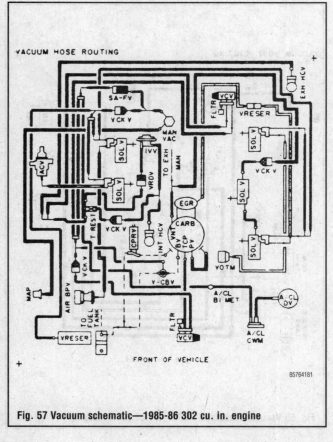

Fig. 57 Vacuum schematic—1985-86 302 cu. in. engine

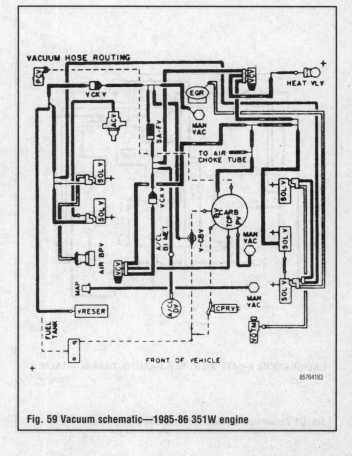

Fig. 59 Vacuum schematic—1985-86 351W engine

5

FUEL SYSTEM

CARBURETED FUEL SYSTEM

Carburetor

The carburetor identification tag is attached to the carburetor. The basic part number for all carburetors is 9510. To obtain replacement parts, it is necessary to know the part number prefix, suffix and, in some cases, the design change code. If the carburetor is ever replaced by a new unit, make sure that the identification tag stays with the new carburetor and the vehicle.

REMOVAL & INSTALLATION

▶ **See Figures 1 thru 8**

1. Remove the air cleaner.
2. Remove the throttle cable or rod from the throttle lever. Disconnect the distributor vacuum line, EGR vacuum line, if so equipped, the inline filter and the choke heat tube at the carburetor.
3. Disconnect the choke clean air tube from the air horn. Disconnect the choke actuating cable, if so equipped.
4. Remove the carburetor retaining nuts then remove the carburetor. Remove the carburetor mounting gasket, spacer (if so equipped), and the lower gasket from the intake manifold.
5. Before installing the carburetor, clean the gasket mounting surfaces of the spacer and carburetor.

6. Place the spacer between two new gaskets and position the spacer and the gaskets on the intake manifold. Position the carburetor on the spacer and gasket and secure it with the retaining nuts. To prevent leakage, distortion or damage to the carburetor body flange, snug the nuts, then alternately tighten each nut in a criss-cross pattern.
7. Connect the inline fuel filter, throttle cable, choke heat tube, distributor vacuum line, EGR vacuum line and choke cable.
8. Connect the choke clean air line to the air horn.
9. Adjust the engine idle speed, the idle fuel mixture and anti-stall dashpot (if so equipped). Install the air cleaner.

ADJUSTMENTS

Idle Mixture

➡**For this procedure, Ford recommends a propane enrichment procedure. This requires special equipment not available to the general public. In lieu of this equipment the following procedure may be followed to obtain a satisfactory idle mixture.**

1. Block the wheels, set the parking brake and run the engine to bring it to normal operating temperature.
2. Disconnect the hose between the emission canister and the air cleaner.

Fig. 1 Disconnect the cruise control cable from the throttle linkage

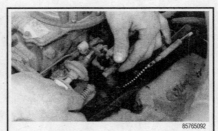

Fig. 2 Disconnect the throttle linkage from the carburetor

Fig. 3 Disconnect the kick-down linkage from the carburetor

Fig. 4 Remove the right front carburetor mounting nut

Fig. 5 Remove the right rear carburetor mounting nut

Fig. 6 Remove the left front carburetor mounting nut

Fig. 7 Remove the left rear carburetor mounting nut

Fig. 8 Carefully lift the carburetor from the intake manifold, you may have to rock it slightly to loosen it

3. On engines equipped with the Thermactor air injection system, the routing of the vacuum lines connected to the dump valve will have to be temporarily changed. Mark them for reconnection to prevent switching them when reconnecting.

4. For valves with one or two vacuum lines at the side, disconnect and plug the lines.

5. For valves with one vacuum line at the top, check the line to see if it is connected to the intake manifold or an intake manifold source such as the carburetor or distributor vacuum line. If not, remove and plug the line at the dump valve and connect a temporary length of vacuum hose from the dump valve fitting to a source of intake manifold vacuum.

6. Remove the limiter caps from the mixture screws by CAREFULLY cutting them with a sharp knife.

7. Place the transmission in neutral and run the engine at 2,500 rpm for 15 seconds.

8. Place the automatic transmission in Drive; the manual in neutral.

9. Adjust the idle speed to the higher of the two figures given on the underhood sticker.

10. Turn the idle mixture screw(s) to obtain the highest possible rpm, leaving the screw(s) in the leanest position that will maintain this rpm.

11. Repeat Steps 7 through 10 until further adjustment of the mixture screw(s) does not increase the rpm.

12. Turn the screw(s) in until the lower of the two idle speed figures is reached. Turn the screw(s) in ¼ turn increments each to insure a balance.

13. Turn the engine off and remove the tachometer. Reinstall all equipment previously removed.

➡**Rough idle, that cannot be corrected by normal service procedures may be caused by leakage between the EGR valve body and diaphragm. To determine if this is the cause: Tighten the EGR bolts to 15 ft. lbs. Connect a vacuum gauge to the intake manifold. Lift to exert a sideways pressure on the diaphragm housing. If the idle changes or the reading on the vacuum gauge varies, replace the EGR valve.**

Float and Fuel Level

CARTER MODEL YF, YFA AND YFA FEEDBACK 1-BBL.

▶ **See Figure 9**

1. Remove the carburetor air horn and gasket from the carburetor.

2. Invert the air horn assembly, and check the clearance from the top of the float to the bottom of the air horn. Hold the air horn at eye level when gauging the float level. The float arm (lever) should be resting on the needle pin. Do not load the needle when adjusting the float. Bend the float arm as necessary to adjust the float level (clearance). Do not bend the tab at the end of the float arm, because it prevents the float from striking the bottom of the fuel bowl when empty.

3. Turn the air horn over and hold it upright and let the float hang free. Measure the maximum clearance from the top of the float to the bottom of the air horn with the float gauge. Hold the air horn at eye level when gauging the dimension. To adjust the float drop, bend the tab at the end of the float arm.

4. Install the carburetor air horn with a new gasket.

Autolite (Motorcraft) Model 2150 2-Bbl. (Wet Adjustment)

1. Operate the engine until it reaches normal operating temperature. Place the vehicle on a level surface and stop the engine.

2. Remove the carburetor air cleaner assembly.

3. Remove the air horn attaching screws and the carburetor identification tag. Temporarily, leave the air horn and gasket in position on the carburetor main body and start the engine. Let the engine idle for a few minutes, then rotate the air horn out of the way and remove the air horn gasket to provide access to the float assembly.

4. While the engine is idling, use a scale to measure the vertical distance from the top machined surface of the carburetor main body to the level of the fuel in the fuel bowl. The measurement must be made at least ¼ inch (6mm) away from any vertical surface to assure an accurate reading, because the surface of the fuel is concave, being higher at the edges than in the center. Care must be exercised to measure the fuel level at the point of contact with the float.

5. If any adjustment is required, stop the engine to minimize the hazard of fire due to spilled gasoline. To adjust the fuel level, bend the float tab contacting the fuel inlet valve upward in relation to the original position to raise the fuel level, and downward to lower it. Each time the float is adjusted, the engine must be started and permitted to idle for a few minutes to stabilize the fuel level. Check the fuel level after each adjustment, until the specified level is obtained.

6. Assemble the carburetor in the reverse order of disassembly, using a new gasket between the air horn and the main carburetor body.

MOTORCRAFT MODEL 7200 VV FEEDBACK 2-BBL.

▶ **See Figures 10 and 11**

1. Remove the upper body assembly and the gasket.

2. Fabricate a gauge to the specified dimensions.

3. With the upper body inverted, place the fuel level gauge on the cast surface of the upper body and measure the vertical distance from the cast surface of the upper body and the bottom of the float.

4. To adjust, bend the float operating lever away from the fuel inlet needle to decrease the setting and toward the needle to increase the setting.

5. Check and/or adjust the float drop using the following procedures.
   a. Fabricate a gauge to the specified dimension.
   b. With the upper body assembly held in the upright position, place the gauge against the cast surface of the upper body and measure the vertical distance between the cast surface of the upper body and the bottom of the float.
   c. To adjust, bend the stop tab on the float lever away from the hinge pin to increase the setting and toward the hinge pin to decrease the setting.

6. Reinstall the upper body assembly and new gasket.

HOLLEY MODEL 4180-C 4-V (DRY ADJUSTMENT)

The float adjustment is a preliminary fuel level adjustment only. The final adjustment (Wet) must be performed after the carburetor has been installed on the engine.

With the fuel bowls and the float assemblies removed, hold the fuel bowls upside down and turn the adjusting nuts until the floats are parallel with the top of the fuel bowls.

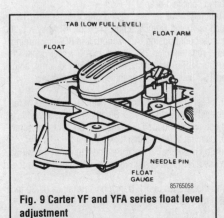

Fig. 9 Carter YF and YFA series float level adjustment

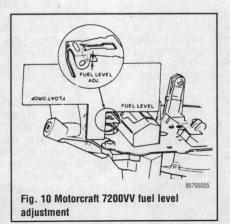

Fig. 10 Motorcraft 7200VV fuel level adjustment

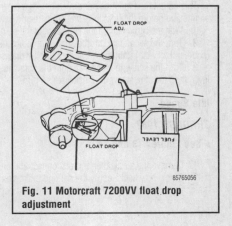

Fig. 11 Motorcraft 7200VV float drop adjustment

HOLLEY MODEL 4180-C 4-V (WET ADJUSTMENT)

▶ **See Figure 12**

➡ **The fuel pump pressure and volume must be to specifications prior to performing the following adjustments.**

1. Operate the engine to normalize engine temperatures and place the vehicle on a flat surface.
2. Remove the air cleaner, and run the engine at 1,000 rpm for about 30 seconds to stabilize the fuel level.
3. Stop the engine and remove the sight plug on the side of the primary carburetor bowl.
4. Check the fuel level. It should be at the bottom of the sight plug hole. If fuel spills out when the sight plug is removed, lower the fuel level. If the fuel level is below the sight glass hole, raise the fuel level.

❋❋ CAUTION

Do not loosen the lock screw or nut, or attempt to adjust the fuel level with the sight glass plug removed or the engine running as fuel may spray out creating a fire hazard.

5. Adjust the front level as necessary by loosening the lock screw, and turning the adjusting nut clockwise to lower fuel level, or counterclockwise to raise fuel level. A ¹⁄₁₆ turn of the adjusting nut will change fuel level approximately ¹⁄₃₂ inch (0.8mm). Tighten the locking screw and install the sight plug, using the old gasket. Start the engine and run for about 30 seconds at 1,000 rpm to stabilize the fuel level.
6. Stop the engine, remove the sight plug and check the fuel level. Repeat step 5 until the fuel level is at the bottom of the sight plug hole, install the sight plug using a new adjusting plug gasket.
7. Repeat steps 3 through 6 for the secondary fuel bowl.

➡ **The secondary throttle must be used to stabilize the fuel level in the secondary fuel bowl.**

8. Install the air cleaner.

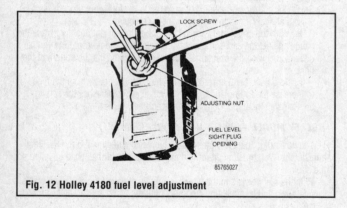

Fig. 12 Holley 4180 fuel level adjustment

Secondary Throttle Plate

This adjustment must be performed before the carburetor is installed on the engine and before the float level wet adjustment.
1. With the carburetor off the engine, hold the secondary throttle plates closed.
2. Turn the secondary throttle shaft lever adjusting screw (stop screw) out (counterclockwise) until the secondary throttle plates seat in the throttle bores.
3. Turn the screw in clockwise until the screw just contacts the secondary lever, then turn the screw in (clockwise) ⅜ turn.

Idle Speed

THROUGH 1982

▶ **See Figures 13 and 14**

1. Remove the air cleaner and disconnect and plug the vacuum lines.
2. Block the wheels, apply the parking brake, turn off all accessories, start the engine and run it to normalize underhood temperatures.

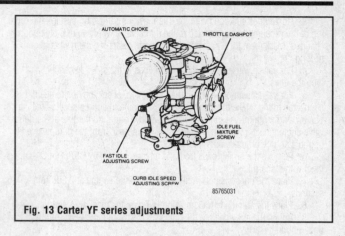

Fig. 13 Carter YF series adjustments

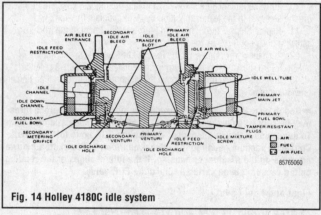

Fig. 14 Holley 4180C idle system

3. Check that the choke plate is fully open and connect a tachometer according to the manufacturer's instructions.
4. Check the throttle stop positioner (TSP) off speed as follows: Collapse the plunger by forcing the throttle lever against it. Place the transmission in neutral and check the engine speed. If necessary, adjust to specified TSP Off speed with the throttle adjusting screw. See the underhood sticker.
5. Place the manual transmission in neutral; the automatic in Drive and make certain the TSP plunger is extended.
6. Turn the TSP until the specified idle speed is obtained.
7. Install the air cleaner and connect the vacuum lines. Check the idle speed. Adjust, if necessary, with the air cleaner on.

1983 AND LATER YFA–IV & YFA–IV–FB

1. Block the wheels and apply the parking brake. Place the transmission in Neutral or Park.
2. Bring engine to normal operating temperature.
3. Place A/C Heat Selector to Off position.
4. Place transmission in specified gear.
5. Check/adjust curb idle RPM as follows: TSP dashpot. Insure that TSP is activated using a ⅜ inch open end wrench, adjust curb idle RPM by rotating the nut directly behind the dashpot housing. Adjust curb idle RPM by turning the idle RPM speed screw. Front mounted TSP (same as A/C kicker on all other calibrations) insure that TSP is activated. After loosening lock nut, adjust curb idle RPM by rotating TSP solenoid until specified RPM is obtained. Tighten locknut.
6. Check/adjust anti-diesel (TSP Off). Manually collapse the TSP by rotating the carburetor throttle shaft lever until the TSP Off adjusting screw contacts the carburetor body. If adjustment is required, turn the TSP Off adjusting screw while holding the lever adjustment screw against the stop.
7. Place the transmission in Neutral or Park. Rev the engine momentarily. Place the transmission in specified position and recheck curb idle rpm. Readjust if required.
8. Check/adjust dashpot clearance to 0.120 inch plus or minus 0.030 inch (3mm plus or minus 0.76mm).

9. If a final curb idle speed adjustment is required, the bowl vent setting must be checked as follows: Stop the engine and turn the ignition key to the On position, so that the TSP dashpot or TSP is activated but the engine is not running (where applicable). Secure the choke plate in the wide open position. Open the throttle, so that the throttle vent lever does not touch the fuel bowl vent rod. Close the throttle, and measure the travel of the fuel bowl vent rod from the open throttle position. Travel of the fuel bowl vent rod should be 0.100–0.150 inch (2.54–3.81mm). If out of specification, bend the throttle vent lever to obtain the required travel. Remove all test equipment, and tighten the air cleaner holddown bolt to specification.

10. Whenever it is required to adjust engine idle speed by more than 50 rpm, the adjustment screw on the AOD linkage lever at the carburetor should also be readjusted.

1983 AND LATER 8-302 (5.0L) 2150–2V FB (FEEDBACK)

1. Set parking brake and block wheels.
2. Place the transmission in Park.
3. Bring the engine to normal operating temperature.
4. Disconnect the electric connector on the EVAP purge solenoid.
5. Disconnect and plug the vacuum hose to the VOTM kicker.
6. Place the transmission in Drive position.
7. Check/adjust curb idle rpm, if adjustment is required: Adjust with the the curb idle speed screw or the saddle bracket adjusting screw, depending on how equipped.
8. Place the transmission in Neutral or Park. Rev the engine momentarily. Place the transmission in Drive position and recheck curb idle rpm. Readjust if required.
9. Remove the plug from the vacuum hose to the VOTM kicker and reconnect.
10. Reconnect the electrical connector on the EVAP purge solenoid.

1983 AND LATER 8-302 (5.0L) 2150–2V (NON-FEEDBACK)

1. Set parking brake and block wheels.
2. Place the transmission in Neutral or Park.
3. Bring engine to normal operating temperature.
4. Place A/C Heat selector to Off position.
5. Disconnect and plug vacuum hose to Thermactor air bypass valve.
6. Place the transmission in specified gear.
7. Check curb idle rpm. Adjust to specification by using the curb idle rpm speed screw or the saddle bracket adjusting screw, depending on how equipped.
8. Place the transmission in Neutral or Park. Rev the engine momentarily. Place the transmission in specified position, and recheck curb idle rpm. Readjust if required.
9. Remove plug from vacuum hose to Thermactor air bypass valve and reconnect.
10. Whenever it is required to adjust engine idle speed by more than 50 rpm, the adjustment screw on the AOD linkage lever at the carburetor should also be readjusted.

1983 AND LATER 8–351 (5.8L) 2150–2V OR 7200 VV

1. Block the wheels and apply parking brake. Place the transmission in Neutral or Park.
2. Bring engine to normal operating temperature.
3. Disconnect purge hose on canister side of evaporator purge solenoid. Check to ensure that purge vacuum is present (solenoid has opened and will require 3 to 5 minute wait after starting engine followed by a short time at part throttle). Reconnect purge hose.
4. Disconnect and plug the vacuum hose to the VOTM kicker.
5. Place the transmission in specified position.
6. Check/adjust curb idle rpm. If adjustment is required, adjust with the curb idle speed screw or the saddle bracket adjusting screw (ensure curb idle speed screw is not touching throttle shaft lever).
7. Place the transmission in Neutral or Park. Rev the engine momentarily. Place the transmission in specified position and recheck curb idle rpm. Readjust if required.
8. Check/adjust throttle position sensor (TPS).
9. Remove the plug from the vacuum hose to the VOTM kicker and reconnect.
10. Apply a slight pressure on top of the nylon nut located on the accelerator pump to take up the linkage clearance.

11. Turn the nylon nut on the accelerator pump rod clockwise until a 0.010 inch plus or minus 0.005 inch (0.254–0.127mm) clearance is obtained between the top of the accelerator pump and the pump lever.
12. Turn the accelerator pump rod nut one turn counterclockwise to set the lever lash preload.
13. If curb idle adjustment exceeds 50 rpm, adjust automatic transmission TV linkage.

1983 AND LATER 8–302 (5.0L) & 351 (5.8L) CANADA 2150–2V

1. Place the transmission in Neutral or Park.
2. Bring engine to normal operating temperature.
3. Place A/C Heat Selector to Off position.
4. Place the transmission in specified gear.
5. Check curb idle rpm. Adjust to specification using the curb idle speed screw or the hex head on the rear of the solenoid or the saddle bracket adjustment screw depending on how equipped.
6. Place the transmission in Neutral or Park. Rev the engine momentarily. Place the transmission in specified position and recheck curb idle rpm. Readjust if required.
7. TSP Off: With transmission in specified gear, collapse the solenoid plunger, and set specified TSP Off speed on the speed screw.
8. Disconnect vacuum hose to decel throttle control modulator and plug (if so equipped).
9. Connect a slave vacuum from manifold vacuum to the decel throttle control modulator (if so equipped).
10. Check/adjust decel throttle control rpm. Adjust if necessary.
11. Remove slave vacuum hose.
12. Remove plug from decel throttle control modulator hose and reconnect.

1983 AND LATER HOLLEY MODEL 4180-C 4V

▶ See Figure 15

1. Block the wheels and apply parking brake.
2. Run engine until normal operating temperature is reached.
3. Place the vehicle in Park or Neutral, A/C in Off position, and set parking brake.
4. Remove air cleaner.
5. Disconnect and plug decel throttle control kicker diaphragm vacuum hose.
6. Connect a slave vacuum hose from an engine manifold vacuum source to the decel throttle control kicker.
7. Run engine at approximately 2,500 rpm for 15 seconds, then release the throttle.
8. If decel throttle control rpm is not within plus or minus 50 rpm of specification, adjust the kicker.
9. Disconnect the slave vacuum hose and allow engine to return to curb idle.
10. Adjust curb idle, if necessary, using the curb idle adjusting screw.
11. Rev the engine momentarily, recheck curb idle and adjust if necessary.
12. Reconnect the decel throttle control vacuum hose to the diaphragm.
13. Reinstall the air cleaner.

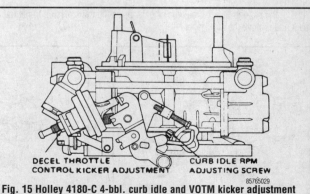

DECEL THROTTLE
CONTROL KICKER ADJUSTMENT

CURB IDLE RPM
ADJUSTING SCREW

85765029

Fig. 15 Holley 4180-C 4-bbl. curb idle and VOTM kicker adjustment locations

Fast Idle Speed

CARTER YF, AND YFA 1-BBL.

▶ See Figure 16

1. Run the engine to normal operating temperature.
2. Remove the air cleaner and attach a tachometer to the engine according to the manufacturer's instructions.
3. Manually rotate the fast idle to the top step while holding the choke plate fully opened.
4. Rotate the cam until the fast idle adjusting screw rests on the cam step specified on the underhood emissions sticker.
5. Turn the fast idle speed adjusting screw to obtain the specified speed.

➡When this operation is performed outdoors in cold weather, all vacuum controls to the distributor and EGR valve must be bypassed. This can be done by connecting a jumper hose from the DIST port on the carburetor to the vacuum advance port of the distributor and by disconnecting and plugging the EGR vacuum source hose.

AUTOLITE (MOTORCRAFT) MODEL 2150 2-BBL.

1. Run the engine to normal operating temperature.
2. Remove the air cleaner and attach a tachometer to the engine according to the manufacturer's instructions.
3. Manually rotate the fast idle to the top step while holding the choke plate fully opened.
4. Rotate the cam until the fast idle adjusting screw rests on the cam step specified on the underhood emissions sticker.
5. Turn the fast idle speed adjusting screw to obtain the specified speed.

➡When this operation is performed outdoors in cold weather, all vacuum controls to the distributor and EGR valve must be bypassed. This can be done by connecting a jumper hose from the DIST port on the carburetor to the vacuum advance port of the distributor and by disconnecting and plugging the EGR vacuum source hose.

MOTORCRAFT MODEL 7200 VV 2-BBL.

▶ See Figure 17

1. Place the transmission in Park or Neutral.
2. Bring the engine to normal operating temperature.
3. Disconnect the purge hose on the canister side of the evaporator purge solenoid. Check to see that purge vacuum is present (solenoid has opened—will require 3 to 5 minute wait after starting the engine) followed by a short time at part throttle. Reconnect the purge hose.
4. Disconnect and plug the vacuum hose at the EGR and purge valves.
5. Place the fast idle lever on the second step of the fast idle cam. (Third step on Calif. models.)
6. Adjust the fast idle rpm to specifications.
7. Reconnect the EGR and purge vacuum hoses.

HOLLEY 4180-C 4V

▶ See Figure 18

1. Set the parking brake, block the wheels, place the transmission in neutral or park and remove the air cleaner.

2. Bring the engine to normal operating temperature.
3. Disconnect the vacuum hoses at the EGR valve and the purge control valves and plug.
4. Place the fast idle adjustment on the specified step of the fast idle cam. Check and adjust the fast idle rpm to the specifications found on the Exhaust Emission Control Decal on the engine.
5. Rev the engine momentarily, place the fast idle adjustment on the specified step and recheck the fast idle rpm.
6. Remove the plug from the EGR valve and the purge control valves and reconnect.

Dashpot

1. Remove the air cleaner.
2. Loosen the anti-stall dashpot locknut.
3. With the choke plate open, hold the throttle plate closed (idle position), and check the clearance between the throttle lever and the dashpot plunger tip with a feeler gauge.

Accelerating Pump Clearance

HOLLEY 4180-C

1. Using a feeler gauge and with the primary throttle plates in the wide open position, there should be 0.015 inch (0.381mm) clearance between the accelerator pump operating lever adjustment screw head and the pump arm when the pump arm is depressed manually.
2. If adjustment is required, hold the adjusting screw locknut and turn the adjusting screw inward to increase the clearance and out to decrease the clearance. One half turn on the adjusting screw is approximately 0.015 inch (0.381mm).

Accelerating Pump Stroke

MOTORCRAFT 2150

▶ See Figure 19

The accelerating pump stroke has been factory set for a particular engine application and should not be readjusted. If the stroke has been

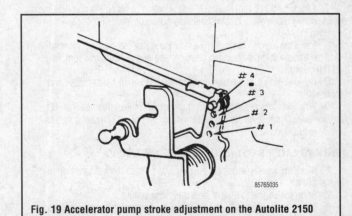

Fig. 19 Accelerator pump stroke adjustment on the Autolite 2150

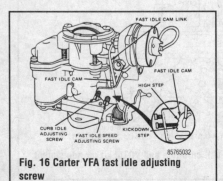

Fig. 16 Carter YFA fast idle adjusting screw

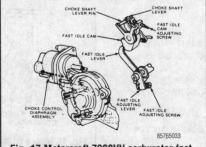

Fig. 17 Motorcraft 7200VV carburetor fast idle adjustment

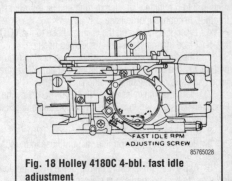

Fig. 18 Holley 4180C 4-bbl. fast idle adjustment

changed from the specified hole reset to specifications by following these procedures.

1. To release the rod from the retaining clip, lift upward on the portion of the clip that snaps over the shaft and then disengage the rod.

2. Position the clip over the specified hole in the overtravel lever and insert the operating rod through the clip and the overtravel lever. Snap the end of the clip over the rod to secure.

HOLLEY 4180-C 4V

♦ See Figure 20

The accelerator pump stroke has been set to help keep the exhaust emission level of the engine within the specified limits. The additional holes provided (if any) for pump stroke adjustment are for adjusting the stroke for specific engine applications. The stroke should not be changed from the specified setting.

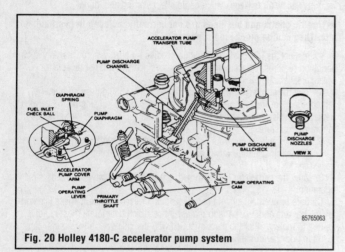

Fig. 20 Holley 4180-C accelerator pump system

Choke Pulldown

CARTER YF, YFA

1. Remove the air cleaner. Remove the choke thermostatic spring housing from the carburetor.

2. Bend a 0.026 inch (0.66mm) diameter wire gauge at a 90 degrees angle approximately ⅛ inch (3mm) from one end. Insert the bent end of the gauge between the choke piston slot and the right hand slot in the choke housing. Rotate the choke piston lever counterclockwise until the gauge is snug in the piston slot.

3. Exert a light pressure on the choke piston lever to hold the gauge in place, then use a drill gauge with a diameter equal to the specified clearance between the lower edge of the choke plate and the carburetor bore to check clearance.

4. To adjust the choke plate pulldown clearance, bend the choke piston lever as required to obtain the specified setting. Remove the choke piston lever for bending to prevent distorting the piston link, causing erratic choke operation.

5. Install the choke thermostatic spring housing and gasket. Set the housing to specifications.

MOTORCRAFT 2150

♦ See Figure 21

1. Set throttle on fast idle cam top step.

2. Note index position of choke bimetallic cap. Loosen retaining screws and rotate cap 90 degrees in the rich (closing) direction.

3. Activate pulldown motor by manually forcing pulldown control diaphragm link in the direction of applied vacuum or by applying vacuum to external vacuum tube.

4. Measure vertical hard gauge clearance between choke plate and center of carburetor air horn wall nearest fuel bowl.

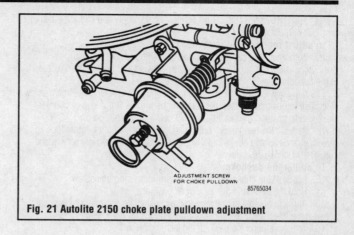

Fig. 21 Autolite 2150 choke plate pulldown adjustment

Pulldown setting should be within specifications for minimum choke plate opening.

If choke plate pulldown is found to be out of specification, reset by adjusting diaphragm stop on end of choke pulldown diaphragm.

If pulldown is reset, cam clearance should be checked and reset if required.

After pulldown check is completed, reset choke bimetallic cap to recommend index position as specified in the Carburetor Specifications Chart. Check and reset fast idle speed to specifications if necessary.

HOLLEY 4180-C

♦ See Figure 22

1. Remove the air cleaner. Then remove the carburetor from the vehicle and cover the intake manifold.

2. Place the carburetor on a stand which allows access to the pulldown diaphragm vacuum passage on the underside of the throttle body.

3. Mark the choke cap and housing. Then remove the choke cap, gasket and retainer.

4. Reinstall the choke cap temporarily with a standard choke cap gasket. Line up the marks made previously on the cap and the housing and rotate the cap 90 degrees counterclockwise from that position. Secure with one screw.

5. With the choke plate in the full closed position, actuate the choke pulldown motor using an outside vacuum source, 17 in.Hg minimum.

6. Using a drill gauge of the specified size check the clearance between the upper edge of the choke plate and the air horn wall.

➡The gauge should fit in such a manner that it contacts the air horn and choke plate but does not move the plate.

7. If the pulldown dimension is out of specification, carefully remove the diaphragm adjustment screw cap with a small sharp punch or screw driver.

8. Turn the adjustment screw with a 5⁄16 inch Allen wrench clockwise to decrease the pulldown set or counterclockwise to increase the pulldown set.

➡Maintain a minimum of 17 in.Hg to the pulldown diaphragm during adjustment. Cycle vacuum from 0–17 in.Hg to verify proper set.

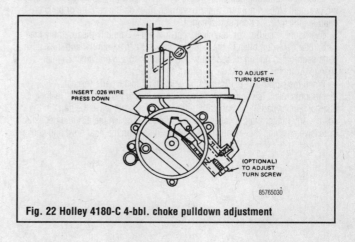

Fig. 22 Holley 4180-C 4-bbl. choke pulldown adjustment

9. Apply RTV sealant to the adjustment screw cavity and check the fast idle cam index adjustment.

To adjust the fast idle cam index:

10. With the choke cap still wrapped, and with vacuum applied to the diaphragm, cycle the throttle. The fast idle screw should rest on the No. 2 step of the fast idle cam.

11. If the fast idle cam requires adjustment, turn the Allen adjustment screw clockwise to position the fast idle screw higher on the No. 2 step or counterclockwise to position the fast idle screw lower on the No. 2 step.

12. Remove the temporary choke plate gasket, install the original locking gasket, choke cap and choke cap retainer. Secure with breakaway screws and check the dechoke adjustment.

To adjust the dechoke:

13. Reinstall the choke cap at the proper index using one screw.

14. Hold the throttle in the wide open position.

15. Apply light closing pressure to the choke plate and measure the gap between the lower edge of the choke plate and the air horn wall.

16. To adjust, bend the pawl on the fast idle lever.

Dechoke

EXCEPT HOLLEY 4180-C-4V

1. Remove the air cleaner.

2. Hold the throttle plate fully open and close the choke plate as far as possible without forcing it. Use a drill of the proper diameter to check the clearance between the choke plate and air horn.

3. If the clearance is not within specification, adjust by bending the arm on the choke trip lever. Bending the arm downward will increase the clearance, and bending it upward will decrease the clearance. Always recheck the clearance after making any adjustment.

4. If the choke plate clearance and fast idle cam linkage adjustment was performed with the carburetor on the engine, adjust the engine idle speed and fuel mixture. Adjust the dashpot (if so equipped).

TROUBLESHOOTING

The best way to diagnose a bad carburetor is to eliminate all other possible sources of the problem. If the carburetor is suspected to be the problem, first perform all of the adjustments given in this Section. If this doesn't correct the difficulty, then check the following. Check the ignition system to make sure that the spark plugs, breaker points, and condenser are in good condition and adjusted to the proper specifications. Examine the emission control equipment to make sure that all the vacuum lines are connected and none are blocked or clogged. Check the ignition timing adjusting. Check all the vacuum lines on the engine for loose connections, splits or breaks. Torque the carburetor and intake manifold attaching bolts to the proper specifications. If, after performing all of these checks and adjustments, the problem is still not solved, then you can safely assume that the carburetor is the source of the problem.

OVERHAUL

Efficient carburetion depends greatly on careful cleaning and inspection during overhaul since dirt, gum, water or varnish in or on the carburetor parts are often responsible for poor performance.

Overhaul the carburetor in a clean, lint-free area. Carefully disassemble the carburetor, referring often to the exploded views. Keep all similar and look-alike parts segregated during disassembly and cleaning to avoid accidental interchange during assembly. Make a note of all jet sizes.

When the carburetor is disassembled, wash all metal parts (except diaphragms, electric choke unit, pump plunger and any other plastic, leather, fiber, or rubber parts) in clean carburetor solvent. Do not leave the parts in the solvent any longer than is necessary to sufficiently loosen the dirt and deposits. Excessive cleaning may remove the special finish from the float bowl and choke valve bodies, leaving these parts unfit for service. Rinse all parts in clean solvent and blow them dry with compressed air or allow them to air dry, while resting on clean, lint-free paper. Wipe clean all cork, plastic, leather and fiber parts with a clean, lint-free cloth.

Blow out all passages and jets with compressed air and be sure that there are no restrictions or blockages. Never use wire or similar tools to clean jets, fuel passages or air bleeds. Clean all jets and valves separately to avoid accidental interchange.

Examine all parts for wear or damage. If wear or damage is found, replace the defective parts. Especially, inspect the following:

1. Check the float needle and seat for wear. If wear is found, replace the complete assembly.

2. Check the float hinge pin for wear and the float(s) for dents or distortion. Replace the float if fuel has leaked into it.

3. Check the throttle and choke shaft bores for wear or an out-of-round condition. Damage or wear to the throttle arm, shaft or shaft bore will often require replacement of the throttle body. These parts require a close tolerance of fit; wear may allow air leakage, which could affect starting and idling.

➡**Throttle shafts and bushings are not normally included in overhaul kits. They can be purchased separately.**

4. Inspect the idle mixture adjusting needles for burrs or grooves. Any such condition requires replacement of the needle, since you will not be able to obtain a satisfactory idle.

5. Test the accelerator pump check valves. They should pass air one way, but not the other. Test for proper seating by blowing and sucking on the valve. Replace the valve as necessary. If the valve is satisfactory, wash the valve again to remove moisture.

6. Check the bowl cover for warped surfaces with a straightedge.

7. Closely inspect the valves and seats for wear and damage, replacing as necessary.

8. After the carburetor is assembled, check the choke valve for freedom of operation.

Carburetor overhaul kits are recommended for each overhaul. These kits contain all gaskets and new parts to replace those which deteriorate most rapidly. Failure to replace all of the parts supplied with the kit (especially gaskets) can result in poor performance later.

➡**Most carburetor rebuilding kits include specific procedures which should be following during overhaul.**

Most carburetor manufacturers supply overhaul kits of these basic types: minor repair; major repair; and gasket kits. Basically, they contain the following:

Minor Repair Kits:
- All gaskets
- Float needle valve
- Mixture adjusting screws
- All diaphragms
- Spring for the pump diaphragm

Major Repair Kits:
- All jets and gaskets
- All diaphragms
- Float needle valve
- Mixture adjusting screws
- Pump ball valve
- Main jet carrier
- Float
- Some float bowl cover holddown screws and washer

Gasket Kits:
- All gaskets

After cleaning and checking all components, reassemble the carburetor, using new parts and referring to the exploded view. When reassembling, make sure that all screws and jets are tight in their seats, but do not overtighten, as the tips will be distorted. Tighten all screws gradually, in rotation. Do not tighten needle valves into their seats; uneven jetting will result. Always use new gaskets. Be sure to adjust the float level.

Carburetor Specifications
Carter Model YF 1-BBL

Year	Engine No. Cyl Displacement (cu in.)	Carb Tag Number	Float Level (in.)	Main Jet (in.)	Pump Jet (in.)	Idle Jet (in.)	Choke System Cap Setting	Choke System Pulldown (in.)	Choke System De-choke (in.)	Dashpot Setting (in.)	Fast Idle Cam Kick-down (in.)
1976	6-300	D5TE-BSB	23/32	0.107	—	—	Index	0.290	0.280	—	0.110
		D5TE-CBA	3/8	0.107	—	—	Index	0.290	0.280	—	0.110
		D5UE-FA	3/8	0.110	—	—	Index	0.290	0.280	—	0.110
		D5TE-APB	23/32	0.110	—	—	Index	0.290	0.280	—	0.110
		D5TE-CAB	23/32	0.107	—	—	Index	0.290	0.280	—	0.110
		D6TE-HA	23/32	0.107	—	—	Index	0.290	0.280	—	0.110
		D5UE-AAB	23/32	0.107	—	—	Index	0.290	0.280	—	0.110
		D5UE-HB	23/32	0.110	—	—	Index	0.290	0.280	—	0.110
		D6TF-DA	23/32	0.107	—	—	Index	0.290	0.280	—	0.110
		D5UE-GB	23/32	0.110	—	—	Index	0.290	0.280	—	0.110
		D5TE-AGA	3/8	0.101	—	—	INR	0.230	0.280	—	0.110
		D5TE-AGB	3/8	0.101	—	—	INR	0.230	0.280	—	0.110
		D5TE-AFA	3/8	0.104	—	—			Manual Choke		0.110
		D5TE-AFB	3/8	0.104	—	—			Manual Choke		0.110
		D5TE-AJA	3/8	0.104	—	—			Manual Choke		0.110
		D5TE-AJB	3/8	0.104	—	—			Manual Choke		0.110

Carburetor Specifications
Autolite Model 4350 4-BBL

Year	Engine No. Cyl Displacement (cu in.)	Carb Tag Number	Carb Model	Float Level (in.)	Main Metering Jet No.	Choke System Cap Setting	Choke System Pull-down (in.)	Choke System Fast Idle Cam (in.)	Choke System De-choke (in.)	Accelerator Pump Operating Rod Hole Position
1976	8-460	D6UE-KA	4350	1.00	421	Index	0.160	0.170	0.300	Inner 2
		D6UE-LA	4350	1.00	421	Index	0.160	0.170	0.300	Inner 2
		D5TE-NA	4350	1.00	421	Index	0.160	0.170	0.300	Inner 2
		D6TE-AU	4350	1.00	421	Index	0.160	0.170	0.300	Inner 2

1979–81 Carburetor Specifications

To determine the applicable carburetor specifications listed in the table below, refer to the engine calibration code on the vehicle's underhood sticker. This method is necessary due to the multiplicity of engine setting variations which are required to meet Federal and California emission regulations.

Calibration Number	Choke Plate Pulldown Setting (inches)	Time for Choke Plate to Rotate (come off) (seconds—maximum)	Air Flow (pounds per minute)	Choke Setting	Fast Idle rpm High Cam	Fast Idle rpm Kick Down	Curb Idle rpm ©A/C Off/On	Curb Idle rpm Non-AC	TSP Off rpm AC	TSP Off rpm Non-AC	Timing rpm
9-51G-RO	.230	80	.06	Index	—	1600	700	700	500	500	500
9-51J-RO	.230	80	.06	Index	—	1600	700	700	500	500	500
9-51K-RO	.230	80	.06	Index	—	1600	700	700	500	500	500
9-51L-RO	.230	80	.06	Index	—	1600	700	700	500	500	500
9-51M-RO	.230	80	.06	Index	—	1600	700	700	500	500	500

Carburetor Specifications
Autolite Model 2150 2-BBL

Year	Engine No. Cyl Displacement (cu in.)	Carb Model	Carb Tag Number	Float Level (Wet) (in.)	Idle Jet (in.)	Main Jet No.	Power Jet (in.)	Pump Jet (in.)	Choke System Cap Setting	Choke System Pull-down (in.)	Choke System Dashpot (in.)	Accelerator Operating Rod Hole Position
1976	8-302	2150	D5TE-BMA	7/8	—	—	—	—	2R	—	—	3
		2150	D5TE-PA	7/8	—	—	—	—	3R	—	—	2
	8-360	2150	D5TE-ABA	0.810	—	47F	—	—	Manual	—	—	4
		2150	D5TE-ASA	7/8	—	57F	—	—	Index	0.179	—	4
		2150	D5TE-ATA	7/8	—	57F	—	—	Index	0.179	—	4
		2150	D5TE-BYA	7/8	—	56F	—	—	2NR	0.140	—	3
		2150	D5TE-AAF	7/8	—	55F	—	—	3NR	0.140	—	3
		2150	D5TE-YF	7/8	—	56F	—	—	2NR	0.140	—	3
		2150	D5TE-ZB	7/8	—	56F	—	—	2NR	0.140	—	3
	8-390	2150	D5TE-BEB	7/8	—	56F	—	—	2NR	0.140	—	3

1979–81 Carburetor Specifications (cont.)

Calibration Number	Choke Plate Pulldown Setting (inches)	Time for Choke Plate to Rotate (come off) (seconds-maximum)	Air Flow (pounds per minute)	Choke Setting	Fast Idle rpm High Cam	Fast Idle rpm Kick Down	Curb Idle rpm ①A/C Off/0n	Curb Idle rpm Non-AC	TSP Off rpm AC	TSP Off rpm Non-AC	Timing rpm
9-51S-RO	.230	80	.06	Index	—	1600	700	700	500	500	500
9-51T-RO	.230	80	.06	Index	—	1600	700	700	500	500	500
9-52G-RO	.230	80	.06	Index	—	1600	550	550	500	500	500
9-52J-RO	.230	80	.06	Index	—	1600	550	550	500	500	500
9-52L-RO	.230	80	.06	Index	—	1600	550	550	500	500	500
9-52M-RO	.230	80	.06	Index	—	1600	550	550	500	500	500
9-53G-RO	.140	235	.085	3 Rich	2000	—	700	700	—	—	550
9-53H-RO	.140	125	.085	3 Rich	2000	—	700	700	—	—	550
9-54G-RO	.145	150	.079	3 Rich	2000	—	600	600	—	—	550
9-54H-RO	.145	150	.079	3 Rich	2000	—	600	600	—	—	550
9-54J-RO	.145	135	.079	2 Rich	2000	—	600	600	—	—	550
9-54R-RO	.145	135	.079	3 Rich	2000	—	600	600	—	—	550
9-54S-RO	.136	75	.080	1 Rich	2400	—	650	650	—	—	550
9-54T-RO	.145	150	.079	3 Rich	2000	—	600	600	—	—	550
9-54U-RO	.136	75	.080	1 Rich	2400	—	650	650	—	—	550
9-59H-RO	.135	84	.074	Index	2000	—	650	650	—	—	650
9-59J-RO	.145	84	.074	Index	2000	—	650	650	—	—	650
9-59K-RO	.145	84	.074	Index	2000	—	650	650	—	—	650
9-59S-RO	.135	84	.07	Index	2000	—	650	650	—	—	650
9-59T-RO	.150	84	.07	Index	2000	—	650	650	—	—	650
9-60G-RO	.145	84	.079	Index	2000	—	550	550	—	—	500
9-60H-RO	.150	84	.08	Index	2000	—	550	550	—	—	500
9-60J-RO	.140	84	.079	Index	2000	—	550	550	—	—	500
9-60L-RO	.150	84	.08	Index	2000	—	550	550	—	—	500
9-60M-RO	.150	84	.08	Index	2000	—	550	550	—	—	500
9-60S-RO	.150	84	—	3 Rich	2100	—	550	550	—	—	500
9-61G-RO	.145	84	.074	Index	2000	—	650	650	—	—	650
9-61H-RO	.135	84	.076	Index	2000	—	650	650	—	—	650
9-62J-RO	.145	85	.079	Index	1900	—	550	550	—	—	550
9-62M-RO	.145	85	.079	Index	1900	—	550	550	—	—	500
9-63H-RO	.190	77	.06	Index	—	1500	800	800	—	—	500
9-64G-RO	.200	67	.06	Index	2200	—	800	600	—	—	500
9-64H-RO	.200	67	.06	Index	2200	—	600	600	500	500	500
9-64S-RO	.200	67	.06	Index	2200	—	600	600	500	500	500
9-66G-RO	.210	130	.09	5 Rich	—	1600	650 ②	650	800 ③	800	650 TSP Off

① Only for A/C-TSP equipped, A/C compressor electromagnetic clutch de-energized.
② Energize A/C electromagnetic clutch.
③ De-energize A/C electromagnetic clutch.

8576508C

1982 Carburetor Specifications Carter YFA

Check the carburetor part number tab to determine which specifications to use for your vehicle

Engine	Part Number	Choke Pulldown Setting	Fast Idle Cam Setting	Dechoke Setting	Choke Plate Come-Off Time	Float Setting (Dry)	Choke Cap Setting	Fast Idle
6-300	E2TE-9510-BZA, BVA	.270	.140	.280	110 sec.	.780	Index	①
	E2TE-9510-AMA E2UE-9510-EA	.230	.140	.280	110 sec.	.780	Index	①
	E2TE-9510-CEA, JA,KA,DA	.320	.140	.330	110 sec.	.780	2NR	①
	E2TE-9510-YA, AAA,MA,ANA	.300	.140	.280	110 sec.	.780	2NR	①
	D5TE-9510-AGB	.230	.110	.280	110 sec.	.875	1NR	①
	D9TE-9510-CA, CB,VB E2TE-9510-ZA EOTE-9510-AMA, AMB,FA,FB	.290	.140	.280	—	.690	Index	①

① Refer to underhood emission sticker

8576509C

Motorcraft 2150

Engine	Part Number	Choke Pulldown Setting	Fast Idle Cam Setting	Dechoke Setting	Float Level (Wet)	Float Level (Dry)	Accelerator Pump Lever Location	Choke Cap Setting	Fast Idle
8-302	E2TE-9510-AYA, BEA,CJA	.130	V-notch	.200	.810	7/16	#2	V-notch	①
	E2TE-9510-BFA, BAA,BBA	.125	V-notch	.200	.810	7/16	#2	V-notch	①
	E2TEP9510-CKA	.120	V-notch	.200	.810	7/16	#2	V-notch	①
	E2TE-9510-JA	.130	V-notch	.200	.875	31/64	#2	V-notch	①
	E3TE-9510-BPA, BRA	.130	V-notch	.250	.875	31/64	#3	V-notch	①
8-351	E2UE-9510-FA E1UE-9510-JA	.120	V-notch	.200	.875	31/64	#3	V-notch	①
	E1UE-9510-KA	.120	V-notch	.200	.875	31/64	#2	V-notch	①
	E2UE-9510-AAA ABA,AKA,ANA,HA, RA,SA	.180	V-notch	.250	.875	31/64	#3	V-notch	①
8-400	E2TE-9510-BGA, BHA	.180	V-notch	.250	.875	31/64	#4	V-notch	①
	E2TE-9510-DCA, DBA	.180	V-notch	.250	.875	31/64	#3	V-notch	①
	E2TE-9510-BJA, BKA	.175	V-notch	.250	.875	31/64	#4	V-notch	①
	E2TE-9510-DDA, DEA	.175	V-notch	.250	.875	31/64	#3	V-notch	①

① Refer to underhood emission sticker

8576510C

Motorcraft 7200

Engine	Part Number	Fast Idle Cam Setting	Float Drop	Float Level (Dry)	Accelerator Pump Lever Lash	Choke Cap Setting	Fast Idle
8-302	All	.355–.365 ②	1.430–1.490	1.010–1.070	.010 ③	Index	①
8-351	All	.355–.365 ②	1.430–1.490	1.010–1.070	.010 ③	Index	①

① Refer to underhood emission sticker
② 2nd highest step
③ Plus one turn counterclockwise

85765511C

Motorcraft 4180

Engine	Part Number	Choke Pulldown Setting	Dechoke Setting	Fuel Level	Choke Cap Setting	Pump Lever Location
8-460	All	.200—.220	.295—.335	sight plug	2NR	#1

85765512C

Motorcraft 2150

Engine	Part Number	Choke Pulldown Setting	Fast Idle Cam Setting	Dechoke Setting	Float Level (Wet)	Float Level (Dry)	Accelerator Pump Lever Location	Choke Cap Setting	Fast Idle
8-302	E3TE-9510-AUA	.142	V-notch	.200	.810	7/16	#3	V-notch	①
	E3TE-9510-BHA	.152	V-notch	.200	.810	7/16	#3	V-notch	①
	E3TE-9510-AYA	.137	V-notch	.250	.810	7/16	#4	V-notch	①
	E3TE-9510-AVA, BEA	.149	V-notch	.250	.810	7/16	#3	V-notch	①
	E3TE-9510-BJA	.157	V-notch	.200	.810	7/16	#4	V-notch	①
	E3TE-9510-BLA, BPA	.157	V-notch	.200	.810	7/16	#3	V-notch	①
	E3TE-9510-BMA	.150	V-notch	.200	.810	7/16	#4	V-notch	①
	E3TE-9510-AZA, BAA, E2TE-9510-BPA, BRA	.130	V-notch	.200	.810	7/16	#3	V-notch	①
8-351	E2UE-9510-CA E2UE-9510-FA	.120	V-notch	.250	.875	31/64	#3	V-notch	①
	E3UE-9510-BA E2UE-9510-KA	.120	V-notch	.200	.875	31/64	#3	V-notch	①
	E3UE-9510-EA, DA E2UE-9510-ANA, AKA	.180	V-notch	.200	.875	31/64	#2	V-notch	①

① Refer to underhood emission sticker

85765514C

Motorcraft 7200

Engine	Part Number	Fast Idle Cam Setting	Float Drop	Float Level (Dry)	Accelerator Pump Lever Lash	Choke Cap Setting	Fast Idle
8-351	All	.355–.365 ②	1.43–1.49	1.010–1.070	.010 ③	Index	①

① Refer to underhood emission sticker
② 2nd highest step
③ Plus one turn counterclockwise

85765515C

1983 Carburetor Specifications Carter YFA

Check the carburetor part number tag to determine which specifications to use for your vehicle

Engine	Part Number	Choke Pulldown Setting	Fast Idle Cam Setting	Dechoke Setting	Choke Plate Come-Off Time	Float Setting (Dry)	Choke Cap Setting	Fast Idle
6-300	E3TE-9510-AMA, APA,YA,ASA,AGA, AHA,AJA,AFA,ANA	.270	.140	.280	90–140 sec.	.780	Red	①
	E3TE-9510-BNA, GA,BDA,ZA,ALA, FA,BKA	.320	.140	.330	90–140 sec.	.780	Red	①
	E3TE-9510-ZA, ABA,BRA,AKA	.300	.140	.280	90–140 sec.	.780	White	①
	E3TE-9510-AAA, ARA	.300	.140	.280	90–140 sec.	.780	Red	①
	D5TE-9510-AGB	.230	.110	.280	—	.375	1NR	①
	EOTE-9510-AMB, FB							①
	E2TE-9510-ZA	.290	.140	.280	—	.690	Index	①

① Refer to underhood emission sticker

85765513C

Motorcraft 4180

Engine	Part Number	Choke Pulldown Setting	Dechoke Setting	Fuel Level	Choke Cap Setting	Pump Lever Location
8-460	All	.210–.230	.300–.330	sight plug	3NR	#1

8576516C

1984 Carburetor Specifications
Carter YFA

Check the carburetor part number tag to determine which specifications to use for your vehicle

Engine	Part Number	Choke Pulldown Setting	Fast Idle Cam Setting	Dechoke Setting	Choke Plate Come-Off Time	Float Setting (Dry)	Choke Cap Setting	Fast Idle
6-300	E4TE-9510-VA, HA,FA,UA,AAA, GA,EA,ZA	.360	.140	.330	90–141 sec.	.780	Red	①
	D5TE-9510-AGB	.230	1NR	.280	—	.375	—	①
	D5TE-9510-AMB, FB	.290	Index	.280	—	.690	Index	①

① Refer to underhood emission sticker

8576517C

Motorcraft 2150

Engine	Part Number	Choke Pulldown Setting	Fast Idle Cam Setting	Dechoke Setting	Float Level (Wet)	Float Level (Dry)	Accelerator Pump Lever Location	Choke Cap Setting	Fast Idle
8-302	E4TE-9510-AMA	.140	V-notch	.250	.875	$^{31}/_{64}$	#3	V-notch	①
	E4TE-9510-AEA	.142	V-notch	.250	.875	$^{31}/_{64}$	#3	V-notch	①
	E4TE-9510-ALA	.125	V-notch	.250	.875	$^{31}/_{64}$	#3	V-notch	①
	E4TE-9510-APA	.145	V-notch	.250	.875	$^{31}/_{64}$	#3	V-notch	①
	E4TE-9510-AKA	.137	V-notch	.250	.875	$^{31}/_{64}$	#3	V-notch	①
	E4TE-9510-AHA	.150	V-notch	.250	.875	$^{31}/_{64}$	#4	V-notch	①
	E4TE-9510-AJA	.150	V-notch	.250	.875	$^{31}/_{64}$	#3	V-notch	①
	E4TE-9510-AFA	.144	V-notch	.250	.875	$^{31}/_{64}$	#3	V-notch	①
	E3TE-9510-BAA, AZA	.130	V-notch	.250	.875	$^{31}/_{64}$	#3	V-notch	①
8-351	E4TE-9510-ADA	.152	V-notch	.250	.810	$^{7}/_{16}$	#4	V-notch	①
	E4TE-9510-ACA	.155	V-notch	.250	.810	$^{7}/_{16}$	#4	V-notch	①
	E3UE-9510-EA, DA	.180	V-notch	.250	.875	$^{31}/_{64}$	#3	V-notch	①

① Refer to underhood emission sticker

8576518C

GASOLINE FUEL INJECTION

Relieving Fuel System Pressure

➡**A special tool is necessary for this procedure.**

1. Make sure the ignition switch is in the OFF position.
2. Disconnect the battery ground.
3. Remove the fuel filler cap.
4. Using EFI Pressure Gauge T80L-9974-A, or equivalent, at the fuel pressure relief valve (located in the fuel line in the upper right corner of the engine compartment) relieve the fuel system pressure. A valve cap must first be removed to gain access to the pressure relief valve.

Air Bypass Valve

REMOVAL & INSTALLATION

1. Disconnect the wiring at the valve.
2. Remove the 2 retaining screws and lift off the valve.
3. Discard the gasket and clean and inspect the mating surfaces.
4. Install the valve with a new gasket, tightening the screws to 102 inch lbs.
5. Connect the wiring.

Air Intake Throttle Body

REMOVAL & INSTALLATION

1. Disconnect the air intake hose.
2. Disconnect the throttle position sensor and air by-pass valve connectors.
3. Remove the four throttle body mounting nuts and carefully separate the air throttle body from the upper intake manifold.
4. Remove and discard the mounting gasket. Clean all mounting surfaces using care not to damage the gasket surfaces of the throttle body and manifold. Do not allow any material to drop into the intake manifold.
5. Install the throttle body in the reverse order of removal. The mounting nuts are tightened to 12-18 ft. lbs.

Fuel Charging Assembly

REMOVAL & INSTALLATION

♦ **See Figures 23 and 24**

1. Relieve the fuel system pressure.
2. Disconnect the battery ground cable and drain the cooling system.

❋❋ CAUTION

When draining the coolant, keep in mind that cats and dogs are attracted by the ethylene glycol antifreeze, and are quite likely to drink any that is left in an uncovered container or in puddles on the ground. This will prove fatal in sufficient quantity. Always drain the

coolant into a sealable container. Coolant should be reused unless it is contaminated or several years old.

3. Label and disconnect the wiring at the:
   a. Throttle position sensor
   b. Air bypass valve
   c. EGR sensor
4. Label and disconnect the following vacuum connectors:
   a. EGR valve
   b. Fuel pressure regulator
   c. Upper intake manifold vacuum tree
5. Disconnect the PCV hose at the upper intake manifold.
6. Remove the throttle linkage at the throttle ball and AOD transmission linkage at the throttle body.
7. Unbolt the cable bracket from the manifold and position the cables and bracket away from the engine.
8. Disconnect the 2 canister purge lines at the throttle body.
9. Disconnect the water heater lines from the throttle body.
10. Remove the EGR tube.
11. Remove the screw and washer which retains the upper intake manifold support bracket to the upper intake manifold.
12. Remove the 6 bolts which retain the upper intake manifold.
13. Remove the upper intake manifold assembly from the lower intake manifold.
14. Remove the distributor. (See Section 3).
15. Disconnect the wiring at the:
   a. Engine coolant temperature sensor
   b. Engine temperature sending unit
   c. Air charge temperature sensor
   d. Knock sensor
   e. Electrical vacuum regulator
   f. Thermactor solenoids
16. Disconnect the injector wiring harness at the main harness.
17. Remove the oxygen sensor ground wire at its intake manifold stud. Note the position of the stud and round wire for installation.
18. Disconnect the fuel supply and return lines from the fuel rails using tool T81P-19623-G or G1.
19. Remove the upper radiator hose.
20. Remove the coolant bypass hose.
21. Disconnect the heater outlet hose at the manifold.
22. Remove the air cleaner bracket.
23. Remove the coil.
24. Noting the location of each bolt, remove the intake manifold retaining bolts.
25. Remove the lower intake manifold from the head.
26. Clean and inspect all mating surfaces. All surfaces MUST be flat and free from debris or damage!
27. Clean and oil all fastener threads.
28. Place a 1/16 inch bead of RTV silicone sealant to the end seals' junctions.

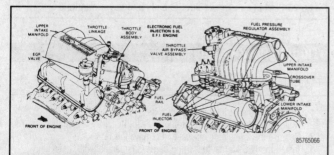

Fig. 23 Ford EFI component location

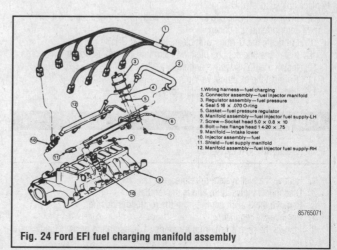

1. Wiring harness—fuel charging
2. Connector assembly—fuel injector manifold
3. Regulator assembly—fuel pressure
4. Seal 5/16 × .070 O-ring
5. Gasket—fuel pressure regulator
6. Manifold assembly—fuel injector fuel supply-LH
7. Screw—Socket head 5.0 × 0.8 × 10
8. Bolt—hex flange head 1.4-20 × .75
9. Manifold—intake lower
10. Injector assembly—fuel
11. Shield—fuel supply manifold
12. Manifold assembly—fuel injector fuel supply-RH

Fig. 24 Ford EFI fuel charging manifold assembly

29. Position the end seals on the block.
30. Install 2 locator pins at opposite corners of the block.
31. Position the lower manifold on the head using new gaskets. Install the bolts and remove the locating pins.
32. Tighten the bolts to 25 ft. lbs. in sequence. Wait ten minutes and retorque the bolts in sequence.
33. Install the coil.
34. Connect the cooling system hoses.
35. Connect the fuel supply and return lines.
36. Connect the wiring at the:
    a. Engine coolant temperature sensor
    b. Engine temperature sending unit
    c. Air charge temperature sensor
    d. Knock sensor
    e. Electrical vacuum regulator
    f. Thermactor solenoids
37. Install the distributor.
38. Position the upper manifold and new gasket on the lower manifold. Install the fasteners finger tight.
39. Install the upper intake manifold support on the manifold and tighten the retaining screw to 30 ft. lbs.
40. Torque the upper-to-lower manifold fasteners to 18 ft. lbs.
41. Install the EGR tube. Torque the fittings to 35 ft. lbs.
42. Install the canister purge lines at the throttle body.
43. Connect the water heater lines at the throttle body.
44. Connect the PCV hose.
45. Install the accelerator cable and throttle linkages.
46. Connect the vacuum hoses.
47. Connect the electrical wiring.
48. Connect the air intake hose, air bypass hose and crankcase vent hose.
49. Connect the battery ground.
50. Refill the cooling system.
51. Install the fuel pressure relief cap. Turn the ignition switch from **OFF** to **ON** at least half a dozen times, **WITHOUT STARTING THE ENGINE**, leaving it in the ON position for about 5 seconds each time. This will build up fuel pressure in the system.
52. Start the engine and allow it to run at idle until normal operating temperature is reached. Check for leaks.

Fuel Injectors

REMOVAL & INSTALLATION

1. Relieve the fuel system pressure.
2. Disconnect the battery ground.
3. Remove the upper intake manifold.
4. Disconnect the wiring at the injectors.
5. Pull upward on the injector body while gently rocking it from side-to-side.
6. Inspect the O-rings on the injector for any sign of leakage or damage. Replace any suspected O-rings.
7. Inspect the plastic cap at the top of each injector and replace it if any sign of deterioration is noticed.
8. Lubricate the O-rings with clean engine oil ONLY!
9. Install the injectors by pushing them in with a gentle rocking motion.
10. Install the fuel supply manifold.
11. Connect the electrical wiring.
12. Install the upper intake manifold.

Fuel Pressure Regulator

REMOVAL & INSTALLATION

1. Relieve the fuel system pressure.
2. Disconnect the vacuum line at the regulator.
3. Remove the 3 allen screws from the regulator housing.
4. Remove the regulator.
5. Inspect the regulator O-ring for signs of deterioration or damage. Discard the gasket.

6. Lubricate the O-ring with clean engine oil ONLY!
7. Make sure that the mounting surfaces are clean.
8. Using a new gasket, install the regulator. Tighten the retaining screws to 40 in. lb.
9. Connect the vacuum line.

Fuel Supply Manifold

REMOVAL & INSTALLATION

♦ See Figure 25

1. Relieve the fuel system pressure.
2. Remove the upper manifold.
3. Disconnect the chassis fuel inlet and outlet lines at the fuel supply manifold using tool T81P-19623-G or G1.
4. Disconnect the fuel supply and return lines at the fuel supply manifold.
5. Remove the 4 fuel supply manifold retaining bolts.
6. Carefully disengage the manifold from the injectors and lift it off.
7. Inspect all components for signs of damage. Make sure that the injector caps are clean.
8. Place the fuel supply manifold over the injectors and seat the injectors carefully in the manifold.
9. Install the 4 bolts and torque them to 20 ft. lbs.
10. Connect the fuel lines.
11. Install the upper manifold.

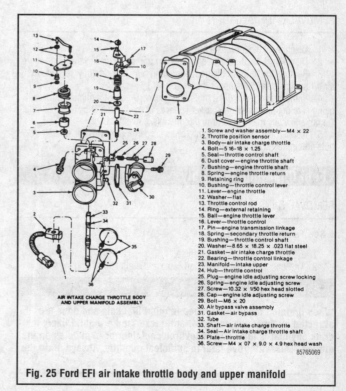

1. Screw and washer assembly—M4 × 22
2. Throttle position sensor
3. Body—air intake charge throttle
4. Bolt—5 16-18 × 1.25
5. Seal—throttle control shaft
6. Dust cover—engine throttle shaft
7. Bushing—engine throttle shaft
8. Spring—engine throttle return
9. Retaining ring
10. Bushing—throttle control lever
11. Lever—engine throttle
12. Washer—flat
13. Throttle control rod
14. Ring—external retaining
15. Ball—engine throttle lever
16. Lever—throttle control
17. Pin—engine transmission linkage
18. Spring—secondary throttle return
19. Bushing—throttle control shaft
20. Washer—8.65 × 18.25 × .023 flat steel
21. Gasket—air intake charge throttle
22. Bearing—throttle control linkage
23. Manifold—intake upper
24. Hub—throttle control
25. Plug—engine idle adjusting screw locking
26. Spring—engine idle adjusting screw
27. Screw—10.32 × 1/50 hex head slotted
28. Cap—engine idle adjusting screw
29. Bolt—M6 × 20
30. Air bypass valve assembly
31. Gasket—air bypass
32. Tube
33. Shaft—air intake charge throttle
34. Seal—Air intake charge throttle shaft
35. Plate—throttle
36. Screw—M4 × 07 × 9.0 × 4.9 hex head wash

85765069

AIR INTAKE CHARGE THROTTLE BODY
AND UPPER MANIFOLD ASSEMBLY

Fig. 25 Ford EFI air intake throttle body and upper manifold

Throttle Position Sensor

REMOVAL & INSTALLATION

1. Disconnect the wiring harness from the TPS.
2. Matchmark the sensor and throttle body for installation reference.
3. Remove the 2 retaining screws and remove the TPS.
4. Install the TPS so that the wiring harness is parallel with the venturi bores, then, rotate the TPS clockwise to align the scribe marks.

Slide the rotary tangs into position over the throttle shaft blade, then rotate the TPS CLOCKWISE ONLY to the installed position. FAILURE TO INSTALL THE TPS IN THIS MANNER WILL RESULT IN EXCESSIVE IDLE SPEEDS!

DIESEL FUEL SYSTEM

Fuel Pump

REMOVAL & INSTALLATION

1. Loosen the threaded connections with the proper size wrench (a flare nut wrench is preferred) and retighten snugly. Do not remove the lines at this time.
2. Loosen the mounting bolts, one to two turns. Apply force with your hand to loosen the fuel pump if the gasket is stuck. Rotate the engine by nudging the starter, until the fuel pump cam lobe is at the low position. At this position, spring tension against the fuel pump bolts will be greatly reduced.
3. Disconnect the fuel supply pump inlet, outlet and fuel return line.

⁂ **CAUTION**

Use care to prevent combustion of the spilled fuel.

4. Remove the fuel pump attaching bolts and remove the pump and gasket. Discard the old gasket.
5. Remove the remaining fuel pump gasket material from the engine and from the fuel pump if you are reinstalling the old pump. Make sure both mounting surfaces are clean.
6. Install the attaching bolts into the fuel supply pump and install a new gasket on the bolts. Position the fuel pump onto the mounting pad. Turn the attaching bolts alternately and evenly and tighten the bolts to the specifications according to the size bolts used on the pump. See the accompanying standard torque chart for reference.

➡ **The cam must be at its low position before attempting to install the fuel supply pump. If it is difficult to start the mounting bolts, remove the pump and reinstall with a lever on the bottom side of the cam.**

7. Install the fuel outlet line. Start the fitting by hand to avoid crossthreading.
8. Install the inlet line and the fuel return line.
9. Start the engine and observe all connections for fuel leaks for two minutes.
10. Stop the engine and check all fuel supply pump fuel line connections. Check for oil leaks at the pump mounting pad.

Glow Plug System

GENERAL INFORMATION

▸ **See Figure 26**

The diesel engine utilizes an electric glow plug system to aid in the start of the engine. The function of this system is to pre-heat the combustion chamber to aid ignition of the fuel.

The system consists of eight glow plugs (one for each cylinder), control switch, power relay, after glow relay, wait lamp latching relay, wait lamp and the eight fusible links located between the harness and the glow plug terminal.

On initial start with cold engine, the glow plug system operates as follows: The glow plug control switch energizes the power relay (which is a magnetic switch) and the power relay contacts close. Battery current energizes the glow plugs. Current to the glow plugs and a wait lamp will be shut off when the glow plugs are hot enough. This takes from 2 to 10 second after the key is first turned on. When the wait lamp goes off, the engine is ready to start. After the engine is started the glow plugs begin an on-off cycle for about 40 to 90 seconds. This cycle helps to clear start-up smoke. The control switch is threaded into the left cylinder head coolant jacket. the control unit senses engine coolant temperature. Since the control unit senses temperature, the glow plug system will not be acti-

5. Tighten the retaining screws to 16 in. lb.

➡ **When correctly installed, the TPS wiring harness should be pointing directly at the air bypass valve.**

6. Connect the wiring.

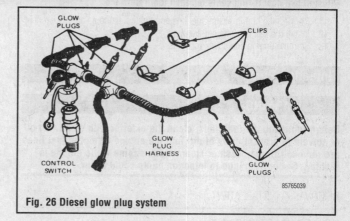

Fig. 26 Diesel glow plug system

vated unless needed. On a restart (warm engine) the glow plug system will not be activated unless the coolant temperature drops below 165°F (91°C).

Since the fast start system utilizes 6 volt glow plugs in a 12 volt system to achieve rapid heating of the glow plug, a cycling device is required in the circuit.

⁂ **CAUTION**

Never bypass the power relay of the glow plug system. Constant battery current (12 volts) to glow plugs will cause them to overheat and fail.

Injection Nozzles

REMOVAL & INSTALLATION

➡ **Before removing the nozzle assemblies, clean the exterior of each nozzle assembly and the surrounding area with clean fuel oil or solvent to prevent entry of dirt into the engine when nozzle assemblies are removed. Also, clean the fuel inlet and fuel leak-off piping connections. Blow dry with compressed air.**

1. Remove the fuel line retaining clamp(s) from the nozzle lines that are to be removed.
2. Disconnect the nozzle fuel inlet (high pressure) and fuel leak-off tees from each nozzle assembly and position out of the way. Cover the open ends of the fuel inlet and outlet or nozzles with protective caps, to prevent dirt from entering.
3. Remove the injection nozzles by turning them counterclockwise. Pull the nozzle assembly, with the copper washer attached, from the engine. Cover the nozzle fuel opening and spray tip, with plastic caps, to prevent the entry of dirt.

➡ **Remove the copper injector nozzle gasket from the nozzle bore with special tool, T71P-19703-C, or equivalent, whenever the gasket does not come out with the nozzle.**

4. Place the nozzle assemblies in a fabricated holder as they are removed from the heads. The holder should be marked with numbers corresponding to the cylinder numbering of the engine. This will allow for reinstallation of the nozzle in the same ports from which they were removed.
5. Thoroughly clean the nozzle bore in cylinder head before reinserting the nozzle assembly with nozzle seat cleaner, special tool T83T-9527-A or equivalent. Make certain that no small particles of metal or carbon remain on the seating surface. Blow out the particles with compressed air.

6. Remove the protective cap and install a new copper gasket on the nozzle assembly, with a small dab of grease.

➡**Anti-seize compound or equivalent should be used on nozzle threads to aid in installation and future removal.**

7. Install the nozzle assembly into the cylinder head nozzle bore.
8. Tighten the nozzle assembly to 33 ft. lbs.
9. Remove the protective caps from nozzle assemblies and fuel lines.
10. Install the leak-off tees to the nozzle assemblies.

➡**Install two new O-ring seals for each fuel return tee.**

11. Connect the high pressure fuel line and tighten, using a flare nut wrench.
12. Install the fuel line retainer clamps.
13. Start the engine and check for leaks.

Injection Pump

✵✵ WARNING

Before removing the fuel lines, clean the exterior with clean fuel oil or solvent to prevent entry of dirt into the engine when the fuel lines are removed. Do not wash or steam clean engine while engine is running. Serious damage to injection pump could occur.

REMOVAL & INSTALLATION

▶ **See Figures 27, 28 and 29**

1. Disconnect battery ground cables from both batteries.
2. Remove the engine oil filler neck.
3. Remove the bolts attaching injection pump to drive gear.
4. Disconnect the electrical connectors to injection pump.
5. Disconnect the accelerator cable and speed control cable from throttle lever, if so equipped.
6. Remove the air cleaner and install clean rags to prevent dirt from entering the intake manifold.
7. Remove the accelerator cable bracket, with cables attached, from intake manifold and position out of the way.

➡**All fuel lines and fittings must be capped using Fuel System Protective Cap Set T83T-9395-A or equivalent, to prevent fuel contamination.**

8. Remove the fuel filter-to-injection pump fuel line and cap fittings.
9. Remove and cap the injection pump inlet elbow and the injection pump fitting adapter.
10. Remove the fuel return line on injection pump, rotate out of the way, And cap all fittings.

➡**It is not necessary to remove injection lines from injection pump. If lines are to be removed, loosen injection line fittings at injection pump before removing it from engine.**

11. Remove the fuel injection lines from the nozzles and cap lines and nozzles.

12. Remove the three nuts attaching the Injection pump to injection pump adapter using Tool T83T-9000-B.
13. If the injection pump is to be replaced, loosen the injection line retaining clips and the injection nozzle fuel lines with Tool T83T-9396-A and cap all fittings at this time with protective cap set T83T-9395-A or equivalent. Do not install the injection nozzle fuel lines until the new pump is installed in the engine.
14. Lift the Injection pump, with the nozzle lines attached, up and out of the engine compartment.

✵✵ WARNING

Do not carry injection pump by Injection nozzle fuel lines as this could cause lines to bend or crimp.

15. Install a new O-ring on the drive gear end of the injection pump.
16. Move the injection pump down and into position.
17. Position the alignment dowel on injection pump into the alignment hole on Drive gear.
18. Install the bolts attaching the injection pump to drive gear and tighten.
19. Install the nuts attaching injection pump to adapter. Align scribe lines on the injection pump flange and the injection pump adapter and tighten to 14 ft. lbs.
20. If the injection nozzle fuel lines were removed from the injection pump install at this time, refer to Fuel Lines-Installation, in this section.
21. Remove the caps from nozzles and the fuel lines and install the fuel line nuts on the nozzles and tighten to 22 ft. lbs.
22. Connect the fuel return line to injection pump and tighten the nuts.
23. Install the injection pump fitting adapter with a new O-ring.
24. Clean the old sealant from the injection pump elbow threads, using clean solvent, and dry thoroughly. Apply a light coating of pipe sealant to the elbow threads.
25. Install the elbow in the injection pump adapter and tighten to a minimum of 6 ft. lbs. Then tighten further, if necessary, to align the elbow with the injection pump fuel inlet line, but do not exceed 360 degrees of rotation or 10 ft. lbs.
26. Remove the caps and connect the fuel filter-to-Injection pump fuel line.
27. Install the accelerator cable bracket to the intake manifold.
28. Remove the rags from the intake manifold and install the air cleaner.
29. Connect the accelerator and speed control cable, if so equipped, to throttle lever.
30. Install the electrical connectors on injection pump.
31. Clean the injection pump adapter and oil filler neck sealing surfaces.
32. Apply a ⅛ inch bead of RTV sealant on the adapter housing.
33. Install the oil filler neck and tighten the bolts.
34. Connect the battery ground cables to both batteries.
35. Run the engine and check for leaks.
36. If necessary, purge high pressure fuel lines of air by loosening connector one half to one turn and cranking engine until solid fuel, free from bubbles flows from connection.

✵✵ CAUTION

Keep eyes and hands away from nozzle spray. Fuel spraying from the nozzle under high pressure can penetrate the skin.

37. Check and adjust injection pump timing as described in this section.

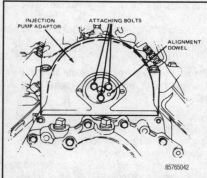

Fig. 27 Diesel injection pump drive gear attaching bolts

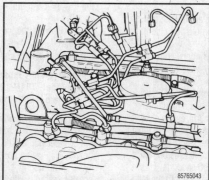

Fig. 28 Diesel injection pump removal. Be careful not to crimp or bend the fuel lines

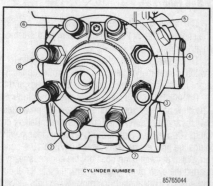

Fig. 29 Injection pump cylinder numbering sequence

Fuel Lines

REMOVAL & INSTALLATION

♦ **See Figure 30**

➡ Before removing any fuel lines, clean the exterior with clean fuel oil, or solvent to prevent entry of dirt into fuel system when the fuel lines are removed. Blow dry with compressed air.

1. Disconnect the battery ground cables from both batteries.
2. Remove the air cleaner and cap intake manifold opening with clean rags.
3. Disconnect the accelerator cable and speed control cable, if so equipped, from the injection pump.
4. Remove the accelerator cable bracket from the intake manifold and position out of the way with cable(s) attached.

❊❊ WARNING

To prevent fuel system contamination, cap all fuel lines and fittings.

5. Disconnect the fuel line from the fuel filter to injection pump and cap all fittings.
6. Disconnect and cap the nozzle fuel lines at nozzles.
7. Remove the fuel line clamps from the fuel lines to be removed.
8. Remove and cap the injection pump inlet elbow.
9. Remove and cap the inlet fitting adapter.
10. Remove the injection nozzle lines, one at a time, from injection pump using Tool T83T-9396-A.

➡ Fuel lines must be removed following this sequence: 5-6-4-8-3-1-7-2. Install caps on each end of each fuel line and pump fittings as it is removed and identify each fuel line accordingly.

11. Install fuel lines on injection pump, one at a time, and Tighten to 22 ft.lbs.

➡ Fuel lines must be installed in the sequence: 2-7-1-3-8-4-6-5.

12. Clean the old sealant from the injection pump elbow, using clean solvent, and dry thoroughly.
13. Apply a light coating of pipe sealant on the elbow threads.

Injection Timing

STATIC TIMING

♦ **See Figure 31**

1. Break the torque of the injection pump mounting nuts (keeping the nuts snug).
2. Rotate the injection pump using Tool T83-9000-C or equivalent to bring the mark on the pump into alignment with the mark on pump mounting adapter.
3. Visually recheck the alignment of the timing marks and tighten injection pump mounting nuts.

DYNAMIC TIMING

♦ **See Figures 32, 33, 34 and 35**

1. Bring the engine up to normal operating temperature.
2. Stop the engine and install a dynamic timing meter, Rotunda 78-0100 or equivalent, by placing the magnetic probe pick-up into the probe hole.
3. Remove the no. 1 glow plug wire and remove the glow plug, install the luminosity probe and tighten to 12 ft.lbs. Install the photocell over the probe.
4. Connect the dynamic timing meter to the battery and adjust the offset of the meter.

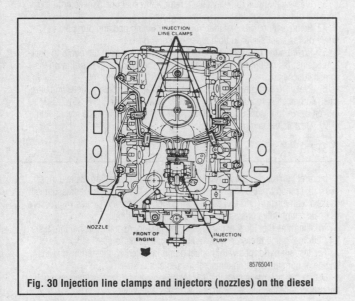

Fig. 30 Injection line clamps and injectors (nozzles) on the diesel

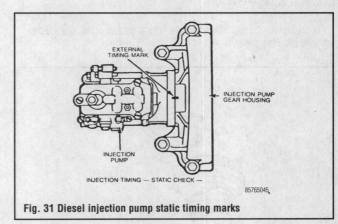

Fig. 31 Diesel injection pump static timing marks

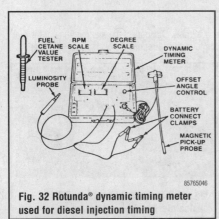

Fig. 32 Rotunda® dynamic timing meter used for diesel injection timing

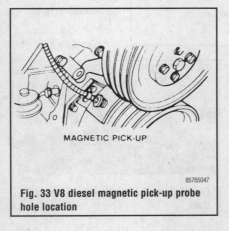

Fig. 33 V8 diesel magnetic pick-up probe hole location

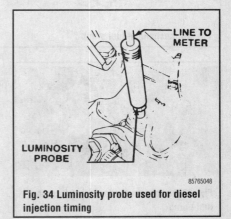

Fig. 34 Luminosity probe used for diesel injection timing

5. Set the transmission in neutral and raise the rear wheels off the ground. Using Rotunda 14-0302, throttle control, set the engine speed to 1,400 rpm with no accessory load. Observe the injection timing on the dynamic timing meter.

➡ **Obtain the fuel sample from the vehicle and check the cetane value using the tester supplied with the Ford special tools 78-0100 or equivalent. Refer to the dynamic timing chart to find the correct timing in degrees.**

6. If the dynamic timing is not within plus or minus 2 degrees of specification, then the injection pump timing will require adjustment.

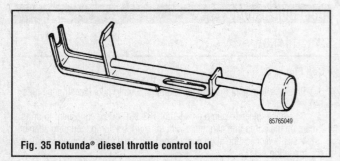

Fig. 35 Rotunda® diesel throttle control tool

7. Turn the engine off. Note the timing mark alignment. Loosen the injection pump-to-adapter nuts.

8. Rotate the injection pump clockwise to retard and counterclockwise to advance timing. Two degrees of dynamic timing is approximately 0.030 inch (0.76mm) of timing mark movement.

9. Start the engine and recheck the timing. If the timing is not within plus or minus 1 degree of specification, repeat steps 7 through 9.

10. Turn off the engine. Remove the dynamic timing equipment. Lightly coat the glow plug thread with anti-seize compound, install the glow plugs and tighten to 12 ft. lbs. Connect the glow plug wires.

Dynamic Timing Specifications

Fuel Cetane Value	Altitude	
	0-3000 Ft ①	Above 3000 Ft ①
38–42	6° ATDC	7° ATDC
43–46	5° ATDC	6° ATDC
47–50	4° ATDC	5° ATDC

① Installation of resetting tolerance for dynamic timing is ± 1°. Service limit is ± 2°.

8576502C

GENERAL FUEL SYSTEM COMPONENTS

Mechanical Fuel Pump

▶ **See Figures 36, 37, 38 and 39**

A mechanical pump is used on carbureted engines. The mechanical fuel pump is camshaft eccentric-actuated and located on the left side of the front cover of the engine.

REMOVAL & INSTALLATION

1. Disconnect the fuel inlet and outlet lines at the fuel pump. Discard the fuel inlet retaining clamp.

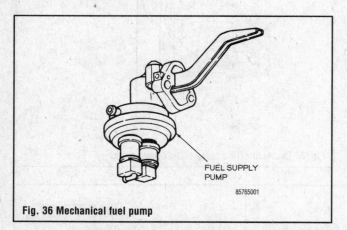

Fig. 36 Mechanical fuel pump

2. Remove the pump retaining bolts then remove the pump assembly and gasket from the engine. Discard the gasket.

3. If a new pump is to be installed, remove the fuel line connector fitting from the old pump and install it in the new pump.

4. Remove all gasket material from the mounting pad and pump flange. Apply oil resistant sealer to both sides of a new gasket.

5. Position the new gasket on the pump flange and hold the pump in position against the mounting pad. make sure that the rocker arm is riding on the camshaft eccentric.

6. Press the pump tight against the pad, install the retaining bolts and alternately torque them to 20-24 ft. lbs. on the 8-302; 14-20 on the 8-351; 19-27 ft. lbs. on the 8-460. Connect the fuel lines. Use a new clamp on the fuel inlet lines.

7. Operate the engine and check for leaks.

TESTING

Incorrect fuel pump pressure and low volume (flow rate) are the two most likely fuel pump troubles that will affect engine performance. Low pressure will cause a lean mixture and fuel starvation at high speeds and excessive pressure will cause high fuel consumption and carburetor flooding.

To determine that the fuel pump is in satisfactory operating condition, tests for both fuel pump pressure and volume should be performed.

The test are performed with the fuel pump installed on the engine and the engine at normal operating temperature and at idle speed.

Before the test, make sure that the replaceable fuel filter has been changed at the proper mileage interval. If in doubt, install a new filter.

Pressure Test

1. Remove the air cleaner assembly. Disconnect the fuel inlet line of the fuel filter at the carburetor. Use care to prevent fire, due to fuel spillage. Place an

Fig. 37 Disconnect the fuel lines from the fuel pump

Fig. 38 Remove the fuel pump mounting bolts

Fig. 39 Pull the fuel pump out of the engine block

absorbent cloth under the connection before removing the line to catch any fuel that might flow out of the line.

2. Connect a pressure gauge, a restrictor and a flexible hose between the fuel filter and the carburetor.

3. Position the flexible hose and the restrictor so that the fuel can be discharged into a suitable, graduated container.

4. Before taking a pressure reading, operate the engine at the specified idle rpm and vent the system into the container by opening the hose restrictor momentarily.

5. Close the hose restrictor, allow the pressure to stabilize and note the reading. The pressure should be 5 psi.

If the pump pressure is not within 4-6 psi and the fuel lines and filter are in satisfactory condition, the pump is defective and should be replaced.

If the pump pressure is within the proper range, perform the test for fuel volume.

Volume Test

1. Operate the engine at the specified idle rpm.

2. Open the hose restrictor and catch the fuel in the container while observing the time it takes to pump 1 pint. 1 pint should be pumped in 20 seconds. If the pump does not pump to specifications, check for proper fuel tank venting or a restriction in the fuel line leading from the fuel tank to the carburetor before replacing the fuel pump.

Electric Fuel Pump

Two electric pumps are used on fuel injected models; a low pressure boost pump mounted in the fuel tank and a high pressure pump mounted on the vehicle frame. Some models equipped with the 8-460 (7.5L) carbureted engines use a single low pressure pump mounted in the fuel tank.

On injected models the low pressure pump is used to provide pressurized fuel to the inlet of the high pressure pump and helps prevent noise and heating problems. The externally mounted high pressure pump is capable of supplying 15.9 gallons of fuel an hour. System pressure is controlled by a pressure regulator mounted on the engine.

With internal fuel tank mounted pumps tank removal is required when servicing the pump. Frame mounted models can be accessed from under the vehicle. Prior to servicing release system pressure (see Fuel Supply Manifold details). Disconnect the negative battery cable prior to pump removal.

REMOVAL & INSTALLATION

In-Tank Pump

▶ See Figures 40, 41 and 42

MID-SHIP FUEL TANK(S)

▶ See Figures 43 and 44

1. Disconnect the negative battery cable.

2. Depressurize the system and drain as much fuel as possible from the tank.

3. Raise the truck and safely support it on jackstands.

4. On trucks with dual tanks, disconnect the ground wire at each tank after draining the tanks.

5. Disconnect the fuel supply, return and vent lines at the tank(s).

6. Disconnect the wiring harness to the fuel pump.

7. Support the fuel tank(s), loosen and remove the mounting straps. Remove the fuel tank(s).

8. Disconnect the lines and harness at the pump flange.

9. Clean the outside of the mounting flange and retaining ring. Turn the fuel pump lock ring counterclockwise and remove.

10. Remove the fuel pump.

11. Clean the mounting surfaces. Put a light coat of grease on the mounting surfaces and on the new sealing ring. Install the new fuel pump.

12. Install components is in the reverse order of removal. Torque the strap bolts to 25-30 ft. lbs. Fill the tank with a least 13 gallons of fuel. Turn the ignition key ON for three seconds. Repeat 6 or 7 times until the fuel system is pressurized. Check for any fitting leaks. Start the engine and check for leaks.

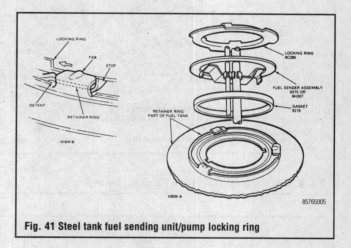

Fig. 41 Steel tank fuel sending unit/pump locking ring

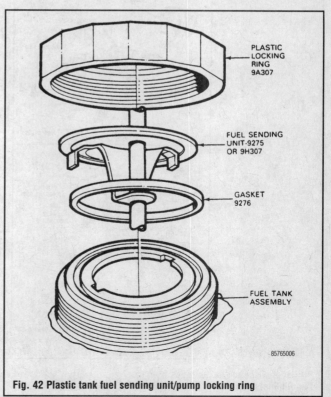

Fig. 42 Plastic tank fuel sending unit/pump locking ring

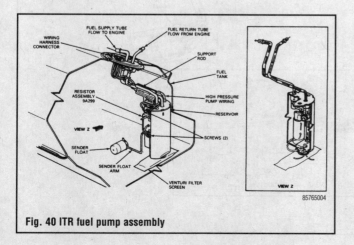

Fig. 40 ITR fuel pump assembly

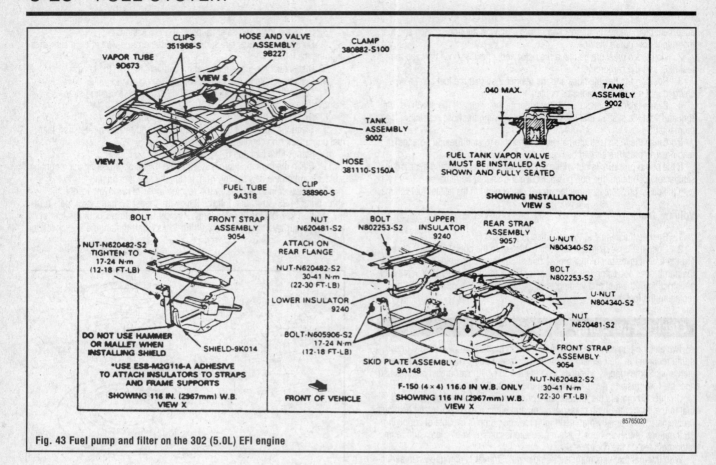

Fig. 43 Fuel pump and filter on the 302 (5.0L) EFI engine

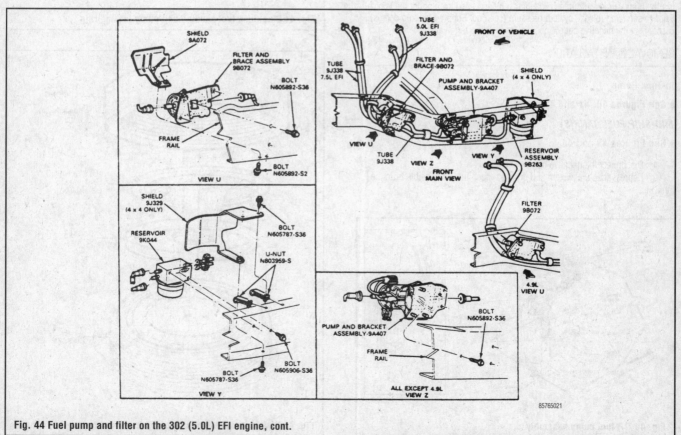

Fig. 44 Fuel pump and filter on the 302 (5.0L) EFI engine, cont.

AFT-OF-AXLE TANK

1. Disconnect the negative battery cable.
2. Depressurize the system and drain as much fuel as possible from the tank.
3. Raise the rear of the truck and safely support it on jackstands.
4. Disconnect the fuel supply, return and vent lines at the tank(s).
5. On trucks with dual tanks, disconnect the ground wire at each tank after draining the tanks.
6. Disconnect the wiring harness to the fuel pump.
7. If you have a metal tank: Support the fuel tank(s), loosen and remove the mounting straps. Remove the fuel tank(s).If you have a plastic tank: Support the tank and remove the bolts attaching the combination skid plate and tank support. Lower the tank and finish removing any hard-to-get-at hoses.
8. Disconnect the lines and harness at the pump flange.
9. Clean the outside of the mounting flange and retaining ring. Turn the fuel pump lock ring counterclockwise and remove.
10. Remove the fuel pump.
11. Clean the mounting surfaces. Put a light coat of grease on the mounting surfaces and on the new sealing ring. Install the new fuel pump.
12. Installation is in the reverse order of removal. Torque the metal tank's strap bolts to 27-37 ft. lbs., using thread locking compound. Torque the plastic tank's attaching bolts to 25-35 ft. lbs., without using thread locking compound. Fill the tank with a least 10 gallons of fuel. Turn the ignition key ON for three seconds. Repeat 6 or 7 times until the fuel system is pressurized. check for any fitting leaks. Start the engine and check for leaks.

External Pump

♦ See Figure 45

1. Disconnect the negative battery cable.
2. Depressurize the fuel system.
3. Raise and support the rear of the vehicle on jackstands.
4. Disconnect the inlet and outlet fuel lines.
5. Remove the pump from the mounting bracket.
6. Install in reverse order, make sure the pump is indexed correctly in the mounting bracket Insulator.

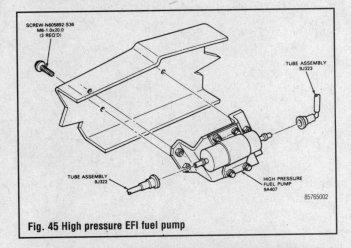

Fig. 45 High pressure EFI fuel pump

Quick-Connect Line Fittings

REMOVAL & INSTALLATION

♦ See Figure 46

➥**Quick-Connect (push) type fittings must be disconnected using proper procedures or the fitting may be damaged. Two types of retainers are used on the push connect fittings. Line sizes of ⅜ inch and ⁵⁄₁₆ inch use a hairpin clip retainer. ¼ inch line connectors use a Duck bill clip retainer.**

Hairpin Clip

1. Clean all dirt and/or grease from the fittings. Spread the two clip legs about an ⅛ inch each to disengage from the fitting and pull the clip outward from the fitting. Use finger pressure only, do not use any tools.
2. Grasp the fittings and hose assembly and pull away from the steel line. Twist the fitting and hose assembly slightly while pulling, if necessary, when a sticking condition exists.
3. Inspect the hairpin clip for damage, replace the clip if necessary. Reinstall the clip in position on the fitting.
4. Inspect the fitting and inside of the connector to insure freedom from dirt or obstruction. Install fitting into the connector and push together. A click will be heard when the hairpin snaps into proper connection. Pull on the line to insure full engagement.

Duck Bill Clip

1. A special tool is available for Ford for removing the retaining clip (Ford Tool No. T82L-9500-AH). If the tool is not available see Step 2. Align the slot on the push connector disconnect tool with either tab on the retaining clip. Pull the line from the connector.
2. If the special clip tool is not available, use a pair of narrow 6 inch locking pliers with a jaw width of 0.2 inch or less. Align the jaws of the pliers with the openings of the fitting case and compress the part of the retaining clip that engages the case. Compressing the retaining clip will release the fitting which may be pulled from the connector. Both sides of the clip must be compressed at the same time to disengage.
3. Inspect the retaining clip, fitting end and connector. Replace the clip if any damage is apparent.
4. Push the line into the steel connector until a click is heard, indicating the clip is in place. Pull on the line to check engagement.

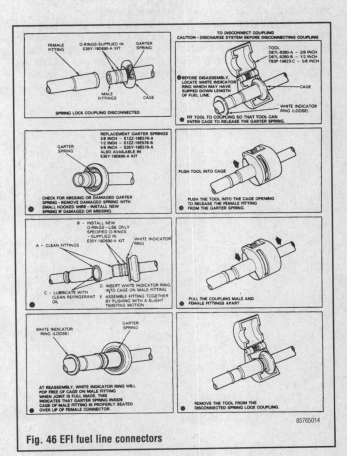

Fig. 46 EFI fuel line connectors

FUEL TANK

Tank Assembly

REMOVAL & INSTALLATION

Mid-Ships Fuel Tank

1. Drain the fuel from the tank into a suitable container by either removing the drain plug, if so equipped, or siphoning through the filler cap opening.
2. Disconnect the fuel gauge sending unit wire and fuel outlet line.
3. Disconnect the air relief tube from the filler neck and fuel tank.
4. Loosen the filler neck hose clamp at the fuel tank and pull the filler neck away from the tank.
5. Remove the retaining strap mounting nuts and bolts and lower the tank to the floor.
6. If a new tank is being installed, change over the fuel gauge sending unit to the new tank.
7. Install the fuel tank in the reverse order of removal. Torque the strap nuts to 30 ft. lbs.

Behind-The-Axle Fuel Tank

1. Raise the rear of the truck.
2. Disconnect the negative battery cable.
3. Disconnect the fuel gauge sending unit wire at the fuel tank.
4. Remove the fuel drain plug or siphon the fuel from the tank into a suitable container.
5. Loosen the fuel line hose clamps, slide the clamps forward and disconnect the fuel one at the fuel gauge sending unit.
6. Loosen the clamps on the fuel filler pipe and vent hose as necessary and disconnect the filler pipe hose and vent hose from the tank.
7. If the tank is the metal type, support the tank and remove the bolts attaching the tank support or skid plate to the frame. Carefully lower the tank or tank/skid plate assembly and disconnect the vent tube from the vapor emission control valve in the top of the tank. Finish removing the filler pipe and filler pipe vent hose if not possible previously. Remove the tank from under the vehicle.

8. If the tank is the plastic type, support the tank and remove the bolts attaching the combination skid plate and tank support to the frame. Carefully lower the tank and disconnect the vent tube from the vapor emission control valve in the top of the tank. Finish removing the filler pipe and filler pipe vent hose if it was not possible previously. Remove the skid plate and tank from under the vehicle. Remove the skid plate from the tank.
9. If the sending unit is to be removed, turn the unit retaining ring counterclockwise and remove the sending unit, retaining ring and gasket. Discard the gasket.
10. Install the tank in the reverse order of removal. With metal tanks, use thread adhesive such as Loctite® on the bolt threads. Torque these bolts to 27-37 ft. lbs. With plastic tanks, DO NOT use thread adhesive. Torque the bolts to 25-35 ft. lbs.

Bronco Fuel Tank

1. Raise and support the rear end on jackstands.
2. Disconnect the negative battery cable.
3. Disconnect the fuel gauge sending unit wire at the fuel tank.
4. Remove the fuel drain plug or siphon the fuel from the tank into a suitable container.
5. Loosen the fuel line hose clamps, slide the clamps forward and disconnect the fuel one at the fuel gauge sending unit.
6. Loosen the clamps on the fuel filler pipe and vent hose as necessary and disconnect the filler pipe hose and vent hose from the tank.
7. Support the tank and remove the bolts lower attaching bolts or skid plate bolts supporting the tank to the frame. Carefully lower the tank or tank/skid plate assembly and disconnect the vent tube from the vapor emission control valve in the top of the tank. Finish removing the filler pipe and filler pipe vent hose if not possible previously. Remove the tank from under the vehicle.
8. If the sending unit is being removed, turn the unit's retaining ring counterclockwise and remove the sending unit, retaining ring and gasket. Discard the gasket.
9. Install the tank in the reverse order of removal. Use thread locking compound on the bolt threads and torque the bolts to 27-37 ft. lbs.

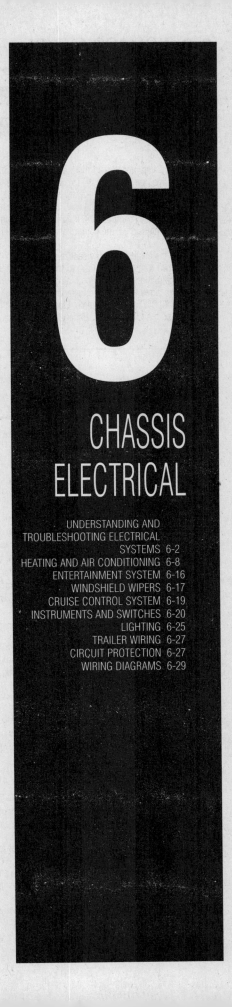

6

CHASSIS ELECTRICAL

UNDERSTANDING AND TROUBLESHOOTING ELECTRICAL SYSTEMS

Basic Electrical Theory

♦ See Figure 1

For any 12 volt, negative ground, electrical system to operate, the electricity must travel in a complete circuit. This simply means that current (power) from the positive (+) terminal of the battery must eventually return to the negative (-) terminal of the battery. Along the way, this current will travel through wires, fuses, switches and components. If, for any reason, the flow of current through the circuit is interrupted, the component fed by that circuit will cease to function properly.

Perhaps the easiest way to visualize a circuit is to think of connecting a light bulb (with two wires attached to it) to the battery—one wire attached to the negative (-) terminal of the battery and the other wire to the positive (+) terminal. With the two wires touching the battery terminals, the circuit would be complete and the light bulb would illuminate. Electricity would follow a path from the battery to the bulb and back to the battery. It's easy to see that with longer wires on

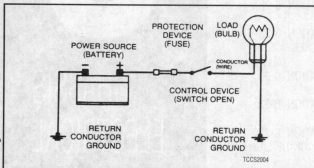

TCCS2004

Fig. 1 This example illustrates a simple circuit. When the switch is closed, power from the positive (+) battery terminal flows through the fuse and the switch, and then to the light bulb. The light illuminates and the circuit is completed through the ground wire back to the negative (-) battery terminal. In reality, the two ground points shown in the illustration are attached to the metal frame of the vehicle, which completes the circuit back to the battery

our light bulb, it could be mounted anywhere. Further, one wire could be fitted with a switch so that the light could be turned on and off.

The normal automotive circuit differs from this simple example in two ways. First, instead of having a return wire from the bulb to the battery, the current travels through the frame of the vehicle. Since the negative (-) battery cable is attached to the frame (made of electrically conductive metal), the frame of the vehicle can serve as a ground wire to complete the circuit. Secondly, most automotive circuits contain multiple components which receive power from a single circuit. This lessens the amount of wire needed to power components on the vehicle.

HOW DOES ELECTRICITY WORK: THE WATER ANALOGY

Electricity is the flow of electrons—the subatomic particles that constitute the outer shell of an atom. Electrons spin in an orbit around the center core of an atom. The center core is comprised of protons (positive charge) and neutrons (neutral charge). Electrons have a negative charge and balance out the positive charge of the protons. When an outside force causes the number of electrons to unbalance the charge of the protons, the electrons will split off the atom and look for another atom to balance out. If this imbalance is kept up, electrons will continue to move and an electrical flow will exist.

Many people have been taught electrical theory using an analogy with water. In a comparison with water flowing through a pipe, the electrons would be the water and the wire is the pipe.

The flow of electricity can be measured much like the flow of water through a pipe. The unit of measurement used is amperes, frequently abbreviated as amps (a). You can compare amperage to the volume of water flowing through a pipe. When connected to a circuit, an ammeter will measure the actual amount of current flowing through the circuit. When relatively few electrons flow through a circuit, the amperage is low. When many electrons flow, the amperage is high.

Water pressure is measured in units such as pounds per square inch (psi); The electrical pressure is measured in units called volts (v). When a voltmeter is connected to a circuit, it is measuring the electrical pressure.

The actual flow of electricity depends not only on voltage and amperage, but also on the resistance of the circuit. The higher the resistance, the higher the force necessary to push the current through the circuit. The standard unit for measuring resistance is an ohm. Resistance in a circuit varies depending on the amount and type of components used in the circuit. The main factors which determine resistance are:

• Material—some materials have more resistance than others. Those with high resistance are said to be insulators. Rubber materials (or rubber-like plastics) are some of the most common insulators used in vehicles as they have a very high resistance to electricity. Very low resistance materials are said to be conductors. Copper wire is among the best conductors. Silver is actually a superior conductor to copper and is used in some relay contacts, but its high cost prohibits its use as common wiring. Most automotive wiring is made of copper.

• Size—the larger the wire size being used, the less resistance the wire will have. This is why components which use large amounts of electricity usually have large wires supplying current to them.

• Length—for a given thickness of wire, the longer the wire, the greater the resistance. The shorter the wire, the less the resistance. When determining the proper wire for a circuit, both size and length must be considered to design a circuit that can handle the current needs of the component.

• Temperature—with many materials, the higher the temperature, the greater the resistance (positive temperature coefficient). Some materials exhibit the opposite trait of lower resistance with higher temperatures (negative temperature coefficient). These principles are used in many of the sensors on the engine.

OHM'S LAW

There is a direct relationship between current, voltage and resistance. The relationship between current, voltage and resistance can be summed up by a statement known as Ohm's law.

Voltage (E) is equal to amperage (I) times resistance (R): $E = I \times R$

Other forms of the formula are $R = E/I$ and $I = E/R$

In each of these formulas, E is the voltage in volts, I is the current in amps and R is the resistance in ohms. The basic point to remember is that as the resistance of a circuit goes up, the amount of current that flows in the circuit will go down, if voltage remains the same.

The amount of work that the electricity can perform is expressed as power. The unit of power is the watt (w). The relationship between power, voltage and current is expressed as:

Power (w) is equal to amperage (I) times voltage (E): $W = I \times E$

This is only true for direct current (DC) circuits; The alternating current formula is a tad different, but since the electrical circuits in most vehicles are DC type, we need not get into AC circuit theory.

Electrical Components

POWER SOURCE

Power is supplied to the vehicle by two devices: The battery and the alternator. The battery supplies electrical power during starting or during periods when the current demand of the vehicle's electrical system exceeds the output capacity of the alternator. The alternator supplies electrical current when the engine is running. Just not does the alternator supply the current needs of the vehicle, but it recharges the battery.

The Battery

In most modern vehicles, the battery is a lead/acid electrochemical device consisting of six 2 volt subsections (cells) connected in series, so that the unit is capable of producing approximately 12 volts of electrical pressure. Each subsection consists of a series of positive and negative plates held a short distance apart in a solution of sulfuric acid and water.

The two types of plates are of dissimilar metals. This sets up a chemical reaction, and it is this reaction which produces current flow from the battery when its positive and negative terminals are connected to an electrical load . The power removed from the battery is replaced by the alternator, restoring the battery to its original chemical state.

The Alternator

On some vehicles there isn't an alternator, but a generator. The difference is that an alternator supplies alternating current which is then changed to direct current for use on the vehicle, while a generator produces direct current. Alternators tend to be more efficient and that is why they are used.

Alternators and generators are devices that consist of coils of wires wound together making big electromagnets. One group of coils spins within another set and the interaction of the magnetic fields causes a current to flow. This current is then drawn off the coils and fed into the vehicles electrical system.

GROUND

Two types of grounds are used in automotive electric circuits. Direct ground components are grounded to the frame through their mounting points. All other components use some sort of ground wire which is attached to the frame or chassis of the vehicle. The electrical current runs through the chassis of the vehicle and returns to the battery through the ground (-) cable; if you look, you'll see that the battery ground cable connects between the battery and the frame or chassis of the vehicle.

➡️ It should be noted that a good percentage of electrical problems can be traced to bad grounds.

PROTECTIVE DEVICES

◗ See Figure 2

It is possible for large surges of current to pass through the electrical system of your vehicle. If this surge of current were to reach the load in the circuit, the surge could burn it out or severely damage it. It can also overload the wiring, causing the harness to get hot and melt the insulation. To prevent this, fuses, circuit breakers and/or fusible links are connected into the supply wires of the electrical system. These items are nothing more than a built-in weak spot in the

system. When an abnormal amount of current flows through the system, these protective devices work as follows to protect the circuit:

- Fuse—when an excessive electrical current passes through a fuse, the fuse "blows" (the conductor melts) and opens the circuit, preventing the passage of current.
- Circuit Breaker—a circuit breaker is basically a self-repairing fuse. It will open the circuit in the same fashion as a fuse, but when the surge subsides, the circuit breaker can be reset and does not need replacement.
- Fusible Link—a fusible link (fuse link or main link) is a short length of special, high temperature insulated wire that acts as a fuse. When an excessive electrical current passes through a fusible link, the thin gauge wire inside the link melts, creating an intentional open to protect the circuit. To repair the circuit, the link must be replaced. Some newer type fusible links are housed in plug-in modules, which are simply replaced like a fuse, while older type fusible links must be cut and spliced if they melt. Since this link is very early in the electrical path, it's the first place to look if nothing on the vehicle works, yet the battery seems to be charged and is properly connected.

✳✳ CAUTION

Always replace fuses, circuit breakers and fusible links with identically rated components. Under no circumstances should a component of higher or lower amperage rating be substituted.

SWITCHES & RELAYS

◗ See Figures 3 and 4

Switches are used in electrical circuits to control the passage of current. The most common use is to open and close circuits between the battery and the various electric devices in the system. Switches are rated according to the amount of amperage they can handle. If a sufficient amperage rated switch is not used in a circuit, the switch could overload and cause damage.

Some electrical components which require a large amount of current to operate use a special switch called a relay. Since these circuits carry a large amount of current, the thickness of the wire in the circuit is also greater. If this large wire were connected from the load to the control switch, the switch would have to carry the high amperage load and the fairing or dash would be twice as large to accommodate the increased size of the wiring harness. To prevent these problems, a relay is used.

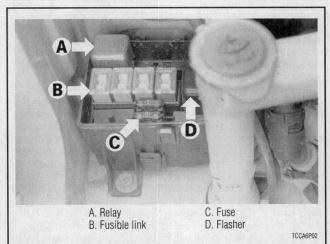

A. Relay
B. Fusible link
C. Fuse
D. Flasher

TCCA6P02

Fig. 3 The underhood fuse and relay panel usually contains fuses, relays, flashers and fusible links

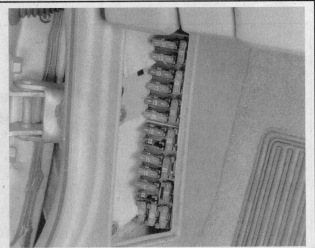

TCCA6P01

Fig. 2 Most vehicles use one or more fuse panels. This one is located on the driver's side kick panel

Relays are composed of a coil and a set of contacts. When the coil has a current passed though it, a magnetic field is formed and this field causes the contacts to move together, completing the circuit. Most relays are normally open, preventing current from passing through the circuit, but they can take any electrical form depending on the job they are intended to do. Relays can be considered "remote control switches." They allow a smaller current to operate devices that require higher amperages. When a small current operates the coil, a larger current is allowed to pass by the contacts. Some common circuits which may

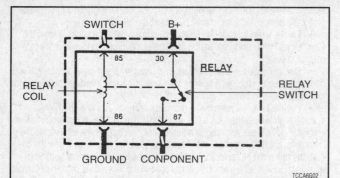

SWITCH   B+

85   30   RELAY

RELAY
COIL   RELAY
SWITCH

86   87

GROUND   COMPONENT

TCCA6G02

Fig. 4 Relays are composed of a coil and a switch. These two components are linked together so that when one operates, the other operates at the same time. The large wires in the circuit are connected from the battery to one side of the relay switch (B+) and from the opposite side of the relay switch to the load (component). Smaller wires are connected from the relay coil to the control switch for the circuit and from the opposite side of the relay coil to ground

use relays are the horn, headlights, starter, electric fuel pump and other high draw ciruits.

LOAD

Every electrical circuit must include a "load" (something to use the electricity coming from the source). Without this load, the battery would attempt to deliver its entire power supply from one pole to another. This is called a "short circuit." All this electricity would take a short cut to ground and cause a great amount of damage to other components in the circuit by developing a tremendous amount of heat. This condition could develop sufficient heat to melt the insulation on all the surrounding wires and reduce a multiple wire cable to a lump of plastic and copper.

WIRING & HARNESSES

The average vehicle contains meters and meters of wiring, with hundreds of individual connections. To protect the many wires from damage and to keep them from becoming a confusing tangle, they are organized into bundles, enclosed in plastic or taped together and called wiring harnesses. Different harnesses serve different parts of the vehicle. Individual wires are color coded to help trace them through a harness where sections are hidden from view.

Automotive wiring or circuit conductors can be either single strand wire, multi-strand wire or printed circuitry. Single strand wire has a solid metal core and is usually used inside such components as alternators, motors, relays and other devices. Multi-strand wire has a core made of many small strands of wire twisted together into a single conductor. Most of the wiring in an automotive electrical system is made up of multi-strand wire, either as a single conductor or grouped together in a harness. All wiring is color coded on the insulator, either as a solid color or as a colored wire with an identification stripe. A printed circuit is a thin film of copper or other conductor that is printed on an insulator backing. Occasionally, a printed circuit is sandwiched between two sheets of plastic for more protection and flexibility. A complete printed circuit, consisting of conductors, insulating material and connectors for lamps or other components is called a printed circuit board. Printed circuitry is used in place of individual wires or harnesses in places where space is limited, such as behind instrument panels.

Since automotive electrical systems are very sensitive to changes in resistance, the selection of properly sized wires is critical when systems are repaired. A loose or corroded connection or a replacement wire that is too small for the circuit will add extra resistance and an additional voltage drop to the circuit.

The wire gauge number is an expression of the cross-section area of the conductor. Vehicles from countries that use the metric system will typically describe the wire size as its cross-sectional area in square millimeters. In this method, the larger the wire, the greater the number. Another common system for expressing wire size is the American Wire Gauge (AWG) system. As gauge number increases, area decreases and the wire becomes smaller. An 18 gauge wire

is smaller than a 4 gauge wire. A wire with a higher gauge number will carry less current than a wire with a lower gauge number. Gauge wire size refers to the size of the strands of the conductor, not the size of the complete wire with insulator. It is possible, therefore, to have two wires of the same gauge with different diameters because one may have thicker insulation than the other.

It is essential to understand how a circuit works before trying to figure out why it doesn't. An electrical schematic shows the electrical current paths when a circuit is operating properly. Schematics break the entire electrical system down into individual circuits. In a schematic, usually no attempt is made to represent wiring and components as they physically appear on the vehicle; switches and other components are shown as simply as possible. Face views of harness connectors show the cavity or terminal locations in all multi-pin connectors to help locate test points.

CONNECTORS

▶ See Figures 5 and 6

Three types of connectors are commonly used in automotive applications—weatherproof, molded and hard shell.

• Weatherproof—these connectors are most commonly used where the connector is exposed to the elements. Terminals are protected against moisture and dirt by sealing rings which provide a weathertight seal. All repairs require the use of a special terminal and the tool required to service it. Unlike standard blade type terminals, these weatherproof terminals cannot be straightened once they are bent. Make certain that the connectors are properly seated and all of the sealing rings are in place when connecting leads.

• Molded—these connectors require complete replacement of the connector if found to be defective. This means splicing a new connector assembly into

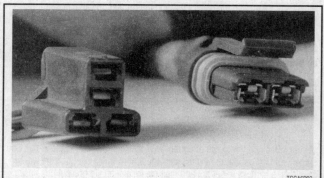

TCCA6P03

Fig. 5 Hard shell (left) and weatherproof (right) connectors have replaceable terminals

TCCA6P04

Fig. 6 Weatherproof connectors are most commonly used in the engine compartment or where the connector is exposed to the elements

the harness. All splices should be soldered to insure proper contact. Use care when probing the connections or replacing terminals in them, as it is possible to create a short circuit between opposite terminals. If this happens to the wrong terminal pair, it is possible to damage certain components. Always use jumper wires between connectors for circuit checking and NEVER probe through weatherproof seals.

• Hard Shell—unlike molded connectors, the terminal contacts in hard-shell connectors can be replaced. Replacement usually involves the use of a special terminal removal tool that depresses the locking tangs (barbs) on the connector terminal and allows the connector to be removed from the rear of the shell. The connector shell should be replaced if it shows any evidence of burning, melting, cracks, or breaks. Replace individual terminals that are burnt, corroded, distorted or loose.

Test Equipment

Pinpointing the exact cause of trouble in an electrical circuit is most times accomplished by the use of special test equipment. The following describes different types of commonly used test equipment and briefly explains how to use them in diagnosis. In addition to the information covered below, the tool manufacturer's instructions booklet (provided with the tester) should be read and clearly understood before attempting any test procedures.

JUMPER WIRES

✸✸ CAUTION

Never use jumper wires made from a thinner gauge wire than the circuit being tested. If the jumper wire is of too small a gauge, it may overheat and possibly melt. Never use jumpers to bypass high resistance loads in a circuit. Bypassing resistances, in effect, creates a short circuit. This may, in turn, cause damage and fire. Jumper wires should only be used to bypass lengths of wire or to simulate switches.

Jumper wires are simple, yet extremely valuable, pieces of test equipment. They are basically test wires which are used to bypass sections of a circuit. Although jumper wires can be purchased, they are usually fabricated from lengths of standard automotive wire and whatever type of connector (alligator clip, spade connector or pin connector) that is required for the particular application being tested. In cramped, hard-to-reach areas, it is advisable to have insulated boots over the jumper wire terminals in order to prevent accidental grounding. It is also advisable to include a standard automotive fuse in any jumper wire. This is commonly referred to as a "fused jumper". By inserting an in-line fuse holder between a set of test leads, a fused jumper wire can be used for bypassing open circuits. Use a 5 amp fuse to provide protection against voltage spikes.

Jumper wires are used primarily to locate open electrical circuits, on either the ground (-) side of the circuit or on the power (+) side. If an electrical component fails to operate, connect the jumper wire between the component and a good ground. If the component operates only with the jumper installed, the ground circuit is open. If the ground circuit is good, but the component does not operate, the circuit between the power feed and component may be open. By moving the jumper wire successively back from the component toward the power source, you can isolate the area of the circuit where the open is located. When the component stops functioning, or the power is cut off, the open is in the segment of wire between the jumper and the point previously tested.

You can sometimes connect the jumper wire directly from the battery to the "hot" terminal of the component, but first make sure the component uses 12 volts in operation. Some electrical components, such as fuel injectors or sensors, are designed to operate on about 4 to 5 volts, and running 12 volts directly to these components will cause damage.

TEST LIGHTS

▶ **See Figure 7**

The test light is used to check circuits and components while electrical current is flowing through them. It is used for voltage and ground tests. To use a 12 volt test light, connect the ground clip to a good ground and probe wherever necessary with the pick. The test light will illuminate when voltage is detected.

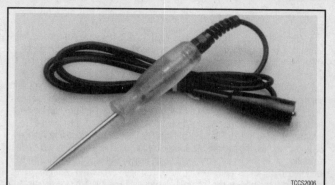
TCCS2006

Fig. 7 A 12 volt test light is used to detect the presence of voltage in a circuit

This does not necessarily mean that 12 volts (or any particular amount of voltage) is present; it only means that some voltage is present. It is advisable before using the test light to touch its ground clip and probe across the battery posts or terminals to make sure the light is operating properly.

✸✸ WARNING

Do not use a test light to probe electronic ignition, spark plug or coil wires. Never use a pick-type test light to probe wiring on computer controlled systems unless specifically instructed to do so. Any wire insulation that is pierced by the test light probe should be taped and sealed with silicone after testing.

Like the jumper wire, the 12 volt test light is used to isolate opens in circuits. But, whereas the jumper wire is used to bypass the open to operate the load, the 12 volt test light is used to locate the presence of voltage in a circuit. If the test light illuminates, there is power up to that point in the circuit; if the test light does not illuminate, there is an open circuit (no power). Move the test light in successive steps back toward the power source until the light in the handle illuminates. The open is between the probe and a point which was previously probed.

The self-powered test light is similar in design to the 12 volt test light, but contains a 1.5 volt penlight battery in the handle. It is most often used in place of a multimeter to check for open or short circuits when power is isolated from the circuit (continuity test).

The battery in a self-powered test light does not provide much current. A weak battery may not provide enough power to illuminate the test light even when a complete circuit is made (especially if there is high resistance in the circuit). Always make sure that the test battery is strong. To check the battery, briefly touch the ground clip to the probe; if the light glows brightly, the battery is strong enough for testing.

➡ **A self-powered test light should not be used on any computer controlled system or component. The small amount of electricity transmitted by the test light is enough to damage many electronic automotive components.**

MULTIMETERS

Multimeters are an extremely useful tool for troubleshooting electrical problems. They can be purchased in either analog or digital form and have a price range to suit any budget. A multimeter is a voltmeter, ammeter and ohmmeter (along with other features) combined into one instrument. It is often used when testing solid state circuits because of its high input impedance (usually 10 megaohms or more). A brief description of the multimeter main test functions follows:

• Voltmeter—the voltmeter is used to measure voltage at any point in a circuit, or to measure the voltage drop across any part of a circuit. Voltmeters usually have various scales and a selector switch to allow the reading of different voltage ranges. The voltmeter has a positive and a negative lead. To avoid damage to the meter, always connect the negative lead to the negative (-) side of the circuit (to ground or nearest the ground side of the circuit) and connect the positive lead to the positive (+) side of the circuit (to the power source or the nearest power source). Note that the negative voltmeter lead will always be black and that the positive voltmeter will always be some color other than black (usually red).

• Ohmmeter—the ohmmeter is designed to read resistance (measured in ohms) in a circuit or component. Most ohmmeters will have a selector switch which permits the measurement of different ranges of resistance (usually the selector switch allows the multiplication of the meter reading by 10, 100, 1,000 and 10,000). Some ohmmeters are "auto-ranging" which means the meter itself will determine which scale to use. Since the meters are powered by an internal battery, the ohmmeter can be used like a self-powered test light. When the ohmmeter is connected, current from the ohmmeter flows through the circuit or component being tested. Since the ohmmeter's internal resistance and voltage are known values, the amount of current flow through the meter depends on the resistance of the circuit or component being tested. The ohmmeter can also be used to perform a continuity test for suspected open circuits. In using the meter for making continuity checks, do not be concerned with the actual resistance readings. Zero resistance, or any ohm reading, indicates continuity in the circuit. Infinite resistance indicates an opening in the circuit. A high resistance reading where there should be none indicates a problem in the circuit. Checks for short circuits are made in the same manner as checks for open circuits, except that the circuit must be isolated from both power and normal ground. Infinite resistance indicates no continuity, while zero resistance indicates a dead short.

✳✳ WARNING

Never use an ohmmeter to check the resistance of a component or wire while there is voltage applied to the circuit.

• Ammeter—an ammeter measures the amount of current flowing through a circuit in units called amperes or amps. At normal operating voltage, most circuits have a characteristic amount of amperes, called "current draw" which can be measured using an ammeter. By referring to a specified current draw rating, then measuring the amperes and comparing the two values, one can determine what is happening within the circuit to aid in diagnosis. An open circuit, for example, will not allow any current to flow, so the ammeter reading will be zero. A damaged component or circuit will have an increased current draw, so the reading will be high. The ammeter is always connected in series with the circuit being tested. All of the current that normally flows through the circuit must also flow through the ammeter; if there is any other path for the current to follow, the ammeter reading will not be accurate. The ammeter itself has very little resistance to current flow and, therefore, will not affect the circuit, but it will measure current draw only when the circuit is closed and electricity is flowing. Excessive current draw can blow fuses and drain the battery, while a reduced current draw can cause motors to run slowly, lights to dim and other components to not operate properly.

Troubleshooting Electrical Systems

When diagnosing a specific problem, organized troubleshooting is a must. The complexity of a modern automotive vehicle demands that you approach any problem in a logical, organized manner. There are certain troubleshooting techniques, however, which are standard:

• Establish when the problem occurs. Does the problem appear only under certain conditions? Were there any noises, odors or other unusual symptoms? Isolate the problem area. To do this, make some simple tests and observations, then eliminate the systems that are working properly. Check for obvious problems, such as broken wires and loose or dirty connections. Always check the obvious before assuming something complicated is the cause.

• Test for problems systematically to determine the cause once the problem area is isolated. Are all the components functioning properly? Is there power going to electrical switches and motors. Performing careful, systematic checks will often turn up most causes on the first inspection, without wasting time checking components that have little or no relationship to the problem.

• Test all repairs after the work is done to make sure that the problem is fixed. Some causes can be traced to more than one component, so a careful verification of repair work is important in order to pick up additional malfunctions that may cause a problem to reappear or a different problem to arise. A

blown fuse, for example, is a simple problem that may require more than another fuse to repair. If you don't look for a problem that caused a fuse to blow, a shorted wire (for example) may go undetected.

Experience has shown that most problems tend to be the result of a fairly simple and obvious cause, such as loose or corroded connectors, bad grounds or damaged wire insulation which causes a short. This makes careful visual inspection of components during testing essential to quick and accurate troubleshooting.

Testing

OPEN CIRCUITS

⧫ **See Figure 8**

This test already assumes the existence of an open in the circuit and it is used to help locate the open portion.

1. Isolate the circuit from power and ground.
2. Connect the self-powered test light or ohmmeter ground clip to the ground side of the circuit and probe sections of the circuit sequentially.
3. If the light is out or there is infinite resistance, the open is between the probe and the circuit ground.
4. If the light is on or the meter shows continuity, the open is between the probe and the end of the circuit toward the power source.

SHORT CIRCUITS

➡**Never use a self-powered test light to perform checks for opens or shorts when power is applied to the circuit under test. The test light can be damaged by outside power.**

1. Isolate the circuit from power and ground.
2. Connect the self-powered test light or ohmmeter ground clip to a good ground and probe any easy-to-reach point in the circuit.
3. If the light comes on or there is continuity, there is a short somewhere in the circuit.
4. To isolate the short, probe a test point at either end of the isolated circuit (the light should be on or the meter should indicate continuity).
5. Leave the test light probe engaged and sequentially open connectors or switches, remove parts, etc. until the light goes out or continuity is broken.
6. When the light goes out, the short is between the last two circuit components which were opened.

VOLTAGE

This test determines voltage available from the battery and should be the first step in any electrical troubleshooting procedure after visual inspection. Many electrical problems, especially on computer controlled systems, can be caused by a low state of charge in the battery. Excessive corrosion at the battery cable terminals can cause poor contact that will prevent proper charging and full battery current flow.

1. Set the voltmeter selector switch to the 20V position.
2. Connect the multimeter negative lead to the battery's negative (-) post or terminal and the positive lead to the battery's positive (+) post or terminal.
3. Turn the ignition switch **ON** to provide a load.
4. A well charged battery should register over 12 volts. If the meter reads below 11.5 volts, the battery power may be insufficient to operate the electrical system properly.

VOLTAGE DROP

⧫ **See Figure 9**

When current flows through a load, the voltage beyond the load drops. This voltage drop is due to the resistance created by the load and also by small resistances created by corrosion at the connectors and damaged insulation on the wires. The maximum allowable voltage drop under load is critical, especially if there is more than one load in the circuit, since all voltage drops are cumulative.

1. Set the voltmeter selector switch to the 20 volt position.
2. Connect the multimeter negative lead to a good ground.
3. Operate the circuit and check the voltage prior to the first component (load).
4. There should be little or no voltage drop in the circuit prior to the first component. If a voltage drop exists, the wire or connectors in the circuit are suspect.
5. While operating the first component in the circuit, probe the ground side of the component with the positive meter lead and observe the voltage readings. A small voltage drop should be noticed. This voltage drop is caused by the resistance of the component.
6. Repeat the test for each component (load) down the circuit.
7. If a large voltage drop is noticed, the preceding component, wire or connector is suspect.

RESISTANCE

♦ See Figures 10 and 11

✳✳ WARNING

Never use an ohmmeter with power applied to the circuit. The ohmmeter is designed to operate on its own power supply. The normal 12 volt electrical system voltage could damage the meter!

1. Isolate the circuit from the vehicle's power source.
2. Ensure that the ignition key is **OFF** when disconnecting any components or the battery.
3. Where necessary, also isolate at least one side of the circuit to be checked, in order to avoid reading parallel resistances. Parallel circuit resistances will always give a lower reading than the actual resistance of either of the branches.

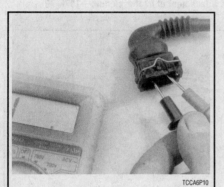

TCCA6P10

Fig. 8 The infinite reading on this multimeter indicates that the circuit is open

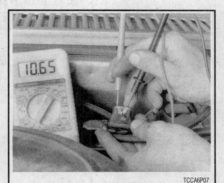

TCCA6P07

Fig. 9 This voltage drop test revealed high resistance (low voltage) in the circuit

TCCA6P08

Fig. 10 Checking the resistance of a coolant temperature sensor with an ohmmeter. Reading is 1.04 kilohms

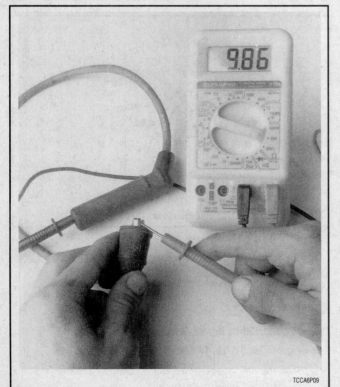

TCCA6P09

Fig. 11 Spark plug wires can be checked for excessive resistance using an ohmmeter

4. Connect the meter leads to both sides of the circuit (wire or component) and read the actual measured ohms on the meter scale. Make sure the selector switch is set to the proper ohm scale for the circuit being tested, to avoid misreading the ohmmeter test value.

Wire and Connector Repair

Almost anyone can replace damaged wires, as long as the proper tools and parts are available. Wire and terminals are available to fit almost any need. Even the specialized weatherproof, molded and hard shell connectors are now available from aftermarket suppliers.

Be sure the ends of all the wires are fitted with the proper terminal hardware and connectors. Wrapping a wire around a stud is never a permanent solution and will only cause trouble later. Replace wires one at a time to avoid confusion. Always route wires exactly the same as the factory.

➡If connector repair is necessary, only attempt it if you have the proper tools. Weatherproof and hard shell connectors require special tools to release the pins inside the connector. Attempting to repair these connectors with conventional hand tools will damage them.

HEATING AND AIR CONDITIONING

Blower Motor

REMOVAL & INSTALLATION

1976

▶ See Figures 12, 13, 14 and 15

1. Disconnect the electrical connectors and the ground wire from the top of the heater.
2. Remove the screws retaining the motor to the plenum chamber and remove the motor assembly.
3. Loosen the blower wheel allen screw and remove the wheel.
4. Remove the motor from the mounting plate.
5. Install the motor to the mounting plate.
6. Install the blower wheel.
7. Position the motor to the plenum chamber. Install the retaining screws.
8. Connect the electrical lead and the ground wire.
9. Check the operation of the blower motor.

1977–79 Standard Heater, Without Air Conditioning

▶ See Figures 12, 13, 14 and 15

1. Disconnect the temperature and function control Bowden cables from the heater housing. This must be done to prevent damage to the cables.
2. Disconnect the wires from the blower resistor.
3. Remove five screws attaching the air inlet (vent) duct to the heater housing.
4. Disconnect the blower wires.
5. Drain the radiator and remove the heater hoses from the heater core.
6. Remove three heater stud retaining nuts and remove heater.
7. Remove gasket between the heater hose ends and the dash panel at core tubes.
8. Remove two screws and two nuts attaching blower to heater.
9. Remove blower fan from motor shaft, and remove motor from mounting plate.

To install:

10. Install new motor on mounting plate and install blower fan on motor shaft.
11. Install blower and motor in heater.
12. Position heater assembly in vehicle and install three stud retaining nuts.
13. Connect heater hoses to heater core and fill radiator.
14. Connect blower motor wires.
15. Place defroster nozzle on heater so that the defroster and heater openings are in the up position and there is no air leak around the seal.
16. Install air inlet (vent) duct to heater. Plush duct firmly against seal on side cowl and tighten five attaching screws.

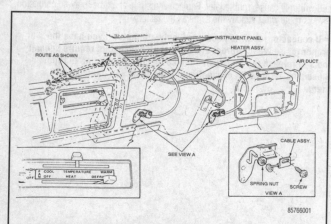

Fig. 12 Heater control cable attachment—1976–79

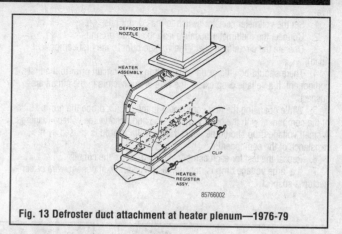

Fig. 13 Defroster duct attachment at heater plenum—1976-79

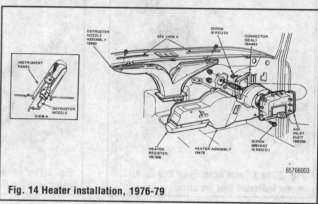

Fig. 14 Heater installation, 1976-79

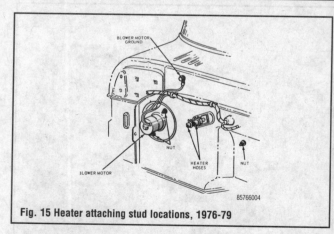

Fig. 15 Heater attaching stud locations, 1976-79

17. Connect wires in blower motor resistor.
18. Connect temperature and function control cables to heater, and adjust the cables.
19. Reinstall gasket between the heater hose ends and the dash panel at core ends.
20. Fill cooling system.

1978–79 Deluxe Hi-Lo Heater, Without Air Conditioning

▶ See Figures 16, 17, 18, 19 and 20

1. Disconnect the battery cable, remove the carburetor air cleaner and partially drain the coolant system.
2. Remove the heater hoses from the heater core.
3. Remove the glove box liner and remove the register duct by pulling from the instrument panel register and releasing the clip at the plenum.

4. Disconnect the right cowl outside air inlet vacuum hose from the outside/recirculating door vacuum motor.

5. Remove the rear housing from under the instrument panel. Remove the outside air inlet duct from the rear housing (4 nuts and 1 bolt) and install one upper nut to retain heater housing-to-dash after rear housing is removed.

6. Remove two screws retaining plenum-to-dash (above transmission tunnel) and two screws to heater housing and remove the plenum.

7. Install a piece of protective tape on A-pillar inner cowl panel, at lower right corner of instrument panel.

8. Remove the lower right instrument panel-to-A-pillar bolt to hold the panel in the rearward position.

9. Remove the heater core (3 screws retaining 2 plates).

10. Remove the temperature blend door (snaps off).

11. Remove the temperature blend door arm support (2 screws) and pivot arm retainer (1 screw).

12. Remove blower motor (2 screws) and remove blower wheel.

To install:

13. Transfer blower to blower motor and panel assembly.

14. Install door arm pivot retainer (1 screw) and door arm support (2 screws).

15. Install the temperature blend door (snaps on).

16. Install heater core.

17. Install the plenum (4 screws).

18. Connect blower wires.

19. Remove heater housing upper retaining nut and install the heater outlet (4 nuts and 1 bolt). Position the air inlet duct.

20. Connect the white vacuum hose to the outside/recirculating door vacuum motor.

21. Reposition the instrument panel, install the retaining bolts and remove the protective tape at the A-pillar inner cowl panel, lower right corner of instrument panel.

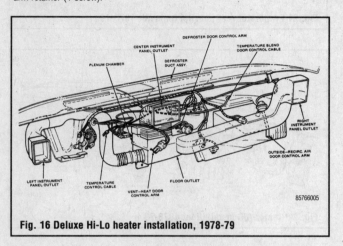

Fig. 16 Deluxe Hi-Lo heater installation, 1978-79

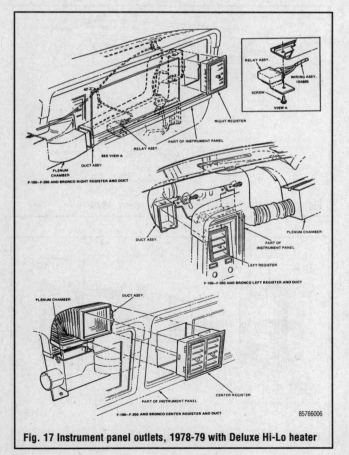

Fig. 17 Instrument panel outlets, 1978-79 with Deluxe Hi-Lo heater

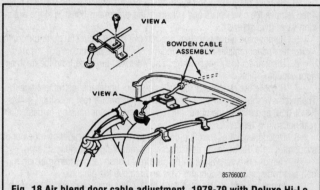

Fig. 18 Air blend door cable adjustment, 1978-79 with Deluxe Hi-Lo heater

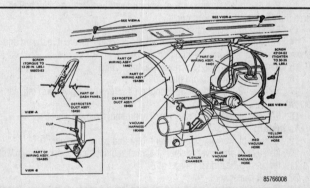

Fig. 19 Plenum chamber and nozzle assembly, 1978-79 with Deluxe Hi-Lo heater

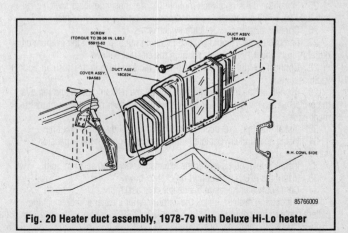

Fig. 20 Heater duct assembly, 1978-79 with Deluxe Hi-Lo heater

22. Install the right register duct assembly and install the glove box liner.

23. Connect heater hoses to the heater core assembly.

24. Fill cooling system, install the air cleaner and connect the battery cable to the battery.

25. Check blower motor operation.

1978–79 With Air Conditioning

▶ See Figures 21, 22, 23, 24 and 25

➡Do not discharge the air conditioning system.

1. Disconnect the battery cable, remove the carburetor air cleaner and partially drain the coolant system.

2. Remove the heater hoses from the heater core.

3. From under the hood, remove A/C hose support bracket from the cowl (one screw).

4. Remove the insulation tape from the expansion valve and sensing bulb. Then remove the cover plate and seal from the evaporator housing at the expansion valve (two screws).

5. Remove the glove box liner and remove the A/C duct by pulling from the instrument panel register and releasing the clip at the plenum.

6. Disconnect the right cowl fresh air inlet vacuum hose from the fresh air door vacuum motor.

7. Remove the evaporator rear housing from under the instrument panel. Then, remove the fresh air inlet tube from the evaporator rear housing (4 nuts and 1 bolt) and install one upper nut to retain evaporator housing-to-dash after rear housing is removed.

8. Disconnect wires from the de-icing switch and pull capillary tube out of evaporator core. Remove the de-icing switch mounting plate (four screws).

9. Remove two screws retaining plenum-to-dash (above transmission tunnel) and two screws to evaporator case and remove the plenum.

10. Install a piece of protective tape on A-pillar inner cowl panel, at lower right corner of instrument panel.

11. Then, remove the lower right instrument panel-to-A-pillar bolt and lower the center instrument panel brace, bolt and nut.

12. Position the instrument panel rearward and install the A-pillar bolt to hold the panel in the rearward position.

13. Remove four evaporator retaining screws.

14. Position the evaporator away from the case and secure it rearward and upward. Remove evaporator sealing grommet.

15. Remove heater core (3 screws retaining 2 plates).

16. Remove A/C-heat door (snaps off).

17. Remove A/C-heat door arm support (2 screws) and pivot arm retainer (1 screw).

18. Remove blower motor (2 screws) and remove blower wheel.

To install:

19. Transfer blower wheel to blower motor and panel assembly.

20. Install door arm pivot retainer (1 screw) and door arm support (2 screws).

21. Install A/C/heat door (snaps on).

22. Install heater core.

23. Remove the retainer that held the evaporator away from the case, install evaporator and tube sealing grommet.

24. Install the plenum (4 screws).

25. Install the de-icing switch mounting plate, install de-icing switch capillary tube back into evaporator core and position blower wire grommet.

26. Connect blower and de-icing switch wires.

27. Remove upper evaporator case retaining nut and install the evaporator outlet (4 nuts and 1 bolt). Then, position the air inlet bellows.

28. Connect the right cowl fresh air inlet vacuum hose to the fresh air door vacuum motor.

29. Reposition the instrument panel, install the retaining bolts and remove the protective tape at the A-pillar inner cowl panel, lower right corner of instrument panel.

30. Install the right A/C duct assembly and install the glove box liner.

31. Install seal and cover plate to the evaporator case at the expansion valve.

32. Install insulation tape over the expansion valve and sensing bulb.

33. Install the A/C hose support bracket-to-cowl.

34. Connect heater hoses to the heater core assembly.

35. Fill cooling system, install the carburetor air cleaner and connect the battery cable to the battery.

36. Check blower motor operation.

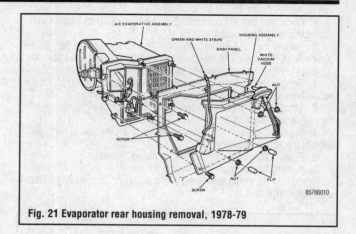

Fig. 21 Evaporator rear housing removal, 1978-79

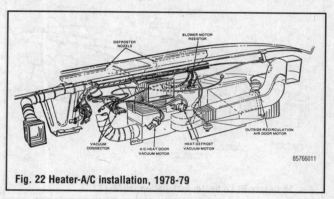

Fig. 22 Heater-A/C installation, 1978-79

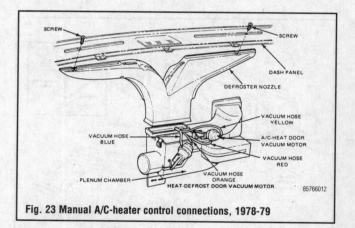

Fig. 23 Manual A/C-heater control connections, 1978-79

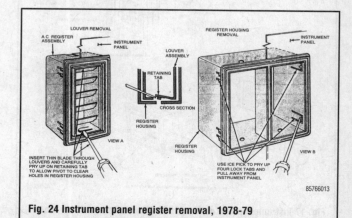

Fig. 24 Instrument panel register removal, 1978-79

Fig. 25 Heater-A/C evaporator case assembly, 1978 Bronco

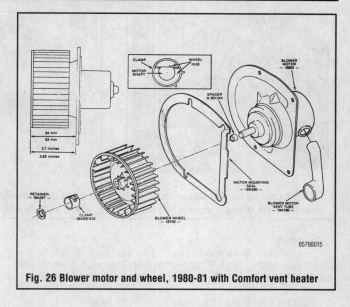

Fig. 26 Blower motor and wheel, 1980-81 with Comfort vent heater

1980–81 Comfort Vent Heaters, Without Air Conditioning

▶ See Figure 26

1. Disconnect the motor wires at the hard shell connectors.
2. Disconnect the blower motor air cooling tube from the motor.
3. Remove four (4) blower motor mounting plate attaching screws and remove the motor and wheel assembly from the blower housing.
4. Remove the hub clamp spring from the blower wheel hub and the retainer from the motor shaft. Then, remove the blower wheel from the motor shaft.

To install:

5. Position the blower wheel on the blower motor shaft. Then, install a new hub clamp spring on the blower hub as shown. The hub clamp spring is included with a new blower wheel but not with the blower motor.
6. Install a new flange gasket on the blower motor flange.
7. Position the blower motor and wheel assembly in the blower housing and install the four (4) attaching screws.

➡ **The wire clamp should be installed under the screw closest to the resistor assembly.**

8. Cement the blower motor air tube on the nipple of the blower housing with RTV silicone adhesive.
9. Connect the blower motor wires at the hard shell connectors.
10. Check the blower motor for proper operation.

1980–86 Standard & High Output Heaters, Without Air Conditioning

▶ See Figures 27 and 28

1. Disconnect the motor wire at the hard shell connector and the ground wire at the ground screw.
2. Remove four (4) screws attaching the blower motor and wheel to the heater case.
3. Remove the blower motor and wheel from the heater case.
4. Remove the blower wheel hub clamp spring and the tab lock washer from the motor shaft. Then, pull the blower wheel from the motor shaft.

To install:

5. Install the blower wheel on the blower motor shaft.
6. Install the hub clamp spring on the blower hub.
7. Position the blower motor and wheel to the heater case, and install the four (4) attaching screws.

1980–86 With Air Conditioning

▶ See Figures 29, 30 and 31

➡ **Do not discharge the air conditioning system.**

1. Disconnect the motor wires at the hard shell connectors.
2. Disconnect the blower motor air cooling tube from the motor.
3. Remove four (4) blower motor mounting plate attaching screws and remove the motor and wheel assembly from the blower housing.
4. Remove the hub clamp spring from the blower wheel hub and the retainer from the motor shaft. Then, remove the blower wheel from the motor shaft.

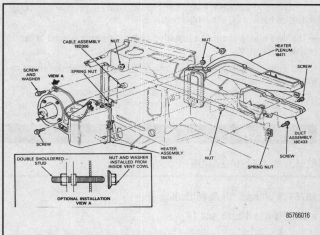

Fig. 27 Heater case and plenum assemblies, 1980 and later standard and high output units without A/C

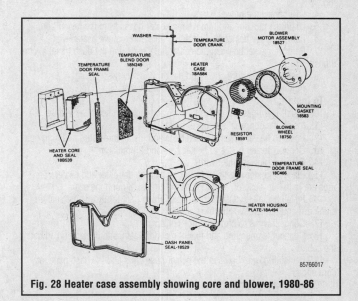

Fig. 28 Heater case assembly showing core and blower, 1980-86

Fig. 29 Removing the four blower motor mounting plate attaching screws, 1980-86

Fig. 30 Removing the blower motor and wheel, 1980-86 with A/C

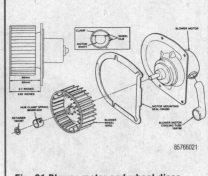

Fig. 31 Blower motor and wheel disassembled, 1980-86 with A/C

To install:

5. Position the blower wheel on the blower motor shaft to the dimension shown. Then, install a new hub clamp spring on the blower hub as shown. The hub clamp spring is included with a new blower wheel but not with the blower motor.

6. Install a new flange gasket on the blower motor flange.

7. Position the blower motor and wheel assembly in the blower housing and install the four (4) attaching screws.

➡**The wire clamp should be installed under the screw closest to the resistor assembly.**

8. Cement the blower motor air tube on the nipple of the blower housing with RTV silicone adhesive.

9. Connect the blower motor wires at the hard shell connectors.

10. Check the blower motor for proper operation.

Heater Core

REMOVAL & INSTALLATION

1976–79 Without Air Conditioning

▶ **See Figures 12, 13 and 14**

1. Disconnect the temperature and function control Bowden cables from the heater housing. This must be done to prevent damage to the cables.

2. Disconnect the wires from the blower resistor.

3. Remove five screws attaching the air inlet (vent) duct to the heater housing.

4. Disconnect the blower wires.

5. Drain the radiator and remove the heater hoses from the heater core.

6. Remove three heater stud retaining nuts and remove heater.

7. Remove gasket between the heater hose ends and the dash panel at core tubes.

8. Remove heater core cover and gasket (four screws).

9. Pull heater core and lower support from heater.

To install:

10. Install foam gaskets on heater core and install in heater assembly.

11. Install the core seal and cover plate.

12. Position heater assembly in vehicle and install three stud retaining nuts.

13. Connect heater hoses to heater core and fill radiator.

14. Connect blower motor wires.

15. Place defroster nozzle on heater so that the defroster and heater openings are in the up position, and there is no air leak around the seal.

16. Install air inlet (vent) duct to heater. Push duct firmly against seal on side cowl and tighten five attaching screws.

17. Connect wires to blower motor resistor.

18. Connect temperature and function control cables to heater, and adjust the cables.

19. Reinstall gasket between the heater hose ends and the dash panel at core ends.

20. Fill Cooling System.

1978–79 Deluxe HI-LO Heater, Without Air Conditioning

1. Disconnect the battery cable, remove the carburetor air cleaner and partially drain the coolant system.

2. Remove the heater hoses from the heater core.

3. Remove the glove box liner and remove the register duct by pulling from the instrument panel register and releasing the clip at the plenum.

4. Disconnect the right cowl outside air inlet vacuum hose from the outside/recirculating door vacuum motor.

5. Remove the rear housing from under the instrument panel. Remove the outside air inlet duct from the rear housing (4 nuts and 1 bolt) and install one upper nut to retain heater housing-to-dash after rear housing is removed.

6. Remove two screws retaining plenum-to-dash (above transmission tunnel) and two screws to heater housing and remove the plenum.

7. Install a piece of protective tape on A-pillar inner cowl panel, at lower right corner of instrument panel.

8. Remove the lower right instrument panel-to-A-pillar bolt and lower the center instrument panel brace, bolt and nut.

9. Position the instrument panel rearward and install the A-pillar bolt to hold the panel in the rearward position.

10. Remove heater core (3 screws retaining 2 plates).

11. Remove the temperature blend door (snaps off).

12. Remove the temperature blend door arm support (2 screws) and pivot arm retainer (1 screw).

13. Remove blower motor (2 screws) and remove blower wheel.

To install:

14. Transfer blower wheel to blower motor and panel assembly.

15. Install door arm pivot retainer (1 screw) and door arm support (2 screws).

16. Install the temperature blend door (snaps on).

17. Install heater core.

18. Install the plenum (4 screws).

19. Connect blower wires.

20. Remove heater housing upper retaining nut and install the heater outlet (4 nuts and 1 bolt). Position the air inlet duct.

21. Connect the white vacuum hose to the outside/recirculating door vacuum motor.

22. Reposition the instrument panel, install the retaining bolts and remove the protective tape at the A-pillar inner cowl panel, lower right corner of instrument panel.

23. Install the right register duct assembly and install the glove box liner.

24. Connect heater hoses to the heater core assembly.

25. Fill cooling system, install the air cleaner and connect the battery cable to the battery.

26. Check blower motor operation.

1978–79 With Air Conditioning

➡**Do not discharge the air conditioning system**

1. Disconnect the battery cable, remove the carburetor air cleaner and partially drain the coolant system.

2. Remove the heater hoses from the heater core.

3. From under the hood, remove A/C hose support bracket from the cowl (one screw).

4. Remove the insulation tape from the expansion valve and sensing bulb. Then remove the cover plate and seal from the evaporator housing at the expansion valve (two screws).

5. Remove the glove box liner and remove the A/C duct by pulling from the instrument panel register and releasing the clip at the plenum.

6. Disconnect the right cowl fresh air inlet vacuum hose from the fresh air door vacuum motor.

7. Remove the evaporator rear housing from under the instrument panel. Then, remove the fresh air inlet tube from the evaporator rear housing (4 nuts and 1 bolt) and install one upper nut to retain evaporator housing-to-dash after rear housing is removed.

8. Disconnect wires from the de-icing switch and pull capillary tube out of evaporator core. Remove the de-icing switch mounting plate (four screws).

9. Remove two screws retaining plenum-to-dash (above transmission tunnel) and two screws to evaporator case and remove the plenum.

10. Install a piece of protective tape on A-pillar inner cowl panel, at lower right corner of instrument panel.

11. Then, remove the lower right instrument panel-to-A-pillar bolt and lower the center instrument panel brace, bolt and nut.

12. Position the instrument panel rearward and install the A-pillar bolt to hold the panel in the rearward position.

13. Remove four evaporator retaining screws.

14. Position the evaporator away from the case and secure it rearward and upward. Remove evaporator sealing grommet.

15. Remove heater core (3 screws retaining 2 plates).

16. Remove A/C-heat door (snaps off).

17. Remove A/C-heat door arm support (2 screws) and pivot arm retainer (1 screw).

To install:

18. Install door arm pivot retainer (1 screw) and door arm support (2 screws).

19. Install A/C-heat door (snaps on).

20. Install heater core.

21. Remove the retainer that held the evaporator away from the case, install evaporator and tube sealing grommet.

22. Install the plenum (4 screws).

23. Install the de-icing switch mounting plate, install de-icing switch capillary tube back into evaporator core and position blower wire grommet.

24. Connect blower and de-icing switch wires.

25. Remove upper evaporator case retaining nut and install the evaporator outlet (4 nuts and 1 bolt). Then, position the air inlet bellows.

26. Connect the right cowl fresh air inlet vacuum hose to the fresh air door vacuum motor.

27. Reposition the instrument panel, install the retaining bolts and remove the protective tape at the A-pillar inner cowl panel, lower right corner of instrument panel.

28. Install the right A/C duct assembly and install the glove box liner.

29. Install seal and cover plate to the evaporator case at the expansion valve.

30. Install insulation tape over the expansion valve and sensing bulb.

31. Install the A/C hose support bracket-to-cowl.

32. Connect heater hoses to the heater core assembly.

33. Fill cooling system, install the carburetor air cleaner and connect the battery cable to the battery.

34. Check blower motor operation.

1980–81 Comfort Vent Heaters, Without Air Conditioning

1. Disconnect the heater hoses from the heater core tubes and plug the hoses with suitable ⅝ inch (16mm) plugs.

2. Remove the glove compartment liner.

3. Remove two (2) spring clips attaching the heater core cover to the plenum along the top edge of the heater core cover.

4. Remove eight (8) screws attaching the heater core cover to the plenum and remove the cover.

5. Remove the heater core from the plenum taking care not to spill coolant from the core.

To install:

6. Install the heater core in the plenum.

7. Install the heater core cover (eight (8) screws and two (2) spring clips along the top edge of the cover).

8. Install the glove compartment liner.

9. Connect the heater hoses to the heater core. Tighten the hose clamps.

10. Add coolant to raise the coolant level to specification.

11. Check the system for proper operation and for coolant leaks.

1980–81 Standard & High Output Heaters, Without Air Conditioning

⬦ **See Figure 28**

1. Disconnect the temperature cable from the temperature blend door and the mounting bracket on top of the heater case.

2. Disconnect the wires from the blower motor resistor and the blower motor.

3. Disconnect the heater hoses from the heater core and plug the hoses with suitable ⅝ inch (16mm) plugs.

4. Working under the instrument panel, remove two (2) nuts retaining the left end of the heater case and the right end of the plenum to the dash panel.

5. In the engine compartment, remove one (1) screw attaching the top center of the heater case to the dash panel.

6. Remove two (2) screws attaching the right end of the heater case to the dash panel, and remove the heater case from the vehicle.

7. Remove nine (9) screws and one (1) bolt and nut attaching the heater housing plate to the heater case, and remove the heater housing plate.

8. Remove three (3) screws attaching the heater core frame to the heater case and remove the frame.

9. Remove the heater core and seal from the heater case.

To install:

10. Position the heater core and seal in the heater case.

11. Install the heater core frame (3 screws).

12. Position the heater housing plate on the heater case and install the nine (9) screws and one (1) bolt and nut.

13. Position the heater case to the dash panel and install the three (3) attaching screws.

14. Working in the passenger compartment, install two (2) nuts to retain the heater case and plenum right end to the dash panel.

15. Connect the heater hoses to the heater core. Tighten the hose clamps.

16. Connect the wires to the blower motor resistor assembly.

17. Connect the blower motor wires.

18. Position (slide) the self-adjusting clip on the temperature cable to a position approximately one 1 inch (25.4mm) from the cable end loop.

19. Snap the temperature cable on the cable mounting bracket of the heater case. Then, position the self-adjusting clip on the door crank arm.

20. Adjust the temperature cable.

21. Check the system for proper operation.

1982–86 Standard & High Output Heaters, Without Air Conditioning

⬦ **See Figure 28**

1. Disconnect the temperature cable from the temperature blend door and the mounting bracket on top of the heater case.

2. Disconnect the wires from the blower motor resistor and the blower motor.

3. Disconnect the heater hoses from the heater core and plug the hoses with suitable ⅝ inch (16mm) plugs.

4. Working under the instrument panel, remove three nuts retaining the left end of the heater case and the right end of the plenum in the dash panel.

5. Remove two screws attaching the right end of the heater case to the dash panel, and remove the heater case from the vehicle.

6. Remove eleven screws and one bolt and nut attaching the heater housing plate to the heater case, and remove the heater housing plate.

7. Remove the heater core and seal from the heater case.

To install:

8. Position the heater core and seal in the heater case.

9. Position the heater housing plate on the heater case and install the eleven screws and one bolt and nut.

10. Position the heater case to the dash panel and install the two attaching screws.

11. Working in the passenger compartment, install three nuts to retain the heater case and plenum right end to the dash panel.

12. Connect the heater hoses to the heater core. Tighten the hose clamps.

13. Connect the wires to the blower motor resistor assembly.

14. Connect the wire harness connector to the blower motor.

15. Position the temperature cable pigtail on the temperature door crank arm with the pigtail up. Be sure a flat washer is placed under the pigtail. Then, install a new pushnut to retain the pigtail on the crank arm.

16. Position the temperature cable flag to the mounting bracket and install the attaching screw.

17. Check the system for proper operation.

1980–86 With Air Conditioning

▶ See Figures 32, 33 and 34

➥ Do not discharge the air conditioning system.

1. Disconnect the heater hoses from the heater core tubes and plug the hoses with suitable 5/8 inch (16mm) plugs.

2. Remove the glove compartment liner.

3. Remove eight (8) screws attaching the heater core cover to the plenum and remove the cover.

4. Remove the heater core from the plenum taking care not to spill coolant from the core.

To install:

5. Install the heater core in the plenum.

6. Install the heater core cover (eight screws).

7. Install the glove compartment liner.

8. Connect the heater hoses to the heater core. Tighten the hose clamps.

9. Add coolant to raise the coolant level to specification.

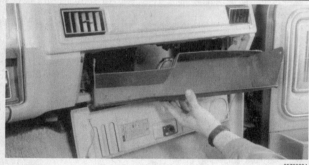

Fig. 32 Removing the glove compartment liner to gain access to the heater core, 1983 F-150 shown with manual A/C

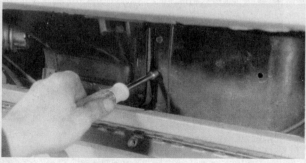

Fig. 33 Removing the heater core cover retaining screws, 1983 F-150 shown with manual A/C

Fig. 34 Removing the heater core cover, 1983 F-150 shown with manual A/C

Control Unit

REMOVAL & INSTALLATION

1976-79

▶ See Figures 35 and 36

1. Disconnect the battery ground.

2. Pull the knob and disc off each radio control shaft.

3. Remove the knob and shaft from the headlight switch.

4. Remove the cluster bezel attaching screws and remove the bezel from the instrument panel.

5. Remove the four heater control attaching screws and pull the control away from the mounting bracket. Disconnect the blower switch and illumination light wires and the two Bowden cables from the control assembly.

6. Installation is the reverse of removal. Check the operation of the unit.

1980-81 with Comfort Vent Heater

▶ See Figure 37

1. Disconnect the battery ground.

2. Remove the two screws attaching the top of the instrument panel center finish panel to the instrument panel pad and pull the center finish panel away from the instrument panel.

3. Remove the knobs from the control assembly by placing a small flat bladed tool between the knob spring retainer and the control assembly. Then, pull on the tool, applying pressure to the spring retainer and pull the knob from the control assembly. Repeat the procedure for each knob.

4. Remove the ash tray, ash tray bracket and the floor register duct.

5. Remove the four heater control attaching screws and pull the control away from the mounting bracket. Disconnect the blower switch and illumination light wires, the vacuum selector switch and the auxiliary fuel tank switch, if so equipped.

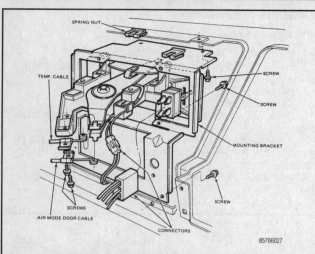

Fig. 35 Rear view of the heater control assembly, 1976-79 without A/C

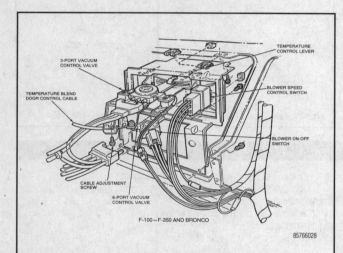

Fig. 36 Rear view of the heater control assembly, 1978-79 Deluxe HI-LO heater without A/C

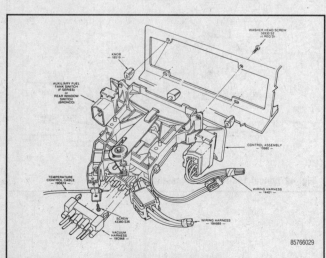

Fig. 37 Rear view of the heater control assembly, 1980-81 with Comfort Control Heater, without A/C

6. Disconnect the vacuum harness connector from the vacuum selector switch.

7. Remove the one screw attaching the temperature cable housing to the control assembly.

8. Remove the spring nut attaching the temperature cable to the temperature lever arm and disconnect the cable from the control assembly.

9. Remove the control assembly.

10. Installation is the reverse of removal. Check the operation of the unit.

1980-86 With Standard and High Output Heater

▶ See Figures 38 and 39

1. Disconnect the battery ground.
2. Pull the knobs from the radio shafts.
3. Remove the two screws attaching the top of the instrument panel center finish panel to the instrument panel pad and pull the center finish panel away from the instrument panel.
4. Remove the knobs from the control assembly by placing a small flat bladed tool between the knob spring retainer and the control assembly. Then, pull on the tool, applying pressure to the spring retainer and pull the knob from the control assembly. Repeat the procedure for each knob.
5. Remove the ash tray and ash tray bracket.
6. Remove the four heater control attaching screws and pull the control away from the mounting bracket. Disconnect the blower switch and illumination light wires, the vacuum selector switch and the auxiliary fuel tank switch, if so equipped.

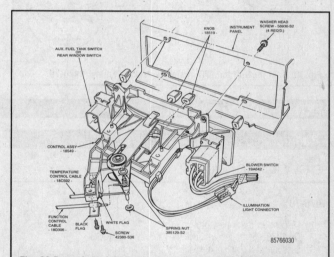

Fig. 38 Rear view of the heater control assembly, 1980-82 with Standard and High Output Heater, without A/C

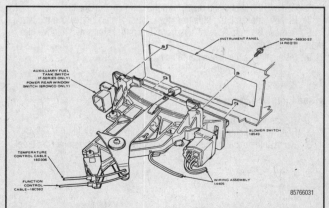

Fig. 39 Rear view of the heater control assembly, 1983-86 with Standard and High Output Heater, without A/C

7. Remove the one screw attaching the temperature cable housing to the control assembly.

8. Remove the spring nut attaching the temperature cable to the temperature lever arm and disconnect the cable from the control assembly.

9. Remove the control assembly.

1976-79

▶ **See Figure 40**

1. Disconnect the battery ground.
2. Remove the instrument cluster.
3. Remove the four heater control attaching screws and pull the control away from the mounting bracket. Disconnect the wire connectors, vacuum lines and cable assembly from the control assembly.
4. Installation is the reverse of removal. Check the operation of the unit.

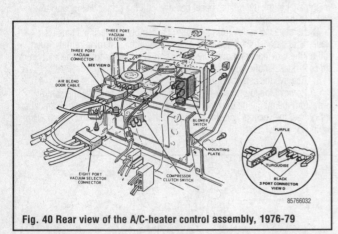

Fig. 40 Rear view of the A/C-heater control assembly, 1976-79

1980-86 With Air Conditioning

▶ **See Figure 41**

1. Remove the instrument panel center finish panel.
2. Remove the control unit knobs by prying on the spring retainer while pulling out on the knob.
3. Remove the 4 control unit attaching screws.
4. Disconnect the wiring and vacuum lines from the control unit.
5. Disengage the temperature cable by depressing the locking tabs on the connector.
6. Rotate the control unit 180° and disconnect the function cable from the control assembly. Remove the control assembly by compressing the locking tabs on the connector.
7. Installation is the reverse of removal. Check the operation of the unit.

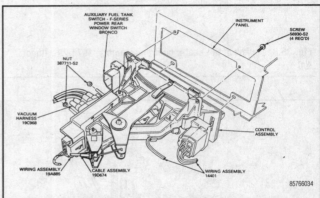

Fig. 41 Rear view of the A/C-heater control assembly, 1983-86

ENTERTAINMENT SYSTEM

Radio

REMOVAL & INSTALLATION

1976-79

1. Disconnect the battery ground cable.
2. On 1978–79 models, remove the ash tray and bracket.
3. Disconnect the antenna, speakers and radio lead.
4. Remove the bolt attaching the radio rear support to the lower edge of the instrument panel.
5. On 1977-78 models equipped with air conditioning, disconnect the left A/C duct hose from the A/C plenum.
6. Remove the knobs and discs from the radio control shafts.
7. Remove the retaining nuts from the control shafts and remove the bezel.
8. Remove the nuts and washers from the control shafts and remove the radio from the panel.
9. Installation is the reverse of removal.

1980-86

▶ **See Figures 42 thru 47**

1. Disconnect the battery ground cable.
2. Remove the knobs and discs from the radio control shafts.
3. Remove the retaining nuts from the control shafts and remove the bezel.

4. Disconnect the antenna, speakers and radio lead.
5. Remove the bolt attaching the radio rear support to the lower edge of the instrument panel.
6. Remove the nuts and washers from the control shafts and remove the radio from the panel.
7. Installation is the reverse of removal.

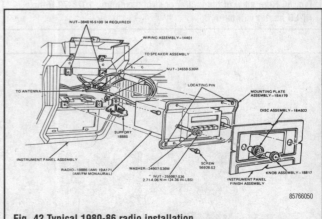

Fig. 42 Typical 1980-86 radio installation

Fig. 43 Removing the knobs and disc from the radio control shaft

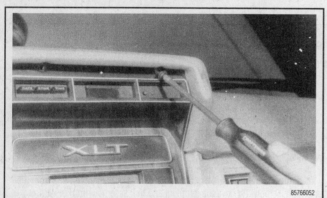

Fig. 44 Removing the cluster bezel retaining screws

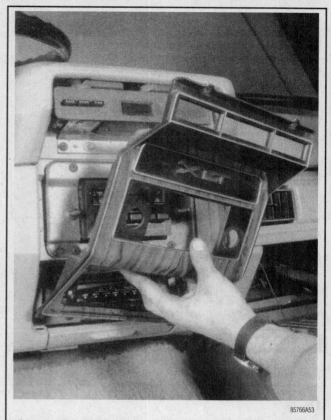

Fig. 45 Removing the cluster bezel from the instrument panel

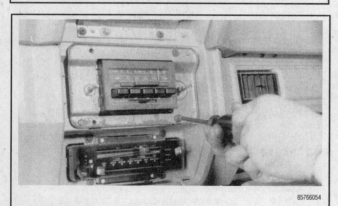

Fig. 46 Removing the radio mounting plate

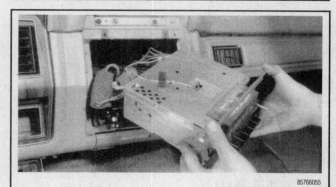

Fig. 47 Carefully pull out the radio and disconnect the antenna, speakers and radio lead

WINDSHIELD WIPERS

Wiper Blade Assembly

Please refer to Section 1 for wiper blade assembly and wiper refill removal and installation procedures.

Wiper Arm Assembly

REMOVAL & INSTALLATION

▶ See Figures 48 and 49

1976–79 F-100-350

Swing the arm and blade away from the windshield and insert a ³⁄₃₂ inch pin through the pin hole. Swinging the assembly away from the windshield will release the spring loaded attaching clip in the arm from the pivot shaft. Inserting the pin will hold it in the released position. The arm can now be pulled off the pivot shaft using a wiper arm removal tool.

⁜ WARNING

Prying off with a screwdriver could damage the pivot shaft.

To replace the arm, hold it in the bent position, slide it on the pivot and remove the pin.

➡Some models do not use the pin type wiper arms. On these models the arm is released by lifting the wiper arm up slightly and releasing the tab under the pivot portion of the arm.

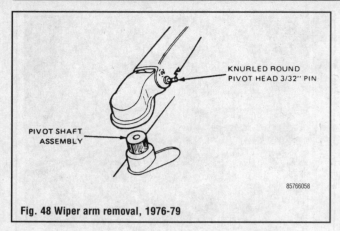

Fig. 48 Wiper arm removal, 1976-79

1980–86

▶ **See Figures 49, 50 and 51**

Raise the blade end of the arm off of the windshield and move the slide latch away from the pivot shaft. This will unlock the wiper arm from the pivot shaft and hold the blade end of the arm off of the glass at the same time. The wiper arm can now be pulled off of the pivot shaft without the aid of any tools.

Windshield Wiper Motor

REMOVAL & INSTALLATION

1976–79

▶ **See Figure 52**

1. Disconnect the battery ground cable.
2. Remove the radio, as outlined earlier in this section.
3. Remove the engine components attached to the lower wiper bracket bolt, if so equipped.
4. Remove the wiper motor bracket attaching bolts.
5. Disconnect the wiper motor wires. Then, disconnect the wiper arm linkage from the motor shaft.
6. Connect the linkage to motor and install motor bracket attaching bolts. Tighten bolts to 8–12 ft. lbs., and install engine components to lower bracket bolts.
7. Connect wiper motor wires.
8. Install radio.
9. Connect battery cable and check wiper motor operation.

1980–86

▶ **See Figures 53, 54 and 55**

1. Disconnect the battery ground cable.
2. Remove both wiper arm and blade assemblies.

3. Remove the cowl grille attaching screws and lift the cowl grille slightly.
4. Disconnect the washer nozzle hose and remove the cowl grille assembly.
5. Remove the wiper linkage clip from the motor output arm.
6. Disconnect the wiper motor's wiring connector.
7. Remove the wiper motor's three attaching screws and remove the motor.
8. Install the motor and attach the three attaching screws. Tighten to 60–85 inch lbs.
9. Connect wiper motor's wiring connector.
10. Install wiper linkage clip to the motor's output arm.
11. Connect the washer nozzle hose and install the cowl assembly and attaching screws.
12. Install both wiper arm assemblies.
13. Connect battery ground cable.

Wiper Linkage

REMOVAL & INSTALLATION

1976–79

▶ **See Figure 52**

1. Open the hood and disconnect the battery ground cable. Remove the arm and blade assemblies from the pivot shafts.
2. Reach under the instrument panel and disconnect the speedometer cable from the rear of the instrument cluster.
3. Remove the instrument cluster bezel.
4. Loosen the three bolts retaining the wiper motor bracket to the cowl. This will allow access between the cowl panel and the link assembly.
5. Remove the clip retaining the motor drive arm to the link assemblies.
6. Through the cluster bezel opening, remove the retaining bolts from the left pivot assembly. Remove the left pivot and link assembly from under the instrument panel.
7. Remove the glove box assembly.
8. Remove the three bolts retaining the right pivot and link assembly to cowl panel.
9. Disconnect the right link assembly from the drive arm and remove the right pivot and link assembly.

To install:

10. Place gaskets on the pivot shafts and position the shafts to the cowl panel and install the retaining bolts.
11. Install the glove box assembly.
12. Position the link assemblies to the motor drive arm and install the retaining clip.
13. Tighten the bolts retaining the motor bracket to the cowl and then install engine components to lower bracket bolt.
14. Install the wiper arm and blade assemblies.
15. Position and install the instrument cluster bezel.
16. Connect the speedometer cable.
17. Connect the battery ground cable and close the hood and check the operation of the wipers.

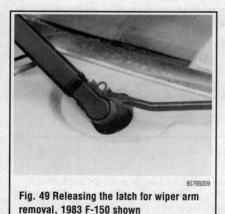

Fig. 49 Releasing the latch for wiper arm removal, 1983 F-150 shown

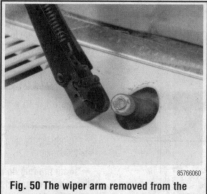

Fig. 50 The wiper arm removed from the shaft, 1983 F-150 shown

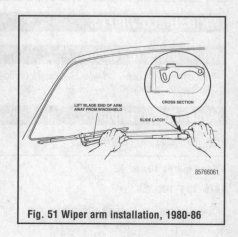

Fig. 51 Wiper arm installation, 1980-86

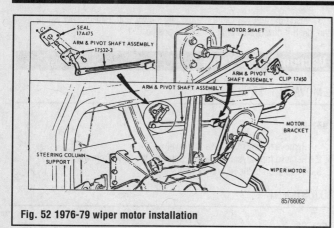

Fig. 52 1976-79 wiper motor installation

1980–86

1. Disconnect the battery ground cable.
2. Remove both wiper arm assemblies.
3. Remove the cowl grille attaching screws and lift the cowl grille slightly.
4. Disconnect the washer nozzle hose and remove the cowl grille assembly.
5. Remove the wiper linkage clip from the motor output arm and pull the linkage from the output arm.
6. Remove the pivot body to cowl screws and remove the linkage and pivot shaft assembly (three screws on each side). The left and right pivots and linkage are independent and can be serviced separately.
To install:
7. Attach the linkage and pivot shaft assembly to cowl with attaching screws.
8. Replace the linkage to the output arm and attach the linkage clip.
9. Connect the washer nozzle hose and cowl grille assembly.
10. Attach cowl grille attaching screws.
11. Replace both wiper arm assemblies.
12. Connect battery ground cable.

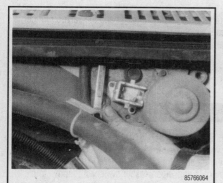

Fig. 53 Removing the upper wiper motor attaching screw, 1983 F-150 shown

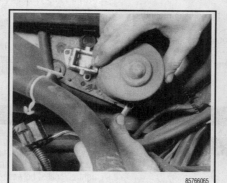

Fig. 54 Removing the lower wiper motor attaching screw, 1983 F-150 shown

Fig. 55 Wiper motor with the electrical connector unfastened, 1983 F-150 shown

CRUISE CONTROL SYSTEM

Speed Sensor

REMOVAL & INSTALLATION

1976-80

1. Unplug the wiring connector leading to the amplifier.
2. Disconnect the upper and lower speedometer cables at the speed sensor.
3. Remove the sensor.
4. Installation is the reverse of removal.

1981-86

1. Unplug the wiring at the sensor on the transmission.
2. Disconnect the speedometer cable from the speed sensor.
3. Remove the retaining bolt and remove the sensor. Remove the drive gear.
4. Installation is the reverse of removal.

Amplifier

REMOVAL & INSTALLATION

1. Disconnect the wiring at the amplifier, located behind the instrument panel.
2. Remove the amplifier mounting bracket attaching screws or nuts and remove the amplifier and bracket.
3. Remove the amplifier from the bracket.
4. Installation is the reverse of removal.

Servo Assembly

REMOVAL & INSTALLATION

1976-80

♦ See Figure 56

1. Disconnect the wiring harness under the hood at the servo.
2. Disconnect the ball chain at the servo.
3. Disconnect the vacuum line at the servo.

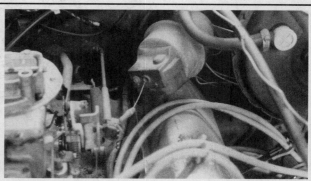

Fig. 56 Servo and bracket assembly, 1978 Bronco shown

4. Remove the pins retaining the servo to its mounting bracket and lift it out.

5. Installation is the reverse of removal.

1981-86

1. Disconnect the wiring at the servo.
2. Disconnect the adjuster from the accelerator cable.
3. Disconnect the vacuum line at the servo.
4. Remove the actuator cable-to-bracket screw.
5. Remove the pins and nuts retaining the servo to its mounting bracket and lift it out.
6. Installation is the reverse of removal.

LINKAGE ADJUSTMENT

1981-86

1. Snap the molded cable retainer over the accelerator cable end fitting attached, to the throttle ball stud.
2. Remove the adjuster retainer clip, if installed, from the adjuster mounting tab.
3. Insert the speed control actuator cable adjuster mounting tab in the slot provided in the accelerator cable support bracket.
4. Pull the cable through the adjuster until a slight tension is felt **without** opening the throttle plate.

INSTRUMENTS AND SWITCHES

Instrument Cluster

REMOVAL & INSTALLATION

1976–79

▶ **See Figures 57 and 58**

1. Disconnect the battery ground cable.
2. Remove the radio knobs from the radio shafts (if so equipped).
3. Remove the fuel gauge switch knob (if so equipped), heater control knobs and wiper/washer knob. Use a hook-shaped tool to release each knob lock tab.
4. Remove the knob and shaft from the light switch.
5. Remove one nut and washer from each radio control shaft, and remove the radio bezel.
6. Remove the cluster trim cover. The attaching screws are located as fol-

5. Insert the adjuster cable retainer clip slowly, until engagement is felt, then, push it downwards until it locks in position.

Vacuum Dump Valve

REMOVAL & INSTALLATION

1981-86

1. Remove the vacuum hose at the valve.
2. Remove the valve and bracket. Separate the valve from the bracket.
3. Installation is the reverse of removal.

ADJUSTMENT

1981-86

The dump valve disconnects the speed control whenever the brake pedal is depressed.

1. Make sure that the brake pedal is fully released and the valve's plunger is in contact with the brake pedal adapter.
2. Move the valve forward in its retaining clip until 3mm (⅛ inch) of the valve plunger is exposed.
3. Make sure that the brake pedal is still in the fully released position, against its stop.

lows: four screws along top of bezel; one screw between the lights and wiper/washer switch, and two screws below the radio. Then, disconnect the A/C duct (if so equipped), and illumination light from the bezel. The illumination light is located between the lights and wiper/washer switches. Remove four cluster attaching screws, disconnect the speedometer cable and wire connector from the printed circuit, and remove the cluster.

To install:

7. Position cluster to opening and connect the multiple connector and the speedometer cable. Connect the A/C duct and A/C illumination light (if so equipped) and install the four cluster retaining screws.
8. Install the trim cover.
9. Install the radio bezel (if so equipped).
10. Install the light switch knob and shaft.
11. Install the heater control knobs and the wiper/washer control knobs.
12. Install the radio knobs, (if so equipped).
13. Connect the battery cable, and check the operation of all gauges, lights and signals.

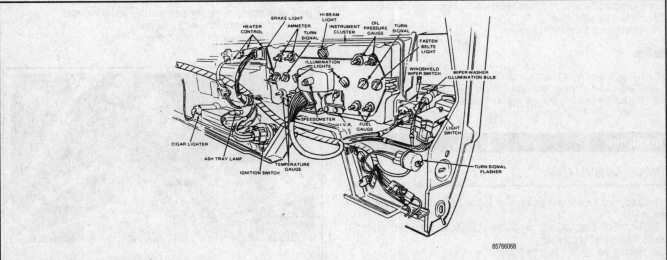

85766068

Fig. 57 1976-79 instrument cluster, rear view

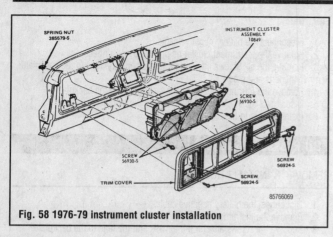

Fig. 58 1976-79 instrument cluster installation

1980–86

▶ **See Figures 59 and 60**

1. Disconnect the battery ground cable.
2. Remove the fuel gauge switch knob (if so equipped), and wiper/washer knob. Use a hook tool to release each knob lock tab.

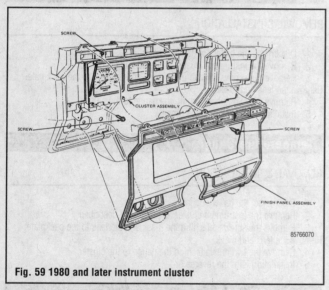

Fig. 59 1980 and later instrument cluster

3. Remove the knob from the headlamp and windshield wiper switch. Remove the fog lamp switch knob, if so equipped.
4. Remove steering column shroud. Care must be taken not to damage transmission control selector indicator (PRNDL) cable on vehicles equipped with automatic transmission.
5. On vehicles equipped with automatic transmission, remove loop on indicator cable assembly from retainer pin. Remove bracket screw from cable bracket and slide bracket out of slot in tube.
6. Remove the cluster trim cover. Remove four cluster attaching screws, disconnect the speedometer cable, wire connector from the printed circuit, 4 × 4 indicator light and remove the cluster.

To install:

7. Position cluster to opening and connect the multiple connector, the speedometer cable and 4 × 4 indicator light. Install the four cluster retaining screws.
8. If so equipped, place loop on transmission indicator cable assembly over retainer on column.
9. Position the tab on steering column bracket into slot on column. Align and attach screw.
10. Place transmission selector lever on steering column into **D** position.
11. Adjust slotted bracket so the pin is within the letter band.
12. Install the trim cover.
13. Install the headlamp switch knob. If so equipped, install the fog lamp switch.
14. Install the wiper/washer control knobs.
15. Connect the battery cable, and check the operation of all gauges, lights and signals.

Speedometer

REMOVAL & INSTALLATION

1. Remove the instrument cluster as previously described.
2. Remove the lens and the mask from the cluster.
3. Disconnect the speedometer cable.
4. Remove the speedometer attaching screws and remove the unit.

To install:

5. Position the speedometer to the pack plate and install the two attaching screws.
6. Examine the square drive hole for sufficient lubrication. If required, apply a ³⁄₁₆ inch dab of lubricant (B5AZ-19581-A or equivalent) in the drive hole.
7. Reconnect the speedometer cable.

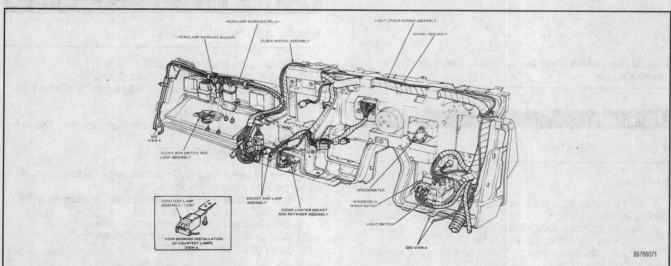

Fig. 60 1980 and later instrument cluster rear view

Speedometer Cable Core

REMOVAL & INSTALLATION

▶ **See Figures 61 and 62**

1. Reach up behind the cluster and disconnect the cable by depressing the quick disconnect tab and pulling the cable away.
2. Remove the cable from the casing. If the cable is broken, raise the vehicle on a hoist and disconnect the cable from the transmission.
3. Remove the cable from the casing.
4. To remove the casing from the vehicle, pull it through the floor pan.
5. To replace the cable, slide the new cable into the casing and connect it at the transmission.
6. Route the cable through the floor pan and position the grommet in its groove in the floor.
7. Push the cable onto the speedometer head.

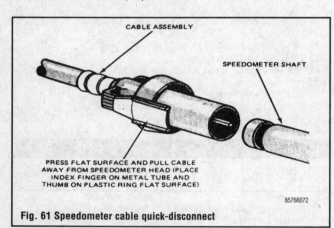

CABLE ASSEMBLY

SPEEDOMETER SHAFT

PRESS FLAT SURFACE AND PULL CABLE AWAY FROM SPEEDOMETER HEAD (PLACE INDEX FINGER ON METAL TUBE AND THUMB ON PLASTIC RING FLAT SURFACE)

85766072

Fig. 61 Speedometer cable quick-disconnect

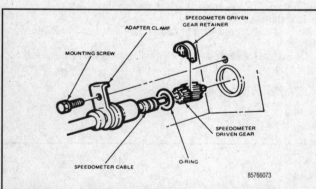

ADAPTER CLAMP

SPEEDOMETER DRIVEN GEAR RETAINER

MOUNTING SCREW

SPEEDOMETER DRIVEN GEAR

O-RING

SPEEDOMETER CABLE

85766073

Fig. 62 Speedometer driven gear-to-transmission installation, all models similar

Tachometer

REMOVAL & INSTALLATION

Mechanical

1. From behind the instrument cluster, disconnect the cable by turning the attaching nut counterclockwise.
2. Snap the light socket out of the tachometer head.
3. Remove the two retaining nuts and bracket.
4. Installation is in the reverse order. Check drive hole and lubricate with a dab of lubricant if necessary.

Electronic

1. Disconnect the battery negative cable.
2. Remove the instrument cluster as previously described.
3. Remove the six screws attaching the mask and the lens to the backplate. Remove the lens and mask.
4. Remove the four nuts attaching the tachometer to the backplate.
5. Disconnect the electrical connector from the tachometer.
6. Installation is in the reverse order.

Oil Pressure Gauge

REMOVAL & INSTALLATION

1. Disconnect the battery negative cable.
2. Remove the instrument cluster as previously described.
3. Remove the screws attaching the mask and the lens to the backplate. Remove the lens and mask.
4. Remove the plastic insulation.
5. Remove the two nuts attaching the gauge to the cluster.
6. Installation is in the reverse order.

Fuel Gauge

REMOVAL & INSTALLATION

1. Disconnect the battery negative cable.
2. Remove the instrument cluster as previously described.
3. Remove the screws attaching the mask and the lens to the backplate. Remove the lens and mask.
4. Remove the two nuts attaching the gauge to the cluster.
5. Installation is in the reverse order.

Temperature Gauge

REMOVAL & INSTALLATION

1. Disconnect the battery negative cable.
2. Remove the instrument cluster as previously described.
3. Remove the screws attaching the mask and the lens to the backplate. Remove the lens and mask.
4. Remove the two nuts attaching the gauge to the cluster.
5. Installation is in the reverse order.

Printed Circuit Board

REMOVAL & INSTALLATION

1. Disconnect the battery negative cable.
2. Remove the instrument cluster as previously described.
3. Unsnap the printed circuit connector buttons from the instrument voltage regulator.
4. Remove the voltage regulator screw.
5. Remove the gauge retaining nuts and the plastic insulators. Remove the light bulbs.
6. Remove the printed circuit.

To install:

7. Carefully position the printed circuit into the back of the cluster and engage it with the plastic locking pins.
8. Install the gauge retaining nuts with the plastic insulators. Install the light bulbs.
9. Install the instrument voltage regulator (one screw).
10. Snap on the connector buttons to the voltage regulator.
11. Install the instrument cluster.

Voltmeter

REMOVAL & INSTALLATION

1. Disconnect the battery negative cable.
2. Remove the instrument cluster as previously described.
3. Remove the screws attaching the mask and the lens to the backplate. Remove the lens and mask.
4. Remove the two nuts attaching the gauge to the cluster.
5. Remove the two wires.
6. Installation is in the reverse order.

Ammeter

REMOVAL & INSTALLATION

1. Disconnect the battery negative cable.
2. Remove the instrument cluster as previously described.
3. Remove the screws attaching the mask and the lens to the backplate. Remove the lens and mask.
4. Remove the two nuts attaching the gauge to the cluster.
5. Remove the plastic insulators.
6. Installation is in the reverse order.

Windshield Wiper/Washer Switch

REMOVAL & INSTALLATION

▶ See Figure 63

1. Disconnect the battery cable.
2. Remove the switch knob, bezel nut and bezel.
3. Pull out the switch from under the instrument panel. Disconnect the plug connector from the switch and remove the switch.
4. Installation is the reverse of the removal procedure.

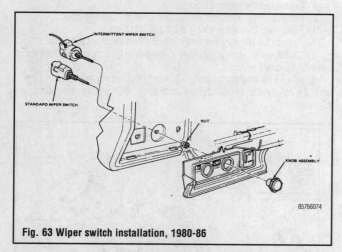

Fig. 63 Wiper switch installation, 1980-86

Headlight Switch

▶ See Figures 64 and 65

REMOVAL & INSTALLATION

1. Disconnect the battery ground cable.
2. Depending on the year and model remove the wiper/washer and fog lamp switch knob if they will interfere with the headlight switch knob removal. Check the switch body (behind dash, see Step 3) for a release button. Press in on the button and remove the knob and shaft assembly. If not equipped with a release button, a hook tool may be necessary for knob removal.

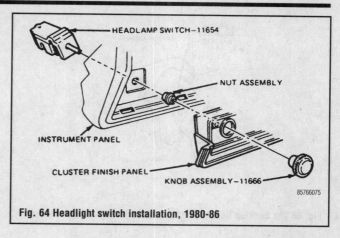

Fig. 64 Headlight switch installation, 1980-86

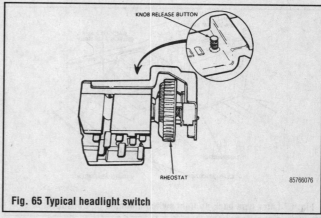

Fig. 65 Typical headlight switch

3. Remove the steering column shrouds and cluster panel finish panel if they interfere with the required clearance for working behind the dash.
4. Unscrew the switch mounting nut from the front of the dash. Remove the switch from the back of the dash and disconnect the wiring harness.
5. Install in reverse order.

Clock

REMOVAL & INSTALLATION

1. Remove the screws retaining the clock assembly to the dash panel.
2. Pull the clock from the dash panel.
3. Disconnect the wiring connector from the back of the clock assembly.
4. Installation is in the reverse order.

Neutral Safety and Back-up Light Switch

REMOVAL & INSTALLATION

Manual Transmission

▶ See Figures 66 and 67

The switch is located on the left side of the transmission case. To remove:
1. Disconnect the negative battery cable.
2. Disconnect the back-up switch harness.
3. Remove the back-up switch and the seal.
4. Installation is the reverse of the removal procedure.

Automatic Transmission

▶ See Figure 68

The switch is located on the left side of the transmission case. To remove:

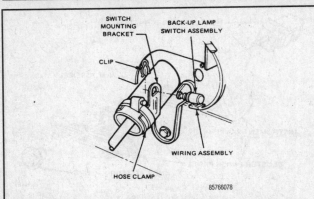

Fig. 66 The back-up light switch is mounted in engine compartment

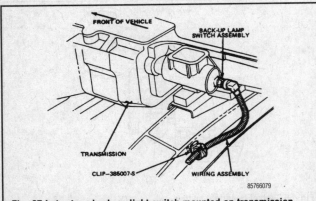

Fig. 67 Later-type back-up light switch mounted on transmission

1. Remove the downshift linkage rod return spring at the low-reverse servo cover.
2. Coat the outer lever attaching nut with penetrating oil. Remove the nut and lever.
3. Remove the 2 switch attaching bolts, disconnect the wiring at the connectors and remove the switch.
To install:
4. Install the switch on the transmission and install the two retaining bolts. With the transmission manual lever in the neutral position, check the position of the switch with a gauge pin (No. 43 drill) in the gauge pin holes.
5. Tighten the attaching bolts to 55–75 inch lbs.
6. Install the outer downshift lever and retaining nut and tighten the nut. Install the downshift linkage rod return spring between the lever and the retaining clip on the low reverse servo cover.
7. Connect the wire multiple connectors and check the operation of the switch.

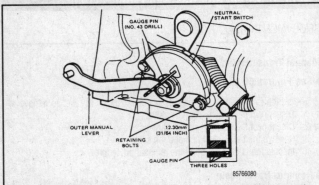

Fig. 68 Neutral start/back-up light switch on vehicles with automatic transmissions

Ignition Switch

REMOVAL & INSTALLATION

1976–79

1. Disconnect the battery ground cable.
2. Turn the ignition key to Accessories and slightly depress the release pin in the face of the lock cylinder.
3. Turn the key counterclockwise and pull the key and lock assembly out of the switch.
4. From under the instrument panel, press in on the rear of the switch ⅛ turn counterclockwise.
5. Remove the bezel and switch. Remove the retainer and spring.
6. Remove the nut from the back of the switch.
7. Remove the accessory and gauge feed wires from the accessory terminal of the switch. Pull the insulated plug from the rear of the switch.
To install:
8. Insert a screwdriver into the lock opening of the switch and turn the slot in the switch to the full counterclockwise position.
9. Connect the insulated plug and wires to the back of the switch. Connect the accessory and gauge wires to the switch and install the retaining nut.
10. Place the bezel and switch in the switch opening, press the switch toward the instrument panel and rotate it ⅛ turn to lock it.
11. Position the spring and retainer on the switch with the open face of the retainer away from the switch. Place the switch in the opening.
12. Press the switch toward the instrument panel and install the bezel.
13. Place the key in the cylinder and turn the key to the accessory position. Place the lock and key in the switch, depress the release pin slightly, and turn the key counterclockwise. Push the new lock cylinder into the switch. Turn the key to check the operation.
14. Connect the battery.

1980–86
♦ See Figure 69

1. Disconnect the battery ground cable.
2. Remove steering column shroud and lower the steering column.
3. Disconnect the switch wiring at the multiple plug.
4. Remove the two nuts that retain the switch to the steering column.
5. Lift the switch vertically upward to disengage the actuator rod from the switch and remove switch.
6. When installing the ignition switch, both the locking mechanism at the top of the column and the switch itself must be in LOCK position for correct adjustment.

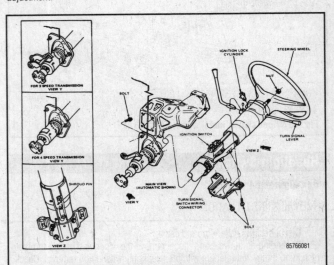

Fig. 69 Blade-type connector ignition switch on steering column, 1980 and later models

To hold the mechanical parts of the column in LOCK position, move the shift lever into PARK (with automatic transmissions) or REVERSE (with manual transmissions), turn the key to LOCK position, and remove the key. New replacement switches, when received, are already pinned in LOCK position by a metal shipping pin inserted in a locking hole on the side of the switch.

7. Engage the actuator rod in the switch.

8. Position the switch on the column and install the retaining nuts, but do not tighten them.

9. Move the switch up and down along the column to locate the mid-position of rod lash, and then tighten the retaining nuts.

10. Remove the locking pin, connect the battery cable, and check for proper start in PARK or NEUTRAL.

Also check to make certain that the start circuit cannot be actuated in the DRIVE and REVERSE position.

11. Raise the steering column into position at instrument panel. Install steering column shroud.

LIGHTING

Headlights

REMOVAL & INSTALLATION

▶ See Figures 70, 71, 72 and 73

✳ CAUTION

On models equipped with halogen headlights, the bulb contains high pressure halogen gas. The bulb may shatter if scratched or dropped! Hold the bulb by its plastic base only. If you touch the glass portion with your fingers, or if any dirt or oily deposits are found on the glass, it must be wiped clean with an alcohol soaked paper towel. Even the oil from your skin will cause the bulb to burn out prematurely due to hot-spotting.

1. Make sure that the headlight switch is **OFF**.

2. Raise the hood and find the bulb base protruding from the back of the head lamp assembly

3. Disconnect the wiring by grasping the connector and pulling it rearward firmly.

4. Remove the headlamp door retaining screws and remove the headlamp door.

5. Remove the headlamp retaining ring screws and remove the retaining ring. Do not disturb the adjustment screws.

6. Pull the headlamp bulb forward and disconnect the wire connector if not done so earlier.

7. Installation is the reverse of removal.

8. Turn the headlights on a check that everything works properly.

ADJUSTMENT

▶ See Figure 74

➡Before making any headlight adjustments, perform the following steps for preparation:

1. Make sure all tires are properly inflated.

2. Take into consideration any faulty wheel alignment or improper rear axle tracking.

3. Make sure there is no load in the truck other than the driver.

4. Make sure all lenses are clean.

Each headlight is adjusted by means of two screws located at the 10 o'clock and 3 o'clock positions on the headlight underneath the trim ring. Always bring each beam into final position by turning the adjusting screws clockwise so that the headlight will be held against the tension springs when the operation is completed.

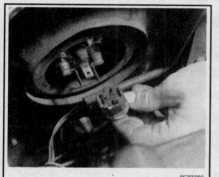

Fig. 70 The wiring connector may be disconnected from under the hood

Fig. 71 Removing the headlight door

Fig. 72 Removing the headlight bulb retaining ring. Do not remove adjusting screws

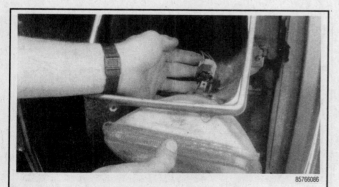

Fig. 73 Detach the connector at the base of the bulb and remove the bulb

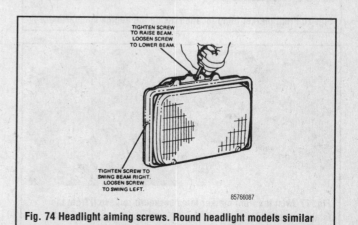

Fig. 74 Headlight aiming screws. Round headlight models similar

Parking Lamps

▶ See Figure 75

REMOVAL & INSTALLATION

1. Remove the head lamp assembly attaching screws.
2. Pull the head lamp assembly out and disconnect the parking lamp socket from the head lamp body.
3. Replace the bulb.
4. Installation is the reverse of removal.

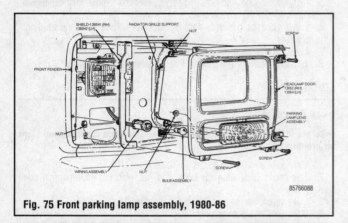

Fig. 75 Front parking lamp assembly, 1980-86

Front Side Marker Lamps

▶ See Figures 76, 77 and 78

REMOVAL & INSTALLATION

1. Remove the two lamp assembly attaching screws. On later models, if only the bulb needs to be replaced the socket can be disconnected from inside the engine compartment without removing the lamp screws as shown.

Fig. 76 Front marker lamp location inside the engine compartment

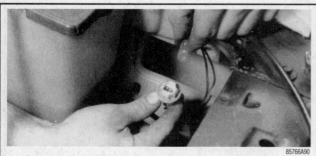

Fig. 77 Twist the front marker lamp socket to remove it from the lamp assembly, then pull out the bulb for replacement

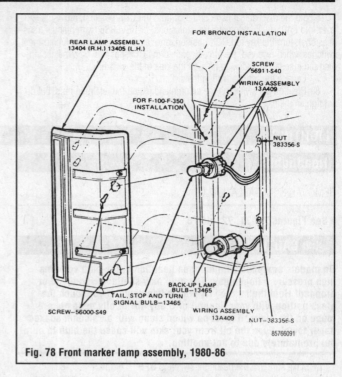

Fig. 78 Front marker lamp assembly, 1980-86

2. Pull the assembly out and disconnect the socket from the lamp body.
3. Replace the bulb.
4. Installation is the reverse of removal.

Rear Lamps

REMOVAL & INSTALLATION

Style Side Pick-Ups and Bronco

▶ See Figures 79, 80, 81 and 82

1. Remove the screws that attach the combination lamp lens assembly and remove the lens.
2. Turn the affected bulb socket counterclockwise to remove the bulb and clockwise to install a new bulb.

Flare Side

The bulbs can be replaced by removing the lens (4 screws). To replace the lamp assembly, remove the 3 nuts from the mounting studs, disconnect the wiring inside the frame rail, unhook the wiring from the retaining clip, pull out the wires and remove the lamp assembly.

Fig. 79 Removing the rear tail lamp assembly retaining screws, Style side pick-up

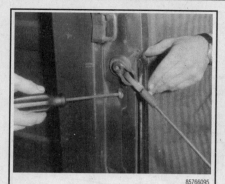

Fig. 80 Removing the rear tail lamp assembly retaining screws

Fig. 81 Removing the bulb and socket from the rear tail lamp assembly

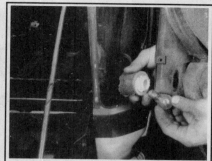

Fig. 82 Removing the bulb from the socket on the rear tail lamp assembly—Style side pick-up shown

Interior Lamps

REMOVAL & INSTALLATION

Dome/Map Lamp

BRONCO

1. Carefully pry the dome lamp lens, at the corners, from the housing.
2. Remove the 2 screws attaching the map lamp lens housing to the lamp base and remove the bulbs. The lamp base is retained to the roof by 4 screws.
3. Installation is the reverse of removal.

F-150/250/350

1. To replace the bulb, snap the lens out of the lamp body and remove the bulb.

2. To remove the lamp body, remove the 4 retaining screws.
3. Installation is the reverse of removal.

Cargo Lamp

REMOVAL & INSTALLATION

F-150/250/350

Remove the 2 lamp retaining screws and remove the lamp. Remove the bulb from the lamp. Installation is the reverse of removal.

Bronco

Carefully unsnap the lamp from the side of the truck, disconnect the wiring and remove the bulb. Installation is the reverse of removal.

TRAILER WIRING

Wiring the truck for towing is fairly easy. There are a number of good wiring kits available and these should be used, rather than trying to design your own. All trailers will need brake lights and turn signals as well as tail lights and side marker lights. Most states require extra marker lights for overly wide trailers. Also, most states have recently required back-up lights for trailers, and most trailer manufacturers have been building trailers with back-up lights for several years.

Additionally, some Class I, most Class II and just about all Class III trailers will have electric brakes.

Add to this number an accessories wire, to operate trailer internal equipment or to charge the trailer's battery, and you can have as many as seven wires in the harness.

Determine the equipment on your trailer and buy the wiring kit necessary. The kit will contain all the wires needed, plus a plug adapter set which included the female plug, mounted on the bumper or hitch, and the male plug, wired into, or plugged into the trailer harness.

When installing the kit, follow the manufacturer's instructions. The color coding of the wires is standard throughout the industry.

One point to note, some domestic vehicles, and most imported vehicles, have separate turn signals. On most domestic vehicles, the brake lights and rear turn signals operate with the same bulb. For those vehicles without separate turn signals, you can purchase an isolation unit so that the brake lights won't blink whenever the turn signals are operated.

One final point, the best kits are those with a spring loaded cover on the vehicle mounted socket. This cover prevents dirt and moisture from corroding the terminals. Never let the vehicle socket hang loosely. Always mount it securely to the bumper or hitch.

➡ **For more information on towing a trailer please refer to Section 1.**

CIRCUIT PROTECTION

Fuses

▶ **See Figures 83 and 84**

On earlier models, the fuse panel is located on the firewall above the driver's left foot.

On later models, the fuse panel is located on the underside of the instrument panel, covered with an access door.

Fuse Link

▶ **See Figure 85**

The fuse link is a short length of special, Hypalon (high temperature) insulated wire, integral with the engine compartment wiring harness and should not

be confused with standard wire. It is several wire gauges smaller than the circuit which it protects. Under no circumstances should a fuse link replacement repair be made using a length of standard wire cut from bulk stock or from another wiring harness.

To repair any blown fuse link use the following procedure:

1. Determine which circuit is damaged, its location and the cause of the open fuse link. If the damaged fuse link is one of three fed by a common No. 10 or 12 gauge feed wire, determine the specific affected circuit.
2. Disconnect the negative battery cable.
3. Cut the damaged fuse link from the wiring harness and discard it. If the fuse link is one of three circuits fed by a single feed wire, cut it out of the harness at each splice end and discard it.
4. Identify and procure the proper fuse link and butt connectors for attaching the fuse link to the harness.
5. To repair any fuse link in a 3-link group with one feed:

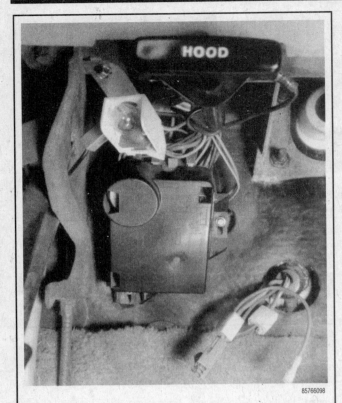

Fig. 83 View of the fuse box located under the hood release lever, 1983 F-150 shown

Fig. 84 Unsnap the cover to access the fuse box, 1983 F-150 shown

a. After cutting the open link out of the harness, cut each of the remaining undamaged fuse links close to the feed wire weld.

b. Strip approximately ½ in. (13mm) of insulation from the detached ends of the two good fuse links. Then insert two wire ends into one end of a butt connector and carefully push one stripped end of the replacement fuse link into the same end of the butt connector and crimp all three firmly together.

➡Care must be taken when fitting the three fuse links into the butt connector as the internal diameter is a snug it for three wires. Make sure to use a proper crimping tool. Pliers, side cutters, etc. will not apply the proper crimp to retain the wires and withstand a pull test.

c. After crimping the butt connector to the three fuse links, cut the weld portion from the feed wire and strip approximately ½ in. (13mm) of insulation from the cut end. Insert the stripped end into the open end of the butt connector and crimp very firmly.

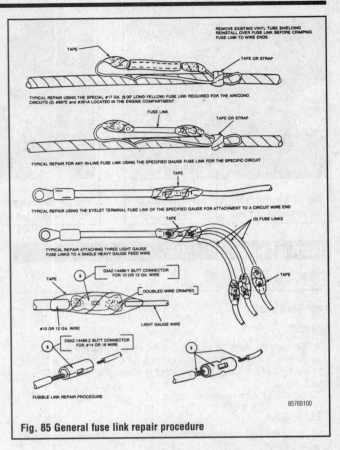

Fig. 85 General fuse link repair procedure

d. To attach the remaining end of the replacement fuse link, strip approximately ½ in. (13mm) of insulation from the wire end of the circuit from which the blown fuse link was removed, and firmly crimp a butt connector or equivalent to the stripped wire. Then, insert the end of the replacement link into the other end of the butt connector and crimp firmly.

e. Using rosin core solder with a consistency of 60 percent tin and 40 percent lead, solder the connectors and the wires at the repairs and insulate with electrical tape.

6. To replace any fuse link on a single circuit in a harness, cut out the damaged portion, strip approximately ½ in. (13mm) of insulation from the two wire ends and attach the appropriate replacement fuse link to the stripped wire ends with two proper size butt connectors. Solder the connectors and wires and insulate the tape.

7. To repair any fuse link which has an eyelet terminal on one end such as the charging circuit, cut off the open fuse link behind the weld, strip approximately ½ in. (13mm) of insulation from the cut end and attach the appropriate new eyelet fuse link to the cut stripped wire with an appropriate size butt connector. Solder the connectors and wires at the repair and insulate with tape.

8. Connect the negative battery cable to the battery and test the system for proper operation.

➡Do not mistake a resistor wire for a fuse link. The resistor wire is generally longer and has print stating, "Resistor: don't cut or splice."

Circuit Breakers

Two circuits are protected by circuit breakers located in the fuse panel: the power windows (20 amp) or power windows and Shift-On-The-Fly (30 amp) and the power door locks (30 amp). The breakers are self-resetting.

Turn Signal and Hazard Flasher Locations

Both the turn signal flasher and the hazard warning flasher are mounted on the fuse panel. The turn signal flasher is mounted on the front of the fuse panel, and the hazard warning flasher is mounted on the rear of the fuse panel.

WIRING DIAGRAMS

WIRING DIAGRAM SYMBOLS

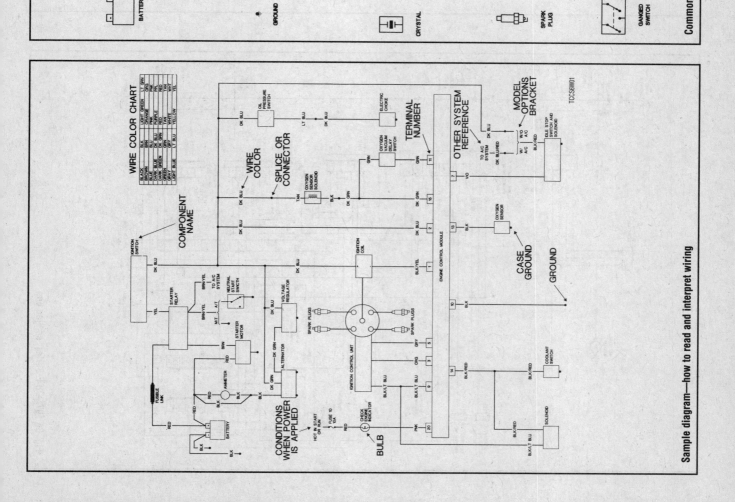

Common wiring diagram symbols

Sample diagram—how to read and interpret wiring

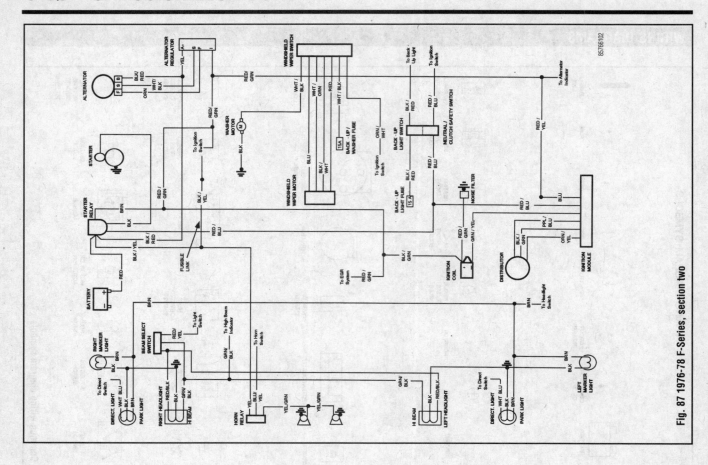

Fig. 87 1976-78 F-Series, section two

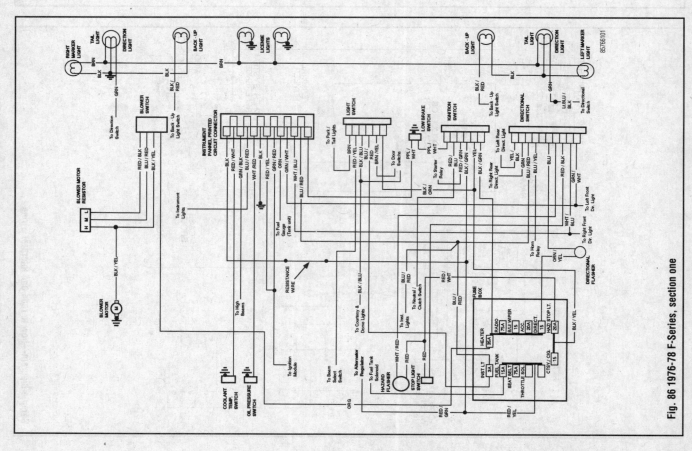

Fig. 86 1976-78 F-Series, section one

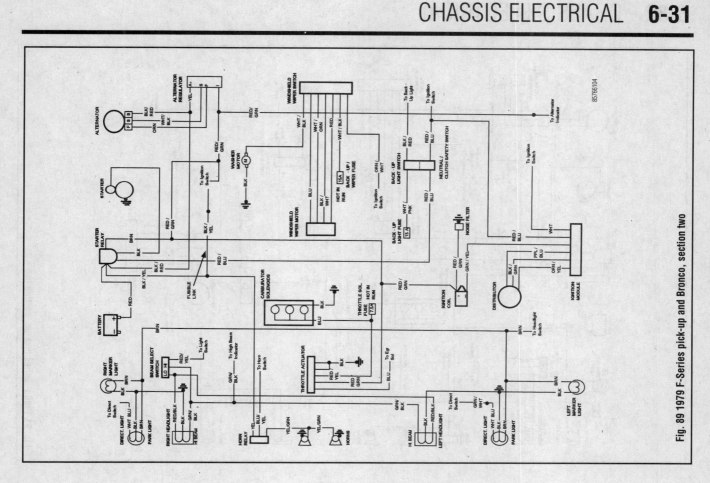

Fig. 89 1979 F-Series pick-up and Bronco, section two

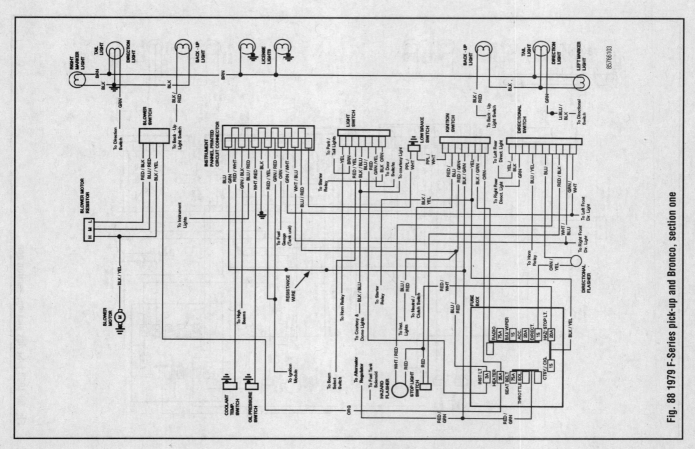

Fig. 88 1979 F-Series pick-up and Bronco, section one

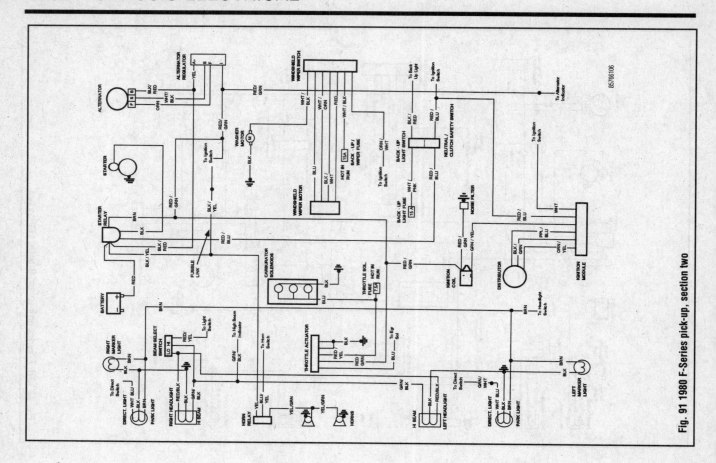

Fig. 91 1980 F-Series pick-up, section two

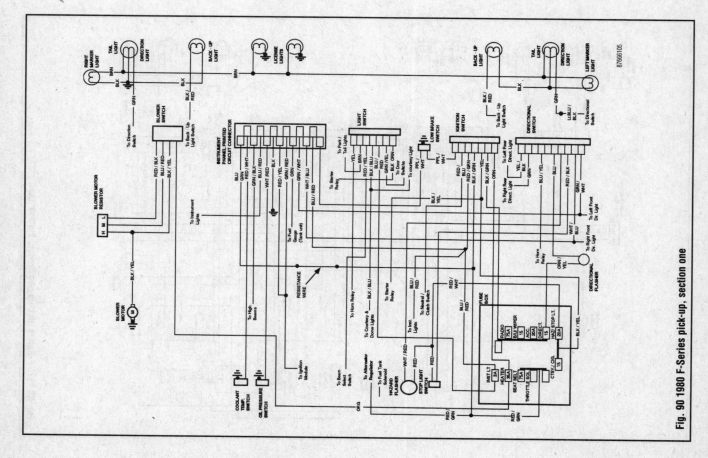

Fig. 90 1980 F-Series pick-up, section one

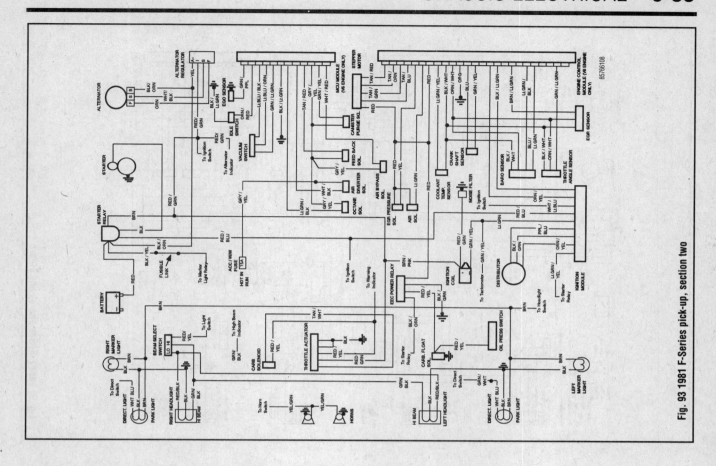

Fig. 93 1981 F-Series pick-up, section two

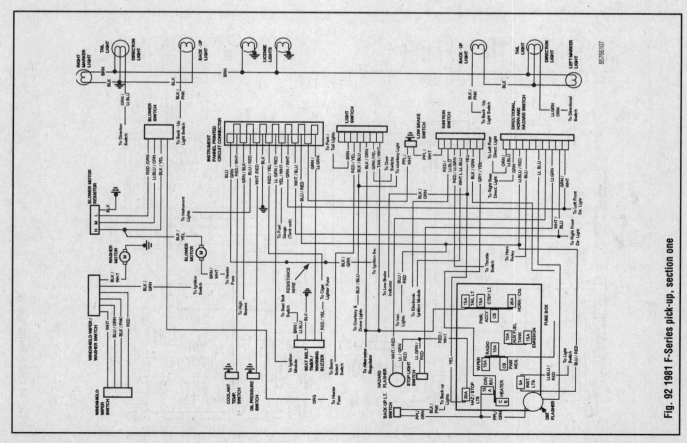

Fig. 92 1981 F-Series pick-up, section one

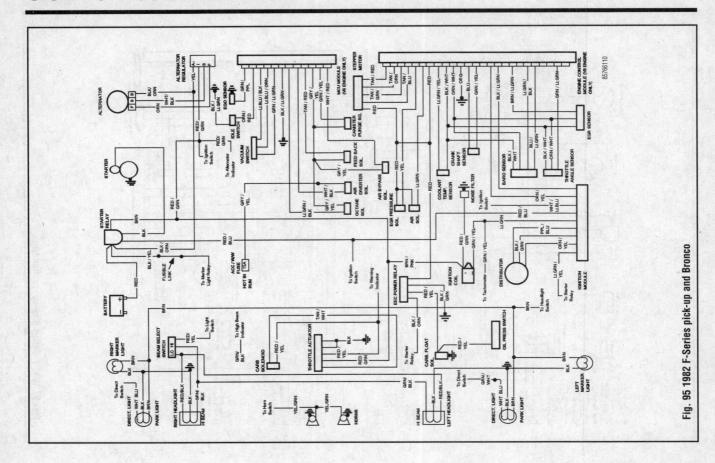

Fig. 95 1982 F-Series pick-up and Bronco

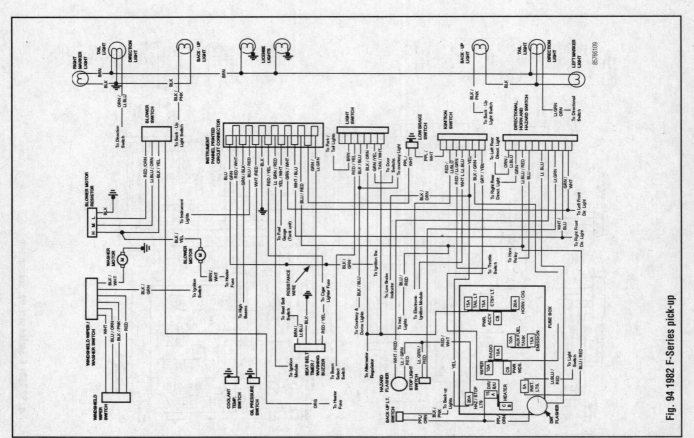

Fig. 94 1982 F-Series pick-up

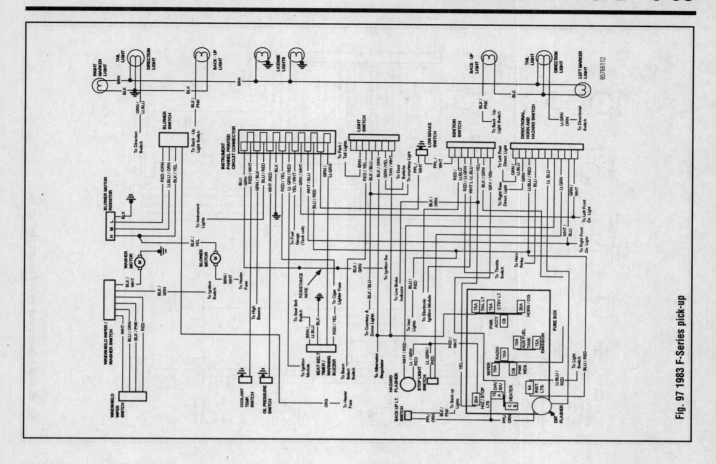

Fig. 97 1983 F-Series pick-up

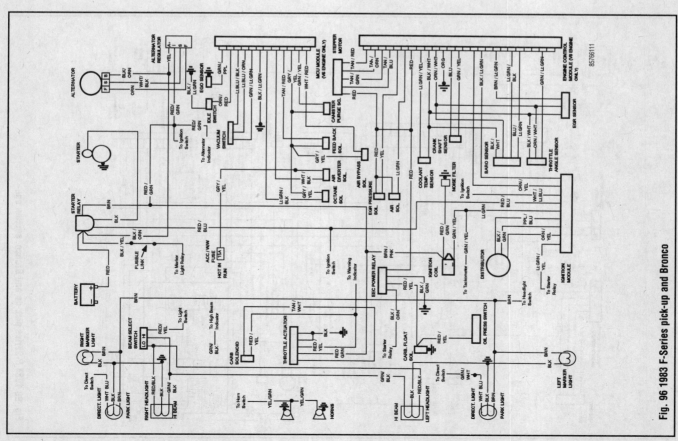

Fig. 96 1983 F-Series pick-up and Bronco

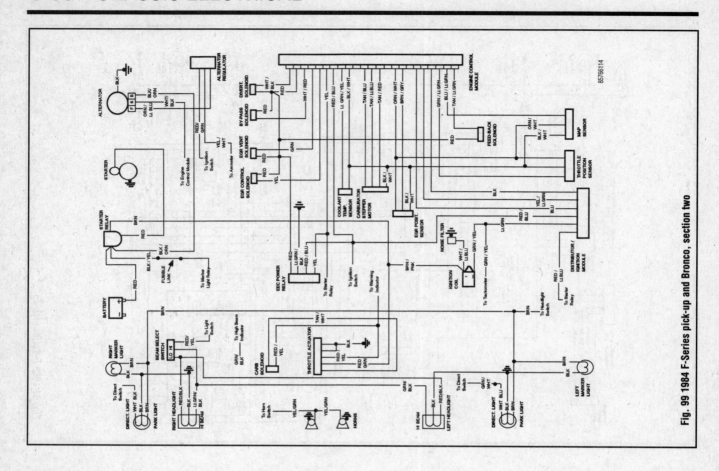

Fig. 99 1984 F-Series pick-up and Bronco, section two

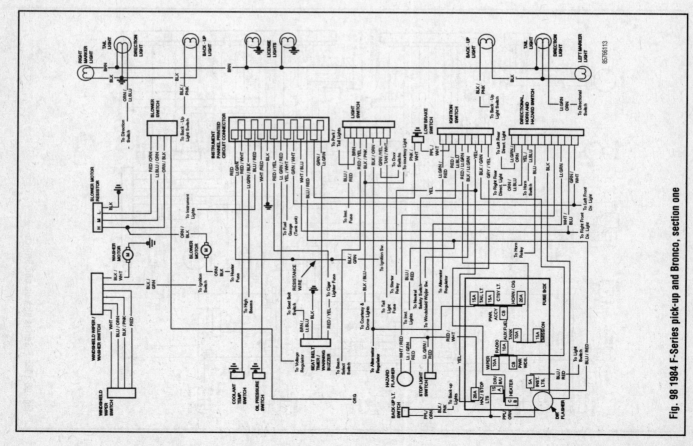

Fig. 98 1984 F-Series pick-up and Bronco, section one

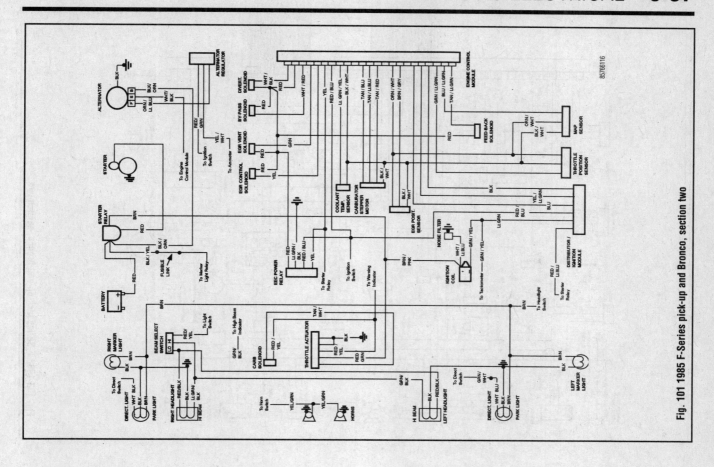

Fig. 101 1985 F-Series pick-up and Bronco, section two

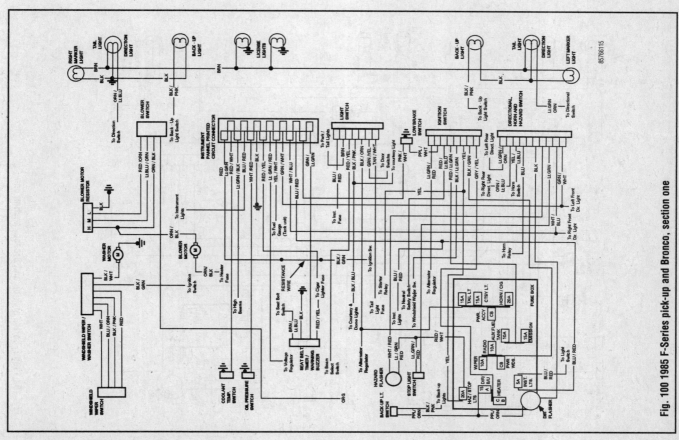

Fig. 100 1985 F-Series pick-up and Bronco, section one

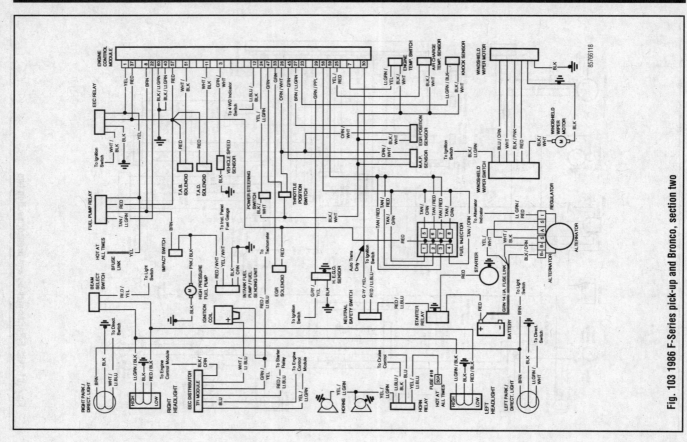

Fig. 103 1986 F-Series pick-up and Bronco, section two

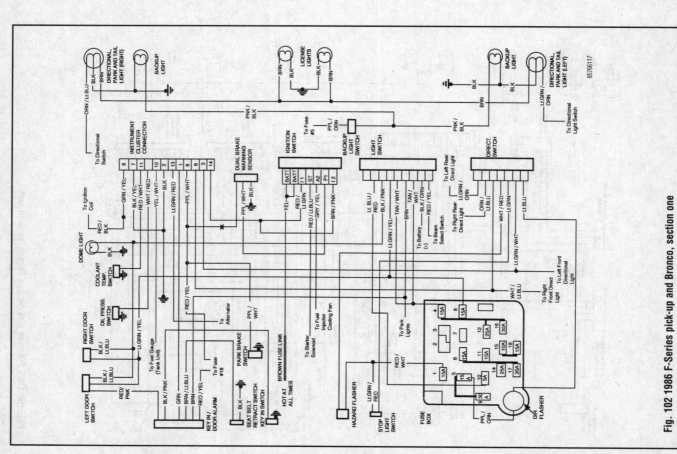

Fig. 102 1986 F-Series pick-up and Bronco, section one

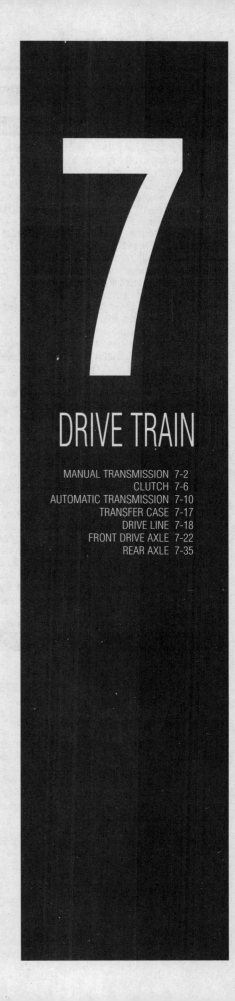

7

DRIVE TRAIN

MANUAL TRANSMISSION

Understanding the Manual Transmission

Because of the way an internal combustion engine breathes, it can produce torque (or twisting force) only within a narrow speed range. Most overhead valve pushrod engines must turn at about 2500 rpm to produce their peak torque. Often by 4500 rpm, they are producing so little torque that continued increases in engine speed produce no power increases.

The torque peak on overhead camshaft engines is, generally, much higher, but much narrower.

The manual transmission and clutch are employed to vary the relationship between engine RPM and the speed of the wheels so that adequate power can be produced under all circumstances. The clutch allows engine torque to be applied to the transmission input shaft gradually, due to mechanical slippage. The vehicle can, consequently, be started smoothly from a full stop.

The transmission changes the ratio between the rotating speeds of the engine and the wheels by the use of gears. 4-speed or 5-speed transmissions are most common. The lower gears allow full engine power to be applied to the rear wheels during acceleration at low speeds.

The clutch driveplate is a thin disc, the center of which is splined to the transmission input shaft. Both sides of the disc are covered with a layer of material which is similar to brake lining and which is capable of allowing slippage without roughness or excessive noise.

The clutch cover is bolted to the engine flywheel and incorporates a diaphragm spring which provides the pressure to engage the clutch. The cover also houses the pressure plate. When the clutch pedal is released, the driven disc is sandwiched between the pressure plate and the smooth surface of the flywheel, thus forcing the disc to turn at the same speed as the engine crankshaft.

The transmission contains a mainshaft which passes all the way through the transmission, from the clutch to the driveshaft. This shaft is separated at one point, so that front and rear portions can turn at different speeds.

Power is transmitted by a countershaft in the lower gears and reverse. The gears of the countershaft mesh with gears on the mainshaft, allowing power to be carried from one to the other. Countershaft gears are often integral with that shaft, while several of the mainshaft gears can either rotate independently of the shaft or be locked to it. Shifting from one gear to the next causes one of the gears to be freed from rotating with the shaft and locks another to it. Gears are locked and unlocked by internal dog clutches which slide between the center of the gear and the shaft. The forward gears usually employ synchronizers; friction members which smoothly bring gear and shaft to the same speed before the toothed dog clutches are engaged.

Adjustments

LINKAGE

Except 4-Speed Overdrive

▶ See Figure 1

1. Place the shifter in the Neutral position and insert a 3/16 inch (4.8mm) gauge pin diameter through the steering column shift levers and the locating hole in the spacer.
2. If the shift rods at the transmission are equipped with threaded sleeves, adjust the sleeves so that they enter the shift levers on the transmission easily with the shift levers in the Neutral position. Now lengthen the rods seven turns of the sleeves and insert them into the shift levers.
3. If the shift rods are slotted, loosen the attaching nut, make sure that the transmission shift levers are in the Neutral position, then retighten the attaching nuts.
4. Remove the gauge pin and check the operation of the shift linkage.

4-Speed Overdrive w/External Linkage

▶ See Figure 2

1. Attach the shift rods to the levers.
2. Rotate the output shaft to determine that the transmission is in neutral.
3. Insert an alignment pin into the shift control assembly alignment hole.

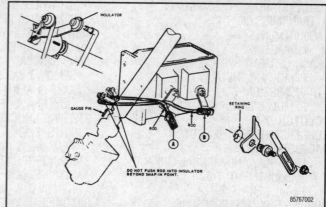

Fig. 1 Three-speed manual transmission shift linkage adjustment—slotted sleeves

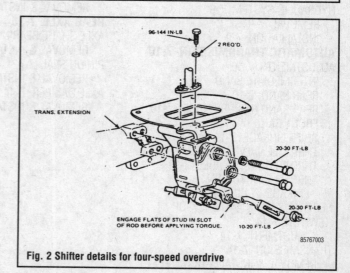

Fig. 2 Shifter details for four-speed overdrive

4. Attach the slotted end of the shift rods over the flats of the studs in the shift control assembly.
5. Install the locknuts and remove the alignment pin.

Back-up Light Switch

REMOVAL & INSTALLATION

The switch is located on the left side of the transmission case. To remove:
1. Disconnect the negative battery cable.
2. Disconnect the back-up switch harness.
3. Remove the back-up switch and the seal.
4. Installation is the reverse of the removal procedure.

Transmission

REMOVAL & INSTALLATION

Ford 3.03 3-Speed

1. Shift the transfer case into Neutral.
2. Remove the bolts attaching the fan shroud to the radiator support, if so equipped.
3. Raise the vehicle on a hoist.

4. Support the transfer case shield with a jack and remove the bolts that attach the shield to the frame side rails. Remove the shield.

5. Drain the transmission and transfer case lubricant. To drain the transmission lubricant, remove the lower extension housing-to-transmission bolt.

6. Disconnect the front and rear driveshafts at the transfer case.

7. Disconnect the speedometer cable at the transfer case.

8. Disconnect the T.R.S. switch, if so equipped.

9. Disconnect the shift rods from the transmission shift levers. Place the First/Reverse gear shift lever into the First gear position and insert the fabricated tool. The tool consists of a length of rod, the same diameter as the holes in the shift levers, which is bent in such a way to fit in the holes in the two shift levers and hold them in the position stated above. More important, this tool will prevent the input shaft roller bearings from dropping into the transmission and output shaft. THIS TOOL IS A MUST.

10. Support the engine with a jack.

11. Remove the two cotter pins, bolts, washers, plate and insulators that secure the crossmember to the transfer case adapter.

12. Remove the crossmember-to-frame side support attaching bolts.

13. Position a transmission jack under the transfer case and remove the upper insulators from the crossmember. Remove the crossmember.

14. Roll back the boot enclosing the transfer case shift linkage. Remove the threaded cap holding the shift lever assembly to the shift bracket. Remove the shift lever assembly.

15. Remove the two lower bolts attaching the transmission to the flywheel housing.

16. Reposition the transmission jack under the transmission and secure it with a chain.

17. Remove the two upper bolts securing the transmission to the flywheel housing. Move the transmission and transfer case rearward and downward out of the vehicle.

18. Move the assembly to a bench and remove the transfer case-to-transmission attaching bolts.

19. Slide the transmission assembly off the transfer case.

To install the transmission:

20. Position the transfer case to the transmission. Apply an oil resistant sealer to the bolt threads and install the attaching bolts. Tighten to 42–50 ft. lbs.

21. Position the transmission and transfer case on a transmission jack and secure them with a chain.

22. Raise the transmission and transfer case assembly into position and install the transmission case to the flywheel housing.

23. Install the two upper and two lower transmission attaching bolts and torque them to 37–42 ft. lbs.

24. Position the transfer case shift lever and install the threaded cap to the shift bracket. Reposition the rubber boot.

25. Raise the transmission and transfer case high enough to provide clearance for installing the crossmember. Position the upper insulators to the crossmember and install the crossmember-to-frame side support attaching bolts.

26. Align the bolt holes in the transfer case adapter with those in the crossmember, then lower the transmission and remove the jack.

27. Install the crossmember-to-transfer case adapter bolts, nuts, insulators, plates and washers. Tighten the nuts and secure them with cotter pins.

28. Remove the engine jack.

29. Remove the fabricated tool and connect each shift rod to its respective lever on the transmission. Adjust the linkage.

30. Connect the speedometer cable.

31. Connect the T.R.S. switch, if so equipped.

32. Install the front and rear driveshafts to the transfer case.

33. Fill the transmission and transfer case to the bottom of the filler hole with the recommended lubricant.

34. Position the transfer case shield to the frame side rails and install the attaching bolts.

35. Lower the vehicle.

36. Install the fan shroud, if so equipped.

37. Check the operation of the transfer case and transmission shift linkage.

Ford RUG 4-Speed OD

1. Raise the vehicle and support it on jackstands.

2. Mark the driveshaft so that it may be installed in the same relative position. Disconnect the driveshaft from the rear U-joint flange. Slide the driveshaft

off the transmission output shaft and install an extension housing seal installation tool, or rags into the extension housing to prevent lubricant leakage.

3. Disconnect the speedometer cable from the extension housing.

4. Remove the retaining clips, flat washers and spring washers that secure the shift rods to the shift levers.

5. Remove the bolts connecting the shift control the transmission extension housing. Remove the nut connecting the shift control to the case.

❊❊ WARNING

A "6" and "8" is stamped on the transmission extension housing by the shift control plate bolts. The "6" and "8" refer to either a 6 or 8 cylinder engine application. The shift plate bolts must be placed in the right holes for proper plate positioning.

6. Remove the rear transmission support connecting bolts attaching the support on the crossmember to the transmission extension housing.

7. Support the engine with a transmission jack and remove the extension housing-to-engine rear support attaching bolts.

8. Raise the rear of the engine high enough to remove the weight from the crossmember. Remove the bolts retaining the crossmember to the frame side supports and remove the crossmember.

9. Support the transmission on a jack and remove the bolts that attach the transmission to the flywheel housing.

10. Move the transmission and jack rearward until the transmission input shaft clears the flywheel housing. If necessary, lower the engine enough to obtain clearance for transmission removal.

❊❊ CAUTION

Do not depress the clutch pedal while the transmission is removed.

To install:

11. Make sure that the mounting surface of the transmission and the flywheel housing are free of dirt, paint, and burrs. Install two guide pins in the flywheel housing lower mounting bolt holes. Move the transmission forward on the guide pins until the input shaft splines enter the clutch hub splines and the case is positioned against the flywheel housing.

12. Install the two upper transmission to flywheel housing mounting bolts snug, and then remove the two guide pins. Install the two lower mounting bolts. Torque all mounting bolts to specifications.

13. Raise the rear of the engine and install the crossmember. Install and torque the crossmember attaching bolts to specifications, then lower the engine.

14. With the transmission extension housing resting on the engine rear support, install the transmission extension housing attaching bolts. Torque the bolts to 42-50 ft. lbs. (57-67 Nm).

15. Position the shift control bracket on the stud on the transmission case and on the bolt attaching holes dependent upon the 6 or 8 cylinder application. See Warning above.

16. Tighten the nut connecting the bracket to the transmission case to 22-30 ft. lbs. Tighten the bolts to 22-30 ft. lbs.

17. Install the retaining clips, flat washers and spring washers that secure the shift rods to the shift levers.

18. Connect the speedometer cable to the extension housing.

19. Remove the extension housing installation tool and slide the forward end of the driveshaft over the transmission output shaft. Connect the driveshaft to the rear U-joint flange.

20. Fill the transmission to the proper level with the specified lubricant.

21. Lower the car. Check the shift and crossover motion for full shift engagement and smooth crossover operation.

NP435

1. Remove the rubber boot and floor mat.

2. Remove the weather pad. It may be necessary first to remove the seat assembly.

3. Disconnect the back-up light switch located in the rear of the gearshift housing cover.

4. Raise the vehicle and position safety stands. Position a transmission jack under the transmission, and disconnect the speedometer cable.

5. Disconnect the parking brake lever from its linkage, and remove the gearshift housing.

6. Disconnect the driveshaft or coupling shaft. Remove the bolts that attach the coupling shaft center support to the crossmember and wire the coupling shaft and driveshaft to one side. Remove the transfer case.

7. Remove the transmission attaching bolts at the clutch housing, and remove the transmission.

Before installing the transmission apply a light film of chassis lubricant to the release lever fulcrum and fork. Do not apply a thick coat of grease to these parts, as it will work out and contaminate the clutch disc.

8. Place the transmission on a transmission jack, and raise the transmission until the input shaft splines are aligned with the clutch disc splines. The clutch release bearing and hub must be properly positioned in the release lever fork.

9. Install guide studs in the clutch housing and slide the transmission forward on the guide studs until it is in position on the clutch housing. Install the attaching bolts or nuts, and tighten them to the following torques:
- 7/16–14; 40–50 ft. lbs.
- 5/8–11; 120–150 ft. lbs.
- 9/16–12; 90–115 ft. lbs.
- 5/8–18C; 120–150 ft. lbs.
- 9/16–18C; 90–115 ft. lbs.

Remove the guide studs and install the two lower attaching bolts.

10. Install the bolts attaching the coupling shaft center support to the crossmember. Tighten the bolts to 40–50 ft. lbs.

11. Connect the driveshaft or coupling shaft and the speedometer cable. Tighten the U-joint nuts.

12. Connect the back-up light switch wire.

13. Install the transmission cover plate. Install the seat assembly if it was removed.

14. Install weather pad, pad retainer, floor mat, and rubber boot.

T-18

1. Open door cover seat.
2. Remove shift knobs.
3. Remove the four screws attaching the transmission shift lever boot assembly.
4. Remove the four screws holding the floor mat.
5. Remove the eleven screws holding the access cover to the floor pan. Place the shift lever in the reverse position and remove the cover.
6. Remove the insulator and dust cover.
7. Remove the transfer case shift lever.
8. Remove the eight bolts holding the shift cover and gasket.
9. Use cardboard or heavy paper to fabricate a suitable cover for the shift cover opening to protect the transmission from dirt during removal.
10. Raise the vehicle on a hoist.
11. Remove the drain pan and drain the transmission.
12. Disconnect the rear driveshaft from the transfer case and wire it out of the way.
13. Disconnect the front driveshaft from the transfer case and wire it out of the way.
14. Remove the cotter key that holds the shift link in place and remove the shift link.
15. Remove the speedometer cable from the transfer case.
16. Position a transmission jack under the transfer case. Remove the six bolts holding the transfer case to the transmission and lower the transfer case from the vehicle.
17. Remove the eight bolts that hold the rear support bracket to the transmission.
18. Position a transmission jack under the transmission and remove the rear support bracket and brace.
19. Remove the four bolts that hold the transmission tot he bell housing.
20. Remove the transmission from the vehicle.
To install:
21. Place the transmission on a transmission jack and install it in the vehicle installing two guide studs in the bell housing top holes, to guide the transmission into position.
22. Install the two lower bolts. Remove the guide studs and install the upper bolts.
23. Place the rear support bracket in position and install the eight retaining bolts.
24. Install the two bolts at the rear support insulator bracket. Remove the transmission jack.

25. Position the transfer case on the transmission jack and install the six retaining bolts and gasket. Position the transfer case on the transmission and tighten the bolts to 50–60 ft. lbs.
26. Install the transfer case shift link and cotter pin.
27. Position and install the speedometer cable.
28. Remove wire and connect front driveshaft.
29. Remove wire and connect rear driveshaft.
30. Fill transfer case and manual transmission with lubricant.
31. Lower vehicle.
32. Remove fabricated dirt shield and prepare gasket area.
33. Position gasket and shift cover.
34. Install two pilot bolts, then install remaining shift cover retaining bolts.
35. Install transfer case shift handle.
36. Install dust cover and insulator.
37. Install access cover to floor pan screws.
38. Install the four floor mat screws.
39. Install the four boot area screws.
40. Install the shift knobs.

T-19

1. Open door cover seat.
2. Remove shift knobs.
3. Remove the four screws attaching the transmission shift lever boot assembly.
4. Remove the four screws holding the floor mat.
5. Remove the eleven screws holding the access cover to the floor pan. Place the shift lever in the reverse position and remove the cover.
6. Remove the insulator and dust cover.
7. Remove the transfer case shift lever.
8. Remove transmission shift lever.
9. Raise the vehicle on a hoist.
10. Remove the drain plug and drain the transmission.
11. Disconnect the rear driveshaft from the transfer case and wire it out of the way.
12. Disconnect the front driveshaft from the transfer case and wire it out of the way.
13. Remove the retainer ring that holds the shift link in place and remove the shift link from transfer case.
14. Remove the speedometer cable from the transfer case.
15. Position a transmission jack under the transfer case. Remove the six bolts holding the transfer case to the transmission and lower the transfer case from the vehicle.
16. Remove the eight bolts that hold the rear support bracket to the transmission.
17. Position a transmission jack under the transmission and remove the rear support bracket and brace.
18. Remove the four bolts that hold the transmission to the bell housing.
19. Remove the transmission from the vehicle.
To install:
20. Place the transmission on a transmission jack and install it in the vehicle installing two guide studs in the bell housing top holes, to guide the transmission into position.
21. Install the two lower bolts. Remove the guide studs and install the upper bolts.
22. Place the rear support bracket in position and install the eight retaining bolts. Torque to 35–50 ft. lbs.
23. Install the two bolts at the rear support insulator bracket. Remove the transmission jack.
24. Position the transfer case on the transmission jack and install the six retaining bolts and gasket. Position the transfer case on the transmission and tighten the bolts to 28–33 ft. lbs.
25. Install the transfer case shift link and retainer ring.
26. Position and install the speedometer cable.
27. Remove wire and connect front driveshaft.
28. Remove wire and connect rear driveshaft.
29. Fill transfer case and transmission.
30. Lower vehicle.
31. Remove fabricated dirt shield and prepare gasket area.
32. Position gasket and shift cover.
33. Install two pilot bolts, then install remaining shift cover retaining bolts.
34. Install transfer case shift handle and transmission shift lever.

35. Install dust cover and insulator.
36. Install access cover to floor pan screws.
37. Install the four floor mat screws.
38. Install the four boot area screws.
39. Install the shift knobs.

Ford Single Rail and TOD (2x4) Overdrive

1. Raise the vehicle and support it on jackstands.
2. Mark the driveshaft so that it may be installed in the same relative position. Disconnect the driveshaft from the rear U-joint flange. Slide the driveshaft off the transmission output shaft and install an extension housing seal installation tool, or rags into the extension housing to prevent lubricant leakage.
3. Disconnect the speedometer cable from the extension housing.
4. Remove three screws securing shift lever to turret assembly.
5. Remove shift lever from turret assembly.
6. Support the engine with a transmission jack and remove the extension housing-to-engine rear support attaching bolts.
7. Raise the rear of the engine high enough to remove the weight from the crossmember. Remove the bolts retaining the crossmember to the frame side supports and remove the crossmember.
8. Support the transmission on a jack and remove the bolts that attach the transmission to the flywheel housing.
9. Move the transmission and jack rearward until the transmission input shaft clears the flywheel housing. If necessary, lower the engine enough to obtain clearance for transmission removal.

✳✳ CAUTION

Do not depress the clutch pedal while the transmission is removed.

To install:

10. Make sure that the mounting surface of the transmission and the flywheel housing are free of dirt, paint, and burrs. Install two guide pins in the flywheel housing lower mounting bolt holes. Move the transmission forward on the guide pins until the input shaft splines enter the clutch hub splines and the case is positioned against the flywheel housing.
11. Install the two upper transmission to flywheel housing mounting bolts snug, and then remove the two guide pins. Install the two lower mounting bolts. Torque all mounting bolts to specifications.
12. Raise the rear of the engine and install the crossmember. Install and torque the crossmember attaching bolts to specifications, then lower the engine.
13. With the transmission extension housing resting on the engine rear support, install the transmission extension housing attaching bolts. Torque the bolts to specifications.
14. Position shift tower to extension housing and secure with three screws.
15. Connect the speedometer cable to the extension housing.
16. Remove the extension housing installation tool and slide the forward end of the driveshaft over the transmission output shaft. Connect the driveshaft to the rear U-joint flange.
17. Fill the transmission to the proper level with the specified lubricant.
18. Lower the car. Check the shift and crossover motion for full shift engagement and smooth crossover operation.

Ford TOD (4x4) Overdrive

1. Raise the vehicle and support it on jackstands.
2. Drain the transmission and/or transfer case.
3. Disconnect the 4WD indicator switch and back-up lamps switch wires at the transmission.
4. Remove the skid plate from the frame, if so equipped.
5. Mark the front and rear driveshaft so they may be installed in the same relative position. Disconnect the rear driveshaft from the transfer case and wire it out of the way.
6. Disconnect the front driveshaft from the transfer case and wire it out of the way.
7. Disconnect the speedometer cable from the transfer case.
8. Remove the retaining clips and shift rod from the transfer case control lever and transfer case shift lever.
9. Disconnect the vent hose from the transfer case.
10. Remove the shift lever from the transmission.

11. Support the transmission with a transmission jack and remove the transmission housing rear support bracket.
12. Raise the rear of the engine high enough to remove the weight from the crossmember. Remove the two nuts connecting the upper gusset to frame on both sides.
13. Remove the nut and bolt assembly connecting the gusset to the support. remove the gusset on the left side.
14. Remove the bolts holding the transmission to the transmission support plate on the crossmember.
15. Raise the transmission with a transmission jack.
16. Remove the nut and bolt assemblies connecting the support plate to the crossmember. Remove the support plate and remove the right gusset.
17. Remove the nut and bolt assemblies connecting the crossmember to the frame and remove the crossmember.
18. Support the transfer case with a transmission jack.
19. Remove the 6 bolts retaining the transfer case to the transmission adapter.
20. Slide the transfer case rearward off the transmission output shaft and lower the transfer case from the vehicle. Remove the gasket between the case and the adapter.
21. Support the transmission on a transmission jack and remove the bolts that attach the transmission to the flywheel housing.
22. Move the transmission and jack rearward until the transmission input shaft clears the flywheel housing. If necessary, lower the engine enough to obtain clearance for transmission removal.

✳✳ CAUTION

Do not depress the clutch pedal while the transmission is removed.

To install:

23. Make sure that the mounting surface of the transmission and the flywheel housing are free of dirt, paint, and burrs. Install two guide pins in the flywheel housing lower mounting bolt holes. Move the transmission forward on the guide pins until the input shaft splines enter the clutch hub splines and the case is positioned against the flywheel housing.
24. Install the two upper transmission to flywheel housing mounting bolts snug, and then remove the two guide pins. Install the two lower mounting bolts. Torque all mounting bolts to specifications.
25. Install the heat shield on the transfer case.
26. Place a new gasket between the transfer case and the transmission adapter. Raise the transfer case on a transmission jack so the transmission output shaft aligns with the splined transfer case input shaft. Slide the transfer case forward on to the transmission output shaft and onto the the adapter. Install the bolts retaining the transfer case to the adapter and tighten to 25-43 ft. lbs. (34-59 Nm).
27. Place the shift rod on the transfer case control lever and transfer case shift lever and attach both the retaining rings.
28. Install the shift lever to the transmission.
29. Connect the speedometer cable to the transfer case.
30. Connect the 4WD indicator switch and back-up lamps switch wires to the transmission.
31. Install the crossmember and transmission support bracket and position the right and left gussets on the bolts in the frame. Install the nuts on the upper gusset to frame bolts and tighten to specifications.
32. Install the crossmember to frame nut and bolt assembly and tighten to specification.
33. Install the nut and bolt assembly connecting the gusset to the crossmember and tighten to specification.
34. Install the nut and bolt assemblies connecting the transmission support bracket to the crossmember and tighten to specification.
35. Lower the transmission onto the support bracket.
36. Install the bolts connecting the transmission support bracket to the transmission and tighten to specification.
37. Install the skid plate to the frame, if so equipped.
38. Remove the transfer case transmission support jack.
39. Connect the rear driveshaft to the to rear output shaft yoke and tighten the nut to 20-28 ft. lbs. (28-33 Nm).
40. Connect the front driveshaft to the to front output yoke and tighten the nut to 8-15 ft. lbs. (11-20 Nm).
41. Fill the transfer case and transmission to the proper level with the correct fluid

CLUTCH

Understanding the Clutch

The purpose of the clutch is to disconnect and connect engine power at the transmission. A vehicle at rest requires a lot of engine torque to get all that weight moving. An internal combustion engine does not develop a high starting torque (unlike steam engines) so it must be allowed to operate without any load until it builds up enough torque to move the vehicle. To a point, torque increases with engine rpm. The clutch allows the engine to build up torque by physically disconnecting the engine from the transmission, relieving the engine of any load or resistance.

The transfer of engine power to the transmission (the load) must be smooth and gradual; if it weren't, drive line components would wear out or break quickly. This gradual power transfer is made possible by gradually releasing the clutch pedal. The clutch disc and pressure plate are the connecting link between the engine and transmission. When the clutch pedal is released, the disc and plate contact each other (the clutch is engaged) physically joining the engine and transmission. When the pedal is pushed in, the disc and plate separate (the clutch is disengaged) disconnecting the engine from the transmission.

Most clutch assemblies consists of the flywheel, the clutch disc, the clutch pressure plate, the throw out bearing and fork, the actuating linkage and the pedal. The flywheel and clutch pressure plate (driving members) are connected to the engine crankshaft and rotate with it. The clutch disc is located between the flywheel and pressure plate, and is splined to the transmission shaft. A driving member is one that is attached to the engine and transfers engine power to a driven member (clutch disc) on the transmission shaft. A driving member (pressure plate) rotates (drives) a driven member (clutch disc) on contact and, in so doing, turns the transmission shaft.

There is a circular diaphragm spring within the pressure plate cover (transmission side). In a relaxed state (when the clutch pedal is fully released) this spring is convex; that is, it is dished outward toward the transmission. Pushing in the clutch pedal actuates the attached linkage. Connected to the other end of this is the throw out fork, which hold the throw out bearing. When the clutch pedal is depressed, the clutch linkage pushes the fork and bearing forward to contact the diaphragm spring of the pressure plate. The outer edges of the spring are secured to the pressure plate and are pivoted on rings so that when the center of the spring is compressed by the throw out bearing, the outer edges bow outward and, by so doing, pull the pressure plate in the same direction — away from the clutch disc. This action separates the disc from the plate, disengaging the clutch and allowing the transmission to be shifted into another gear. A coil type clutch return spring attached to the clutch pedal arm permits full release of the pedal. Releasing the pedal pulls the throw out bearing away from the diaphragm spring resulting in a reversal of spring position. As bearing pressure is gradually released from the spring center, the outer edges of the spring bow outward, pushing the pressure plate into closer contact with the clutch disc. As the disc and plate move closer together, friction between the two increases and slippage is reduced until, when full spring pressure is applied (by fully releasing the pedal) the speed of the disc and plate are the same. This stops all slipping, creating a direct connection between the plate and disc which results in the transfer of power from the engine to the transmission. The clutch disc is now rotating with the pressure plate at engine speed and, because it is splined to the transmission shaft, the shaft now turns at the same engine speed.

The clutch is operating properly if:
1. It will stall the engine when released with the vehicle held stationary.
2. The shift lever can be moved freely between 1st and reverse gears when the vehicle is stationary and the clutch disengaged.

Adjustments

FREE-PLAY AND MANUAL LINKAGE ADJUSTMENT

▶ **See Figures 3, 4 and 5**

1. Measure the clutch pedal free-play by depressing the pedal slowly until the free-play between the release bearing assembly and the pressure plate is removed. Note this measurement. The difference between this measurement and when the pedal is not depressed is the free-play measurement.
2. If the free-play measurement is less than ½–¾ inch (12.7–19.05mm), the clutch linkage must be adjusted.

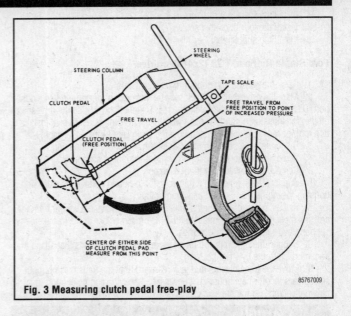

Fig. 3 Measuring clutch pedal free-play

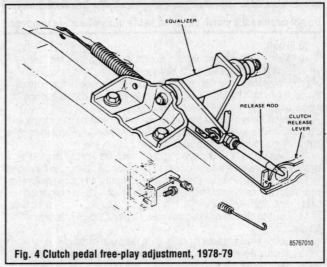

Fig. 4 Clutch pedal free-play adjustment, 1978-79

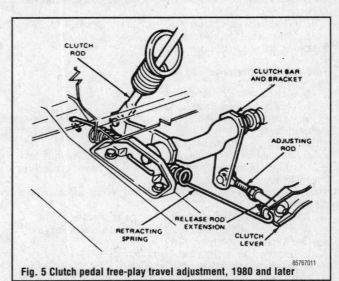

Fig. 5 Clutch pedal free-play travel adjustment, 1980 and later

3. Loosen the two jam nuts on the release rod under the truck and back off both nuts several turns.

4. Loosen or tighten the first jam nut (nearest the release lever) against the bullet (rod extension) until a free-play measurement of ¾–1½ inch (19.05–38.1mm) is obtained. A free-play measurement closer to 1½ inch (38.1mm) is more desirable.

5. When the correct free-play measurement is obtained, hold the first jam nut in position and securely tighten the other nut against the first.

6. Recheck the free-play adjustment. Total pedal travel is fixed and is not adjustable.

PEDAL HEIGHT

1976–79

1. Measure the clutch pedal free travel using a steel tape. Measure the distance from the clutch pedal pad to the steering wheel rim. Depress the pedal slowly until the free travel between the release bearing assembly and the pressure plate assembly is taken up. Note this measurement. The difference between the two measurements is the free travel.

2. If the free travel measurement is less than ½ inch (12.7mm) on 1978 models or ¾ inch (19.05mm) on 1979 models, or greater than 2 inches (51mm) on 1978 models or 1½ inches (38mm) 1979 models, the clutch linkage must be adjusted.

3. With retracting spring removed, hold the release rod firmly against release lever, eliminating lever free play.

4. Position first jam nut 0.062 inch (1.6mm) from the bar while holding needle firmly against release lever.

5. Position second jam nut finger tight against the first nut, while holding second nut. Lock the first nut with 15–20 ft. lbs. torque. This gives ¾–1½ inch (19–38mm) at pedal pad with 1½ inch (38mm) preferred.

6. Check adjustment with retracting spring in place.

1980–86

1. Measure the clutch pedal free travel using a steel tape. Measure the distance from the clutch pedal pad to the steering wheel rim. Depress the pedal slowly until the free travel between the release bearing assembly and the pressure plate assembly is taken up. Note this measurement. The difference between the two measurements is the free travel.

2. If the free travel measurement is less than ½ inch (12.7mm) or more than 2 inch (51mm), the clutch linkage must be adjusted.

3. Remove the retracting spring.

4. Loosen the two jam nuts on the release rod assembly and back off both nuts several turns.

5. Slide the release rod extension (bullet) firmly against the release lever. Push the release rod forward against the equalizer bar lever to eliminate all free-play from the linkage system.

6. Insert 0.135 inch (3.4mm) thick gauge between the jam nut and bullet. Tighten the first jam nut finger tight against the gauge with all free-play eliminated.

7. Tighten the second jam nut finger tight against the first jam nut. Hold the first nut and tighten the second jam nut to 15–20 ft. lbs. Free-play should measure ¾–1½ inch (19–38mm) at the pedal.

8. With the recommended free travel obtained, and holding the first jam nut, position and securely tighten the second jam nut against the first jam nut.

9. Recheck the pedal free travel.

Driven Disc and Pressure Plate

REMOVAL & INSTALLATION

✳✳ CAUTION

The clutch driven disc may contain asbestos, which has been determined to be a cancer causing agent. Never clean clutch surfaces with compressed air! Avoid inhaling any dust from clutch surface! When cleaning clutch surfaces, use a commercially available brake cleaning fluid.

1976–79

▶ See Figures 6 and 7

1. Disconnect the release lever retracting spring and pushrod assembly at the lever.

2. Refer to the appropriate transmission part of this chapter for instructions and remove the transmission from the vehicle.

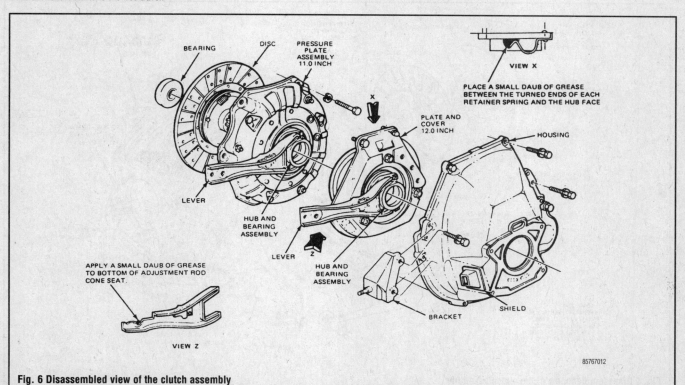

Fig. 6 Disassembled view of the clutch assembly

85767012

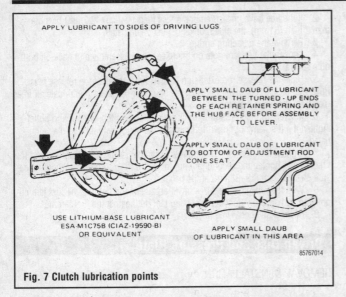

APPLY LUBRICANT TO SIDES OF DRIVING LUGS

APPLY SMALL DAUB OF LUBRICANT BETWEEN THE TURNED - UP ENDS OF EACH RETAINER SPRING AND THE HUB FACE BEFORE ASSEMBLY TO LEVER.

APPLY SMALL DAUB OF LUBRICANT TO BOTTOM OF ADJUSTMENT ROD CONE SEAT.

USE LITHIUM-BASE LUBRICANT ESA-M1C75B (C1AZ-19590-B) OR EQUIVALENT

APPLY SMALL DAUB OF LUBRICANT IN THIS AREA

85767014

Fig. 7 Clutch lubrication points

3. If the clutch housing is not provided with a dust cover, remove the starting motor. Remove the flywheel housing attaching bolts and remove the housing.

4. If the flywheel housing is provided with a dust cover, remove it from the housing. Remove the release lever and release bearing from the clutch housing.

5. Mark the pressure plate and cover assembly and the flywheel, so that the parts can be reinstalled in the same relative position.

6. Loosen the pressure plate and cover attaching bolts evenly until the pressure plate springs are expanded, and remove the bolts.

7. Remove the pressure plate and cover assembly and the clutch disc from the flywheel or through the opening in the bottom of the clutch housing. Remove the pilot bearing only for replacement.

To install:

8. Position the clutch disc on the flywheel so that the pilot tool can enter the clutch pilot bearing and align the disc.

9. When installing the original pressure plate and cover assembly, align the assembly and flywheel according to the marks made during the removal operations. Position the pressure plate and cover assembly on the flywheel, align the pressure plate and disc, and install the retaining bolts that fasten the assembly to the flywheel. Tighten the bolts to 20–30 ft. lbs. and remove the clutch disc pilot tool.

10. With the clutch fully released, apply a light film of lithium base grease ESA-M1C75-B or equivalent on the sides of the driving lugs.

11. Position the clutch release bearing and the bearing hub on the release lever. Install the release lever on the trunnion in the flywheel housing. Apply a light film of lithium base grease ESA-M1C75-B or equivalent to the release lever fingers and to the lever trunnion or fulcrum. Fill the annular groove of the release bearing hub with grease.

12. If the flywheel housing has been removed, position it against the engine rear cover plate, and install the attaching bolts. Tighten the bolts to 40–50 ft. lbs.

13. Install the starter motor. Install the transmission assembly on the clutch housing. Tighten the bolts to 50–60 ft. lbs.

14. Install the slave cylinder on vehicles so equipped, and tighten the bolts.

15. Adjust the release lever pushrod assembly. Connect the release lever retracting spring.

16. Install the clutch housing dust cover if so equipped.

1980–86

♦ See Figure 8

1. Disconnect the release lever retracting spring and pushrod assembly at the lever. Remove starter.

2. Refer to the appropriate transmission part of this chapter for instructions and remove the transmission from the vehicle.

3. If the clutch housing is not provided with a dust cover, remove the starter. Remove the flywheel housing attaching bolts and remove the housing.

4. If the flywheel housing is provided with a dust cover, remove it from the housing. Remove the release lever and release bearing from the clutch housing.

5. Loosen the pressure plate and cover attaching bolts evenly until the pressure plate springs are expanded, and remove the bolts.

6. Remove the pressure plate and cover assembly and the clutch disc from the flywheel or through the opening in the bottom of the clutch housing. Remove the pilot bearing only for replacement.

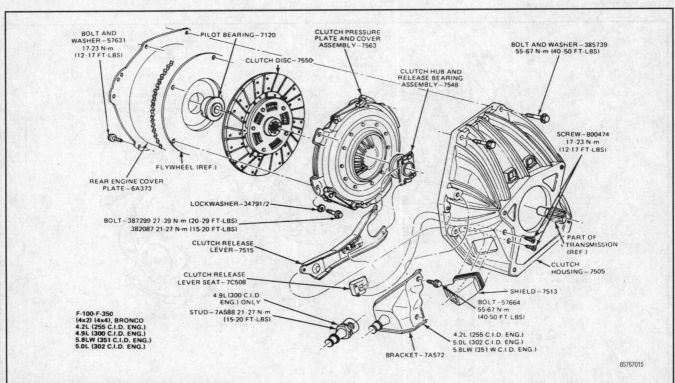

BOLT AND WASHER – 57631 17-23 N·m (12-17 FT-LBS)

PILOT BEARING – 7120

CLUTCH PRESSURE PLATE AND COVER ASSEMBLY – 7563

BOLT AND WASHER – 385739 55-67 N·m (40-50 FT-LBS)

CLUTCH DISC – 7550

CLUTCH HUB AND RELEASE BEARING ASSEMBLY – 7548

SCREW – 800474 17-23 N·m (12-17 FT-LBS)

FLYWHEEL (REF.)

REAR ENGINE COVER PLATE – 6A373

LOCKWASHER – 34791/2

BOLT 387299 27-39 N·m (20-29 FT-LBS) 382087 21-27 N·m (15-20 FT-LBS)

CLUTCH RELEASE LEVER – 7515

CLUTCH RELEASE LEVER SEAT – 7C508

4.9L (300 C.I.D. ENG.) ONLY

STUD – 7A588 21-27 N·m (15-20 FT-LBS)

PART OF TRANSMISSION (REF.)

CLUTCH HOUSING – 7505

SHIELD – 7513

BOLT – 57664 55-67 N·m (40-50 FT LBS)

4.2L (255 C.I.D. ENG.) 5.0L (302 C.I.D. ENG.) 5.8LW (351 W C.I.D. ENG.)

BRACKET – 7A572

F-100-F-350 (4x2) (4x4), BRONCO 4.2L (255 C.I.D. ENG.) 4.9L (300 C.I.D. ENG.) 5.8LW (351 C.I.D. ENG.) 5.0L (302 C.I.D. ENG.)

85767015

Fig. 8 Disassembled view of the clutch assembly

To install:

7. Position the clutch disc on the flywheel so that the pilot tool can enter the clutch pilot bearing and align the disc.

8. When installing the original pressure plate and cover assembly, align the assembly and flywheel according to the marks made during the removal operations. Position the pressure plate and cover assembly on the flywheel, align the pressure plate and disc, and install the retaining bolts that fasten the assembly to the flywheel. Tighten the bolts to 20–30 ft. lbs., and remove the clutch disc pilot tool.

9. Position the clutch release bearing and the bearing hub on the release lever. Install the release lever on the pivot bar pedestal in the flywheel housing. Apply a light film of lithium base grease ESA-M1C75-B or equivalent to the release lever fingers and to the lever pivot ball. Fill the annular groove of the release bearing hub with grease.

10. If the flywheel housing has been removed, position it against the engine rear cover plate and install the attaching bolts. Tighten the bolts to 40–50 ft. lbs.

11. Install the starter motor. Install the transmission assembly on the clutch housing. Tighten the bolts.

12. Adjust the release lever pushrod assembly. Connect the release lever retracting spring.

13. Install the clutch housing dust cover if so equipped.

Hydraulic System

▶ **See Figure 9**

➥**This applies to 1983-1984 models with 6.9L diesel engines, 7.5L (460cu. in.) gas engines, and all 1985-86 models with manual transmissions.**

The hydraulic clutch system operates much like a hydraulic brake system. When you push down (disengage) the clutch pedal, the mechanical clutch pedal movement is converted into hydraulic fluid movement, which is then converted back into mechanical movement by the slave cylinder to actuate the clutch release lever.

The system consists of a combination clutch fluid reservoir/master cylinder assembly, a slave cylinder mounted on the bellhousing, and connecting tubing.

Fluid level is checked at the master cylinder reservoir. The hydraulic clutch system continually remains in adjustment, like a hydraulic disc brake system, so not clutch linkage or pedal adjustment is necessary.

REMOVAL

The clutch hydraulic system is serviced as a complete assembly and is pre-filled and bled. Individual components are not available.

❋❋ WARNING

Prior to any vehicle service that requires removal of the slave cylinder, such as transmission and/or clutch housing removal, the clutch master cylinder pushrod must be disconnected from the clutch pedal. Failure to do this may damage the slave cylinder if the clutch pedal is depressed while the slave cylinder is disconnected.

1. From inside the truck cab, remove the cotter pin retaining the clutch master cylinder pushrod to the clutch pedal lever. Disconnect the pushrod and remove the bushing.

2. Remove the two nuts retaining the clutch reservoir and master cylinder assembly to the firewall.

3. From the engine compartment, remove the clutch reservoir and master cylinder assembly from the firewall. Note here how the clutch tubing routes to the slave cylinder.

4. Push the release lever forward to compress the slave cylinder.

5. On all engines except the diesel and the 7.5L gasoline engines, remove the plastic clip that retains the slave cylinder to the bracket. Remove the slave cylinder.

6. On the diesel and the 7.5L, the steel retaining clip is permanently attached to the slave cylinder. Remove the slave cylinder by prying on the clip to free the tangs while pulling the cylinder clear.

7. Remove the release lever by pulling it outward.

8. Remove the clutch hydraulic system from the truck.

INSTALLATION

1. Position the clutch pedal reservoir and master cylinder assembly into the firewall from inside the cab, and install the two nuts and tighten.

2. Route the clutch tubing and slave cylinder to the bell housing, taking care that the nylon lines are kept away from any hot exhaust system components.

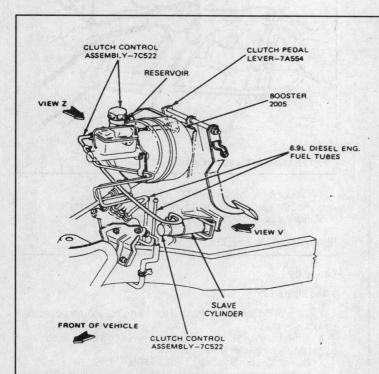
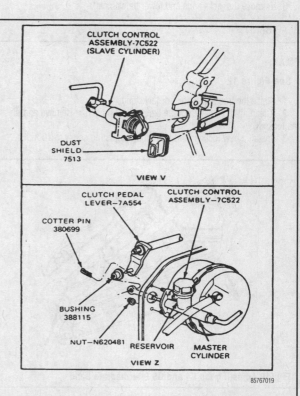

Fig. 9 Hydraulic clutch system, 1983-86

85767019

3. Install the slave cylinder by pushing the slave cylinder pushrod into the cylinder. Engage the pushrod into the release lever and slide the slave cylinder into the bell housing lugs. Seat the cylinder into the recess in the lugs.

➡ **When installing a new hydraulic system, you'll notice that the slave cylinder contains a shipping strap that propositions the pushrod for installation, and also provides a bearing insert. Following installation of the new slave cylinder, the first actuation of the clutch pedal will break the shipping strap and give normal clutch action.**

AUTOMATIC TRANSMISSION

The automatic transmission allows engine torque and power to be transmitted to the rear wheels within a narrow range of engine operating speeds. It will allow the engine to turn fast enough to produce plenty of power and torque at very low speeds, while keeping it at a sensible rpm at high vehicle speeds (and it does this job without driver assistance). The transmission uses a light fluid as the medium for the transmission of power. This fluid also works in the operation of various hydraulic control circuits and as a lubricant. Because the transmission fluid performs all of these functions, trouble within the unit can easily travel from one part to another.

Adjustments

INTERMEDIATE BAND

C4, C5 and C6

▶ **See Figures 10 and 11**

1. Raise the truck on a hoist or jackstands.
2. Clean all dirt away from the band adjusting screw. Remove and discard the locknut.
3. Install a new locknut and tighten the adjusting screw to 10 ft. lbs.
4. Back off the adjusting screw EXACTLY 1¾ turns for the C4, 4¼ turns for the C5 and 1½ turns for the C6.
5. Hold the adjusting screw from turning and tighten the locknut to 35-40 ft. lbs.
6. Remove the jackstands and lower the vehicle.

REAR BAND

FMX

▶ **See Figure 12**

1. Raise the truck on a hoist or jackstands.
2. Clean all dirt away from the band adjusting screw. Remove and discard the locknut.
3. Install a new locknut and tighten the adjusting screw to 10 ft. lbs.

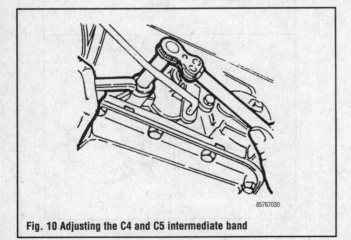

Fig. 10 Adjusting the C4 and C5 intermediate band

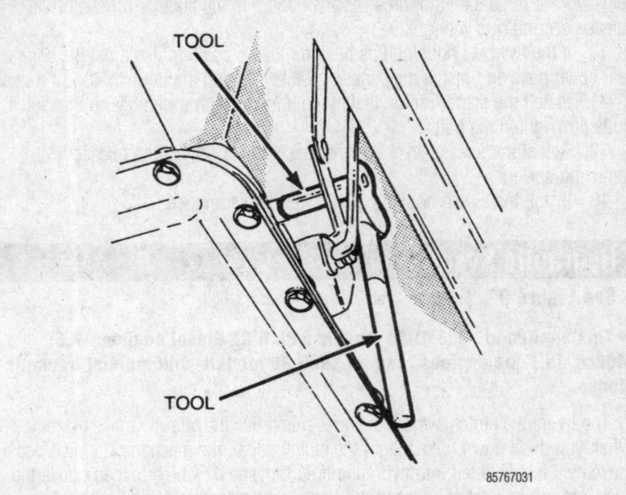

4. Clean the master cylinder pushrod bearing and apply a light film of SAE 30 engine oil.
5. From inside the cab, install the bushing on the clutch pedal lever. Connect the clutch master cylinder pushrod to the clutch pedal lever and install the cotter pin.
6. Check the clutch reservoir and add fluid if required. Depress the clutch pedal at least ten times to verify smooth operation and proper clutch release.

Fig. 11 Adjusting the C6 intermediate band

Fig. 12 Adjusting the FMX rear band

4. Back off the adjusting screw EXACTLY 1½ turns.
5. Hold the adjusting screw from turning and tighten the locknut to 35-40 ft. lbs.
6. Remove the jackstands and lower the vehicle.

REAR BAND (LOW/REVERSE)

C4 and C5

▶ **See Figure 13**

1. Clean all dirt from around the band adjusting screw and remove and discard the locknut.
2. Install a new locknut on the adjusting screw. Using a torque wrench, tighten the adjusting screw to 10 ft. lbs.
3. Back off the adjusting screw EXACTLY 3 FULL TURNS.
4. Hold the adjusting screw steady and tighten the locknut to 35–45 ft. lbs.

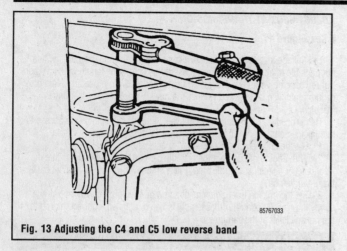

Fig. 13 Adjusting the C4 and C5 low reverse band

FRONT BAND

FMX

▶ **See Figure 14**

1. Remove the transmission oil pan.
2. Loosen the front servo adjusting screw locknut
3. Pull back on the actuating rod, and insert a ¼ inch spacer between the adjusting screw and the servo piston stem.
4. Tighten the adjusting screw to 10 inch lbs.
5. Remove the spacer and tighten the adjusting screw an additional ¾ turn.
6. Hold the adjusting screw stationary and tighten the locknut to 20-25 ft. lbs.
7. Install the oil pan and a new gasket in the reverse order of removal.

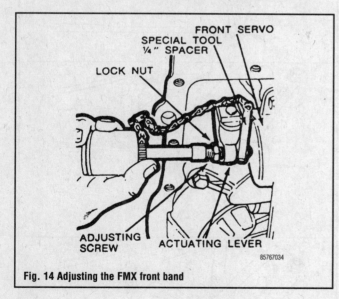

Fig. 14 Adjusting the FMX front band

SHIFT LINKAGE

▶ **See Figure 15**

1. With the engine stopped, place the transmission selector lever at the steering column in the D or OD (AOD trans.), position against the D or OD (AOD trans.) stop.
2. Loosen the shift rod adjusting nut at the transmission lever point "A".
3. Shift the manual lever at the transmission all the way rearward to the **D or OD** position, then two detents forward.

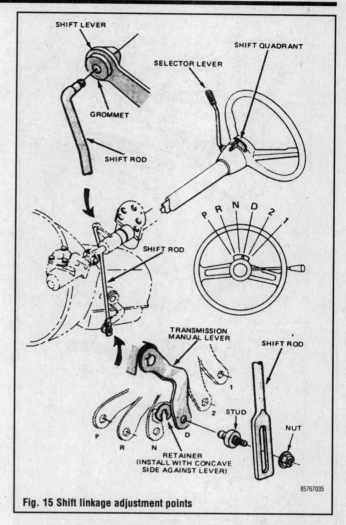

Fig. 15 Shift linkage adjustment points

4. With the selector lever and transmission manual lever in the D or OD position, tighten the adjusting nut at point "A" to 12-18 ft. lbs. Do not allow the rod or shift lever to move while tightening the nut.
5. Check the operation of the shift linkage.

THROTTLE VALVE LINKAGE

AOD Transmission With Carburetor

▶ **See Figure 16**

ADJUSTMENT AT THE CARBURETOR

The TV control linkage may be adjusted at the carburetor using the following procedure:
1. Check that engine idle speed is set at the specification.
2. De-cam the fast idle cam on the carburetor so that the throttle lever is at its idle stop. Place shift lever in N (neutral), set park brake (engine off).
3. Back out linkage lever adjusting screw all the way (screw end if flush with lever face).
4. Turn in adjusting screw until a thin shim (0.005 inch max.) or piece of writing paper fits snugly between end of screw and Throttle Lever. To eliminate effect of friction, push linkage lever forward (tending to close gap) and release before checking clearance between end of screw and throttle lever. Do not apply any load on levers with tools or hands while checking gap.
5. Turn in adjusting screw an additional four turns. (Four turns are preferred. Two turns minimum is permissible if screw travel is limited).

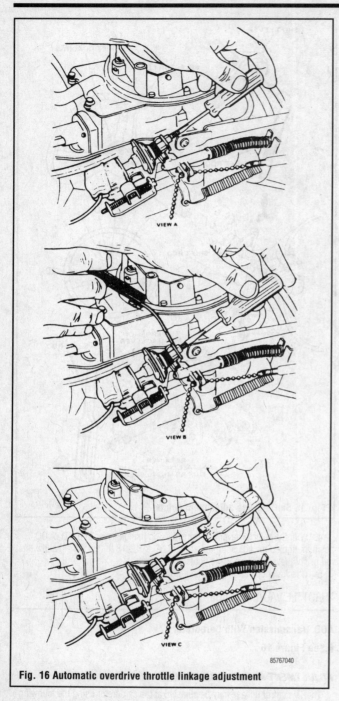

Fig. 16 Automatic overdrive throttle linkage adjustment

6. If it is not possible to turn in adjusting screw at least two addition turns or if there was sufficient screw adjusting capacity to obtain an initial gap in Step 2 above, refer to Linkage Adjustment at Transmission. Whenever it is required to adjust idle speed by more than 50 rpm, the adjustment screw on the linkage lever at the carburetor should also be readjusted as shown.

Idle Speed Change/Turns on Linkage Lever Adjustment Screw
• Less than 50 rpm: No change required
• 50 to 100 rpm increase: 1½ turns out
• 50 to 100 rpm decrease: 1½ turns in
• 100 to 150 rpm increase: 2½ turns out
• 100 to 150 rpm decrease: 2½ turns in

After making any idle speed adjustments, always verify the linkage lever and throttle lever are in contact with the throttle lever at its idle stop and the shift lever is in N (neutral).

ADJUSTMENT AT TRANSMISSION

▶ **See Figure 17**

The linkage lever adjustment screw has limited adjustment capability. It is not possible to adjust the TV linkage using this screw, the length of the TV control rod assembly must be readjusted using the following procedure. This procedure must also be followed whenever a new TV control rod assembly is installed.

This procedure requires placing the vehicle on jackstands to give access to the linkage components at the transmission TV control lever.

1. Set the engine curb idle speed to specification.
2. With engine off, de-cam the fast idle cam on the carburetor so that the throttle lever is against the idle stop. Place shift lever in Neutral and set park brake (engine off).
3. Set the linkage lever adjustment screw at its approximately mid-range.
4. If a new TV control rod assembly is being installed, connect the rod to the linkage lever at the carburetor.

✶✶ CAUTION

The following steps involve working in proximity to the exhaust system. Allow the exhaust system to cool before proceeding.

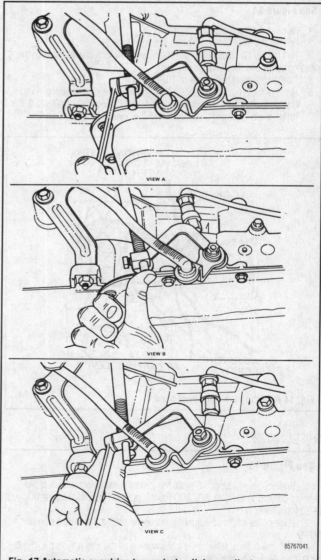

Fig. 17 Automatic overdrive transmission linkage adjustment

5. Raise the vehicle on the hoist.

6. Using a 13mm box end wrench, loosen the bolt on the sliding trunnion block on the TV control rod assembly. Remove any corrosion from the control rod and free-up the trunnion block so that it slides freely on the control rod. Insert pin into transmission lever grommet.

7. Push up on the lower end of the control rod to insure that the linkage lever at carburetor is firmly against the throttle lever. Release force on rod. Rod must stay up.

8. Push the TV control lever on the transmission up against its internal stop with a firm force (approximately 5 pounds) and tighten the bolt on the trunnion block. do not relax force on lever until nut is tightened.

9. Lower the vehicle and verify that the throttle lever is still against the idle stop. If not, repeat steps 2 through 9.

THROTTLE VALVE CABLE

▶ **See Figures 18 and 19**

AOD Transmission with EFI Fuel System

ADJUSTMENT WITH ENGINE OFF

1. Set the parking brake and put the selector lever in **N**.
2. Remove the protective cover from the cable.
3. Make sure that the throttle lever is at the idle stop. If it isn't, check for binding or interference. NEVER ATTEMPT TO ADJUST THE IDLE STOP!
4. Make sure that the cable is free of sharp bends or is not rubbing on anything throughout its entire length.
5. Lubricate the TV lever ball stud with chassis lube.

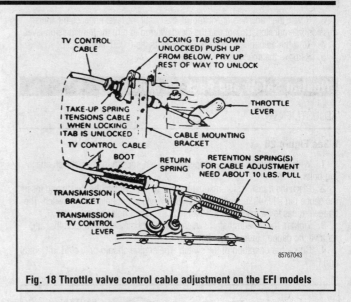

Fig. 18 Throttle valve control cable adjustment on the EFI models

THROTTLE KICKDOWN LINKAGE

1. Move the carburetor throttle linkage to the wide open position.
2. Insert a 0.060 inch thick spacer between the throttle lever and the kickdown adjusting screw.

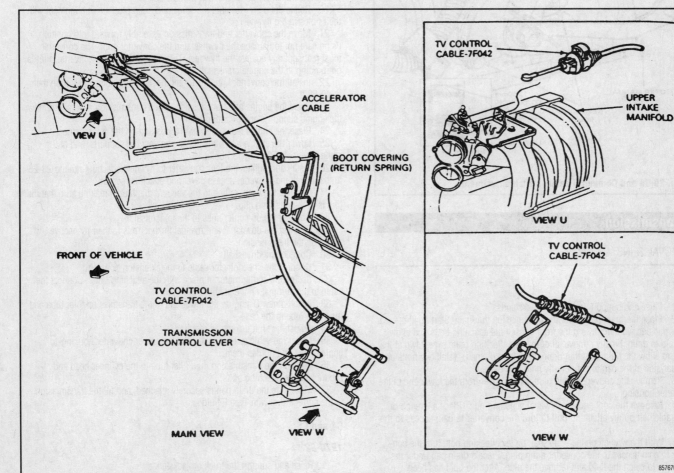

Fig. 19 Throttle valve control cable adjustment on the EFI models

3. Rotate the transmission kickdown lever until the lever engages the transmission internal stop. Do not use the kickdown rod to turn the transmission lever.

4. Turn the adjusting screw until it contacts the 0.060 inch spacer.

5. Remove the spacer.

Neutral Safety and Back-Up Switch

ADJUSTMENT

▶ **See Figure 20**

1. With the manual linkage properly adjusted, loosen the two switch attaching bolts.

2. Place the transmission manual lever in neutral. Rotate the switch and insert the gauge pin (No. 43 drill shank end) into the gauge pin holes of the switch. The gauge pin has to be inserted a full $^{31}/_{64}$ inch into the 3 holes of the switch.

3. Tighten the 2 neutral start switch attaching bolts to 55-75 inch lbs. and remove the gauge pin from the switch.

4. Check the operation of the switch. The engine should only start in Neutral and Park.

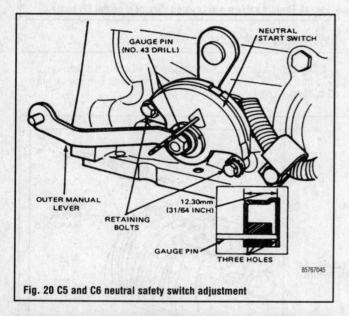

Fig. 20 C5 and C6 neutral safety switch adjustment

Transmission

REMOVAL & INSTALLATION

FMX

1. Raise and support the truck on jackstands.

2. Place the drain pan under the transmission fluid pan. Starting at the rear of the pan and working toward the front, loosen the attaching bolts and allow the fluid to drain. Finally remove all of the pan attaching bolts except two at the front, to allow the fluid to further drain. With fluid drained, install two bolts on the rear side of the pan to temporarily hold it in place.

3. Remove the converter drain plug access cover from the lower end of the converter housing.

4. Remove the converter-to-flywheel attaching nuts. Place a wrench on the crankshaft pulley attaching bolt to turn the converter to gain access to the nuts.

5. With the wrench on the crankshaft pulley attaching bolt, turn the converter to gain access to the converter drain plug. Place a drain pan under the converter to catch the fluid and remove the plug. After the fluid has been drained, reinstall the plug.

6. Disconnect the driveshaft from the rear axle and slide shaft rearward from the transmission. Install a seal installation tool in the extension housing to prevent fluid leakage.

7. Disconnect the speedometer cable from the extension housing.

8. Disconnect the downshift and manual linkage rods from the levers at the transmission.

9. Disconnect the oil cooler lines from the transmission.

10. Remove the vacuum hose from the vacuum diaphragm unit. Remove the vacuum line retaining clip.

11. Disconnect the cable from the terminal on the starter motor. Remove the three attaching bolts and remove the starter motor.

12. Position a transmission jack to support the transmission. Install the safety chain to hold the transmission on the jack.

13. With the transmission jack, raise the transmission high enough to remove the engine rear supports.

14. Lower the engine against a floor stand or engine support bar until the converter housing is clear of the crossmember when all weight is off the transmission jack.

15. Remove the remaining converter housing to engine attaching bolts.

16. Move the converter and transmission assembly toward the rear and lower it, leaving the flywheel attached to the crankshaft. If additional clearance is needed, tilt the rear of the assembly upright slightly and to the rear enough to allow removal of the six flywheel to crankshaft bolts. Move the assembly to the rear and remove it.

To install:

17. Tighten the converter drain plug to 15-28 ft. lbs.

18. Position the converter on the transmission making sure the converter drive flats are fully engaged in the pump gear.

19. With the converter properly installed, place the transmission on the jack. Secure the transmission on the jack with the chain.

20. Rotate the converter until the studs and drain plug are in alignment with their holes in the flywheel.

21. Move the converter and transmission assembly forward into position, using care not to damage the flywheel and the converter pilot. The converter must rest squarely against the flywheel. This indicates that the converter pilot is not binding in the engine crankshaft.

22. Install the converter housing-to-engine attaching bolts and torque them to 40-50 ft. lbs.

23. Raise the engine and transmission with a transmission jack, and remove the engine support stand or support bar.

24. Place the engine rear supports in a position on the crossmember.

25. Lower the engine and transmission against the supports, and at the same time install the support bolts.

26. Install and tighten the four converter to flywheel attaching nuts to 23-28 ft. lbs. Install the converter access cover and attaching screws.

27. Connect the vacuum line to the vacuum diaphragm making sure that the line is in the retaining clip.

28. Connect the oil cooler lines to the transmission.

29. Connect the downshift and manual linkage rods to their respective levers on the transmission.

30. Connect the driveshaft.

31. Connect the speedometer cable to the extension housing.

32. Secure the starter motor in place with the attaching bolts. Connect the cable to the terminal on the starter.

33. Install a new O-ring on the lower end of the transmission filler tube and insert the tube in the case.

34. Adjust the shift linkage as required.

35. Lower the vehicle. Then install the two upper converter housing-to-engine bolts and tighten them.

36. Position the transmission fluid filler tube to the cylinder head and secure with the attaching bolts.

37. Make sure the drain pan is securely attached, and fill the transmission to the correct level with Type F fluid.

C4 and C5

1976-82

1. Raise and support the truck on jackstands.

2. Place the drain pan under the transmission fluid pan. Starting at the rear of the pan and working toward the front, loosen the attaching bolts and allow

the fluid to drain. Finally remove all of the pan attaching bolts except two at the front, to allow the fluid to further drain. With fluid drained, install two bolts on the rear side of the pan to temporarily hold it in place.

3. Remove the converter drain plug access cover from the lower end of the converter housing.

4. Remove the converter-to-flywheel attaching nuts. Place a wrench on the crankshaft pulley attaching bolt to turn the converter to gain access to the nuts.

5. With the wrench on the crankshaft pulley attaching bolt, turn the converter to gain access to the converter drain plug. Place a drain pan under the converter to catch the fluid and remove the plug. After the fluid has been drained, reinstall the plug.

6. On 2-wheel drive models, disconnect the driveshaft from the rear axle and slide shaft rearward from the transmission. Install a seal installation tool in the extension housing to prevent fluid leakage.

7. Disconnect the speedometer cable from the extension housing.

8. Disconnect the downshift and manual linkage rods from the levers at the transmission.

9. Disconnect the oil cooler lines from the transmission.

10. Remove the vacuum hose from the vacuum diaphragm unit. Remove the vacuum line retaining clip.

11. Disconnect the cable from the terminal on the starter motor. Remove the three attaching bolts and remove the starter motor.

12. Position a transmission jack to support the transmission. Install the safety chain to hold the transmission on the jack.

13. Remove the two engine rear support crossmember to frame attaching bolts.

14. Remove the two engine rear support and insulator assembly-to-extension housing attaching bolts.

15. Raise the transmission with a transmission jack and remove the rear support.

16. Remove the six converter housing to engine attaching bolts.

17. Move the converter and transmission away from the engine. Lower the jack and remove the converter and transmission assembly from under the vehicle.

To install:

18. Tighten the converter drain plug to 15-28 ft. lbs.

19. Position the converter on the transmission making sure the converter drive flats are fully engaged in the pump gear.

20. With the converter properly installed, place the transmission on the jack. Secure the transmission on the jack with the chain.

21. Rotate the converter until the studs and drain plug are in alignment with their holes in the flywheel.

22. Move the converter and transmission assembly forward into position, using care not to damage the flywheel and the converter pilot. The converter must rest squarely against the flywheel. This indicates that the converter pilot is not binding in the engine crankshaft.

23. Install the converter housing-to-engine attaching bolts and torque them to 40-50 ft. lbs.

24. Install the converter to flywheel attaching nuts and tighten to 20-34 ft. lbs.

25. Position the engine rear support and insulator assembly above the crossmember. Install the rear support and insulator assembly-to-extension housing mounting bolts and tighten the bolts to 45 ft. lbs.

26. Secure the starter motor in place with the attaching bolts and tighten to 20-30 ft. lbs. Connect the cable to the terminal on the starter.

27. Lower the transmission and remove the jack.

28. Install a new O-ring on the lower end of the transmission filler tube and insert the tube in the case.

29. Connect the speedometer cable to the extension housing.

30. Connect the downshift and manual linkage rods to their respective levers on the transmission.

31. Connect the driveshaft.

32. Connect the vacuum line to the vacuum diaphragm making sure that the line is in the retaining clip.

33. Install the converter housing access cover and secure it with the attaching bolts.

34. Adjust the shift linkage as required.

35. Lower the vehicle. Then install the two upper converter housing-to-engine bolts and tighten them.

36. Position the transmission fluid filler tube to the cylinder head and secure with the attaching bolts.

37. Make sure the drain pan is securely attached, and fill the transmission to the correct level with Type F fluid for the C4 and Ford Type H fluid for the C5.

C5

1983-86

1. Raise and support the truck on jackstands.

2. Place the drain pan under the transmission fluid pan. Starting at the rear of the pan and working toward the front, loosen the attaching bolts and allow the fluid to drain. Finally remove all of the pan attaching bolts except two at the front, to allow the fluid to further drain. With fluid drained, install two bolts on the rear side of the pan to temporarily hold it in place.

3. Remove the converter drain plug access cover from the lower end of the converter housing.

4. Remove the converter-to-flywheel attaching nuts. Place a wrench on the crankshaft pulley attaching bolt to turn the converter to gain access to the nuts.

5. With the wrench on the crankshaft pulley attaching bolt, turn the converter to gain access to the converter drain plug. Place a drain pan under the converter to catch the fluid and remove the plug. After the fluid has been drained, reinstall the plug.

6. Disconnect the driveshaft from the rear axle and slide shaft rearward from the transmission. Install a seal installation tool in the extension housing to prevent fluid leakage.

7. Disconnect the cable from the terminal on the starter motor. Remove the three attaching bolts and remove the starter motor.

8. Remove the two rear mount to crossmember insulator attaching nuts and the two crossmember to frame attaching bolts. Remove the right and left gussets

9. Remove the two engine rear support and insulator assembly-to-extension housing attaching bolts.

10. Disconnect the downshift and manual linkage rods from the levers at the transmission.

11. Remove the two bolts securing the bellcrank bracket to the converter housing.

12. Position a transmission jack to support the transmission.

13. Raise the transmission with the transmission jack to provide clearance to remove the crossmember. Remove the rear mount from the crossmember and remove the crossmember from the side supports.

14. Lower the transmission to gain access and disconnect the oil cooler lines from the transmission.

15. Disconnect the speedometer cable from the extension housing.

16. Remove the bolt and remove the filler tube from the block and lift the filler tube and the dipstick from the block.

17. Install the safety chain to hold the transmission on the jack.

18. Remove the six converter housing to engine attaching bolts.

19. Move the converter and transmission away from the engine. Lower the jack and remove the converter and transmission assembly from under the vehicle.

To install:

20. Tighten the converter drain plug to 12-17 ft. lbs.

21. Position the converter on the transmission making sure the converter drive flats are fully engaged in the pump gear.

22. With the converter properly installed, place the transmission on the jack. Secure the transmission on the jack with the chain.

23. Rotate the converter until the studs and drain plug are in alignment with their holes in the flywheel.

24. Move the converter and transmission assembly forward into position, using care not to damage the flywheel and the converter pilot. The converter must rest squarely against the flywheel. This indicates that the converter pilot is not binding in the engine crankshaft.

25. Install the converter housing-to-engine attaching bolts and torque them to 40-50 ft. lbs.

26. Install the converter to flywheel attaching nuts and tighten to 20-34 ft. lbs.

27. Remove the safety chain from around the transmission. lbs.

28. Install a new O-ring on the lower end of the transmission filler tube and insert the tube in the case.

29. Connect the speedometer cable to the extension housing.

30. Connect the oil cooler lines to right side of the case.

31. Position the crossmember on the side supports. Position the rear mount insulator to the crossmember and install the attaching bolts and nuts and tighten to 50-70 ft. lbs.

32. Secure the engine rear support to the extension housing and tighten the bolts to 60-80 ft. lbs.

33. Lower the transmission and remove the jack.

34. Secure the crossmember to the side supports with the attaching bolts and tighten the bolts to 65-88 ft. lbs.

35. Install the two bolts and secure the bellcrank bracket to the converter housing.

36. Connect the downshift and manual linkage rods to their respective levers on the transmission.

37. Install the converter to flywheel attaching nuts and tighten to 20-34 ft. lbs.

38. Install the converter housing access cover and secure it with the attaching bolts.

39. Secure the starter motor in place with the attaching bolts and tighten to 20-30 ft. lbs. Connect the cable to the terminal on the starter.

40. Connect the driveshaft.

41. Adjust the shift and throttle linkage as required.

42. Lower the vehicle. Then install the two upper converter housing-to-engine bolts and tighten them.

43. Position the transmission fluid filler tube to the cylinder head and secure with the attaching bolts.

44. Make sure the drain pan is securely attached, and fill the transmission to the correct level with Ford Type H fluid or equivalent.

C6

1. From in the engine compartment, remove the two upper converter housing-to-engine bolts.

2. Disconnect the neutral switch wire at the in-line connector.

3. Remove the bolt securing the fluid filler tube to the engine cylinder head.

4. Raise and support the truck on jackstands.

5. Place the drain pan under the transmission fluid pan. Starting at the rear of the pan and working toward the front, loosen the attaching bolts and allow the fluid to drain. Finally remove all of the pan attaching bolts except two at the front, to allow the fluid to further drain. With fluid drained, install two bolts on the rear side of the pan to temporarily hold it in place.

6. Remove the converter drain plug access cover from the lower end of the converter housing.

7. Remove the converter-to-flywheel attaching nuts. Place a wrench on the crankshaft pulley attaching bolt to turn the converter to gain access to the nuts.

8. With the wrench on the crankshaft pulley attaching bolt, turn the converter to gain access to the converter drain plug. Place a drain pan under the converter to catch the fluid and remove the plug. After the fluid has been drained, reinstall the plug.

9. On 2-wheel drive models, disconnect the driveshaft from the rear axle and slide shaft rearward from the transmission. Install a seal installation tool in the extension housing to prevent fluid leakage.

10. Disconnect the speedometer cable from the extension housing.

11. Disconnect the downshift and manual linkage rods from the levers at the transmission.

12. Disconnect the oil cooler lines from the transmission.

13. Remove the vacuum hose from the vacuum diaphragm unit. Remove the vacuum line retaining clip.

14. Disconnect the cable from the terminal on the starter motor. Remove the three attaching bolts and remove the starter motor.

15. On 4-wheel drive models remove the transfer case.

16. Remove the two engine rear support and insulator assembly attaching bolts.

17. Remove the two engine rear support and insulator assembly-to-extension housing attaching bolts.

18. Remove the eight bolts (1976-81) or six bolts (1982-86) securing the No. 2 crossmember to the frame side rails.

19. Raise the transmission with a transmission jack and remove both crossmembers.

20. Secure the transmission to the jack with the safety chain.

21. Remove the remaining converter housing-to-engine attaching bolts.

22. Move the transmission away from the engine. Lower the jack and remove the converter and transmission assembly from under the vehicle.

To install:

23. Tighten the converter drain plug.

24. Position the converter on the transmission making sure the converter drive flats are fully engaged in the pump gear.

25. With the converter properly installed, place the transmission on the jack. Secure the transmission on the jack with the chain.

26. Rotate the converter until the studs and drain plug are in alignment with their holes in the flywheel.

27. Move the converter and transmission assembly forward into position, using care not to damage the flywheel and the converter pilot. The converter must rest squarely against the flywheel. This indicates that the converter pilot is not binding in the engine crankshaft.

28. Install the converter housing-to-engine attaching bolts and torque them to 65 ft. lbs. for the diesel; 50 ft. lbs. for gasoline engines.

29. Remove the transmission jack safety chain from around the transmission.

30. Position the No. 2 crossmember to the frame side rails. Install and tighten the attaching bolts.

31. Install transfer case on 4-wheel drive models.

32. Position the engine rear support and insulator assembly above the crossmember. Install the rear support and insulator assembly-to-extension housing mounting bolts and tighten the bolts to 45 ft. lbs.

33. Lower the transmission and remove the jack.

34. Secure the engine rear support and insulator assembly to the crossmember with the attaching bolts and tighten them to 80 ft. lbs.

35. Connect the vacuum line to the vacuum diaphragm making sure that the line is in the retaining clip.

36. Connect the oil cooler lines to the transmission.

37. Connect the downshift and manual linkage rods to their respective levers on the transmission.

38. Connect the speedometer cable to the extension housing.

39. Secure the starter motor in place with the attaching bolts. Connect the cable to the terminal on the starter.

40. Install a new O-ring on the lower end of the transmission filler tube and insert the tube in the case.

41. Secure the converter-to-flywheel attaching nuts and tighten them to 30 ft. lbs.

42. Install the converter housing access cover and secure it with the attaching bolts.

43. Connect the driveshaft.

44. Adjust the shift linkage as required.

45. Lower the vehicle. Then install the two upper converter housing-to-engine bolts and tighten them.

46. Position the transmission fluid filler tube to the cylinder head and secure with the attaching bolts.

47. Make sure the drain pan is securely attached, and fill the transmission to the correct level with Type F fluid for 1976 and Dexron®II fluid for 1977-86.

AOD

1. Raise the vehicle on hoist or stands.

2. Place the drain pan under the transmission fluid pan. Starting at the rear of the pan and working toward the front, loosen the attaching bolts and allow the fluid to drain. Finally remove all of the pan attaching bolts except two at the front, to allow the fluid to further drain. With fluid drained, install two bolts on the rear side of the pan to temporarily hold it in place.

3. Remove the converter drain plug access cover from the lower end of the converter.

4. Remove the converter-to-flywheel attaching nuts. Place a wrench on the crankshaft pulley attaching bolt to turn the converter to gain access to the nuts.

5. Place a drain pan under the converter to catch the fluid. With the wrench on the crankshaft pulley attaching bolt, turn the converter to gain access to the converter drain plug and remove the plug. After the fluid has been drained, reinstall the plug.

6. On 2-wheel drive models, matchmark and disconnect the driveshaft from the rear axle and slide shaft rearward from the transmission. Install a seal installation tool in the extension housing to prevent fluid leakage.

7. Disconnect the cable from the terminal on the starter motor. Remove the three attaching bolts and remove the starter motor. Disconnect the neutral start switch wires at the plug connector.

8. Remove the rear mount-to-crossmember attaching bolts and the two crossmember-to-frame attaching bolts.

9. Remove the two engine rear support-to-extension housing attaching bolts.

10. Disconnect the TV linkage rod from the transmission TV lever. Disconnect the manual rod from the transmission manual lever at the transmission.

11. Remove the two bolts securing the bellcrank bracket to the converter housing.

12. On 4-wheel drive models, remove the transfer case.

13. Raise the transmission with a transmission jack to provide clearance to remove the crossmember. Remove the rear mount from the crossmember and remove the crossmember from the side supports.

14. Lower the transmission to gain access to the oil cooler lines.

15. Disconnect each oil line from the fittings on the transmission.

16. Disconnect the speedometer cable from the extension housing.

17. Remove the bolt that secures the transmission fluid filler tube to the cylinder block. Lift the filler tube and the dipstick from the transmission.

18. Secure the transmission to the jack with the chain.

19. Remove the converter housing-to-cylinder block attaching bolts.

20. Carefully move the transmission and converter assembly away from the engine and, at the same time, lower the jack to clear the underside of the vehicle.

21. Remove the converter and mount the transmission in a holding fixture.

22. Tighten the converter drain plug.

23. Position the converter on the transmission, making sure the converter drive flats are fully engaged in the pump gear by rotating the converter.

24. With the converter properly installed, place the transmission on the jack. Secure the transmission to the jack with a chain.

25. Rotate the converter until the studs and drain plug are in alignment with the holes in the flywheel.

26. Move the converter and transmission assembly forward into position, using care not to damage the flywheel and the converter pilot. The converter must rest squarely against the flywheel. This indicates that the converter pilot is not binding in the engine crankshaft.

27. Install and tighten the converter housing-to-engine attaching bolts to 40-50 ft. lbs.

28. Remove the safety chain from around the transmission.

29. Install a new O-ring on the lower end of the transmission filler tube. Insert the tube in the transmission case and secure the tube to the engine with the attaching bolt.

30. Connect the speedometer cable to the extension housing.

31. Connect the oil cooler lines to the right side of transmission case.

32. Position the crossmember on the side supports. Torque the bolts to 55 ft. lbs. Position the rear mount on the crossmember and install the attaching nuts to 90 ft. lbs.

33. On 4-wheel drive models, install the transfer case.

34. Secure the rear support to the extension housing and tighten the bolts to 80 ft. lbs.

35. Lower the transmission and remove the jack.

36. Make sure the drain pan is securely attached, and fill the transmission to the correct level with Dexron®II fluid.

TRANSFER CASE

The transfer case used in 1976 F-100 is the Dana 21 2-speed unit. In 1976–79 models, the New Process 205 part time and the new Process 203 full time units were available. In 1980–86 models, the New Process 208 and Borg-Warner 1345 units were used.

Adjustments

SHIFT LEVER

➡**Only the NP-203 requires adjustment.**

NP-203

1. Place shift lever in neutral position.

2. Remove two adjusting stud nuts.

3. Install ¼ inch (6.35mm) diameter alignment pin, 1¼ inch (31¾mm) long, through shifter assembly.

4. Align the two transfer case levers as follows:

   a. Bottom lever, (Lock lever): Rotate clockwise to the forward position.

   b. Top lever, (Range lever): Place in the Mid-position or Neutral position.

5. Reposition the two shift rods and tighten new adjusting stud nuts to 15–20 ft. lbs.

6. Remove alignment pin from shifter assembly.

Transfer Case

REMOVAL & INSTALLATION

Dana 21

1. Shift the transfer case into Neutral.

2. Remove the bolts attaching the fan shroud to the radiator support.

3. Raise the vehicle on a hoist.

4. Support the transfer case shield with a jack and remove the bolts that attach the shield to the frame side rails. Remove the shield.

5. Drain the transmission and transfer case lubricant.

6. Disconnect the front and rear driveshafts at the transfer case.

7. Disconnect the speedometer cable at the transfer case.

8. If equipped with a manual transmission, disconnect the shift rods from the transmission shift lever. Then, place the First/Reverse gear shift lever in to the First gear position and insert the fabricated tool. (See transmission removal and installation.) This tool will prevent the input shaft roller bearings from dropping into the transmission case when separating the transfer case from the transmission and output shaft.

9. Support the engine with a jack.

10. Remove the two cotter pins, bolts, washers, plates and insulators that secure the crossmember to the transfer case adapter.

11. Remove the crossmember to frame side support attaching bolts.

12. Raise the transmission and remove the upper insulators from the crossmember. Remove the crossmember.

13. Remove the carpet from around the shift levers. Remove the bolts holding the shifter to the transmission adapter. Remove the boot from the bottom of the shifter. Bend up the left side of the floor opening as required to remove the shifter assemb

14. Secure the transfer case to a transmission jack and remove the transfer case adapter-to-transmission attaching bol

15. Move the transfer case and jack rearward until it clears the transmission output shaft. Lower the transfer ca

16. Installation is the reverse of the removal procedure.

New Process 203

1. Drain the transfer case by removing the power take-off lower bolts and the front output rear cover lower bolts.

2. Disconnect the front axle driveshaft from the flange at the transfer case.

3. Disconnect the shift rods from the transfer case.

4. Disconnect the speedometer cable and lockout lamp switch wire from the transfer case rear output shaft housing.

5. Remove the transfer case-to-transmission adapter attaching bolts. Disconnect the rear axle driveshaft at the transfer case flange.

6. Position a transmission jack under the transfer case and secure it to the jack.

7. Remove the transfer case mounting bracket support to frame crossmember nuts, bolts, spacers and upper absorbers and remove the transfer case.

8. Using a chain fall, place the transfer case on a suitable work bench.

   To install:

9. Using a chain fall, secure the transfer case on a transmission jack.

10. Position the transfer case in the truck, aligning the mounting bracket supports with the lower absorbers. Align the transfer case-to-transmission attaching bolts.

11. Install the transfer case mounting bracket support to frame crossmember bolts with upper absorbers and spacers. Tighten all mounting bolts to 40–50 ft. lbs.

12. Remove the transmission jack.

13. Connect the speedometer cable and the lockout switch wire to the transfer case.

14. Connect the rear axle driveshaft to the transfer case rear output flange.

15. Install the shift rods on the transfer case and adjust the shift linkage.

16. Connect the front axle driveshaft to the transfer case flange.

17. Fill the transfer case with SAE 80W/90 oil. Tighten the filler plug to 25–35 ft. lbs.

New Process 205

1. Drain the transfer case. Disconnect the rear axle driveshaft and front driveshaft from the flange at the transfer case.

2. Disconnect the shift selector rod steady rest and the speedometer cable at the transfer case.

3. Secure the transfer case to a transmission jack, and remove the mounting bolts.

4. Remove transfer case, and place it on a floor stand or work bench.

To install:

5. Remove the transfer case from the floor stand or bench and place it on the transmission jack.

6. Raise the transfer case into position and attach the mounting bolts. Tighten the bolts and nuts to 20–40 ft. lbs.

7. Connect the shift selector rod, the speedometer cable, and steady rest.

8. Connect the front and rear axle driveshafts and tighten the universal joint U-bolt nuts.

9. Fill the transfer case to filler plug level with SAE 80W/90 oil. Tighten drain plug to 25–35 ft. lbs.

New Process 208

1. Raise vehicle on a hoist.

2. Place a drain pan under transfer case, remove drain plug and drain fluid from transfer case.

3. Disconnect four wheel drive indicator switch wire connector at transfer case.

4. Disconnect speedometer driven gear from transfer case rear bearing retainer.

5. Remove nut retaining transmission shift lever assembly to transfer case.

6. If so equipped, remove skid plate from frame.

7. Remove heat shield from frame.

❋❋ CAUTION

Catalytic converter is located beside the heat shield. Be careful when working around catalytic converter because of the extremely high temperatures generated by the converter.

8. Support transfer case with transmission jack.

9. Disconnect front driveshaft from front output shaft yoke.

10. Disconnect rear driveshaft from rear output shaft yoke.

11. Remove the bolts retaining transfer case to transmission adapter. Remove gasket between transfer case and adapter.

12. Lower transfer case from vehicle.

To install:

13. Place a new gasket between transfer case and adapter.

14. Raise transfer case with transmission jack so transmission output shaft aligns with splined transfer case input shaft. Install bolts retaining transfer case to adapter. Tighten bolts to 30–40 ft. lbs.

15. Connect rear driveshaft to rear output shaft yoke.

16. Connect front driveshaft to front output yoke.

17. Remove transmission jack from transfer case.

18. Position heat shield to frame crossmember and mounting lug on transfer case. Install and tighten bolts and screw to 11–16 ft. lbs.

19. Install skid plate to frame. Tighten nuts and bolts.

20. Install shift lever to transfer case. Install retaining nut.

21. Connect speedometer driven gear to transfer case.

22. Connect 4-wheel drive indicator switch wire connector at transfer case.

23. Install drain plug. Remove filler plug, and install 2.8 liters (six pints) of automatic transmission fluid Ford type CJ or Dexron®II, Series D or equivalent. Install filler plug.

24. Lower vehicle.

Borg-Warner Model 1345

1. Raise and support the truck on jackstands.

2. Drain the fluid from the transfer case.

3. Disconnect the four wheel drive indicator switch wire connector at the transfer case.

4. Remove the skid plate from the frame, if so equipped.

5. Matchmark and disconnect the front driveshaft from the front output yoke.

6. Matchmark and disconnect the rear driveshaft from the rear output shaft yoke.

7. Disconnect the speedometer driven gear from the transfer case rear bearing retainer.

8. Remove the retaining rings and shift rod from the transfer case shift lever.

9. Disconnect the vent hose from the transfer case.

10. Remove the heat shield from the frame.

11. Support the transfer case with a transmission jack.

12. Remove the bolts retaining the transfer case to the transmission adapter.

13. Lower the transfer case from the vehicle.

To install:

14. When installing place a new gasket between the transfer case and the adapter.

15. Raise the transfer case with the transmission jack so that the transmission output shaft aligns with the splined transfer case input shaft. Install the bolts retaining the transfer case to the adapter.

16. Remove the transmission jack from the transfer case.

17. Connect the rear driveshaft to the rear output shaft yoke. Torque the bolts to 15 ft. lbs.

18. Install the shift lever to the transfer case and install the retaining nut.

19. Connect the speedometer driven gear to the transfer case.

20. Connect the four wheel drive indicator switch wire connector at the transfer case.

21. Connect the front driveshaft to the front output yoke. Torque the bolts to 15 ft. lbs.

22. Position the heat shield to the frame crossmember and the mounting lug on the transfer case. Install and tighten the retaining bolts.

23. Install the skid plate to the frame.

24. Install the drain plug. Remove the filler plug and install six pints of Dexron®II type transmission fluid or equivalent.

25. Lower the vehicle.

DRIVE LINE

Driveshaft

▶ **See Figures 21, 22, 23, and 24**

REMOVAL & INSTALLATION

Single Type U-Joint

REAR ONE-PIECE DRIVESHAFT

1. Matchmark the driveshaft yoke and axle pinion flange.

2. Remove the U-bolt nuts and U-bolts attaching the yoke to the axle flange.

3. Separate the yoke from the flange. It may be necessary to pry it free with a small prybar. Immediately after separation, wrap tape around the U-joint caps to keep them from falling off.

4. Slip the driveshaft off the transmission splines.

5. Installation is the reverse of removal. Align the yoke-to-flange matchmarks. Torque the U-bolt nuts to 15 ft. lbs.

FRONT DRIVESHAFT

1. Matchmark the driveshaft yoke and axle pinion flange.

2. Matchmark the driveshaft yoke and transfer case flange.

3. Remove the U-bolt nuts and U-bolts attaching the yoke to the axle flange.

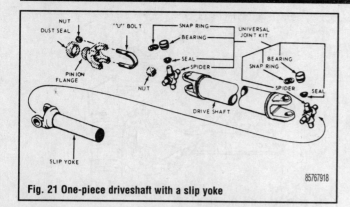

Fig. 21 One-piece driveshaft with a slip yoke

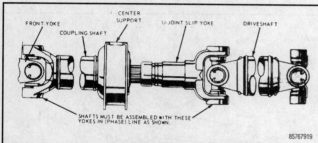

Fig. 22 Two-piece driveshaft with a slip yoke at the transmission end

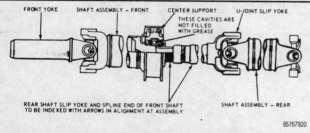

Fig. 23 Two-piece driveshaft with a fixed yoke at the transmission end

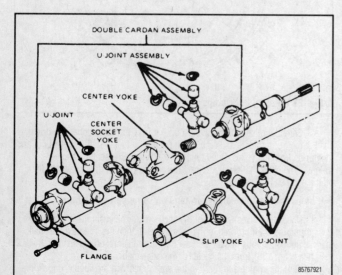

Fig. 24 Rear driveshaft components on the Bronco and F-150 4x4

4. Separate the yoke from the flange. It may be necessary to pry it free with a small prybar. Immediately after separation, wrap tape around the U-joint caps to keep them from falling off.

5. Remove the U-bolts and nuts (bolts for the F-350) and disconnect the driveshaft from the transfer case. It may be necessary to pry it free with a small prybar. Immediately after separation, wrap tape around the U-joint caps to keep them from falling off.

→**Avoid separating the driveshaft parts at the slip joint. If the driveshaft should become separated or if you wish to separate it, see the procedure, below.**

6. Installation is the reverse of removal. Align the yoke-to-flange matchmarks. Torque the U-bolt nuts to 15 ft. lbs. Torque the F-350 bolts to 20–28 ft. lbs.

TWO-PIECE DRIVESHAFT/COUPLING SHAFT EXC. MOTOR HOME CHASSIS

1. Matchmark the driveshaft yoke and axle pinion flange.
2. Remove the U-bolt nuts and U-bolts attaching the yoke to the axle flange.
3. Separate the yoke from the flange. It may be necessary to pry it free with a small prybar. Immediately after separation, wrap tape around the U-joint caps to keep them from falling off.
4. Slip the driveshaft off the coupling shaft splines.
5. Remove the center bearing.
6. Slide the coupling shaft from the transmission shaft splines.
7. Clean all parts and check for damage. Do not remove the blue plastic coating from the male splines.
8. Installation is the reverse of removal. Coat the splines with chassis lube. Torque the center bearing support bolts to 50 ft. lbs. Align the yoke-to-flange matchmarks. Torque the U-bolt nuts to:
   - $5/16$ in.-18: 15 ft. lbs.
   - $3/8$ in.-18: 17–26 ft. lbs.
   - $7/16$ in.-20: 30–40 ft. lbs.

TWO OR THREE-PIECE DRIVESHAFT—MOTOR HOME CHASSIS

1. Matchmark the driveshaft yoke and axle pinion flange.
2. Remove the U-bolt nuts and U-bolts attaching the yoke to the axle flange.
3. Separate the yoke from the flange. It may be necessary to pry it free with a small prybar. Immediately after separation, wrap tape around the U-joint caps to keep them from falling off.
4. Slip the driveshaft off the coupling shaft splines.
5. Remove the rearmost center bearing.
6. Remove the center driveshaft from its mating yoke.
7. Remove the next center bearing.
8. Remove the front driveshaft from the transmission splines.
9. Clean all parts and check for damage. Do not remove the blue plastic coating from the male splines.
10. Installation is the reverse of removal. Coat the splines with chassis lube. Torque the center bearing support bolts to 50 ft. lbs. Align the yoke-to-flange matchmarks. Torque the U-bolt nuts to:
    - $5/16$ in.-18: 15 ft. lbs.
    - $3/8$ in.-18: 17–26 ft. lbs.
    - $7/16$ in.-20: 30–40 ft. lbs.

Double Cardan Type U-Joint

BRONCO REAR DRIVESHAFT

1. Matchmark the rear yoke and axle flange.
2. Matchmark the front cardan joint and the transfer case yoke.
3. Remove the U-bolt nuts and U-bolts attaching the yoke to the axle flange.
4. Separate the yoke from the flange. It may be necessary to pry it free with a small prybar. Immediately after separation, wrap tape around the U-joint caps to keep them from falling off.
5. Remove the cardan joint-to transfer case yoke bolts and separate the cardan joint from the yoke.
6. Installation is the reverse of removal. Align the matchmarks. Torque the U-bolt nuts to 15 ft. lbs.; the cardan joint bolts to 25 ft. lbs.

F-350 FRONT DRIVESHAFT

1. Matchmark the front yoke and front axle flange.
2. Matchmark the cardan joint and the transfer case yoke.

3. Remove the U-bolt nuts and U-bolts attaching the yoke to the axle flange.

4. Separate the yoke from the flange. It may be necessary to pry it free with a small prybar. Immediately after separation, wrap tape around the U-joint caps to keep them from falling off.

5. Remove the cardan joint-to transfer case yoke bolts and separate the cardan joint from the yoke.

6. Installation is the reverse of removal. Align the matchmarks. Torque the U-bolt nuts to 15 ft. lbs.; the cardan joint bolts to 25 ft. lbs.

FRONT DRIVESHAFT SEPARATION

1. Remove the driveshaft and place it on a workbench.
2. Using side cutters, cut the boot bands. Discard them.
3. Pull the 2 sections apart.
4. Remove and inspect the boot. If it is in any way damaged, replace it.

➡**If the boot was split or torn, the grease will probably be contaminated, so thoroughly clean all old grease from the parts and replace it with fresh grease.**

5. Install the boot on the splined shaft as far as it will go.
6. Install a new small clamp and crimp it with crimping pliers. Use only crimp type clamps as hose type clamps can throw the shaft out of balance.
7. Coat the splines with chassis lube.
8. Place about 10 grams of chassis lube in the boot.
9. Place a new large crimp clamp on the rear yoke.
10. Align the blind splines and push the rear yoke onto the driveshaft splines.
11. Remove the excess grease and position the rear end of the boot in the slip yoke boot groove. On trucks with single type U-joints at each end, move the yoke in or out as required to obtain a total driveshaft length of:
   - F-150, 250 and Bronco; C6: 892mm
   - AOD trans.: 917mm

This measurement is made between the centerlines of the U-joints.
   - F-350; C6 trans.: 819mm

This measurement is made between the centerlines of the U-joints with the shaft fully collapsed.

12. Make sure that the boot has stayed in its groove, dispel any trapped air from the boot and crimp the clamp in place.

DRIVESHAFT BALANCING

▸ **See Figures 25, 26, and 27**

Driveline vibration or shudder, felt mainly on acceleration, coasting or under engine braking, can be caused, among other things, by improper driveshaft installation or imbalance.

If the condition follows driveshaft replacement or installation after disconnection, try disconnecting the driveshaft at the axle and rotating it 180°. Then, reconnect it. If that doesn't work, try the following procedure:

1. Raise and support the truck on jackstands so that all wheels are off the ground and free to rotate. The truck must be as level as possible.

2. Remove the wheels. Install the lug nuts to retain the brake drums or rotors.

3. Start the engine, place the transmission in gear and increase engine speed to the point at which the vibration is most severe. Record this speedometer speed as a reference point.

4. Shift into neutral and shut off the engine.

5. Check all driveshaft attachment fasteners, U-joint bearing caps, U-joint cap retaining rings or cap locating lugs. Tighten any loose fasteners, replace any missing, damaged or shaved retaining rings or lugs. If worn U-joints are suspected, replace them. If everything is normal, or if any corrections made do not solve the problem, continue.

6. Start the engine, place the transmission in gear and increase engine speed to an indicated road speed of 40–50 mph (64–80 kmh). Maintain this speed with some sort of accelerator control, such as a weight on the pedal, or have an assistant hold the pedal.

☀ CAUTION

The following procedure can be dangerous! Be careful when approaching the spinning driveline parts!

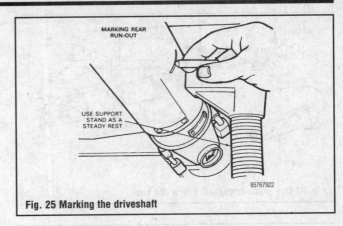

Fig. 25 Marking the driveshaft

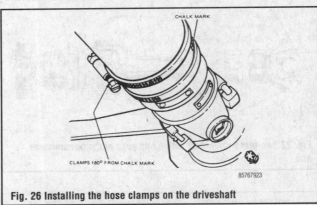

Fig. 26 Installing the hose clamps on the driveshaft

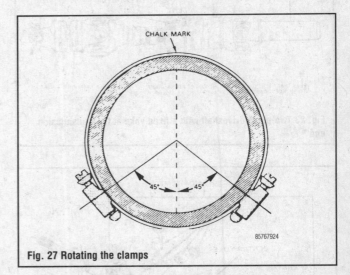

Fig. 27 Rotating the clamps

7. Carefully raise a piece of chalk until it **just barely** touches the driveshaft at the front, middle and rear. At either end, try touching the shaft about an inch or so from the yokes. Don't touch any existing driveshaft balancing weights. The chalk marks will indicate the heavy points of the driveshaft. Shut off the engine.

➡**It helps greatly to steady your hand on some sort of support.**

8. Check the driveshaft end of the shaft first. If the chalk mark is continuous around the shaft proceed to the opposite end, then the middle. If the chalk mark is not continuous, install 2 screw-type hose clamps on the shaft so that their heads are 180° from the center of the chalk mark.

9. Start the engine and run it to the speed recorded previously. If the vibration persists, stop the engine and move the screw portions of the clamps 45° from each other. Try the run test again.

✳✳ WARNING

Check the engine temperature!

10. If the vibration persists, move the screw portions of the clamps apart in small increments until the vibration disappears. If this doesn't cure the problem, proceed to the other end, then the middle, performing the operation all over again. If the problem persists, investigate other driveline components.

U-JOINT OVERHAUL

♦ **See Figures 28 thru 33**

Except Double Cardan Universal

1. Remove the driveshaft from the vehicle and place it in a vise, being careful not to damage it.
2. Remove the snaprings which retain the bearings in the flange and in the driveshaft.
3. Remove the driveshaft tube from the vise and position the U-joint in the vise with a socket smaller than the bearing cap on one side and a socket larger than the bearing cap on the other side.
4. Slowly tighten the jaws of the vise so that the smaller socket forces the U-joint spider and the opposite bearing into the larger socket.
5. Remove the other side of the spider in the same manner (if applicable) and remove the spider assembly from the driveshaft. Discard the spider assemblies.
6. Clean all foreign matter from the yoke areas at the end of the driveshaft(s).
7. Start the new spider and one of the bearing cap assemblies into a yoke by positioning the yoke in a vise with the spider positioned in place with one of the bearing cap assemblies positioned over one of the holes in the yoke.

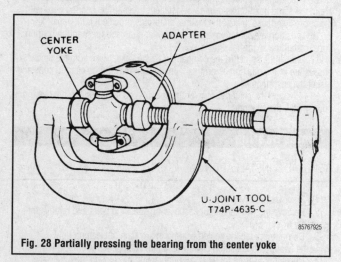

Fig. 28 Partially pressing the bearing from the center yoke

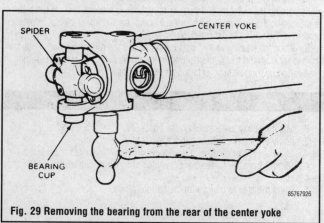

Fig. 29 Removing the bearing from the rear of the center yoke

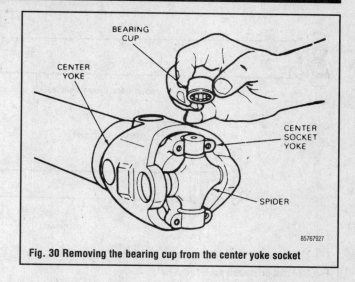

Fig. 30 Removing the bearing cup from the center yoke socket

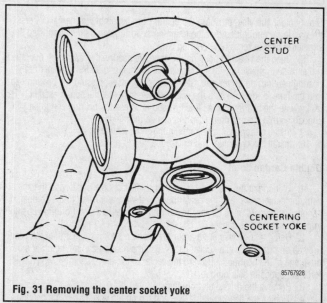

Fig. 31 Removing the center socket yoke

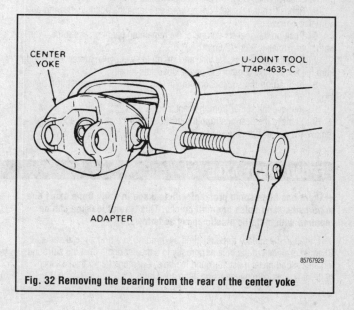

Fig. 32 Removing the bearing from the rear of the center yoke

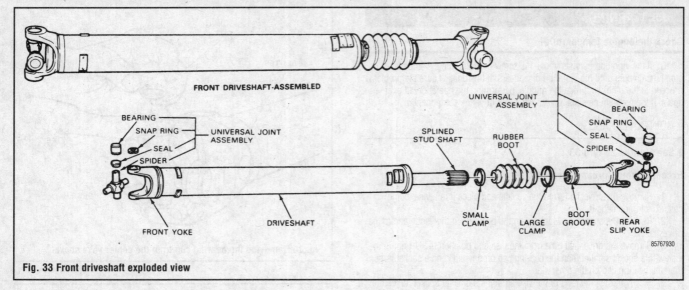

FRONT DRIVESHAFT-ASSEMBLED

BEARING
SNAP RING
SEAL
SPIDER
UNIVERSAL JOINT ASSEMBLY

UNIVERSAL JOINT ASSEMBLY
BEARING
SNAP RING
SEAL
SPIDER

SPLINED STUD SHAFT
RUBBER BOOT

SMALL CLAMP
LARGE CLAMP
BOOT GROOVE
REAR SLIP YOKE

FRONT YOKE
DRIVESHAFT

85767930

Fig. 33 Front driveshaft exploded view

Slowly close the vise, pressing the bearing cap assembly in the yoke. Press the cap in far enough so that the retaining snapring can be installed. Use the smaller socket to recess the bearing cap.

8. Open the vise and position the opposite bearing cap assembly over the proper hole in the yoke with the socket that is smaller than the diameter of the bearing cap located on the cap. Slowly close the vise, pressing the bearing cap into the hole in the yoke with the socket. Make sure that the spider assembly is in line with the bearing cap as it is pressed in. Press the bearing cap in far enough so that the retaining snapring can be installed.

9. Install all remaining U-joints in the same manner.

10. Install the driveshaft and grease the new U-joints.

Double Cardan Joint

1. Working at the rear axle end of the shaft, mark the position of the spiders, the center yoke, and the centering socket yoke as related to the companion flange. The spiders must be assembled with the bosses in their original position to provide proper clearances.

2. Using a large vise or an arbor press and a socket smaller than the bearing cap on one side and a socket larger than the bearing cap on the other side, drive one of the bearings in toward the center of the universal joint, which will force the opposite bearing out.

3. Remove the driveshaft from the vise.

4. Tighten the bearing in the vise and tap on the yoke to free the bearing from the center yoke. Do not tap on the driveshaft tube.

5. Reposition the sockets on the yoke and force the opposite bearing outward and remove it.

6. Position the sockets on one of the remaining bearings and force it outward approximately ⅜in. (9.5mm).

7. Grip the bearing in the vise and tap on the weld yoke to free the bearing from the center yoke. Do not tap on the driveshaft tube.

8. Reposition the sockets on the yoke to press out the remaining bearing.

9. Remove the spider from the center yoke.

10. Remove the bearings from the driveshaft yoke as outlined above and remove the spider from the yoke.

FRONT DRIVE AXLE

➡ **There has been some problem with leakage in early Dana axles due to porosity, sand holes or small cracks. This type of leakage can be repaired with metallic plastic epoxy as follows:**

1. Clean the surface to be repaired by grinding to a bright metal surface. Chamfer or undercut the hole or porosity to a greater depth than the surrounding area. Solid metal must surround the hole. Openings larger than ¼ inch (6.35mm) must be repaired using a threaded plug.

11. Insert a suitable tool into the centering ball socket located in the companion flange and pry out the rubber seal. Remove the retainer, three piece ball seat, washer and spring from the ball socket.

12. Inspect the centering ball socket assembly for worn or damaged parts. If any damage is evident replace the entire assembly.

13. Insert the spring, washer, three piece ball seat and retainer into the ball socket.

14. Using a suitable tool, install the centering ball socket seal.

15. Position the spider in the driveshaft yoke. Make sure the spider bosses are in the same position as originally installed. Press in the bearing cups with the sockets and vise. Install the internal snaprings provided in the repair kit.

16. Position the center yoke over the spider ends and press in the bearing cups. Install the snaprings.

17. Install the spider in the companion flange yoke. Make sure the spider bosses are in the position as originally installed. Press on the bearing cups and install the snaprings.

18. Position the center yoke over the spider ends and press on the bearing cups. Install the snaprings.

Center Bearing

REMOVAL & INSTALLATION

1. Remove the driveshafts.

2. Remove the two center support bearing attaching bolts and remove the assembly from the vehicle.

3. Do not immerse the sealed bearing in any type of cleaning fluid. Wipe the bearing and cushion clean with a cloth dampened with cleaning fluid.

4. Check the bearing for wear or rough action by rotating the inner race while holding the outer race. If wear or roughness is evident, replace the bearing. Examine the rubber cushion for evidence of hardening, cracking, or deterioration. Replace it if it is damaged in any way.

5. Place the bearing in the rubber support and the rubber support in the U-shaped support and install the bearing in the reverse order of removal. Torque the bearing to support bracket fasteners to 50 ft. lbs.

2. Mix the epoxy as directed on the container.

3. Apply the repair mixture with a clean tool.

4. Allow the repair mixture to harden by drying with a heat lamp placed 12 inch (305mm) from the surface for 5 minutes or by air drying at above 50°F for 3–4 hours.

5. Grind the area to blend with the surroundings.

Front Hub

REMOVAL & INSTALLATION

1976–79 Bronco and F-100–F-250

INTERNAL TYPE

▶ **See Figures 34 thru 40**

1. Remove the free running hub bolts and washers.
2. Remove the hub ring and the knob. Wipe the parts clean.
3. Remove the internal snapring from the groove in the hub.
4. Remove the cam body ring and clutch retainer from the hub.

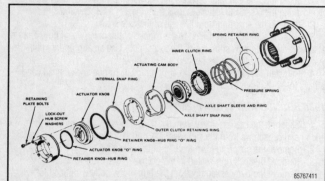

Fig. 34 Free running hub–internal type—1979 Bronco and F-100–F-250

5. Remove the axle shaft snapring. For easier snapring removal, push inward on the axle shaft sleeve ring and at the same time, pull out on the axle shaft with a bolt.
6. Remove the axle shaft sleeve ring, and the inner clutch ring. A slight rocking of the hub may make extraction easier.

➡**Use caution once the spring retainer is removed. Occasionally the spring will release and unexpectedly exit the hub assembly.**

7. Remove the pressure spring and the spring retainer ring.
To install:
8. Grease the hub inner spline with Moly grease or equivalent.
9. Install the spring retainer ring, positioned with recessed undercut area going in first. Be sure ring seats against the bearing.
10. Install the coil spring, with the large end of the spring entering first.
11. Grease with Moly grease or equivalent and install the axle shaft sleeve and ring and the inner clutch ring. Be sure that the teeth are meshed together in a locked position for easy assembly. Rocking the hub back and forth may be required to align the spline. Keep the 2 gears in the locked position.
12. Install the axle shaft snapring. Push inward on gear and, if necessary, push out axle shaft to allow groove clearance on shaft for the snapring. Be sure snapring is fully seated in the snapring groove on the shaft.
13. Install the actuating cam body ring into the outer clutch retaining ring. Assemble into the hub.
14. Install the internal snapring. Be sure that the snapring is fully seated in the snapring groove in the hub.
15. Apply a small amount of Moly grease or equivalent on the ears of the cam. Apply a small amount of Parker O-ring lube or an equivalent lube in groove of actuating knob before assembling outer O-ring.
16. Assemble knob in hub ring and assemble to axle with knob in **LOCK** position. Assemble screws and washers alternately and evenly, making sure the retainer ring is not cocked in the hub.
17. Tighten the six hub bolts to 30 to 35 inch lbs. Be sure the washers are under each retaining screw. Each free running hub will fit either wheel. Do not

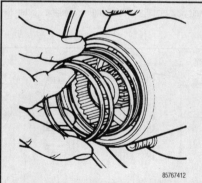

Fig. 35 Coil spring insertion–internal type hub–1979 Bronco and F-100–F-250

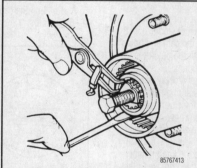

Fig. 36 Installing axle shaft snapring–internal type hub–1979 Bronco and F-100–F-250

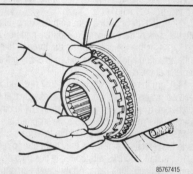

Fig. 37 Axle shaft sleeve and ring and inner clutch ring installation–internal type hub—1979 Bronco and F-100–F-250

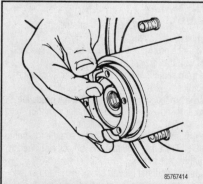

Fig. 38 Installing cam body ring–internal type hub–1979 Bronco and F-100–F-250

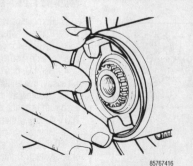

Fig. 39 Installing internal snapring–internal type hub–1979 Bronco and F-100–F-250

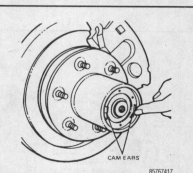

Fig. 40 Apply grease on ears of cam–internal type hub–1979 Bronco and F-100–F-250

drive vehicle until you are sure that both free running hubs are engaged or disengaged.

EXTERNAL TYPE—F-250 ONLY

▶ See Figure 41

1. Remove the free-running hub cap screws and washers.
2. Loosen the gear hub housing and slide it away from the hub and drum assembly.
3. Remove the snapring while holding pressure on the clutch gear. Ease the clutch gear and pressure spring out of the assembly. The actuator knob should be in the lock position for this step.
4. Turn the actuator knob to the free position. With a drift, drive the cam lock pin out of the assembly. Remove the actuating cam from the knob.
5. Remove the knob retainer snapring and remove the knob retainer. Using a capscrew, pull out slightly on the axle shaft and remove the snapring which retains the bushing and inner clutch gear assembly. Remove these parts.
6. Inspect the components for wear or damage and replace components as required.
   To install:

➡Before assembly, inspect the splines of the axle shaft to make sure that they are free of any possible nicks or burs. Threaded holes in the wheel hub should be cleaned before assembling new retainer screws. These holes can be cleaned by directing compressed air into the threaded holes.

7. Apply Moly XL hi-speed grease to the back face of the bushing, also to the splines of the inner clutch gear.
8. Assemble the inner clutch gear into the bushing. Install the bushing and inner clutch gear onto the axle shaft. Install the snapring.
9. Apply a small amount of Parker O-ring lubricant on the actuator knob, making sure the knob is lubricated.
10. Assemble O-ring onto actuator knob. Install the actuating knob into the knob retainer with the arrow pointing to the free position.
11. Install the knob retainer snapring. Make sure the snapring is positioned into the groove in the knob.
12. Install the actuating cam onto the knob, aligning the ears of the cam with the slots of the retainer. Position the parts on a small piece of wood.
13. Assemble the cam locking pin through the grooves of the cam and holes in the actuating knob. Be sure the ends of the pin are flush with the outside diameter of the cam.
14. Turn the actuator knob to the lock position. Apply a small amount of Moly hi-speed grease to both grooves of the cam. Install the pressure spring and outer clutch gear. Compress the pressure spring by forcing down on the clutch gear and assemble the snapring. Make sure the snapring is secure in the groove of the cam.
15. Turn the actuator knob to the free position. Assemble the 6 dished washers to the 6 retainer screws as they were during removal.
16. Install 2 screws with correctly positioned washers into the knob retainer to properly line up the parts. Apply a small amount Moly hi-speed grease to the outer spline and the teeth of the outer clutch gear. Remove any excess lubricant from the gasket surface of the retainer.
17. Install a new outer retainer gasket. Assemble the gear hub housing by aligning the splines of the housing with those on the outer clutch gear. Then install a new inner metal gasket on hub housing.

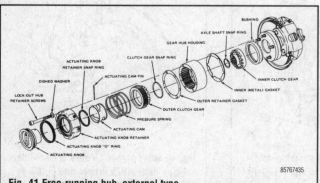

Fig. 41 Free-running hub–external type

18. Position the free-running hub subassembly to axle assembly using 2 new retainer screws as pilots to align the holes of the gasket to the holes of the wheel hub. Tighten the retainer screws to secure the free-running hub. Turn the actuator knob to the lock position.
19. Install the remaining 4 new retainer screws with washers. Tighten the screws evenly to 30–35 ft. lbs. The free-running hub may be hard to engage and disengage, however, after use they should loosen up for easier operation.

➡Do not drive the vehicle until both free-running hubs are either engaged or disengaged.

Manual Locking Hubs

1980–85 BRONCO AND F-150–F-250

▶ See Figure 42

1. To remove the hub, first separate the cap assembly from the body assembly by removing the 6 socket head capscrews from the cap assembly and slip apart.
2. Remove the snapring from the end of the axle shaft.
3. Remove the lock ring seated in the groove of the outer wheel hub. The body assembly will now slide out of the wheel hub. Use an appropriate puller to remove the body assembly, as needed.
4. Reinstall the hub in reverse order of removal. Torque socket head capscrews to 30–35 inch lbs.

1986 BRONCO AND F-150–F-250

1. Separate the cap assembly from the body assembly by removing the 6 Allen head capscrews from the cap assembly and slip apart.
2. Remove the snapring from the end of the axle shaft.
3. Remove the lock ring seated in the groove of the outer wheel hub.
4. Remove the body assembly from the hub. If the body is difficult to remove, install 2 capscrews and pull the body from the hub.
   To install:
5. Insert the body assembly into the hub. Install the lock ring in the groove to retain the body in the hub.
6. Install the snapring that retains the axle shaft to the body.
7. Position the cap onto the body. Install the retaining screws and tighten to 40–60 inch lbs.

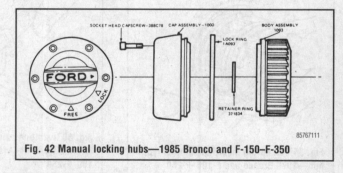

Fig. 42 Manual locking hubs—1985 Bronco and F-150–F-350

Automatic Locking Hubs

1980–84 F-250–F-350

1. Remove capscrews and remove hub cap assembly from the spindle.
2. Remove capscrew from end of axle shaft.
3. Remove lock ring seated in the groove of the wheel hub with a knife blade or with a small sharp awl with the tip bent in a hook.
4. Remove body assembly from spindle. If body assembly does not slide out easily, use an appropriate puller.
5. Unscrew all three set screws in the spindle locknut until the heads are flush with the edge of the locknut. Remove outer spindle locknut with tool T80T-4000-V, Automatic Hub Lock Nut Wrench or equivalent.
6. Reinstall in reverse order of removal. Tighten the outer spindle locknut to 15–20 ft. lbs. with special tool T80T-4000-V, Automatic Hub Lock Nut Wrench or equivalent. Tighten down all three set screws.
7. Firmly push in body assembly until the friction shoes are on top of the spindle outer locknut. Install the capscrews into the axle shaft and tighten to 35–50 inch lbs.

8. Place cap on spindle and install capscrews. Tighten to 35–50 inch lbs. Turn dial firmly from stop to stop, causing the dialing mechanism to engage the body spline.

➡**Be sure both hub dials are in the same position, AUTO or LOCK.**

1985–86 F-250–F-350

▶ **See Figures 43 and 44**

1. To remove the hub, separate the cap assembly from the body assembly by removing the 5 capscrews, using Torx R bit TX25, from the cap assembly. Remove the cover.

➡**Do not drop the ball bearing, bearing retainer or retainer race during removal.**

2. Remove the rubber seal. Remove the steal bridge retainer from the retainer ring space.

3. Remove the retainer ring by closing the ends with needle nose pliers while pulling the hub lock from the wheel hub.

To install:

4. Start the lock hub assembly into the hub making sure the large tangs are lined up with the lock washer and the outside diameter and inside diameter splines are in line with the hub and axle shaft splines.

5. Install retainer ring by closing the ends with needle nose pliers and at the same time push the hub lock assembly into the hub.

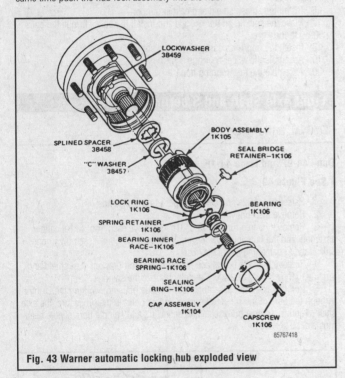

Fig. 43 Warner automatic locking hub exploded view

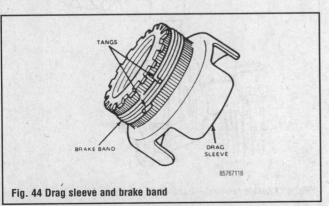

Fig. 44 Drag sleeve and brake band

6. Install the seal bridge retainer with narrow end first. Install the rubber seal over the hub lock.

7. Install the cover making sure the ball bearing, bearing race and retainer are in place. Tighten the 5 screws to 40–50 inch lbs. in sequence, torque one, skip one, etc. until all screws are tight.

Axle Shafts, Spindle and Joints

REMOVAL & INSTALLATION

Dana 44 IFS, Dana 44 IFS-HD and Dana 50 IFS

▶ **See Figures 45, 46 and 47**

1. Raise and support the front end on jackstands.
2. Remove the front wheels.
3. Remove the calipers.
4. Remove the hub/rotor assemblies.
5. Remove the nuts retaining the spindle to the steering knuckle. Tap the spindle with a plastic mallet to remove it from the knuckle.
6. Remove the splash shield.
7. On the left side, pull the shaft from the carrier, through the knuckle.
8. On the right side, remove and discard the keystone clamp from the shaft and joint assembly and the stub shaft. Slide the rubber boot onto the shaft and pull the shaft and joint assembly from the splines of the stub shaft.
9. Place the spindle in a soft-jawed vise clamped on the second step of the spindle.
10. Using a slidehammer and bearing puller, remove the needle bearing from the spindle.
11. Inspect all parts. If the spindle is excessively corroded or pitted it must be replaced. If the U-joints are excessively loose or don't move freely, they must be replaced. If any shaft is bent, it must be replaced.

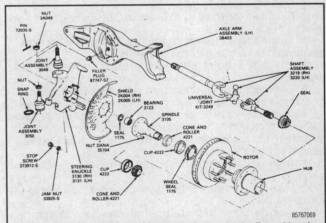

Fig. 45 Spindle, left shaft and joint installation for the Dana 44 and 50 front axles

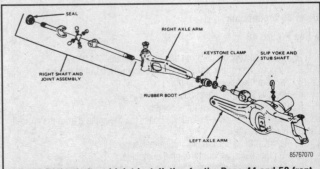

Fig. 46 Right shaft and joint installation for the Dana 44 and 50 front axles

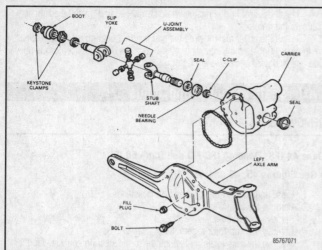

Fig. 47 Carrier and slip yoke, stub shaft installation on the Dana 44 and 50 IFS

12. Clean all dirt and grease from the spindle bearing bore. The bore must be free of nicks and burrs.

To install:

13. Insert a new spindle bearing in its bore with the printing facing outward. Drive it into place with drive T80T-4000-S for F-150 and Bronco and F-250, or T80T-4000-R for the F-350, or their equivalents. Install a new bearing seal with the lip facing away from the bearing.

14. Pack the bearing and hub seal with grease. Install the hub seal with a driver.

15. Place the thrust washer on the axle shaft.

16. Place a new slender on the axle shaft.

17. Install the rubber V-seal on the slinger. The seal lip should face the spindle.

18. Install the plastic spacer on the axle shaft. The chamfered side of the spacer should be inboard against the axle shaft.

19. Pack the thrust face of the seal in the spindle bore and the V-seal on the axle shaft with heavy duty, high temperature, waterproof wheel bearing grease.

20. On the right side, install the rubber boot and new keystone clamps on the stub shaft and slip yoke. The splines permit only one way of meshing so you'll have to properly align the missing spline in the slip yoke with the gapless male spline on the shaft. Slide the right shaft and joint assembly into the slip yoke, making sure that the splines are fully engaged. Slide the boot over the assembly and crimp the keystone clamp.

21. On the left side, slide the shaft and joint assembly through the knuckle and engage the splines in the carrier.

22. Install the splash shield and spindle on the knuckle. Tighten the spindle nuts to 60 ft. lbs.

23. Install the rotor on the spindle. Install the outer wheel bearing into the cup. Make sure that the grease seal lip totally encircles the spindle.

24. Install the wheel bearing, locknut, thrust bearing, snapring and locking hubs.

25. Install the caliper.

Dana 60 Monobeam

▶ **See Figure 48**

1. Raise and support the front end on jackstands.
2. Remove the caliper from the knuckle and wire it out of the way.
3. Remove the free-running hub.
4. Remove the front wheel bearing.
5. Remove the hub and rotor assembly.
6. Remove the spindle-to-knuckle bolts. Tap the spindle from the knuckle using a plastic mallet.
7. Remove the splash shield and caliper support.
8. Pull the axle shaft out through the knuckle.
9. Using a slidehammer and bearing cup puller, remove the needle bearing from the spindle.

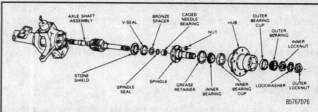

Fig. 48 Axle shaft components for the Dana 60 Monobeam front axle

10. Clean the spindle bore thoroughly and make sure that it is free of nicks and burrs. If the bore is excessively pitted or scored, the spindle must be replaced.

11. Insert a new spindle bearing in its bore with the printing facing outward. Drive it into place with driver T80T-4000-R, or its equivalent. Install a new bearing seal with the lip facing away from the bearing.

12. Pack the bearing with waterproof wheel bearing grease.

13. Pack the thrust face of the seal in the spindle bore and the V-seal on the axle shaft with waterproof wheel bearing grease.

14. Carefully guide the axle shaft through the knuckle and into the housing. Align the splines and fully seat the shaft.

15. Place the bronze spacer on the shaft. The chamfered side of the spacer must be inboard.

16. Install the splash shield and caliper support.

17. Place the spindle on the knuckle and install the bolts. Torque the bolts to 50-60 ft. lbs.

18. Install the hub/rotor assembly on the spindle.

19. Assemble the wheel bearings.

20. Assemble the free-running hub.

Front Axle Shaft and Steering Knuckle

REMOVAL & INSTALLATION

Dana 44-9F and Dana 44-1F

▶ **See Figure 49**

1. Raise the vehicle and safely support it on jackstands.
2. Remove the front wheels.
3. Remove the free running hubs. Then remove each front wheel caliper assembly and the hub and rotor assembly. Secure the brake assembly to one side to avoid damaging the brake hose.
4. Remove the nuts that attach the brake support bracket, dust shield and spindle to the steering knuckle. Carefully remove the spindle.
5. Pull the axle shaft assembly from the axle housing, working the U-joint through the bore of the steering knuckle. At this point in the procedure, the axle shaft, U-joints, spindle bore seals and deflectors and spindle bore needle bearings can be serviced.

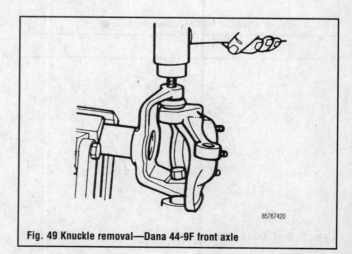

Fig. 49 Knuckle removal—Dana 44-9F front axle

➡️**Use care to prevent damage to the seal. If the seal is bumped against the knuckle bore, it can be damaged.**

6. Disconnect the steering connecting rod end from the steering knuckle. Refer to Section 8 for more information, if required.

7. Remove the cotter key from the upper ball socket. Loosen the nuts from the upper and lower ball sockets. Discard the nut from the bottom socket after the knuckle breaks loose from the yoke. This nut is of the torque-prevailing design and is NOT to be reused.

8. Remove the knuckle from the yoke. In the event that the top socket should remain in the yoke, remove it by hitting on top of the stud with a rawhide hammer. Discard the socket and remove and discard the adjusting sleeve.

9. Remove the bottom socket by removing the clamps and puller jaws from the T of the T71T-3010-P or equivalent, using only the T forcing screw to push out the bottom socket. Discard the socket. Remove and discard the adjusting sleeve.

10. If the top ball joint remained in the knuckle, drive it from the knuckle at this point.

To install:

11. Place the knuckle in a vise. Position the new lower ball joint in the knuckle and force the ball joint into the knuckle.

12. Make sure that the ball joint shoulder is seated against the knuckle. Try placing a 0.0015 inch (0.038mm) feeler gauge between the ball joint and the knuckle. The feeler should not enter at the area of minimum contact.

13. Install the snapring.

14. In a similar manner, press the new top ball joint into place.

15. Make sure that the ball joint is seated against the steering knuckle. Use a 0.0015 inch feeler gauge between the socket and knuckle. The gauge is not to enter at minimum area of contact.

16. Assemble a new adjusting sleeve into the top of the yoke. Leave approximately 2 threads exposed to protect the threads in the yoke.

17. Assemble the knuckle with the sockets to the yoke. Install a new nut onto the bottom socket. Tighten the nut finger tight.

18. Place a spanner wrench and step plate over the adjusting sleeve. Locate the puller so it will pull the knuckle assembly into the yoke. Turn the forcing screw and carefully pull the knuckle assembly into the yoke. With torque still applied, tighten the lower ball joint nut to 70–90 ft. lbs. If the bottom stud should turn with the nut, add more torque to the forcing screw. Remove the puller, step plate and holding plate.

19. Tighten the adjusting sleeve to 40 ft. lbs. Once tightened, remove the spanner wrench.

20. Install the upper ball joint nut and torque it to specifications as listed in Section 8 of this manual. Line up the cotter key hole in the castellation nut with the hole in the stud by tightening, not loosening the nut.

21. Install a new cotter key.

22. Attach a pull scale to the knuckle and check the turning effort. Pull should not exceed 26 lbs. If it does, the ball joints will have to be replaced.

23. Connect the steering linkage to the knuckle. Tighten it to specifications as listed in Section 8 of this manual.

24. Make sure that the seal and deflector are properly installed on the axle shaft assembly. Assemble the seal on the shoulder of the deflector. Position the wheel bearing spacer and apply a small amount of wheel bearing lubricant to the exposed face of the spacer.

25. Slide the axle shaft back into the housing, taking great care to avoid damage to the seal.

26. Install the backing plate, lubricate the spindle using C1AZ-19590-B lubricant or equivalent, install the spindle. Tighten the retaining screws and tighten to 30–40 ft. lbs.

27. Install the wheel, hub and drum as an assembly. Fill the axle with the proper grade and quantity of lubricant, as required.

Dana 60–7F

♦ See Figures 50 thru 63

1. Raise the vehicle and safely support it on jackstands.

2. Remove the front wheels.

3. Remove the caliper assembly and position out of the way. Remove the hub assembly.

4. Remove the inner wheel bearing and seal. Remove the nuts attaching the spindle shaft to the knuckle. Remove the spindle by lightly tapping with a rawhide hammer.

5. Place the spindle in a vise and remove the needle bearings using tool OTC 960, needle bearing remover or equivalent.

6. Remove the axle shaft joint assembly and the tie rod. Refer to Section 8 if more information is required.

7. Remove the 4 nuts on the steering arm in an alternate pattern as the compression springs will force the steering arm up.

8. Remove the steering arm, compression spring and gasket. Discard the gasket, replace gasket with a new one during assembly.

9. Remove 4 capscrews on the bearing cap. Remove the kingpin tapered bushing and knuckle from yoke. Remove kingpin felt seal and kingpin from the steering knuckle.

10. Remove the kingpin bearing cup, grease retainer, and seal all at the same time. Discard the seal and replace with new one at time of assembly. Inspect the grease retainer and replace with new one at time of assembly.

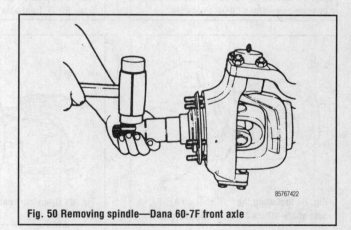

Fig. 50 Removing spindle—Dana 60-7F front axle

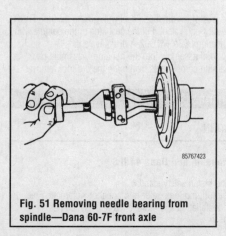

Fig. 51 Removing needle bearing from spindle—Dana 60-7F front axle

Fig. 52 Removing nuts from steering—Dana 60-7F front axle

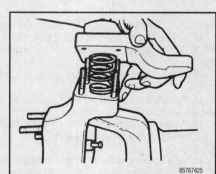

Fig. 53 Removing steering arm, compression spring and gasket—Dana 60-7F front axle

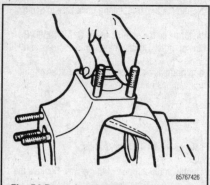

Fig. 54 Removing kingpin tapered bushing—Dana 60-7F front axle

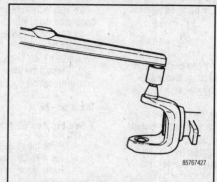

Fig. 55 Installing kingpin—Dana 60-7F front axle

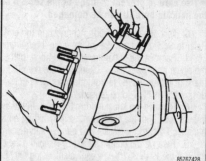

Fig. 56 Installing knuckle and tapered bushing over kingpin—Dana 60-7F front axle

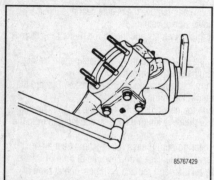

Fig. 57 Tightening the cap screws of the bearing cap—Dana 60-7F front axle

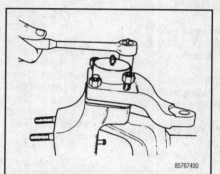

Fig. 58 Tightening bolts on steering cap over compression spring and gasket—Dana 60-7F front axle

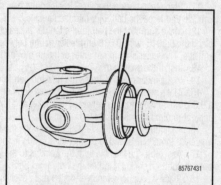

Fig. 59 Removing the "V" seal on front axle shaft—Dana 60-7F front axle

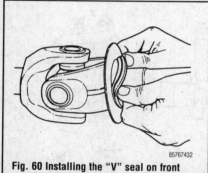

Fig. 60 Installing the "V" seal on front axle shaft—Dana 60-7F front axle

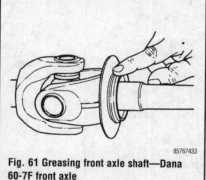

Fig. 61 Greasing front axle shaft—Dana 60-7F front axle

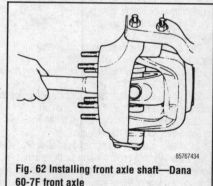

Fig. 62 Installing front axle shaft—Dana 60-7F front axle

To install:

11. Assembly new grease retainer and kingpin bearing cup.

12. Fill the area in the grease retainer with Ford lubricant specification ESA MIC92-A or equivalent. Grease the bearing cone and install. Install new kingpin bearing oil seal.

13. Install kingpin and tighten to specifications as listed in Section 8 of this manual.

14. Assemble bearing cap with 4 cap screws. Tighten cap screws alternately and evenly. Tighten the cap screws to 70–90 ft. lbs.

15. Assemble compression spring on kingpin bushing. Assemble the steering arm with new gasket, over the 4 studs. Tighten nut alternately and evenly to 70–90 ft. lbs.

16. Assemble new neddle bearings into the spindle.

17. Some axles are equipped with a "V" seal which is assembled to the axle shaft stone shield. If the seal is worn, remove and replace with a new one.

18. Assemble "V" seal to axle shaft stone shield. Lip of the seal is directed towards the spindle.

19. Pack the thrust face area of the shaft and seal with grease meeting Ford specifications ESA-M1C92-A or equivalent. Fill the seal area of the spindle with grease meeting Ford specifications ESA-M1C92-A or equivalent.

20. Assemble axle shaft joint assembly into the housing. Assemble new bronze spacer and the remaining components, reversing the order of removal.

Front Wheel Bearings

REMOVAL & INSTALLATION

Dana 50, Dana 60 Monobeam and Dana 44 IFS

1. Raise the vehicle and install safety stands.

2. If equipped with free running hubs refer to Manual or Automatic Free Running Hub Removal and Installation and remove the hub assemblies.

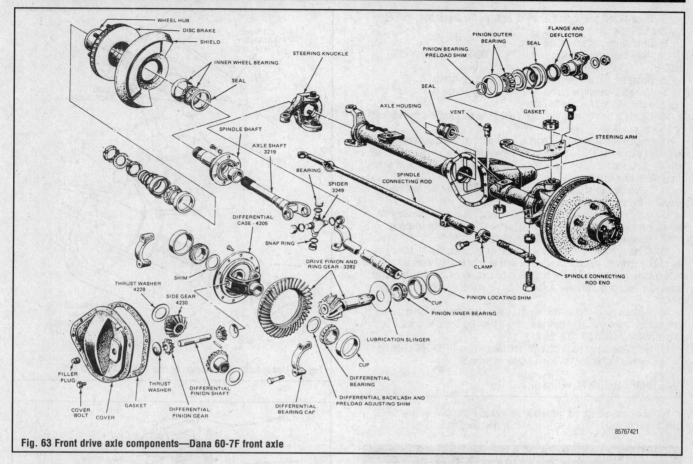

Fig. 63 Front drive axle components—Dana 60-7F front axle

3. If equipped, remove the adjusting nut using spanner wrench, Tool T59T-1197-B, or equivalent.

4. If equipped with Dana 50 or Dana 60 Monobeam front axle, remove the outer locknut, lockwasher and inner locknut with spanner wrench D85T-1197-A or equivalent.

5. Remove the caliper and suspend it out of the way. See Section 9.

6. Slide the hub and disc assembly off of the spindle. The outer wheel bearing will slide out as the hub is removed, so be prepared to catch it.

7. Lay the hub on a clean work surface. Carefully remove the inner bearing cone and grease seal out of the hub using the appropriate puller.

8. Inspect the bearing cups for pits or cracks. If necessary, remove them with a drift. If new cups are installed, install new bearings.

To install:

9. Lubricate the bearings with Multi-Purpose Lubricant Ford Specification, ESA-MIC7-B or equivalent. Clean all old grease from the hub. Pack the cones and rollers. If a bearing packer is not available, work as much lubricant as possible between the rollers and the cages.

10. Drive new cups into place with a driver, making sure that they are fully seated.

11. Position the inner bearing cone and roller in the inner cup and install the grease retainer.

12. Carefully position the hub and disc assembly on the spindle.

13. Install the outer bearing cone and roller, and the adjusting nut or locknuts and washers.

14. If equipped with a Dana 44 IFS of 44 IFS HD front driving axle, adjust bearings as follows:

a. Using Tool T59T-1197-B and a torque wrench, tighten the bearing adjusting nut to 50 ft. lbs., while rotating the wheel back and forth to seat the bearings.

b. Back off the adjusting nut approximately 60°.

c. Retighten the adjusting nut to 15 ft. lbs. Remove the tool and the torque wrench.

d. Inspect the end-play of the wheel on the spindle. It should be 0.00–0.006 in. If excess end-play is present, retorque the bearings.

15. If equipped with a Dana 50 IFS and Dana 60 Monobeam front driving axle, adjust bearings as follows:

a. With the outer locknut and lock washer removed, tighten the inner locknut to 50 ft. lbs. while rotating the wheel back and forth to seat the bearings.

b. Back off the adjusting nut and retighten to 31–39 ft. lbs.

c. While rotating the hub, back off the locknut 135-150°.

d. Install the lockwasher so the key is positioned in the spindle groove. Rotate the inner locknut so the pin is aligned into the nearest lock washer hole.

e. Install the outer locknut and tighten to 160-205 ft. lbs. using spanner wrench.

f. Inspect the end-play of the wheel on the spindle. It should be 0.00–0.006 in. If excess end-play is present, retorque the bearings.

16. Assemble the hub parts.

17. Install the caliper.

18. Remove the safety stands and lower the vehicle.

Right Side Slip Yoke and Stub Shaft, Carrier, Carrier Oil Seal and Bearing

REMOVAL & INSTALLATION

Dana 44-IFS and Dana 50-IFS

➡**This procedure requires the use of special tools.**

1. Raise and support the front end on jackstands.

2. Disconnect the front driveshaft from the carrier and wire it up out of the way.

3. Remove the left and right axle shafts and both spindles.

4. Support the carrier with a floor jack and unbolt the carrier from the support arm.

5. Place a drain pan under the carrier, separate the carrier from the support arm and drain the carrier.

6. Remove the carrier from the truck.

7. Place the carrier in holding fixture T57L-500-B with adapters T80T-4000-B.

8. Rotate the slip yoke and shaft assembly from the carrier.

9. Using a slidehammer/puller remove the caged needle bearing and oil seal as a unit. Discard the oil seal bearing.

10. Clean the bearing bore thoroughly and make sure that it is free of nicks and burrs.

11. Insert a new bearing in its bore with the printing facing outward. Drive it into place with driver T83T-1244-A, or its equivalent. Install a new bearing seal with the lip facing away from the bearing. Coat the bearing and seal with waterproof wheel bearing grease.

12. Install the slip yoke and shaft assembly into the carrier so that the groove in the shaft is visible in the differential case.

13. Install the snapring in the groove in the shaft. It may be necessary to force the snapring into place with a small prybar. Don't strike the snapring!

14. Remove the carrier from the holding fixture.

15. Clean all traces of sealant from the carrier and support arm. Make sure the mating surfaces are clean. Apply a ¼ inch wide bead of RTV sealant to the mating surface of the carrier. The bead must be continuous and should not pass through or outside of the holes. Install the carrier with 5 minutes of applying the sealer.

16. Position the carrier on the jack and raise it into position using guide pins to align it if you'd like. Install and hand-tighten the bolts. Torque the bolts in a circular pattern to 30-40 ft. lbs.

17. Install the support arm tab bolts and torque them to 85-100 ft. lbs.

18. Install all other parts in reverse order of removal.

AXLE SHAFT U-JOINT OVERHAUL

Follow the procedures outlined under Axle Shaft Removal & Installation to gain access to the U-joints. Overhaul them as described under U-joints.

Steering Knuckle and Ball Joints

REMOVAL & INSTALLATION

▶ **See Figures 64, 65 and 66**

Independent Front Axles

1. Raise and support the front end on jackstands.

2. Remove the spindles and left and right shafts and joint.

3. Remove the tie rod nut and disconnect the tie rod from the steering arm.

4. Remove the cotter pin from the top ball joint stud. Remove the nut from the top stud and loosen the nut on the lower stud inside the knuckle.

5. Hit the top stud sharply with a plastic mallet to free the knuckle from the axle arm. Remove and discard the bottom nut. New nuts should be used at assembly.

6. Note the positioning of the camber adjuster carefully for reassembly. Remove the camber adjuster. If it's hard to remove, use a puller.

7. Place the knuckle in a vise and remove the snapring from the bottom ball joint. Not all ball joints will have this snapring.

8. Remove the plug from C-frame tool T74P-4635-C and replace it with plug T80T-3010-A. Assemble C-frame tool T74P-4635-C and receiving cup D79T-3010-G (Bronco, F-150 and 250) or T80T-3010-A2 (F-250HD and F-350). on the knuckle.

9. Turn the forcing screw inward until the ball joint is separated from the knuckle.

10. Assemble the C-frame tool with receiving cup D79P-3010-BG on the upper ball joint and force it out of the knuckle.

▶**Always force out the bottom ball joint first.**

11. Clean the ball joint bores thoroughly.

12. Insert the lower joint into its bore as straight as possible.

13. On the Bronco, F-150 and F-250, assemble the C-frame tool, receiving cup T80T-3010-A3 and installing cup D79T-3010-BF onto the lower ball

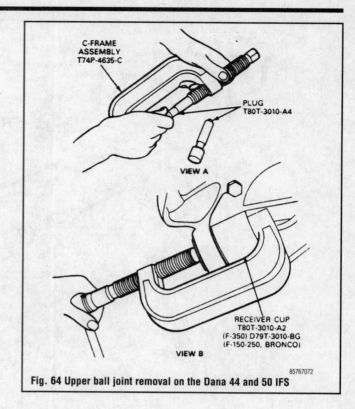

Fig. 64 Upper ball joint removal on the Dana 44 and 50 IFS

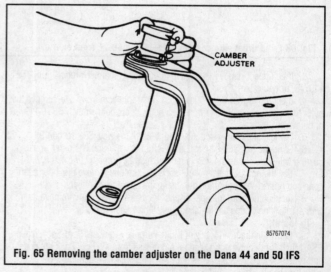

Fig. 65 Removing the camber adjuster on the Dana 44 and 50 IFS

joint. On the F-250HD and F-350, assemble the C-frame tool, receiving cup T80T-3010-A3 and receiving cup D79T-3010-BG on the lower ball joint.

14. Turn the screw clockwise until the ball joint is firmly seated.

➡**If the ball joint cannot be installed to the correct depth, you'll have to realign the receiving cup on the tool.**

15. On all models, assemble the C-frame, receiving cup T80T-3010-A3 and replacer T80T-3010-A1 on the upper ball joint.

16. Turn the screw clockwise until the ball joint is firmly seated.

➡**If the ball joint cannot be installed to the correct depth, you'll have to realign the receiving cup on the tool.**

17. Place the knuckle into position on the axle arm. Install the camber adjuster on the upper ball joint stud with the arrow point to positive or negative as noted before disassembly.

18. Install a new nut on the bottom stud, finger tight. Install a new nut on the top stud finger tight.

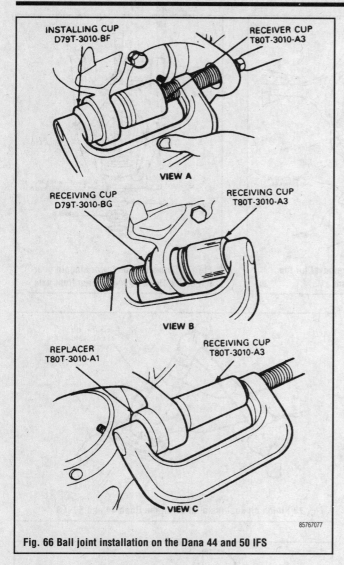

Fig. 66 Ball joint installation on the Dana 44 and 50 IFS

19. Tighten the bottom nut to 80 ft. lbs.
20. Tighten the top nut to 100 ft. lbs., then, (tighten) advance the nut until the cotter pin hole align with the castellations. Install a new cotter pin.
21. Again tighten the bottom nut, this time to 110 ft. lbs.
22. Install the remaining components.

Steering Knuckle and Kingpins

REMOVAL & INSTALLATION

◆ **See Figures 67 thru 72**

Monobeam Front Axle

➡For this job you'll need a torque wrench with a capacity of at least 600 ft. lbs.

1. Raise and support the front end on jackstands.
2. Remove the axle shafts.
3. Alternately and evenly remove the 4 bolts that retain the spindle cap to the knuckle. This will relieve spring tension.
4. When spring tension is relieved, remove the bolts.
5. Remove the spindle cap, compression spring and retainer. Discard the gasket.
6. Remove the 4 bolts securing the lower kingpin and retainer to the knuckle. Remove the lower kingpin and retainer.

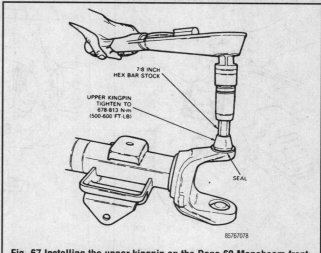

Fig. 67 Installing the upper kingpin on the Dana 60 Monobeam front axle

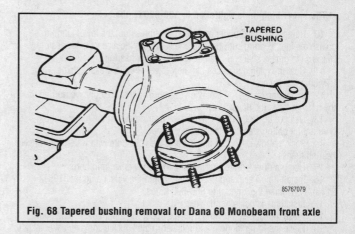

Fig. 68 Tapered bushing removal for Dana 60 Monobeam front axle

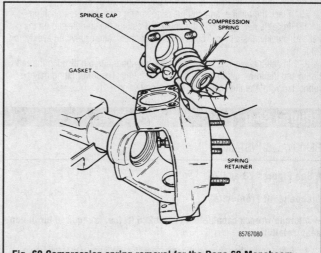

Fig. 69 Compression spring removal for the Dana 60 Monobeam front drive axle

7. Remove the tapered bushing from the top of the upper kingpin.
8. Remove the knuckle from the axle yoke.
9. Remove the upper kingpin from the axle yoke with a piece of ⅞ inch hex-shaped case hardened metal bar stock, or, with a ⅞ inch hex socket. Discard the upper kingpin and seal.

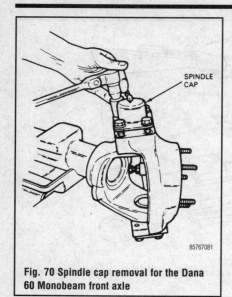

Fig. 70 Spindle cap removal for the Dana 60 Monobeam front axle

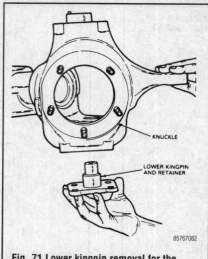

Fig. 71 Lower kingpin removal for the Dana 60 Monobeam front axle

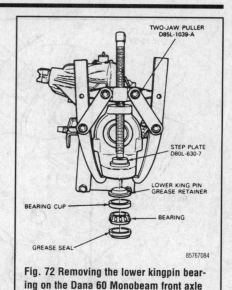

Fig. 72 Removing the lower kingpin bearing on the Dana 60 Monobeam front axle

➡ The upper kingpin is tightened to 500-600 ft. lbs.

10. Using a 2-jawed puller and step plate, press out the lower kingpin grease retainer, bearing cup, bearing and seal from the axle yoke lower bore. Discard the grease seal and retainer, and the lower bearing cup.

11. Coat the mating surfaces of a new lower kingpin grease retainer with RTV silicone sealer.

12. Install the retainer in the axle yoke bore so that the concave portion of the retainer faces the upper kingpin.

13. Using a bearing driver, drive a new bearing cup in the lower kingpin bore until it bottoms against the grease retainer.

14. Pack the lower kingpin bearing and the yoke bore with waterproof wheel bearing grease.

15. Using a driver, drive a new seal into the lower kingpin bore.

16. Install a new seal and upper kingpin into the yoke using tool T86T-3110-AH. Tighten the kingpin to 500-600 ft. lbs.

17. Install the knuckle on the yoke.

18. Place the tapered bushing over the upper kingpin in the knuckle bore.

19. Place the lower kingpin and retainer in the knuckle and axle yoke. Install the 4 bolts and tighten them, alternately and evenly, to 90 ft. lbs.

20. Place the retainer and compression spring on the tapered bushing.

21. Install a new gasket on the knuckle. Position the spindle cap on the gasket and knuckle. Install the 4 bolts and tighten them, alternately and evenly, to 90 ft. lbs.

22. Install the axle shafts and lubricate the upper kingpin through the zerk fitting and the lower fitting through the flush fitting. The lower fitting may be lubricated with Alemite adapter #6783, or equivalent.

Pinion Seal

REMOVAL & INSTALLATION

◆ See Figures 73 and 74

Independent Front Axle

➡ A torque wrench capable of at least 225 ft. lbs. is required for pinion seal installation.

1. Raise and safely support the vehicle with jackstands under the frame rails. Allow the axle to drop to rebound position for working clearance.

2. Mark the companion flanges and U-joints for correct reinstallation position.

3. Remove the driveshaft. Use a suitable tool to hold the companion flange. Remove the pinion nut and companion flange.

4. Use a slide hammer and hook or sheet metal screw to remove the oil seal.

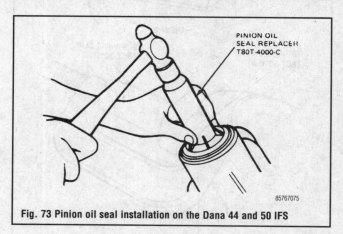

Fig. 73 Pinion oil seal installation on the Dana 44 and 50 IFS

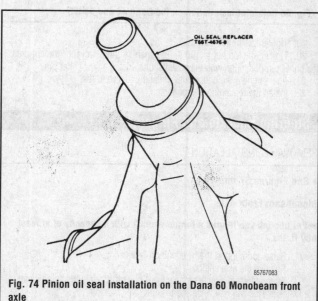

Fig. 74 Pinion oil seal installation on the Dana 60 Monobeam front axle

5. Install a new pinion seal after lubricating the sealing surfaces. Use a suitable seal driver. Install the companion flange and pinion nut. Tighten the nut to 200-220 ft. lbs.

Monobeam Front Axle

➡**A torque wrench capable of at least 300 ft. lbs. is required for pinion seal installation.**

1. Raise and support the truck on jackstands.
2. Allow the axle to hang freely.
3. Matchmark and disconnect the driveshaft from the front axle.
4. Using a tool such as T75T-4851-B, or equivalent, hold the pinion flange while removing the pinion nut.
5. Using a puller, remove the pinion flange.
6. Use a puller to remove the seal, or punch the seal out using a pin punch.
7. Thoroughly clean the seal bore and make sure that it is not damaged in any way. Coat the sealing edge of the new seal with a small amount of 80W/90 oil and drive the seal into the housing using a seal driver.
8. Coat the inside of the pinion flange with clean 80W/90 oil and install the flange onto the pinion shaft.

9. Install the nut on the pinion shaft and tighten it to 250-300 ft. lbs.
10. Connect the driveshaft.

Axle Unit

REMOVAL & INSTALLATION

Independent Front Axles

◆ **See Figures 75 and 76**

1. Raise and support the front end on jackstands placed under the radius arms.
2. Remove the wheels.
3. Remove the calipers and wire them out of the way. Don't disconnect the brake lines.

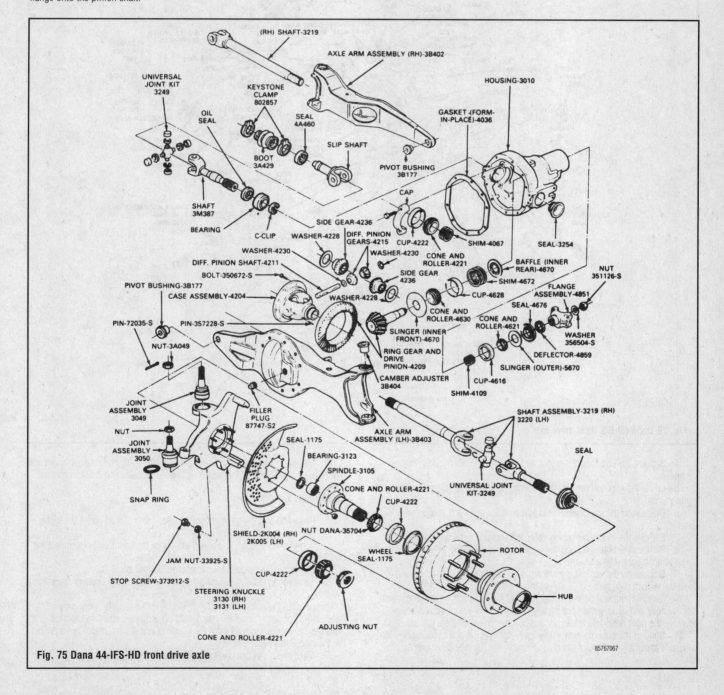

Fig. 75 Dana 44-IFS-HD front drive axle

85767067

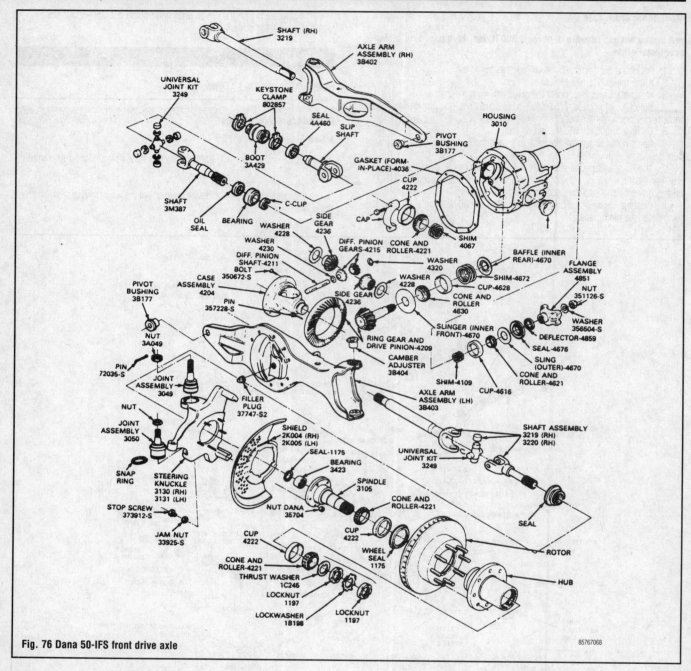

Fig. 76 Dana 50-IFS front drive axle

85767068

4. Support the axle arm with a jack and remove the upper coil spring retainers.

5. Lower the jack and remove the coil springs, spring cushions and lower spring seats.

6. Disconnect the shock absorbers at the radius arms and upper mounting brackets.

7. Remove the studs and spring seats at the radius arms and axle arms.

8. Remove the bolts securing the upper attachment to the axle arm and the lower attachment to the axle arm.

9. Disconnect the vent tube at the housing. Remove the vent fitting and install a ⅛ inch pipe plug.

10. Remove the pivot bolt securing the right side axle arm to the crossmember. Remove and discard the boot clamps and remove the boot from the shaft. Remove the right drive axle assembly and pull the axle shaft from the slip shaft.

11. Support the housing with a floor jack. Remove the bolt securing the left side axle assembly to the crossmember. Remove the left side drive axle assembly.

12. Installation is, basically, a reversal of the removal procedure. Always use new boot clamps. Observe the torque values listed in Section 8 of this manual.

Monobeam Axle

1. Raise and support the front end on jackstands placed under the frame.
2. Remove the wheels.
3. Remove the calipers and wire them out of the way. Don't disconnect the brake lines.
4. Disconnect the stabilizer links at the stabilizer bar.
5. Remove the U-bolts securing the stabilizer bar and mounting brackets to the axle.
6. Remove the cotter pins and nuts securing the spindle connecting rod to the steering knuckles. Separate the connecting rod to the steering knuckles. Separate the connecting rods from the knuckles with a pitman arm puller. Wire the steering linkage to the spring.
7. Matchmark and disconnect the driveshaft from the front axle.

8. Disconnect the vent tube at the axle and plug the fitting.

9. On the right side, disconnect the track bar from the right spring cap.

10. Raise the front end and position jackstands under front springs at a point about half way between the axle and spring rear hanger. Remove the jackstands from the front of the frame and lower the truck onto the stands under the springs. Make sure that the truck is securely supported.

11. Support the axle with a floor jack.

12. Remove the U-bolts securing the springs to the axle.

13. Lower the axle from the truck.

14. Installation is the reverse of removal. Observe the suspension components torque values listed in Section 8 of this manual. Tighten the components listed as follows:

• Driveshaft-to-flange: 15-20 ft. lbs.
• Spindle connecting rod-to-knuckle: 70-100 ft. lbs.

REAR AXLE

Axle Shaft, Bearing and Seal

REMOVAL & INSTALLATION

◆ **See Figures 77 thru 83**

Ford 9 Inch Removable Carrier

➥The following procedure requires the use of special tools, including a shop press.

1. Jack up the vehicle and support it on jackstands.

2. Remove the wheel.

3. Working through the hole in the flange, remove the nuts that secure the wheel bearing retainer.

4. Pull the axle assembly out of the axle housing.

5. Whenever an axle shaft is removed the oil seal should be replaced. Install one nut to hold the brake backing plate in place and remove the oil seal with a slide hammer and adapter.

6. If the wheel bearing is to be replaced, the inner retaining ring must be loosened. Never use heat to do this.

7. Nick the retaining ring deeply with a cold chisel in several places. It will then slide off the axle.

8. The use of a shop press is necessary for the removal of the bearing.

To install:

9. Lightly coat the wheel bearing bores with axle lubricant.

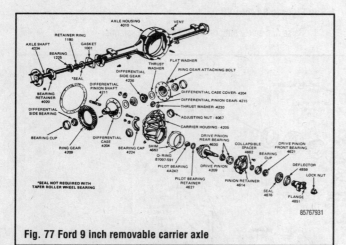

Fig. 77 Ford 9 inch removable carrier axle

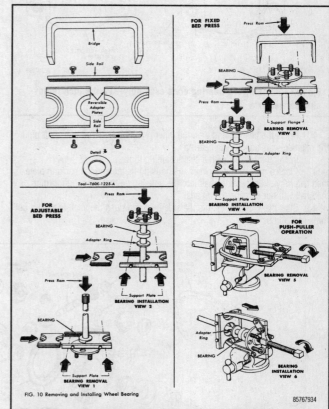

Fig. 80 Removing and installing the wheel bearing—Ford 9 inch removable carrier axle

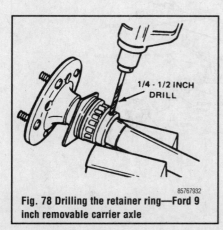

Fig. 78 Drilling the retainer ring—Ford 9 inch removable carrier axle

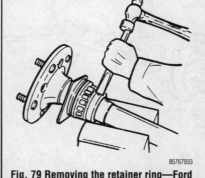

Fig. 79 Removing the retainer ring—Ford 9 inch removable carrier axle

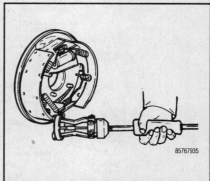

Fig. 81 Removing the bearing race—Ford 9 inch removable carrier axle

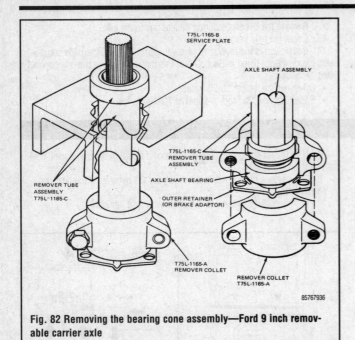

Fig. 82 Removing the bearing cone assembly—Ford 9 inch removable carrier axle

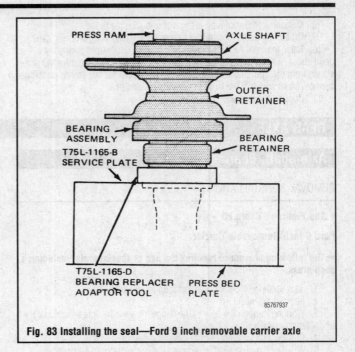

Fig. 83 Installing the seal—Ford 9 inch removable carrier axle

10. Press the bearing and then the inner retaining ring onto the shaft until the retainer seats against the bearing.

11. Install the oil seal with a seal installing tool.

12. Place a new gasket between the housing flange and the backing plate, then carefully slide the axle shaft into the housing so that the rough forging of the shaft will not damage the oil seal.

13. Start the axle splines into the side gear and push the shaft in until it bottoms in the housing.

14. Install the bearing retainer plate and nuts.
15. Install the brake drum and wheel.

Ford 8.8 in. (223.5mm) Ring Gear Integral Carrier Ford 10.25 in. (260.35mm) Ring Gear, Semi-Floating Integral Carrier

◆ **See Figures 84 thru 88**

1. Raise and safely support the vehicle on jackstands.

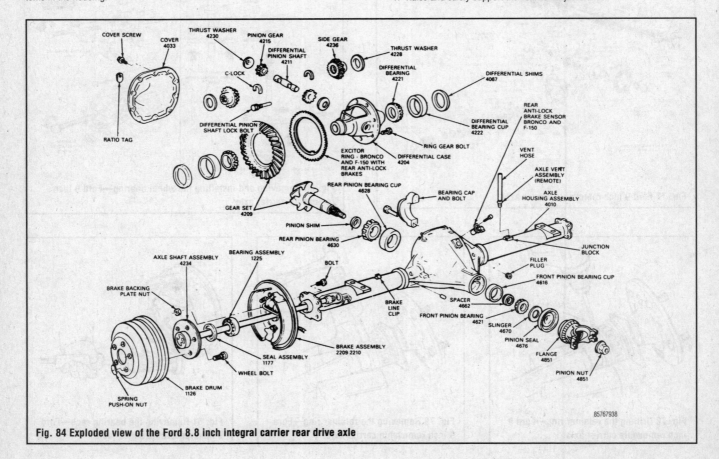

Fig. 84 Exploded view of the Ford 8.8 inch integral carrier rear drive axle

2. Remove the wheels from the brake drums.

3. Place a drain pan under the housing and drain the lubricant by loosening the housing cover.

4. Remove the locks securing the brake drums to the axle shaft flanges and remove the drums.

5. Remove the housing cover and gasket.

6. Remove the side gear pinion shaft lockbolt and the side gear pinion shaft.

7. Push the axle shafts inward and remove the C-locks from the inner end of the axle shafts. Temporarily replace the shaft and lockbolt to retain the differential gears in position.

8. Remove the axle shafts with a slide hammer. Be sure the seal is not damaged by the splines on the axle shaft.

9. Remove the bearing and oil seal from the housing. Both the seal and bearing can be removed with a slide hammer

10. Two types of bearings are used on some axles, one requiring a press fit and the other a loose fit. A loose fitting bearing does not necessarily indicate excessive wear.

11. Inspect the axle shaft housing and axle shafts for burrs or other irregularities. Replace any work or damaged parts. A light yellow color on the bearing

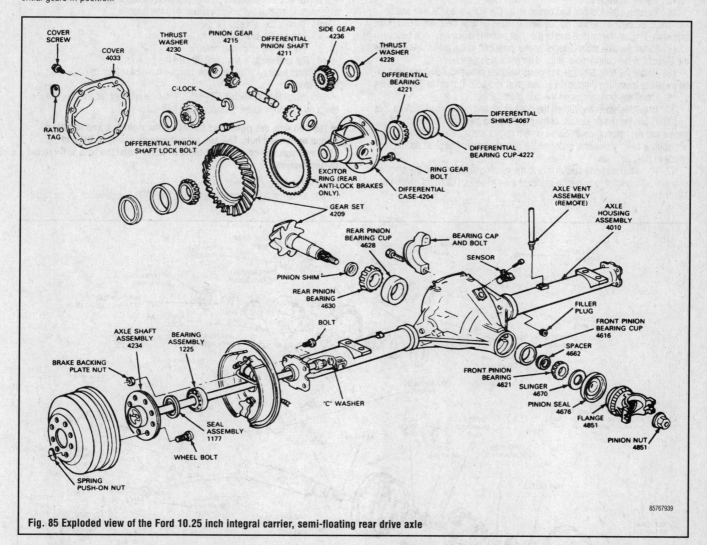

Fig. 85 Exploded view of the Ford 10.25 inch integral carrier, semi-floating rear drive axle

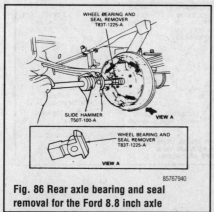

Fig. 86 Rear axle bearing and seal removal for the Ford 8.8 inch axle

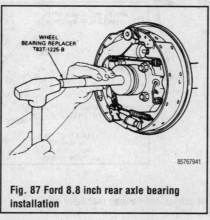

Fig. 87 Ford 8.8 inch rear axle bearing installation

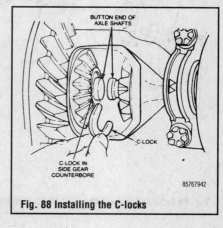

Fig. 88 Installing the C-locks

journal of the axle shaft is normal, and does not require replacement of the axle shaft. Slight pitting and wear is also normal.

12. Lightly coat the wheel bearing rollers with axle lubricant. Install the bearings in the axle housing until the bearing seats firmly against the shoulder.

13. Wipe all lubricant from the oil seal bore, before installing the seal.

14. Inspect the original seals for wear. If necessary, these may be replaced with new seals, which are prepacked with lubricant and do not require soaking.

To install:

15. Install the oil seal.

16. Rπemove the lockbolt and pinion shaft. Carefully slide the axle shafts into place. Be careful that you do not damage the seal with the splined end of the axle shaft. Engage the splined end of the shaft with the differential side gears.

17. Install the axle shaft C-locks on the inner end of the axle shafts and seat the C-locks in the counterbore of the differential side gears.

18. Rotate the differential pinion gears until the differential pinion shaft can be installed. Install the differential pinion shaft lockbolt. Tighten to 15–22 ft. lbs.

19. Install the brake drum on the axle shaft flange.

20. Install the wheel and tire on the brake drum and tighten the attaching nuts.

21. Clean the gasket surface of the rear housing and install a new cover gasket and the housing cover. Some covers do not use a gasket. On these models, apply a bead of silicone sealer on the gasket surface. The bead should run inside of the bolt holes.

22. Raise the rear axle so that it is in the running position. Add the amount of specified lubricant to bring the lubricant level to ½ in. (12.7mm) below the filler hole.

Ford 10.25 in. (260.35mm) Ring Gear, Full Floating Integral Carrier

♦ **See Figures 89 thru 98**

The wheel bearings on the full floating rear axle are packed with wheel bearing grease. Axle lubricant can also flow into the wheel hubs and bearings, however, wheel bearing grease is the primary lubricant. The wheel bearing grease provides lubrication until the axle lubricant reaches the bearings during normal operation.

1. Set the parking brake and loosen the axle shaft bolts.

2. Raise the rear wheels off the floor and place jackstands under the rear axle housing so that the axle is parallel with the floor.

3. Remove the wheels.

4. Remove the brake drums.

5. Remove the axle shaft bolts.

6. Remove the axle shaft and discard the gaskets.

7. With the axle shaft removed, remove the gasket from the axle shaft flange studs.

8. Install Hub Wrench T85T–4252–AH, or equivalent, so that the drive tangs on the tool engage the slots in the hub nut.

➡**The hub nuts are right hand thread on the right hub and left hand thread on the left hub. The hub nuts should be stamped RH and LH. Never use power or impact tools on these nuts! The nuts will ratchet during removal.**

9. Remove the hub nut.

10. Install step plate adapter tool D80L–630–7, or equivalent, in the hub.

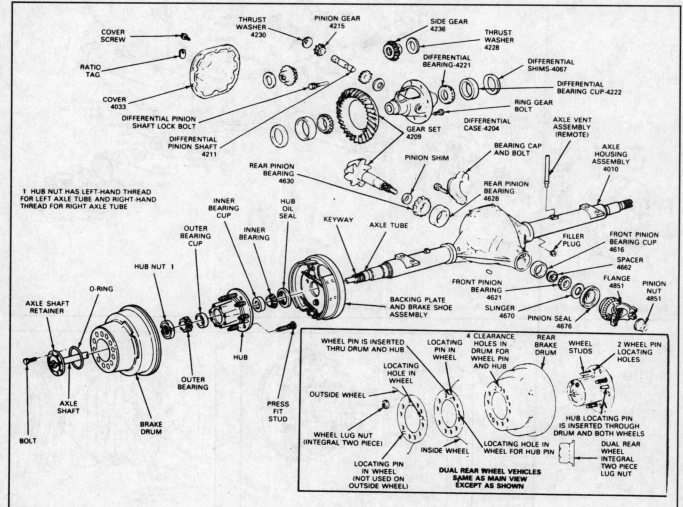

Fig. 89 Exploded view of the Ford 10.25 inch integral carrier, full-floating rear drive axle

85767943

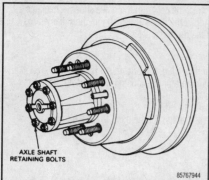

Fig. 90 Rear axle shaft retaining bolts on the Ford 10.25 inch full-floating rear axle

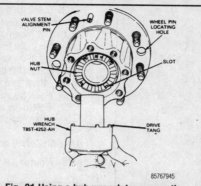

Fig. 91 Using a hub wrench to remove the hub nuts on the 10.25 inch full-floating axle

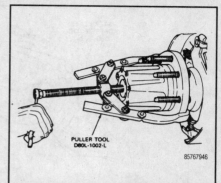

Fig. 92 Loosening the hub on the 10.25 inch full-floating axle

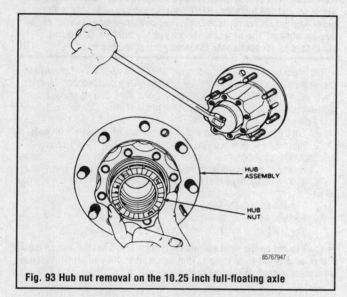

Fig. 93 Hub nut removal on the 10.25 inch full-floating axle

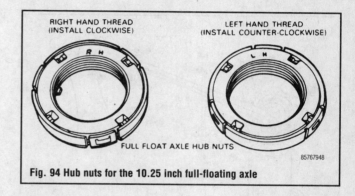

Fig. 94 Hub nuts for the 10.25 inch full-floating axle

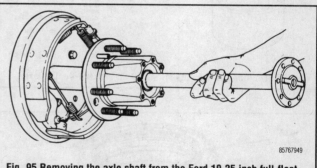

Fig. 95 Removing the axle shaft from the Ford 10.25 inch full-floating rear axle

11. Install puller D80L–1002–L, or equivalent and loosen the hub to the point of removal. Remove the puller and step plate.

12. Remove the hub, taking care to catch the outer bearing as the hub comes off.

13. Install the hub in a soft-jawed vise and pry out the hub seal.

14. Lift out the inner bearing.

15. Drive out the inner and outer bearing races with a drift.

16. Wash all the old grease or axle lubricant out of the wheel hub, using a suitable solvent.

17. Wash the bearing races and rollers and inspect them for pitting, galling, and uneven wear patterns. Inspect the roller for end wear. Replace any bearing and race that appears in any way damaged. Always replace the bearings and races as a set.

18. Coat the race bores with a light coat of clean, waterproof wheel bearing grease and drive the races squarely into the bores until they are fully seated. A good indication that the race is seated is when you notice the grease from the bore squashing out under the race when it contact the shoulder. Another indication is a definite change in the metallic tone when you seat the race. Just be very careful to avoid damaging the bearing surface of the race!

19. Pack each bearing cone and roller with a bearing packer or in the manner outlined in Section 1 for the front wheel bearings on 2-Wheel Drive trucks.

To install:

20. Place the inner bearing cone and roller assembly in the wheel hub.

➡ **When installing the new seal, the words OIL SIDE must go inwards towards the bearing!**

21. Place the seal squarely in the hub and drive it into place. The best tool for the job is a seal driver such as T85T–1175–AH, which will stop when the seal is at the proper depth.

➡ **If the seal is misaligned or damaged during installation, a new seal must be installed.**

22. Clean the spindle thoroughly. If the spindle is excessively pitted, damaged or has a predominately bluish tint (from overheating), it must be replaced.

23. Coat the spindle with 80W/90 oil.

24. Pack the hub with clean, waterproof wheel bearing grease.

25. Pack the outer bearing with clean, waterproof wheel bearing grease in the same manner as you packed the inner bearing.

26. Place the outer bearing in the hub and install the hub and bearing together on the spindle.

27. Install the hub nut on the spindle. Make sure that the nut tab is located in the keyway prior to thread engagement. Turn the hub nut onto the threads as far as you can by hand, noting the thread direction.

28. Install the hub wrench tool and tighten the nut to 55–65 ft. lbs. Rotate the hub occasionally during nut tightening.

29. Ratchet the nut back 5 teeth. **Make sure that you hear 5 clicks!**

30. Inspect the axle shaft Q-ring seal and replace it if it looks at all bad.

31. Install the axle shaft.

32. Coat the axle shaft bolt threads with waterproof seal and install them by hand until they seat. **Do not tighten them with a wrench at this time!**

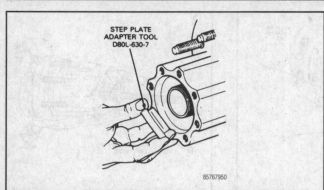

Fig. 96 Installing the step plate adapter tool on the 10.25 inch full-floating axle

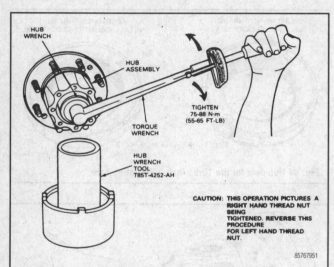

Fig. 97 Installing the hub nuts for the 10.25 inch full-floating axle

33. Check the diameter across the center of the brake shoes. Check the diameter of the brake drum. Adjust the brake shoes so that their diameter is 0.030 in. (0.76mm) less than the drum diameter.

34. Install the brake drum

35. Install the wheel.

36. Loosen the differential filler plug. If lubricant starts to run out, retighten the plug. If not, remove the plug and fill the housing with 80W/90 gear oil.

37. Lower the truck to the floor.

38. Tighten the wheel lugs to 140 ft. lbs.

39. Now tighten the axle shaft bolts. Torque them to 60–80 ft. lbs.

Dana Model 60 or 70

▶ See Figures 99 thru 103

✳✳ CAUTION

New Dual Rear Wheel models have flat-faced lug nut replacing the old cone-shaped lug nuts. NEVER replace these new nuts with the older design! Never replace the newer designed wheels with older design wheels! The newer wheels have lug holes with special shoulders to accommodate the newly designed lug nuts.

The wheel bearings on full floating rear axles are packed with wheel bearing grease. Axle lubricant can also flow into the wheel hubs and bearings, however, wheel bearing grease is the primary lubricant. The wheel bearing grease provides lubrication until the axle lubricant reaches the bearings during normal operation.

1. Set the parking brake and loosen -do not remove- the axle shaft bolts.

2. Raise the rear wheels off the floor and place jackstands under the rear axle housing so that the axle is parallel with the floor. Release the parking brake.

3. Remove the axle shaft bolts and lockwashers. They should not be re-used.

4. Place a heavy duty wheel dolly under the wheels and raise them so that all weight is off the wheel bearings.

5. Remove the axle shaft and gasket(s).

6. Remove the caliper. See Section 9.

7. Using a special hub nut wrench, remove the hub nut.

➡**The hub nut on the right spindle is right hand thread; the one on the left spindle is left hand thread. They are marked RH and LH. NEVER use an impact wrench on the hub nut!**

8. Remove the outer bearing cone and pull the wheel straight off the axle.

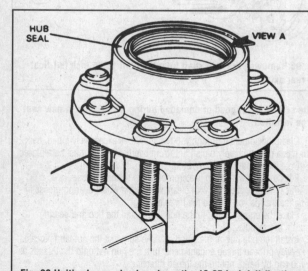

Fig. 98 Unitized rear wheel seals on the 10.25 inch full-floating axle

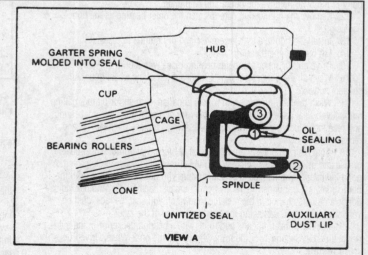

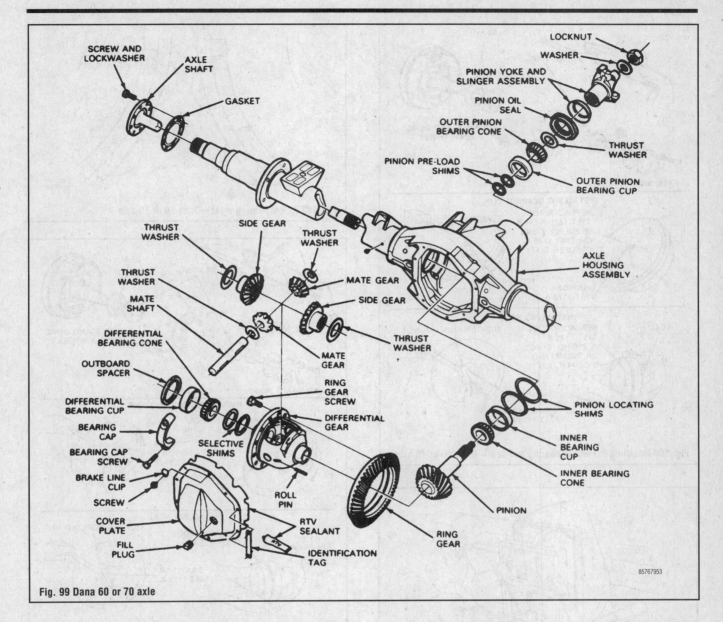

Fig. 99 Dana 60 or 70 axle

9. With a piece of hardwood or a brass drift which will just clear the outer bearing cup, drive the inner bearing cone and inner seal out of the wheel hub.

10. Wash all the old grease or axle lubricant out of the wheel hub, using a suitable solvent.

11. Wash the bearing cups and rollers and inspect them for pitting, galling, and uneven wear patterns. Inspect the roller for end wear.

12. If the bearing cups are to be replaced, drive them out with a brass drift. Install the new cups with a block of wood and hammer or press them in.

13. If the bearing cups are properly seated, a 0.0015 in. (0.038mm) feeler gauge will not fit between the cup and the wheel hub. The gauge should not fit beneath the cup. Check several places to make sure the cups are squarely seated.

14. Pack each bearing cone and roller with a bearing packer or in the manner outlined for the front wheel bearings in Section 1. Use a multi-purpose wheel bearing grease.

15. Place the inner bearing cone and roller assembly in the wheel hub. Install a new inner seal in the hub with a seal installation tool.

16. Wrap the threads of the spindle with tape and carefully slide the hub straight on the spindle. Take care to avoid damaging the seal! Remove the tape.

17. Install the outer bearing. Start the hub nut, making sure that the hub tab is engaged with the keyway prior to threading.

18. Tighten the nut to 6575 ft. lbs. while rotating the wheel.

➡**The hub will ratchet at torque is applied. This ratcheting can be avoided by using Ford tool No. T88T-4252-A. Avoiding ratcheting will give more even bearing preloads.**

19. Back off (loosen) the adjusting nut 90° (¼ turn). Then, tighten it to 1520 ft. lbs.

20. Using a dial indicator, check endplay of the hub. No endplay is permitted.

21. Clean the hub bolt holes thoroughly. Replace the hub if any cracks are found around the holes or if the threads in the holes are in any way damaged.

22. Install the axle shaft, new flange gasket, lock washers and new shaft retaining bolts. Coat the bolt threads with thread adhesive. Tighten them snugly, but not completely.

23. Install the drums and wheels.

24. Lower the truck to the ground.

25. Tighten the wheel lug nuts.

26. Tighten the axle shaft bolts to 70–85 ft. lbs.

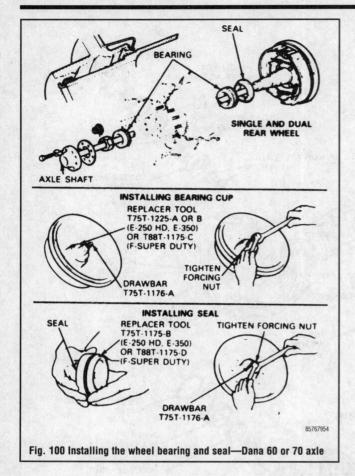

Fig. 100 Installing the wheel bearing and seal—Dana 60 or 70 axle

Fig. 101 Heavy duty wheel dolly

Pinion Seal

REMOVAL & INSTALLATION

Ford 9 inch Removable Carrier Axle

➡A torque wrench capable of at least 225 ft. lbs. is required for pinion seal installation.

1. Raise and safely support the vehicle with jackstands under the frame rails. Allow the axle to drop to rebound position for working clearance.
2. Remove the rear wheels and brake drums. No drag must be present on the axle.

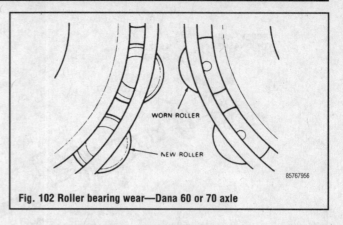

Fig. 102 Roller bearing wear—Dana 60 or 70 axle

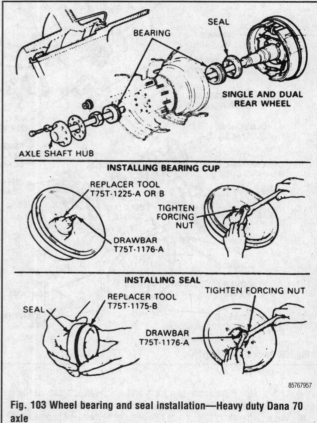

Fig. 103 Wheel bearing and seal installation—Heavy duty Dana 70 axle

3. Mark the companion flanges and U-joints for correct reinstallation position.
4. Remove the driveshaft.
5. Using an inch pound torque wrench and socket on the pinion yoke nut measure the amount of torque needed to maintain differential rotation through several clockwise revolutions. Record the measurement.
6. Use a suitable tool to hold the companion flange. Remove the pinion nut.
7. Place a drain pan under the differential, clean the area around the seal, and mark the yoke-to-pinion relation.
8. Use a 2-jawed puller to remove the pinion.
9. Remove the seal with a small prybar.
To install:
10. Thoroughly clean the oil seal bore.

➡If you are not absolutely certain of the proper seal installation depth, the proper seal driver must be used. If the seal is misaligned or damaged during installation, it must be removed and a new seal installed.

11. Drive the new seal into place with a seal driver such as T83T–4676–A. Coat the seal lip with clean, waterproof wheel bearing grease.

12. Coat the splines with a small amount of wheel bearing grease and install the yoke, aligning the matchmarks. Never hammer the yoke onto the pinion!

13. Install a NEW nut on the pinion.

14. Hold the yoke with a holding tool. Tighten the pinion nut, taking frequent turning torque readings until the original preload reading is attained. If the original preload reading, that you noted before disassembly, is lower than the original reading, keep tightening the pinion nut until the specified reading is reached. If the original preload reading is higher than 8-14 inch lbs., torque the nut just until the original reading is reached.

✷✷ WARNING

Under no circumstances should the nut be backed off to reduce the preload reading! If the preload is exceeded, the yoke and bearing must be removed and a new collapsible spacer must be installed. The entire process of preload adjustment must be repeated.

15. Install the driveshaft using the matchmarks. Torque the nuts to 15 ft. lbs.

Ford 8.8 in. (223.5mm) Ring Gear Integral Carrier Axle

➡**A torque wrench capable of at least 225 ft. lbs. is required for pinion seal installation.**

1. Raise and safely support the vehicle with jackstands under the frame rails. Allow the axle to drop to rebound position for working clearance.

2. Remove the rear wheels and brake drums. No drag must be present on the axle.

3. Mark the companion flanges and U-joints for correct reinstallation position.

4. Remove the driveshaft.

5. Using an inch pound torque wrench and socket on the pinion yoke nut measure the amount of torque needed to maintain differential rotation through several clockwise revolutions. Record the measurement.

6. Use a suitable tool to hold the companion flange. Remove the pinion nut.

7. Place a drain pan under the differential, clean the area around the seal, and mark the yoke-to-pinion relation.

8. Use a 2-jawed puller to remove the pinion.

9. Remove the seal with a small prybar.

To install:

10. Thoroughly clean the oil seal bore.

➡**If you are not absolutely certain of the proper seal installation depth, the proper seal driver must be used. If the seal is misaligned or damaged during installation, it must be removed and a new seal installed.**

11. Drive the new seal into place with a seal driver such as T83T–4676–A. Coat the seal lip with clean, waterproof wheel bearing grease.

12. Coat the splines with a small amount of wheel bearing grease and install the yoke, aligning the matchmarks. Never hammer the yoke onto the pinion!

13. Install a NEW nut on the pinion.

14. Hold the yoke with a holding tool. Tighten the pinion nut to at least 160 ft. lbs., taking frequent turning torque readings until the original preload reading is attained.If the original preload reading, that you noted before disassembly, is lower than the specified reading of 8–14 inch lbs. for used bearings; 16–29 inch lbs. for new bearings, keep tightening the pinion nut until the specified reading is reached.If the original preload reading is higher than the specified values, torque the nut just until the original reading is reached.

✷✷ WARNING

Under no circumstances should the nut be backed off to reduce the preload reading! If the preload is exceeded, the yoke and bearing must be removed and a new collapsible spacer must be installed. The entire process of preload adjustment must be repeated.

15. Install the driveshaft using the matchmarks. Torque the nuts to 15 ft. lbs.

Ford 10.25 in. (260.35mm) Ring Gear Integral Carrier Axle

➡**A torque wrench capable of at least 225 ft. lbs. is required for pinion seal installation.**

1. Raise and safely support the vehicle with jackstands under the frame rails. Allow the axle to drop to the rebound position for working clearance.

2. Remove the rear wheels and brake drums. No drag must be present on the axle.

3. Mark the companion flanges and U-joints for correct reinstallation position.

4. Remove the driveshaft.

5. Using an inch pound torque wrench and socket on the pinion yoke nut measure the amount of torque needed to maintain differential rotation through several clockwise revolutions. Record the measurement.

6. Use a suitable tool to hold the companion flange. Remove the pinion nut.

7. Place a drain pan under the differential, clean the area around the seal, and mark the yoke-to-pinion relation.

8. Use a 2-jawed puller to remove the pinion.

9. Remove the seal with a small prybar.

To install:

10. Thoroughly clean the oil seal bore.

➡**If you are not absolutely certain of the proper seal installation depth, the proper seal driver must be used. If the seal is misaligned or damaged during installation, it must be removed and a new seal installed.**

11. Drive the new seal into place with a seal driver such as T83T–4676–A. Coat the seal lip with clean, waterproof wheel bearing grease.

12. Coat the splines with a small amount of wheel bearing grease and install the yoke, aligning the matchmarks. Never hammer the yoke onto the pinion!

13. Install a NEW nut on the pinion.

14. Hold the yoke with a holding tool. Tighten the pinion nut to at least 160 ft. lbs., taking frequent turning torque readings until the original preload reading is attained.If the original preload reading, that you noted before disassembly, is lower than the specified reading of 8–14 inch lbs. for used bearings; 16–29 inch lbs. for new bearings, keep tightening the pinion nut until the specified reading is reached.If the original preload reading is higher than the specified values, torque the nut just until the original reading is reached.

✷✷ WARNING

Under no circumstances should the nut be backed off to reduce the preload reading! If the preload is exceeded, the yoke and bearing must be removed and a new collapsible spacer must be installed. The entire process of preload adjustment must be repeated.

15. Install the driveshaft using the matchmarks. Torque the nuts to 15 ft. lbs.

Dana 60

➡**A torque wrench capable of at least 300 ft. lbs. is required for pinion seal installation.**

1. Raise and support the van on jackstands.

2. Allow the axle to hang freely.

3. Matchmark and disconnect the driveshaft from the axle.

4. Using a tool such as T75T4851B, or equivalent, hold the pinion flange while removing the pinion nut.

5. Using a puller, remove the pinion flange.

6. Use a puller to remove the seal, or punch the seal out using a pin punch.

7. Thoroughly clean the seal bore and make sure that it is not damaged in any way. Coat the sealing edge of the new seal with a small amount of 80W/90 oil and drive the seal into the housing using a seal driver.

8. Coat the inside of the pinion flange with clean 80W/90 oil and install the flange onto the pinion shaft.

9. Install the nut on the pinion shaft and tighten it to 250300 ft. lbs.

10. Connect the driveshaft.

Dana 70

➡ **A torque wrench capable of at least 500 ft. lbs. is required for pinion seal installation.**

1. Raise and safely support the vehicle with jackstands under the frame rails. Allow the axle to drop to the rebound position for working clearance.

2. Remove the rear wheels and brake drums. No drag must be present on the axle.

3. Mark the companion flanges and U-joints for correct reinstallation position.

4. Remove the driveshaft.

5. Use a suitable tool to hold the companion flange. Remove the pinion nut.

6. Place a drain pan under the differential, clean the area around the seal, and mark the yoke-to-pinion relation.

7. Use a 2-jawed puller to remove the pinion.

8. Remove the seal with a small prybar.

9. Thoroughly clean the oil seal bore.

➡ **If you are not absolutely certain of the proper seal installation depth, the proper seal driver must be used. If the seal is misaligned or damaged during installation, it must be removed and a new seal installed.**

10. Coat the new oil seal with wheel bearing grease. Install the seal using oil seal driver T56T4676B. After the seal is installed, make sure that the seal garter spring has not become dislodged. If it has, remove and replace the seal.

11. Install the yoke, using flange replacer tool D81T4858A if necessary to draw the yoke into place.

12. Install a new pinion nut and washer. Torque the nut to 440500 ft. lbs.

13. Connect the driveshaft. Torque the fasteners to 1520 ft. lbs.

Axle Damper

REMOVAL & INSTALLATION

This device is a large, heavy weight attached to a mounting flange on the differential carrier. Its purpose is to suppress driveline vibrations.

To remove/install the damper, simply support it and remove/install the bolts. Bolt torque is 40–60 ft. lbs.

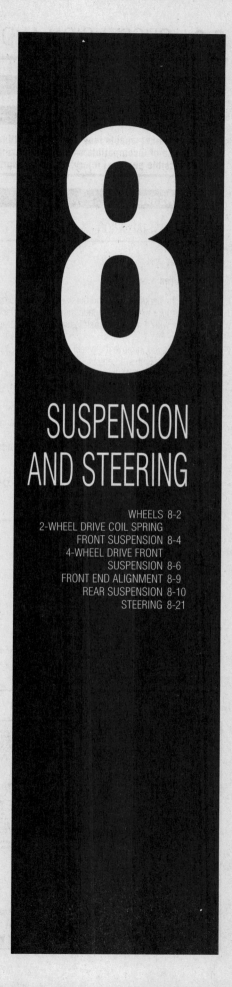

8

SUSPENSION
AND STEERING

WHEELS

❊❊ CAUTION

Some aftermarket wheels may not be compatible with these vehicles. The use of incompatible wheels may result in equipment failure and possible personal injury! Use only approved wheels!

Wheel Assembly

REMOVAL & INSTALLATION

Front Wheel

▶ See Figures 1 and 2

1. Set the parking brake and block the opposite wheel.
2. On trucks with an automatic transmission, place the selector lever in **P**. On trucks with a manual transmission, place the transmission in reverse gear.
3. If equipped, remove the wheel cover.
4. Break loose the lug nuts.
5. Raise the truck until the tire is clear of the ground.
6. Remove the lug nuts and remove the wheel.

To install:

7. Clean the wheel lugs and brake drum or hub of all foreign material.
8. Position the wheel on the hub or drum and hand-tighten the lug nuts. Make sure that the coned ends face inward.
9. Using the lug wrench, tighten all the lugs, in a criss-cross fashion until they are snug.
10. Lower the truck. Tighten the nuts, in the sequence shown, to the specification shown in the Torque Chart at the end of this Section.

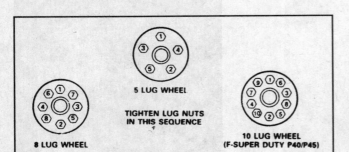

Fig. 1 Wheel lug torque sequences

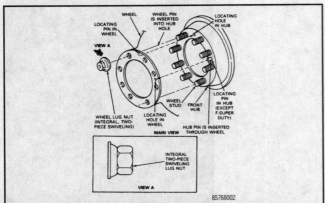

Fig. 2 Front wheel installation for F-350 w/dual rear wheels. The 10-lug wheel is identical except for the number of wheel lugs

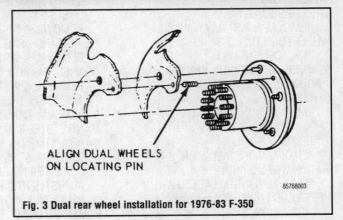

Fig. 3 Dual rear wheel installation for 1976-83 F-350

Rear Wheel

1976-83 F-350 WITH DUAL REAR WHEELS

▶ See Figure 3

1. Set the parking brake and block the opposite wheel.
2. On trucks with an automatic transmission, place the selector lever in **P**. On trucks with a manual transmission, place the transmission in reverse.
3. If equipped, remove the wheel cover.
4. Break loose the lug nuts.
5. Raise the truck until the tire is clear of the ground.
6. Remove the lug nuts and remove the wheel.

To install:

7. Clean the wheel lugs and brake drum or hub of all foreign material.
8. Position the wheel on the hub or drum and hand-tighten the lug nuts.
9. Using the lug wrench, tighten all the lugs, in a criss-cross fashion until they are snug.
10. Lower the truck. Tighten the nuts, in the sequence shown, to the figure shown in the Torque Chart at the end of this Section.

1984-86 F-350 WITH DUAL REAR WHEELS

▶ See Figure 4

❊❊ CAUTION

During the 1984 model year, Ford changed to a 2-piece wheel lug nut. Use only integral 2-piece, swiveling lug nuts. Do not attempt to use cone-shaped, one-piece lugs. The use of cone-shaped nuts will cause the nuts to come loose during vehicle operation! Do not

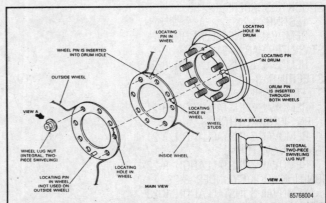

Fig. 4 Dual rear wheel installation for 1984-86 F-350 with 2-piece lug nuts

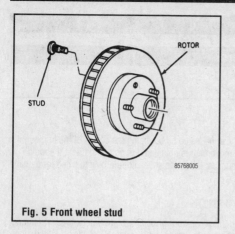

Fig. 5 Front wheel stud

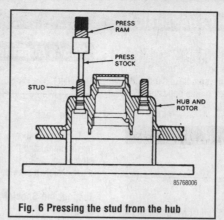

Fig. 6 Pressing the stud from the hub

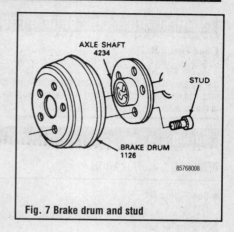

Fig. 7 Brake drum and stud

attempt to use older-style wheels that use cone-shaped lug nuts. This practice will also cause the wheels to come loose!

1. Set the parking brake and block the opposite wheel.
2. On trucks with an automatic transmission, place the selector lever in **P**. On trucks with a manual transmission, place the transmission in reverse.
3. If equipped, remove the wheel cover.
4. Break loose the lug nuts.
5. Raise the truck until the tire is clear of the ground.
6. Remove the lug nuts and remove the wheel(s).

To install:

7. Clean the wheel lugs and brake drum or hub of all foreign material.
8. Mount the inner wheel on the hub with the dished (concave) side inward. Align the wheel with the small indexing hole located in the wheel between the stud holes with the alignment pin on the hub. Make sure that the wheel is flush against the hub.
9. Install the outer wheel so that the protruding (convex) side is flush against the inner wheel. Make sure that the alignment pin is protruding through the wheel index hole.
10. Hand-tighten the lug nuts.
11. Using the lug wrench, tighten all the lugs, in a criss-cross fashion until they are snug.
12. Lower the truck. Tighten the nuts, in the sequence shown, to the figure given in the Torque Chart at the end of this Section.

✳✳ CAUTION

The lug nuts on dual rear wheels should be retightened after the first 100 miles of new-vehicle operation. The lug nuts on dual rear wheels should be retightened at an interval of 500 miles after anytime a wheel has been removed and installed for any reason! Failure to observe this procedure may result in the wheel coming loose during vehicle operation!

Wheel Lug Stud

REPLACEMENT

▶ See Figures 5, 6, 7 and 8

Front Wheels

USING A PRESS

1. Remove the wheel.
2. Place the hub/rotor assembly in a press, supported by the hub surface. NEVER rest the assembly on the rotor!

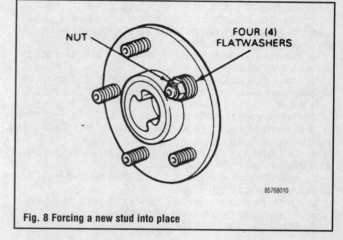

Fig. 8 Forcing a new stud into place

3. Press the stud from the hub.
4. Position the new stud in the hub and align the serrations. Make sure it is square and press it into place.

USING A HAMMER AND DRIVER

1. Remove the wheel.
2. Support the hub/rotor assembly on a flat, hard surface, resting the assembly on the hub. NEVER rest the assembly on the rotor!
3. Position a driver, such as a drift or broad punch, on the outer end of the stud and drive it from the hub.
4. Turn the assembly over, coat the serrations of the new stud with liquid soap, position the stud in the hole, aligning the serrations, and, using the drift and hammer, drive it into place until fully seated.

Rear Wheels

1. Remove the wheel.
2. Remove the drum or rotor from the axle shaft or hub studs.
3. Using a large C-clamp and socket, press the stud from the drum or rotor.
4. Coat the serrated part of the stud with liquid soap and place it in the hole. Align the serrations.
5. Place 3 or 4 flat washers on the outer end of the stud and thread a lug nut on the stud with the flat side against the washers. Tighten the lug nut until the stud is drawn all the way in.

✳✳ WARNING

Do not use an impact wrench!

2-WHEEL DRIVE COIL SPRING FRONT SUSPENSION

▶ See Figure 9

Trucks with 2-Wheel Drive and coil springs use two I-beam type front axles; one for each wheel. One end of each axle is attached to the spindle and a radius arm, and the other end is attached to a frame pivot bracket on the opposite side of the truck.

Springs

REMOVAL & INSTALLATION

▶ See Figure 9

1. Raise the front of the vehicle and place jackstands under the frame and a jack under the axle.
2. Remove the wheels.
3. Disconnect the shock absorber from the lower bracket.
4. Remove one bolt and nut and remove the rebound bracket.
5. Remove the two spring upper retainer attaching bolts from the top of the spring upper seat and remove the retainer.
6. Remove the nut attaching the spring lower retainer to the lower seat and axle and remove the retainer.
7. Place a safety chain through the spring to prevent it from suddenly coming loose. Slowly lower the axle and remove the spring.

To install:

8. Place the spring in position and raise the front axle.
9. Position the spring lower retainer over the stud and lower seat, and install the two attaching bolts.
10. Position the upper retainer over the spring coil and against the spring upper seat, and install the two attaching bolts.
11. Tighten the upper retaining bolts to the specifications given in the Torque Chart at the end of this Section.
12. Connect the shock absorber to the lower bracket. Torque the bolt and nut to the specifications given at the end of this Section.
13. Remove the jack and safety stands.

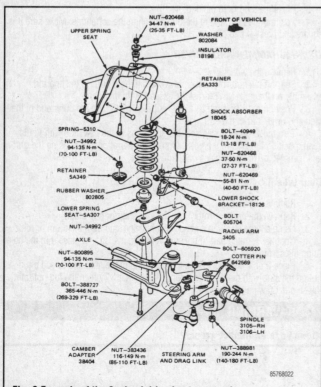

Fig. 9 Example of the 2-wheel drive front suspension

Shock Absorbers

TESTING

Bounce Test

Each shock absorber can be tested by bouncing the corner of the truck until maximum up and down movement is obtained. Let go of the truck. It should stop bouncing in 1-2 bounces. If not, the shock should be inspected for damage and possibly replaced.

Inspect the Shock Mounts

Check the shock mountings for worn or defective grommets, loose mounting nuts, interference or missing bump stops. If no apparent defects are noted, continue testing.

Inspecting Shocks for Leaks

Disconnect each shock lower mount and pull down on the shock until it is fully extended. inspect for leaks in the seal area. Shock absorber fluid is very thin and has a characteristic odor and dark brown color. Don't confuse the glossy paint on some shocks with leaking fluid. A slight trace of fluid is a normal condition; they are designed to seep a certain amount of fluid past the seals for lubrication. If you are in doubt as to whether the fluid on the shock is coming from the shock itself or from some other source, wipe the seal area clean and manually operate the shock (see the following procedure). Fluid will appear if the unit is leaking.

Manually Operating the Shocks

It may be necessary to fabricate a holding fixture for certain types of shock absorbers. If a suspected problem is in the front shocks, disconnect both front shock lower mountings.

➡**When manually operating air shocks, the air line must be disconnected at the shock.**

Grip the lower end of the shock and pull down (rebound stroke) and then push up (compression stroke). The control arms will limit the movement of front shocks during the compression stroke. Compare the rebound resistance of both shocks and compare the compression resistance. Usually any shock showing a noticeable difference will be the one at fault.

If the shock has internal noises, extend the shock fully then exert an extra pull. If a small additional movement is felt, this usually means a loose piston and the shock should be replaced. Other noises that are cause for replacing shocks are a squeal after a full stroke in both directions, a clicking noise on fast reverse and a lag at reversal near mid-stroke.

REMOVAL & INSTALLATION

▶ See Figure 9

To replace the front shock absorber, remove the self-locking nut, steel washer, and rubber bushings at the upper end of the shock absorber. Remove the bolt and nut at the lower end and remove the shock absorber.

When installing a new shock absorber, use new rubber bushings. Position the shock absorber on the mounting brackets with the stud end at the top.

Install the steel washer, rubber bushing, steel washer and self-locking nut at the upper end, and the bolt and nut at the lower end. Tighten the fasteners to the specifications given at the end of this Section.

Front Wheel Spindle

REMOVAL & INSTALLATION

1. Jack up the front of the truck and safely support it with jackstands.
2. Remove the wheels.

3. Remove the front brake caliper assembly and hold it out of the way with a piece of wire. Do not disconnect the brake line.

4. Remove the brake rotor from the spindle.

5. Remove the inner bearing cone and seal. discard the seal, as you'll be fitting a new one during installation.

6. Remove the brake dust shield.

7. Disconnect the steering linkage from the spindle arm using a tie rod removal tool.

8. Remove the cotter from the upper and lower ball joint stud nuts. Discard the cotter pins, as new ones should be installed during reassembly.

9. Remove the upper ball joint nut and loosen the lower ball joint nut to the end of the threads.

10. Strike the inside area or the spindle as shown in the illustration to pop the ball joints loose from the spindle.

❋❋ WARNING

Do not use a forked ball joint removal tool to separate the ball joints as this damage the seal and ball joint socket.

11. Remove the nut. Remove the spindle.

12. Before reassembly, note that new cotter pins should be used on the ball joints, and that new bearing seal(s) should also be used. Also, make sure the upper and lower ball joint seals are in place.

13. Place the spindle over the ball joints.

14. Install the nuts on the lower ball joint stud and tighten to the specifications shown in the Torque Chart at the end of this Section. Turn the castellated nut until you are able to install the cotter pin.

15. Install the camber adapter in the upper spindle over the upper ball joint stud. Be sure the adapter is aligned properly.

➡ **If camber adjustment is necessary special adapters must be installed.**

16. Install the nut on the upper ball joint stud. Hold the camber adapter with a wrench to keep the ball stud from turning. If the ball stud turns, tap the adapter deeper into the spindle. Tighten the nut to the specifications given in the Torque Chart at the end of this Section and continue tightening the castellated nut until it lines up with the hole in the stud. Install the cotter pin.

17. Tighten the lower nut to the specifications given at the end of this Section. Advance the nut to install a new cotter pin.

18. Install the brake dust shield.

19. Pack the inner and outer bearing cone with a quality wheel bearing grease by hand, working the grease through the cage behind the roller.

20. Install the inner bearing cone and seal. Install the hub and rotor on the spindle.

21. Install the outer bearing cone, washer, and nut. Adjust the bearing endplay and install the nut retainer, cotter pin and dust cap.

22. Install the brake caliper. connect the steering linkage to the spindle. Tighten the nut to the specifications given in the Torque Chart at the end of this Section and advance the nut as far necessary to install the cotter pin.

23. Install the wheels. Lower the truck and adjust toe-in if necessary.

Upper and Lower Ball Joints

INSPECTION

1. Before an inspection of the ball joints, make sure the front wheel bearings are properly packed and adjusted.

2. Jack up the front of the truck and safely support it with jackstands, placing the stands under the I-beam axle beneath the spring.

3. Have a helper grab the lower edge of the tire and move the wheel assembly in and out.

4. While the wheel is being moved, observe the lower spindle arm and the lower part of the axle jaw (the end of the axle to which the spindle assembly attaches). If there is 1/32 in. or greater movement between the lower part of the axle jaw and the lower spindle arm, the lower ball must be replaced.

5. To check upper ball joints, grab the upper edge of the tire and move the wheel in and out. If there is 1/32 in. or greater movement between the upper spindle arm and the upper part of the jaw, the upper ball joint must be replaced.

REMOVAL

1. Remove the spindle as previously described.

2. Remove the snapring from the ball joints. Assemble the C-frame assembly T74P-4635-C and receiver cup D81T-3010-A, or equivalents, on the upper ball joint. Turn the forcing screw clockwise until the ball joint is removed from the axle.

3. Repeat step 2 on the lower ball joint.

➡ **The upper ball joint must always be removed first. DO NOT heat the ball joint or spindle!**

INSTALLATION

➡ **The lower ball joint must be installed first.**

1. To install the lower ball joint, assemble the C-frame with ball joint receiver cup D81T-3010-A5 and installation cup D81T-3010-A1, and turn the forcing screw clockwise until the ball joint is seated. DO NOT heat the ball joint to aid in installation!

2. Install the snapring onto the ball joint.

3. Install the upper ball joint in the same manner as the lower ball joint.

4. Install the spindle assembly.

Radius Arm

REMOVAL & INSTALLATION

➡ **A torque wrench with a capacity of at least 350 ft. lbs. is necessary, along with other special tools, for this procedure.**

1. Raise the front of the vehicle and place safety stands under the frame and a jack under the wheel or axle. Remove the wheels.

2. Disconnect the shock absorber from the radius arm bracket.

3. Remove the two spring upper retainer attaching bolts from the top of the spring upper seat and remove the retainer.

4. Remove the nut which attached the spring lower retainer to the lower seat and axle and remove the retainer.

5. Lower the axle and remove the spring.

6. Remove the spring lower seat and shim from the radius arm. The, remove the bolt and nut which attach the radius arm to the axle.

7. Remove the cotter pin, nut and washer from the radius arm rear attachment.

8. Remove the bushing from the radius arm and remove the radius arm from the vehicle.

9. Remove the inner bushing from the radius arm.

To install:

10. Position the radius arm to the axle and install the bolt and nut finger-tight.

11. Install the inner bushing on the radius arm and position the arm to the frame bracket.

12. Install the bushing, washer, and attaching nut. Tighten the nut to the specifications given in the Torque Chart at the end of this Section and install the cotter pin.

13. Tighten the radius arm-to-axle bolt to the specifications given in the Torque Chart at the end of this Section.

14. Install the spring seat and insulator on the radius arm so that the hole in the seat fits over the arm-to-axle nut.

15. Install the spring.

16. Connect the shock absorber. Torque the nut and bolt to the specifications given in the Torque Chart at the end of this Section.

17. Install the wheels.

Stabilizer Bar

REMOVAL & INSTALLATION

1. Raise and support the front end on jackstands.

2. Disconnect the right and left stabilizer bar ends from the link assembly.

3. Disconnect the retainer bolts and remove the stabilizer bar.
4. Disconnect the stabilizer link assemblies by loosening the right and left locknuts from their respective brackets on the I-beams.
To install:
5. Loosely install the entire assembly. The links are marked with an **R** and **L** for identification.
6. Tighten the link-to-stabilizer bar and axle bracket fasteners to the specifications given in the Torque Chart at the end of this Section.
7. Check to make sure that the insulators are properly seated and the stabilizer bar is centered.
8. Tighten all fasteners to the specifications given in the Torque Chart at the end of this Section.

Twin I-Beam Axles

REMOVAL & INSTALLATION

➡ **A torque wrench with a capacity of at least 350 ft. lbs. is necessary, along with other special tools, for this procedure.**

4-WHEEL DRIVE FRONT SUSPENSION

♦ **See Figures 10 and 11**

The 1976-79 front suspension consists of a driving axle which is attached to the vehicle frame with two coil springs, two radius arms, and a track bar.

The 1980-86 suspension of an F-150 and Bronco consists of a Dana 44-IFS independent driving axle attached to the frame with two coil springs, two radius arms, and a stabilizer bar.

The 1980-86 front suspension on an F-250 consists of a Dana 44- or 50-IFS independent driving axle attached to the frame with two semi-elliptic leaf springs. Each spring is clamped to the axle with two U-bolts. The front of the spring rests in a front shackle bracket and the rear is attached to a frame bracket.

The front suspension on an F-350 consists of a Dana 60 Monobeam one-piece driving axle attached to the frame with two semi-elliptic leaf springs. Each spring is clamped to the axle with two U-bolts. The front of the spring rests in a front shackle bracket and the rear is attached to a frame bracket. On the right spring cap a track bar is attached with the other end mounted on the crossmember.

➡ **The 1976–79 radius arm and cap are matched sets and should never be mixed with other sets. They are identified by numbers 1 through 100. The numbers should be together when installing the radius arm and cap.**

Springs

REMOVAL & INSTALLATION

1976–79

1. Raise the vehicle and remove the shock absorber-to-lower bracket attaching bolt and nut.
2. Remove two spring lower retainer attaching bolts from inside of the spring coil.
3. Remove two spring upper retainer attaching bolts and nuts and remove the upper retainer.
4. Position safety stands under the frame side rails and lower the axle enough to relieve tension from the spring. Remove the spring, lower retainer, and lower the spring from the vehicle.
5. Position the spring, spring lower seat, and lower retainer to the frame spring pocket and the radius arm. Position the spring seat and the lower retainer.
6. Position the upper retainer over the spring coil and loosely install the two attaching bolts and nuts.
7. Install the two lower retainer attaching bolts and tighten to 80–120 ft. lbs.
8. Tighten the upper retainer attaching bolts to 20–30 ft. lbs.
9. Position the shock absorber to the lower bracket and install the attaching

1. Raise and support the front end on jackstands.
2. Remove the spindles.
3. Remove the springs.
4. Remove the stabilizer bar.
5. Remove the lower spring seats from the radius arms.
6. Remove the radius arm-to-axle bolts.
7. Remove the axle-to-frame pivot bolts and remove the axles.
To install:
8. Position the axle on the pivot bracket and loosely install the bolt/nut.
9. Position the other end on the radius arm and install the bolt. Torque the bolt to the specifications given in the Torque Chart at the end of this Section.
10. Install the spring seats.
11. Install the springs.
12. Torque the axle pivot bolts to the specifications given in the Torque Chart at the end of this Section.
13. Install the spindles.
14. Install the stabilizer bar.

bolt and nut. Tighten the bolt and nut to 40–60 ft. lbs. Remove safety stands and lower the vehicle.

1980-86 F-150 and Bronco

1. Raise and support the front end on jackstands.
2. Remove the shock absorber lower attaching bolt and nut.
3. Remove the spring lower retainer nuts from inside of the spring coil.
4. Remove the upper spring retainer by removing the attaching screw.
5. Position safety stands under the frame side rails and lower the axle on a floor jack just enough to relieve tension from the spring.

➡ **The axle must be supported on the jack throughout spring removal, and must not be permitted to hang from the brake hose. If the length of the brake hose does not provide sufficient clearance it may be necessary to remove and support the brake caliper.**

6. Remove the spring lower retainer and lower the spring from the vehicle.
7. To install place the spring in position and slowly raise the front axle. Make sure the springs are positioned correctly in the upper spring seats.
8. Install the lower spring retainer and torque the nut to the specifications given in the Torque Chart at the end of this Section.
9. Position the upper retainer over the spring coil and tighten the attaching screws to the specifications given in the Torque Chart at the end of this Section.
10. Position the shock absorber to the lower bracket and torque the attaching bolt and nut to the specifications given in the Torque Chart at the end of this Section.
11. Remove the safety stands and lower the vehicle.

1980-86 F-250 and F-350

1. Raise the vehicle frame until the weight is off the front spring with the wheels still touching the floor. Support the axle to prevent rotation.
2. Disconnect the lower end of the shock absorber from the U-bolt spacer. Remove the U-bolts, U-bolt cap and spacer. On F-350 models, remove the 2 bolts retaining the track bar to the spring cap and the track bar bracket.
3. Remove the nut from the hanger bolt retaining the spring at the rear and drive out the hanger bolt.
4. Remove the nut connecting the front shackle and spring eye and drive out the shackle bolt and remove the spring.
5. To install position the spring on the spring seat. Install the shackle bolt through the shackle and spring. Torque the nuts to the specifications shown in the Torque Chart at the end of this Section.
6. Position the rear of the spring and install the hanger bolt. Torque the nut to the specifications shown in the Torque Chart at the end of this Section.
7. Position the U-bolt spacer and place the U-bolts in position through the holes in the spring seat cap. Install but do not tighten the U-bolt nut. On the F-

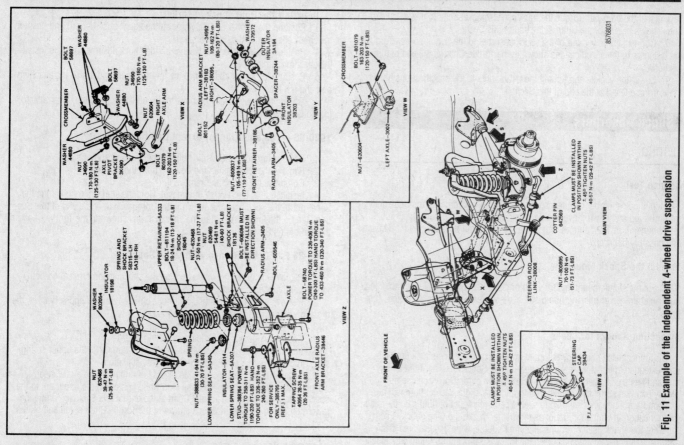

Fig. 11 Example of the independent 4-wheel drive suspension

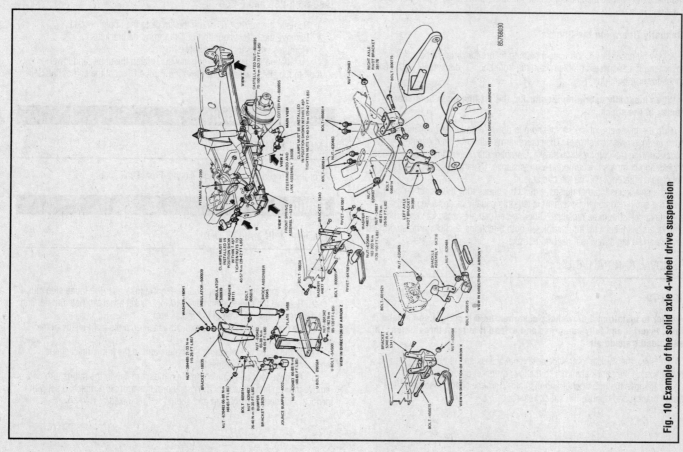

Fig. 10 Example of the solid axle 4-wheel drive suspension

350, install the track bar. Torque the track bar-to-bracket bolts to the specifications shown in the Torque Chart at the end of this Section.

8. Connect the lower end of the shock absorber to the U-bolt spacer. Torque the fasteners to the specifications shown in the Torque Chart at the end of this Section.

9. Lower the vehicle and tighten the U-bolt nuts to the specifications shown in the Torque Chart at the end of this Section.

Shock Absorbers

TESTING

Bounce Test

Each shock absorber can be tested by bouncing the corner of the truck until maximum up and down movement is obtained. Let go of the truck. It should stop bouncing in 1-2 bounces. If not, the shock should be inspected for damage and possibly replaced.

Inspect the Shock Mounts

Check the shock mountings for worn or defective grommets, loose mounting nuts, interference or missing bump stops. If no apparent defects are noted, continue testing.

Inspecting Shocks for Leaks

Disconnect each shock lower mount and pull down on the shock until it is fully extended. inspect for leaks in the seal area. Shock absorber fluid is very thin and has a characteristic odor and dark brown color. Don't confuse the glossy paint on some shocks with leaking fluid. A slight trace of fluid is a normal condition; they are designed to seep a certain amount of fluid past the seals for lubrication. If you are in doubt as to whether the fluid on the shock is coming from the shock itself or from some other source, wipe the seal area clean and manually operate the shock (see the following procedure). Fluid will appear if the unit is leaking.

Manually Operating the Shocks

It may be necessary to fabricate a holding fixture for certain types of shock absorbers. If a suspected problem is in the front shocks, disconnect both front shock lower mountings.

➡ When manually operating air shocks, the air line must be disconnected at the shock.

Grip the lower end of the shock and pull down (rebound stroke) and then push up (compression stroke). The control arms will limit the movement of front shocks during the compression stroke. Compare the rebound resistance of both shocks and compare the compression resistance. Usually any shock showing a noticeable difference will be the one at fault.

If the shock has internal noises, extend the shock fully then exert an extra pull. If a small additional movement is felt, this usually means a loose piston and the shock should be replaced. Other noises that are cause for replacing shocks are a squeal after a full stroke in both directions, a clicking noise on fast reverse and a lag at reversal near mid-stroke.

REMOVAL & INSTALLATION

1976-79

➡ Prior to installing a new shock absorber, hold it upright and extend it fully. Invert it and fully compress and extend it at least three times. This will bleed trapped air.

1. Raise the vehicle to provide additional access and remove the bolt and nut attaching the shock absorber to the lower bracket on the radius arm.

2. Remove the nut, washer and insulator from the shock absorber at the frame bracket and remove the shock absorber.

To install the front shock absorber:

3. Position the washer and insulator on the shock absorber rod and position the shock absorber to the frame bracket.

4. Position the insulator and washer on the shock absorber rod and install the attaching nut loosely.

5. Position the shock absorber to the lower bracket and install the attaching bolt and nut loosely.

6. Tighten the lower attaching bolts to 40–60 ft. lbs., and the upper attaching bolts to 15–25 ft. lbs.

1980-86 F-150 and Bronco, except Quad Shocks

1. Remove the upper nut while holding the shock absorber stem.
2. Remove the lower mounting bolt/nut from the bracket.
3. Compress the shock and remove it.
4. Installation is the reverse of removal. Hold the stud while tightening the upper nut to the specifications shown in the Torque Chart at the end of this Section. Torque the lower bolt/nut to the specifications shown in the Torque Chart at the end of this Section.

1980-86 F-150 and Bronco with Quad Shocks

1. Remove the upper nut while holding the shock absorber stem on both forward and rearward shocks.
2. Remove the lower mounting bolt/nut from the rearward shock bracket; the nut and washer from the forward shock bracket.
3. Compress the shocks and remove them.
4. Cut the insulators from the upper spring seat.
5. Install new one piece insulators into the top surface of the upper spring seat. Coat them with a soap solution to aid in installation.
6. Installation of the shocks is the reverse of removal. Use a new steel washer under the upper nut. Hold the stud while tightening the upper nut to the specifications shown in the Torque Chart at the end of this Section. Torque the lower bolt/nut to the specifications shown in the Torque Chart at the end of this Section.

1980-86 F-250 and F-350

1. Remove the nut/bolt retaining the shock to the upper bracket.
2. Remove the lower mounting bolt/nut from the bracket.
3. Compress the shock and remove it.
4. Installation is the reverse of removal. Tighten the upper and lower nut/bolt to the specifications shown in the Torque Chart at the end of this Section.

Front Wheel Spindle

REMOVAL & INSTALLATION

For this procedure, see Section 7 under Front Drive Axle.

Radius Arm

REMOVAL & INSTALLATION

1976–79

1. Raise the vehicle and position safety stands under the frame side rails.
2. Remove the shock absorber-to-lower bracket attaching bolt and nut and pull the shock absorber free of the radius arm.
3. Remove two spring lower retainer attaching bolts from inside of the spring coil.
4. Remove the nut attaching the radius arm to the frame bracket and remove the radius arm rear insulator.
5. Remove four bolts attaching the radius arm cap to the radius arm and remove the cap and insulator. The cap and radius arm are a matched set with identical numbers on each part and should not be mixed.

6. Move the axle forward and remove the radius arm and insulator from the axle. Then, pull the radius arm from the frame bracket.The radius arm and cap must be identified by a T on each piece in addition to a number (1 through 100).

7. Position the washer and insulator on the rear of the radius arm and insert the radius arm and insulator into the frame bracket.

8. Position the rear insulator and washer on the radius arm and loosely install the attaching nut.

9. Position the insulator on the axle and position the radius arm to the insulator and axle.

10. Position the front insulator to the axle and install the radius arm cap with the numbers on the radius arm and cap together. Tighten the attaching bolts diagonally in pairs to 90–110 ft. lbs.

11. Position the spring lower seat and retainer to the spring and axle. Install the two attaching bolts. Tighten the bolts to 45–55 ft. lbs.

12. Tighten the radius rod rear attaching nut to 80–120 ft. lbs.

13. Position the shock absorber to the lower bracket and install the attaching bolt and nut. Tighten the nut to 40–60 ft. lbs. Remove safety stands and lower the vehicle.

1980-86 F-150 and Bronco

1. Raise the vehicle and position safety stands under the frame side rails.
2. Remove the shock absorber lower attaching bolt and nut and pull the shock absorber free of the radius arm.
3. Remove the lower spring retaining bolt from the inside of the spring coil.
4. Loosen the axle pivot bolt.
5. Remove the nut attaching the radius arm to the frame bracket and remove the radius arm rear insulator. Lower the axle and allow the axle to move forward.

➡The axle must be supported on a floor jack throughout this procedure, and must not be permitted to hang from the brake hose. If the length of the brake hose does not provide sufficient clearance it may be necessary to remove and support the brake caliper.

6. Remove the spring as described above.
7. Remove the bolt and stud attaching the radius arm and bracket to the axle.
8. Move the axle forward and remove the radius arm from the axle. Then, pull the radius arm from the frame bracket.
9. Install the components in the reverse order of removal. Install new bolts and stud type bolts which attach the radius arm and bracket to the axle. Torque all fasteners the specifications shown in the Torque Chart at the end of this Section.

Stabilizer Bar

REMOVAL & INSTALLATION

1978–79

1. Remove locknut, washers, and insulator to remove link assemblies from stabilizer bar. Remove nuts, bolts, and washers connecting link assemblies to frame.
2. Remove nuts on U-bolts to remove stabilizer bar from retainers. Remove stabilizer bar. Remove U-bolts, brackets and retainers.
3. Place bracket assemblies on axle aligning holes in brackets with alignment pins on axles.
4. Install U-bolts through bracket assembly. Position stabilizer bar on brackets. Install retainer and tighten nuts to 35–55 ft. lbs.
5. Install link assemblies on frame. Connect link assemblies to stabilizer bar. Tighten link to stabilizer bar nuts to 18–25 ft. lbs. Tighten link to frame nuts to 40–60 ft. lbs.

1980-86 F-150 and Bronco

1. Unbolt the stabilizer bar from the connecting links.
2. Unbolt the stabilizer bar retainers.
3. If you have to remove the stabilizer bar mounting bracket, remove the coil springs as described above.
4. Installation is the reverse of removal. Torque the retainer nuts to the specifications shown in the Torque Chart at the end of this Section, then torque all other nuts at the links to the specifications shown in the Torque Chart at the end of this Section.

1980-86 F-250 and F-350

1. Remove the bolts, washers and nuts securing the links to the spring seat caps.On models with the Monobeam axle, remove the nut, washer and bolt securing the links to the mounting brackets. Remove the nuts, washers and insulators connecting the links to the stabilizer bar. Remove the links.
2. Unbolt and remove the retainers from the mounting brackets.
3. Remove the stabilizer bar.
4. Installation is the reverse of removal. Torque the connecting links-to-spring seat caps to the specifications shown in the Torque Chart at the end of this Section. Torque the nuts securing the connecting links to the stabilizer bar to the specifications shown in the Torque Chart at the end of this Section. Torque the retainer-to-mounting bracket nuts to the specifications shown in the Torque Chart at the end of this Section.

FRONT END ALIGNMENT

If the tires are worn unevenly, if the vehicle is not stable on the highway or if the handling seems poor, the wheel alignment should be checked. If an alignment problem is suspected, first check for improper tire inflation and other possible causes. These can be worn suspension or steering components, accident damage or even unmatched tires. If any worn or damaged components are found, they must be replaced before the wheels can be properly aligned. Wheel alignment requires very expensive equipment and involves minute adjustments which must be accurate; it should only be performed by a trained technician. Take your vehicle to a properly equipped shop.

Following is a description of the alignment angles which are adjustable on most vehicles and how they affect vehicle handling. Although these angles can apply to both the front and rear wheels, usually only the front suspension is adjustable.

CASTER

◆ See Figure 12

Looking at a vehicle from the side, caster angle describes the steering axis rather than a wheel angle. The steering knuckle is attached to the axle yoke through ball joints or king pins. The wheel pivots around the line between these points to steer the vehicle. When the upper point is tilted back, this is described as positive caster. Having a positive caster tends to make the wheels self-cen-

tering, increasing directional stability. Excessive positive caster makes the wheels hard to steer, while an uneven caster will cause a pull to one side. Overloading the vehicle or sagging rear springs will affect caster, as will raising the rear of the vehicle. If the rear of the vehicle is lower than normal, the caster becomes more positive.

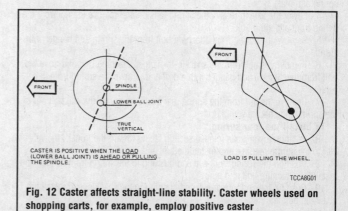

TCCA8G01

Fig. 12 Caster affects straight-line stability. Caster wheels used on shopping carts, for example, employ positive caster

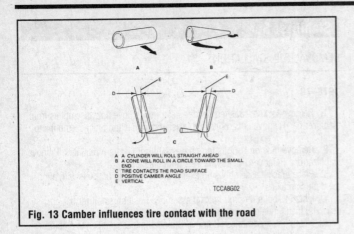

A A CYLINDER WILL ROLL STRAIGHT AHEAD
B A CONE WILL ROLL IN A CIRCLE TOWARD THE SMALL
  END
C TIRE CONTACTS THE ROAD SURFACE
D POSITIVE CAMBER ANGLE
E VERTICAL

TCCA8G02

Fig. 13 Camber influences tire contact with the road

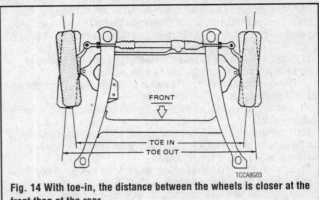

TCCA8G03

Fig. 14 With toe-in, the distance between the wheels is closer at the front than at the rear

CAMBER

♦ See Figure 13

Looking from the front of the vehicle, camber is the inward or outward tilt of the top of wheels. When the tops of the wheels are tilted in, this is negative camber; if they are tilted out, it is positive. In a turn, a slight amount of negative camber helps maximize contact of the tire with the road. However, too much negative camber compromises straight-line stability, increases bump steer and torque steer.

TOE

♦ See Figure 14

Looking down at the wheels from above the vehicle, toe angle is the distance between the front of the wheels relative to the distance between the back of the wheels. If the wheels are closer at the front, they are said to be toed-in or to have negative toe. A small amount of negative toe enhances directional stability and provides a smoother ride on the highway.

REAR SUSPENSION

Semi-elliptic, leaf type springs are used at the rear axle. The front end of the spring is attached to a spring bracket on the frame side member. The rear end of the spring is attached to the bracket on the frame side member with a shackle. Each spring is attached to the axle with two U-bolts. A spacer is located between the spring and the axle on some applications to obtain a level ride position.

Springs

REMOVAL & INSTALLATION

♦ See Figures 15 thru 34

1976–79

1. Raise the vehicle and install jackstands under the frame. The vehicle must be supported in such a way that the rear axle hangs free with the tire a few inches off the ground. Place a hydraulic floor jack under the center of the axle housing.
2. Disconnect the shock absorber from the axle.
3. Remove the U-bolt attaching nuts and remove the two U-bolts and the spring clip plate.
4. Lower the axle to relieve the spring tension and remove the nut from the spring front attaching bolt.
5. Remove the spring front attaching bolt from the spring and hanger with a drift.
6. Remove the nut from the shackle-to-hanger attaching bolt and drive the bolt from the shackle and hanger with a drift and remove the spring from the vehicle.
7. Remove the nut from the spring rear attaching bolt. Drive the bolt out of the spring and shackle with a drift:
   To install the rear spring:
8. Position the shackle (closed section facing toward the front of the vehicle) to the spring rear eye and install the bolt and nut.
9. Position the spring front eye and bushing to the spring front hanger, and install the attaching bolt and nut.
10. Position the spring rear eye and bushing to the shackle, and install the attaching bolt and nut.

11. Raise the axle to the spring and install the U-bolts and spring clip plate.
12. Torque the U-bolt nuts and spring front and rear attaching bolt nuts to 45–60 ft. lbs.
13. Remove the jackstands and lower the vehicle.

➡Squeaky rear springs can be corrected by tightening the front and rear eye bolts to 150–204 ft. lbs., then raising and supporting the rear of the vehicle so that the rear springs hang, spreading the leaves. Apply a silicone based lubricant for a distance of 3inch (76mm) in from each leaf tip.

1980–86

1. Raise the vehicle by the frame until the weight is off the rear spring with the tires still on the floor.
2. Remove the nuts from the spring U-bolts and drive the U-bolts from the U-bolt plate. Remove the auxiliary spring and spacer, if so equipped.
3. Remove the spring-to-bracket nut and bolt at the front of the spring.
4. Remove the upper and lower shackle nuts and bolts at the rear of the spring and remove the spring and shackle assembly from the rear shackle bracket.
5. Remove the bushings in the spring or shackle, if they are worn or damaged, and install new ones.

➡When installing the components, snug down the fasteners. Don't apply final torque to the fasteners until the vehicle is back on the ground.

6. Position the spring in the shackle and install the upper shackle-to-spring nut and bolt with the bolt head facing outward.
7. Position the front end of the spring in the bracket and install the nut and bolt.
8. Position the shackle in the rear bracket and install the nut and bolt.
9. Position the spring on top of the axle with the spring center bolts centered in the hole provided in the seat. Install the auxiliary spring and spacer, if so equipped.
10. Install the spring U-bolts, plate and nuts.
11. Lower the vehicle to the floor and tighten the attaching hardware the specifications shown in the Torque Chart at the end of this section.

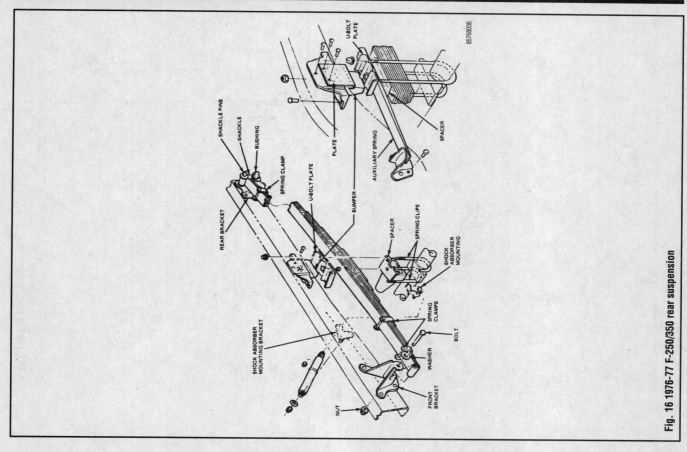

Fig. 16 1976-77 F-250/350 rear suspension

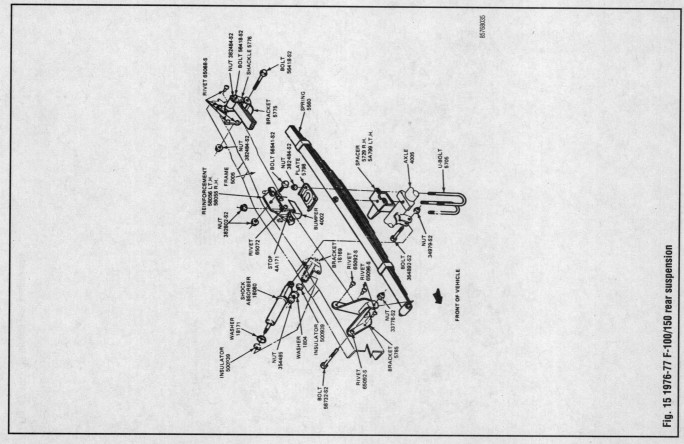

Fig. 15 1976-77 F-100/150 rear suspension

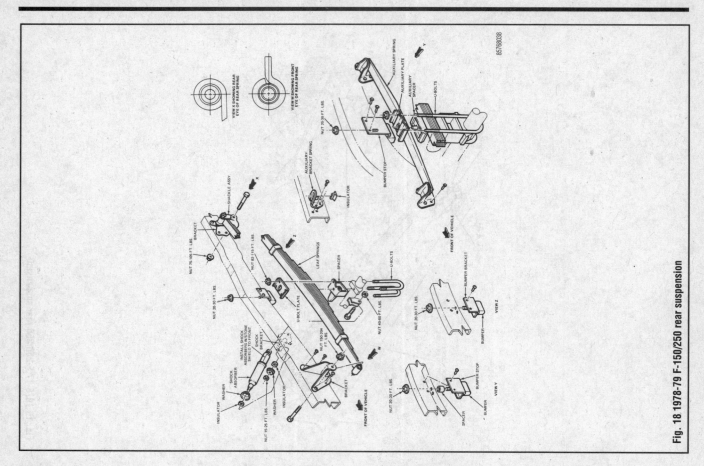

Fig. 18 1978-79 F-150/250 rear suspension

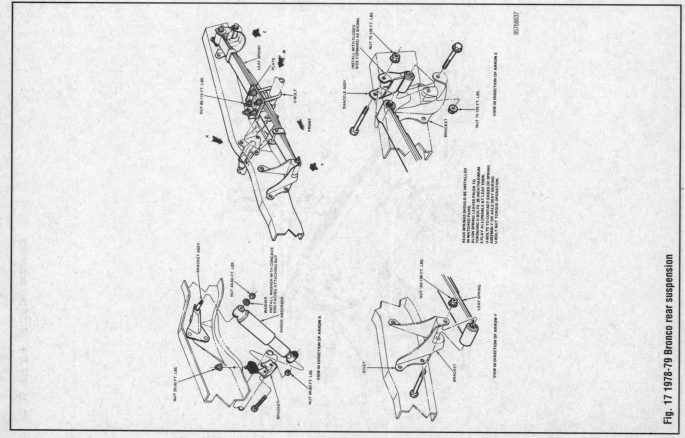

Fig. 17 1978-79 Bronco rear suspension

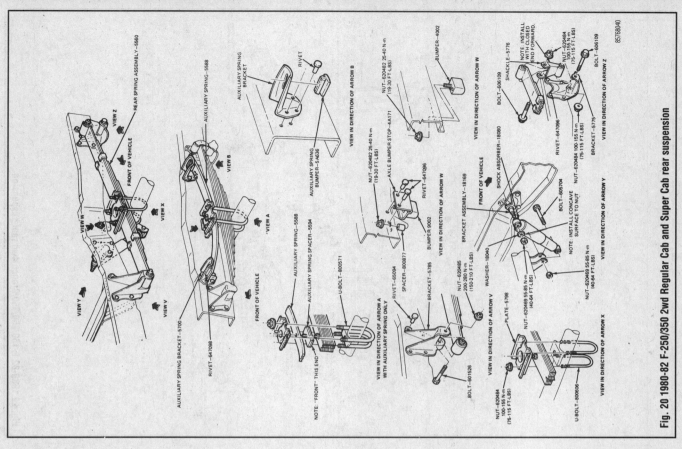

Fig. 20 1980-82 F-250/350 2wd Regular Cab and Super Cab rear suspension

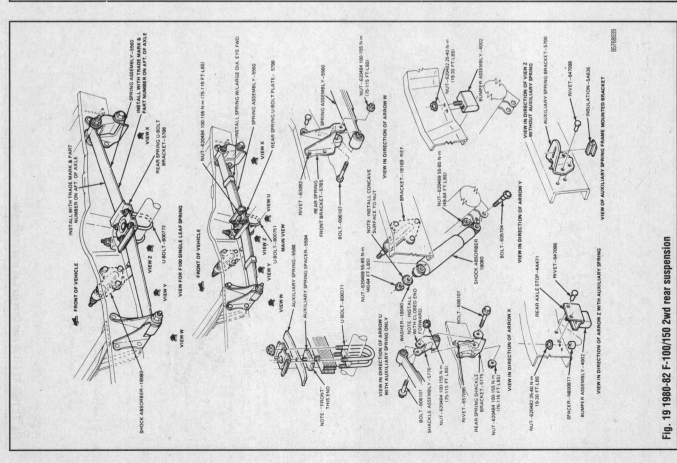

Fig. 19 1980-82 F-100/150 2wd rear suspension

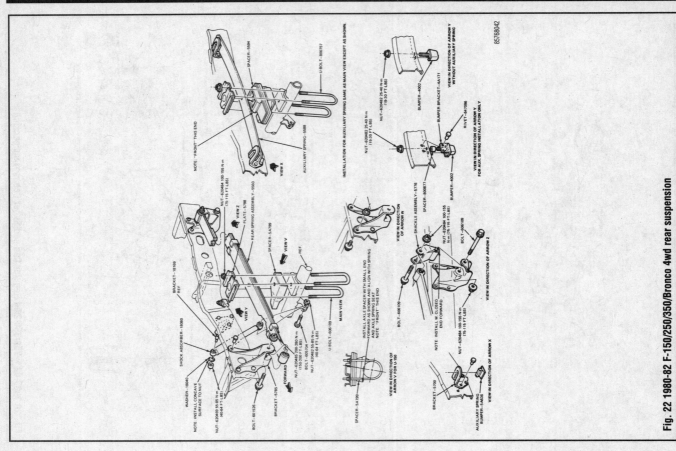

Fig. 22 1980-82 F-150/250/350/Bronco 4wd rear suspension

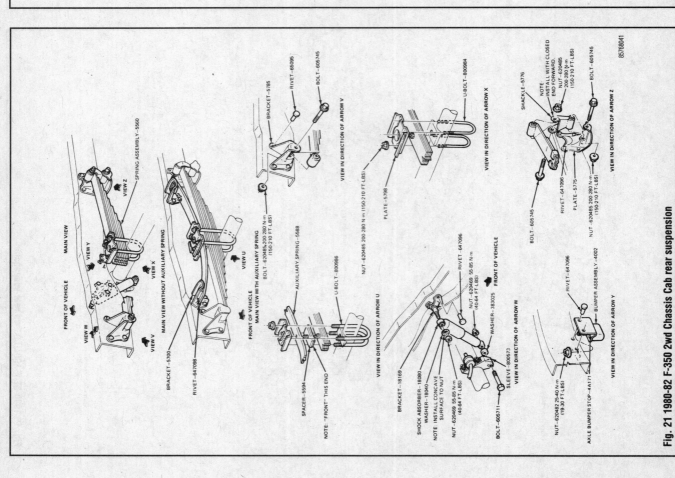

Fig. 21 1980-82 F-350 2wd Chassis Cab rear suspension

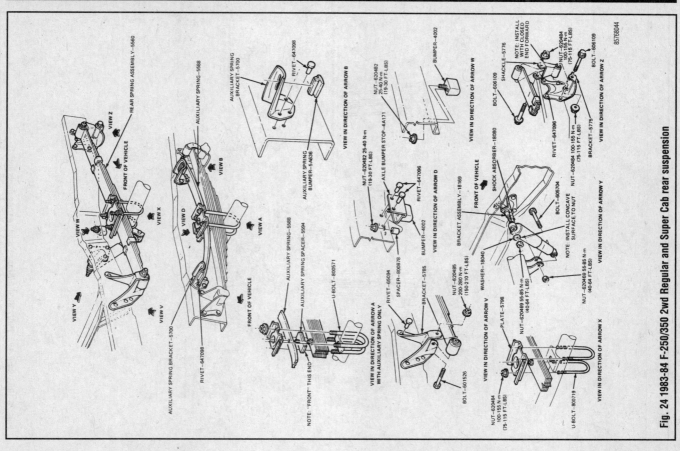

Fig. 24 1983-84 F-250/350 2wd Regular and Super Cab rear suspension

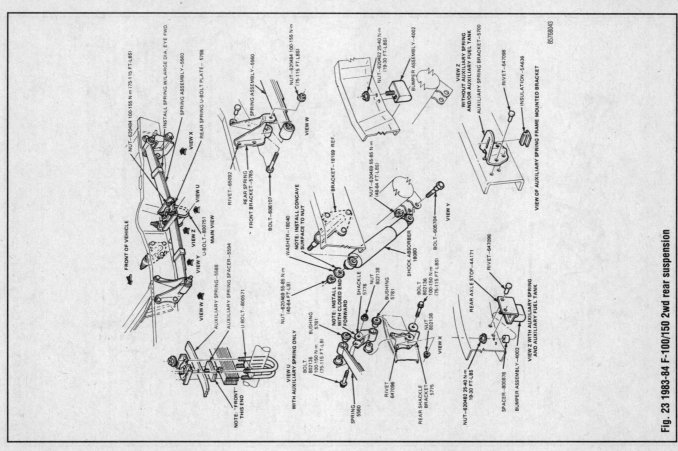

Fig. 23 1983-84 F-100/150 2wd rear suspension

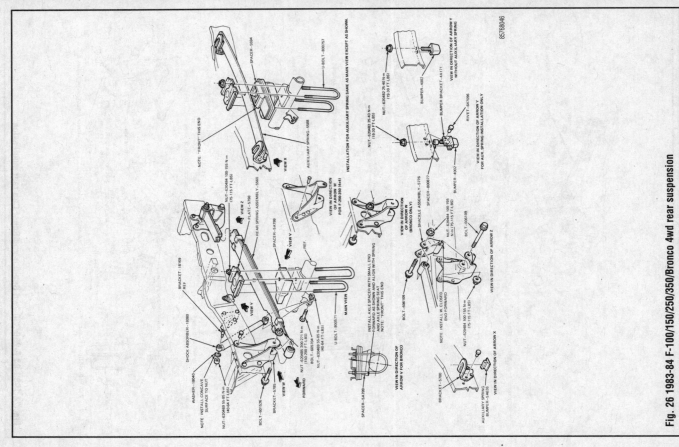

Fig. 26 1983-84 F-100/150/250/350/Bronco 4wd rear suspension

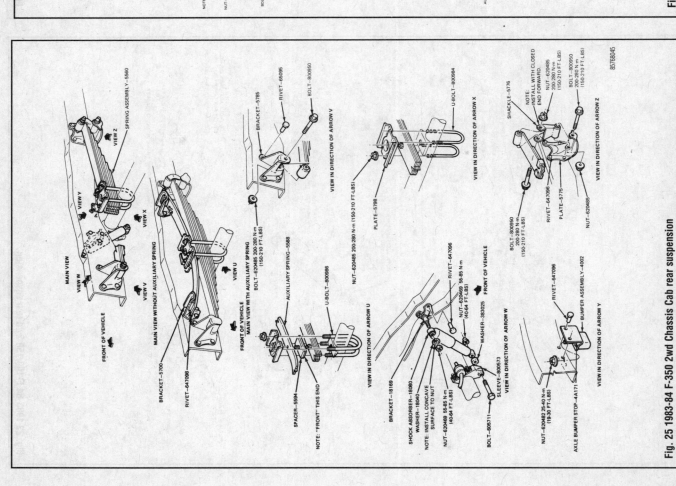

Fig. 25 1983-84 F-350 2wd Chassis Cab rear suspension

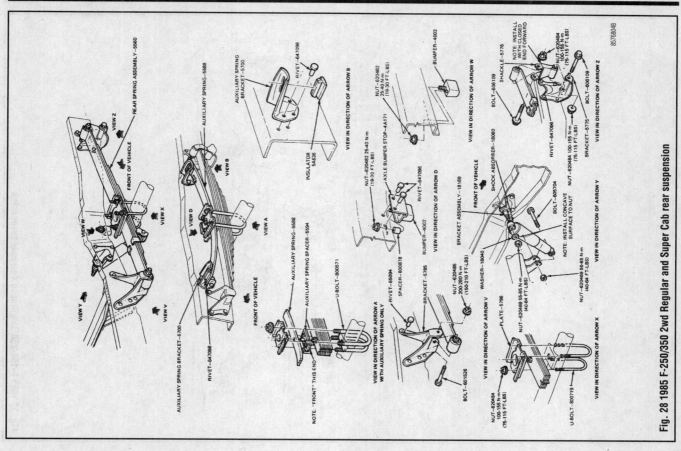

Fig. 28 1985 F-250/350 2wd Regular and Super Cab rear suspension

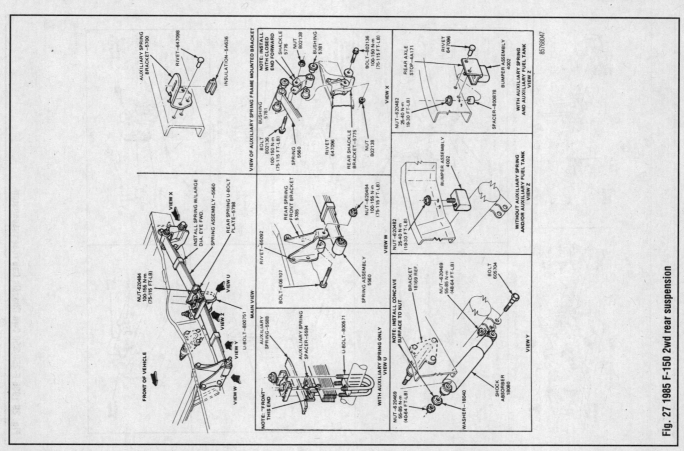

Fig. 27 1985 F-150 2wd rear suspension

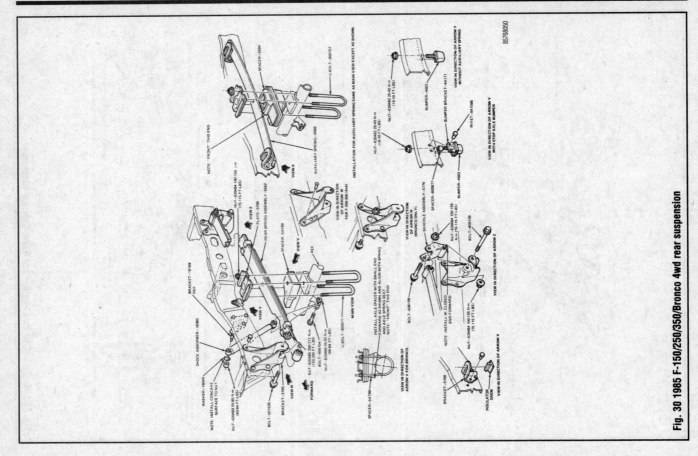

Fig. 30 1985 F-150/250/350/Bronco 4wd rear suspension

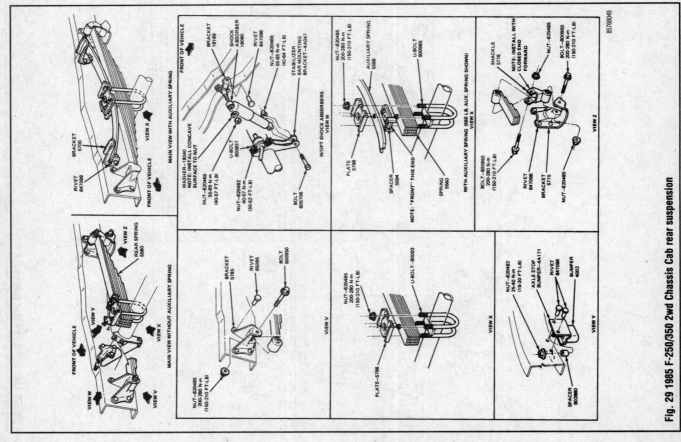

Fig. 29 1985 F-250/350 2wd Chassis Cab rear suspension

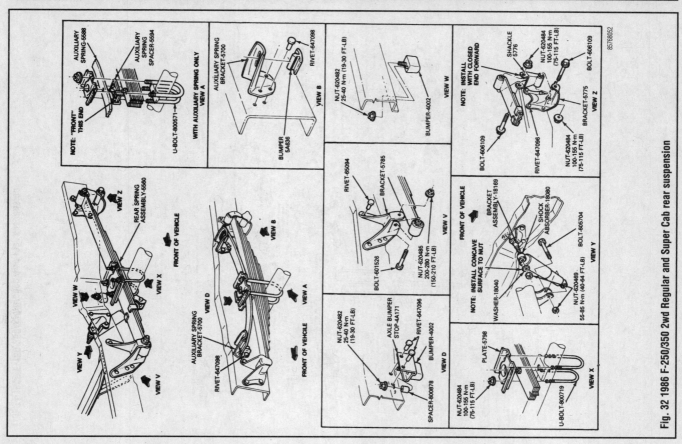

Fig. 32 1986 F-250/350 2wd Regular and Super Cab rear suspension

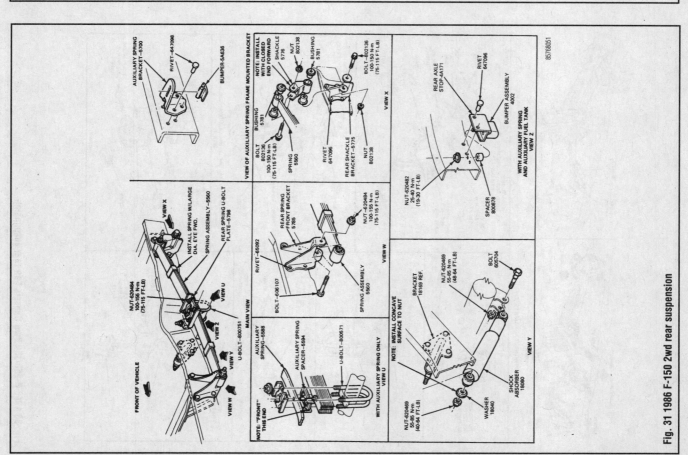

Fig. 31 1986 F-150 2wd rear suspension

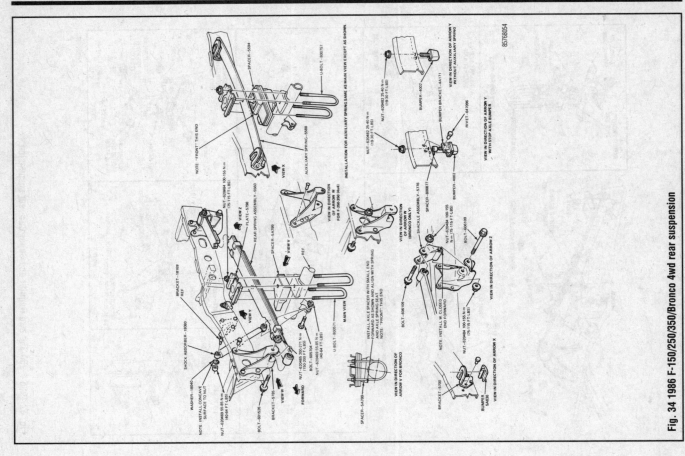

Fig. 34 1986 F-150/250/350/Bronco 4wd rear suspension

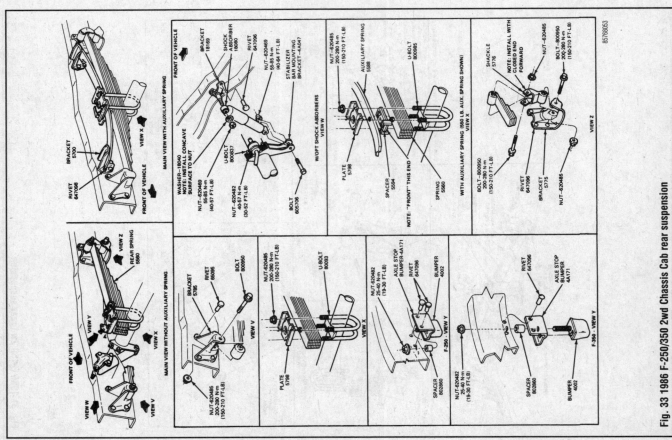

Fig. 33 1986 F-250/350 2wd Chassis Cab rear suspension

Shock Absorbers

TESTING

Check, inspect and test the rear shock absorbers in the same manner as outlined for the front shock absorbers.

REMOVAL & INSTALLATION

♦ See Figures 15 thru 34

1976-79

➥**Prior to installing a new shock absorber, hold it right side up and extend it fully. Turn it upside down and fully compress and extend it at least three times. This will bleed any trapped air.**

1. Raise the vehicle and place jackstands under the frame.
2. Remove the shock absorber-to-upper bracket attaching nut and washers, and bushing from the shock absorber rod.
3. Remove the shock absorber-to-axle attaching bolt. Drive the bolts from the axle bracket and shock absorber with a brass drift and remove the shock absorber.
4. Position the washers and bushing on the shock absorber rod and position the shock absorber at the upper bracket.
5. Position the bushing and washers on the shock absorber rod and install the attaching nut loosely.
6. Position the shock absorber at the axle housing bracket and install the

attaching bolt and nut. Tighten the fasteners to the specifications given in the Torque Chart at the end of this Section.

1980-86

To replace the rear shock absorber, remove the self-locking nut, steel washer, and rubber bushings at the upper and lower ends and remove the shock absorber.

When a new shock absorber is installed, use new rubber bushings. Position the shock on the mounting brackets with the large hole at the top.

Install the steel washer, rubber bushings, steel washer, and self-locking nuts. Tighten the nut until it rests against the shoulder of the stud. Tighten the upper and lower nuts to the specifications shown in the Torque Chart at the end of this Section.

Stabilizer Bar

REMOVAL & INSTALLATION

♦ See Figures 15 thru 34

1. Remove the nuts from the lower ends of the stabilizer bar link.
2. Remove the outer washers and insulators.
3. Disconnect the bar from the links.
4. Remove the inner insulators and washers.
5. Unbolt the link from the frame.
6. Remove the U-bolts, brackets and retainers.
7. Installation is the reverse of removal. Observe the torque figures the specifications shown in the Torque Chart at the end of this Section.

STEERING

Steering Wheel

REMOVAL & INSTALLATION

♦ See Figure 35, 36, 37, 38 and 39

1. Set the front wheel in the straight ahead position and make chalk marks on the column and steering wheel hub for alignment purposes during installation.
2. Disconnect the negative battery cable.
3. Remove the one screw from the underside of each steering wheel spoke, and lift the horn switch assembly (steering wheel pad) from the steering wheel. On vehicles equipped with the sport steering wheel option, pry the button cover off with a screwdriver.
4. Disconnect the horn switch wires at the connector and remove the switch assembly. On trucks equipped with speed control, squeeze the J-clip ground wire terminal firmly and pull it out of the hole in the steering wheel. Don't pull the wire out without squeezing the clip.
5. Remove the horn switch assembly.
6. Remove the steering wheel retaining nut and remove the steering wheel with a puller.

✳✳ WARNING

Never hammer on the wheel or shaft to remove it! Never use a knock-off type puller.

7. Install the steering wheel in the reverse order of removal. Tighten the shaft nut to the specifications shown in the Torque Chart at the end of this Section.

Turn Signal Switch

REMOVAL & INSTALLATION

1976–77

1. Disconnect the horn and turn signal wires at the connectors located behind the instrument panel. Remove the steering column wires and terminals from the connectors by inserting a small screwdriver or similar tool in the

Fig. 35 Removing the horn pad screws

Fig. 36 Marking the wheel for installation

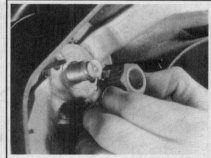
Fig. 37 Removing the steering wheel nut

Fig. 38 Removing the steering wheel with a puller

Fig. 39 Steering wheel removed

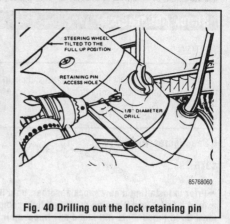

Fig. 40 Drilling out the lock retaining pin

opposite end from which the wire is inserted and depress the tang on the wire. The wire can then be removed from the connector.

➡Be sure to record the color code and location of each wire before removing it from the connector plug. Tape a pull-through wire or cord to one of the wire ends.

2. Remove the steering wheel.
3. Turn the signal switch lever counterclockwise to remove it. Remove the screws and retainer which hold the turn signal switch and wire assembly to the steering column, and pull the assembly from the column. Disconnect the pull-through wire or cord from the end of the wire to which it was taped.

To install:
4. Tape the loose ends of the new turn signal switch wires to the pull-through wire or cord. Carefully pull the wires through the steering column, while guiding the turn signal switch into position. Install the switch retainer screws.
5. Assemble the rest of the steering column in the reverse order of disassembly.

1978-86
1. Disconnect the battery ground cable.
2. Remove the steering wheel.
3. Remove the turn signal lever by unscrewing it from the steering column.
4. Disconnect the turn signal indicator switch wiring connector plug by lifting up the tabs on the side of the plug and pulling it apart.
5. Remove the switch assembly attaching screws.
6. On trucks with a fixed column, lift the switch out of the column and guide the connector plug through the opening in the shift socket.
7. On trucks with a tilt column, remove the connector plug before removing the switch from the column. The shift socket opening is not large enough for the plug connector to pass through.
8. Install the turn signal switch in the reverse order of removal. Check turn signal switch for proper operation.

Ignition Switch

REMOVAL & INSTALLATION

▶ See Figures 40 thru 46

Column Mounted Switches

➡For dash mounted switches, see Section 6.

1. Disconnect the battery ground cable.
2. Remove the steering column shroud and lower the steering column.
3. Disconnect the switch wiring at the multiple plug.
4. Remove the two nuts that retain the switch to the steering column.
5. Lift the switch vertically upward to disengage the actuator rod from the switch and remove the switch.
6. When installing the ignition switch, both the locking mechanism at the top of the column and the switch itself must be in the LOCK position for correct adjustment. To hold the mechanical parts of the column in the LOCK position, move the shift lever into PARK (with automatic transmissions) or REVERSE (with manual transmissions), turn the key to the LOCK position, and remove the key. New replacement switches, when received, are already pinned in the LOCK position by a metal shipping pin inserted in a locking hole on the side of the switch.
7. Engage the actuator rod in the switch.
8. Position the switch on the column and install the retaining nuts, but do not tighten them.
9. Move the switch up and down along the column to locate the mid-position of rod lash, and then tighten the retaining nuts.
10. Remove the locking pin, connect the battery cable, and check for proper start in PARK or NEUTRAL. Also check to make certain that the start circuit cannot be actuated in the DRIVE and REVERSE position.
11. Raise the steering column into position at instrument panel. Install steering column shroud.

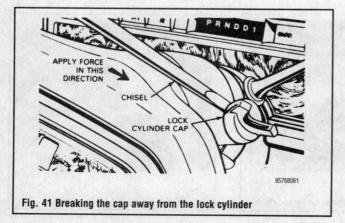

Fig. 41 Breaking the cap away from the lock cylinder

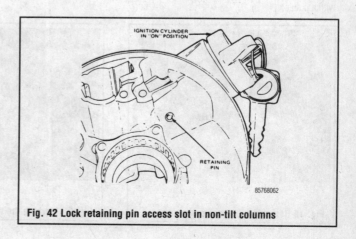

Fig. 42 Lock retaining pin access slot in non-tilt columns

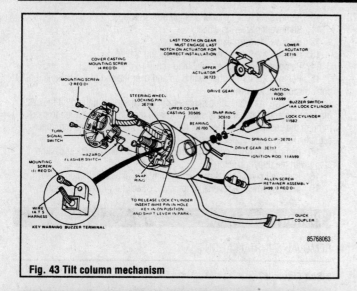

Fig. 43 Tilt column mechanism

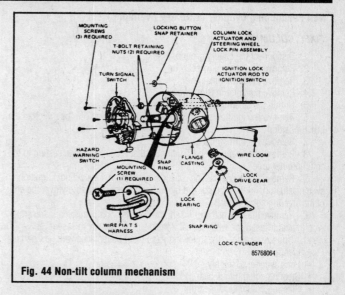

Fig. 44 Non-tilt column mechanism

Ignition Lock Cylinder

REMOVAL & INSTALLATION

◆ **See Figures 40 thru 46**

➡ **For trucks with dash mounted switches, see Section 6.**

With Key

1. Disconnect the battery ground.
2. On tilt columns, remove the upper extension shroud by unsnapping the shroud from the retaining clip at the 9 o'clock position.

3. Remove the trim shroud halves.
4. Unplug the wire connector at the key warning switch.
5. Place the shift lever in PARK and turn the key to ON.
6. Place a ⅛ in. wire pin in the hole in the casting surrounding the lock cylinder and depress the retaining pin while pulling out on the cylinder.
7. When installing the cylinder, turn the lock cylinder to the RUN position and depress the retaining pin, then insert the lock cylinder into its housing in the flange casting. Assure that the cylinder is fully seated and aligned in the interlocking washer before turning the key to the OFF position. This will allow the cylinder retaining pin to extend into the cylinder cast housing hole.
8. The remainder of installation is the reverse of removal.

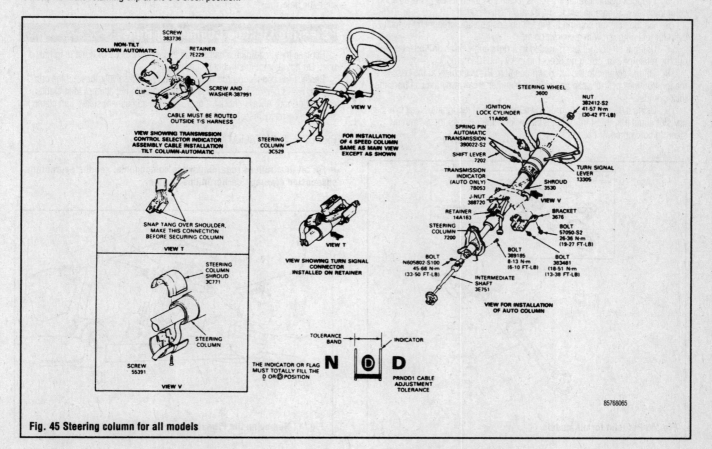

Fig. 45 Steering column for all models

Non-Functioning Cylinder or No Key Available

FIXED COLUMNS

1. Disconnect the battery ground.
2. Remove the steering wheel.
3. Remove the turn signal lever.
4. Remove the column trim shrouds.
5. Unbolt the steering column and lower it carefully.
6. Remove the ignition switch and warning buzzer and pin the switch in the LOCK position.
7. Remove the turn signal switch.
8. Remove the snapring and T-bolt nuts that retain the flange casting to the column outer tube.
9. Remove the flange casting, upper shaft bearing, lock cylinder, ignition switch actuator and the actuator rod by pulling the entire assembly over the end of the steering column shaft.
10. Remove the lock actuator insert, the T-bolts and the automatic transmission indicator insert, or, with manual transmissions, the key release lever.
11. Upon reassembly, the following parts must be replaced with new parts:
   • Flange
   • Lock cylinder assembly
   • Steering column lock gear
   • Steering column lock bearing
   • Steering column upper bearing retainer
   • Lock actuator assembly
12. Assembly is a reversal of the disassembly procedure. It is best to install a new upper bearing. Check that the vehicle starts only in PARK and NEUTRAL.

TILT COLUMNS

1. Disconnect the battery ground.
2. Remove the steering column shrouds.
3. Using masking tape, tape the gap between the steering wheel hub and the cover casting. Cover the entire circumference of the casting. Cover the seat and floor area with a drop-cloth.
4. Pull out the hazard switch and tape it in a downward position.
5. The lock cylinder retaining pin is located on the outside of the steering column cover casting adjacent to the hazard flasher button.
6. Tilt the steering column to the full up position and prepunch the lock cylinder retaining pin with a sharp punch.
7. Using a ⅛ in. drill bit, mounted in a right angle drive drill adapter, drill out the retaining pin, going no deeper than ½ in. (12.7mm).
8. Tilt the column to the full down position. Place a chisel at the base of the ignition lock cylinder cap and using a hammer break away the cap from the lock cylinder.
9. Using a ⅜ in. drill bit, drill down the center of the ignition lock cylinder key slot about 1¾ in. (44mm), until the lock cylinder breaks loose from the steering column cover casting.

10. Remove the lock cylinder and the drill shavings.
11. Remove the steering wheel.
12. Remove the turn signal lever.
13. Remove the turn signal switch attaching screws.
14. Remove the key buzzer attaching screw.
15. Remove the turn signal switch up and over the end of the column, but don't disconnect the wiring.
16. Remove the 4 attaching screws from the cover casting and lift the casting over the end of the steering shaft, allowing the turn signal switch to pass through the casting. The removal of the casting cover will expose the upper actuator. Remove the upper actuator.
17. Remove the drive gear, snapring and washer from the cover casting along with the upper actuator.
18. Clean all components and replace any that appear damaged or worn.
19. Installation is the reverse of removal. Check for proper operation.

Pitman Arm

REMOVAL & INSTALLATION

▸ **See Figure 47**

All Models

1. Place the wheels in a straight-ahead position.
2. Disconnect the drag link at the Pitman arm. You'll need a puller such as a tie rod end remover.
3. Remove the Pitman arm-to-gear nut and washer.
4. Matchmark the Pitman arm and gear housing for installation purposes.
5. Using a 2-jawed puller, remove the Pitman arm from the gear.
6. Installation is the reverse of removal. Align the matchmarks when installing the Pitman arm. Torque the Pitman arm nut to the specifications shown in the Torque Chart at the end of this section; torque the drag link ball stud nut to the specifications shown in the Torque Chart at the end of this section, advancing the nut to align the cotter pin hole. Never back off the nut to align the hole.

Steering Linkage Connecting Rods

Replace the drag link if a ball stud is excessively loose or if the drag link is bent. Do not attempt to straighten a drag link.

Replace the connecting rod if the ball stud is excessively loose, if the connecting rod is bent or if the threads are stripped. Do not attempt to straighten connecting rod. Always check to insure that the adjustment sleeve and clamp stops are correctly installed on the Bronco.

REMOVAL & INSTALLATION

➥**For all illustrations regarding these components, see the appropriate suspension coverage earlier in this section.**

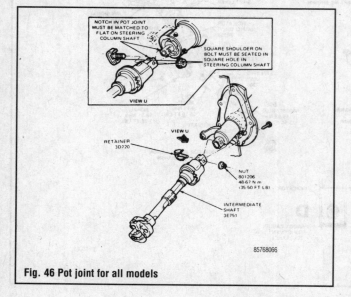

Fig. 46 Pot joint for all models

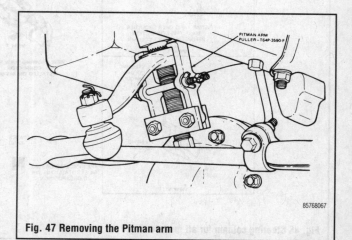

Fig. 47 Removing the Pitman arm

1976–79

1. Remove the cotter pins and nuts from the drag link, ball studs and from the right connecting rod ball stud.
2. Remove the right connecting rod ball stud from the drag link.
3. Remove the drag link ball studs from the spindle and the Pitman arm.
4. Position the new drag link, ball studs in the spindle, and Pitman arm and install nuts.
5. Position the right connecting rod ball stud in the drag link and install nut.
6. Tighten the nuts as follows and install the cotter pins. Drag link studs, 50–75 ft. lbs. Ball studs, 50–60 ft. lbs. Connecting rod studs, 35–45 ft. lbs.
7. Remove the cotter pin and nut from the connecting rod.
8. Remove the ball stud from the mating part.
9. Loosen the clamp bolt and turn the rod out of the adjustment sleeve.
10. Lubricate the threads of the new connecting rod, and turn it into the adjustment sleeve to about the same distance the old rods were installed. This will provide an approximate toe-in setting. Position the connecting rod ball studs in the spindle arms.
11. Install the nuts on to the connecting rod ball studs, tighten the nut to specification and install the cotter pin.
12. Check the toe-in and adjust, if necessary. After checking or adjusting toe-in, center the adjustment sleeve clamps between the locating nubs, positions the clamps and tighten the nuts to 35–45 ft. lbs.

Tie Rod and Drag Link

REMOVAL & INSTALLATION

▶ See Figures 48, 49 and 50

1980–86

EXCEPT RUBBERIZED BALL SOCKET LINKAGE

1. Place the wheels in a straight-ahead position.
2. Remove the cotter pins and must from the drag link and tie rod ball studs.
3. Remove the drag link ball studs from the right hand spindle and pitman arm.
4. Remove the tie rod ball studs from the left hand spindle and drag link.
5. Installation is the reverse of removal. Seat the studs in the tapered hole before tightening the nuts. This will avoid wrap-up of the rubber grommets during tightening of the nuts. Torque the nuts to the specifications shown in the Torque Chart at the end of this Section. Always use new cotter pins.
6. Have the front end alignment checked.

RUBBERIZED BALL SOCKET LINKAGE

1. Raise and support the front end on jackstands.
2. Place the wheels in the straight-ahead position.
3. Remove the nuts connecting the drag link ball studs to the connecting rod and pitman arm.
4. Disconnect the drag link using a tie rod end remover.

5. Loosen the bolts on the adjuster clamp. Count the number of turns it take to remove the drag link from the adjuster.
6. Installation is the reverse of removal. Install the drag link with the same number of turns it took to remove it. Make certain that the wheels remain in the straight-ahead position during installation. Seat the studs in the tapered hole before tightening the nuts. This will avoid wrap-up of the rubber grommets during tightening of the nuts. Torque the all fasteners to the specifications shown in the Torque Chart at the end of this Section.
7. Have the front end alignment checked.

Connecting Rod

REMOVAL & INSTALLATION

1980–86

➡For all illustrations regarding these components, see the appropriate suspension coverage earlier in this section.

RUBBERIZED BALL SOCKET LINKAGE

1. Raise and support the front end on jackstands.
2. Place the wheels in the straight-ahead position.
3. Disconnect the connecting rod from the drag link by removing the nut and separating the two with a tie rod end remover.
4. Loosen the bolts on the adjusting sleeve clamps. Count the number of turns it takes to remove the connecting rod from the connecting rod from the adjuster sleeve and remove the rod.
5. Installation is the reverse of removal. Install the connecting rod the exact number of turns noted during removal. Torque all fasteners to the specifications shown in the Torque Chart at the end of this Section.
6. Have the front end alignment checked.

Tie Rod Ends

➡For all illustrations regarding these components, see the appropriate suspension coverage earlier in this section.

REMOVAL & INSTALLATION

1980–86

RUBBERIZED BALL SOCKET LINKAGE

1. Raise and support the front end on jackstands.
2. Place the wheels in a straight-ahead position.
3. Remove the ball stud from the pitman arm using a tie rod end remover.
4. Loosen the nuts on the adjusting sleeve clamp. Remove the ball stud from the adjuster, or the adjuster from the tie rod. Count the number of turns it takes to remove the sleeve from the tie rod or ball stud from the sleeve.
5. Install the sleeve on the tie rod, or the ball in the sleeve the same number of turns noted during removal. Make sure that the adjuster clamps are in the

Fig. 48 Measure the length of the assembled removable end

85768068

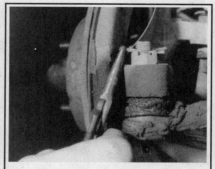

Fig. 49 Removing the cotter pin from the ball stud

85768069

Fig. 50 Separating the tie rod end ball stud from the knuckle

85768070

correct position and torque the clamp bolts to the specifications shown in the Torque Chart at the end of this Section.

6. Keep the wheels straight ahead and install the ball studs. Torque the nuts to the specifications shown in the Torque Chart at the end of this Section. Use new cotter pins.

7. Install the drag link and connecting rod.

8. Have the front end alignment checked.

Manual Steering Gear

ADJUSTMENT

1976–79

1. Be sure that the steering column is properly aligned and is not causing excessive turning effort.

2. The steering gear must be removed from the truck.

3. Be sure that the ball nut assembly and the sector gear are properly adjusted as follows to maintain minimum steering shaft endplay and backlash between the sector gear and ball nut (preload adjustment).

4. Loosen the sector shaft adjusting screw locknut and tighten worm bearing adjuster screw until all endplay is removed.

5. Measure the worm bearing preload by attaching an in.lb. torque wrench to the input shaft. Measure the torque required to rotate the input shaft all the way to the right and then turn back about one half turn. The worm bearing preload should be 10–16 in.lb.

6. Turn the sector shaft adjusting screw clockwise until the specified pull is obtained to rotate the worm past its center. With the steering gear in the center position, hold the sector shaft to prevent rotation and check the lash between the ball nuts, balls and worm shaft by applying a 15 in.lb. torque on the steering gear input shaft, in both right and left turn directions. Total travel of the wrench should not exceed 1¼ inch (32mm) when applying a 15 in.lb. torque on the steering shaft.

7. Tighten the sector shaft adjusting screw locknut, and recheck the backlash adjustment.

1980 and Later

PRELOAD AND MESHLOAD CHECK

1. Raise and support the front end on jackstands.

2. Disconnect the drag link from the pitman arm.

3. Lubricate the wormshaft seal with a drop of automatic transmission fluid.

4. Remove the horn pad from the steering wheel.

5. Turn the steering wheel slowly to one stop.

6. Using an inch-pound torque wrench on the steering wheel nut, check the amount of torque needed to rotate the steering wheel through a 1½ turn cycle. The preload should be 5-9 inch lbs. If not, proceed with the rest of the steps.

7. Rotate the steering wheel from stop-to-stop, counting the total number of turns. Using that figure, center the steering wheel (½ the total turns).

8. Using the inch-pound torque wrench, rotate the steering wheel 90° to either side of center, noting the highest torque reading over center. The meshload should be 9-14 inch lbs., or at least 2 inch lbs. more than the preload figure.

PRELOAD AND MESHLOAD ADJUSTMENT

1. Remove the steering gear.

2. Torque the sector cover bolts on the gear to 40 ft. lbs.

3. Loosen the preload adjuster nut and tighten the worm bearing adjuster nut until all endplay has been removed. Lubricate the wormshaft seal with a few drops of automatic transmission fluid.

4. Using an 1⁄16 in., 12 point socket and an inch-pound torque wrench, carefully turn the wormshaft all the way to the right.

5. Turn the shaft back to the left and measure the torque over a 1½ turn cycle. This is the preload reading.

6. Tighten or loosen the adjuster nut to bring the preload into range (7-9 inch lbs.).

7. Hold the adjuster nut while torquing the locknut to 187 ft. lbs.

8. Rotate the wormshaft stop-to-stop counting the total number of turns and center the shaft (½ the total turns).

9. Using the torque wrench and socket, measure the torque required to turn the shaft 90° to either side of center.

10. Turn the sector shaft adjusting screw as needed to bring the meshload torque within the 12-14 inch lbs. range, or at least 4 inch lbs. higher than preload torque.

11. Hold the adjusting screw while tightening the locknut to 25 ft. lbs.

12. Install the gear.

REMOVAL & INSTALLATION

▶ **See Figures 51, 52 and 53**

1976–79

1. Raise the vehicle on a hoist and remove the Pitman arm attaching nut and lockwasher.

2. Remove the Pitman arm from the sector shaft using Tool T64P-3590-F.

3. Remove bolts, nuts and flat washers that attach the steering gear to the frame side rail, and lower the vehicle.

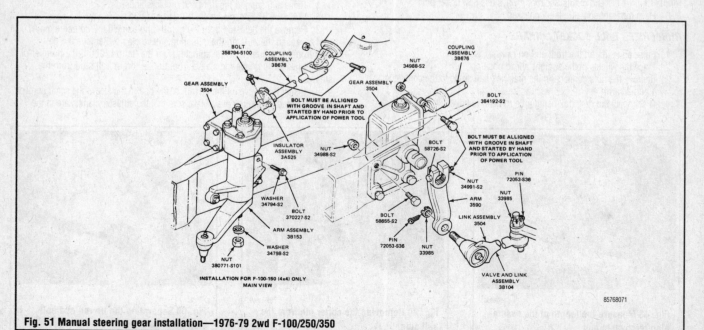

85768071

Fig. 51 Manual steering gear installation—1976-79 2wd F-100/250/350

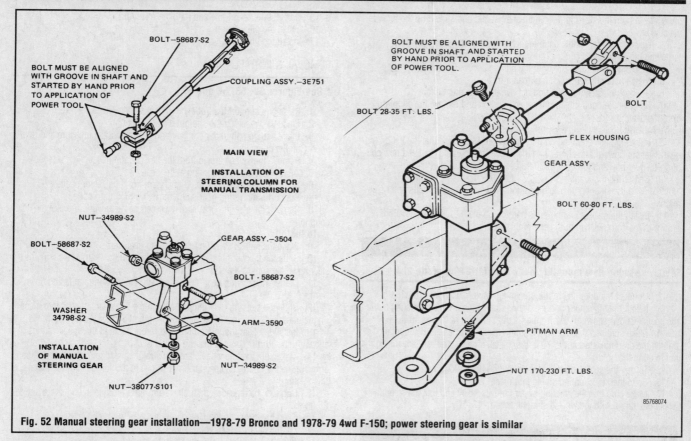

Fig. 52 Manual steering gear installation—1978-79 Bronco and 1978-79 4wd F-150; power steering gear is similar

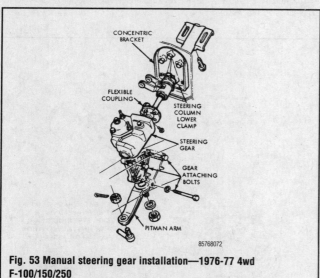

Fig. 53 Manual steering gear installation—1976-77 4wd F-100/150/250

4. Remove the flex coupling bolt and nut from the coupling clamp. Loosen the clamp from the coupling at the end of the steering column and separate the coupling from the steering gear input shaft by pushing the steering shaft toward the steering column. Discard the clamp, bolt, and nut.

5. Remove and discard the flex coupling clamp from the steering gear input shaft, and remove the steering gear from the frame side rail.

6. Place the steering gear on the frame side rail and install the attaching bolts, nuts, and flat washers.

7. Place the flex coupling and a new clamp on the steering gear input shaft and install the clamp bolt and nut. Tighten the bolt and nut to 28–35 ft. lbs.

8. Install a new steering shaft clamp at the end of the steering column and tighten the bolt and nut to 20–30 ft. lbs.

9. Raise the vehicle and tighten the steering gear attaching bolts and nuts to 60–80 ft. lbs.

10. Place the Pitman arm on the sector shaft and install the washer and attaching nut. Tighten the nut to 170–230 ft. lbs., lower the vehicle, and fill the gear with lubricant SAE-90EP Oil.

1980-86

▶ See Figure 54

1. Raise and support the front end on jackstands.
2. Place the wheels in a straight-ahead position. Disengage the flex cou-

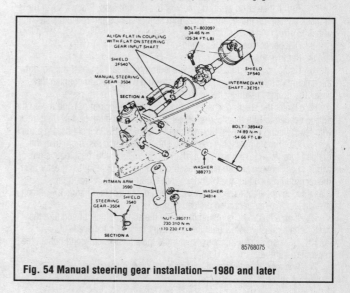

Fig. 54 Manual steering gear installation—1980 and later

pling shield from the steering gear input shaft shield and slide it up the intermediate shaft.

3. Disconnect the flexible coupling from the steering shaft flange by removing the 2 nuts.

4. Disconnect the drag link from the pitman arm.

5. Matchmark and remove the pitman arm.

6. Support the steering gear and remove the attaching bolts.

7. Remove the coupling-to-gear attaching bolt and remove the coupling from the gear.

To install:

8. Install the flex coupling on the input shaft. Make sure that the flat on the gear is facing upward and aligns with the flat on the coupling. Install a new coupling-to-gear bolt and torque it to 30 ft. lbs.

9. Center the input shaft.

10. Place the steering gear into position. Make sure that all bolts and holes align.

11. Install the gear mounting bolts and torque them to the specifications shown in the Torque Chart at the end of this Section.

> ❄❄ **CAUTION**
>
> **If you are using new mounting bolts they MUST be grade 9!**

12. Connect the drag link to the pitman arm and hand-tighten the nut.

13. Install the pitman arm on the sector shaft. Torque the sector shaft nut to the specifications shown in the Torque Chart at the end of this Section.

14. Make sure that the wheels are still in the straight-ahead position and tighten the drag link stud nut to 70 ft. lbs. Install a new cotter pin, advancing the nut to align the hole.

15. Torque the sector shaft-to-flex coupling nuts to 20 ft. lbs.

16. Snap the flex coupling shield into place.

17. Make sure that the steering system moves freely and that the steering wheel is straight with the wheels straight-ahead.

Power Steering Gear

ADJUSTMENTS

Meshload

1. Raise and support the front end on jackstands.

2. Matchmark the pitman arm and gear housing.

3. Set the wheels in a straight-ahead position.

4. Disconnect the pitman arm from the sector shaft.

5. Disconnect the fluid RETURN line at the pump reservoir and cap the reservoir nipple.

6. Place the end of the return line in a clean container and turn the steering wheel lock-to-lock a few times to expel the fluid from the gear.

7. Turn the steering wheel all the way to the right stop. Place a small piece of masking tape on the steering wheel rim as a reference and rotate the steering wheel 45° from the right stop.

8. Disconnect the battery ground.

9. Remove the horn pad.

10. Using an inch-pound torque wrench on the steering wheel nut, record the amount of torque needed to turn the steering wheel ⅛ turn counterclockwise. The preload reading should be 4-9 inch lbs.

11. Center the steering wheel (½ the total lock-to-lock turns) and record the torque needed to turn the steering wheel 90° to either side of center. On a truck with fewer than 5,000 miles, the meshload should be 15-25 inch lbs. On a truck with 5,000 or more miles, the meshload should be 7 inch lbs. more than the preload torque. On trucks with fewer than 5,000 miles, if the meshload is not within specifications, it should be reset to a figure 14-18 inch lbs. greater than the recorded preload torque. On trucks with 5,000 or more miles, if the meshload is not within specifications, it should be reset to a figure 10-14 inch lbs. greater than the recorded preload torque.

12. If an adjustment is required, loosen the adjuster locknut and turn the sector shaft adjuster screw until the necessary torque is achieved.

13. Once adjustment is completed. hold the adjuster screw and tighten the locknut to 45 ft. lbs.

14. Recheck the adjustment readings and reset if necessary.

15. Connect the return line and refill the reservoir.

16. Install the pitman arm.

17. Install the horn pad.

REMOVAL & INSTALLATION

▶ **See Figures 52, 55, 56 and 57**

1. Raise and support the front end on jackstands.

2. Place the wheels in the straight-ahead position.

3. Place a drain pan under the gear and disconnect the pressure and return lines. Cap the openings.

4. Remove the splash shield from the flex coupling.

5. Disconnect the flex coupling at the gear.

6. Matchmark and remove the pitman arm from the sector shaft.

7. Support the steering gear and remove the mounting bolts.

8. Remove the steering gear. It may be necessary to work it free of the flex coupling.

To install:

9. Place the splash shield on the steering gear lugs.

10. Slide the flex coupling into place on the steering shaft. Make sure the steering wheel spokes are still horizontal.

11. Center the steering gear input shaft with the indexing flat facing downward.

12. Slide the steering gear input shaft into the flex coupling and into place on the frame side rail. Install the flex coupling bolt and torque it to 30 ft. lbs.

13. Install the gear mounting bolts and torque them to the specifications shown in the Torque Chart at the end of this Section.

14. Make sure that the wheels are still straight ahead and install the pitman arm. Torque the nut to the specifications shown in the Torque Chart at the end of this Section.

15. Connect the pressure, then, the return lines. Torque the pressure line to 25 ft. lbs.

16. Snap the flex coupling shield into place.

17. Fill the steering reservoir.

18. Run the engine and turn the steering wheel lock-to-lock several times to expel air. Check for leaks.

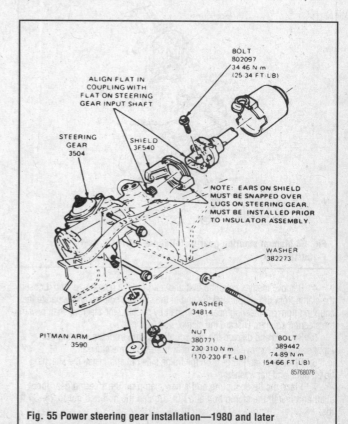

Fig. 55 Power steering gear installation—1980 and later

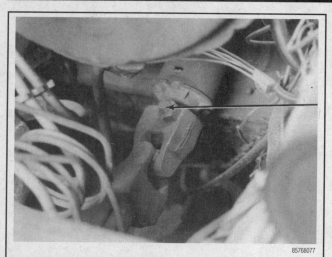

Fig. 56 Intermediate shaft-to-steering column upper joint connection. Remove the pinchbolt shown to disconnect

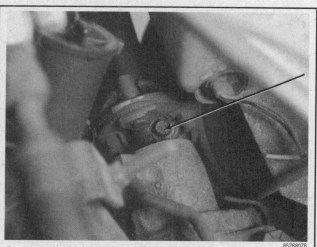

Fig. 57 Intermediate shaft-to-steering gear joint connection. Remove the pinchbolt shown to disconnect

Power Steering Pumps

REMOVAL & INSTALLATION

1. Disconnect the return line at the pump and drain the fluid into a container.
2. Disconnect the pressure line from the pump.
3. Loosen the pump bracket nuts and remove the drive belt. On the 8-302 with a serpentine drive belt, remove belt tension by lifting the tensioner out of position.
4. Remove the nuts and lift out the pump/bracket assembly.
5. If a new pump or bracket is being installed, you'll have to remove the pulley from the present pump. This is best done with a press and adapters.
6. Installation is the reverse of removal. Note the torques shown in the Torque Chart at the end of this Section.

Quick-Connect Pressure Line

Some pumps will have a quick-connect fitting for the pressure line. This fitting may, under certain circumstances, leak and/or be improperly engaged resulting in unplanned disconnection.

The leak is usually caused by a cut O-ring, imperfections in the outlet fitting inside diameter, or an improperly machined O-ring groove.

Improper engagement can be caused by an improperly machined tube end, tube nut, snapring, outlet fitting or gear port.

If a leak occurs, the O-ring should be replaced with new O-rings. Special O-rings are made for quick-disconnect fittings. Standard O-rings should never be used in their place. If the new O-rings do not solve the leak problem, replace the outlet fitting. If that doesn't work, replace the pressure line.

Improper engagement due to a missing or bent snapring, or improperly machined tube nut, may be corrected with a Ford snapring kit made for the purpose. If that doesn't work, replace the pressure hose.

When tightening a quick-connect tube nut, always use a tube nut wrench; never use an open-end wrench! Use of an open-end wrench will result in deformation of the nut! Tighten quick-connect tube nuts to 15 ft. lbs. maximum.

Swivel and/or endplay of quick-connect fittings is normal.

TORQUE SPECIFICATIONS
WHEELS/HUBS/BEARINGS

Component	U.S.	Metric
Wheel lug nuts ①		
1976-77 ①		
F-100/150/250	90 ft. lbs.	122 Nm
F-350 w/5200 lb. axle	90 ft. lbs.	122 Nm
F-350 w/drw and 6800 lb. axle ②	135 ft. lbs.	184 Nm
F-350 w/drw and 7400 lb. axle ②	210 ft. lbs.	286 Nm
1978-79 ①		
F-100/150/250/Bronco	90 ft. lbs.	122 Nm
F-350 w/srw	135 ft. lbs.	184 Nm
F-350 w/drw, exc. 7400 lb. axle	145 ft. lbs.	197 Nm
F-350 w/drw and 7400 lb. axle ②	220 ft. lbs.	299 Nm
1980-82		
Bronco, F-150/250	65-115 ft. lbs.	88-156 Nm
F-350 w/srw	115-175 ft. lbs.	156-238 Nm
F-350 w/drw	175-260 ft. lbs.	238-354 Nm
1983		
Bronco, F-150, 250 under 8500 GVW	85-115 ft. lbs.	88-156 Nm
F-250 8500+ GVW, F-350 w/srw	115-175 ft. lbs.	156-238 Nm
F-350 w/drw	175-260 ft. lbs.	238-354 Nm
1984-85		
Bronco, F-150, 250 under 8500 GVW	85-115 ft. lbs.	88-156 Nm
F-250, 8500+ GVW, F-350 w/srw	115-175 ft. lbs.	156-238 Nm
F-350 w/drw & 2-piece lug nuts	125-155 ft. lbs.	170-211 Nm
1986		
All 5-lug wheels	90-110 ft. lbs.	122-150 Nm
All 8-lug wheels	130-150 ft. lbs.	177-204 Nm
Front wheel bearing seating torque ③		
2-wheel drive ③		
1976-77	17-25 ft. lbs.	23-34 Nm
1978-86	22-25 ft. lbs.	30-34 Nm
4-wheel drive		
1976-83	50 ft. lbs. ④	68 Nm
1984-85		
Dana 44IFS/IFS-HD	50 ft. lbs. ④	68 Nm ⑤
Dana 50IFS		
1986		
Dana 44IFS/IFS-HD	70 ft. lbs. ④⑤	95 Nm ⑤
Dana 50IFS, 60 Monobeam		
Front wheel bearing outer locknut		
4-wheel drive		
1976	80-100 ft. lbs.	109-136 Nm
1977	50-70 ft. lbs.	68-95 Nm
1978-79	50-80 ft. lbs.	68-109 Nm
1980-81	50 ft. lbs.	68 Nm
1982	150 ft. lbs.	204 Nm
1983		
Bronco/F-150	150 ft. lbs.	204 Nm
F-250/350	65 ft. lbs.	88 Nm
1984-85		
Dana 44IFS/IFS-HD	150 ft. lbs.	204 Nm
Dana 50IFS	65 ft. lbs.	88 Nm
1986		
Dana 44IFS	—	—
Dana 50IFS, 60 Monobeam	160-205 ft. lbs.	218-279 Nm

85768299

TORQUE SPECIFICATIONS
WHEELS/HUBS/BEARINGS

Component	U.S.	Metric
Manual locking hub retainer cap		
1976-82	30-35 inch lbs.	3-4 Nm
1983-85	35-55 inch lbs.	4-6 Nm
1986	40-60 inch lbs.	4.5-6.5 Nm
Automatic locking hubs		
1980-81		
Outer spindle locknut	15-20 ft. lbs.	20-27 Nm
Axle shaft capscrew	35-50 ft. lbs.	48-68 Nm
Retainer cover capscrews	35-50 inch lbs.	4-5.5 Nm
1982-86		
Cover capscrews	40-50 inch lbs.	4.5-5.5 Nm
Rear wheel bearing (full floating axle)		
Adjusting nut		
1976 ⑦	120-140 ft. lbs.	163-189 Nm
1977-81 ⑦	50-80 ft. lbs.	68-109 Nm
1982-86 ⑦	120-140 ft. lbs.	163-189 Nm
Locknut		
1976-79	90-110 ft. lbs.	122-150 Nm
Axle shaft retaining bolts (full floating)		
1976-86	40-50 ft. lbs.	54-68 Nm

srw: single rear wheels
drw: dual rear wheels

① Back-off ⅓ turn
② Dual rear wheels only: retorque the lug nuts after 500 miles (805km)
③ Single rear wheel lug nuts are black in color; dual rear wheel lug nuts are zinc plate in color. The lug nuts should not be mixed.
④ The dual rear wheel lug nuts are left hand threads for left rear wheels only.
⑤ After tightening, back off ⅛-¼ turn so that nylon insert above keyway is uncut.
⑥ Back-off ⅛ turn and install cotter pin
⑦ Back off 1976-81: 90 deg. 1982-85: 45 deg.

① 1. Tighten to 50 ft. lbs. (68 Nm)
  2. Back off completely and retorque to 31-39 ft. lbs. (42-53 Nm)
  3. While rotating the hub, back off ⅜-½ turn tighten; it will ratchet.
② After 70 ft. lbs. (95 Nm), the nut will no longer tighten, then tighten to 15 ft. lbs. (20 Nm).

85768298

TORQUE SPECIFICATIONS — STEERING

Component	U.S.	Metric
Steering shaft or coupling-to-gear		
1976-77	33-37 ft. lbs.	45-64 Nm
1978-79 All	40-60 ft. lbs.	54-82 Nm
Coupling shaft-to-upper steering shaft		
1976-79	40-60 ft. lbs.	54-82 Nm
1980-85	45-60 ft. lbs.	61-82 Nm
1986	35-50 ft. lbs.	48-68 Nm
Steering wheel-to-column		
1976-86	30-45 ft. lbs.	41-54 Nm
Steering column support bracket		
1976-79	8-18 ft. lbs.	11-24 Nm
1980-81	13-38 ft. lbs.	18-52 Nm
1982-86	13-20 ft. lbs.	18-27 Nm
Flange assy-to-steering column		
1976-77	11-21 ft. lbs.	15-29 Nm
1978		
F-250 4wd	11-21 ft. lbs.	15-29 Nm
F-150/Bronco	28-35 ft. lbs.	38-48 Nm
1979	11-21 ft. lbs.	15-29 Nm
Flange assy-to-steering gear		
1976-86	28-35 ft. lbs.	38-48 Nm
Flange assy-to-coupling shaft		
1976-79	11-21 ft. lbs.	15-29 Nm
1980	17-21 ft. lbs.	23-29 Nm
1981-86	14-21 ft. lbs.	19-29 Nm
Power steering adjusting bracket-to-engine		
1976-86	40-50 ft. lbs.	54-68 Nm
Power steering pump-to-bracket		
1976-78		
F-100/150/250/Bronco	40-50 ft. lbs.	54-68 Nm
F-350	15-20 ft. lbs.	20-27 Nm
1979-86		
6-cyl.	46-65 ft. lbs.	63-88 Nm
8-cyl.	30-45 ft. lbs.	41-61 Nm
Power steering cooler-to-compressor		
1976-78	20-30 ft. lbs.	27-41 Nm
Power steering support bracket-to-engine		
1976-78	40-50 ft. lbs.	54-68 Nm
1979-86	30-45 ft. lbs.	41-61 Nm
Power steering hose couplings		
1976-86		
5/16 in. nuts	16-25 ft. lbs.	22-34 Nm
3/8 in. nuts	20-30 ft. lbs.	27-41 Nm
Toe adjustment sleeve bolts		
1976-79	25-35 ft. lbs.	34-48 Nm
Drag link-to-pitman arm		
1979 F-250 4wd	50-75 ft. lbs.	68-102 Nm
Tie rod-to-axle		
1979 F-250 4wd	50-75 ft. lbs.	68-102 Nm

85768296

TORQUE SPECIFICATIONS — STEERING

Component	U.S.	Metric
Steering gear-to-frame		
1976		
F-100/250/350 2wd	55-75 ft. lbs.	75-102 Nm
F-100 4wd	60-80 ft. lbs.	82-109 Nm
F-250 4wd	50-65 ft. lbs.	68-88 Nm
1977		
F-250 4wd	50-65 ft. lbs.	68-88 Nm
All others	55-75 ft. lbs.	75-102 Nm
1978		
All 2wd	50-65 ft. lbs.	68-88 Nm
F-150/Bronco	60-85 ft. lbs.	82-116 Nm
F-250	95-125 ft. lbs.	129-170 Nm
1979		
F-150/250 4wd Super Cab, & F-250 4wd Regular Cab	95-125 ft. lbs.	129-170 Nm
F-100/250/350 2wd	50-65 ft. lbs.	68-88 Nm
F-150 Regular Cab and Bronco	60-85 ft. lbs.	82-116 Nm
1980		
2-wheel drive	65-75 ft. lbs.	88-102 Nm
4-wheel drive	95-125 ft. lbs.	129-170 Nm
1981-86		
All	65-75 ft. lbs.	88-102 Nm
Pitman arm-to-steering gear		
1976		
F-100/250/350 2wd	170-230 ft. lbs.	231-313 Nm
F-100 4wd	105-135 ft. lbs.	143-184 Nm
F-250 4wd	130-170 ft. lbs.	177-231 Nm
1977		
F-250 4wd	130-170 ft. lbs.	177-231 Nm
All others	170-230 ft. lbs.	231-313 Nm
1978-86		
All	170-230 ft. lbs.	231-313 Nm
Spindle connecting rod studs		
1976-97	60-70 ft. lbs.	82-95 Nm
Drag link/tie rod end studs		
1980-86	50-75 ft. lbs.	68-102 Nm
Spindle connecting rod clamps		
1976-79		
Bronco/F-100/250	35-45 ft. lbs.	48-61 Nm
F-350	40-60 ft. lbs.	54-82 Nm
Linkage adjusting sleeve clamp		
1980-86	30-42 ft. lbs.	41-57 Nm
Steering damper		
To brackets		
1976-79	15-25 ft. lbs.	20-34 Nm
To frame		
1976-79	10-15 ft. lbs.	14-20 Nm
Bracket-to-drag link		
1976-79	10-15 ft. lbs.	14-20 Nm
To right shock bracket		
1979 F-250	40-50 ft. lbs.	54-68 Nm

85768297

TORQUE SPECIFICATIONS
TWIN I-BEAM FRONT SUSPENSION

Component	U.S.	Metric
Spring		
Upper retainer-to-seat		
1976–79	18-25 ft. lbs.	24-34 Nm
1980–86	13-18 ft. lbs.	18-24 Nm
Lower retainer-to-seat	30-70 ft. lbs.	41-95 Nm
To-lower retainer nut		
1984–86	70-100 ft. lbs.	95-136 Nm
Shock absorber		
Stud-to-upper seat		
1976–83	15-25 ft. lbs.	20-34 Nm
1984–86		
F-150	25-35 ft. lbs.	34-48 Nm
Lower end bolt		
F-250/350	15-25 ft. lbs.	20-34 Nm
1976–86	40-60 ft. lbs.	54-82 Nm
Lower bracket-to-radius arm		
1976–79	70-90 ft. lbs.	95-122 Nm
1980–86	27-37 ft. lbs.	37-50 Nm
Radius arm		
To front axle and bracket		
1976–82	240-320 ft. lbs.	326-435 Nm
1983		
Forged I-beam	240-320 ft. lbs.	326-435 Nm
Stamped steel I-beam	269-329 ft. lbs.	366-447 Nm
1984–86		
F-150	269-329 ft. lbs.	366-447 Nm
F-250/350	240-320 ft. lbs.	326-435 Nm
To rear bracket		
1976–80	80-120 ft. lbs.	109-163 Nm
1981–82	80-100 ft. lbs.	109-136 Nm
1983–86	80-210 ft. lbs.	109-163 Nm
Rear bracket-to-frame①		
1976–79	70-90 ft. lbs.	95-122 Nm
1980–86	77-110 ft. lbs.	105-150 Nm
Axle-to-pivot Bracket		
1976–86	120-150 ft. lbs.	163-204 Nm
Axle pivot bracket (left) to upper frame nut		
1984–86	104-149 ft. lbs.	141-203 Nm
Axle pivot bracket (left) side retainer-to-frame nut		
1984–86	104-149 ft. lbs.	141-203 Nm
Stabilizer bar		
Link-to-bracket		
1976–79	40-60 ft. lbs.	54-82 Nm
1980–82	48-65 ft. lbs.	65-88 Nm
1983		
Forged I-beam	—	—
Stamped steel I-beam	52-74 ft. lbs.	71-101 Nm
1984–86	52-74 ft. lbs.	71-101 Nm
Link-to-bar		
1976–79	15-25 ft. lbs.	20-34 Nm
1980–82	48-65 ft. lbs.	65-88 Nm

85768295

TORQUE SPECIFICATIONS
TWIN I-BEAM FRONT SUSPENSION

Component	U.S.	Metric
1983		
Stamped steel I-beam	52-75 ft. lbs.	71-101 Nm
Forged I-beam	—	—
1984–86	52-74 ft. lbs.	71-101 Nm
Bar retainer-to-frame		
1976–79	15-25 ft. lbs.	20-34 Nm
1980–82	27-37 ft. lbs.	37-50 Nm
1983		
Stamped steel I-beam	27-37 ft. lbs.	37-50 Nm
Forged I-beam	—	—
1984–86	27-37 ft. lbs.	37-50 Nm
Spindle pin lock bolt nut		
1976–82	38-62 ft. lbs.	52-84 Nm
1983–86		
Forged I-beam	38-62 ft. lbs.	52-84 Nm
Stamped steel I-beam		
Spindle steering arm-to-rod and link		
1976–79	50-75 ft. lbs.	68-102 Nm
1980–82	70-100 ft. lbs.	95-136 Nm
1983		
Stamped steel I-beam	52-73 ft. lbs.	71-99 Nm
Forged I-beam	70-100 ft. lbs.	95-136 Nm
1984–86	70-100 ft. lbs.	95-136 Nm
Spindle plug		
1976–82	35-50 ft. lbs.	48-68 Nm
1983–86		
Stamped steel I-beam	—	—
Forged I-beam	35-50 ft. lbs.	48-68 Nm
Ball joint nuts		
Upper	85-110 ft. lbs.	116-150 Nm
Lower		
1976–82	140-180 ft. lbs.	190-245 Nm
1983		
Part No. 388981	140-180 ft. lbs.	190-245 Nm
Part No. 33850	104-146 ft. lbs.	141-199 Nm
1984–86	140-180 ft. lbs.	190-245 Nm

① 1979 F-250 conventional cab, 7800-8000 GVW (3538kg-3629kg) and F-250 Super Cab, exc. 8100 GVW (3674kg): 47-70 ft. lbs. (64-95 Nm)
The following models have a riveted radius arm rear bracket:
F-350 Conventional Cab
F-250 Camper and 140 inch (355.6cm) wheel base Style side
F-250 Super Cab w/8100 lb. GVW (3674kg)
F-350 Super Cab w/9350 lb. GVW (4241kg)

85768294

TORQUE SPECIFICATIONS
4-WHEEL DRIVE FRONT SUSPENSION

Component	U.S.	Metric
Spring-to-axle U-bolt		
1976-77 F-250	100-135 ft. lbs.	136-184 Nm
1978-79 F-250	120-155 ft. lbs.	163-211 Nm
1980-86 F-250/350	85-120 ft. lbs.	116-163 Nm
Spring-to-front hanger bracket		
F-250		
1976-77	90-130 ft. lbs.	122-177 Nm
1978-79	150-204 ft. lbs.	204-277 Nm
F-250/350		
1980-86	120-150 ft. lbs.	163-204 Nm
Spring shackle-to-bracket & spring		
F-250		
1976-79	90-130 ft. lbs.	122-177 Nm
F-250/350		
1980-86	150-210 ft. lbs.	204-286 Nm
Spring-to-shackle		
F-250/350	120-150 ft. lbs.	163-204 Nm
Jounce bumper-to-frame		
F-250		
1976-77	20-30 ft. lbs.	27-41 Nm
1978-83	15-25 ft. lbs.	20-34 Nm
1984-85	13-18 ft. lbs.	18-24 Nm
1986	20-30 ft. lbs.	27-41 Nm
Radius arm-to-bracket		
1976-80	80-120 ft. lbs.	109-163 Nm
1981-86	80-100 ft. lbs.	109-136 Nm
Radius arm bracket-to-frame	77-110 ft. lbs.	105-150 Nm
Spring retainer-to-upper seat		
1976-77	20-30 ft. lbs.	27-41 Nm
1978-79		
F-100/150		
Bronco/F-150		
Bolt	20-30 ft. lbs.	27-41 Nm
Lockbolt	18-24 ft. lbs.	24-33 Nm
1980-86		
Bronco/F-150	13-18 ft. lbs.	18-24 Nm
Track bar pivot-to-frame		
1976-77 F-100/150	110-130 ft. lbs.	150-177 Nm
1978-79 Bronco/F-150	119-161 ft. lbs.	162-219 Nm
1986 F-350	77-110 ft. lbs.	105-150 Nm
Track bar pivot-to-axle		
1976-79 All	155-205 ft. lbs.	211-279 Nm
1986 F-350	120-150 ft. lbs.	163-204 Nm
Spring lower seat-to-radius arm		
F-100/150/Bronco		
1976-79	45-55 ft. lbs.	61-75 Nm
1980	41-94 ft. lbs.	56-128 Nm
1981-82	30-70 ft. lbs.	41-95 Nm
1983-86	70-100 ft. lbs.	95-136 Nm

8576293

TORQUE SPECIFICATIONS
4-WHEEL DRIVE FRONT SUSPENSION

Component	U.S.	Metric
Axle cap-to-radius arm		
1976		
F-100	90-110 ft. lbs.	122-150 Nm
1977		
F-100/150	83-116 ft. lbs.	113-158 Nm
1978-79		
Bronco/F-150	90-110 ft. lbs.	122-150 Nm
Axle pivot bracket-to-frame		
1983	120-150 ft. lbs.	163-204 Nm
1984-86	77-110 ft. lbs.	105-150 Nm
Shock absorber lower bracket-to-frame		
F-250		
1976-77	30-40 ft. lbs.	41-54 Nm
1978-79	35-45 ft. lbs.	48-61 Nm
F-250/350		
1980-83	48-65 ft. lbs.	65-88 Nm
1984-86	52-74 ft. lbs.	71-101 Nm
Shock absorber upper end		
1976-77		
F-100/150	40-60 ft. lbs.	54-82 Nm
F-250	15-25 ft. lbs.	20-34 Nm
1978-82	15-25 ft. lbs.	20-34 Nm
All		
1983-85	25-35 ft. lbs.	34-48 Nm
All		
1986	25-35 ft. lbs.	34-48 Nm
Bronco/F-150/250		
F-350	52-74 ft. lbs.	71-101 Nm
Shock absorber lower end		
F-100/150/Bronco	40-60 ft. lbs.	54-82 Nm
F-250/350		
1976-79	15-25 ft. lbs.	20-34 Nm
1980-82	48-65 ft. lbs.	65-88 Nm
1983-86	52-74 ft. lbs.	71-101 Nm
Track bar-to-frame		
1976-77		
F-100/150		
9/16-12 nut	50-70 ft. lbs.	68-95 Nm
7/16-14 nut	30-40 ft. lbs.	41-54 Nm
1978-79		
Bronco/F-150		
9/16-12 nut	50-70 ft. lbs.	68-95 Nm
7/16-14 nut	20-30 ft. lbs.	27-41 Nm
Retainer-to-radius arm bracket		
1978-79		
Bronco/F-150	80-120 ft. lbs.	109-163 Nm
Retainer-to-axle bracket U-bolt nuts		
1978-97		
Bronco/F-150	35-45 ft. lbs.	48-61 Nm

8576292

TORQUE SPECIFICATIONS
REAR LEAF SUSPENSION

Component	U.S.	Metric
Stabilizer bar		
Bar-to-link nuts	15–25 ft. lbs.	20–34 Nm
Bar-to-axle U-bolts		
1976–83		
F-150/Bronco	40–50 ft. lbs.	54–68 Nm
F-250/350	35–50 ft. lbs.	48–68 Nm
1984–86		
All	30–42 ft. lbs.	41–57 Nm
Link-to-frame nuts		
1976–83	50–60 ft. lbs.	68–82 Nm
1984–86 2wd	40–60 ft. lbs.	54–82 Nm
Link bracket-to-frame		
1984–86 4wd	20–30 ft. lbs.	27–41 Nm
Link-to-bracket		
1984–86 4wd	40–60 ft. lbs.	54–82 Nm
Shock absorber upper end		
1976		
F-100 all, F-250 2wd	15–25 ft. lbs.	20–34 Nm
F-250 4wd, F-350 all	40–60 ft. lbs.	54–82 Nm
1977		
F-100/150 all, F-250 2wd	15–25 ft. lbs.	20–34 Nm
F-250 4wd, F-350 all	15–25 ft. lbs.	20–34 Nm
1978–79		
F-100/150/250/350	15–5 ft. lbs.	20–34 Nm
Bronco	40–60 ft. lbs.	54–82 Nm
1980		
All	40–60 ft. lbs.	54–82 Nm
1981–86		
All	40–65 ft. lbs.	54–88 Nm
Shock absorber lower end		
1976–86	40–60 ft. lbs.	54–82 Nm
Spring-to-axle U-bolt		
1976		
F-100 all, F-250 2wd		
½-13 nut	45–70 ft. lbs.	61–95 Nm
9/16-12 nut	85–115 ft. lbs.	116–156 Nm
F-250 4wd, F-350 all	150–190 ft. lbs.	204–258 Nm
1977		
F-100/150 all, F-250 2wd		
½-13 nut	74–107 ft. lbs.	101–146 Nm
9/16-12 nut	82–115 ft. lbs.	112–156 Nm
F-250 4wd, F-350 all	110–160 ft. lbs.	150–218 Nm
1978–79		
Bronco/F-150/250	85–115 ft. lbs.	116–156 Nm
F-350	110–160 ft. lbs.	150–218 Nm
1980–81		
Bronco/F-150/F-250	75–115 ft. lbs.	102–156 Nm
F-350	110–160 ft. lbs.	150–218 Nm
1982–83		
Bronco/F-150/250	75–100 ft. lbs.	102–136 Nm
F-350	150–210 ft. lbs.	204–286 Nm

85766290

TORQUE SPECIFICATIONS
REAR LEAF SUSPENSION

Component	U.S.	Metric
1984–86		
Bronco/F-150, F-250 under 8500 GVW	75–115 ft. lbs.	102–156 Nm
F-250 8500+ GVW, F-350	150–210 ft. lbs.	204–286 Nm
Spring-to-front hanger		
1976–77	75–105 ft. lbs.	102–143 Nm
1978–81		
F-100, 2wd F-150	75–105 ft. lbs.	102–143 Nm
Bronco, 4wd F-150, F-250/350	150–200 ft. lbs.	204–272 Nm
1982–86		
F-150 2wd	75–115 ft. lbs.	102–156 Nm
All others	150–200 ft. lbs.	204–272 Nm
Spring-to-rear hanger		
1976		
F-100	75–105 ft. lbs.	102–143 Nm
F-250/350	150–190 ft. lbs.	204–258 Nm
1977		
F-100/150	75–107 ft. lbs.	102–146 Nm
F-250/350	110–160 ft. lbs.	150–218 Nm
1978–79		
All	75–105 ft. lbs.	102–143 Nm
1980		
All	75–115 ft. lbs.	102–156 Nm
1981–83		
F-150/250/350/Bronco	75–115 ft. lbs.	102–156 Nm
F-359 w/136.8 & 160.8 in. WB	150–200 ft. lbs.	204–272 Nm
1984–86		
All exc. 2wd F-250/350 Chassis Cab	75–115 ft. lbs.	102–156 Nm
2wd F-250/350 Chassis Cab	150–210 ft. lbs.	204–286 Nm
Rear spring shackle-to-frame		
All exc. 2wd F-250/350 Chassis Cab	75–115 ft. lbs.	102–156 Nm
2wd F-250/350 Chassis Cab	150–210 ft. lbs.	204–286 Nm
Axle bumper-to-frame	20–30 ft. lbs.	27–41 Nm

85766291

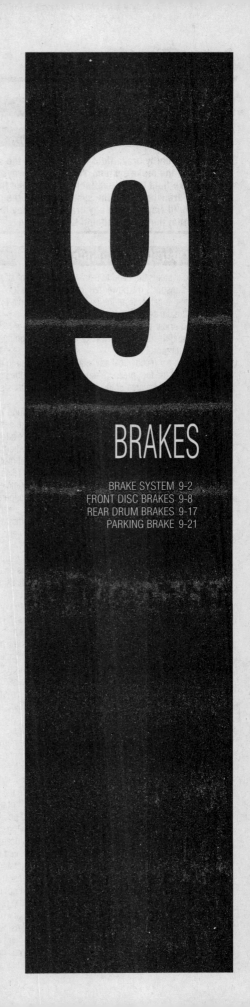

9

BRAKES

BRAKE SYSTEM

❊❊ WARNING

Clean, high quality brake fluid is essential to the safe and proper operation of the brake system. You should always buy the highest quality brake fluid that is available. If the brake fluid becomes contaminated, drain and flush the system and fill the master cylinder with new fluid. Never reuse any brake fluid. Any brake fluid that is removed from the system should be discarded.

Basic Operating Principles

Hydraulic systems are used to actuate the brakes of all modern automobiles. The system transports the power required to force the frictional surfaces of the braking system together from the pedal to the individual brake units at each wheel. A hydraulic system is used for two reasons.

First, fluid under pressure can be carried to all parts of an automobile by small pipes and flexible hoses without taking up a significant amount of room or posing routing problems.

Second, a great mechanical advantage can be given to the brake pedal end of the system, and the foot pressure required to actuate the brakes can be reduced by making the surface area of the master cylinder pistons smaller than that of any of the pistons in the wheel cylinders or calipers.

The master cylinder consists of a fluid reservoir along with a double cylinder and piston assembly. Double type master cylinders are designed to separate the front and rear braking systems hydraulically in case of a leak. The master cylinder coverts mechanical motion from the pedal into hydraulic pressure within the lines. This pressure is translated back into mechanical motion at the wheels by either the wheel cylinder (drum brakes) or the caliper (disc brakes).

Steel lines carry the brake fluid to a point on the vehicle's frame near each of the vehicle's wheels. The fluid is then carried to the calipers and wheel cylinders by flexible tubes in order to allow for suspension and steering movements.

In drum brake systems, each wheel cylinder contains two pistons, one at either end, which push outward in opposite directions and force the brake shoe into contact with the drum.

In disc brake systems, the cylinders are part of the calipers. At least one cylinder in each caliper is used to force the brake pads against the disc.

All pistons employ some type of seal, usually made of rubber, to minimize fluid leakage. A rubber dust boot seals the outer end of the cylinder against dust and dirt. The boot fits around the outer end of the piston on disc brake calipers, and around the brake actuating rod on wheel cylinders.

The hydraulic system operates as follows: When at rest, the entire system, from the piston(s) in the master cylinder to those in the wheel cylinders or calipers, is full of brake fluid. Upon application of the brake pedal, fluid trapped in front of the master cylinder piston(s) is forced through the lines to the wheel cylinders. Here, it forces the pistons outward, in the case of drum brakes, and inward toward the disc, in the case of disc brakes. The motion of the pistons is opposed by return springs mounted outside the cylinders in drum brakes, and by spring seals, in disc brakes.

Upon release of the brake pedal, a spring located inside the master cylinder immediately returns the master cylinder pistons to the normal position. The pistons contain check valves and the master cylinder has compensating ports drilled in it. These are uncovered as the pistons reach their normal position. The piston check valves allow fluid to flow toward the wheel cylinders or calipers as the pistons withdraw. Then, as the return springs force the brake pads or shoes into the released position, the excess fluid reservoir through the compensating ports. It is during the time the pedal is in the released position that any fluid that has leaked out of the system will be replaced through the compensating ports.

Dual circuit master cylinders employ two pistons, located one behind the other, in the same cylinder. The primary piston is actuated directly by mechanical linkage from the brake pedal through the power booster. The secondary piston is actuated by fluid trapped between the two pistons. If a leak develops in front of the secondary piston, it moves forward until it bottoms against the front of the master cylinder, and the fluid trapped between the pistons will operate the rear brakes. If the rear brakes develop a leak, the primary piston will move forward until direct contact with the secondary piston takes place, and it will force the secondary piston to actuate the front brakes. In either case, the brake pedal moves farther when the brakes are applied, and less braking power is available.

All dual circuit systems use a switch to warn the driver when only half of the brake system is operational. This switch is usually located in a valve body which is mounted on the firewall or the frame below the master cylinder. A hydraulic piston receives pressure from both circuits, each circuit's pressure being applied to one end of the piston. When the pressures are in balance, the piston remains stationary. When one circuit has a leak, however, the greater pressure in that circuit during application of the brakes will push the piston to one side, closing the switch and activating the brake warning light.

In disc brake systems, this valve body also contains a metering valve and, in some cases, a proportioning valve. The metering valve keeps pressure from traveling to the disc brakes on the front wheels until the brake shoes on the rear wheels have contacted the drums, ensuring that the front brakes will never be used alone. The proportioning valve controls the pressure to the rear brakes to lessen the chance of rear wheel lock-up during very hard braking.

Warning lights may be tested by depressing the brake pedal and holding it while opening one of the wheel cylinder bleeder screws. If this does not cause the light to go on, substitute a new lamp, make continuity checks, and, finally, replace the switch as necessary.

The hydraulic system may be checked for leaks by applying pressure to the pedal gradually and steadily. If the pedal sinks very slowly to the floor, the system has a leak. This is not to be confused with a springy or spongy feel due to the compression of air within the lines. If the system leaks, there will be a gradual change in the position of the pedal with a constant pressure.

Check for leaks along all lines and at wheel cylinders. If no external leaks are apparent, the problem is inside the master cylinder.

DISC BRAKES

Instead of the traditional expanding brakes that press outward against a circular drum, disc brake systems utilize a disc (rotor) with brake pads positioned on either side of it. An easily-seen analogy is the hand brake arrangement on a bicycle. The pads squeeze onto the rim of the bike wheel, slowing its motion. Automobile disc brakes use the identical principle but apply the braking effort to a separate disc instead of the wheel.

The disc (rotor) is a casting, usually equipped with cooling fins between the two braking surfaces. This enables air to circulate between the braking surfaces making them less sensitive to heat buildup and more resistant to fade. Dirt and water do not drastically affect braking action since contaminants are thrown off by the centrifugal action of the rotor or scraped off the by the pads. Also, the equal clamping action of the two brake pads tends to ensure uniform, straight line stops. Disc brakes are inherently self-adjusting. There are three general types of disc brake:
1. A fixed caliper.
2. A floating caliper.
3. A sliding caliper.

The fixed caliper design uses two pistons mounted on either side of the rotor (in each side of the caliper). The caliper is mounted rigidly and does not move.

The sliding and floating designs are quite similar. In fact, these two types are often lumped together. In both designs, the pad on the inside of the rotor is moved into contact with the rotor by hydraulic force. The caliper, which is not held in a fixed position, moves slightly, bringing the outside pad into contact with the rotor. There are various methods of attaching floating calipers. Some pivot at the bottom or top, and some slide on mounting bolts. In any event, the end result is the same.

DRUM BRAKES

Drum brakes employ two brake shoes mounted on a stationary backing plate. These shoes are positioned inside a circular drum which rotates with the wheel assembly. The shoes are held in place by springs. This allows them to slide toward the drums (when they are applied) while keeping the linings and drums in alignment. The shoes are actuated by a wheel cylinder which is mounted at the top of the backing plate. When the brakes are applied, hydraulic pressure forces the wheel cylinder's actuating links outward. Since these links bear directly against the top of the brake shoes, the tops of the shoes are then forced against the inner side of the drum. This action forces the bottoms of the two shoes to contact the brake drum by rotating the entire assembly slightly (known as servo action). When pressure within the wheel cylinder is relaxed, return springs pull the shoes back away from the drum.

Most modern drum brakes are designed to self-adjust themselves during application when the vehicle is moving in reverse. This motion causes both shoes to rotate very slightly with the drum, rocking an adjusting lever, thereby causing rotation of the adjusting screw. Some drum brake systems are designed to self-adjust during application whenever the brakes are applied. This on-board adjustment system reduces the need for maintenance adjustments and keeps both the brake function and pedal feel satisfactory.

Adjustments

➧ See Figures 1 and 2

DRUM BRAKES

The drum brakes are self-adjusting and require a manual adjustment only after the brake shoes have been replaced, or when the length of the adjusting screw has been changed while performing some other service operation, as i.e., taking off brake drums.

To adjust the brakes, follow the procedures given below:

Drum Installed

1. Raise and support the rear end on jackstands.
2. Remove the rubber plug from the adjusting slot on the backing plate.
3. Insert a brake adjusting spoon into the slot and engage the lowest possible tooth on the starwheel. Move the end of the brake spoon downward to move the starwheel upward and expand the adjusting screw. Repeat this operation until the brakes lock the wheels.
4. Insert a small screwdriver or piece of firm wire (coat hanger wire) into the adjusting slot and push the automatic adjusting lever out and free of the starwheel on the adjusting screw and hold it there.

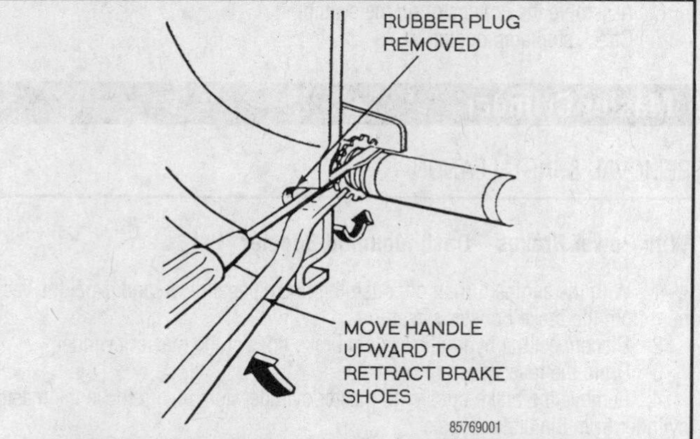

Fig. 1 Positioning and operation of the brake adjusting tools while backing off the rear brake shoes, 1976-79 F-100-250, 1978-79 Bronco, 1980-86 F-100-150 and Bronco

5. Engage the topmost tooth possible on the starwheel with the brake adjusting spoon. Move the end of the adjusting spoon upward to move the adjusting screw starwheel downward and contract the adjusting screw. Back off the adjusting screw starwheel until the wheel spins freely with a minimum of drag. Keep track of the number of turns that the starwheel is backed off, or the number of strokes taken with the brake adjusting spoon.
6. Repeat this operation for the other side. When backing off the brakes on the other side, the starwheel adjuster must be backed off the same number of turns to prevent side-to-side brake pull.
7. When the brakes are adjusted make several stops while backing the vehicle, to equalize the brakes at both of the wheels.
8. Remove the safety stands and lower the vehicle. Check brake fluid level. Road test the vehicle.

Drum Removed

➧ See Figures 3 and 4

⁂ CAUTION

Brake shoes contain asbestos, which has been determined to be a cancer causing agent. Never clean the brake surfaces with compressed air! Avoid inhaling any dust from any brake surface! When cleaning brake surfaces, use a commercially available brake cleaning fluid.

1. Make sure that the shoe-to-contact pad areas are clean and properly lubricated.
2. Using and inside caliper check the inside diameter of the drum. Measure across the diameter of the assembled brake shoes, at their widest point.
3. Turn the adjusting screw so that the diameter of the shoes is 0.030 inch (0.76mm) less than the brake drum inner diameter.
4. Install the drum.

Brake Light Switch

REMOVAL & INSTALLATION

1976-79 Without Speed Control

➧ See Figure 5

1. Spread the plastic connector tabs and pull the electrical connector from the end of the switch body.
2. Unscrew the switch assembly from the retainer.
3. To install the switch, screw the switch into the retainer until it bottoms out.
4. Install the wire harness connector to the switch.
5. Adjust the switch by pulling the brake pedal firmly back to the normal rest position. If the stoplamps remain on after the adjustment, rotate the switch assembly one turn towards the plunger.
6. Check stoplamp operation.

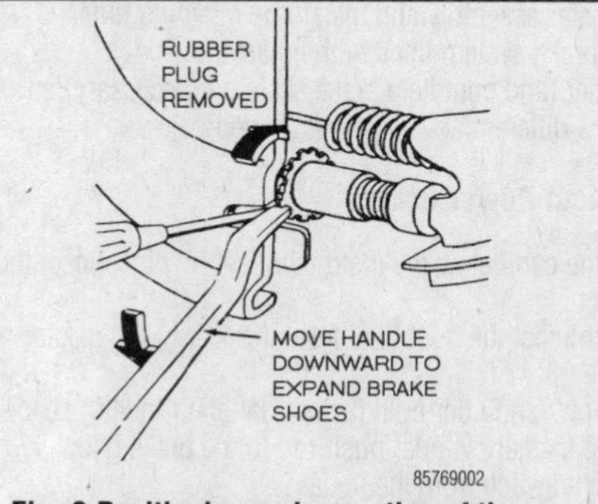

Fig. 2 Positioning and operation of the brake adjusting tools while expanding the rear brake shoes, 1976-86 F-250-350

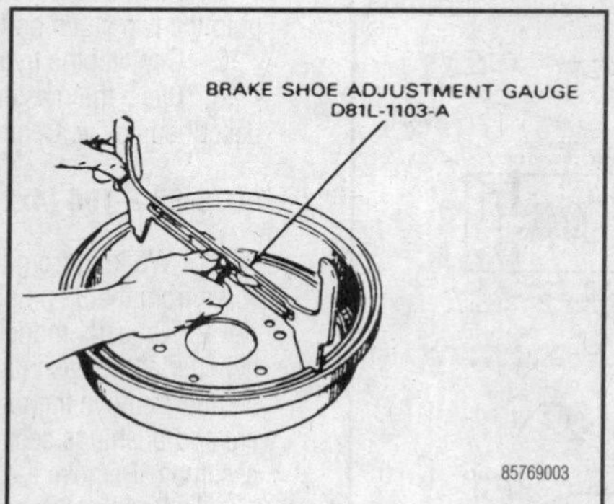

Fig. 3 Measuring drum

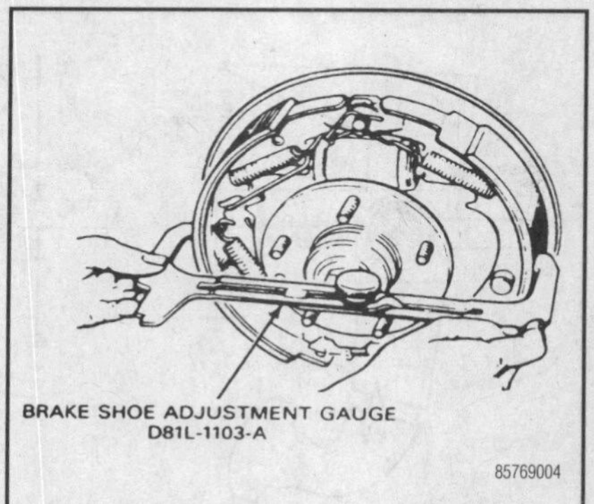

Fig. 4 Measuring shoes

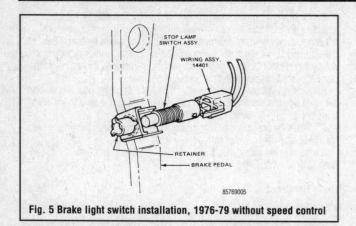

Fig. 5 Brake light switch installation, 1976-79 without speed control

1976-79 With Speed Control

♦ See Figure 6

1. Disconnect the switch wiring connector from the switch.
2. Remove the hairpin retainer, slide the stoplamp switch, pushrod and nylon washers and bushings off of the pedal. Remove the washer, then the switch by sliding it up or down.
3. To install the switch, refer to the illustration and install in reverse of removal.

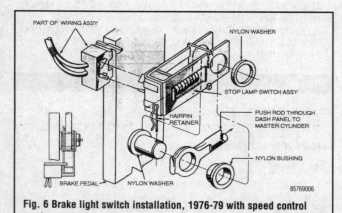

Fig. 6 Brake light switch installation, 1976-79 with speed control

1980-86

♦ See Figures 7 and 8

1. Lift the locking tab on the switch connector and disconnect the wiring.
2. Remove the hairpin retainer, slide the stoplamp switch, pushrod and nylon washer off of the pedal. Remove the washer, then the switch by sliding it up or down.

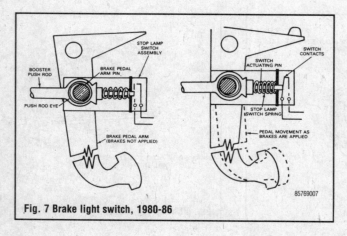

Fig. 7 Brake light switch, 1980-86

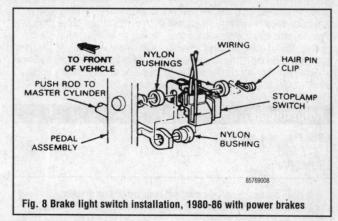

Fig. 8 Brake light switch installation, 1980-86 with power brakes

➡On vehicles equipped with speed control, the spacer washer is replaced by the dump valve adapter washer.

3. To install the switch, position it so that the U-shaped side is nearest the pedal and directly over/under the pin.
4. Slide the switch up or down, trapping the master cylinder pushrod and bushing between the switch side plates.
5. Push the switch and pushrod assembly firmly towards the brake pedal arm. Assemble the outside white plastic washer to the pin and install the hairpin retainer.

✳✳ CAUTION

Don't substitute any other type of retainer. Use only the Ford specified hairpin retainer.

6. Assemble the connector on the switch.
7. Check stoplamp operation.

Master Cylinder

REMOVAL & INSTALLATION

With Power Brakes—Dash Mounted Booster

1. With the engine turned off, push the brake pedal down and expel the vacuum from the brake booster system.
2. Disconnect the hydraulic system brake lines at the master cylinder.
3. Drain the reservoir.
4. Remove the brake booster to master cylinder nuts then remove the master cylinder from the brake booster.
   To install:
5. Before installing measure the distance from the outer end of the booster assembly push rod to the front face of the brake booster assembly. Turn the push rod adjusting screw in or out as required to obtain the specified length.
6. Position the master cylinder assembly over the booster push rod and onto the two studs on the booster assembly and install the retaining nuts.
7. Connect the hydraulic brake system lines to the master cylinder.
8. Bleed the master cylinder (and complete brake system if necessary) as described below. Centralize the differential valve as described below.

1976-85 F-100 (4x2) Without Power Brakes

1. Working from inside the cab below the instrument panel, disconnect the wires from the stop light switch.
2. On early models, disconnect the dust boot from the rear of the master cylinder at the dash panel.
3. Remove the retaining nut, shoulder bolt, (or pin on later models) spacers and bushings securing the master cylinder push rod to the brake pedal assembly. Remove the stoplight switch from the pedal.
4. Remove the boot from the master cylinder push rod.
5. Disconnect the hydraulic system brake lines at the master cylinder.
6. Remove the master cylinder retaining nuts and remove the master cylinder.

To install:

7. Position master cylinder on the dash panel in the engine compartment and install the retaining nuts.

8. Loosely connect the hydraulic system brake lines to the master cylinder.

9. Working from inside the cab on early models, position the boot over the push rod and secure the boot to the master cylinder.

10. Install the retaining nut, shoulder bolt, (or pin on later models) stoplight switch. spacers and bushings securing the master cylinder push rod to the brake pedal assembly.

11. The push rod should extend past the face of the booster as follows:
- 1976: 0.880-0.895 in.
- 1977-81: 0.931-0.946 in.
- 1982-86: 0.980-0.995 in.

OVERHAUL

♦ **See Figure 9**

The most important thing to remember when rebuilding the master cylinder is cleanliness. Work in clean surroundings with clean tools and clean cloths or paper for drying purposes. Have plenty of clean alcohol and brake fluid on hand to clean and lubricate the internal components. There are service repair kits available for overhauling the master cylinder.

1. Clean the outside of the master cylinder and remove the filler cap and gasket (diaphragm). Pour out any fluid that remains in the cylinder reservoir. Do not use any fluids other than brake fluid or alcohol to clean the master cylinder.

2. Unscrew the piston stop from the bottom of the cylinder body. Remove the O-ring seal from the piston stop. Discard the seal.

3. Remove the pushrod boot, if so equipped, from the groove at the rear of the master cylinder and slide the boot away from the rear of the master cylinder.

4. Remove the snaping retaining the primary and secondary piston assemblies within the cylinder body.

5. Remove the pushrod (if so equipped) and primary piston assembly from the master cylinder. Discard the piston assembly, including to boot (if so equipped).

6. Apply an air hose to the rear brake outlet port of the cylinder body and carefully blow the secondary piston out of the cylinder body.

7. Remove the return spring, spring retainer, cap protector, and cups from the secondary piston. Discard the cup protector and cups.

8. Clean all of the remaining parts in clean isopropyl alcohol and inspect the parts for chipping, excessive wear or damage. Replace them as required.

➡ **When using a master cylinder repair kit, install all the parts supplied in the kit.**

9. Check all recesses, openings and internal passages to be sure they are open and free from foreign matter. Use compressed air to blow out dirt and cleaning solvent remaining after the parts have been cleaned in the alcohol. Place all the parts on a clean pan, lint free cloth, or paper to dry.

10. Dip all the parts, except the cylinder body, in clean brake fluid.

11. Assemble the two secondary cups, back-to-back, in the grooves near the end of the secondary piston.

12. Install the secondary piston assembly in the master cylinder.

13. Install a new O-ring on the piston stop, and start the stop into the cylinder body.

14. Position the boot, snaping and pushrod retainer on the pushrod. Make sure the pushrod retainer is seated securely on the ball end of the rod. Seat the pushrod in the primary piston assembly.

15. Install the primary piston assembly in the master cylinder. Push the primary piston inward and tighten the secondary piston stop to retain the secondary piston in the bore.

16. Press the pushrod and pistons inward and install the snaping in the cylinder body.

17. Before the master cylinder is installed on the vehicle, the unit must be bled: support the master cylinder body in a vise, and fill both fluid reservoirs with brake fluid.

18. Loosely install plugs in the front and rear brake outlet bores. Depress the primary piston several times until air bubbles cease to appear in the brake fluid.

19. Tighten the plugs and attempt to depress the piston. The piston travel should be restricted after all air is expelled.

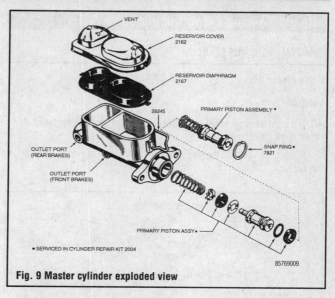

Fig. 9 Master cylinder exploded view

20. Remove the plugs. Install the cover and gasket (diaphragm) assembly, and make sure the cover retainer is tightened securely.

21. Install the master cylinder in the vehicle and bleed the hydraulic system.

Pressure Differential Valve

REMOVAL & INSTALLATION

1. Raise the vehicle on a hoist. Disconnect the brake warning lamp wire from the valve assembly switch.

➡ **To avoid damaging the brake warning switch wire connector, expand the plastic lugs so that the shell wire connector may be removed from the switch body.**

2. Disconnect the brake hydraulic lines from the differential valve assembly.

3. Remove the screw retaining the pressure differential, metering and proportioning valve assembly to the frame side rail or support bracket and remove the valve assembly.

To install:

4. Mount the combination brake differential valve assembly on the frame side rail or support bracket and tighten the attaching screw.

5. Connect the brake hydraulic system lines to the differential valve assembly and tighten the tube nuts securely.

6. Connect the shell wire connector to the brake warning lamp switch. Make sure that the plastic lugs on the connector hold the connector securely to the switch.

7. Bleed the brakes and centralize the pressure differential valve.

CENTRALIZING THE PRESSURE DIFFERENTIAL VALVE

After any repair or bleeding of the primary (front brake) or secondary (rear brake) system, the dual brake system warning light will usually remain illuminated due to the pressure differential valve remaining in the offcenter position.

To centralize the pressure differential valve and turn off the warning light after the systems have been bled, follow the procedure below.

1. Turn the ignition switch to the ACC or ON position.

2. Check the fluid level in the master cylinder reservoirs and fill them to within ¼ inch (6.35mm) of the top with brake fluid, if necessary.

3. Depress the brake pedal and the piston should center itself causing the brake warning light to go out.

4. Turn the ignition switch to the OFF position.

5. Before driving the vehicle, check the operation of the brakes and be sure that a firm pedal is obtained.

Height Sensing Proportioning Valve

REMOVAL & INSTALLATION

♦ See Figure 10

1985-86

➡The height sensing valve is not repairable and must be replaced if found to be defective.

1. Raise and support the rear and allow the rear suspension and axle to hang in the full rebound position.

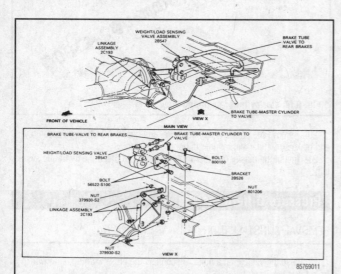

Fig. 10 Height sensing proportioning valve installation

➡The rear shock absorbers must be connected to the rear axle.

2. Remove both rear wheels.
3. Disconnect both hydraulic brake lines from the sensing valve.
4. Disconnect the linkage from the sensing valve.

➡If the linkage is damaged a new sensing valve and new linkage must be installed.

5. Remove the valve sensing valve from its bracket.
To install:
6. Place the new valve on the bracket and tighten the mounting bolts
7. Install the two brake tubes to the sensing valve.
8. Connect the linkage to the sensing valve shaft. Squeeze the plastic bushing of the link assembly onto the serrated section of the valve shaft using large groove joint pliers

➡The pivot joint of the linkage must face towards the rear of the vehicle.

9. Install the nut securing the link to the valve shaft and tighten to 8 ft. lbs. (10 Nm).
10. Bleed the brake system.
11. Install both rear wheels.
12. Lower the vehicle and check for proper operation.

➡The sensing valve will automatically become operational when the suspension is in the empty vehicle position.

Brake Hoses and Lines

Metal lines and rubber brake hoses should be checked frequently for leaks and external damage. Metal lines are particularly prone to crushing and kinking under the vehicle. Any such deformation can restrict the proper flow of fluid and therefore impair braking at the wheels. Rubber hoses should be checked for cracking or scraping; such damage can create a weak spot in the hose and it could fail under pressure.

Any time the lines are removed or disconnected, extreme cleanliness must be observed. Clean all joints and connections before disassembly (use a stiff bristle brush and clean brake fluid); be sure to plug the lines and ports as soon as they are opened. New lines and hoses should be flushed clean with brake fluid before installation to remove any contamination.

REMOVAL & INSTALLATION

♦ See Figures 11, 12, 13 and 14

1. Disconnect the negative battery cable.
2. Raise and safely support the vehicle on jackstands.
3. Remove any wheel and tire assemblies necessary for access to the particular line you are removing.
4. Thoroughly clean the surrounding area at the joints to be disconnected.
5. Place a suitable catch pan under the joint to be disconnected.
6. Using two wrenches (one to hold the joint and one to turn the fitting), disconnect the hose or line to be replaced.
7. Disconnect the other end of the line or hose, moving the drain pan if necessary. Always use a back-up wrench to avoid damaging the fitting.
8. Disconnect any retaining clips or brackets holding the line and remove the line from the vehicle.

➡If the brake system is to remain open for more time than it takes to swap lines, tape or plug each remaining clip and port to keep contaminants out and fluid in.

To install:
9. Install the new line or hose, starting with the end farthest from the master cylinder. Connect the other end, then confirm that both fittings are correctly threaded and turn smoothly using finger pressure. Make sure the new line will not rub against any other part. Brake lines must be at least 1/2 in. (13mm) from the steering column and other moving parts. Any protective shielding or insulators must be reinstalled in the original location.

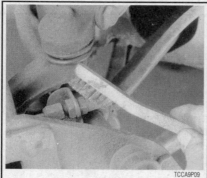

Fig. 11 Use a brush to clean the fittings of any debris

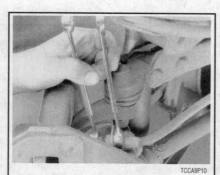

Fig. 12 Use two wrenches to loosen the fitting. If available, use flare nut type wrenches

Fig. 13 Any gaskets/crush washers should be replaced with new ones during installation

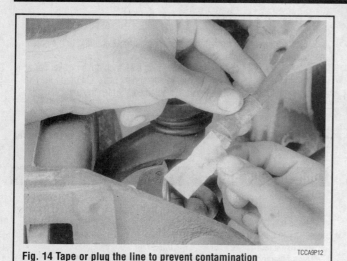

Fig. 14 Tape or plug the line to prevent contamination

TCCA9P12

✷✷ WARNING

Make sure the hose is NOT kinked or touching any part of the frame or suspension after installation. These conditions may cause the hose to fail prematurely.

10. Using two wrenches as before, tighten each fitting.
11. Install any retaining clips or brackets on the lines.
12. If removed, install the wheel and tire assemblies, then carefully lower the vehicle to the ground.
13. Refill the brake master cylinder reservoir with clean, fresh brake fluid, meeting DOT 3 specifications. Properly bleed the brake system.
14. Connect the negative battery cable.

Power Booster

REMOVAL & INSTALLATION

▶ See Figure 15

1. Disconnect the negative battery cable. Working inside the vehicle below the instrument panel, disconnect the booster valve operating rod from the brake pedal assembly.
2. Disconnect the wires from the stoplight switch.
3. Disconnect the manifold vacuum hose from the booster unit.
4. Unbolt and remove the master cylinder from the booster, without disconnecting the brake lines. Support the master cylinder out of the way.
5. Remove the four bracket-to-dash panel attaching bolts.
6. Remove the booster and bracket assembly from the dash panel, sliding the valve operating rod out from the engine side of the dash panel.
7. Mount the booster and bracket assembly to the dash panel by sliding the valve operating rod in through the hole in the dash panel, and installing the attaching bolts.
8. Connect the manifold vacuum hose to the booster.
9. Install the master cylinder.
10. Connect the stop light switch wires.
11. Working inside the vehicle below the instrument panel, install the rubber boot on the valve operating rod at the passenger side of the dash panel.
12. Connect the valve operating rod to the brake pedal with the bushings, eccentric shoulder bolt, and nut.
13. Reconnect the negative battery cable. Check operation of stop-lights and brake system.

PUSHROD ADJUSTMENT

▶ See Figure 16

The pushrod has an adjustment screw to maintain the correct relationship between the booster control valve plunger and the master cylinder piston. If the

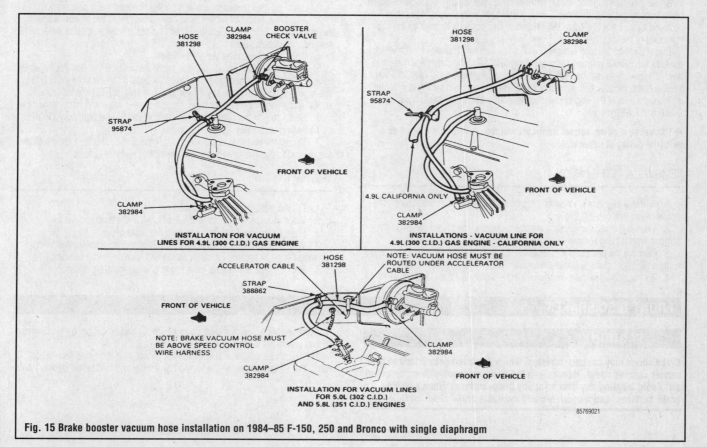

Fig. 15 Brake booster vacuum hose installation on 1984–85 F-150, 250 and Bronco with single diaphragm

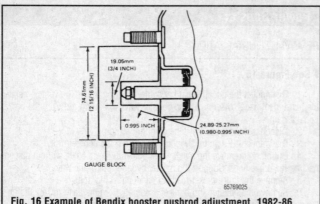

Fig. 16 Example of Bendix booster pushrod adjustment, 1982-86 shown

plunger is too long it will prevent the master cylinder piston from completely releasing hydraulic pressure, causing the brakes to drag. If the plunger is too short it will cause excessive pedal travel and an undesirable clunk in the booster area. Remove the master cylinder for access to the booster pushrod. Adjust to the following specifications:

- 1976: 0.880-0.895 in.
- 1977-81: 0.931-0.946 in.
- 1982-86: 0.980-0.995 in.

To check the alignment of the screw, fabricate a gauge (from cardboard, following the dimensions in the above illustration) and place it against the master cylinder mounting surface of the booster body. Adjust the pushrod screw by turning it until the end of the screw just touches the inner edge of the slot in the gauge. Install the master cylinder and bleed the system.

Brake Booster Vacuum Pump

Unlike gasoline engines, diesel engines have little vacuum available to power brake booster systems. The diesel is thus equipped with a vacuum pump, which is driven by a single belt off of the alternator. This pump is located on the top right side of the engine.

Diesel pickups are also equipped with a low vacuum indicator switch which actuates the BRAKE warning lamp when available vacuum is below a certain level. The switch senses vacuum through a fitting in the vacuum manifold that intercepts the vacuum flow from the pump. The low vacuum switch is mounted on the right side of the engine compartment, adjacent to the vacuum pump on F-250 and F-350 models.

➡The vacuum pump cannot be disassembled. It is only serviced as a unit (the pulley is separate).

REMOVAL & INSTALLATION

1. Remove the hose clamp and disconnect the pump from the hose on the manifold vacuum outlet fitting.
2. Loosen the vacuum pump adjustment bolt and the pivot bolt. Slide the pump downward and remove the drive belt from the pulley.
3. Remove the pivot and adjustment bolts and the bolts retaining the pump to the adjustment plate. Remove the vacuum pump and adjustment plate.
4. To install, install the pump-to-adjustment plate bolts and tighten to 11-18

ft. lbs. Position the pump and plate on the vacuum pump bracket and loosely install the pivot and adjustment bolts.
5. Connect the hose from the manifold vacuum outlet fitting to the pump and install the hose clamp.
6. Install the drive belt on the pulley. Place a ⅜ inch drive breaker bar or ratchet into the slot on the vacuum pump adjustment plate. Lift up on the assembly until the proper belt tension is obtained. Tighten the pivot and adjustment bolts to 11-18 ft. lbs.
7. Start the engine and make sure the brake system functions properly.

➡The BRAKE light will glow until brake vacuum builds up to the normal level.

Bleeding the Brakes

When any part of the hydraulic system has been disconnected for repair or replacement, air may get into the lines and cause spongy pedal action (because air can be compressed and brake fluid cannot). To correct this condition, it is necessary to bleed the hydraulic system after it has been properly connected to be sure that all air is expelled from the brake cylinders and lines.

When bleeding the brake system, bleed one brake cylinder at a time, beginning at the cylinder with the longest hydraulic line (farthest from the master cylinder) first. keep the master cylinder reservoir filled with brake fluid during bleeding operation. Never use brake fluid that has been drained from the hydraulic system, no matter how clean it is.

It will be necessary to centralize the pressure differential valve after a brake system failure has been corrected and the hydraulic system has been bled.

The primary and secondary hydraulic brake systems are individual systems and are bled separately. During the entire bleeding operation, do not allow the reservoir to run dry. Keep the master cylinder reservoirs filled with brake fluid.

WHEEL CYLINDERS AND CALIPERS

1. Clean all dirt from around the master cylinder fill cap, remove the cap and fill the master cylinder with brake fluid until the level is within ¼ inch of the top of the edge of the reservoir.
2. Clean off the bleeder screws at the wheel cylinders and calipers.
3. Attach the length of rubber hose over the nozzle of the bleeder screw at the wheel to be done first. Place the other end of the hose in a glass jar, submerged in new brake fluid.
4. Open the bleed screw valve ½-¾ turn.
5. Have an assistant slowly depress the brake pedal. Close the bleeder screw valve and tell your assistant to allow the brake pedal to return slowly. Continue this pumping action to force any air out of the system. When bubbles cease to appear at the end of the bleeder hose, close the bleed valve and remove the hose.
6. Check the master cylinder fluid level and add fluid accordingly. Do this after bleeding each wheel.
7. Repeat the bleeding operation at the remaining 3 wheels, ending with the one closest to the master cylinder. Fill the master cylinder reservoir.

MASTER CYLINDER

1. Fill the master cylinder reservoirs.
2. Place absorbent rags under the fluid lines at the master cylinder.
3. Have an assistant depress and hold the brake pedal.
4. With the pedal held down, slowly crack open the hydraulic line fitting, allowing the air to escape. Close the fitting and have the pedal released.
5. Repeat Steps 3 and 4 for each fitting until all the air is released.

FRONT DISC BRAKES

❊ CAUTION

Brake shoes may contain asbestos, which has been determined to be a cancer causing agent. Never clean the brake surfaces with compressed air! Avoid inhaling any dust from any brake surface! When cleaning brake surfaces, use a commercially available brake cleaning fluid.

There are two types of sliding calipers, the LD sliding caliper unit is operated by one piston per caliper.

The HD slider caliper unit contains two pistons on the same side of the rotor. The caliper slides on the support assembly and is retained by a key and spring.

Brake Pads

INSPECTION

Remove the brake pads as described below and measure the thickness of the lining. If the lining at any point on the pad assembly is less than 0.0625 inch (1/16 inch or 1.5mm) for LD brakes or 0.03125 inch (1/32 inch or 0.794mm) for HD brakes, thick (above the backing plate or rivets), or there is evidence of the lining being contaminated by brake fluid or oil, replace the brake pad.

REMOVAL & INSTALLATION

➡NEVER REPLACE THE PADS ON ONE SIDE ONLY! ALWAYS REPLACE PADS ON BOTH WHEELS AS A SET!

1976-83 with LD Sliding Caliper (Single Piston)

◗ See Figures 17 thru 36

1. To avoid overflowing of the master cylinder when the caliper pistons are pressed into the caliper cylinder bores, siphon or dip some brake fluid out of the larger reservoir.
2. Jack up the front of the vehicle and remove the wheels.
3. Dip out a part of the fluid from the larger portion of the master cylinder.
4. Jack up the front of the vehicle and support it on jackstands.
5. Remove the front wheel.
6. Using an 8 inch (203mm) C-clamp, bottom the caliper piston by positioning the fixed end of the clamp against the inner side of the caliper and tightening the clamp against the outer pad.
7. Remove the clamp. Remove the key retaining screw.
8. Using a brass drift and light hammer, drive out the caliper support key, and caliper support spring.
9. It is not necessary to disconnect the brake hose.

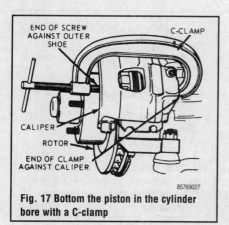
Fig. 17 Bottom the piston in the cylinder bore with a C-clamp

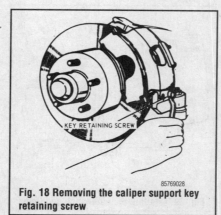
Fig. 18 Removing the caliper support key retaining screw

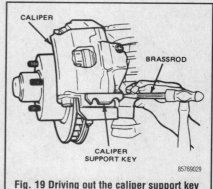
Fig. 19 Driving out the caliper support key with a drift

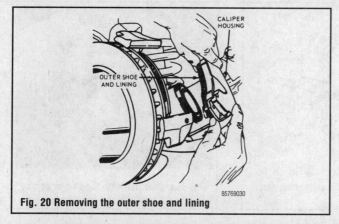
Fig. 20 Removing the outer shoe and lining

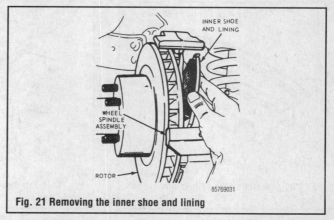
Fig. 21 Removing the inner shoe and lining

Fig. 22 Assembled view of the LD sliding caliper front brake assembly, 1983 shown

Fig. 23 Removing the caliper support key retaining screw, 1983 shown

Fig. 24 Driving out the caliper support key with a drift, 1983 shown

Fig. 25 Support the caliper assembly with a wire, 1983 shown

Fig. 26 Removing the outer shoe and lining, 1983 shown

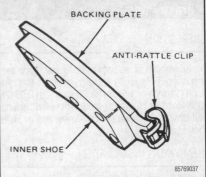

Fig. 27 Installing the anti-rattle clip on the inner shoe

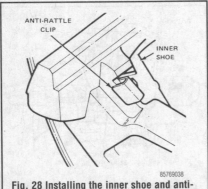

Fig. 28 Installing the inner shoe and anti-rattle clip

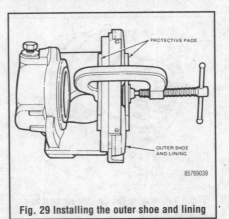

Fig. 29 Installing the outer shoe and lining

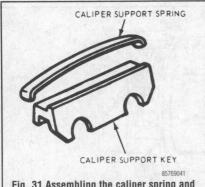

Fig. 30 Holding the upper machined surface of the spindle assembly in preparation for installing the caliper support spring and key

Fig. 31 Assembling the caliper spring and key

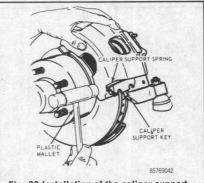

Fig. 32 Installation of the caliper support spring and key

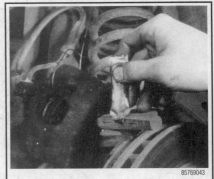

Fig. 33 Lightly lubricate the sliding portion of the caliper with brake caliper grease

Fig. 34 Positioning the caliper assembly on the spindle, 1983 shown

Fig. 35 Inserting the caliper support spring and key, 1983 shown

Fig. 36 Installing the caliper support spring and key, 1983 shown

10. Remove the caliper from its support assembly by pushing downward toward the spindle and rotating the upper end upward and out of the spindle assembly. Support the caliper with a length of wire so that no stress is placed upon the brake hose.

11. Remove the outer pad. It may be necessary to tap it loose. Remove the inner pad and anti-rattle clip.

12. Clean and inspect the caliper assembly.

To install:

13. Place a new anti-rattle clip on the lower end of the inner pad. Be sure that the clip tabs are positioned properly and that the clip is fully seated.

14. Place the inner pad in the caliper, with the loop type spring of the clip away from the rotor.

15. Place the outer pad in the caliper. Press the tabs into place with fingers or a C-clamp.

16. Place the caliper on the spindle by pivoting it around the support upper mounting surface. Be careful not to tear the boot as it slips over the inner pad.

17. Use a screwdriver to hold the upper machined surface of the caliper against the surface of the support assembly, and install a new caliper support spring and key assembly. Drive the key and spring into position with a plastic mallet. Install the key retaining screw and tighten to 20 ft. lbs.

18. When pads have been installed on both front wheels, lower the vehicle and check the fluid level in the master cylinder. Fill as necessary.

19. Depress the pedal several times until a firm pedal is achieved. Do not drive the vehicle until the pedal is firm.

1984-86 with LD Sliding Caliper (Single Piston)

▶ **See Figures 37 thru 42**

The LD Light Duty sliding caliper disc brake assembly is used on the F-150, F-250 below 6900 GVWR and Bronco.

1. Place an 8 inch (203mm) C-clamp on the caliper and tighten the clamp to bottom the caliper piston in the cylinder bore. Remove the C-clamp.

2. Clean the excess dirt from around the caliper pin tabs.

3. Drive the upper caliper pin inward until the tabs on the pin touch the spindle.

4. Insert a small prybar into the slot provided behind the pin tabs on the inboard side of the pin.

5. Using needlenosed pliers, compress the outboard end of the pin while, at the same time, prying with the prybar until the tabs slip into the groove in the spindle.

6. Place the end of a $7/16$ inch (11mm) punch against the end of the caliper pin and drive the pin out of the caliper slide groove.

7. Repeat this procedure for the lower pin.

8. Lift the caliper off of the rotor.

9. Remove the brake pads and anti-rattle spring.

➡ **Do not allow the caliper to hang by the brake hose.**

To install:

10. Thoroughly clean the areas of the caliper and spindle assembly which contact each other during the sliding action of the caliper.

11. Place a new anti-rattle clip on the lower end of the inboard shoe. Make sure that the tabs on the clip are positioned correctly and the loop-type spring is away from the rotor.

12. Place the lower end of the inner brake pad in the spindle assembly pad abutment, against the anti-rattle clip, and slide the upper end of the pad into position. Be sure that the clip is still in position.

13. Check and make sure that the caliper piston is fully bottomed in the cylinder bore. Use a large C-clamp to bottom the piston, if necessary.

14. Position the outer brake pad on the caliper, and press the pad tabs into place with your fingers. If the pad cannot be pressed into place by hand, use a C-clamp. Be careful not to damage the lining with the clamp. Bend the tabs to prevent rattling.

15. Position the caliper on the spindle assembly. Lightly lubricate the caliper sliding grooves with caliper pin grease.

16. Position the a new upper pin with the retention tabs next to the spindle groove.

➡ **Don't use the bolt and nut with the new pin.**

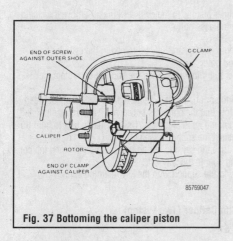

Fig. 37 Bottoming the caliper piston

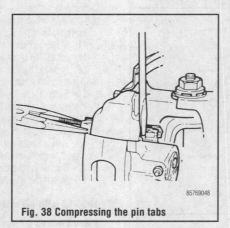

Fig. 38 Compressing the pin tabs

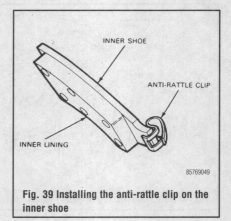

Fig. 39 Installing the anti-rattle clip on the inner shoe

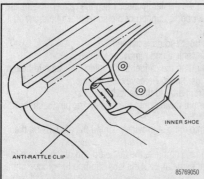

Fig. 40 Installing the inner shoe and the anti-rattle clip

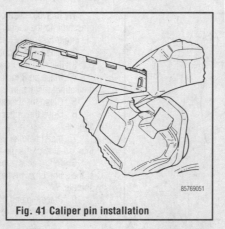

Fig. 41 Caliper pin installation

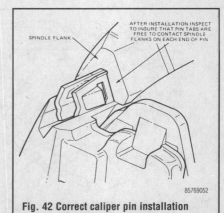

Fig. 42 Correct caliper pin installation

17. Carefully drive the pin, at the outboard end, inward until the tabs contact the spindle face.

18. Repeat the procedure for the lower pin.

✳✳ WARNING

Don't drive the pins in too far, or it will be necessary to drive them back out until the tabs snap into place. The tabs on each end of the pin MUST be free to catch on the spindle sides!

19. Install the wheels.

1976-83 with HD Sliding Caliper (Two Piston)

▶ **See Figures 43 thru 46**

1. To avoid overflowing of the master cylinder when the caliper pistons are pressed into the caliper cylinder bores, siphon or dip some brake fluid out of the larger reservoir.

2. Raise and support the front end on jackstands.

3. Jack up the front of the vehicle and remove the wheels.

4. Remove the key retaining screw.

5. Using a brass drift and light hammer, drive out the caliper support key, and caliper support spring.

6. It is not necessary to disconnect the brake hose.

7. Remove the caliper from its support assembly by rotating the key and spring end out and away from the rotor. Slide the opposite end of the caliper clear of the slide in the support and off the rotor. Lay the tie rod on the tie rod or axle. Do not let the hang by the brake hose.

8. Remove the caliper brake shoe anti-rattle spring and the inner and outer shoe and lining assemblies.

9. Clean and inspect the caliper assembly. Thoroughly clean the area of the caliper and support that contact during the sliding action of the caliper.

10. Place a C-clamp on the caliper housing mid-way between between the piston bores, and using the inner shoe and lining over the pistons, tighten the

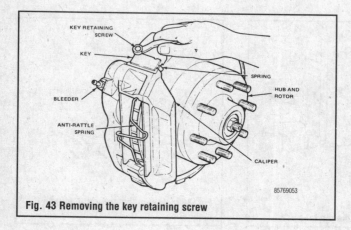

Fig. 43 Removing the key retaining screw

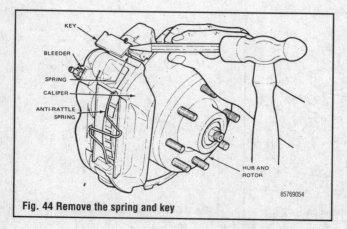

Fig. 44 Remove the spring and key

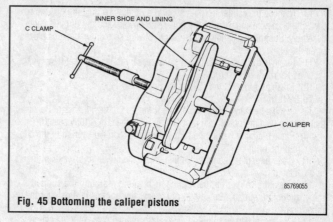

Fig. 45 Bottoming the caliper pistons

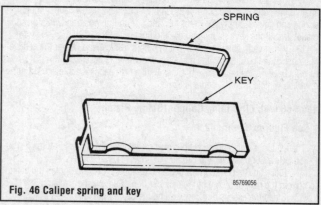

Fig. 46 Caliper spring and key

C-clamp to bottom the caliper pistons in the cylinder bores. Remove the clamp and the inner shoe and lining assembly.

To install:

11. Make sure the caliper pistons are fully bottomed in the cylinder bore.

12. Install the inner and outer shoe.

13. Position the caliper rail into the slide on the support and rotate the caliper onto the rotor.

14. Position the key and spring, and hand start the sub-assembly between the caliper and support. Note that the spring is between the key and caliper and that the spring tangs overlap the ends of the key. Use a suitable tool to hold up the caliper, if required, against the support assembly.

15. Using a hammer, drive the key and spring into position aligning the correct notch with the existing hole in the support.

16. Secure the the key to the support with the key retaining screw.

17. Install the wheels.

1984-86 with HD sliding Caliper (Two Piston)

▶ **See Figures 47 thru 51**

1. To avoid overflowing of the master cylinder when the caliper pistons are pressed into the caliper cylinder bores, siphon or dip some brake fluid out of the larger reservoir.

2. Raise and support the front end on jackstands.

3. Jack up the front of the vehicle and remove the wheels.

4. Place an 8 inch (203mm) on the caliper and tighten the clamp to bottom the caliper pistons in the cylinder bores. Remove the C-clamp.

5. Clean the excess dirt from around the caliper pin tabs.

6. Drive the upper caliper pin inward until the tabs on the pin touch the spindle.

7. Insert a small prybar into the slot provided behind the pin tabs on the inboard side of the pin.

8. Using needlenosed pliers, compress the outboard end of the pin while, at the same time, prying with the prybar until the tabs slip into the groove in the spindle.

9. Place the end of a 7/16 inch (11mm) against the end of the caliper pin and drive the pin out of the caliper slide groove.

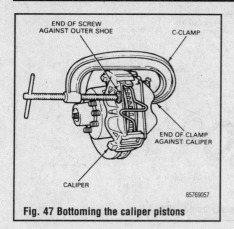

Fig. 47 Bottoming the caliper pistons

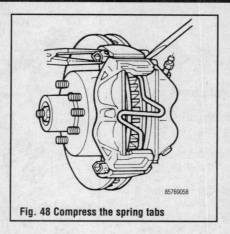

Fig. 48 Compress the spring tabs

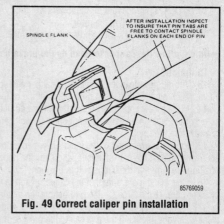

Fig. 49 Correct caliper pin installation

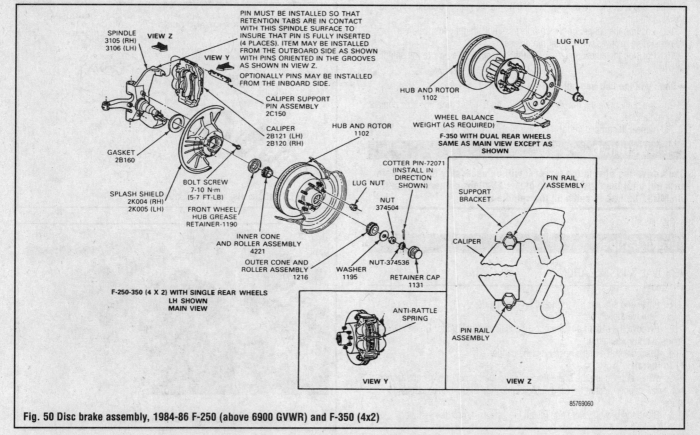

Fig. 50 Disc brake assembly, 1984-86 F-250 (above 6900 GVWR) and F-350 (4x2)

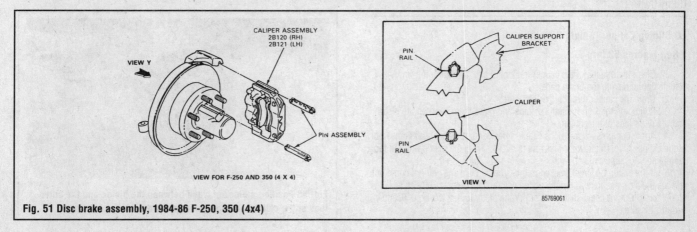

Fig. 51 Disc brake assembly, 1984-86 F-250, 350 (4x4)

10. Repeat this procedure for the lower pin.
11. Lift the caliper off of the rotor.
12. Remove the brake pads and anti-rattle spring.

➡ **Do not allow the caliper to hand by the brake hose.**

To install:

13. Thoroughly clean the areas of the caliper and spindle assembly which contact each other during the sliding action of the caliper.

14. Place a new anti-rattle clip on the lower end of the inboard shoe. Make sure that the tabs on the clip are positioned correctly and the loop-type spring is away from the rotor.

15. Place the lower end of the inner brake pad in the spindle assembly pad abutment, against the anti-rattle clip, and slide the upper end of the pad into position. Be sure that the clip is still in position.

16. Check and make sure that the caliper piston is fully bottomed in the cylinder bore. Use a large C-clamp to bottom the piston, if necessary.

17. Position the outer brake pad on the caliper, and press the pad tabs into place with your fingers. If the pad cannot be pressed into place by hand, use a C-clamp. Be careful not to damage the lining with the clamp. Bend the tabs to prevent rattling.

18. Position the caliper on the spindle assembly. Lightly lubricate the caliper sliding grooves with caliper pin grease.

19. Position the a new upper pin with the retention tabs next to the spindle groove.

➡ **Don't use the bolt and nut with the new pin.**

20. Carefully drive the pin, at the outboard end, inward until the tabs contact the spindle face.
21. Repeat the procedure for the lower pin.

✳✳ WARNING

Don't drive the pins in too far, or it will be necessary to drive them back out until the tabs snap into place. The tabs on each end of the pin MUST be free to catch on the spindle sides!

22. Install the wheels.

Brake Caliper

REMOVAL & INSTALLATION

1. Raise and support the front end on jackstands.
2. Remove the wheels.
3. Remove the caliper and the brake pads as outlined under Disc Brake Pad Removal and Installation.
4. Disconnect the brake hose from the caliper.

To install:

5. When connecting the brake fluid hose to the caliper, it is recommended that a new copper washer be used at the connection of the brake hose and caliper.

6. Bleed the brake system and install the wheels. Lower the vehicle.

OVERHAUL

LD Sliding Caliper (Single Piston)

▸ **See Figures 52 thru 57**

1. Clean the outside of the caliper in alcohol after removing it from the vehicle and removing the brake pads.
2. Drain the caliper through the inlet port.
3. Roll some thick shop cloths or rags and place them between the piston and the outer legs of the caliper.
4. Apply compressed air to the caliper inlet port until the piston comes out of the caliper bore. Use low air pressure to avoid having the piston pop out too rapidly and possible causing injury.
5. If the piston becomes cocked in the cylinder bore and will not come out, remove the air pressure and tap the piston with a soft hammer to try and straighten it. Do not use a sharp tool or pry the piston out of the bore. Reapply the air pressure.

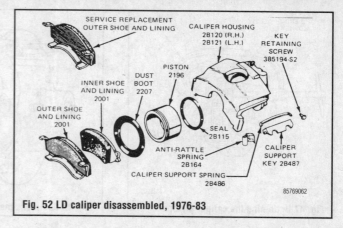

Fig. 52 LD caliper disassembled, 1976-83

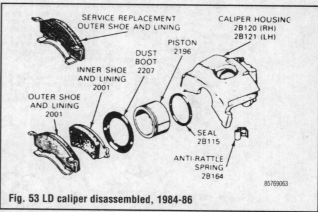

Fig. 53 LD caliper disassembled, 1984-86

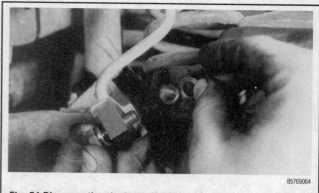

Fig. 54 Disconnecting the brake line from the caliper

Fig. 55 Position a block of wood between the piston and the outer legs of the caliper and apply compressed air to the inlet port

Fig. 56 Remove the boot from the caliper piston bore

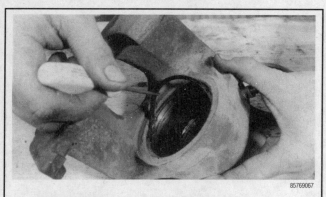

Fig. 57 Remove the seal from the caliper piston bore

6. Remove the boot from the piston and seal from the caliper cylinder bore.

7. Clean the piston and caliper in alcohol.

8. Lubricate the piston seal with clean brake fluid, and position the seal in the groove in the cylinder bore.

9. Coat the outside of the piston and both of the beads of dust boot with clean brake fluid. Insert the piston through the dust boot until the boot is around the bottom (closed end) of the piston.

10. Hold the piston and dust boot directly above the caliper cylinder bore, and use your fingers to work the bead of dust boot into the groove near the top of the cylinder bore.

11. After the bead is seated in the groove, press straight down on the piston until it bottoms in the bore. Be careful not to cock the piston in the bore. Be careful not to cock the piston in the bore. Use a C-clamp with a block of wood inserted between the clamp and the piston to bottom the piston, if necessary.

12. Install the brake pads and install the caliper. Bleed the brake hydraulic system and recenter the pressure differential valve. Do not drive the vehicle until a firm brake pedal is obtained.

HD Sliding Caliper (Two Piston)—1976-79

▶ **See Figure 58**

1. Disconnect and plug the flexible brake hose.

2. Remove the front shoe and lining assemblies.

3. Drain the fluid from the cylinders.

4. Secure the caliper in a vise and place a block of wood between the caliper bridge and the cylinders.

5. Apply low pressure air to the brake hose inlet and the pistons will be forced out to the wood block.

6. Remove the block of wood and remove the pistons.

7. Remove the bolts and washers that attach the caliper to the cylinder housing and separate the caliper from the housing.

8. Remove the piston seals.

9. Lubricate the new piston seals with clean brake fluid and install them in the seal grooves in the cylinder bores.

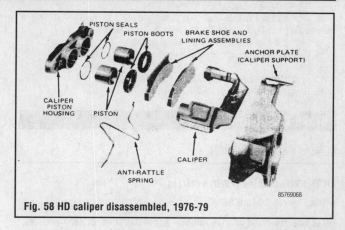

Fig. 58 HD caliper disassembled, 1976-79

10. Lubricate the retaining lips of the dust boots with clean brake fluid and install them in the grooves of the cylinder bores.

11. Apply a film of clean brake fluid to the pistons.

12. Insert the pistons into the dust boots and start them into the cylinders by hand until they are beyond the piston seals. Be careful not to dislodge or damage the piston seals.

13. Place a block of wood over one piston and press the piston into the cylinder. Be careful not to cock the piston in the cylinder bore.

14. Install the second piston in the same manner.

15. Place the piston housing on the caliper and install the piston housing to caliper mounting bolts to 155-185 ft. lbs.

16. Install the brake shoe assemblies and anti-rattle clip in the caliper assembly.

17. Install the brake hose. Torque the fitting to 25 ft. lbs.

18. Install the caliper and bleed the system.

HD Sliding Caliper (Two Piston)—1980-86

▶ **See Figure 59**

1. Disconnect and plug the flexible brake hose.

2. Remove the front shoe and lining assemblies.

3. Drain the fluid from the cylinders.

4. Secure the caliper in a vise and place a block of wood between the caliper bridge and the cylinders.

5. Apply low pressure air to the brake hose inlet and the pistons will be forced out to the wood block.

6. Remove the block of wood and remove the pistons.

7. Remove the piston seals.

8. Lubricate the new piston seals with clean brake fluid and install them in the seal grooves in the cylinder bores.

9. Lubricate the retaining lips of the dust boots with clean brake fluid and install them in the grooves of the cylinder bores.

10. Apply a film of clean brake fluid to the pistons.

11. Insert the pistons into the dust boots and start them into the cylinders by hand until they are beyond the piston seals. Be careful not to dislodge or damage the piston seals.

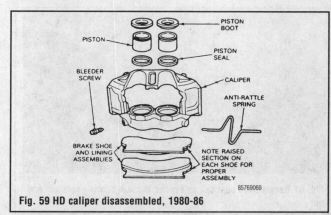

Fig. 59 HD caliper disassembled, 1980-86

12. Place a block of wood over one piston and press the piston into the cylinder. Be careful not to cock the piston in the cylinder bore.

13. Install the second piston in the same manner.

14. Install the brake shoe assemblies and anti-rattle clip in the caliper assembly.

15. Install the brake hose. Torque the fitting to 25 ft. lbs.

16. Install the caliper and bleed the system.

Brake Disc (Rotor)

REMOVAL & INSTALLATION

All Two Wheel Drive (2WD) Vehicles

▶ See Figures 60 thru 68

➡ **For hub, rotor and bearing removal and installation for 4WD vehicles, please refer to Section 7.**

1. Jack up the front of the vehicle and support it with jackstands. Remove the front wheel.

2. Remove the caliper assembly and support it on the frame with a piece of wire without disconnecting the brake fluid hose.

3. Remove the hub and rotor assembly as described in Section 1 for all 2WD vehicles.

4. Install the rotor in the reverse order of removal, and adjust the wheel bearing as outlined in Section 1.

INSPECTION

If the rotor is deeply scarred or has shallow cracks, it may be refinished on a disc brake rotor lathe. Also, if the lateral run-out exceeds 0.010 in. (0.25mm) within a 6 in. (152mm) radius when measured with a dial indicator, with the stylus 1 in. (25mm) in from the edge of the rotor, the rotor should be refinished or replaced.

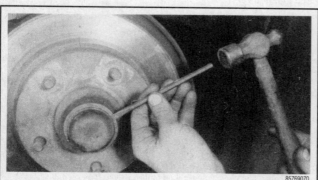

Fig. 60 Use a hammer and light chisel to tap the dust cap off the hub and rotor assembly

Fig. 61 Remove the dust cap to expose the hub bearing retainer and nut

Fig. 62 Remove the cotter pin from the retainer

Fig. 63 Remove the the retainer to expose the nut

Fig. 64 Remove the retaining nut

Fig. 65 Remove the outer bearing retaining washer

Fig. 66 Lift the hub and rotor assembly off the spindle

Fig. 67 Carefully pry out the grease seal from the hub and rotor assembly

Fig. 68 Driving out the inner bearing from the hub and rotor assembly

A maximum of 0.020 in. (0.5mm) of material may be removed equally from each friction surface of the rotor. If the damage cannot be corrected when the rotor has been machined to the minimum thickness shown on the rotor, it should be replaced.

The finished braking surfaces of the rotor must be parallel within 0.007 in. (0.18mm) for an integral hub and rotor and 0.0010 (0.0254 mm) for a separate hub and rotor and lateral run-out must not be more than 0.003 in. (0.076mm) on the inboard surface in a 5 in. (127mm) radius.

REAR DRUM BRAKES

❊❊ CAUTION

Brake shoes may contain asbestos, which has been determined to be a cancer causing agent. Never clean the brake surfaces with compressed air! Avoid inhaling any dust from any brake surface! When cleaning brake surfaces, use a commercially available brake cleaning fluid.

Brake Drums

INSPECTION

Check that there are no cracks or chips in the braking surface. Excessive bluing indicates overheating and a replacement drum is needed. The drum can be machined to remove minor damage and to establish a rounded braking surface on a warped drum. Never exceed the maximum oversize of the drum when machining the braking surface. The maximum inside diameter is stamped on the rim of the drum.

REMOVAL & INSTALLATION

Bronco, F-150, and F-250 Light Duty

1. Raise the vehicle so that the wheel to be worked on is clear of the floor and install jackstands under the vehicle.
2. Remove the wheel. Remove the three retaining nuts and remove the brake drum. It may be necessary to back off the brake shoe adjustment in order to remove the brake drum. This is because the drum might be grooved or worn from being in service for an extended period of time.
3. Before installing a new brake drum, be sure to remove any protective coating with carburetor degreaser.
4. Install the brake drum in the reverse order of removal and adjust the brakes.

F-250HD, F-350

1. Raise the vehicle and install jackstands.
2. Remove the wheel. Loosen the rear brake shoe adjustment.
3. Remove the rear axle retaining bolts and lockwashers, axle shaft, and gasket.
4. Remove the wheel bearing locknut, lockwasher, and adjusting nut.
5. Remove the hub and drum assembly from the axle.
6. Remove the brake drum-to-hub retaining screws, bolts or bolts and nut. Remove the brake drum from the hub.
   To install:
7. Place the drum on the hub and attach it to the hub with the attaching nuts and bolts.
8. Place the hub and drum assembly on the axle and start the adjusting nut.
9. Adjust the wheel bearing nut and install the wheel bearing lockwasher and locknut.
10. Install the axle shaft with a new gasket and install the axle retaining bolts and lockwashers.
11. Install the wheel and adjust the brake shoes. Remove the jackstands and lower the vehicle.

Brake Shoes

REMOVAL & INSTALLATION

Bronco, F-150

◆ **See Figures 69 thru 81**

1. Raise and support the vehicle and remove the wheel and brake drum from the wheel to be worked on.

➡**If you have never replaced the brakes on a vehicle before and you are not too familiar with the procedures involved, only dissemble and assemble one side at a time, leaving the other side intact as a reference during reassembly.**

2. Install a clamp over the ends of the wheel cylinder to prevent the pistons of the wheel cylinder from coming out, causing loss of fluid and much grief.

3. Contract the brake shoes by pulling the self-adjusting lever away from the starwheel adjustment screw and turn the starwheel up and back until the pivot nut is drawn onto the starwheel as far as it will come.

4. Pull the adjusting lever, cable and automatic adjuster spring down and toward the rear to unhook the pivot hook from the large hole in the secondary shoe web. Do not attempt to pry the pivot hook from the hole.

5. Remove the automatic adjuster spring and the adjusting lever.

6. Remove the secondary shoe-to-anchor spring with a brake tool. (Brake tools are very common implements and are available to auto parts stores). Remove the primary shoe-to-anchor spring and unhook the cable anchor. Remove the anchor pin plate.

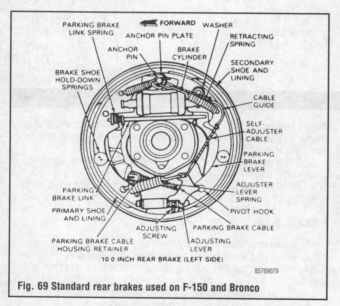

Fig. 69 Standard rear brakes used on F-150 and Bronco

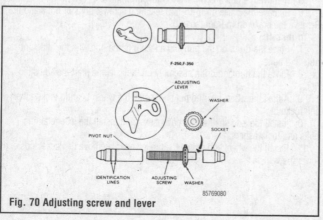

Fig. 70 Adjusting screw and lever

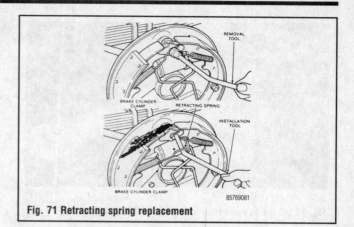

Fig. 71 Retracting spring replacement

Fig. 72 Unhooking the adjusting spring from the the pivot hook

Fig. 73 Pull the adjusting lever down and unhook the pivot hook from the large hole in the secondary shoe web

Fig. 74 Attach a pair of locking pliers to the lighter secondary shoe retracting spring and unhook from the anchor pin

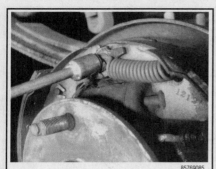

Fig. 75 Using a brake spring removal tool to disengage the primary shoe retracting spring

Fig. 76 Using a brake spring removal tool to remove the primary shoe retracting spring

Fig. 77 Remove the cable guide from the secondary shoe

Fig. 78 Remove the secondary shoe hold-down spring

Fig. 79 Remove the adjuster assembly

Fig. 80 Disconnect the parking brake cable from the lever

Fig. 81 Disconnect the parking brake link and spring

7. Remove the cable guide from the secondary shoe.

8. Remove the shoe holddown springs, shoes, adjusting screw, pivot nut, and socket. Note the color of each holddown spring for assembly. To remove the holddown springs, reach behind the brake backing plate and place one finger on the end of one of the brake holddown spring mounting pins. Using a pair of pliers, grasp the washer type retainer on top of the holddown spring that corresponds to the pin which you are holding. Push down on the pliers and turn them 90 degrees to align the slot in the washer with the head on the spring mounting pin. Remove the spring and washer retainer and repeat this operation on the hold down spring on the other shoe.

9. Remove the parking brake link and spring. Disconnect the parking brake cable from the parking brake lever.

10. After removing the rear brake secondary shoe, disassemble the parking brake lever from the shoe by removing the retaining clip and spring washer.

11. Assemble the parking brake lever to the secondary shoe and secure it with the spring washer and retaining clip.

12. Apply a light coating of Lubriplate® at the points where the brake shoes contact the backing plate.

13. Position the brake shoes on the backing plate, and install the holddown spring pins, springs, and spring washer type retainers. On the rear brake, install the parking brake link, spring and washer. Connect the parking brake cable to the parking brake lever.

14. Install the anchor pin plate, and place the cable anchor over the anchor pin with the crimped side toward the backing plate.

15. Install the primary shoe-to-anchor spring with the brake tool.

16. Install the cable guide on the secondary shoe web with the flanged holes fitted into the hole in the secondary shoe web. Thread the cable around the cable guide groove.

17. Install the secondary shoe-to-anchor (long) spring. Be sure that the cable end is not cocked or binding on the anchor pin when installed. All of the parts should be flat on the anchor pin. Remove the wheel cylinder piston clamp.

18. Apply Lubriplate® to the threads and the socket end of the adjusting starwheel screw. Turn the adjusting screw into the adjusting pivot nut to the limit of the threads and then back off ½ turn.

➡ **Interchanging the brake shoe adjusting screw assemblies from one side of the vehicle to the other would cause the brake shoes to retract rather than expand each time the automatic adjusting mechanism is operated. To prevent this, the socket end of the adjusting screw is stamped with an "R" or an "L" for "RIGHT" or "LEFT". The adjusting pivot nuts can be distinguished by the number of lines machined around the body of the nut; one line indicates left hand nut and two lines indicate a right hand nut.**

19. Place the adjusting socket on the screw and install this assembly between the shoe ends with the adjusting screw nearest to the secondary shoe.

20. Place the cable hook into the hole in the adjusting lever from the backing plate side. The adjusting levers are stamped with an **R** (right) or a **L** (left) to indicate their installation on the right or left hand brake assembly.

21. Position the hooked end of the adjuster spring in the primary shoe web and connect the loop end of the spring to the adjuster lever hole.

22. Pull the adjuster lever, cable and automatic adjuster spring down toward the rear to engage the pivot hook in the large hole in the secondary shoe web.

23. After installation, check the action of the adjuster by pulling the section of the cable guide and the adjusting lever toward the secondary shoe web far enough to lift the lever past a tooth on the adjusting screw starwheel. The lever should snap into position behind the next tooth, and release of the cable should cause the adjuster spring to return the lever to its original position. This return action of the lever will turn the adjusting screw starwheel one tooth. The lever should contact the adjusting screw starwheel one tooth above the centerline of the adjusting screw.

If the automatic adjusting mechanism does not perform properly, check the following:

24. Check the cable and fittings. The cable ends should fill or extend slightly beyond the crimped section of the fittings. If this is not the case, replace the cable.

25. Check the cable guide for damage. The cable groove should be parallel to the shoe web, and the body of the guide should lie flat against the web. Replace the cable guide if this is not so.

26. Check the pivot hook on the lever. The hook surfaces should be square with the body on the lever for proper pivoting. Repair or replace the hook as necessary.

27. Make sure that the adjusting screw starwheel is properly seated in the notch in the shoe web.

F-250 HD, F-350

▶ **See Figures 82, 83 and 84**

1. Raise and support the vehicle.
2. Remove the wheel and drum.
3. Remove the parking brake lever assembly retaining nut from behind the backing plate and remove the parking brake lever assembly.
4. Remove the adjusting cable assembly from the anchor pin, cable guide, and adjusting lever.
5. Remove the brake shoe retracting springs.
6. Remove the brake shoe holddown spring from each shoe.
7. Remove the brake shoes and adjusting screw assembly.
8. Disassembly the adjusting screw assembly.
9. Clean the ledge pads on the backing plate. Apply a light coat of Lubriplate® to the ledge pads (where the brake shoes rub the backing plate).
10. Apply Lubriplate® to the adjusting screw assembly and the holddown and retracting spring contacts on the brake shoes.
11. Install the upper retracting spring on the primary and secondary shoes and position the shoe assembly on the backing plate with the wheel cylinder pushrods in the shoe slots.

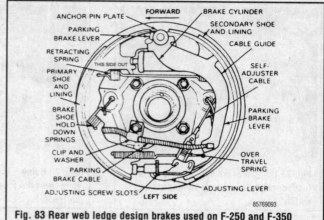

Fig. 83 Rear web ledge design brakes used on F-250 and F-350 models

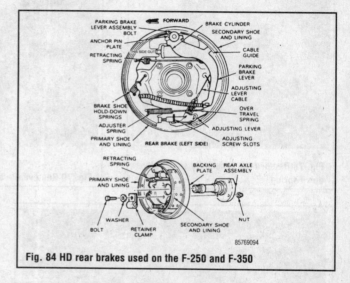

Fig. 84 HD rear brakes used on the F-250 and F-350

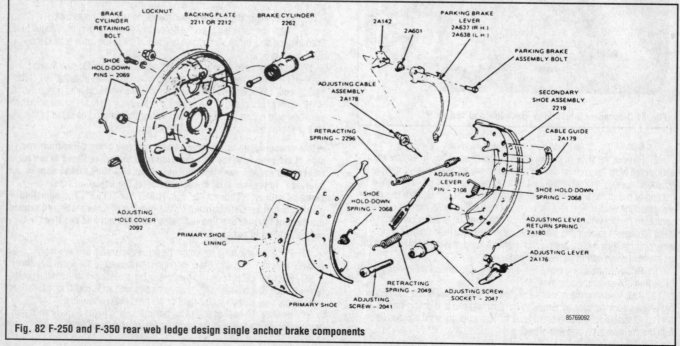

Fig. 82 F-250 and F-350 rear web ledge design single anchor brake components

12. Install the brake shoe holddown springs.

13. Install the brake shoe adjustment screw assembly with the slot in the head of the adjusting screw toward the primary shoe, lower retracting spring, adjusting lever spring, adjusting lever assembly, and connect the adjusting cable to the adjusting lever. Position the cable in the cable guide and install the cable anchor fitting on the anchor pin.

14. Install the adjusting screw assemblies in the same locations from which they were removed. Interchanging the brake shoe adjusting screws from one side of the vehicle to the other will cause the brake shoes to retract rather than expand each time the automatic adjusting mechanism is operated. To prevent incorrect installation, the socket end of each adjusting screw is stamped with an **R** or an **L** to indicate their installation on the right or left side of the vehicle. The adjusting pivot nuts can be distinguished by the number of lines machined around the body of the nut. Two lines indicate a right hand nut; one line indicates a left hand nut.

15. Install the parking brake assembly in the anchor pin and secure with the retaining nut behind the backing plate.

16. Adjust the brakes before installing the brake drums and wheels. Install the brake drums and wheels.

17. Lower the vehicle and road test the brakes. New brakes may pull to one side or the other before they are seated. Continued pulling or erratic braking should not occur.

Wheel Cylinders

REMOVAL & INSTALLATION

1. Remove the brake drum.
2. Remove the brake shoes.
3. Loosen the brake line at the wheel cylinder.

4. Remove the wheel cylinder attaching bolt and unscrew the cylinder from the brake line.

5. Installation is the reverse of removal. Bleed the brake system.

OVERHAUL

♦ See Figure 85

Purchase a brake cylinder repair kit. Remove and disassemble the wheel cylinder. Follow the instructions in the kit. Never repair only one cylinder. Repair both at the same time.

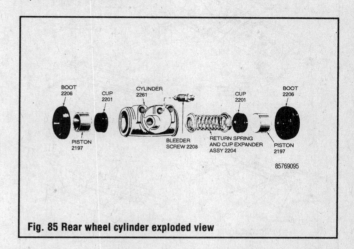

BOOT 2206   CUP 2201   CYLINDER 2261   CUP 2201   BOOT 2206

PISTON 2197   BLEEDER SCREW 2208   RETURN SPRING AND CUP EXPANDER ASSY 2204   PISTON 2197

85769095

Fig. 85 Rear wheel cylinder exploded view

PARKING BRAKE

➡**Before making any parking brake adjustment, make sure that the drum brakes are properly adjusted.**

Cables

ADJUSTMENT

♦ See Figures 86 thru 91

1. Raise and support the rear end on jackstands.
2. The brake drums should be cold.

3. Make sure that the parking brake pedal is fully released.

4. While holding the tension equalizer, tighten the equalizer nut 6 full turns past its original position.

5. Fully depress the parking brake pedal. Using a cable tension gauge, check rear cable tension. Cable tension should be 350 lbs. minimum.

6. Fully release the parking brake. No drag should be noted at the wheels.

7. If drag is noted on F-250 and F-350 models, you'll have to remove the drums and adjust the clearance between the parking brake lever and cam plate. Clearance should be 0.015 inch. Clearance is adjusted at the parking brake equalizer adjusting nut. If the tension limiter on the F-150 and Bronco doesn't release the drag, the tension limiter will have to be replaced.

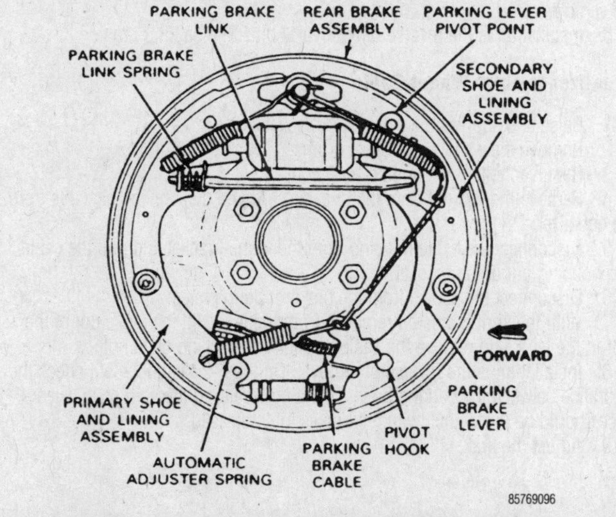

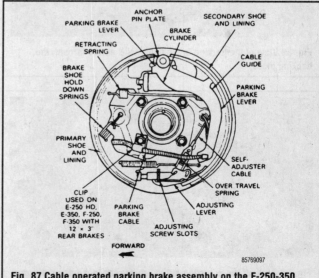

85769096

Fig. 86 Cable operated parking brake assembly on the F-150 and Bronco

85769097

Fig. 87 Cable operated parking brake assembly on the F-250-350 H.D. brakes

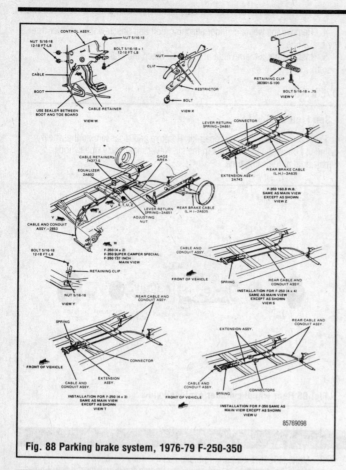

Fig. 88 Parking brake system, 1976-79 F-250-350

Fig. 89 View of the parking brake cable as it enters through the backing plate

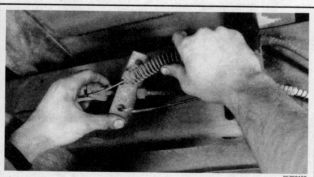

Fig. 90 Back off the adjusting nut to release the tension and disconnect the spring from the equalizer

Fig. 91 Back off the adjusting nut to release the tension and also disconnect the cable from the equalizer

Initial Adjustment When the Tension Limiter Has Been Replaced

1. Raise and support the front end on jackstands.
2. Depress the parking brake pedal fully.
3. Hold the tension limiter, install the equalizer nut and tighten it to a point 2½ inch plus or minus ⅛ inch up the rod.
4. Check to make sure that the cinch strap has 1⅜ inch remaining.

REMOVAL & INSTALLATION

▸ See Figures 86 thru 91

Parking Brake Control

1. Raise and support the rear end on jackstands.
2. Loosen the adjusting nut at the equalizer.
3. Working in the engine compartment, remove the nuts attaching the parking brake control to the firewall.
4. Remove the cable from the control assembly clevis by compressing the conduit end prongs.
5. Installation is the reverse of removal. Torque the attaching nuts to 15 ft. lbs.

Equalizer-to-Control Assembly Cable

1. Raise and support the rear end on jackstands.
2. Back off the equalizer nut and disconnect the cable from the tension limiter.
3. Remove the parking brake cable from the mount.
4. Disconnect the forward end of the cable from the control assembly.
5. Using a cord attached to the upper end of the cable, pull the cable from the vehicle.
6. Installation is the reverse of removal. Adjust the parking brake.

Equalizer-to-Rear Wheel Cable

1. Raise and support the rear end on jackstands.
2. Remove the wheels and brake drums.
3. Remove the tension limiter.
4. Remove the locknut from the threaded rod and disconnect the cable from the equalizer.
5. Disconnect the cable housing from the frame bracket and pull the cable and housing out of the bracket.
6. Disconnect the cables from the brake backing plates.
7. With the spring tension removed from the lever, lift the cable out of the slot in the lever and remove the cable through the backing plate hole.
8. Installation is the reverse of removal. On the F-250 and F-350, check the clearance between the parking brake operating lever and the cam plate. Clearance should be 0.015 inch with the brakes fully released.
9. Adjust the brakes.

BRAKE SPECIFICATIONS
All measurements in inches unless noted.

Year	Model	Master Cylinder Bore	Brake Disc Original Thickness	Brake Disc Minimum Thickness	Maximum Runout	Brake Drum Diameter Original Inside Diameter	Brake Drum Diameter Max. Wear Limit	Brake Drum Diameter Maximum Machine Diameter	Minimum Lining Thickness Front	Minimum Lining Thickness Rear
1976	F-100, 150	1.000	1.185	1.180	①	11.03	—	11.09	—	②
	F-250	1.062	1.185	1.120	①	12.00	—	12.06	—	②
	F-350	1.062	1.185	1.120	①	12.00	—	12.06	—	②
1977	F-100, 150	1.000	1.185	1.180	①	11.03	—	11.09	—	②
	F-250	1.062	1.185	1.120	①	12.00	—	12.06	—	②
	F-350	1.062	1.185	1.120	①	12.00	—	12.06	—	②
1978	F-100, 150, Bronco	1.000	1.185	1.180	①	11.03	—	11.09	—	②
	F-250	1.062	1.185	1.120	①	12.00	—	12.06	—	②
	F-350	1.062	1.185	1.120	①	12.00	—	12.06	—	②
1979	F-100, 150, Bronco	1.000	1.185	1.180	①	11.03	—	11.09	—	②
	F-250	1.062	1.185	1.120	①	12.00	—	12.06	—	②
	F-350	1.062	1.185	1.120	①	12.00	—	12.06	—	②
1980	F-100, 150, Bronco	1.000	1.185	1.180	①	11.03	—	11.09	—	②
	F-250	1.062	1.185	1.120	①	12.00	—	12.06	—	②
	F-350	1.062	1.185	1.120	①	12.00	—	12.06	—	②
1981	F-100 ③	1.000	—	0.810	④	11.03	—	11.09	—	②
	Bronco, F-150 (4 x 4)	1.062	—	1.120	④	11.03	—	11.09	—	②
	F-250 (4 x 4)	1.062	—	1.180	④	12.00	—	12.06	—	②
	F-100, 150, 250, 350 ⑥	1.062	—	⑤	④	12.00	—	12.06	—	②
1982	F-100 ③	1.000	—	0.810	④	11.03	—	11.09	—	②
	Bronco, F-150 (4 x 4)	1.062	—	1.120	④	11.03	—	11.09	—	②
	F-250 (4 x 4)	1.062	—	1.180	④	12.00	—	12.06	—	②
	F-100, 150, 250, 350 ⑥	1.062	—	⑤	④	12.00	—	12.06	—	②
1983	F-100 ③	1.000	—	0.810	④	11.03	—	11.09	—	②
	Bronco, F-150 (4 x 4)	1.062	—	1.120	④	11.03	—	11.09	—	②
	F-250 (4 x 4)	1.062	—	1.180	④	12.00	—	12.06	—	②
	F-100, 150, 250, 350 ⑥	1.062	—	⑤	④	12.00	—	12.06	—	②
1984	Bronco, F-150 (4 x 4)	1.000	—	1.120	④	11.03	—	11.09	—	②
	F-250 (4 x 4)	1.062	—	1.180	④	12.00	—	12.06	—	②
	F-150, 250, 350 ⑥	1.062	—	⑤	④	12.00	—	12.06	—	②
1985	Bronco, F-150 (4 x 4)	1.000	—	1.120	④	11.03	—	11.09	—	②
	F-250 (4 x 4)	1.062	—	1.180	④	12.00	—	12.06	—	②
	F-150, 250, 350 ⑥	1.062	—	⑤	④	12.00	—	12.06	—	②
1986	Bronco, F-150 (4 x 4)	1.000	—	1.120	④	11.03	—	11.09	—	②
	F-150, 250, 350	1.062	—	⑤	④	12.00	—	12.06	—	②

① Integral hub and disc: 0.003 in.
  Separate hub and disc: 0.005 in.
② 1/32 inch within rivet
③ 4650/4900 GVWR with power brakes
④ Integral hub and disc: 0.003 inch
  Separate hub and disc: 0.0010 inch
⑤ Integral hub and disc L.D.: 1.12 inch
  Integral hub and disc H.D.: 1.18 inch
  Separate hub and disc: 1.18 inch
⑥ 6200/6900 GVWR

85769C02

TORQUE SPECIFICATIONS

Component	U.S.	Metric
Front Disc Brake Calipers		
LD sliding caliper		
Key retaining screw		
1976–86:	14–22 ft. lbs.	19–29 Nm
HD sliding caliper		
Key retaining screw		
1976–83:	12–20 ft. lbs.	17–27 Nm
Brake hose to caliper bolt:	17–25 ft. lbs.	23–34 Nm
Anchor plate to spindle:	74–102 ft. lbs.	101–138 Nm
Piston housing to caliper bolts		
1976–79 with HD sliding caliper:	155–185 ft. lbs.	210–251 Nm
Master cylinder to booster:	13–25 ft. lbs.	18–33 Nm
Booster to dash panel:	12–25 ft. lbs.	18–33 Nm
Brake booster vacuum pump		
With 6.9L diesel engine		
Pump to adj. plate:	11–18 ft. lbs.	15–25 Nm
Adj. and pivot bolts:	11–18 ft. lbs.	15–25 Nm

85769C01

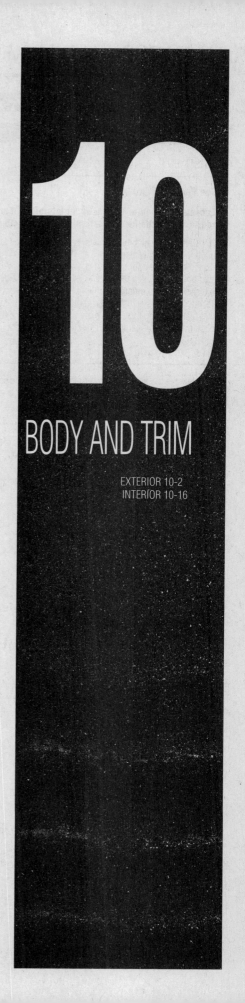

10

BODY AND TRIM

EXTERIOR

Doors

ADJUSTMENT

▶ **See Figures 1 and 2**

➡ **Loosen the hinge-to-door bolts for lateral adjustment only. Loosen the hinge-to-body bolts for both lateral and vertical adjustment.**

1. Determine which hinge bolts are to be loosened and back them out just enough to allow movement.

2. To move the door safely, use a padded pry bar. When the door is in the proper position, tighten the bolts to 24 ft. lbs. and check the door operation. There should be no binding or interference when the door is closed and opened.

3. Door closing adjustment can also be affected by the position of the lock striker plate. Loosen the striker plate bolts and move the striker plate just enough to permit proper closing and locking of the door.

REMOVAL & INSTALLATION

1. Remove the upper and lower hinge access hole cover plates, if so equipped and matchmark the hinge-to-body and hinge-to-door locations. Support the door either on jackstands or have somebody hold it for you.

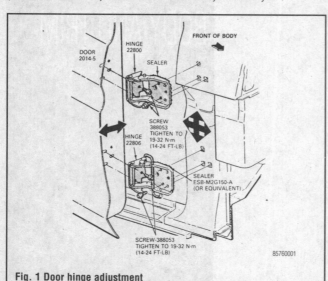

Fig. 1 Door hinge adjustment

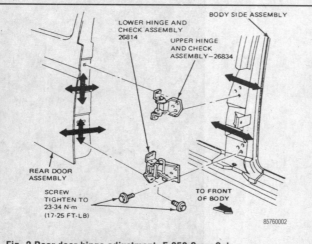

Fig. 2 Rear door hinge adjustment, F-350 Crew Cab

2. Remove the lower hinge-to-door bolts.

3. Remove the upper hinge-to-door bolts and lift the door off the hinges.

4. If the hinges are being replaced, remove them from the door pillar.

To install:

5. Install the door and hinges with the bolts finger tight.

6. Adjust the door and torque the hinge bolts to 24 ft. lbs.

Hood

REMOVAL & INSTALLATION

➡ **You'll need an assistant for this job.**

1976-79

▶ **See Figure 3**

1. Open the hood and remove the hood hinge bolts and with the aid of a helper lift the hood off the hinges.

2. If the hood is to be replaced, transfer the hood latch components and ornaments to the new hood.

3. With the aid of a helper position the hood on the hinges and install the hinge bolts snug.

4. Adjust the hood for proper fit and tighten the hinge bolts securely.

5. Adjust the hood latch for proper alignment.

1980-86

▶ **See Figure 4**

1. Open the hood.

2. Remove the 2 link assembly bolts.

3. Matchmark the hood-to-hinge position.

4. Remove the hood-to-hinge bolts and lift off the hood.

5. Installation is the reverse of removal. Loosely install the hood and align the matchmarks. Torque all bolts to 20 ft. lbs.

ADJUSTMENT

1. Open the hood and matchmark the hinge and latch positions.

2. Loosen the hinge-to-fender bolts just enough to allow movement of the hood.

3. Move the hood as required to obtain the proper fit and alignment between the hood and the top of the cowl panel. Tighten the bolts to 34 ft. lbs.

4. Loosen the 2 latch attaching bolts.

5. Loosen the hinge-to-hood bolts just enough to allow movement of the hood.

6. Move the hood forward/backward and/or side-to-side to obtain a proper hood fit.

7. Tighten the hood-to-hinge bolts to 20 ft. lbs.

8. Move the latch from side-to-side to align the latch with the striker. Torque the latch bolts.

9. Lubricate the latch and hinges and check the hood fit (open and close it) several times.

Hood Latch

▶ **See Figures 5, 6, 7 and 8**

ADJUSTMENT

1. Make sure that the hood is properly aligned.

2. Open the hood.

3. Loosen the hood latch attaching bolts just enough to move the latch.

4. Move the latch until it is aligned with the hood latch striker. Tighten the bolts.

5. Make sure full engagement of the striker occurs. If not, re-adjust the latch.

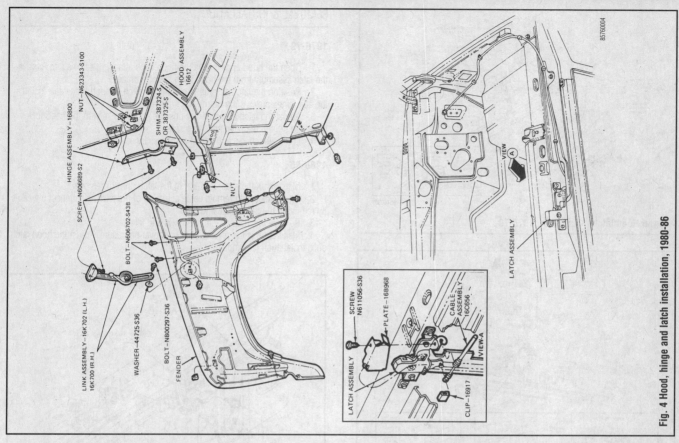

Fig. 4 Hood, hinge and latch installation, 1980-86

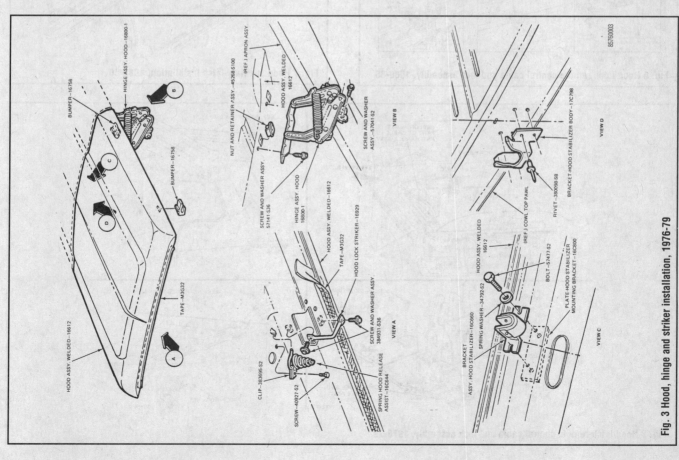

Fig. 3 Hood, hinge and striker installation, 1976-79

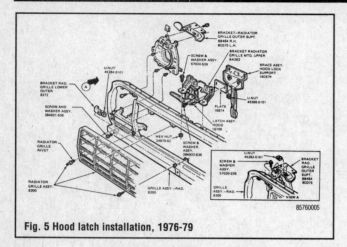

Fig. 5 Hood latch installation, 1976-79

REMOVAL & INSTALLATION

1976-79

1. Open the hood and remove the hood latch attaching screws and remove the latch assembly from the hood latch support brace.
2. Position the latch assembly to the hood latch support brace and install the attaching screws snug but do not tighten.
3. Adjust the latch assembly for positive engagement with the hood lock hook and tighten the latch attaching screws.
4. Lubricate, check, and adjust as necessary as necessary.

1980-86

1. Matchmark the exact location of the latch prior to removal.
2. On vehicles with remote cable actuation of the latch, disconnect the cable by removing the cable plate and clip.
3. Remove the latch attaching screws and latch.
4. Installation is the reverse of the removal procedure. Adjust the hood latch once installation is complete.

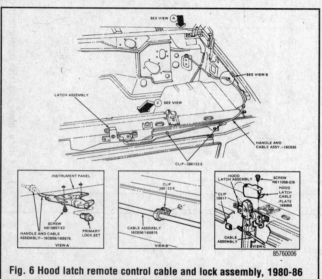

Fig. 6 Hood latch remote control cable and lock assembly, 1980-86

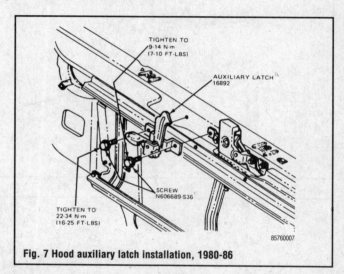

Fig. 7 Hood auxiliary latch installation, 1980-86

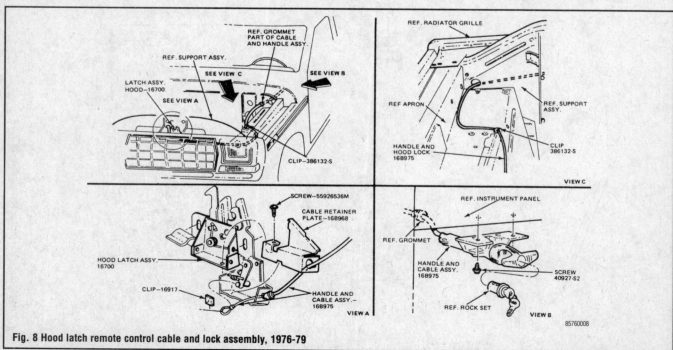

Fig. 8 Hood latch remote control cable and lock assembly, 1976-79

Tailgate

REMOVAL & INSTALLATION

▶ See Figure 9

1978-86 Bronco

1. Lower the tailgate.
2. Disconnect the left and right cable assemblies at the tailgate.
3. Disconnect the tailgate window motor wire at the connector the connector.
4. Pull the wiring from the tailgate body rail.
5. Have someone support the tailgate and remove the torsion bar retainer from the body.

6. Remove the three screw and washer assemblies that secure the left and right hinge assemblies.
7. Remove the tailgate and hinge assemblies from the vehicle.
8. Installation is the reverse of removal.

Styleside Pick-up

1976-79

▶ See Figure 10

1. Open and support the tailgate assembly and remove the hinge attaching screws on each side of the tailgate.
2. Carefully raise the lower portion of the tailgate upward and disengage it from the tailgate latch brackets.
3. Installation is the reverse of removal.

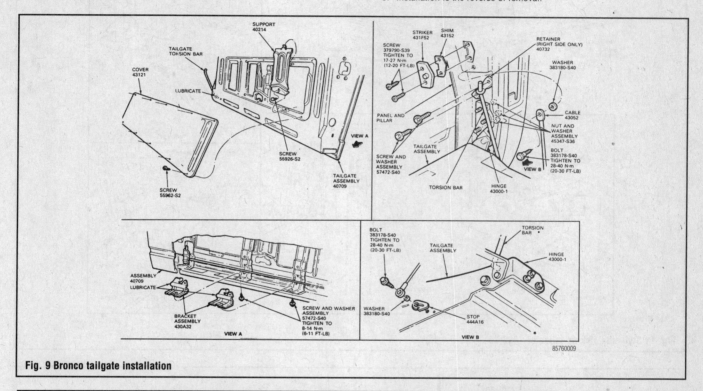

Fig. 9 Bronco tailgate installation

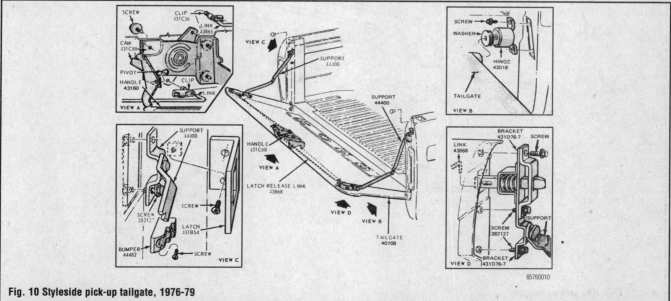

Fig. 10 Styleside pick-up tailgate, 1976-79

1980-86

♦ See Figure 11

1. Remove the tailgate support strap at the pillar T-head pivot.
2. Lift off the tailgate at the right hinge.
3. Pull off the left hinge.
4. Installation is the reverse of removal.

Flareside Pick-up

♦ See Figure 12

1. Unhook the chain.
2. Remove the movable pivot-to-body bolts and remove the pivot.
3. Slide the tailgate off the stationary pivot.
4. Installation is the reverse of removal.

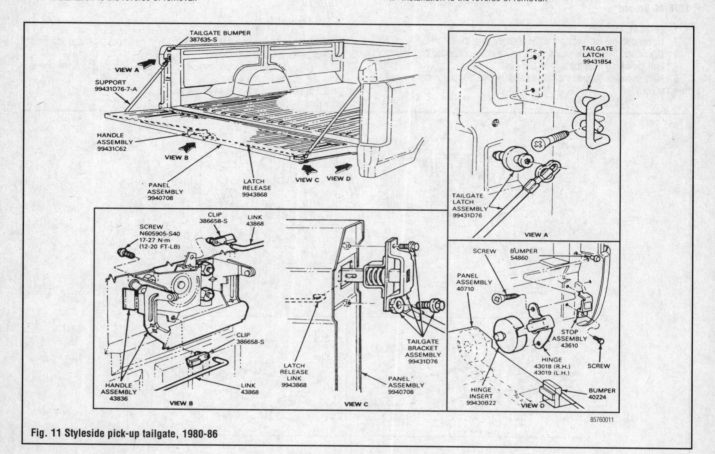

Fig. 11 Styleside pick-up tailgate, 1980-86

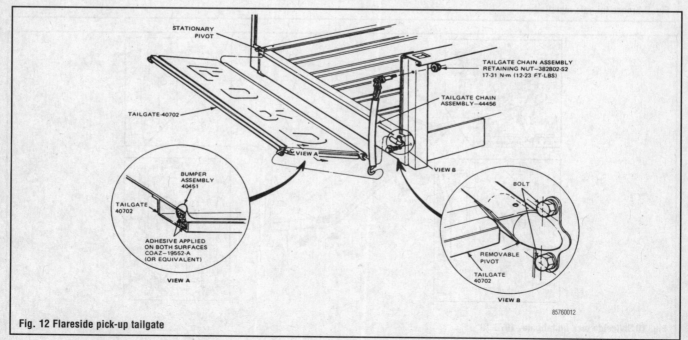

Fig. 12 Flareside pick-up tailgate

Tailgate Latch Release Handle and Lock Release Control Assemblies

REMOVAL & INSTALLATION

1978-86 Bronco

▶ **See Figure 13**

1. Lower the tailgate and remove the inner access cover.
2. Remove the 2 screws securing the handle to the tailgate.
3. Remove the rod from the clip that holds the handle rod to the lock control.
4. Remove the handle and rod assembly.
5. Disconnect the latch release links and latch control rod.
6. Disconnect the wiring from the interlock switch.
7. Remove the 3 lock control-to-tailgate retaining screws.
8. Remove the lock control from the tailgate.

To install:

9. Install the lock control and tighten the screws to 11 ft. lbs.
10. Connect the wires.
11. Place the latch control rod in position and install the clip.
12. Place the latch release links in position and install the clips.
13. Place the handle and rod assembly in the tailgate. Connect the rod to the lock control and install the clip.
14. Install and tighten the handle attaching screws.
15. Install the access cover.

Grille

REMOVAL & INSTALLATION

1976-79

▶ **See Figure 14**

1. To remove the outer shell, remove the six screws attaching each end of the grille to the fender.

2. Remove the lower retaining screws at the lower corners of the grille.
3. Remove the grille outer support bracket-to-radiator support bolts at each end of the grille.
4. Remove the upper mounting bracket-to-grille bolts.
5. Remove the retaining screw at the lower center bracket to grille screw.
6. Disconnect the parking light and headlamp wires and remove the grille.

To install:

7. Transfer all U-nuts, clips and mounting brackets, etc. to a new grille if the grille is to be replaced. Position the new grille..
8. Connect the parking light and headlamp wires.
9. Install the upper mounting bracket-to-grille bolts.
10. Install the grille outer support bracket-to-radiator support bolts at each end of the grille.
11. Install the lower retaining screws at the lower corners of the grille.
12. Install the retaining screw at the lower center bracket to grille screw.
13. Install the six screws attaching each end of the grille to the fender.

1980-86

▶ **See Figure 15**

1. Remove the one grille attaching screw at the hood latch support brace at the lower center of the grille.
2. Remove the two screws on the right side and left side of the grille at the radiator grille support on each side.
3. Remove the three remaining screws which fasten the upper grille moulding to the moulding retainer and remove the grille.
4. Installation is the reverse of removal.

Front Fender

REMOVAL & INSTALLATION

1976-79

▶ **See Figure 16**

1. Clean all fender fasteners and liberally apply penetrating oil, such as Liquid Wrench®, WD-40®, or equivalent.

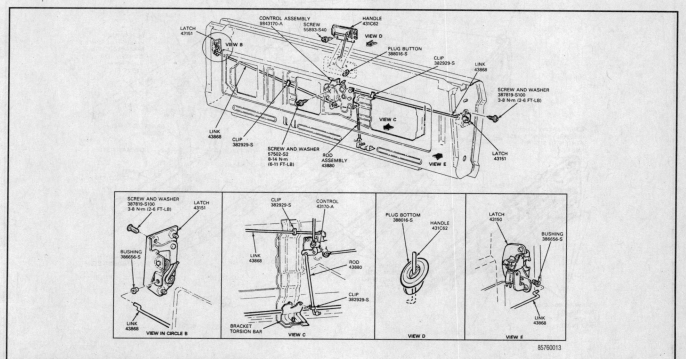

85760013

Fig. 13 Tailgate latch release and lock control, 1978-86 Bronco

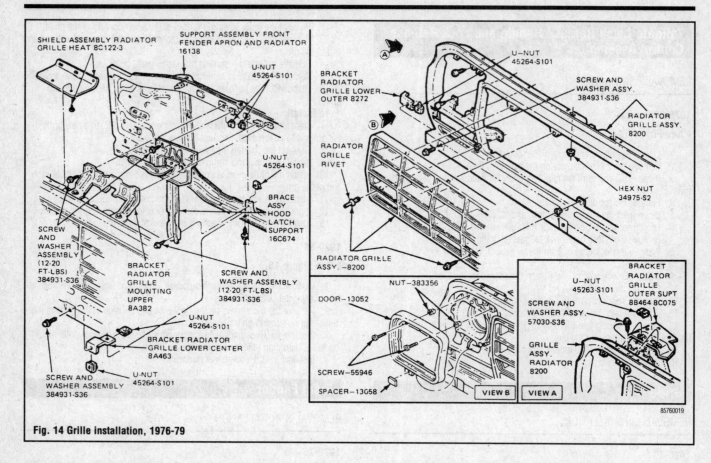

Fig. 14 Grille installation, 1976-79

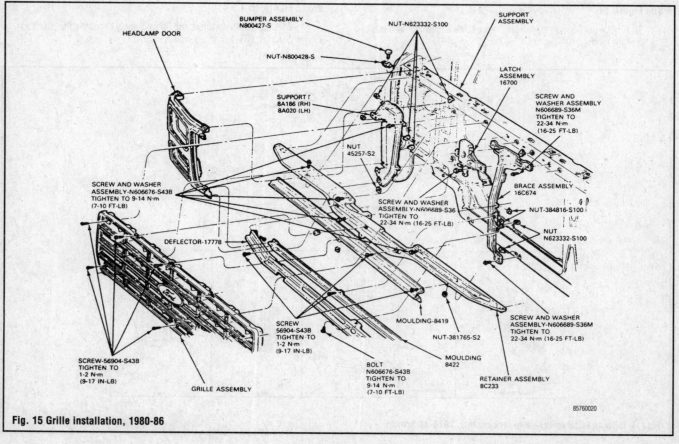

Fig. 15 Grille installation, 1980-86

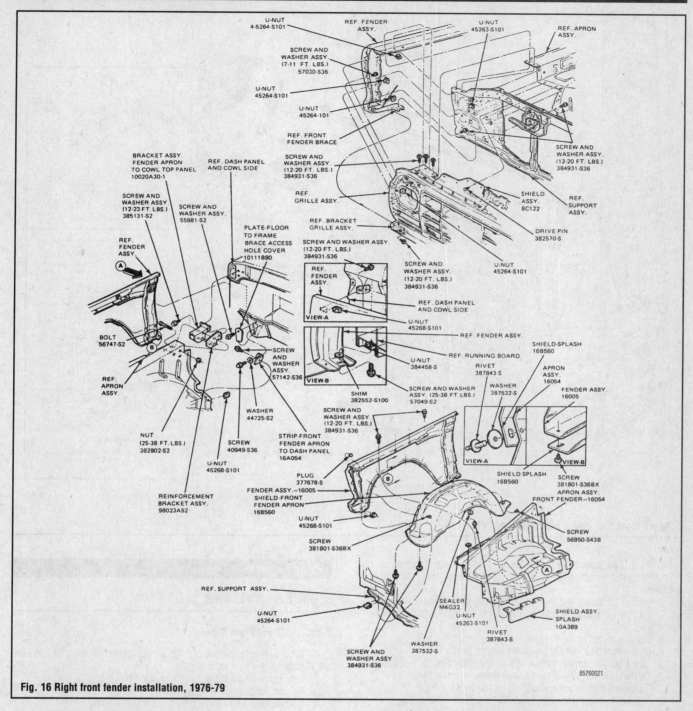

Fig. 16 Right front fender installation, 1976-79

2. Remove the grille and headlamp assemblies.

3. Remove the fender-to-radiator support screws.

4. Remove the screw attaching the rear lower end of the fender to the lower corner of the cab and remove the one pin retaining the seal to the lower corner of the cab.

5. Remove the screw inside the cab attaching the top of the rear corner of the fender to the cowl.

6. Remove the screws attaching the top edge of the fender to the fender apron and radiator support and remove the fender from the vehicle.

7. Remove the pins attaching the seal to the fender and remove the seal from the fender.

8. Remove the nuts and retainers from the fender.

To install:

9. Position the seal to the fender and install the attaching pins.

10. Apply sealer to the upper edge of the apron.

11. Position the fender on the vehicle and loosely install all screws nuts and bolts.

12. Go around the fender and check its fit. Position the fender for even fit with all adjoining panels and tighten all the fasteners.

13. Install all parts removed previously.

1980-86

◆ See Figure 17

1. Clean all fender fasteners and liberally apply penetrating oil, such as Liquid Wrench®, WD-40®, or equivalent.

2. Remove the headlamp assemblies.

3. Remove the fender-to-radiator support screws.

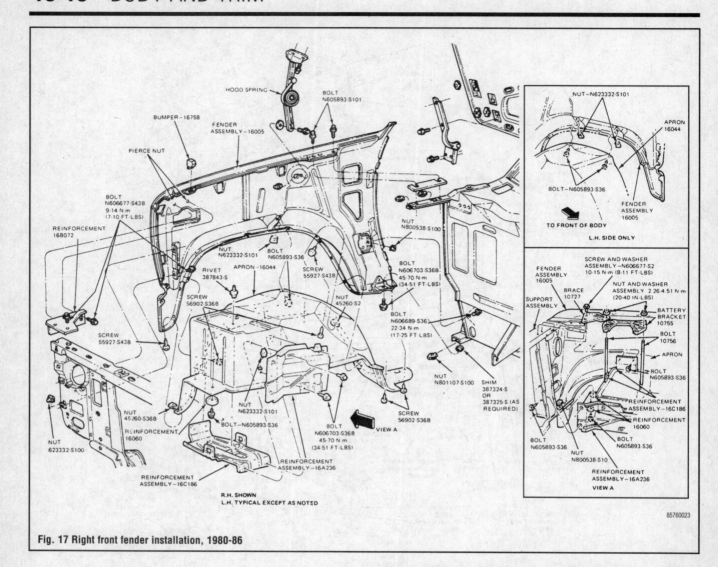

Fig. 17 Right front fender installation, 1980-86

4. Remove the screw attaching the fender to the lower corner of the cab.

5. Remove the screw inside the cab attaching the lower end of the fender to the cowl.

6. Remove the screws attaching the top edge of the fender to the cowl extension.

7. Remove the screws that attach the fender to the apron, around the wheel opening.

8. Remove the top fender-to-apron bolts.

9. On the right side, remove the battery and the battery tray.

10. On the left side, remove the auxiliary battery and/or tool box both options.

11. On the right side, detach the main wiring harness from the fender.

12. On the left side, detach the hood latch cable from the fender.

13. Remove the hood prop spring from the fender.

14. Remove the fender.

To install:

15. Apply sealer to the upper edge of the apron.

16. Position the fender on the vehicle and loosely install all screws nuts and bolts.

17. Go around the fender and check its fit. Position the fender for even fit with all adjoining panels and tighten all the fasteners.

18. Install all parts removed previously.

Rear Fender

REMOVAL & INSTALLATION

F-150, 250, 350 Flare Side

1. Clean all fender fasteners and liberally apply penetrating oil, such as Liquid Wrench®, WD-40®, or equivalent.

2. Remove the fender brace-to-fender nut and bolt.

3. Remove the 12 fender-to-body nuts.

4. Remove the 3 fender-to-running board nuts and bolts.

5. Remove the fender.

To install:

6. Clean the body mounting points.

7. Position the fender and loosely install all fasteners.

8. Go around the fender and check for proper clearance. Position the fender for even fit with all adjoining panels and tighten all the fasteners.

F-350 with Dual Rear Wheels

1. Clean all fender fasteners and liberally apply penetrating oil, such as Liquid Wrench®, WD-40®, or equivalent.
2. Remove the fender brace to fender nut and bolt.
3. Remove the 12 fender-to-body nuts and bolts.
4. Remove the three nuts and bolts attaching the running board to the fender and remove the fender.

To install:

5. Clean the body mounting points.
6. Position the fender and loosely install all fasteners.
7. Go around the fender and check its fit. Position the fender for even fit with all adjoining panels and tighten all the fasteners.

Body and Chassis Mounts

REPLACEMENT

▶ **See Figures 18, 19, 20, 21 and 22**

To replace or service body and chassis mounts, use the accompanying illustrations. When installing body mounts, do not use **any** lubricants on the mounts!

Mirrors

REMOVAL & INSTALLATION

All mirrors are remove by removing the mounting screws and lifting off the mirror and gasket.

Antenna

REMOVAL & INSTALLATION

1976-79

▶ **See Figure 23**

1. Disconnect the antenna cable at the radio by pulling it straight out of the set.
2. Working under the instrument panel, disengage the cable from its retainers.

➡ **On some models, it may be necessary to remove the glove box get at the cable.**

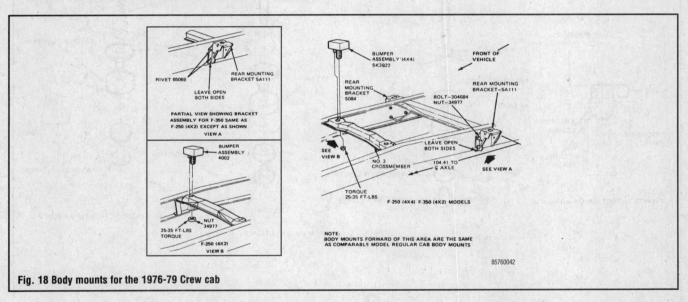

Fig. 18 Body mounts for the 1976-79 Crew cab

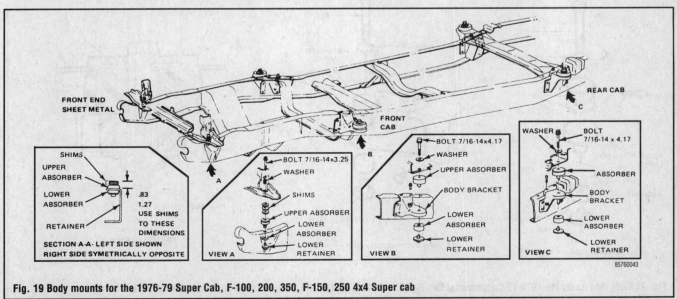

Fig. 19 Body mounts for the 1976-79 Super Cab, F-100, 200, 350, F-150, 250 4x4 Super cab

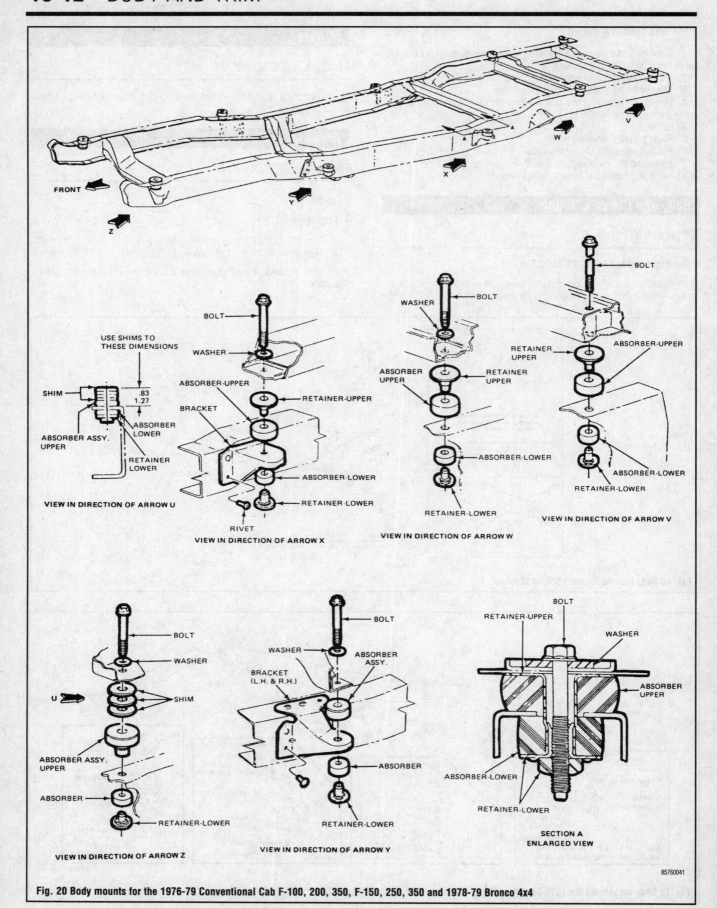

Fig. 20 Body mounts for the 1976-79 Conventional Cab F-100, 200, 350, F-150, 250, 350 and 1978-79 Bronco 4x4

85760041

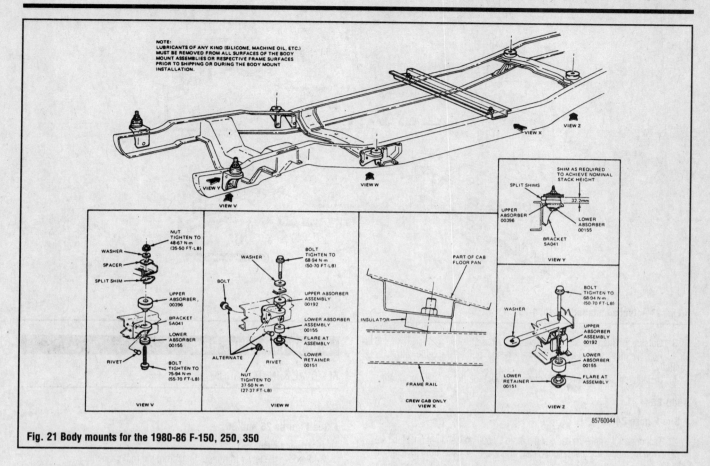

Fig. 21 Body mounts for the 1980-86 F-150, 250, 350

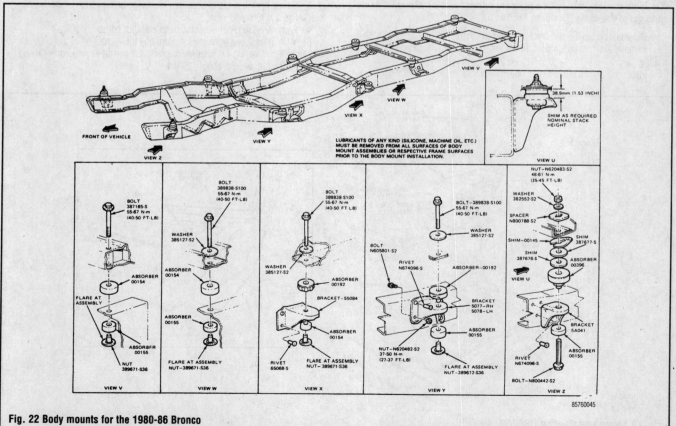

Fig. 22 Body mounts for the 1980-86 Bronco

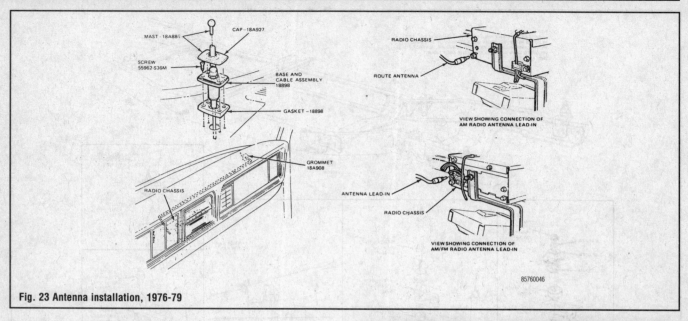

Fig. 23 Antenna installation, 1976-79

3. Outside, unsnap the cap from the antenna base.
4. Remove the 4 screws and lift off the antenna, pulling the cable with it, carefully.
5. Installation is the reverse of removal. Check radio for proper operation.

1980-86

▶ See Figure 24

1. Disconnect the antenna cable at the radio by pulling it straight out of the set.
2. Working under the instrument panel, disengage the cable from its retainers.

➡ **On some models, it may be necessary to remove the instrument panel pad to get at the cable. (Refer to Section 6).**

3. Outside, unsnap the cap from the antenna base.
4. Remove the 4 screws and lift off the antenna, pulling the cable with it, carefully.
5. Installation is the reverse of removal. Check radio for proper operation.

Bronco Fiberglass Roof

REMOVAL & INSTALLATION

Roof

▶ See Figures 25 and 26

1. Lower the tailgate.
2. Remove the lower trim mouldings from the roof panels.
3. Scribe the locations of each trim moulding bracket and number each bracket as it is removed.
4. Remove all the roof attaching bolts and trim bolts.
5. With at least one other person, carefully lift the roof off of the body. Be careful to avoid tearing the weather-stripping. Be careful to avoid over-flexing the roof. The roof weighs about 120 lbs.

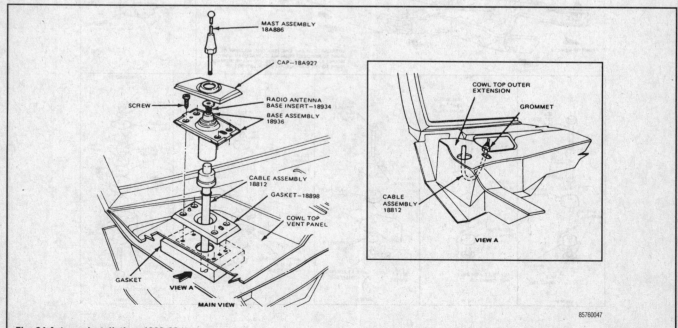

Fig. 24 Antenna installation, 1980-86

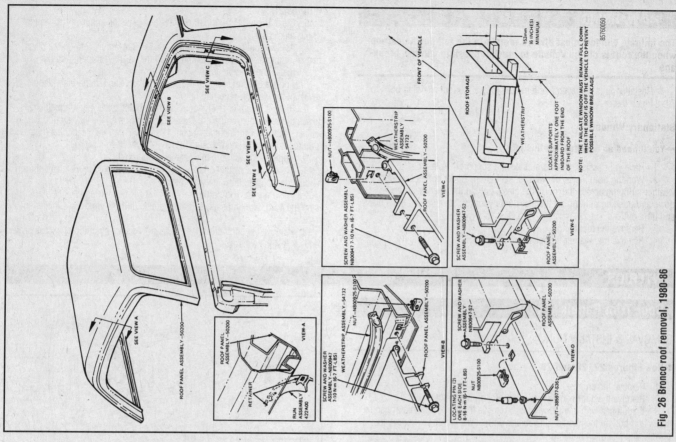

Fig. 26 Bronco roof removal, 1980-86

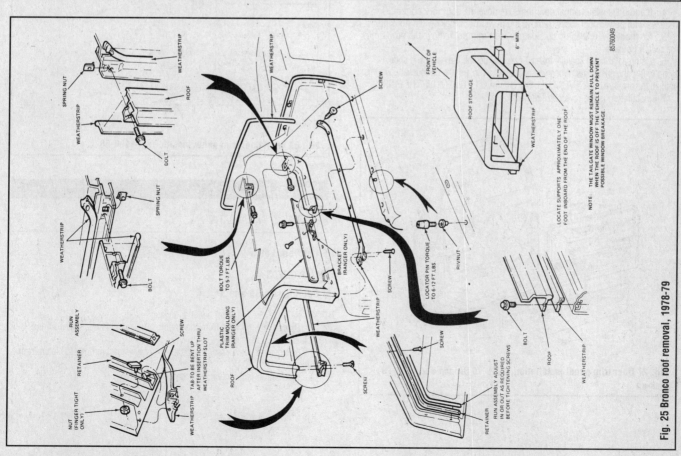

Fig. 25 Bronco roof removal, 1978-79

✳ WARNING

The tailgate window must always remain in the full down position when the roof is off the vehicle to prevent possible window breakage

6. Installation is the reverse of removal. Torque the roof retaining bolts to 72–84 inch lbs.

Stationary Window

➡ **You'll need an assistant for this job.**

1. Have your assistant stand outside and support the glass.
2. Working from inside the vehicle, start at one upper corner and work the weather-stripping across the top of the glass, pulling the weather-stripping down and pushing outward on the glass until your assistant can grab the glass and lift it out.
3. Remove the mouldings.
4. Remove the weather-stripping from the glass.

To install:

5. Clean the weather-stripping, glass and glass opening with solvent to remove all old sealer.
6. Apply liquid butyl sealer C9AZ–19554–B, or equivalent, in the glass channel of the weather-stripping and install the weather-stripping on the glass.
7. Install the mouldings.
8. Apply a bead of sealer to the opening flange and in the inner flange crevice of the weather-stripping lip.
9. Place a length of strong cord, such as butcher's twine, in the flange crevice of the weather-stripping. The cord should go all the way around the weather-stripping with the ends, about 18 in. (457mm) long each, hanging down together at the bottom center of the window.
10. Apply soapy water to the weather-stripping lip.
11. Have your assistant position the window assembly in the channel from the outside, applying firm inward pressure.
12. From inside, you guide the lip of the weather-stripping into place using the cord, working each end alternately, until the window is locked in place.
13. Remove the cord, clean the glass and weather-stripping of excess sealer and leak test the window.

INTERIOR

Door Trim Panels

REMOVAL & INSTALLATION

▶ **See Figures 27, 28 and 29**

1. Remove the armrest.
2. Remove the door handle screw and pull off the handle.
3. If equipped with manual windows, remove the window regulator handle screw and pull off the handle. On vehicles with power windows, remove the power window switch housing.
4. If equipped with manual door locks, remove the door lock control. On vehicles with power door locks, remove the power door lock switch housing.
5. On models with electric outside rear view mirrors, remove the power mirror switch housing.
6. Using a flat wood spatula, insert it carefully behind the panel and slide it along to find the push-pins. When you encounter a pin, pry the pin outward. Do this until all the pins are out. NEVER PULL ON THE PANEL TO REMOVE THE PINS!
7. Installation is the reverse of removal.

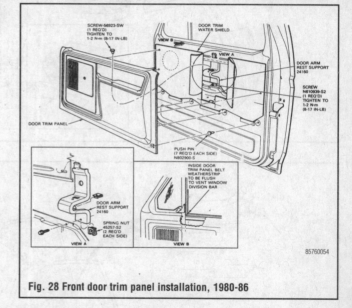

Fig. 28 Front door trim panel installation, 1980-86

Manual Door Locks

REMOVAL & INSTALLATION

Front Door Latch

ALL MODELS

▶ **See Figures 30 and 31**

1. Remove the door trim panel and watershield.
2. Disconnect the rods from the handle and lock cylinder, and from the remote control assembly.
3. Remove the latch assembly attaching screws and remove the latch from the door.
4. Installation is the reverse of removal.

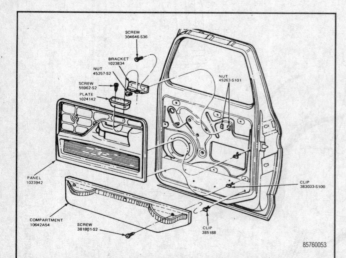

Fig. 27 Door trim panel installation, 1978-79 Bronco and 1976-79 pick-up

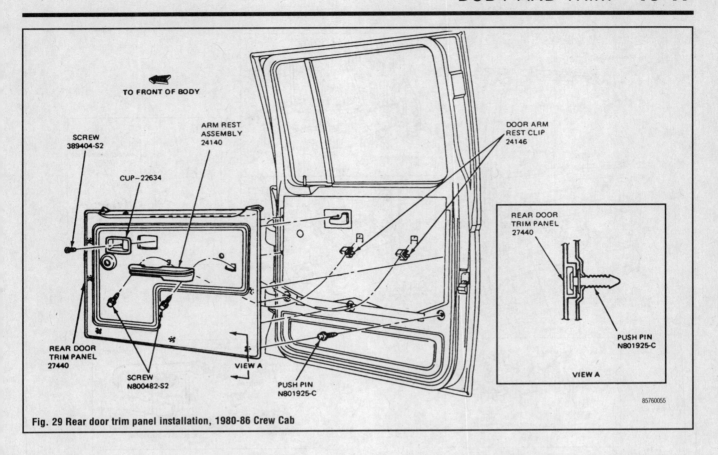

Fig. 29 Rear door trim panel installation, 1980-86 Crew Cab

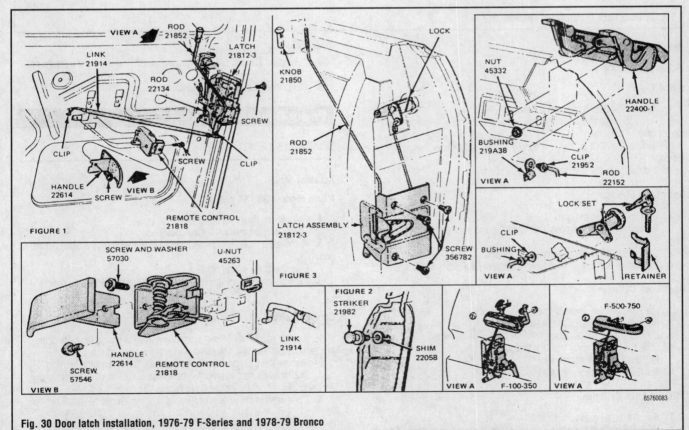

Fig. 30 Door latch installation, 1976-79 F-Series and 1978-79 Bronco

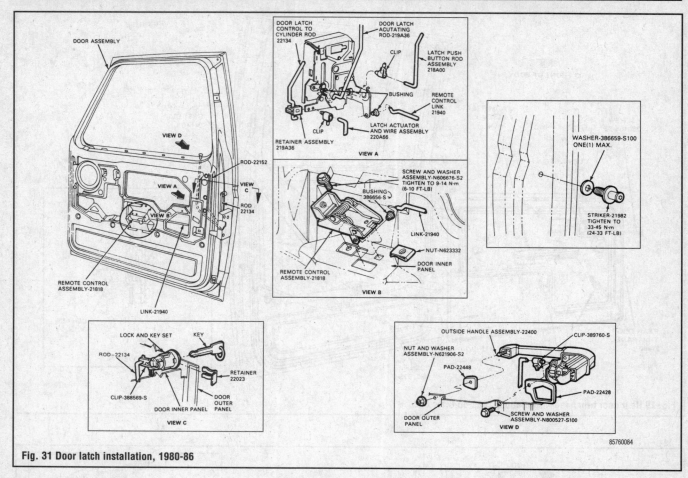

Fig. 31 Door latch installation, 1980-86

Rear Door Latch

F-350 CREW CAB

▶ **See Figure 32**

1. Remove the door trim panel and watershield.
2. Disconnect the rods from the handle and lock cylinder, and from the remote control assembly.
3. Remove the latch assembly attaching screws and remove the latch from the door.
4. Installation is the reverse of removal.

Door Lock Linkage

1. Remove the door trim panels.
2. Remove the door lock control attaching screws and remove the control from the door.
3. Disconnect the linkage rod from the control.
4. Installation is the reverse of removal. Transfer the clip to the new linkage.

Door Lock Cylinder

1. Place the window in the UP position.
2. Remove the trim panel and watershield.
3. Disconnect the actuating rod from the lock control link clip.
4. Slide the retainer away from the lock cylinder.
5. Pull the cylinder from the door.
6. Installation is the reverse of removal.

Tailgate Lock Cylinder

1. Remove the tailgate access cover.
2. Raise the glass. If the glass can't be raised, remove it as described below.

3. Remove the lock cylinder retainer.
4. Disengage the lock cylinder from the switch and remove it from the tailgate.
5. Installation is the reverse of removal.

Power Door Locks

REMOVAL & INSTALLATION

Actuator Motor

▶ **See Figures 33, 34 and 35**

1. Remove the door trim panel.
2. Disconnect the motor from the door latch.
3. Remove the motor and swivel bracket from the door by drilling out the pop rivet.
4. Disconnect the wiring harness.
5. Installation is the reverse of removal. Make sure that the pop rivet is tight.

Control Switch

1. Insert a small, thin-bladed screwdriver into the spring tab slots at the front and rear of the switch housing, and pop the housing out.
2. Remove the 3 connector attaching screws from the switch housing.
3. The switch is held in place by the electrical contact pins. Carefully pry the switch away from the connector to remove it.
4. Installation is the reverse of removal. The switch can be install only one way.

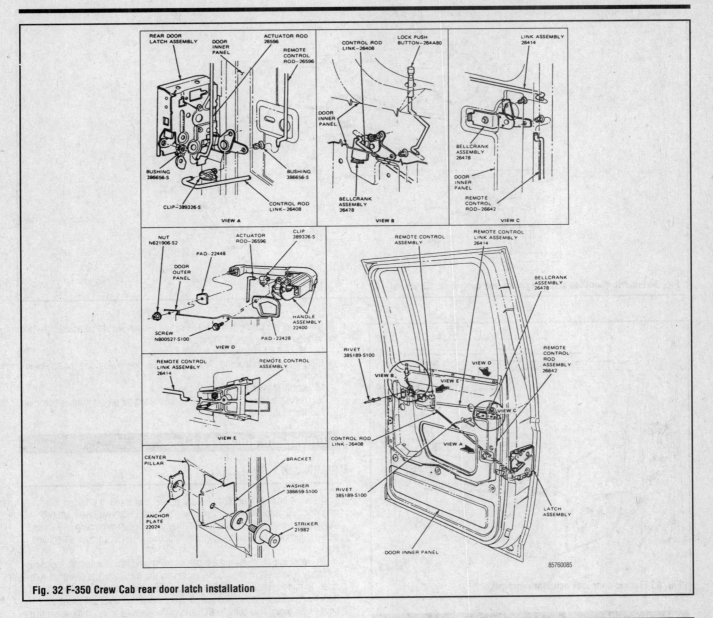

Fig. 32 F-350 Crew Cab rear door latch installation

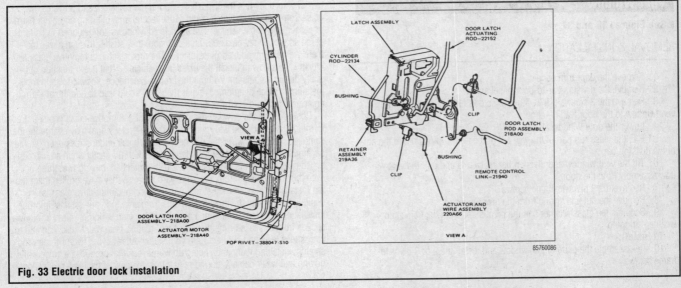

Fig. 33 Electric door lock installation

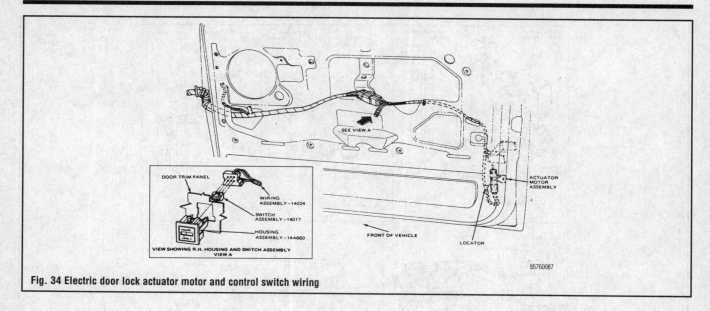

Fig. 34 Electric door lock actuator motor and control switch wiring

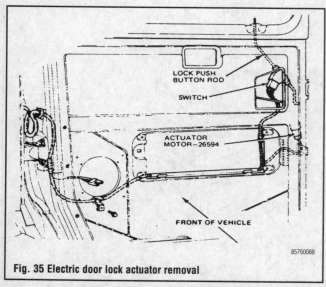

Fig. 35 Electric door lock actuator removal

Vent Window

▶ **See Figures 36 and 37**

REMOVAL & INSTALLATION

1. Remove the door trim panel.
2. Remove the division bar-to-door panel screw.
3. Remove the 3 screws (1976-79) or 2 screws (1980-86) retaining the vent window to the door leading edge.
4. Lower the door window all the way.
5. Pull the glass run part of the way out of the door run retainer in the area of the division bar.
6. Tilt the vent window and division bar rearwards and pull the vent window assembly from the door.
7. Remove the 2 pivot-to-frame screws.
8. Remove the nut and spring from the lower pivot.
9. Separate the glass retainer and the pivot stops from the frame and weather-stripping.
To install:
10. Re-assemble the parts of the window and install the 2 or 3 pivot-to-frame screws.

11. Install the spring and nut. The spring tension should be adjusted so that the window will stay open at highway speeds.
12. Place the run assembly in the vent assembly.
13. Place the window and division bar in the door. Make sure the spacer is in position.
14. Install the window-to-door edge screws.
15. Install the division bar screw. Adjust the run for proper window operation.
16. Install the door trim.

Windshield and Fixed Glass

REMOVAL & INSTALLATION

If your windshield, or other fixed window, is cracked or chipped, you may decide to replace it with a new one yourself. However, there are two main reasons why replacement windshields and other window glass should be installed only by a professional automotive glass technician: safety and cost.

The most important reason a professional should install automotive glass is for safety. The glass in the vehicle, especially the windshield, is designed with safety in mind in case of a collision. The windshield is specially manufactured from two panes of specially-tempered glass with a thin layer of transparent plastic between them. This construction allows the glass to "give" in the event that a part of your body hits the windshield during the collision, and prevents the glass from shattering, which could cause lacerations, blinding and other harm to passengers of the vehicle. The other fixed windows are designed to be tempered so that if they break during a collision, they shatter in such a way that there are no large pointed glass pieces. The professional automotive glass technician knows how to install the glass in a vehicle so that it will function optimally during a collision. Without the proper experience, knowledge and tools, installing a piece of automotive glass yourself could lead to additional harm if an accident should ever occur.

Cost is also a factor when deciding to install automotive glass yourself. Performing this could cost you much more than a professional may charge for the same job. Since the windshield is designed to break under stress, an often life saving characteristic, windshields tend to break VERY easily when an inexperienced person attempts to install one. Do-it-yourselfers buying two, three or even four windshields from a salvage yard because they have broken them during installation are common stories. Also, since the automotive glass is designed to prevent the outside elements from entering your vehicle, improper installation can lead to water and air leaks. Annoying whining noises at highway speeds from air leaks or inside body panel rusting from water leaks can add to your stress level and subtract from your wallet. After buying two or three windshields, installing them and ending up with a leak that produces a noise while driving and water damage during rainstorms, the cost of having a professional

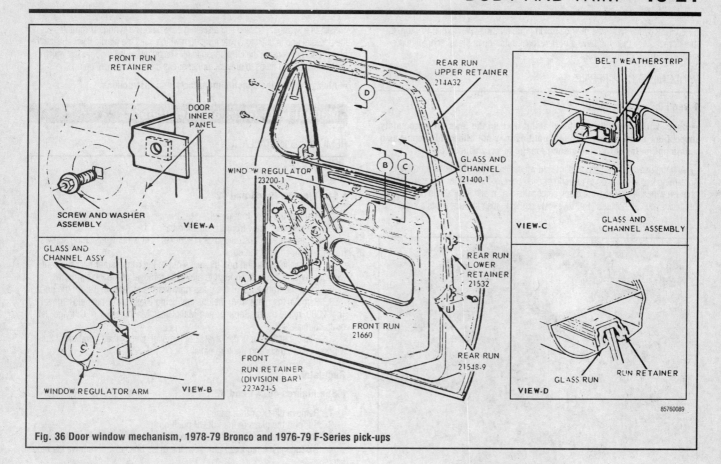

Fig. 36 Door window mechanism, 1978-79 Bronco and 1976-79 F-Series pick-ups

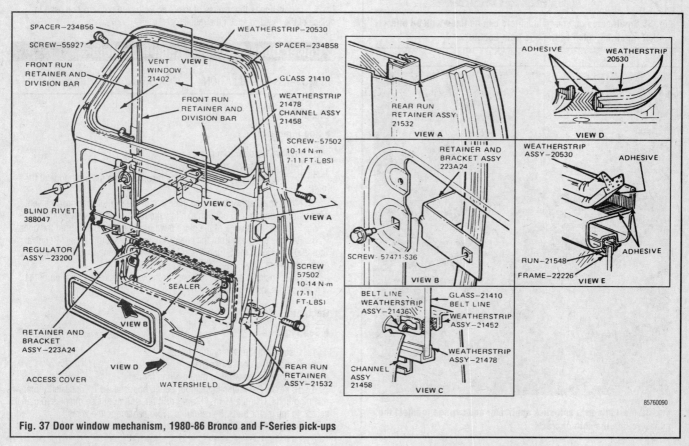

Fig. 37 Door window mechanism, 1980-86 Bronco and F-Series pick-ups

do it correctly the first time may be much more alluring. We here at Chilton, therefore, advise that you have a professional automotive glass technician service any broken glass on your vehicle.

WINDSHIELD CHIP REPAIR

▶ See Figures 38 and 39

➡Check with your state and local authorities on the laws for state safety inspection. Some states or municipalities may not allow chip repair as a viable option for correcting stone damage to your windshield.

Although severely cracked or damaged windshields must be replaced, there is something that you can do to prolong or even prevent the need for replacement of a chipped windshield. There are many companies which offer windshield chip repair products, such as Loctite's® Bullseye™ windshield repair kit. These kits usually

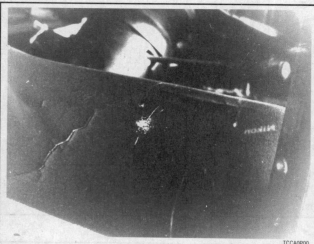

TCCA0P00

Fig. 38 Small chips on your windshield can be fixed with an after-market repair kit, such as the one from Loctite®

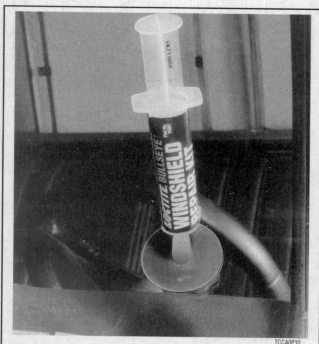

TCCA0P10

Fig. 39 Most kits us a self-stick applicator and syringe to inject the adhesive into the chip or crack

consist of a syringe, pedestal and a sealing adhesive. The syringe is mounted on the pedestal and is used to create a vacuum which pulls the plastic layer against the glass. This helps make the chip transparent. The adhesive is then injected which seals the chip and helps to prevent further stress cracks from developing

➡Always follow the specific manufacturer's instructions.

Manual Door Glass and Regulator

REMOVAL & INSTALLATION

Glass

▶ See Figures 40, 41 and 42

1. Remove the door trim panel.
2. Remove the screw from the division bar.
3. Remove the 2 (1980-86) or 3 (1976-79) vent window attaching screws from the front edge of the door.
4. Lower the glass and pull the glass out of the run retainer near the vent window division bar, just enough to allow the removal of the vent window.
5. Push the front edge of the glass downward and remove it from the door.
6. Remove the glass from the channel using Glass and Channel Removal Tool 2900, made by the Sommer and Mala Glass Machine Co. of Chicago, ILL., or its equivalent.
7. Glass installation is the reverse of removal. Check the operation of the window before installing the trim panel.

Regulator

▶ See Figures 40, 41 and 42

1. Remove the door trim panel.
2. Support the glass in the full UP position.
3. Drill out the regulator attaching rivets using a ¼ in. (6mm) drill bit.
4. Disengage the regulator arm from the glass bracket and remove the regulator.
5. Installation is the reverse of removal. Bolts and nuts may be used in place of the rivets to attach the regulator.

Power Door Glass and Regulator Motor

REMOVAL & INSTALLATION

Glass

▶ See Figure 41

1. Remove the door trim panel.
2. Remove the screw from the division bar.
3. Remove the 2 vent window attaching screws from the front edge of the door.
4. Lower the glass and pull the glass out of the run retainer near the vent window division bar, just enough to allow the removal of the vent window.
5. Push the front edge of the glass downward and remove it from the door.
6. Remove the glass from the channel using Glass and Channel Removal Tool 2900, made by the Sommer and Mala Glass Machine Co. of Chicago, ILL., or its equivalent.
7. Glass installation is the reverse of removal. Check the operation of the window before installing the trim panel.

Regulator

▶ See Figure 43

1. Disconnect the battery ground.
2. Remove the door trim panel.
3. Disconnect the window motor wiring harness.
4. There are 2 dimples in the door panel, opposite the 2 concealed motor retaining bolts. Using a ½ in. (13mm) drill bit, drill out these dimples to gain access to the motor bolts. Be careful to avoid damage to the wires.
5. Remove the 3 motor mounting bolts.

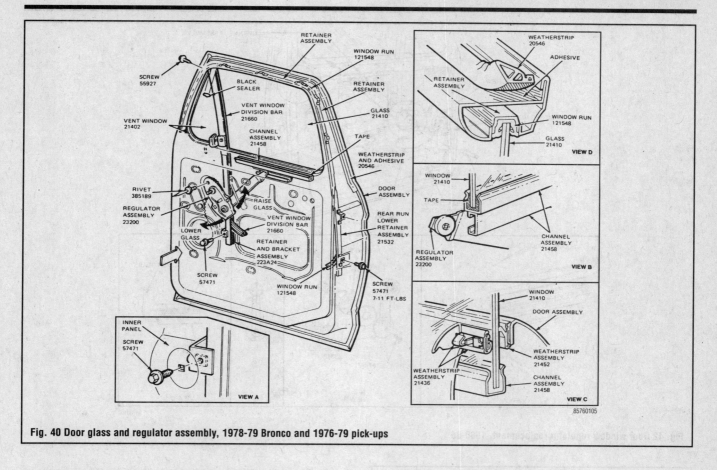

Fig. 40 Door glass and regulator assembly, 1978-79 Bronco and 1976-79 pick-ups

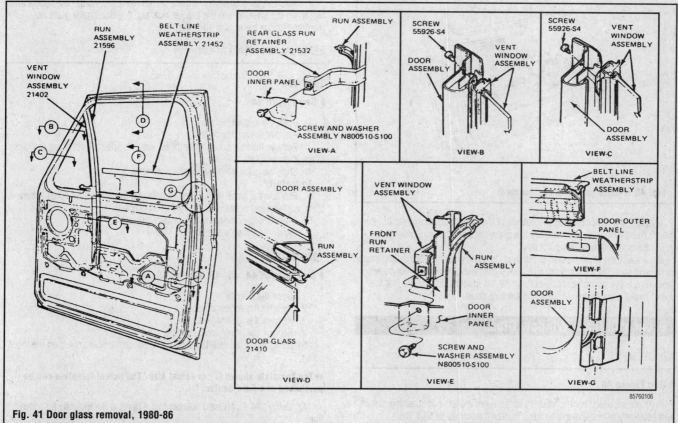

Fig. 41 Door glass removal, 1980-86

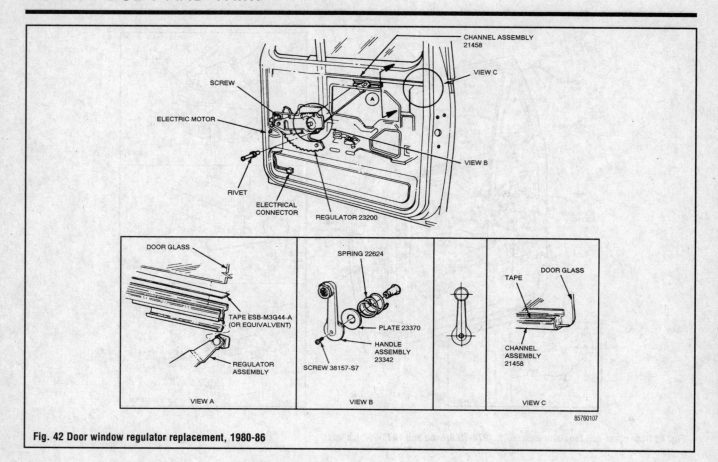

Fig. 42 Door window regulator replacement, 1980-86

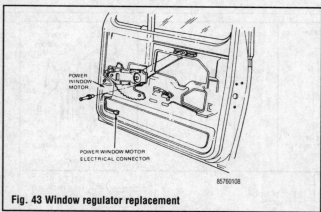

Fig. 43 Window regulator replacement

6. Push the motor towards the outside of the door to disengage it from the gears. You'll have to support the window glass once the motor is disengaged.

7. Remove the motor from the door.

8. Installation is the reverse of removal. To avoid rusting in the drilled areas, prime and paint the exposed metal, or, cover the holes with waterproof body tape. Torque the motor mounting bolts to 50–85 inch lbs. Make sure that the motor works properly before installing the trim panel.

Bronco Tailgate Window Glass

ADJUSTMENT

▶ See Figure 44

1. Fore-aft adjustment is made by loosening the glass run attaching screws and positioning the glass as required. Tighten the screws to 10 ft. lbs.

2. Side-to-side adjustment is made by removing the inside cover panel and loosening the glass-to-window bracket nuts and positioning the glass as required. Torque the nuts to 10 ft. lbs.

REMOVAL & INSTALLATION

1978-79

▶ See Figure 44

1. Open the tailgate.
2. Remove the access cover.
3. Remove the four screw assemblies, washers and nuts attaching the glass to the glass brackets.
4. Slide the glass from the tailgate assembly.
To install:
5. Position the glass in the open tailgate and install the four screw assemblies, washers and nuts to the window glass brackets.
6. Check the operation and adjust as necessary.
7. Install the inside access cover.

1980-86

▶ See Figures 44, 45, 46, 47 and 48

1. Open the tailgate.
2. Remove the access cover.
3. Remove the watershield.
4. Remove the cover panel support.
5. Using the template illustrated, centerpunch the holes noted on the inner panel.

➥The template shown is not actual size. The actual template can be purchased at a Ford dealer.

6. Using a ⅝ in. (16mm) holesaw, cut 4 holes at the template hole location.

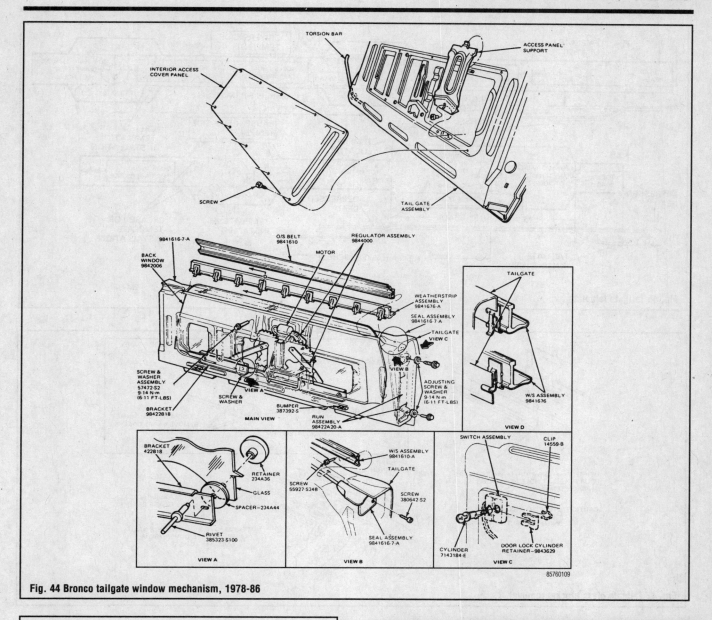

Fig. 44 Bronco tailgate window mechanism, 1978-86

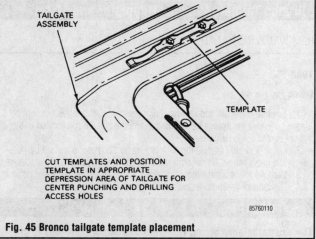

CUT TEMPLATES AND POSITION
TEMPLATE IN APPROPRIATE
DEPRESSION AREA OF TAILGATE FOR
CENTER PUNCHING AND DRILLING
ACCESS HOLES

Fig. 45 Bronco tailgate template placement

> ※ **WARNING**
>
> **Cover the glass with protective padding prior to cutting the holes.**

7. Working through the holes, remove the 4 glass bracket retaining nuts.

8. Using a $\frac{5}{16}$ in. (8mm) drift punch, remove the glass bracket C-channel from the glass and bracket.

9. Remove the padding and drillings.

10. Grasp the glass at the 2 bottom cutouts and slide it to the half-open position. Disconnect the rear window grid wire, if so equipped, and remove the glass from the tailgate.

11. Make sure that you remove all the drillings from the tailgate. Vacuuming them out is a good idea. These drillings, if left in the tailgate will lead to rusting of the surrounding metal. Prime and paint the drilled out holes to prevent rusting.

12. Installation is the reverse of removal. Torque the four retaining nuts to 10 ft. lbs.

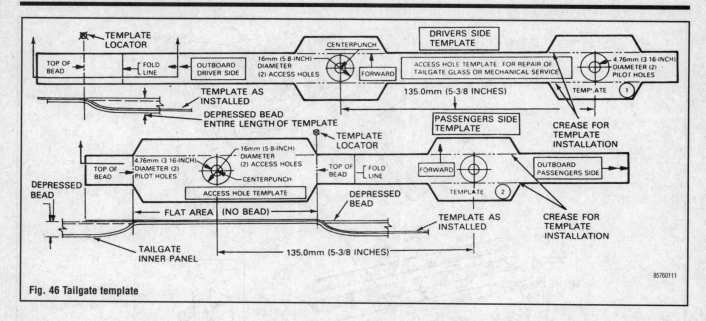

Fig. 46 Tailgate template

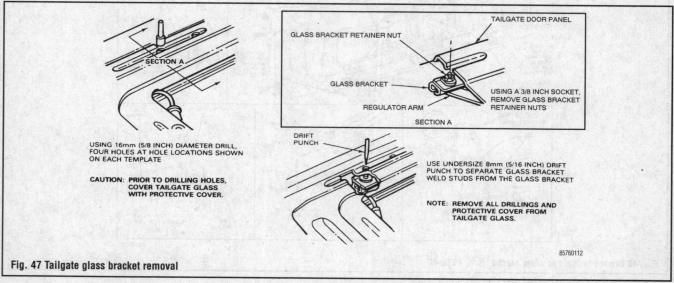

Fig. 47 Tailgate glass bracket removal

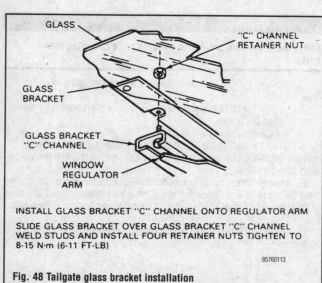

INSTALL GLASS BRACKET "C" CHANNEL ONTO REGULATOR ARM

SLIDE GLASS BRACKET OVER GLASS BRACKET "C" CHANNEL WELD STUDS AND INSTALL FOUR RETAINER NUTS TIGHTEN TO 8-15 N·m (6-11 FT-LB)

Fig. 48 Tailgate glass bracket installation

Bronco Tailgate Window Regulator and Motor

REMOVAL & INSTALLATION

1980-86

▸ See Figure 44

1. Lower the tailgate and remove the access panel. If the glass cannot be lowered, remove the access panel and depress the lockout rod located in the bottom center of the tailgate.
2. Using a jumper to the tailgate motor, raise the glass to the full up position. If the glass cannot be raised it will have to be removed as outlined above.
3. Remove the regulator mounting bolts and nuts and lift out the regulator.
4. Disconnect the motor harness.

✳✳ CAUTION

The counterbalance spring is under considerable tension. To prevent injury from sudden movement of the regulator components, clamp or lock the gear sectors prior to removing the components!

5. Detach the motor from the tailgate and remove it.
6. Installation is the reverse of removal. Torque the regulator mounting bolts to 10 ft. lbs.

Inside Rear View Mirror

REMOVAL & INSTALLATION

The mirror is held in place with a single setscrew. Loosen the screw and lift the mirror off. Repair kit for damaged mirrors are available at most auto parts stores.

Front Bench Seat

REMOVAL & INSTALLATION

♦ See Figures 49 and 50

1. Remove the 4 seat track-to-floor pan bolts.
2. Carefully lift the seat and remove from the vehicle.

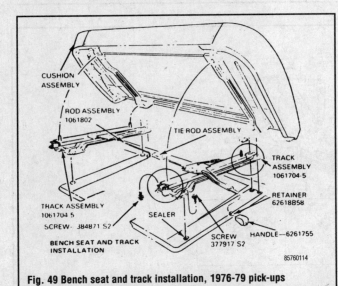

Fig. 49 Bench seat and track installation, 1976-79 pick-ups

To install:
3. Apply sealer to the mounting hole areas.
4. Install the seat in the vehicle and adjust position.
5. Install the mounting bolts and torque to 30 ft. lbs.

Driver's Bucket Seat

REMOVAL & INSTALLATION

♦ See Figures 51 and 52

1. Remove the 4 seat track-to-floor pan bolts.
2. Lift the seat and remove from the vehicle.
3. To install, apply sealer to the hole areas and position seat in the vehicle. Install and torque the mounting bolts to 30 ft. lbs.

Driver's Captain's Chair

REMOVAL & INSTALLATION

1. Remove the 4 seat track-to-floor pan bolts and lift out the seat.
2. Apply sealer to the hole areas and install the seat. Torque the bolts to 30 ft. lbs.

Passenger's Bucket Seat or Captain's Chair

REMOVAL & INSTALLATION

♦ See Figure 52

1. Remove the 2 front bolts retaining the passenger's seat and support assembly to the floor pan.
2. Move the seat release lever rearward allowing the seat to pop-up and fold forward.
3. Remove the 2 rear seat assembly-to-floor pan bolts.
4. Disengage one end of the passenger's seat support stop cable.
5. Move the seat and support assembly rearward until the seat back clears the instrument panel when folded forward.
6. Fold the seat fully forward and disengage the ends of the 3 assist springs from their retainers. NEVER TRY TO REMOVE THE SEAT WITH THE SPRINGS ATTACHED!
7. Return the seat to the upright position and push the seat back down firmly until the seat is latched.
8. Remove the seat from the vehicle.

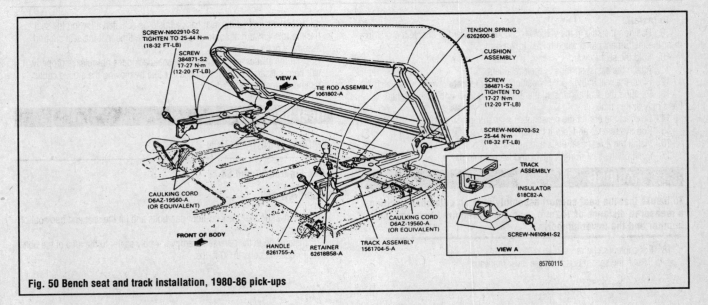

Fig. 50 Bench seat and track installation, 1980-86 pick-ups

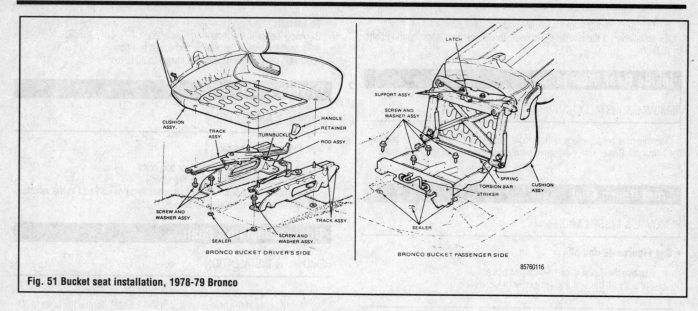

Fig. 51 Bucket seat installation, 1978-79 Bronco

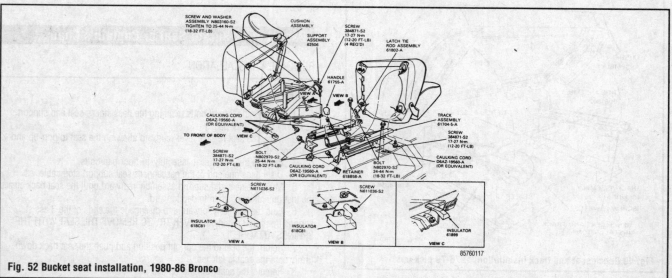

Fig. 52 Bucket seat installation, 1980-86 Bronco

To install:

9. Position the seat in the vehicle far enough rearward to enable the seat to clear the instrument panel when folded forward.

10. Fold the seat forward.

11. Attach the assist springs to their retainers.

12. Place the seat in the upright position. Push the seat down firmly to latch it.

13. Position the seat and install the 2 front holddown bolt. Hand-tighten them only at this time.

14. Connect the end of the passenger's seat support stop cable.

15. Pop the seat up and fold it forward.

16. Install the 2 rear seat bolts and tighten all 4 bolts to 30 ft. lbs.

17. Position the seat upright again and latch it into place.

❋❋ WARNING

To insure that the seat support assembly is in an unlatched position, a measured distance of 102mm, or more, is required between the bumper and the lower support.

18. For captain's chairs:
   a. Push the seat support release lever rearward.

b. Make sure that the seat back adjuster is actuated allowing the seat back to fold forward at approximately the same time that the seat support assembly pops up.

c. If the seat assembly and/or the seat back does not release properly, it will be necessary to adjust the release cable by moving the slotted cable retainer fore or aft as needed.

Rear Bench Seat

REMOVAL & INSTALLATION

▶ **See Figures 53 and 54**

F-350 Crew Cab

1. Remove the seat track-to-floor pan bolts and lift the seat and track out of the vehicle.

2. Installation is the reverse of removal. Apply sealer to the area of the bolt holes. Torque the bolts to 30 ft. lbs.

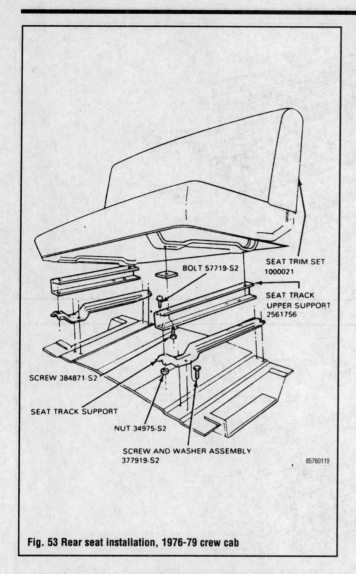

Fig. 53 Rear seat installation, 1976-79 crew cab

Folding Rear Seat

REMOVAL & INSTALLATION

F-Series Pickups

♦ **See Figures 55, 56 and 57**

The side-facing seats are held in place with 2 bolts. The forward facing seat is held down with 4 bolts. When replacing the seat, use sealer in the bolt hole areas. Torque the bolts to 30 ft. lbs.

Bronco

To remove the folding rear seat, fold down the seat back and unlatch the seat from the floor. Fold the seat forward and remove the seat track-to-floor bolts. Torque the bolts to 60 ft. lbs.

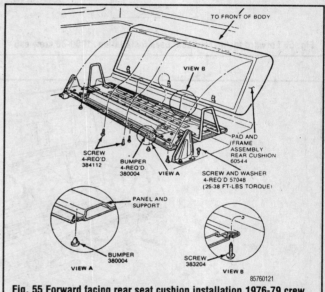

Fig. 55 Forward facing rear seat cushion installation,1976-79 crew cab

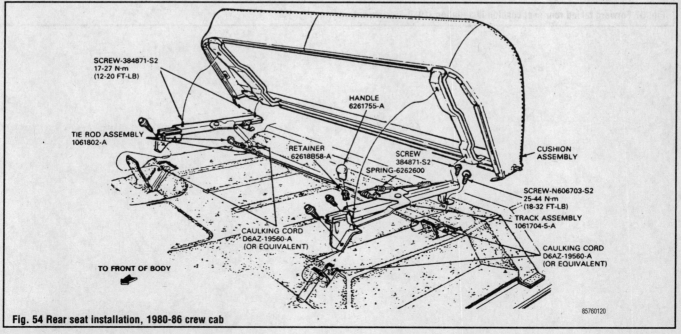

Fig. 54 Rear seat installation, 1980-86 crew cab

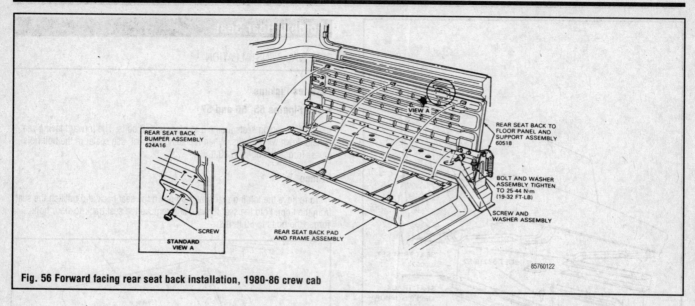

Fig. 56 Forward facing rear seat back installation, 1980-86 crew cab

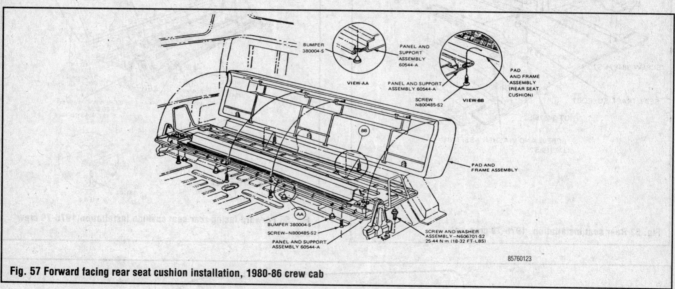

Fig. 57 Forward facing rear seat cushion installation, 1980-86 crew cab

GLOSSARY

AIR/FUEL RATIO: The ratio of air-to-gasoline by weight in the fuel mixture drawn into the engine.

AIR INJECTION: One method of reducing harmful exhaust emissions by injecting air into each of the exhaust ports of an engine. The fresh air entering the hot exhaust manifold causes any remaining fuel to be burned before it can exit the tailpipe.

ALTERNATOR: A device used for converting mechanical energy into electrical energy.

AMMETER: An instrument, calibrated in amperes, used to measure the flow of an electrical current in a circuit. Ammeters are always connected in series with the circuit being tested.

AMPERE: The rate of flow of electrical current present when one volt of electrical pressure is applied against one ohm of electrical resistance.

ANALOG COMPUTER: Any microprocessor that uses similar (analogous) electrical signals to make its calculations.

ARMATURE: A laminated, soft iron core wrapped by a wire that converts electrical energy to mechanical energy as in a motor or relay. When rotated in a magnetic field, it changes mechanical energy into electrical energy as in a generator.

ATMOSPHERIC PRESSURE: The pressure on the Earth's surface caused by the weight of the air in the atmosphere. At sea level, this pressure is 14.7 psi at 32°F (101 kPa at 0°C).

ATOMIZATION: The breaking down of a liquid into a fine mist that can be suspended in air.

AXIAL PLAY: Movement parallel to a shaft or bearing bore.

BACKFIRE: The sudden combustion of gases in the intake or exhaust system that results in a loud explosion.

BACKLASH: The clearance or play between two parts, such as meshed gears.

BACKPRESSURE: Restrictions in the exhaust system that slow the exit of exhaust gases from the combustion chamber.

BAKELITE: A heat resistant, plastic insulator material commonly used in printed circuit boards and transistorized components.

BALL BEARING: A bearing made up of hardened inner and outer races between which hardened steel balls roll.

BALLAST RESISTOR: A resistor in the primary ignition circuit that lowers voltage after the engine is started to reduce wear on ignition components.

BEARING: A friction reducing, supportive device usually located between a stationary part and a moving part.

BIMETAL TEMPERATURE SENSOR: Any sensor or switch made of two dissimilar types of metal that bend when heated or cooled due to the different expansion rates of the alloys. These types of sensors usually function as an on/off switch.

BLOWBY: Combustion gases, composed of water vapor and unburned fuel, that leak past the piston rings into the crankcase during normal engine operation. These gases are removed by the PCV system to prevent the buildup of harmful acids in the crankcase.

BRAKE PAD: A brake shoe and lining assembly used with disc brakes.

BRAKE SHOE: The backing for the brake lining. The term is, however, usually applied to the assembly of the brake backing and lining.

BUSHING: A liner, usually removable, for a bearing; an anti-friction liner used in place of a bearing.

CALIPER: A hydraulically activated device in a disc brake system, which is mounted straddling the brake rotor (disc). The caliper contains at least one piston and two brake pads. Hydraulic pressure on the piston(s) forces the pads against the rotor.

CAMSHAFT: A shaft in the engine on which are the lobes (cams) which operate the valves. The camshaft is driven by the crankshaft, via a belt, chain or gears, at one half the crankshaft speed.

CAPACITOR: A device which stores an electrical charge.

CARBON MONOXIDE (CO): A colorless, odorless gas given off as a normal byproduct of combustion. It is poisonous and extremely dangerous in confined areas, building up slowly to toxic levels without warning if adequate ventilation is not available.

CARBURETOR: A device, usually mounted on the intake manifold of an engine, which mixes the air and fuel in the proper proportion to allow even combustion.

CATALYTIC CONVERTER: A device installed in the exhaust system, like a muffler, that converts harmful byproducts of combustion into carbon dioxide and water vapor by means of a heat-producing chemical reaction.

CENTRIFUGAL ADVANCE: A mechanical method of advancing the spark timing by using flyweights in the distributor that react to centrifugal force generated by the distributor shaft rotation.

CHECK VALVE: Any one-way valve installed to permit the flow of air, fuel or vacuum in one direction only.

CHOKE: A device, usually a moveable valve, placed in the intake path of a carburetor to restrict the flow of air.

CIRCUIT: Any unbroken path through which an electrical current can flow. Also used to describe fuel flow in some instances.

CIRCUIT BREAKER: A switch which protects an electrical circuit from overload by opening the circuit when the current flow exceeds a predetermined level. Some circuit breakers must be reset manually, while most reset automatically.

COIL (IGNITION): A transformer in the ignition circuit which steps up the voltage provided to the spark plugs.

COMBINATION MANIFOLD: An assembly which includes both the intake and exhaust manifolds in one casting.

COMBINATION VALVE: A device used in some fuel systems that routes fuel vapors to a charcoal storage canister instead of venting them into the atmosphere. The valve relieves fuel tank pressure and allows fresh air into the tank as the fuel level drops to prevent a vapor lock situation.

COMPRESSION RATIO: The comparison of the total volume of the cylinder and combustion chamber with the piston at BDC and the piston at TDC.

CONDENSER: 1. An electrical device which acts to store an electrical charge, preventing voltage surges. 2. A radiator-like device in the air conditioning system in which refrigerant gas condenses into a liquid, giving off heat.

CONDUCTOR: Any material through which an electrical current can be transmitted easily.

CONTINUITY: Continuous or complete circuit. Can be checked with an ohmmeter.

COUNTERSHAFT: An intermediate shaft which is rotated by a mainshaft and transmits, in turn, that rotation to a working part.

CRANKCASE: The lower part of an engine in which the crankshaft and related parts operate.

CRANKSHAFT: The main driving shaft of an engine which receives reciprocating motion from the pistons and converts it to rotary motion.

CYLINDER: In an engine, the round hole in the engine block in which the piston(s) ride.

CYLINDER BLOCK: The main structural member of an engine in which is found the cylinders, crankshaft and other principal parts.

CYLINDER HEAD: The detachable portion of the engine, usually fastened to the top of the cylinder block and containing all or most of the combustion chambers. On overhead valve engines, it contains the valves and their operating parts. On overhead cam engines, it contains the camshaft as well.

DEAD CENTER: The extreme top or bottom of the piston stroke.

DETONATION: An unwanted explosion of the air/fuel mixture in the combustion chamber caused by excess heat and compression, advanced timing, or an overly lean mixture. Also referred to as "ping".

DIAPHRAGM: A thin, flexible wall separating two cavities, such as in a vacuum advance unit.

DIESELING: A condition in which hot spots in the combustion chamber cause the engine to run on after the key is turned off.

DIFFERENTIAL: A geared assembly which allows the transmission of motion between drive axles, giving one axle the ability to turn faster than the other.

DIODE: An electrical device that will allow current to flow in one direction only.

DISC BRAKE: A hydraulic braking assembly consisting of a brake disc, or rotor, mounted on an axle, and a caliper assembly containing, usually two brake pads which are activated by hydraulic pressure. The pads are forced against the sides of the disc, creating friction which slows the vehicle.

DISTRIBUTOR: A mechanically driven device on an engine which is responsible for electrically firing the spark plug at a predetermined point of the piston stroke.

DOWEL PIN: A pin, inserted in mating holes in two different parts allowing those parts to maintain a fixed relationship.

DRUM BRAKE: A braking system which consists of two brake shoes and one or two wheel cylinders, mounted on a fixed backing plate, and a brake drum, mounted on an axle, which revolves around the assembly.

DWELL: The rate, measured in degrees of shaft rotation, at which an electrical circuit cycles on and off.

ELECTRONIC CONTROL UNIT (ECU): Ignition module, module, amplifier or igniter. See Module for definition.

ELECTRONIC IGNITION: A system in which the timing and firing of the spark plugs is controlled by an electronic control unit, usually called a module. These systems have no points or condenser.

END-PLAY: The measured amount of axial movement in a shaft.

ENGINE: A device that converts heat into mechanical energy.

EXHAUST MANIFOLD: A set of cast passages or pipes which conduct exhaust gases from the engine.

FEELER GAUGE: A blade, usually metal, or precisely predetermined thickness, used to measure the clearance between two parts.

FIRING ORDER: The order in which combustion occurs in the cylinders of an engine. Also the order in which spark is distributed to the plugs by the distributor.

FLOODING: The presence of too much fuel in the intake manifold and combustion chamber which prevents the air/fuel mixture from firing, thereby causing a no-start situation.

FLYWHEEL: A disc shaped part bolted to the rear end of the crankshaft. Around the outer perimeter is affixed the ring gear. The starter drive engages the ring gear, turning the flywheel, which rotates the crankshaft, imparting the initial starting motion to the engine.

FOOT POUND (ft. lbs. or sometimes, ft.lb.): The amount of energy or work needed to raise an item weighing one pound, a distance of one foot.

FUSE: A protective device in a circuit which prevents circuit overload by breaking the circuit when a specific amperage is present. The device is constructed around a strip or wire of a lower amperage rating than the circuit it is designed to protect. When an amperage higher than that stamped on the fuse is present in the circuit, the strip or wire melts, opening the circuit.

GEAR RATIO: The ratio between the number of teeth on meshing gears.

GENERATOR: A device which converts mechanical energy into electrical energy.

HEAT RANGE: The measure of a spark plug's ability to dissipate heat from its firing end. The higher the heat range, the hotter the plug fires.

HUB: The center part of a wheel or gear.

HYDROCARBON (HC): Any chemical compound made up of hydrogen and carbon. A major pollutant formed by the engine as a byproduct of combustion.

HYDROMETER: An instrument used to measure the specific gravity of a solution.

INCH POUND (inch lbs.; sometimes in.lb. or in. lbs.): One twelfth of a foot pound.

INDUCTION: A means of transferring electrical energy in the form of a magnetic field. Principle used in the ignition coil to increase voltage.

INJECTOR: A device which receives metered fuel under relatively low pressure and is activated to inject the fuel into the engine under relatively high pressure at a predetermined time.

INPUT SHAFT: The shaft to which torque is applied, usually carrying the driving gear or gears.

INTAKE MANIFOLD: A casting of passages or pipes used to conduct air or a fuel/air mixture to the cylinders.

JOURNAL: The bearing surface within which a shaft operates.

KEY: A small block usually fitted in a notch between a shaft and a hub to prevent slippage of the two parts.

MANIFOLD: A casting of passages or set of pipes which connect the cylinders to an inlet or outlet source.

MANIFOLD VACUUM: Low pressure in an engine intake manifold formed just below the throttle plates. Manifold vacuum is highest at idle and drops under acceleration.

MASTER CYLINDER: The primary fluid pressurizing device in a hydraulic system. In automotive use, it is found in brake and hydraulic clutch systems and is pedal activated, either directly or, in a power brake system, through the power booster.

MODULE: Electronic control unit, amplifier or igniter of solid state or integrated design which controls the current flow in the ignition primary circuit based on input from the pick-up coil. When the module opens the primary circuit, high secondary voltage is induced in the coil.

NEEDLE BEARING: A bearing which consists of a number (usually a large number) of long, thin rollers.

OHM: (Ω) The unit used to measure the resistance of conductor-to-electrical flow. One ohm is the amount of resistance that limits current flow to one ampere in a circuit with one volt of pressure.

OHMMETER: An instrument used for measuring the resistance, in ohms, in an electrical circuit.

OUTPUT SHAFT: The shaft which transmits torque from a device, such as a transmission.

OVERDRIVE: A gear assembly which produces more shaft revolutions than that transmitted to it.

OVERHEAD CAMSHAFT (OHC): An engine configuration in which the camshaft is mounted on top of the cylinder head and operates the valve either directly or by means of rocker arms.

OVERHEAD VALVE (OHV): An engine configuration in which all of the valves are located in the cylinder head and the camshaft is located in the cylinder block. The camshaft operates the valves via lifters and pushrods.

OXIDES OF NITROGEN (NOx): Chemical compounds of nitrogen produced as a byproduct of combustion. They combine with hydrocarbons to produce smog.

OXYGEN SENSOR: Use with the feedback system to sense the presence of oxygen in the exhaust gas and signal the computer which can reference the voltage signal to an air/fuel ratio.

PINION: The smaller of two meshing gears.

PISTON RING: An open-ended ring with fits into a groove on the outer diameter of the piston. Its chief function is to form a seal between the piston and cylinder wall. Most automotive pistons have three rings: two for compression sealing; one for oil sealing.

PRELOAD: A predetermined load placed on a bearing during assembly or by adjustment.

PRIMARY CIRCUIT: the low voltage side of the ignition system which consists of the ignition switch, ballast resistor or resistance wire, bypass, coil, electronic control unit and pick-up coil as well as the connecting wires and harnesses.

PRESS FIT: The mating of two parts under pressure, due to the inner diameter of one being smaller than the outer diameter of the other, or vice versa; an interference fit.

RACE: The surface on the inner or outer ring of a bearing on which the balls, needles or rollers move.

REGULATOR: A device which maintains the amperage and/or voltage levels of a circuit at predetermined values.

RELAY: A switch which automatically opens and/or closes a circuit.

RESISTANCE: The opposition to the flow of current through a circuit or electrical device, and is measured in ohms. Resistance is equal to the voltage divided by the amperage.

RESISTOR: A device, usually made of wire, which offers a preset amount of resistance in an electrical circuit.

RING GEAR: The name given to a ring-shaped gear attached to a differential case, or affixed to a flywheel or as part of a planetary gear set.

ROLLER BEARING: A bearing made up of hardened inner and outer races between which hardened steel rollers move.

ROTOR: 1. The disc-shaped part of a disc brake assembly, upon which the brake pads bear; also called, brake disc. 2. The device mounted atop the distributor shaft, which passes current to the distributor cap tower contacts.

SECONDARY CIRCUIT: The high voltage side of the ignition system, usually above 20,000 volts. The secondary includes the ignition coil, coil wire, distributor cap and rotor, spark plug wires and spark plugs.

SENDING UNIT: A mechanical, electrical, hydraulic or electro-magnetic device which transmits information to a gauge.

SENSOR: Any device designed to measure engine operating conditions or ambient pressures and temperatures. Usually electronic in nature and designed to send a voltage signal to an on-board computer, some sensors may operate as a simple on/off switch or they may provide a variable voltage signal (like a potentiometer) as conditions or measured parameters change.

SHIM: Spacers of precise, predetermined thickness used between parts to establish a proper working relationship.

SLAVE CYLINDER: In automotive use, a device in the hydraulic clutch system which is activated by hydraulic force, disengaging the clutch.

SOLENOID: A coil used to produce a magnetic field, the effect of which is to produce work.

SPARK PLUG: A device screwed into the combustion chamber of a spark ignition engine. The basic construction is a conductive core inside of a ceramic insulator, mounted in an outer conductive base. An electrical charge from the spark plug wire travels along the conductive core and jumps a preset air gap to a grounding point or points at the end of the conductive base. The resultant spark ignites the fuel/air mixture in the combustion chamber.

SPLINES: Ridges machined or cast onto the outer diameter of a shaft or inner diameter of a bore to enable parts to mate without rotation.

TACHOMETER: A device used to measure the rotary speed of an engine, shaft, gear, etc., usually in rotations per minute.

THERMOSTAT: A valve, located in the cooling system of an engine, which is closed when cold and opens gradually in response to engine heating, controlling the temperature of the coolant and rate of coolant flow.

TOP DEAD CENTER (TDC): The point at which the piston reaches the top of its travel on the compression stroke.

TORQUE: The twisting force applied to an object.

TORQUE CONVERTER: A turbine used to transmit power from a driving member to a driven member via hydraulic action, providing changes in drive ratio and torque. In automotive use, it links the driveplate at the rear of the engine to the automatic transmission.

TRANSDUCER: A device used to change a force into an electrical signal.

TRANSISTOR: A semi-conductor component which can be actuated by a small voltage to perform an electrical switching function.

TUNE-UP: A regular maintenance function, usually associated with the replacement and adjustment of parts and components in the electrical and fuel systems of a vehicle for the purpose of attaining optimum performance.

TURBOCHARGER: An exhaust driven pump which compresses intake air and forces it into the combustion chambers at higher than atmospheric pressures. The increased air pressure allows more fuel to be burned and results in increased horsepower being produced.

VACUUM ADVANCE: A device which advances the ignition timing in response to increased engine vacuum.

VACUUM GAUGE: An instrument used to measure the presence of vacuum in a chamber.

VALVE: A device which control the pressure, direction of flow or rate of flow of a liquid or gas.

VALVE CLEARANCE: The measured gap between the end of the valve stem and the rocker arm, cam lobe or follower that activates the valve.

VISCOSITY: The rating of a liquid's internal resistance to flow.

VOLTMETER: An instrument used for measuring electrical force in units called volts. Voltmeters are always connected parallel with the circuit being tested.

WHEEL CYLINDER: Found in the automotive drum brake assembly, it is a device, actuated by hydraulic pressure, which, through internal pistons, pushes the brake shoes outward against the drums.

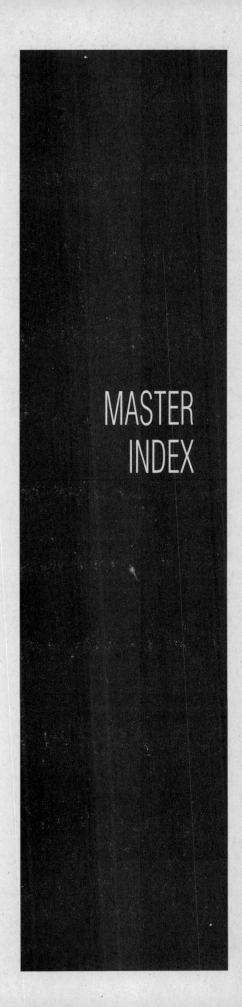

MASTER
INDEX